ISBN 978-0-282-86735-5
PIBN 10870641

1 MONTH OF
FREE
READING

at
www.ForgottenBooks.com

By purchasing this book you are eligible for one month membership to ForgottenBooks.com, giving you unlimited access to our entire collection of over 1,000,000 titles via our web site and mobile apps.

To claim your free month visit:
www.forgottenbooks.com/free870641

English
Français
Deutsche
Italiano
Español
Português

www.forgottenbooks.com

Mythology Photography **Fiction**
Fishing Christianity **Art** Cooking
Essays Buddhism Freemasonry
Medicine **Biology** Music **Ancient
Egypt** Evolution Carpentry Physics
Dance Geology **Mathematics** Fitness
Shakespeare **Folklore** Yoga Marketing
Confidence Immortality Biographies
Poetry **Psychology** Witchcraft
Electronics Chemistry History **Law**
Accounting **Philosophy** Anthropology
Alchemy Drama Quantum Mechanics
Atheism Sexual Health **Ancient History**
Entrepreneurship Languages Sport
Paleontology Needlework Islam
Metaphysics Investment Archaeology
Parenting Statistics Criminology
Motivational

THE

LIFE AND LETTERS

OF

TANIST OF CARBERY,

WITH SOME PORTION OF

"THE HISTORY OF THE ANCIENT FAMILIES OF THE SOUTH OF IRELAND,"

COMPILED SOLELY FROM

UNPUBLISHED DOCUMENTS IN HER MAJESTY'S
STATE PAPER OFFICE.

BY

OF GLEANN-A-CHROIM.

LONDON:
LONGMANS, GREEN, READER, AND DYER.
DUBLIN: HODGES AND SMITH.
1867.

LONDON :
PRINTED BY HARRISON AND SONS, ST. MARTIN'S LANE.

TO

THAT SEPT OF THE RACE OF HEBER

WHICH HAVING BEEN THE MOST EXALTED IS THE MOST HUMBLED,

TO

THE DESCENDANTS, RICH AND POOR,

OF

DERMOD MACCARTHY, KING OF DESMOND,

This Volume is Dedicated

AS A TRIBUTE OF LOVE AND REVERENCE,

BY

THE AUTHOR.

Winsley Manor House,
Wilts.

INTRODUCTION.

"The Venerable Charles O'Conor (in a letter to Bryan O'Conor, Kerry, in 1755), describes this great Irish Sept (the MacCarthys) as the most eminent by far of all the noble families of the South, and Sovereigns of all that part of Ireland, including the greatest part of the county of Cork.

"I am really anxious (wrote Mr. O'Conor,) for a good account of the celebrated Florence McCarthy, who assumed the title of *More*, by the unanimous suffrages of Tirone, the Clergy, and the people, and was kept prisoner eleven years in the Tower of London; after which he escaped, and joined in the Tirone war."

"Mr. O'Conor wished for a history of the ancient families of the South of Ireland; but in that he was disappointed."

Hardiman's Irish Minstrelsy. Vol. II, page 418.

More than a century has elapsed since there was thus placed on record the declaration of one of the most eminent of our scholars, that "a Life of Florence MacCarthy was wanting to our literature, and that he greatly desired to see such a deficiency supplied:" this declaration, and this desire have been many times since repeated by scholars scarcely less eminent, whose lives have been dedicated, in other, and more important departments, to their country's literature. The vacancy, and the invitation to supply it, have remained a barren tradition till this day!

To accept what has been an open challenge for more than a hundred years would be presumptuous in the writer —of no repute—who now assumes it, had the silence of our students proceeded from any difficulty, other than the remoteness of the materials from their homes, and the time necessary for their collection from amidst many thousands of letters and despatches, most of them utterly illegible without long, and irksome study. In truth the documents

A 2

necessary for this work, as they exist only in Her Majesty's State Paper Office, in London, lay beyond the convenient reach of our Irish scholars, and none other have cared to concern themselves about them; hence, the presumption that might seem to attach to such an undertaking, is the less, in that, at the very time Mr. O'Conor was lamenting this void in our national literature, "a good account of Florence MacCarthy" was already written, and needed but the time and toil requisite for compiling, and placing it before the reader! It was written in alternate chapters by himself, by Sir Robert Cecyll, Sir George Carewe, by successive Deputies, and Presidents of Munster, and by countless correspondents of the English Ministers and the Privy Council, during the entire period of his career. It is the Life thus written that is now offered to the public, and with it so much of "the history of the ancient families of the South of Ireland," as comprised the great struggle with which terminated the Rights, Chiefries, and recognised succession of elective chiefs, and the separate existence of the mere Irish in Septs.

It may with safety be affirmed that little is generally known of Florence MacCarthy beyond what is written in the Pacata Hibernia, and the histories of Cork, Kerry, and Waterford, by Smith; even Mr. O'Conor, in part misled by the latter writer, has, in the few lines he has quoted, fallen into two inaccuracies! Florence did not escape from the Tower of London; nor can it be said that he joined in the Tirone war! The archives of Her Majesty's State Paper Office contain the Life, public and private, of this remarkable mere Irishman, from the age of 12 to 76; a period of 64 years, of which—for what reason the reader will eventually be well able to judge—48 had been already, at the period when this biography closes, spent in state prisons; the Tower, the Gatehouse, the Marshalsea, and other jails; or on parole, under heavy recognizances, within a few miles of London. The same documents that were laid before Burghley, Walsyngham, Cecyll, and Queen Elizabeth, and before every successive Minister, and the Privy Council, for a further period of 40 years, are now, for the first time printed, and offered to the favourable notice of the reader.

Mention of distinct portions of the pedigrees of the numerous Sept of the MacCarthys will unavoidably be of frequent occurrence throughout the following pages; for the descent, and great alliances of Florence were the incessant, and most hurtful charges which his adversaries could make against him. Not only his personal enemies, but the English authorities in Munster, were at the pains of collecting, and sending home to the Privy Council, evidences of his descent from the ancient Kings of Ireland, and the minutest details of his alliances with the nobility of his own day, as proofs of *the danger to the State of allowing liberty to "a man of such greatness."*

It may be needful, and it will be sufficient, to render this descent, and these alliances intelligible to the reader, to state that the Sept of the M.C.s had for several centuries been divided into three great stems, each subdivided into several minor, and dependent, but still powerful branches. The main line was known amongst the Irish, as that of M.C. Mor, the second as M.C. Reagh, and the third, and probably the wealthiest, as M.C. of Muskerry. In the middle of the 16th century, the head of the main line, and chief of his race, was Donal, Earl of Clancar; the chief of Muskerry, was Sir Cormac McTeig, who had been declared by an English Lord Deputy, " the rarest man that was ever born of his race;" and the chieftain of Carbery, was Sir Donogh MacCarthy Reagh, the father of Florence, 9th in descent from Dermod of Cille-Baine (so called a loco occisionis) whom the Normans found King of Cork or Desmond, when they first set foot in Ireland. For several generations the descendants of Dermod, in the main line, were styled " Kings of Desmond;" and the MacCarthy Reaghs, " Princes of Carbery;" not only in the Irish chronicles, but in letters, and patents from the Kings of England. One such instance, amongst many, occurs in the close rolls, preserved in the Tower of London, amongst which is one exceedingly curious; it is an order, made in the first year of the reign of Hen. III, A.D. 1217, to the Justiciary of

Ireland, "to cause payment to be made, without delay, to Petronilla de Bloet, a Norman Lady, of her dower, which had been given to her by her brother, Thomas de Bloet, on her marriage to Dermot MacCarthy, King of Cork!" Dermod was born A.D. 1098! He was 73 years of age when "he defeated the Danes of Limerick, in a battle in which several of their bravest commanders were slain, including Torna, son of Giolla-Cainniah, and Torcar, son of Treni; burned the market place, and demolished the greater part of the fortress."—(Cronnelly, Irish Fam. Hist.) The Normans arrived at this time; and in 1172, King Hen. II. himself landed in Ireland. If Petronilla accompanied him, Dermod may have been not more than 74 when he married her; if she waited till Norman rule was established with some security in Ireland, she may have married him at any time between 1172 and 1185, at which period he was killed, as it is asserted, by treachery of the English, under FitzWalter, with whom he was holding conference. He was at the time 87 years of age.

It is surprising that the marriage of the old King with this young Norman damsel should have escaped mention by the chroniclers of Ireland! that they should not have attributed to the power of her charms his submission to Henry, the consequent rebellion of his subjects, his deposition in favour of his son Cormac Liathanach, and his recovery of his kingdom by the aid of Norman troops, under Raymond le Gros.

This close roll throws some suggestive twilight upon the tame submission of this warlike Prince, and upon the rebellion of his son, and of his subjects.

Close Rolls, 302.
Mandatu' est G. Marisc Justic Hibn qd sn dilone hre faciat Petronillæ Bloet Maritagiu suu quod Thom: Bloet Frat ejus eide Petronillæ dedit cu Dermot Magarthy Rege de Corke viro suo.
"T. Com ut supª.

An. I. Hen. III. A.D. 1217.

The maritagium, or dower, of this lady must have been withheld by her own people, or by Dermot's successors, for at least 22, and probably not less than 30 years. Elsewhere in the same rolls, Thomas de Bloet is styled Lord of Thyvernail. The family is frequently mentioned in the Rolls of Hen. III., during whose reign different members of it appear to have been attached to the Royal Household.

Before committing the following pages to the benevolence of all who may condescend to peruse them, the author is desirous to avert the possible censure of those of his readers, who, happily for themselves, may know little of the men who were sent to rule and civilize Ireland in the 16th century, and who may think that he has written of them with undue severity! He has done far otherwise! he has again and again revised these pages, with the resolution to remove from them every word of reproach; but he has found it impossible to write a single chapter of Anglo-Irish history on such terms: not only must he have suppressed every expression of detestation for treachery and rapacity, but he must have supressed also every official document containing the narrative written by the actors themselves, of the events he has had to record: on these documents—the real accusers—be the blame! should the reader still feel disposed to attach any.

There remains but one more object of solicitude with the writer of this biography, and it forces him to address a few earnest words to those of his countrymen who—however reluctantly—have given credence to two severe accusations against the subject of this memoir, viz., 1st, that when hardest pressed by the English Government, and in a weak moment, when he thought that he could purchase his freedom by it, Florence had—to use the words of an eminent scholar of our own day and country—"*boasted that he had caused the ruin of the Earl of Desmond,*" and—as implied—the failure of the great effort made in 1600, for the nation's "liberty, and religion!" And secondly, that "*he had advised the Government to bribe the bards to bring over the Gentlemen of Ireland to British interests.*"

These cruel reproaches have not only been made in print by writers who would willingly have overlooked much in a man who had suffered much for his race and nation, but they have been made subject of frequent remonstrance with this author, as if all that he could say to endear the memory of Florence to his countrymen must be vain words, in face of so unworthy an acknowledgment! To these of his readers he would earnestly appeal to judge kindly, as well as justly! Had Florence chosen to take the part that was taken by the Earl of Thomond, no price that Elizabeth could offer would have been thought too great to purchase, or reward him. To make him merely *a good subject* Cecyll offered the Earldom that had been given to his father-in-law: what would have been denied to him if he had entered zealously into English interests when Norreys and Carewe were successively cooped up in Cork, and trembling for the loss of Munster?

These accusations had their origin in a letter seen by few, read carelessly, and preserved where it is beyond reach of convenient reference. This author hopes he has for ever disposed of this cruel reproach against the fair fame of a distinguished man, and justice authorizes him to claim, in reparation for a great wrong, that henceforth at least, our writers cease to countenance so defamatory a tradition.

Finally, the author of the following pages foresees that he can scarcely escape two objections to the manner in which he has accomplished his task. The first is that he has allowed this volume to grow into larger dimensions than he needed, by the introduction into it of much biography of other men! and the second, that the insertion of so many contemporary documents is both tedious, and useless! since the complement of the work itself has required the repetition of the narrative contained in them.

In reply to the first objection he must request his reader's permission to refer to the wish of Mr. O'Conor, and to add that he knew no better way for furnishing some "history of the ancient families of the South of Ireland," for which that great national scholar was "so really anxious," and which this writer has considered within the scope and conditions of his undertaking. To the second, and graver charge, he must reply that our Irish scholars consider these State Papers as fountains unsullied of true history, and look upon such para-

phrases as these of this author as tending but to trouble the
clearness, and purity of their waters; and hence that they
value more the publishing of one such document than all that
he has written, or could write; but better favour than either
of these apologies may deserve, he trusts to receive from the
benevolence of his reader.

It is now several years since it was first proposed to the
writer to compile this biography of Florence MacCarthy. The
late learned Dr. O'Donovan, who knew so well the abundance
of the materials accessible for the illustration of our history,
and the vacancies yet left in our biographical literature, urged
upon him the wish so long on record, of the venerable Charles
O'Conor, and it was in compliance with this often repeated
solicitation that the work was undertaken; during its first
few pages the writer had the encouragement of that learned
scholar. Subsequently that of the late lamented John
Windele, Esq., of Mr. Cronnelly, the author of " Irish family
histories," and of Herbert F. Hore, Esq. All of these eminent
Irish scholars are taken! and this author grieves that it has
not been permitted to him to offer his completed task to their
kindly criticism.

The earlier chapters of this Life were published in the
Journal of the Kilkenny and South of Ireland Archæological
Society; and for the great space that was allotted to it in
those pages—where the room could be ill spared—the writer
is much indebted to the kindness of the learned, and courteous
Editor, the Rev. James Graves, M.A., &c.

With names so respected, so warmly and justly cherished,
it is a pleasing duty to associate that of one other gentleman,
to whom, in the course of this work, the author has been
under much obligation—John Maclean, Esquire, of the War
Office, an accomplished genealogist and antiquarian, the
learned and accurate editor of " The Life and Times of Sir
Peter Carewe," and " The Letters of Sir Robert Cecil," than
which few works of our own time are more interesting, or more
useful to the student of Irish history.

It would be an ungracious act to place these numerous
State Papers in the hands of his readers, and not express his

great admiration of the copious and accurate calendar of them by Hans Claude Hamilton, Esq. This author spent nearly twelve months in the State Paper Office ; and, but for the assistance he derived from Mr. Hamilton's great work, his labour would have been immense, and the result but little! They only who have laboured to discover, in the staggering oghams of the hundreds of correspondents of the Ministers of Elizabeth, some acknowledged alphabetic form, can have an idea of the toil required to decipher them ; they only who have followed the track of Mr. Hamilton through these papers, and under his guidance, can duly appreciate the ability and truthfulness of the analysis of the many thousand documents that have passed through his hands; "to this patient, learned, and accurate writer every student of Anglo-Irish history is under lasting obligations."

These last few words were spoken years ago, by the late Dr. O'Donovan to this author, and he has much pleasure in repeating them.

———————————

"The seal, of which a drawing is presented on the cover of this volume, was exhibited to the Royal Irish Academy, by the late Dr. Petrie, about 30 years ago, upon occasion of his reading to that learned body an ' Essay on the Seals of Irish Chiefs.' 'This seal,—said that eminent antiquarian,— which is from my own cabinet, is, as the inscription shows, the seal of Donal Oge, the son of Donal Roe Mac Carthy, who, as appears from the notices in the Irish and English authorities, became King or Lord of Desmond, by the murder of his father, Donal Roe, in 1306, or, as some accounts state, in 1302, and was himself killed in 1309. The legend runs thus :—

S. Dovenaldi: Og: Fili: D: Roth Macarthy.

"The name of this Prince appears in the pedigree of the MacCarthy family as 15th in ascent from the last Earl of Clancarty, and the thirtieth in descent from their great ancestor Olioll Olum."

At the death of Dr. Petrie this seal passed to the Museum of the Royal Irish Academy.

ERRATUM.

When too late for correction in its own place, the author discovered the error into which he was led by the mutilated passage at page 435 in the letter of Daniel MacCarthy to Lord Dorchester. The reader is requested to gather from that passage that Donal did, *for a small som of money*, himself marry the daughter of Malcolm Hamilton, then lately deceased, who had succeeded Miler McGrath as Archbishop of Cashel.

LIFE AND LETTERS

OF

FLORENCE MACCARTHY MOR.

CHAPTER I.

In the autumn of the year 1575, a memorable Vice-regal progress was made through the accessible parts of Ireland by Sir Henry Sidney, and the diary of that political excursion has been transmitted to us in a series of spirited, and extremely curious letters, written by the Lord Deputy himself to the Lords of the Privy Council in England. As he passed along from city to city, he collected and took with him in his train the great nobles of the land, as well "the commendable and orderly Lords of the Pale" as the native chieftains of countries into which neither the Queen's writ nor the Queen's Deputy might venture. The object of Sir Henry Sidney in traversing Ireland with so much display, was to overawe, to conciliate, and to make personal acquaintance with the provincial magnates, on whose behaviour must depend the success of his Government. The character and loyalty, as well as the condition of the vast estates of the men whom he visited, were keenly observed and graphically sketched for the information of the Queen and her Ministers. Two days before Christmas the stately train of the Deputy made its entry into the city of Cork. By this time it had collected every personage of note from the counties through which it had passed; and never since the days of Henry II, had the land witnessed so large an assembly of English and Irish nobles on terms of amity. Sir Henry and his company "were received by the citizens of Cork with all joyfulness, tokens, and shows, the best they could express of their dutiful thanksgiving to Her Majesty. He was for the time of his continuance there, very honourably attended, and accompanied by the Earls of Desmond, Thomond, and Clancar, &c., &c. Besides the above mentioned, were divers of the Irishry not yet nobilitated. The Lord of Carbry, called

14

Sir Donell (Donogh) MacCarthy, and the Lord of Muskery, called Sir Cormac MacTeig; neither of these, but in respect of his territories, were able to be a viscount; and truly I wish them both to be made barons; for they be both good subjects, and in especial the latter, who for his obedience to Her Majesty, and her laws, and disposition to civility, is the rarest man that ever was born of the Irish ; but of him I intend to write especially before it be long; for truly he is a special man . . . and the better to furnish out the beauty and filling of the city, all these principal lords had with them their wives during all the Christmas, who truly kept very honourable, at least very plentiful houses ; and, to be brief, many widow-ladies were there also, who erst had been wives to earls, and others of good note and account."

It thus chanced that, in addition to the rival houses of Ormond and Desmond, with the choicest gentlemen of their blood, this visit of the Deputy assembled within the city of Cork the three great chiefs of the Sept of the MacCarthys, with their wives and families. The Earl of Clancar, by the Irish styled MacCarthy Mor, was accompanied by his countess, the sister of the Earl of Desmond, and his infant children, the Baron of Valentia and the Lady Ellen. No less than fourteen lords of counties, most of them of his own race, attended him. The Lord of Muskery, the wealthiest chief-tain of the Sept, with a less attendance, and the Lord of the fertile lands of Carbery, Sir Donogh MacCarthy Reagh, both in especial favour with the Lord Deputy, were also there, the latter accompanied by his two sons, Florence and Dermod Moyle, and escorted by O'Mahone Finn of Evaghe, O'Driscoll More, O'Donovan, O'Daly, O'Crowly, and others of less note.

During six weeks all was festivity in Cork; and at the end of that time the Lord Deputy, and those nobles whose political feelings and interests were especially English, swept onward in imposing state to renew in Limerick the shows and tokens which had welcomed them to Waterford and Cork. Gradually the great lords and chieftains, whose countries were in the neighbourhood, took their departure also ; the Earl of Desmond to Dungarvan, the Earl of Clancar to the Palice, Sir Cormac MacTeige to Blarney, and Sir Donogh MacCarthy Reagh to Kilbrittain Castle.

Of the 160 castles built in the county of Cork, says our greatest local antiquarian, the learned Mr. Windele, in his "South of Ireland," fifty-six were erected by Irish chieftains, twenty-six by the MacCarthys alone. Of these castles four, viz., the Palice, Castle-Logh, Ross-i-Donogho, and Killorgan,

were described by Sir George Carewe as " built on the edge
of Logh Lene, and the river of Lawne, and might stop all
the passages of Desmond." " The Lawne," says Mr. Windele,
" is a river abounding in salmon and white trout ; in it is also
frequently found the pearl fish, some fine pearls from which
have been repeatedly taken. The tract of country lying
along its banks, and at the mountain's foot, to some considerable distance, is still called MacCarthy Mor's country, as containing the ancient residence of the chief of that name. The
mensal demesne was, however, more extensive, extending
southward over Inveragh, its western boundary being the
ocean. The Castle of Palice, otherwise Caislean-Va-Cartha,
stood, a naked ruin, on an eminence, a little to the north of
the lake, and in view of Lawne Bridge ; a few scattered trees
point out its site. The green field in front is still called
Park-an-Croh, the gallows-field, that being the place where
MacCarthy executed his justice on delinquents."

Relative to Kilbrittain, the chief residence of the Mac-
Carthy Reaghs, Smith, in his history of Cork, writes—" When
this castle was up, it was a stately building, environed with
a large bawn, fortified with six turrets on the walls. It was
pleasantly situated on a mount, between greater hills ; the
sea flows (almost up to it) through the harbour of Court Mac-
Sherry." Not far from it, on the sea-coast, lies Coolmain,
another castle of MacCarthy Reagh. To this chieftain belonged also the castles of Kilgobhan, Cariganass, and Dun
Daniel.

"Blarney," says Mr. Windele, "is a well-known village,
castle, and demesne, five miles west of Cork, near the junc-
tion of several rivulets. It was, until the Revolution of
1688, the principal residence of that branch of the Royal
house of MacCarthy, ennobled under English rule by the
titles of Lords of Muskerry and Earls of Clan Carthy, &c."
Its wonder-working "stone" enjoys an. universal reputation,
and has been kissed and sung "a thousand times repeated!"
The enormous wealth of this branch of the MacCarthys may
be supposed from a passage of Mr. Windele's account of the
last Earl of Clancarthy. "With the fortunes of King James
(he says) fell those of Clancarthy. His property, which, upon
a loose calculation made in the middle of the last century,
was supposed to be worth £150,000 per annum, and in 1796
about £200,000, was confiscated!" He was taken prisoner on
the surrender of Cork, and exiled ; he subsequently received
his pardon from the Government of William, and would have
been restored to his estates but, it is alleged, for the interfer-

ence of Sir R. Cox. *A pension of £300 was all he could obtain!* and with this he retired to Altona; he died at Hamburgh in 1734."

A brief period of tranquillity succeeded the Vice-regal visit to Munster. A great danger was supposed to have been averted by the policy of Sir Henry Sidney; the citizens of Cork resumed their commercial occupations with renewed confidence, and the native chieftains returned to rule their vast territories with laws of their own, and as unquestioned a supremacy as if Deputy or Queen had never been heard of in Ireland.

Finin or Florence, the subject of this biography, the eldest son of Sir Donogh MacCarthy, was at this time about 12 years of age. How he is likely to have spent the years of his boyhood; at what time and from what sources he derived the education that made him the accomplished man, the astute politician, the fair scholar that he afterwards became, is matter for interesting inquiry. That his early years were passed in the seclusion of Carbery, chiefly in companionship, with the sons of his uncle, Sir Owen, and the youths of the various minor chieftains subordinate to his father, all of whom in after life became stubborn and daring rebels, there can be no doubt. The pursuits of these young wild lads it is not difficult to imagine ; their days would be spent upon the waves that beat against the walls of Kilbrittain Castle ; in the woods, or on the mountains with hound and hawk, for which their country was celebrated. Pursuits of a more exciting nature, however, occasionally gave variety to these recreations, and brought them into some slight collision with laws which they neither recognised nor respected. Amongst the many devices of the English authorities by which they strove to place some limits to the power of the native lords over their followers, and, if possible, to win from them to themselves some portion of the attachment which constituted their strength, was an attempt to extend to the tenant protection against the payment of duties, which English law looked upon as extortions, but which, in fact, were the conditions by which, *in lieu of rent*, the follower held his lands. Scores of duties and rights, of which few English knew even the names, were exacted by the Irish chiefs, and had been paid by their dependants time out of mind without a murmur. Against some of these customs, such, for example, as coyne and livery, the English loudly protested; they made it punishable in the lords to exact them, and promised protection and redress to the tenant who would have the courage to refuse to pay them. From that moment these rights were claimed with tenfold rigour, usually paid as a grievance, and sometimes resisted. Woe to the man who replied to his chief or his chief's officer with an allusion to English law! Yet occasionally such men were found; and the two presentments following, made by Cork juries in the time of Sir William Drury, will show how the Irish chiefs dealt, and taught their children to deal with men thus ill advised; and give us, moreover, some insight into the training which led the youth of Ireland to look to themselves for redress, and to consider English law as an English enemy.

" We present that Owen MacCarthy and Donell MacCarthy, brethren to MacCarthy Reagh, and Finin (Florence) MacCarthy, son to the said MacCarthy Reagh, daily at their pleasure, take meat and drink, with force and extortion for themselves, and their train of horsemen, galloglass and kerne, of the freeholders and inhabitants of Carbry; and besides, they take of the same freeholders, and inhabitants, a sum of money called *cowe*, (*cua*, flesh-meat, a tax raised by the Lord's son to buy meat for his feasts), to the number of five marks of half-face money yearly in every people [Sept] within Carbry, against the will of the freeholders, and inhabitants, and also of the cessor of the county."

" We present that Donel-na-pipie, and MacCarthy Reagh's young son Finin, the 15th of May last, in the year of the reign of our Sovereign Lady Queen Elizabeth that now is the 18th, wrongfully came with force of arms, &c., to Erdyrie Lemerarie in Carbry in the county of Cork, and then and there have forcibly taken and rered the sum of £8 17 9 s^{ts} of the proper goods and chattels of Finin Mac Dermodie of le Clynyne-Crymmyne, and their poor tenants in the name of the said extortion called Cowe."

Smith, in his history of Cork, thus explains the origin of this nick-name fixed upon Donal, and borne by him through life. " This Donal ni-Pipy was so called, because in his time some pipes of wine were cast on shore at Burrin ; and consequently were his right, being a wreck, and accordingly he had them, which in those superstitious times was reckoned very fortunate, the wreck being esteemed (as the Cornish men's phrase is) God's goods." That this designation was *in some way* connected with pipes of wine thrown on shore as wreck, would seem very probable ; but the above presentation of the Cork jurors proves that Smith's account is not absolutely accurate ; for there we see Donal bearing the name during the chieftainship of his uncle, Sir Donogh, who, and not he, would have had right to these pipes of wine if thrown on shore as wreck. Donal may perhaps have been the first to discover them, and for this reason have received the designation, or they may have been cast ashore on such lands as were assigned to him by his uncle, but not on that account his property.

At the time of these raids upon his father's freeholders, Florence was but twelve years of age; they were his first exploits on his return to his home after taking leave of Sir Henry Sidney in Cork. What came of these presentments of the Cork jurors it is easy to guess; simply nothing! for a quarrel with the Lord of Carbery, so especial and rare a man, one of the few native chieftains who supported the English Government, was too serious a matter to be encountered for the sake of Finin MacDermodie, his own follower, the chief of a small Sept of the MacCarthys, called Mac-Ineen-Cro-meen. What was the natural effect of such stern discipline upon the minds of boys purposely trained to enforce it, the rebellion which shortly followed, amply reveals to us; that it left no trace upon the character of Florence is to be attributed to his subsequent, and a far different discipline. Let it not be supposed that an Irish chieftain possessed no means of providing for his children better employment than the pursuits complained of. He might, as many of them did, send his sons to the English Universities, or to schools of good repute in Dublin, or the provincial towns, or he might, if it so pleased him, maintain, as did "the commendable lords of the Pale," a domestic tutor; but the Irish chieftain well knew that in sending his son from him, he gave a hostage to his rulers, and that in domesticating a tutor within his family he maintained a spy. There were other resources, viz., the bards or rhymers, and the priests; and to them it is evident that Sir Donogh trusted for the tuition of his son. Florence has sufficiently proved by his letters, and by a very remarkable treatise on the history of his country, the only work of a literary kind which, as far as we know, he ever wrote, that he possessed a rare and intimate acquaintance with the ancient language, written history, traditions, poems, and pedigrees of his country, precisely the kind of lore which O'Daly, the hereditary bard of MacCarthy Reagh, perhaps as well as any man living, could have taught him; but shrewder and abler teachers than the Munster bard were to be found constantly flitting between Ireland and every Catholic court in Europe; from such masters as Father Archer, Edmund Campion, and MacEggan, Cecyll himself might have learned something. From these men, or men like them, Florence may have derived the intimate knowledge which, beyond all men of his day, he possessed of the state of his own country, its strength and weakness, the alliances and power of its chiefs, the personal character of every man of note sent out from England, the jealousies, the contentions, the dishonesty that prevailed amongst the Lords Justices—many of them men whose fingers crept as instinctively towards the unlawful half-face coin current beyond the Pale, as towards the fresh-minted money imported by the undertaker. Much of this his own sagacity might in time have enabled him to arrive at; but it needed able tuition, and the keenest wit that ever issued from Rome or Rheims, to indoctrinate him in the mysteries of a sublime dissimulation that should bear him harmless through all perils, safe from all adversaries, save the mere ruffian of politics, the man who could pledge the honour and word of his Sovereign, and violate both! Such a man had not yet been met with in Spain or Rome; no such man appeared even in Ireland, till Florence had foiled the last resources of Carewe, and when fourteen days more of his freedom, it was thought, would imperil English rule in Munster.

The sketch of the education of Florence is not yet complete. He appeared before the world a linguist, a scholar, a subtile politician; fortunately for himself he was also a lawyer! From his father's brehon he might have learned, he probably did, Irish law sufficient to have enabled him to rule Carbery, or Ireland itself, in the days of Donal Reagh, his ancestor; but it was to be his lot for fifty long years, to fight for his patrimony in English courts of law; and but for one of the curious presentments made by the Cork juries, it must have remained a mystery to us how his familiarity with English law had been acquired. Amongst many grievances of these worthy men appeared the following:—

" We present that all the lords of this county, to colour and maintain their own extortions, have wrought such a policy to entertain all the lawyers of the province, whereby no freeholder, nor poor man, can have a lawyer to speak in his cause, be it never no just."

The most striking circumstance attending the career of Florence Mac Carthy is the personal influence which he ac— quired over every one to whom he could gain access. Not a single great personage whose good will was of importance to him, from Her Majesty downwards, including Burghley and Cecyl, Ormond, Raleigh, Stanhope, Fitzwilliams, St. Leger, Norreys, nay Carewe himself, but acknowledged in their turns the power of this influence. They each and all knew him to be ambitious; they believed him to be false; they could judge harshly of him in his absence; they could confiscate his property; seize his person; write upon paper excellent reasons for prosecuting him to the uttermost; but when all was done, when in a paroxysim of wrath the Queen had desired Sir Thomas Norreys, then Vice-President of Munster, to appre-

hend him, we see first his captor, after a few weeks' intercourse with him, writing letters to the Minister in his favour;
then Lord Burghley throwing open the doors of the Tower
for his exit, and presenting him to the Queen; next, Elizabeth
showering upon him " great gifts and graces;" and finally,
the Lords of the Privy Council more zealous in the restitution
than they had been in the confiscation of his property!
Superadded to all that he had learned from priest, and bard,
and lawyer, Florence derived from early association with the
young eaglets of England—those majestic birds of prey
which, early jostled by elder brothers out of the maternal
nest, winged with unerring instinct their flight from every
province of their native land, to seek their fortunes at Court,
and find them in Ireland—the knowledge which they alone
could teach him. From them he learned to keep the impulses
of his Irish blood in subjection, and to mask with a serene
brow, and polished ease of manner, whatever passions might
be in commotion within. He was quick to perceive the peculiarities of the English mind; to appreciate and appropriate
to himself the calm courtesy of demeanour which distinguished the cadets of the noble families who flocked to
Ireland as to an El Dorado. In them he was enabled to
study thoroughly the character of the rival race, and by comparison to estimate the strength and weakness of his own.
Little that was good was he likely to learn from those young
courtiers and adventurers; personal bravery he had no cause
to seek exclusively from them, for the meanest of his father's
followers would have been as able a teacher; but cruelty and
rapacity, haughtiness and contempt for the people whose
lands they coveted, hollow loyalty, peculation, and craft
scarcely covered by an exterior of seeming frankness and
good fellowship—all this he might have learned; and if the
taint of any one of these vices had blotted his character, it
would have been fair to remember who, at the early age of
15, had been his associates.

Scarcely had the Cork festivities terminated, and the Lord
Deputy returned to Dublin, when ominous sounds betokened
the reawakening of the volcano in Munster, the pleasant light
paled, and presently passed away altogether from Sir Henry
Sidney's despatches, and he was compelled to write in the
style of his predecessors :—" The Earl of Desmond did not a
little sturr, and fall into disallowable heats and passions,
blowing out words of evil digestion:"—"The Earl of Desmond
was again becoming troublesome; he was committing many
murders, making grievous spoils, taking the Queen's castles,

and had burned a church!" The validity of the professions
so recently made to the Deputy was at once put to the proof;
and few indeed of the men whose loyal intentions he had
extolled, stood by the Government in the struggle that followed—a struggle that was to endure for eight years; for so
long it took the whole power of Elizabeth to conquer this
single rebel. Amongst the few, however, were two men,
respecting whom Sir Henry Sidney had not erred when he
called them "especial and rare men;" they were not nobilitated when he mentioned them, nor were they when they
brought the whole force of their countries to assist the
Government in its hour of need. One of these was Sir Cormack MacCarthy, Lord of Muskerry, the other, Sir Donogh
MacCarthy Reagh, Lord of Carbery. In the long and gloomy
struggle that ensued these two men were found faithful. Sir
Donogh well knew that the sympathies of his people were
not with the Queen's cause; and as the strongest pledge he
could offer of his own earnestness and loyalty, he came himself, and brought his eldest son Florence, then scarcely more
than twelve years of age, to do service with the English army.
In after life, when borne down by a multitude of evil wishers,
and when his own loyalty was a subject of much ambiguity,
Florence found it important to appeal to his father's services,
and his own; and to the words of that appeal, which will
appear in its time, we are indebted for our knowledge of the
part acted by Sir Donogh in this long and sanguinary
struggle. How important it was to the English Government
to secure the services of the great Sept of the MacCarthys
and their dependents, may be judged from the following list
of their forces left us by Sir George Carewe:—

LIST OF THE IRISH FORCES IN DESMOND.

	Horse.	Galloglas.	Kerne.
MacCarthy More, Prince of that portion	40	160	2000
MacCarthy Reagh, Lord of Carbry	60	80	2000
Donogh MacCarthy of Dowallie	24	80	200
Teig MacCormac of Muskry	40	80	200
O'Keefe	12	0	100
McAwliffe	80	0	60
O'Donovan	6	0	60
O'Driscols of Collimore and Baltimore	6	0	200
O'Mahon of Ivaghe	26	0	120
O'Sullevan Beare and Bantry	10	0	200
O'Donough More of Lough Lene	12	0	200
O'Mahoni of Brin	46	0	100
O'Dwyre of Kil-na-managhe	12	0	100
McTeig McPhilip of Kilnaloghengarty	6	0	40

The last two were not followers of MacCarthy.

In the third year of the great Desmond rebellion Sir Donogh MacCarthy died. In what terms Sir Henry Sidney had spoken of him the reader has seen, and that he had recommended him to be "nobilitated." Had this recommendation been complied with, it is doubtful whether, beyond a change of designation when in contact with the English, any effect would have been produced in the circumstances of the heir of Sir Donogh. A few years earlier the Earl of Clancar had been nobilitated; O'Neill himself had been nobilitated, with no perceptible advantage to any one save the Heralds who registered their patents. The titles imposed upon these Irish chiefs had not added a man to their followers, and the Government that bestowed them might have estimated the efficacy of their gift by the fact that the acceptance of them had not made their recipients the less trusted by their own people; indeed, amongst the mere Irish these titles were simply ignored; for the Earl of Clancar remained still MacCarthy Mor, the Earl of Tyrone was still O'Neill, and Sir Donogh would have remained MacCarthy Reagh to the end of his days. Any English title must have descended lineally; whereas the Captaincies of the Irish Septs passed, by Tanistry, collaterally, to "the eldest cousin of the blood." Florence did not succeed to his father's country; and had the Queen created him Baron or Earl of Carbery, his uncle Sir Owen, would have been his Lord none the less; and, but for the prudent management of his private possessions by his father, he might have been left dependent for subsistence on the caprice of his Chief. The value which the Earl of Tyrone set upon his English title we may conjecture from a passage in a letter from Carewe to Cecyll, in which he writes:—

"Which humour hath long smothered in his breast, having evermore had a thirsty desire to be called *O'Neill*, a name more in price with him than to be entituled Cæsar."

The Irish chroniclers have not allowed Sir Donogh MacCarthy to pass away without the eulogy that was his due. Under the date of 1576 his demise is thus noticed in the " Annals of the Four Masters :"

" MacCarthy Reagh (Donogh, son of Donell, son of Finin) died._-A cause of lamentation to the chiefs, of sadness to the husbandmen, and of sorrow to the farmers of his own territory; a man who outshone his seniors, and who was not excelled by his juniors. He was interred in the burial-place of his father and grandfather at Timoleague, and his brother Owen MacCarthy was inaugurated as his successor."

On the 1st of the following June an inquisition was held

at Cork, in the presence of Sir William Drury and others, from which we learn the extent of the private possessions of Sir Donogh MacCarthy, and the fact that Florence was at the time but fifteen years of age.

(Lambeth M.S., vol. 613, page 61.)

1576. *June 1st. An Inquisition taken upon the Death of* SIR DONOGH MACCARTY *in Anno* 19 *Eliz.*

" Inquisito capta apud civitatem Cork in le Guildhall ejusdem civitatis in com' Corke, die Veneris pxime post festū Penticostes viz. primo die mensis Junii anno Regni Regine nře invict' Elizabethe decimo nono, corā Willmo Drury milit' Dūo presidente totius provinciæ Momoniæ, et uno de Privato concilio dict' Dñæ Reginæ in regno suo Hiberniæ, et sociis suis commissionariis prædict' Dñæ Regine p totam provinciam p̄dictam, tam infra libertates quā extra, ad inquirend de omnibus et singulis ter' tenement' reddit' proficuis comoditatibus emolumentis wardiis marritagiis releviis escaetis juribus forisfacturis et aliis hereditamentis quibuscumque eidem Dñæ Reginæ, vel aliquibus progenitorum suorum ratione concessionis donationis attinctur' forisfactur', actûs parliamenti, escaeti mortis alicujus personæ vel aliter qualitercunque spectantibus, vel pertinent', et ad alia faciend' et inquirend' prout in lřeris patentibus dictæ Dñæ Reginæ inde eis confecte gerentes dat' apud Wexford nono die Aprilis año Regni p̄dictæ Dñæ Reginæ decimo nono magis liquett per sacramentum juratorum subscriptorum, viz.

" David Martell de Martellston Gen.   Jchˢ Barry de Donboige Gen. Willme Mallefunte de Courteston Gen.   David McShane de Midestowne Gen.   Jacobi Hoare de Money Gen.   Florentii OMahowny de OMahowne-castle Gen.   Johⁿⁱˢ Skiddi e de Frissellcastle Gen.   Donaldi McOwen de Drisshane Gen.   Daniell O'Herlihie de Ballyworny Gen.   Jacobi Oge Rooch de Knyvre Gen.   Petri Cogan de Ballenecourtey Gen.   Fynen McCormac de Bellemᵉlashy Gen.

" Qui jurat' dicunt p sacřum suum quod Donatus alˢ Donogh MacCarty, nup de Kilbirtane in com̄ Corke Miles Seisitus fuit in Dominico suo ut de Feodo, de una carucata terræ in Knock-ne-gaple in com̄ Corke, de duabus carucat' terræ et dimid' caŗucat' in Rathharowc in com̄ p̄dict', de una carucat' vocat' Ballenveny in com̄ præd', de una carucat' terræ vocat' Currymvir in com̄ præd', de una carucat' terræ vocat' Langestowne in com̄ præd', de duabus carucat' terræ vocat' Kildare in com̄ præd', de una carucat' terræ vocat' Cloghane in com̄ præd', de duabus carucat' terræ vocat' Rath-droughtie in com̄ præd', de una carucat' terræ· vocat' Killinstie in com̄ præd', de medietate unius carucat' terræ in Ballerviellen in com̄-præd', de duabus carucat' terræ in Killinvarra in com̄ præd', de medietate unius carucat' terr in Knockbrowne in com̄ præd', de una carucat' terræ in Barra-liegh in com̄ præd', de medietate unius carucat' terræ in Martlesknocke in com̄ præd', de tertia parte unius carucat' terr' in Gortinenige in com̄ præd', de duabus partibus unius carucat' terræ in Garan Rieugh in com̄ præd', de una carucat' terræ in Ardgehan in com̄ præd', de medietate unius carucat' terræ in Ballenagornagh in com̄ præd', de medietate unius carucat' terræ in Castle Iwer in com̄ præd', et de una carucat' terræ vocat' Curry-I-Cruwolley in eodem com̄ Corke, et quod omnia et singťa præd' terras et tenementa tenuit de præd' Dña Regina p que servitia penitus ignorant. Ac etiam dictus Donatus sit seisitus de omnibus et singulis p̄missis 24 die Januarii anno Regni dictæ Dñæ Reginæ, decimo nono obiit sic inde seisitus, Et qd

omnia et singula præmissa valent per annum quinq̃ Libr' Et quod Florentius al⁸ Fynen Mac Carty est Filius et Heres dicti Donati, et infra etatem
vizᵗ de etate quinq̃ decem annorem.
    " In cujus rei testimoñ tam prd' commissionarii quam juratores predicti
huic Inquisitioni sigilla sua apposuerunt, die et anno prius supra script'.
                                Exʳ p Wᵐ MARWOOD,
                                    " Deptˢ. R. R."

    The character of Sir Owen MacCarthy has been sketched
in few words by a shrewd observer of men, the veteran
St. Leger, whose business it was to watch, and report upon
his conduct. He informed his Government that, "though
specious in shew, he was a very hypocrite, being badly bent,
and a notorious Papist, and who would be in rebellion if he
dared." We shall find, when death transferred the white rod
of his chieftainship to other, feebler, and far worse hands,
that the chroniclers of Carbery spoke of him in very different language. Such as he was, however, Sir Owen succeeded his brother, and his very first act, viz., that of his
Inauguration, brought upon him a scowl of ill-humour from
the authorities of Munster. Succession by Tanistry was a
custom in especial disfavour with the English Government;
and the ceremonies attending the election of the chiefs, like
many of the rights inherent in their office, were pronounced
illegal, and an usurpation of the Queen's authority, " to whom
alone it belonged to appoint to any dignity or office within
the realm." But by the Septs themselves these ceremonies
were considered of as much importance as the election; indeed, without them the election was ineffective. In a note
to the pedigree of the O'Mahonys at Lambeth, Carewe
writes:—

    " O'Mahon's country doeth follow the ancient Tanist law of Ireland;
and unto whom Mac Carthy Reagh shall give a white rod, he is O'Mahon,
or Lord of the Country; but the giving of the rod avails nothing except
he be chosen by the followers, nor yet the election without the rod."

    The MacCarthy Reagh was inaugurated with the same
ceremonial with which he inaugurated the O'Mahon and other
dependent chiefs. There was a grievance attached to this,
and it did not escape the keen eyes of the Cork juries, who
presented—

    " That when any Lord or Gentleman of the Irishry within this county,
is made Lord or Captain of his name or kindredtie, he taketh of every inhabitant, freeholder, and tenant under him, a cow to be paid for erecting a
rod in that name."

    Could Sir Owen have followed his own inclinations, there
is little doubt but that he would have at once transferred

every soldier he maintained, every follower he possessed,
from the Queen to the rebel Earl of Desmond; but his castles
were garrisoned, his country filled with English soldiers, so
that he had little choice left him of the part he must take, or
at least countenance, till the troubles should be ended; hence,
he contented himself with taking careful note of the charges
for "cess, and maintenance of the Queen's troops," to which
his country was subjected, to be presented for payment, or
compensation, when opportunity should be fitting; and allowed
his young nephew, a boy of fifteen, to take the command of
the followers that had been his father's.

As a minor, Florence legally fell under the guardianship
of Sir William Drury. In ordinary circumstances, a ward of
his condition would either have been domesticated in the
family of his guardian, or sent to Dublin, or England, or elsewhere, under the eyes of the Government, for his education;
and it is not a little remarkable that so young a lad should
have been permitted to live amongst his own people, by whom
many essentials of English education were held in slight
esteem. It was, perhaps, thought that his association with
English officers would be the surest means of attaching him
to the cause in which his father had endeavoured to train
him. His whole life was certainly affected by this early
companionship. Amongst these young soldiers were some,
who, by their own conduct in after life, added renown to
names already illustrious; there were others so deeply tainted
with the vices of the detestable school which sent them to
Ireland to enrich or distinguish themselves by any means,
that they became men of intrigue, loose in their loyalty, and
made wreck of name and fame alike. How Florence served
the Queen during the whole of the rebellion that was raging
at the time when he assumed the command of the Carbery
forces, we shall eventually see in his own words. The last
desperate struggles of the Earl of Desmond tested his activity
and fidelity, and, in all probability, his diplomatic ingenuity
also: for the Earl of Clancar, the head of his house, was
drifting on to ruin almost as certainly as his brother-in-law
of Desmond. Justly an object of suspicion to the Government, his wife and only son had long since been seized as
pledges for his behaviour; nothing could be more deplorable
than his own position, and that of the country which he so
ill governed. Desmond had become a vast wilderness; the
tenants and freeholders, harassed alike by friend and foe,
were disgusted with the indecision of their Lord, which deprived them of the excitement of open action, whilst it left

them a prey to the fugitives who took shelter amongst them, and to the troops who pursued them; yet it is not to be supposed that they, or their kinsmen of Carbery, could wish to see the head of their race involved in the destruction which was coming swiftly over the Earl of Desmond; nor can it be imagined that there were wanting amongst the Irish allies of the Government, men willing to offer him a word of counsel in season. So utterly hopeless had become, at last, the condition of the unfortunate Desmond, that a man of greater courage, of higher principles than Donal Earl of Clancar, might have thought it time to take steps to sever himself from his falling relative, and abandon him to his evil fortunes. With this object, and, doubtless, under the guidance of a head shrewder than his own, he-wrote in plaintive wise a letter to the Queen, which is not without dignity and pathos :—

"1583. *May 28th.* THE EARL OF CLANCAR *to* QUEEN ELIZABETH.

"After moste humble duetie remembred, may yt please your most Excellent Mātie, whereas I Daniell (whom your Princely goodnes created Erle of Clancarthie) considering how farr I am bounde to y^r Highnes (whose long life, prosperous raigne, and happie estate I have alwayes, and doe most humbly and hartely wishe and pray for) unfainedly served against the unnaturall traitors, to the uttermoste of my power, ptely wth Sir John Parrott (then Lord President of Mounster) at the taking of Castlemaing, and all times els when occasion was given, nevertheles I (being suspected wthout cause, uppon the countrys enormities) was driven, not only to maintaine my wife twoe yeares at Cork as a pledge, but also to send my sonn from scoole to the Castle of Dublin, remaining there nowe the space of three yeares, without learning, to my intollerable grief and hindrance. Besides that I sustained many wrongs by the late Capteine Zouche, Capteine Smithe, and others (ptely mencioned in a note here inclosed) by meanes whereof I am greivouslie combred on every side; for the traitors doe not not spare me; the soldiers in like case doe take what they can finde; alleadging that it is better for them so to doe then to leave it for the traytors: but Moste Gracious and Soveraigne Lady, I am sure it happeneth farr contrary to your Highnes upright pleasure, and moste myld disposition, that they (under culloure of Desmond), shoulde seeke my destruction, as yf they had bene mortall enemyes; which imboldeth me the rather moste humblie to beseche your Excellent Matie (of your pity towardes the oppressed) to have compassion of me in reforming these wrongfull abuses, and uppon continuance of my trueth, (wch alwayes hitherto hath bene performed) to vouchesafe thenlargement of my sonn, that the childe may be the better reduced in his tender yeares to acknowledge his duty towardes God, and loyalty to your Highnes, whom I beseche thAlmighty to prosper in all wisdom and understanding, to the comeforte of your true and faithfull subjects, and suppression of your enemies. Thus (beseeching your Highness to perdon the necessity of my boldnes) I moste humbly take leave.

"From Clonmell the 28th of Maij 1583.
Your Highnes moste loyall subiect
"DANYELL CLANCARTHYE."

The Earl wrote at the same time to Ormond, then Lieutenant-General of her Majesty's forces, to explain his helpless
condition, and to request that troops might be sent into his
country to expel his unfortunate brother-in-law, and to rescue
from final ruin the followers whom his own misrule had
brought to extremity. These letters were written not a day
too soon; they were, however, effective, and he had the
affliction to see English captains take possession of his
country, and the consolation of knowing that he had saved
himself by his timely abandonment of his relative! The last
throes of the death-struggle of the Earl of Desmond, the
"Ingens rebellibus Exemplar," are best described in the
words of the stern man whose perseverance at last hunted
him, and a single faithful follower, to the cabin beside the
Maing, where the sword of a wretched kerne spilled the blood
of this great Geraldine.

1583. *April 42th.* ORMOND *to the* QUEEN.

"There have been six score traitors put to the sword, and executed
since my coming. Desmond being long since fled over the mountaine into
Kerrye, is nowe gon to seke relife by suche spoiles as he can take from the
Erle of Clancartie (his brother-in-law), Capt^en Barkley having followed
him thether to ayde th Erle of Clancartie. I have sent Sir Cormok
McTeig and Sir William Stanley towards Castlemaing, to lye for him
therabout (if, in the mean tyme, they mete him not). Myself wth my
horsemen intend to lye out, this side the mountaine, for him. I finde
your Majestie's opinion provethe true, for sins I kept him from the counties
of Waterford and Tipprary his men have bene forced many tymes to eat
horses and caren; and being nowe kept from cowes in the mountains of
Desmond, famyn will destroy them, as daily hit dothe. God send them
all the plague I wish them, and blesse your Majesty wth a moste happy
raigne."
"Cork 24th April, 1583.
"THO^s ORMOND & OSS."

1583. *Nov. 15th.* ORMOND *to the* PRIVY COUNCIL.

"In my way nowe from Dublin I receved l^res of the killing of the
traitors Gorehe, McSwiny (Capten of Galloglass) the onely man that relived
th Erle of Desmond in his extreme misery; and the next day after my coming hither to Kilkenny, I receved certaine word that Donill McImorier-
taghe (of whom, at my last being in Kerry, I toke assuraunce to sarve
against Desmond), being accompanied with 25 kerne of his owne sept, and
6 of the ward of Castlemaigne, the 11th of this moneth at night, assaulted
th Erle in his cabban, in a place called Glaneguicntye nere the river of the
Maigne, and slew him, whose heade I have sent for, and appointed his
boddy to be hanged up in chaines at Cork.
"From Kilkenny 15 Novr 1583.
"THO^s ORMOND ET OSS."

Within a fortnight from the date of this letter the great rebellion which had wasted Munster for eight years, was concluded; its chief had fallen; and Ormond, as if the simple tidings would be too good to be credible in England, discovered a means of removing all doubt from the mind of the Queen; he wrote—

ORMOND *to* WALSINGHAM.

" I do send Her Highnes (for profe of the good successe of the service, and the happy ende thereof) by this berrer, the principall traitor Desmond's heade, as the best token of the same, and profe of my faithfull service and travaile ; whearby her charges may be deminished, as to her princelie pleasure shalbe thought meete
"Novr 28^h 1583.
"THOMAS ORMŌD ET OSS."

Never since the time of Miles de Cogan, Robert Fitzstephen, and Philip de Braos,—the undertakers of their day, —had there been such a feast for the vultures, such spoil for the undertakers of Elizabeth! Half a million and more of acres lapsed, by English law, to the Crown, by the death of a rebel to whom, by law, they had never belonged! There was, indeed, a feeble voice raised, a cry that had been heard years before, from a man urging, what everybody knew, that the Palatinate of the Geraldines was by inheritance *his;* that the dainty token sent by Ormond to the Queen had worn a coronet usurped from an elder brother! but that voice was drowned amidst the shrieks, and the clangour of wings of the ravenous birds that were fighting over their prey. Had the claimant, Sir Thomas of Desmond, been himself a mart of land, he would assuredly have fallen to the lot of Raleigh or Barkely, Phyton or Courtney, Popham or Herbert, or others of that fortunate company! A few years after the division of the lands forfeited by the Earl of Desmond, a return was called for by the Government, of the various Seignories in the hands of these undertakers, with the amount of rent paid for them to the Queen, and the number of people they had placed upon their lands. The list was made by Sir Edward Phyton, himself a fortunate possessor of a large tract of country, and by the Attorney-General, Sir John Popham, who, with his son-in-law, had imported labourers and farm implements *before securing his grant,* and then had the mortification to find that "there was no room for him," and had been compelled to send back his yeomen to Wiltshire and Somersetshire. We shall meet with him again hereafter, making another attempt to introduce his Penates and rural deities into Munster, invading certain carucates of Carbery belonging to Florence MacCarthy, and exerting his powerful legal influence to ruin the man whom he failed to plunder.

"This was the relation and state of English in Munster given to Her Majesty's Attorney-General (Sir John Popham) and Sir Edward Phyton the last summer, and sithence—

TABLE OF UNDERTAKERS IN FEBR^r., 1589.

In Kerry and Desmond at Eight Pence an Acre.

	Acres.	People.	Rent.
Sir Valentine Browne....	6000	20	£100
Sir Edwd Denny	6000	„	100
Sir William Herbert and } Sir Charles Herbert }	18000	„	300

Conelogh [Connilloe] at 4 pence the Acre.

Mr. Trencher	12000	37	150
Sir Willm Courtney	12000	„	150
Mr. Oughtread....	12000	22	150
Mr. Billingsby	12000	137	150
Sir Edwd Barkley	12000	„	150

Cork at one penny the Acre.

Hugh Cuffe	12000	74	66 13 4
Arthur Hyde	6000	24	23 6 8
Phaane Beacher	12000	12	66 13 4
Hugh Worthe	12000	„	66 13 4
Sir Warham St Leger, and } Sir Richd Grynfield }	12000	„	33 6 8
Arthur Robyns....	4000	„	22 4 5
George Robynson	4000	12	22 4 5
Mr. Read	3000	„	16 14 4

Limerick at 2^d. ob. (2½).
Tipperary and Waterford at 1^d. q^r. (1^d¼).

Sir Edward Phyton, and Rich^d } Bould, and Thos Preston }	11000	60	80
Richd Phyton and } Alex^r Phyton }	2000	20	
The Earl of Uremont (Ormond) } (he entered but lately) }	3000	„	16 13 4
Thomas Fleetwood	3000	22	16 13 4
Marmaduke Redman, but now } dispossessed by Patrick Con- } don. His petition is with } Mr. Secretary }	3000	22	16 13 4
Sir Walter Raleigh and } his associates }	36000		
My Lord Chancellor	6000	200	33 6 8

C

"Mr. Attorney (Popham), Mr. Edward Rogers (Popham's son-in-law), and Mr. Warre have had above sixty Englishmen there these two years, and now for want of land are driven to call them home again; besides there were divers women and servants. Also Sir Warham St. Leger, Sir Walter Raleigh, Sir Edwd Denny, Sir William Herbert, Sir Thomas Norreys, Sir George Bourchier, Sir Edwd Barclay, Denzill Hollis, Arthur Robyns, and Mr. Read have no English people numbered by us, because we have not been informed of them.

"Also that the Rent of Sir Walter Raleigh, Sir Edwd Denny, Denzill Hollis, and Rich^d and Alex^r Phyton are not rated, because we know them not.

"Note also, the chargeable lands are not valued, nor many other parcels lying dispersed.

" E. PHYTON.
" J. POPHAM.

"People, 661.
" £1674 14 10."

Before the patents were signed for this list of grants,— before the country which the Geraldines had held for nearly four centuries was, by a magnificent application of Sir Henry Sidney's "fixed principle," dispersed amongst English subjects,—a young man presented himself at the court of Elizabeth to claim a simple act of justice. It was James Fitzgerald, the eldest son of Sir Thomas of Desmond, well enough known, a few years later, as James Fitz Thomas, or the Sougaun Earl. His father had long ago resigned himself to the obscurity of private life, and the usurpation of his birthright; but this youth, with the chivalrous daring of his race, and the vernal simplicity of his years, came to plead against the huge iniquity of this confiscation. He informed the Queen, what the Queen knew already as well as he did, that his father was the eldest son of James, the fifteenth Earl of Desmond; that the traitor whose headless body was waving upon the Cork gibbet, had been the usurper of his brother's rights before he was a rebel: that the Queen could not by any law, English or Irish, inherit estates from a man who legally possessed none; that the Earldom granted by Edward III. to the eldest sons in succession could not be forfeited by the rebellion of a younger brother, to whom it belonged not; nor the blood of an innocent man be attainted because a cadet of his family had been a traitor. The reply he received to this fanciful suit will be given later in his own words; the patents were signed for the undertakers, and James Fitz-Thomas returned to his native land to abide his time.

And now the bill of charges which, it has been mentioned, Sir Owen MacCarthy had kept with admirable exactness, during the past years of trouble, failed not to find its way to the notice of her Majesty. We lay it before the reader, for it will give him some idea of the wealth of an Irish chieftain, and the resources of an Irish country, in which Sir Henry Sidney "found more idle vagabonds kept than good cattle bred."

1583. *July 25th.* SIR OWEN MAC CARTHY REAGH *to* HER MAJESTY.

"My moste humble and bounden duetie to yor Excellent Majestie premissed. I thought it goode to signifie unto yor Highnes whate I and my contrey have employd for the better furtherance of yor Majesties service during the rebellion in Mounster, the particulers wherof appeareth in a schedule herein inclosed ; and as Ceptaine Barkley may certifie the same unto yor M$_a$^{tie}, who behaued himselfe verie well in the said contrey ; not doubting but yor Highnes (according your accustomed bountie) will haue consideracion of the same, moste humby beseching your royall Majestie to grant unto me suche resonable requests as mine agents will pticulerly declare to yor Highnes on my behalf ; and thus (with all due reverence) I moste humbly take my leave. At Your M$_a$^{ties} citie of Cork the 25th of July, 1583.
 "Yo^r Highnes' Faithful Subiect,
 "OWEN CARTY."

A *briefe selection* of suche payments as Sir Owen McCarthy Knight and his countrey of Caribrie in the Countie of Cork haue paid for the furtherance of Her M$_a$^{ties} Service sence the first of the Rebelion of James Fitz Mores.

In primes. In the tyme of the Governement of Sir John Perot Lord psident of Mounster, for the better mainteynance of Hir M$_a$^{ties} Garisons being then here, paid in byfs, and cesse taken upp of the said countrey, the som of a thousand Pounds st^g.
 Item, after to the Earle of Ormonde, being then L. Genl of Mounster, in money and byfs taken upp of the said contrey, the sum of £700 st^g.
 Item, to Sir William Drury L. psident of Mounster for cesse of 16 horsmen, being towe yeares in the said contrey, viz. to every horsman 5^s. st. per diem, amountith to the som of £1147 st^g.
 Item, more to the said Sr William in money towards Hir M$_a$^{ties} charges, and to be released of the cesse of the said horsmen £1000 st^g.
 Item, the said Sir Owen McCartie paid to Patrick Shearlock of Waterford for the nomber of thrie score kerne cessed upon his said contrey £50.
 Item, besedes the pmisses the said Sir Owen (of his owne goode will) for the better furtherance of Hir M$_a$^{ties} Service, have kept in his contrey aforesaid sence the begynning of the rebellion of the Earle of Desmond 100 Englishe soldiers footmen, and paid there Capteyns yearly £1200 vizt.

Item to Capteyn William Apsley	....	....	....	£1200
Item to Capteyn Fenton	....	....	....	1200
Item to Capteyn Barkley	....	....	....	1200
The totall Som amounteth to....	....	....	....	£7497

For the distending of this document, the chieftain of
c 2

Carbery was doubtless indebted to the skill of his lawyer; a little later the reader will meet with a genuine specimen of Sir Owen's own unaided style of letter writing.

From the first outbreak of the Desmond rebellion, Florence served with the royal forces. At its close, at the age of twenty, with a sound reputation for loyalty, if for little else, he repaired to the English court. Of his personal appearance at this time no notice has reached us, except that he was taller by the head and shoulders than most men, but whether favoured by nature in form and countenance, or not, it is certain that he possessed in an eminent degree a power of winning the good-will of all to whom he had access.

On his arrival in England he was at once taken by the hand by Lord Burghley and presented to the Queen, "who most graciously and bountifully rewarded him, presenting him at once with a gift of a thousand marks, and settling on him an annuity of two hundred marks." In the saloons of the minister he met daily the companions of his Munster campaigns; and had it pleased him, he might have turned away his thoughts from the contentions of his native land, and, living in the radiance of court favour, have aspired to as lofty fortunes as the Queen had bestowed upon any of his countrymen. Could he have allied himself with an English heart to the policy of Lord Burghley, and brought his able mind, and great influence, to aid in the subjugation of Ireland, it would have been impossible for him to miss a career of safe distinction. But whatever dreams his ambition might indulge in, certainly none of them were to arrive at greatness by making himself a model of loyalty, or a champion of English policy in his native country. There were moments in his career when he appeared to falter in a course of a very opposite nature, and to lend himself for a while to the purposes of the governors of Munster; but it will be found that such conduct was traceable to a motive very different from attachment to England.

For four or five years little attention, certainly little jealousy, seems to have been bestowed upon Florence. He went and came unobserved between Carbery and London. When in Munster, he was in frequent attendance on the Vice-President; and when in London, at the court. His position was not one of sufficient mark to excite any peculiar vigilance as to his mode of life; he had not succeeded in the Captaincy of Carbery, and therefore, though the inheritor of vast estates, he was of no political importance. A few years later the keenest eyes of Munster watched his slightest movement,

and then it was discovered that "he had long affected the
company of Spaniards, and had learned their language; that
he had so won upon the affections of the old Lord de Courcy
as to obtain from that nobleman vast portions of his lands, and
especially the fortress of Down M'Patrick (the Old Head of
Kinsale), which commanded the harbour of Kinsale, and
mostly tending towards Spain." But a proceeding which
chiefly attracted the alarm of the Munster Government was
a certain negotiation of Florence relative to the succession of
Carbery. Sir Henry Sidney had written to the Privy Council
that "*his fixed principle was the dissipation of the great lordships*; to distribute the lands, if among English, the better;
if not, yet that they be dissipated."

To this *fixed principle* the barbarous usage of Tanistry,
" not deserving the name of law," was in direct opposition;
and to the abolition of this usage the utmost endeavours of
the Government were directed. It was not, however, attempted by violence; a statute, merely permissive, invited
the great Lords to surrender their countries to the Queen, and
receive them back by Letters Patent, to hold, at a nominal
rent, *by English tenure*; that is, with succession by lineal
descent, and, in failure of male heirs, revertible to the Crown.
Some Irish chieftains, desirous of securing the succession of
their Captaincies to their sons, had fallen in with this English
offer. An ancestor of the MacCarthy Reagh had done so;
and so also, more recently, had the Earl of Clancar, when he
consented to exchange for his Peerage the honoured title of
his forefathers, that, namely, of MacCarthy Mor. This interruption of the national usage seldom extended beyond one
generation: the brothers, as of immemorial usage, stepped
into the vacancy caused by the demise of the Chief; and the
son, in spite of his Letters Patent, was put aside, to wait till,
in the course of nature, his turn should come for the succession. Sir Donogh, the father of Florence, had succeeded to
his elder brother, although that elder brother had left sons;
he was in turn succeeded by Sir Owen MacCarthy; and Sir
Owen was aware that his sons were fated not to succeed him.
The heir of Carbery was Donal, called na-Pipy; and the heir
to Donal was, not Donal's son, nor a son of Sir Owen, but
Florence, the son of Sir Donogh, the elder brother of Sir
Owen.

About the time that Sir Owen sent in his bill of charges
to the Government, it was known that he was about to repair
to court; Donal-na-Pipy instantly took the alarm; he well
knew that Sir Owen had little love for him, and he naturally

imagined that the purpose of this visit was the surrender of his lands, and the resuming them to hold by English tenure. He at once invited a family meeting on the subject, the result of which was, that Sir Owen consented to leave matters as they were, on the condition that Donal would pledge himself, nay, bind himself, in securities of £10,000, to Florence, that he would take no steps to divert the succession from him. We shall see in what light this family compact was afterwards misrepresented to Florence's prejudice; and his own account of the transaction.

At the time of the surrender of his lands to Queen Elizabeth, and resuming them by Letters Patent, the Earl of Clancar had no brothers to dispute the succession. An only son stood in the way of extinction of the elder branch of the MacCarthys, and the Earl may have thought that this surrender, and the acceptance of an English Earldom in lieu of his hereditary title, was a lighter punishment for a life of disloyalty, than he might have expected: the letter written by him, towards the close of the Desmond rebellion, has shown us that his son was then living in Dublin Castle, a pledge for the good behaviour of the father. All that we know further of the brief career of this youth is contained in the following despatches :—

1584. *July* 9*th.* *From* TREASURER WALLOP *to* Sir F. WALSINGHAM.

"My Lo. Deputie hath sent the Earls of Desmond and Clancarty their sonnes to the Court by two of my men, whom I beseeche you to discharge of them as sone as they come to the Court wth them."

1584. *Nov.* 28*th.* WATERHOUSE *to* WALSINGHAM.

"The two other letters are from the Earl of Clanrickarde ; the one, as I learn (both from himselfe and Sir Richard), is to exhort his son, the Baron of Dunkellin, to beware of such advice as hath been given to the young Baron of Valentia, for his undutiful *departure into France.*"

1585. *January* 19*th.*

" I have no other newes besydes those I sent you lately, save that one Barry, who was the enticer and conveyer away of the Lord of Valentia from here, is of late taken by the Earl of Glencarre, who had intelligence of his coming over into the country, disguised like a beggar, to see how he could procure some relief for the young Lord. I have given order to have him safely sent hither unto me : when I have him, I will learn of him what I may.

" From the Castle of Dublin."

1585. *Feb.* 12. NICHOLAS SKIDDIE *to* WALSINGHAM.

"R^t hon. : My humble and most bonden duty premised. Finding this bearer, my cousin, James Meagher, repairing towards the Court, I thought good to write your Honor these few lines, declaring that William Barry, the man that brought the Earl of Clancarre's son into France, is apprehended in Desmond, and now brought to Cork. I offered to bring him to your Honor, wherein I could not prevail, by reason that my Lo. Deputie did write for him ; and it is meant that the said Barry shall be sent to Dublin."

Of this boyish escapade, and of the truly Irish device of Barry, we hear no more. It appears that after the death of the Earl of Desmond, the young Valentia had been sent to England, detained there a very short time, sent back to Dublin Castle, and thence, with or without the consent of his father, spirited away to France.

Neither his subsequent adventures, nor his death, which must have taken place within a few months of this last date, receive any notice from the correspondents of the English Minister.

It would seem that the Earl found means to persuade the Irish authorities that he had had no part in the singular frolic of his son and heir ; and Florence MacCarthy had not yet earned the credit of suggesting every irregularity committed by any of his name and race ; for we find, from the " Annals of the Four Masters," *sub anno*, that at this precise period the Earl, Florence, and his uncle and cousins, were summoned to the Parliament held at Dublin by Sir John Perrott in 1585.

" Annals of the Four Masters," An. 1585. Translation by Dr. O'Donovan. " To this Parliament repaired some of the Chiefs of the descendants of Eoghan More, with their dependents, namely MacCarthy More,* (Donell, the son of Douell, son of Cormac Ladrach), MacCarthy Cairbreach (Owen, son of Donnell, son of Fineen, son of Donnell, son of Dermotan-Duna), and the sons of his two brothers, namely, Donnell, son of Cormac-na-h'aine, and Fineen (Florence), the son of Donogh."

By the terms of the Earl's surrender, his lands must at his demise, failing male issue, lapse to the Queen. He had indeed a daughter, and it was presumable that on her marriage, with the Queen's approbation, she would receive the same grant that had been made to him and his son at the time of his creation.

The English policy, " the fixed principle," was indeed *the dissipation of the great countries;* but even the inventor of this great engine of state policy had left on record a warning " that it was perilous, and bred such a number of inconve-

* MacCarthy More. He is entered in the list next after "The Earle of Tomond " as " The Earle of Clancare," that being an Anglicised abbreviation of "Clann Carthia," and *not* Glencare, the vale of the river Carthach, in the county of Kerry, as ignorantly assumed by most Anglo-Irish writers.—Dr. O'D.

niences as could hardly be cured." Whatever Elizabeth might choose to do with the heiress and her lands, might be matter of conjecture; what she would *not* do, was a perfect certainty: she would *not* allow the extensive country of the Earl to fall into the hands of any other Irish Chief, and thus augment estates which it was her chief object to break up.

It would seem that upon the death of his son, and in the uncertainty of what might befall his estates after his own demise, the Earl no longer placed any restraint upon his extravagance. The English undertakers had introduced to his notice the convenience of raising money upon his lands by mortgage, and into this ready way of supplying the requirements of an unbounded licentiousness and unthrift, the Earl plunged headlong. The same recklessness that characterized his political conduct prevailed in his money transactions. There was a gentleman of the name of Browne, originally from Lancashire, who had served the Irish Government in various capacities, but chiefly as a surveyor of lands, to which the Queen, on one pretext or another, made claim. In an evil hour for his own peace, he made the acquaintance of the Earl of Clancar, and was induced to lend him money. Of the recklessness of the Earl, the reader may form an idea from the fact, that for the loan of three several sums of £421 1s. 2d., £121 13s. 3d., and £80, he made over to the lender his lands at Molahiff, of the yearly value of £1,000. These lands were not, as in cases of ordinary mortgage, mere security for the money lent, but, in addition, their entire yearly proceeds were made over to the lender in lieu of any stated interest, until the Earl should repay the original sums, which, unfortunately, there was expressly reserved to him the right of doing. A day came when all the lands of the Earl passed into other hands; repayment of this loan was then offered; it was refused! and then began a grand legal contest for the possession of these lands—which had grown into a signory—destined to endure nearly half a century.

Whatever consequences might arise from these ruinous modes of supplying his wants, they were in the obscurity of the distant future; and the Earl was prepared to sell more than his lands for money. There was another person who, for motives far different from the motives of Sir Valentine Browne, dealt with the Earl in his traffic of mortgages. Florence MacCarthy inherited, as we have seen, great wealth; and, before the attention of the President of Munster had been directed to his private transactions, he had possessed himself, by mortgage also, of the principal fortresses of the

Earl's country, especially of Castle Lough, one of the three great mansions, "the owner of which, if a MacCarthy, might always look to be MacCarthy More."

Thus stood matters in the year 1587, when the first rumour was heard of the Earl's intention "to prefer his daughter in marriage."

CHAPTER II.

THAT the Queen had a right to control the marriage of the heiress of MacCarthy Mor, seems to have been a fixed conviction in the minds of all men—who had no concern in the matter —that she had at any time singled out any individual by name, to whom she would *not* consent to see her united, is scarcely probable; it is, however, certain that no Englishman would have dared to seek her hand without previously securing the consent of her Majesty. The rumour of the Earl's intention to seek a fitting match for his daughter, naturally attracted the notice of the authorities in Munster; and Sir Warham St. Leger suggested to Sir Thomas Norreys, then Vice-President of Munster, to make offer for the hand of the young lady; promising all his influence to obtain for him, not only the Queen's consent, but a grant of succession to the Earl's country. Sir Thomas at first "entertained the idea with some favour, but, after some little trouble taken, he in the end misliked of it." Sir Valentine Browne was at this time seated at Molahiff, in the centre of the Earl's country: the capabilities of the desolate wilderness around him were known better to him than to any man; and, that dreams of corn-fields and orchards spreading over that improvable waste, of peaceful, well-clad, hard-working English yeomen enlivening his landscape, should present themselves to the mind of the Surveyor, is not surprising. He had a son, also, for whose "preferment in marriage" he was solicitous; and the settlement of this son may well have connected itself, in his imagination, with those other pleasing dreams of civilizing the land in which he had cast his lot.

He stood well with the authorities of his own province, though not so well as he fancied; he had some credit at court, though that also he overrated; but he had influence in one quarter concerning which he could make no mistake: he resolved to seek for his son Nicholas the prize which Sir Thomas Norreys had timorously relinquished. Sir Valentine knew the Earl thoroughly; and his dealing with him was direct, and practical. It was presently rumoured abroad " that the Earl had agreed, *for money*, to give his daughter in marriage to Mr. Nicholas Browne!" it was also asserted that her Majesty's consent had been obtained; and, what was of more importance, the consent, *also for money*, of the great officers of the Earl! Bitter was the humiliation, fierce the wrath, united and resolute the protest, of the Chieftains of the entire Sept, when the tale of this unworthy traffic reached them! The indignation even of the poor oppressed Countess of Clancar was raised.

"As there is nothing," wrote Sir Warham St. Leger, "that the Irishe more esteme then the nobilitie of bloud, preferringe it farre before eyther vertue or wealth, so abhorre they nothinge more then disparagement, more odious unto them then death."

The pedigree of Browne is preserved at Lambeth, in the collections of Carewe; and Lord Burghley, if he ever saw the document, must have felt some sympathy with this cry of shame, and abhorrence from a Royal Sept. All this emotion was, however, unnecessary: the dignity of the united blood of the Geraldines and of MacCarthy Mor was in no danger of attaint. Whatever had been the early nature of this transaction, the issue was a masterpiece of levity on the part of the Earl, and of address in another individual whose name had not hitherto been connected with it. The Countess, perhaps even her daughter, the Vice-President of Munster, the shrewd St. Leger, Browne and his son, Burghley, and the Queen, were alike the sport of a mind, the fertility of whose invention was at that time little suspected. Florence Mac-Carthy was then "at the court;" removed from all suspicion of complicity either in the bargain of the Earl, or the opposition of the Sept. Thither, too, the Earl repaired, possibly to avoid the storm which he had raised. It would almost pass credibility that he should have so far compromised himself with the Brownes, as to permit them to make application for the Queen's consent, and yet never seriously have intended to allow this marriage at all! It is difficult, however, to believe but that such was the case : for when all the details of this curious transaction came to light, it was found that a regular marriage contract, legally drawn up, sealed and witnessed, had been signed by the Earl, by which nearly the whole of his country, including—with a malicious specialty —the lands of Molahiff, were settled on his daughter on her marriage.

Shortly after the Earl's arrival in London, Florence quitted the Court, and returned to Ireland. He presented himself to the Vice-President of Munster, Sir Thomas Norreys, and, with the aspect of an injured man, complained of the conduct of the Earl towards him. He exhibited documents relative to various loans made by him on security of the Earl's lands, and declared that the Earl had broken faith with him and forfeited those securities. The benefit of these forfeitures he offered to make over to Sir Thomas; but finding that he was not willing to take advantage of the offer, he requested from him letters of authority into Desmond, to enable him to take possession of the lands legally his security. The letters were given, and he took his departure. A few days later, Munster was startled by the intelligence that the great heiress of MacCarthy Mor was married to her kinsman Florence ! The details of this romantic story will be best told in the words of Sir Warham St. Leger, to whose lot it fell, in the temporary absence of the Vice-President, to send the unwelcome tale to England. There now burst suddenly upon the mind of this far-sighted statesman the full magnitude of the ambition of Florence: and in order that the Queen might see it as clearly as he saw it, he did not content himself with the recital of "the contemptuous action," but laid a detailed statement before her of all the consequences to be dreaded from this alliance. Even this he thought insufficient, and composed an elaborate treatise on the state of the province, which, in the form of three Tracts, were sent for the grave considera- tion of the Lords of the Privy Council. These documents were forwarded, the letter on the 14th of May, the first moment that the news reached him, and the Tracts followed it with all speed.

Sir Warham St. Leger has, in the following documents, furnished us incidentally with a considerable portion of the history of the families of the South of Ireland, which Mr. O'Conor so much desired. Two or three facts concerning Florence are well worthy of note. "He was much embrased in his countrie, and in the whole province ! he was fervent in the old religion ! and he was during seven or eight years much addicted to the company of Spaniards !" It is very curious that there should have been "company of Spaniards" for him to frequent: we are left to conjecture whether these Spaniards were merchants or ecclesiastics, or gentlemen who had accompanied Philip into England in the last reign; or spies employed by the Spanish Government to report on the sincerity, and actual resources of the great Irish chiefs, who were in constant treaty for aid of arms and money to enable them to continue their opposition to the Queen's government. Of whatever denomination they might be, the circumstance

of their existence in Cork, in any considerable number, is
unexpected, and difficult to account for. Respecting Florence's
designs on the succession to Carbery after Sir Owen's death,
St. Leger needlessly alarmed himself. Donal-na-Pipy stood
before him by usage of Tanistry, and, as we shall see, it was
Donal, not Florence, who contemplated turning the succession
from its lawful course.

"1588. *May* 14. *From* SIR WARHAM ST. LEGER *to the* LORDS
OF HER MAT⁸ PRIVY COUNCIL.

*The Marriage of Florence Mac Carthy with the Earl of Clancar's
Daughter.*

"Certaine perticuler matters to be imparted to the Queene's
Moste Excellent Ma'tie.

" Florence, alis Fynan Mackkertie, hath latelie espoused
the onlie daughter and child legittimate of the Earle of Clankertie, by a cunning practise contrived betweene yᵉ Countesse,
mother to the said childe, and the said Fynan, without her
husband's consent, as yt is here given out by those that be
favourers of that action (howe likelie the same ys to be treue,
that a woman durste adventure to make such a match withoute her husbandes knowledge, I referr to her Ma'tie's deepe
conceipte) ; for my owne parte, I do thinke in my conscyence
yt is a secret practyse betweene the Earle and his wyfe; and
the matter concluded in Englande before Phineans cominge
thence, entendinge thereby to prevente the bestowinge of
her by Her Highnes dyrections, and soe ys the generall op-
pynion of sundrie of her good and sounde subiects here, that
are jelyous of the match as far forthe as myselfe.

" The Perills that may accrue by the match are these,
vizᵗ.:—1st. The saied Florence, alias Fynian, is dyscended
of the Doughter of Morrys of Desmonde, uncle of the' late
wicked Earle of Desmonde, cousyn germain to James Fytz
Morrys sonne nowe in Spayne, and likewise to Morrys of
Desmonde, Traytor, also in Spaine.

" 2d. He is alsoe cosyn germain to him that is nowe Lo: of
Muskerye, whoe is sonne to the said Fynian's mother's syster.

" 3d. He is also cousyn germain to the L. Rotche that
now is, whoe haith married the syster of the saied Fynian's
mother ; by which kyndred he is stronglie allyed.

" 4th. He is alsoe lyke, after the decease of Sir Owen
Makertie, whoe is a man in yeares, and growne latelie sicklie,
and thereby not likelie to lyve manye yeares, to have by

Tanyshipp the goverment of the countrie of Carburye; unlesse he be prevented thereof by Her Ma'tie's assystinge
Donell Mack Kertie, whoe in right ought by Tanyshipp to
have the goverment of Carburie before him, in as much as
he cometh of the elder brother of the Macke Kerties of Carburye, and besides that his tytle of Tanyshipp, he ought to
have the countrie before Finian, in so much as he sheweth a
Pattente from Her Ma^{ts} predecessors, whoe graunted the
saied countrie to the heirs males of the Mack Kertie of Carburye, to hould the same by English Tenure; the which
Pattente the saied Donell now maketh chalendge unto, beinge
descended of the elder brother, and is in question with Sir
Owen Macke Kertie for the enioying the benefytt of the saied
Patente (much to the dyslike of the saied Sir Owen and
Finian, whoe join together againste the saied Donell). Notwthstanding the saied Sir Owen ys uncle to the said Donell
as well as to Finian, by the which yt is here generally
thought that the marke Sir Owen Mack Kertie and Fynian
shooteth at ys to dysappoynte Donell, and Finian to take
the place of the goverment of Carburye after Sir Owen's
deathe, by Tanyshipp; and then atcheavinge to that, together
withe the marriage of the Earle of Clancarties daughter, yf he
maye, by his frinds in Englande, wynne by his match to suc-
ceade the Earle of Clankertie, as heire unto his countrye;
howe perillous that maye be to make him soe greate, together
wth the allyaunces before recyted, and the allyaunce he is like
to have by this marryage, by which all the Clan Kerties and
there followers are to be at his devotion, I referr to her
Ma'ties deepe consideraçon what maye growe thereof, if he
should become undutyfull! of which, althoughe there be good
hope to the contrarie, yet what yll counsell maye doe, he
beinge greatly addicted to the brute sorte of those remote
pties, and his mother in lawe, whoe is the chief contryver of
this marriage, and whoe haith ben but a badd subiect unto
Her Highnes, may worke on him, I lykewise referr to Her
Ma'tie.

"5th. The yonge man is greatlie embrased in his countie,
as also in this provynce; he haith ben anye tyme this seven
or eight yeares greatlie addicted to learne the Spanysh tonge;
and haith ben verey desierous, synce I have known him, to
have the companye of Spanyerdes; the which tonge he haith
obteyned. He is fervente in the olde Relygion, without
which his mother in lawe woulde never have condyscended
to have matcht her daughter with him; and I verelye thinke
(yf it were duly examyned) he was marryed with a masse,

and not by suche iniunctions as be sett downe by Her Highnes;
nor yet had the lysence of the Bysshopp of this Dyocesse, to
marrie without lawfull Banes asked; for there were verey .
fewe either of Carburye or Desmonde that were at the marryage. Either Sir Owen O'Syllyvan, or O'Sullevan Moore, I
cannot tell whether one of them, was the onlye Gentleman
that were at the solempnisinge thereof. It was verey secretlie
done; and after the solempnizinge thereof (they thinckinge
that it shoulde not be knowne), they sent l^res to overtake a
messinger latelie sente from hence to the Earle of Clankertie,
whoe shoulde have ben stayed yf he had not ben gone to the
sea, before their messinger came to staye the former messinger.

" 6th. The waye to prevente this, their cunynge practyse,
is for Her Ma'tie to staye grauntynge the Earle of Clankerties enioyeing of his countrye to him, and to his heirs geñall,
and let him remayne as he doeth, whereby the countrie maye
returne unto Her Highnes disposicõn whensoever yt shall
please God to call him out of this lyfe (not leavinge yssue
male behinde him).

" 7th. Another meane to cutt this youth from growinge
to greate is for Her Ma'tie to allowe of Donell Mac Kerthies
Pattente graunted by her predecessors, yf the Pattente be
good, wherein Her Highnes shall not onlye doe Justyce, but
withall cutt of Finyan's growinge to be to greate (the which
is one of the greateste myscheives that doeth hurte in this her
realme,) for they have alreadye enough, and a great deall
more then they can well govern. In this my plaine wrytinge,
I humblie beseech Her Ma'tie to graunte me pardon, protestinge to God, I do not wryte thus muche for mallyce to anye
person, but onlye of mere zeall I professe to the safe Goverment of this Her Realme; for were yt not therefore, I coulde
wyshe the Gentleman as much good as anie he that loves
him beste. And so wyshinge all to fall out for the beste I
leave; with my prayer to God to sende Her Ma'tie longe lyfe,
with prosperous successe in all her doinges.

"From Corke, this 14th May, 1588.
" WARHAM SENT LEGER."

Endorsed—" Sir Warham St. Leger's declaration to Her
Majesty of the many inconveniences that may arise to the
state of Ireland by the late marriage of Florence MacCarthy
with the daughter and heir of the Earl of Clancar."

·*Extracted from the first of three Tracts sent to Lord Burleigh.*

" The Earle of Glyncarr, before Her Ma'tie created him

Earle, was by Inheritance Mc Cartie Moore; by the wch amonge the Irishe he was accounted the cheefest in this Province, as descended from them that before they weare subdued to the Crowne of England, weare the Kinges of the greater parte thereof; and at the tyme of his creaĉon, and surrender of his formĺ titles, he had, and ever synce claymeth under his juris-dicĉon and dominion *fourteene several countries*, beside som of lesse quantitie; most of them possessed by such as have de-scended out of his house; from every of wch he demandeth sondrie duties and services, whereof many are abolyshed by statute.

" The First is the countrey of Mc Donochoe (called Duallo), wch hath w^thin it thre other countreis. O'Chalachan's coun-trey, McAunlief's countrey, and O'Keit's countrey. He claymeth in these countreis the gevinge of the Rodd to the chieffe Lords at their first entrie, who by receivinge a whit wande at his handes, for wch they are to paie him a certen dutie, are therby declared from thenceforthe to be Lords of those countreis. He claymeth allso that they are to *rise out* wth him when he makes warre; to maintaine for him seaven and twentie Galleglasses, besides to finde him for a certen tyme, when he cometh to their countreis.

" The Second—the countrey of Muskerie, a very large countrey, wherin *five other* countreis are conteyned; he claym-eth of them *risinge out*, the keapinge of *thirtie galleglass*, and findinge of him for a certen tyme. The Lordes of this coun-trey, by takinge L^res Patents of the Kings of England, have exempted themsealves from him, as they affyrme.

" The Third countrey is O'Sulivan Moore's. It conteyneth two hundred ploughlandes. He claymeth there the geavinge of the Rodd, the findinge of Fiftie Gallyglasses, Risinge out, and in yearely spendinge the value of £20.

" The Fourth is O'Sulivan Beare's countrey, which contey-neth allso 160 ploughlands; he claymethe there Risinge out, the findinge of 50 Galleyglas, the geavinge of the Rodd, and to the value of £40 a yeare in spendings and refeccons.

" The Fyft is O'Donochoe Moore's countrey. It conteyneth 45 ploughlands, and it is nowe all in the Earle's hands, by Her Ma^ts gyft.

" The Sixt is the Lord of Cosmaignes countrey. It con-teyneth 84 ploughlands. It is now all in the Earle's hands by Her M^ts gift, or ye most part thereof.

" The Seaventh is the Lord of Kerslawny's (cois leamhna) countrey, otherwise called Slight Cormak. It conteyneth 35 ploughlands, whereof some are in the Ile of Valentia. He claymeth there the geaving of the Rodd, Risinge out, the findinge of 40 Galleyglas, and to the value of £40 a yeare in spendinge.

"The Eight is the Countrey of [Mac] Gelecuddè. It contayneth 46 ploughlands He claymeth there Risinge out, the gevinge of the Rodde, the findinge of 30 Galleglas, and to the value of £20 a yeare in spendinge.

"The Ninethe is Mac Fynin's Countrey [in Glenaraught, Co. Kerry]. It conteyneth 28 ploughlands. He claymeth the givinge of the Rodd, the findinge of 15 Galleyglas, Risinge out, and to the value of £24 yearely in spendinge.

"The Tenthe is the Countrey of Clandonoroe. It contayneth 24 Ploughlands. He claymeth theare Risinge out, and it is in the Erle's hands by Her M^{ts} Gyfte.

"The Eleaventh is the Countrey of O'Donocho-Glañ (O' Donoghue of Glenflesk, in Kerry). He hath there no other dutie but onlly six and fortie shillings fourpence of yearelie Rent. The countrey conteyneth 20 ploughlands.

"The Twelueth is the Countrey of Clan Dermonde. It conteyneth 28 ploughlands. He claymeth Risinge out, the keepinge of 16 Galleyglas, and in yearlie spendinge to the value of £40.

"The Thirteenth is Clanlawra's [in O'Sullevan Beare's country]. This countrie conteyneth 32 ploughlands. It is all in the Earle's hands by Her Ma^{ts} gift.

"The Fourteenthe is the Countrey of Loughlegh (loghlaoighech) [in Kerry] or of Teignitowin. It conteyneth 32 Ploughlands. The Earle claymeth it to be excheated unto him for want of Heires right and legitimate.

"Moreover, the Earle hath in Chiefe Rents yssuinge out of Barrett's Countrey, by the cyttie of Corke, £11 a yeare; out of the Abbey of Killaha, £4 a yeare or thereabouts; out of Ballenskellig yearly as much. Out of certen churchland in Beare the like some; besides he hath in Demayne land in the hundreds of Maygonie and Euraught about his Castle of the Pallace [in Kerry], his Castle of Ballicarbery, Castle Lough, and the Abbey of Vriett [Muckrus], three score ploughlands or thereabouts. In O'Suliuan Beares Countrey, Muskery, and Duallo, or in Donochoe's Countrey, certen ploughlands; also in eache of them Demayne lands.

"All his Lands and Territories lieth in the Counties of Desmond and Cork, and some parte in the county of Kerrie. The most parte of his land is waste and uninhabited, wch hath growne partly by the calamities of the late warres, partly by the exaccons that he hath used uppon his tenñants.

D

"It is of great consequence and importance unto our in-
habitacon there, that the Earle's Estate be not enlarged, to
the ende that after his decease, Englishe Gentlemen may be
there planted, and all his dependences brought to hould
onely of Her Ma'tie; unlesse it so weare that by Her Highnes
fav^r and good likinge, his daughter weare maried to som
worthy English Gentleman, and his lands assured after his
deceasse to the heires males of their two bodies. In w^{ch}
case allso I wishe the keapinge of Galleyglas, Risinge out,
and ceassinge of souldiors, to be wholly extinguished, the
spendings and Refeccons to be reduced to som money rent;
the gevinge *of the Rodd to be abolished*, and all those meane
Lords to hould their lands of Her Highnes."

"*As there is nothinge that the Irishe more esteme then the nobilitie of bloud, pferringe it 'farre before eyther vertue or wealth,
so abhorre they nothinge more then disparagem^t, more odious unto
them then Death;* wch well apeared in that late communicacon
of mariadge betwene the Earle of Glyncarr's daughter, and
supposed heire, and Sir Valentine Browne's yonger sonne,
wch both by the Earle assented unto *for money*, and for
reward by certen of his men negotiated in the countrey very
earnestlie, as well for the matter, as for the maner of atchy-
vinge, wrought generally in those parts a bitter discontentment, so much the deepelier printed in their myndes, by how
much the earnestlier it was borne them in hande (by those that
undertooke to effect it), that it must needes take place, for
that it was intended by the state; soe well liked of by Her
Majestie, and so resolved upon by the Earle. The Countesse
and yonge Lady came unto me, and div^s of the Gentlemen
of the countrey to acquaint me wth their discontentment;
and some others of the best of those partes discovered their
grieffes by their l^{res}. Their mynde all then seemed to tende
to the dislike of that place, and to desire that she mought be
matched to some one of a noble howse; wherein they made
great ptestacons they would be much psuaded by me. I wthall
understood by some that weare privye to their myndes that
(fearinge that matche should be forced upon them) they had
an intencon to convay the yonge Lady into O'Ruirk's countrey (in the *north* part of Conaght), who not long synce is
maried to the Cowntesse of Glyncarrs sister.

I held it best, in respect of the tyme, to lessen theyr discontentment what I mought, and to assure them that it
stoode not wth the course of Her Mats most blessed Government; neyther would the lawes of England pmitt that any
should be forced to marie against their wills, and that they

weare to feare nó such matter. I did besides, both by letters
and message, deale with Sir Thomas Norrys, Vice President
of Mounster, whom I then thought disposed to seate himselfe
in these partes, that yf he could like of such a matche, and
would to that ende become a petytioner unto Her Ma'tie for
the renuinge of the Earle's letters Patents into a further
estate, I would assist him to the uttermost of my small endeavour, and no whit doubted but the countrey should most
readilie assent unto it. After some paines taken, he in the
ende mysliked of it, beinge, as it seemed, otherwise disposed
to bestowe himselfe. So the Countesse and the rest of those
partes cóntynuinge in the feare of the former matche, and
beinḡe in no hope of anie better, concluded soddenlie a
mariage wth Florence Mc Cartie, who cam wᵗh the Vice
President's warrants into the countrey to take possession of
a Castle morgadged unto him by the Earle of Glycarre; of
wᶜh matche the efficient cause I take to have byn a fonde
feare, and a fonde desire: the instrumentall cause to have
byn fonde cowncell: the feare was, that she must needes ells
have byn maried to Mr. Browne: the desire was to contynue
the Howse in the name, wᶜh by this matche they weare in a
dooble hope to performe; fyrst, by Petiĉon unto Her Ma'tie,
hopinge that Florence Mc Cartye had those frends, and that
favoʳ wᵗh Her Highnes, that his suite for the landes should be
easilie obtayned; secondly, yf their petiĉons fayled, they
hoped on their power; for that Florence Mc Cartie was like to
be Mc Carthy Reoghe, and so by forces of both countreis,
might attayne his pretended Rights; especially upon such
opportunities as trobles in England, or disturbances here
might produce; a matter of some consequence, and verie piu-
diciall to the acĉon we here undertake, and so much the
more to be looked unto, by howe much the Mc Carties
ptende to have Right to the most of Mounster, wherof sometimes they weare Lords, and phrps aspire to be Lords againe
by meanes of this yonge Gentleman, beinge by the Father's
side a Mc Cartye, and by the mother's side a Giraldyné, and
therefore likelier to be favored in these partes.

This newe matche, the new settlinge of the Englishe (the
English undertakers on the lands forfeited by the Earl of
Desmond), the discontentment of the Irishe, the present state
of the Province, the expectaĉon of some trouble in England,
puttinge them in hope of due meanes and opportunities.
The counsell herein, both evill given, and followed, proceeded
(yf not higher) from the Lords of Countries wthin Desmond,
and principall officers about the Earle of Glyncarre, who,

heretofore accustomed to extorĉons, oppressions, and spoiles,' by the wᶜh they weare wont to be enriched, now bridled and; restrayned, they longe for their former estate, and are ympa-' tient of justice, and good Government. The chiefe of those in this acĉon were *O'Sullivan Moore*, Lord of a great Coun- trey, the Earle's Seneschall and Marshall, married to Florens; McCarthy's sister, able to make a hundred swords : *Mac Fy-* *nine,* Lord of a lesse Countrey, but more fruitfull, of lesse power then the other, maried to the Earle of Glyncarrs base' daughter; Donell Mac Tybert, the Earle's Constable of his' Castle of the Pallace, and chieffe officer of his lands, beinge principall of a populous Sept called the *Mergies* (?), and foster father to the yonge Lady; Hugh McOwen, Captaine of the Earle's Galleyglasse, and som others of their sorte. The remedies and pvenĉons of their hopes and intents, in my simple conceipt, will be to take order that Carberie shall des-; cende accordinge to the lʳᵉˢ Patents of Her Highnes most renowned Father to Donell Mc Cartye, otherwise calle Donell Pipi, and his heires lawfully begotten; and the agree ment amonge themselves, made contrarie to the purport o the Letters pattents, to contynue no longer then duringe Sir Owen McCarties liefe. Secondly, Her Maᵗie to graunt no further estate of the Earle of Glyncarrs lands, but after his, deceasse to plant therein English Genᵗ and Inhabitants. Thirdly, in the meane tyme to cause good pledgs and assur-' ans to be taken of Florence MᶜCartye, and the rest of the contrivers of this mariadge, of their loyaltie and good de- meanure, wᶜh is in part allready don. Fourthly, to contynue the Earle of Glyncarr wᵗhin the boundes of Lawe & justice,' that he oppresse not his countrie, sellinge their landes and spoylinge their goodes, against all right ; whereby the people,' findinge their safetie in Her Maᵗies government, may the more affect it, and havinge amongst them fewe discontented, may the lesse be disposed to innovasions."

"The above document is apparently (says Mr. Hamilton,' in his Calendar) by Sir Warham St. Leger, and addressed to Lord Burghley."

Extracted from the Second Tract. 1588. *June* 12.

"That, as the Mariadge of Florence McCartie to the Earle of Glyncarr's daughter tendeth to the disturbance of these partes yf it be not prevented, so, as great and as dangerous trobles will growe otherwise if it be not looked into in tyme!

" Synce the discoverie of Florence Mc Carte's dryft, to joyne in himsealfe Desmond and Carberie, and so to erect againe the greatnes and tyranny of the McCarties, a counterpractise to the sealffe same ende, but by other meanes, partely for the hatred borne to our newe Inhabitaçon, partely for the malice and dislike borne to Florence McCartie, but chieffely for ye desire to greaten their faction, and mayntayne the name and force of Mc Cartie Moore, hath byn entered into: the chieffe doer whereof was Sir Owen O'Sulivan of Beerhaven, he bearinge an impatient mynd of our neighbourhood, and thinkinge himsealfe wronged by Florence Mc Carty, who promised to mary his daughter, and fearinge some diminution of his owne estate by the suite of his nephewe Donell O'Sulivan, and desirous to have a frend of a Mc Carty, and so to make his partie good howsoever the world went; havinge on the one syde the Lorde Barrye, his brother-in-lawe and firme frend, who is but too great, contryved furthwyth first to enter into a league wth Donell Mc Cartie, the Earle of Glyncarr's base sonne, whom that countrey doth much favo^r, and would fayne have to be Mc Cartie. Secondly, to allie himsealffe with the Knights of Kerrie's sonne and Heyre, the Chieffe of the Giraldines in these partes, likliest to drawe evill humo^{rs} unto him, and to growe to badd action, beinge not able to recover what his father hath sould, but by force and stronge hande. These purposes Sir Owen (O'Sullevan Beare) did so pertinently pursue, that wthin few daies after that mariadge he sayled from his countrey to Desmonde, and there entringe into a league wth his greatest enemye before, Donell Mc Carty, the Earle of Glyncarres base sonne, thence came to Kerrie, and concluded a mariadge betwene his yonger daughter and the Knight of Kerrie's sonne & heire; hopinge, no doubt, that they two should drawe untoe them all the evill disposed of Kerrie and Desmonde; and he ioyninge wth them his forces out of Beare, Bantrie, and other partes of the cowntie of Corke, should be able, when they sawe their tyme, to do in those partes what they thought good, wch their purpose I hould no less requisite to be prevented, then the former drift of Florence Mc Cartie to the like ende.

" The remedies seeme unto me to be these:—Sir Owen O'Sulivan committed to Warde, tyll he put in good pledgs and assurances for his Loyaltie! The apprehension of the Earle of Glyncarr's base sonne, and the *execution of him* by Justice, or by martiall Lawe, for breakinge Her Mat^s prison, and livinge ever synce wthout pardon or protection, not sub-

mittinge himselfe to due Authoritie; or the imployment of
him in some service out of these partes; the geving of Justice
to the Inhabitants of Desmonde, that neyther by the Earle of
Clancarties unlawfull graunts they be deprived of their lands,
nor by the payment of his debtes spoyled of their goods; so,
finding the sweete of her Mats government they shall repose
themselves theron most contentidly, and will not be drawne
to any tumult, wch the Earle doubtles in favour of his base
sonne would gladly urge them unto when tyme favoured;
and thereuntoe his dealings seeme untoe me to tende, directed
by others that looke beyonde the present."

The effect produced by this daring contempt of the Queen's
authority may be judged by the fact, that, as early as the 3rd
of June, Elizabeth sent orders to Sir Thomas Norreys to ap-
prehend Florence, and make earnest, instant inquiry into
" the means and manner by which he had accomplished the
said marriage;" and also, quickly following upon this imperious announcement of the royal will, went another letter from
Walsyngham, commanding the arrest of the Countess of Clancartie, of the bride, and of as many as could be found to have
had any share in the matter; and further, pressing a most
searching investigation into every detail of the transaction.
The result of these inquiries, with what passages Sir Thomas
Norreys could himself relate of his own intercourse with
Florence, is now laid before the reader; and, perhaps, in the
entire mass of State Papers of the period, there is nothing
more curious than the correspondence which arose out of this
first development of Florence's plans for his future career.
The equanimity with which he could encounter this sudden
burst of royal indignation, the surprising adroitness with
which he could turn aside its arrowy sleet from himself, and
withdraw his young wife from its mischief, will appear in the
sequel, but not until the requirements of his position had
urged him to the committal of a second action, equally
"contemptuous" and more defiant of the Queen, by which
his purpose was fairly accomplished. From this moment
come into operation the unrivalled tact, and personal address,
which the reader may be prepared to trace through every
phase of his future life.

"1588. *July* 1. SIR THO^s NORREYS *to* WALSYNGHAM.

" Rt: Hon: my most bounden dewty remembred. Whereas
Her Ma'tie, by her l^res of 3d of June last past, gave me in

cõmandent to comitt the body of Florence Mac Carthy, and
thereupon to certifye Her Highnes of my doings therein, as
also of the meanes and man^r by which the sayd Florence
compassed the mariage wth the Earle of Clancarties daughter;
for that the circumstances thereof doe inforce a tedious recitall, I presumed not to trouble Her Highnes wth the parti-
cularities, but thought them rather meet to be advᵗized to yor
H^o. (who hade alsoe written to me touching ye same) to thend
that by yor meanes the knowledg thereof might be delivered
to Her Ma'ty at her good pleasure.

" Upon the first arrivall of the sayd Florence here, cõming
unto me he gave no signe of any such purpose, as sithens fell
out; but to give color (as semes) to his intent, and to draw
me ye further from suspicõn thereof, through his ṣeeming conceived unkyndnes against ye Earle, he then discoṽed unto me
some ill dealing of the sayd Earle towards him, namely how,
that being bownd to him in great bands for assurance of
certein lands, and for pformance of some other condictions,
amongst wch one was, that he should give him his daughter
in ᵗnariage, he neverthelesse had broken wth him, and therefore offered me (Yf I should so lyke) the benefitt of the forfeitures of the sayd lands : wch speaches (as sithens as I have
conceived) seeme to have proceded of some further matter in
ye secret of his harte, those his words being so contrary to
that wch he eftesoones did attempt. But the very grownd
thereof (as I am informed, and as by many strong circumstances may be gathered) proceded from ye Earle himselfe,
however sithens he would fynd himself grieved therewith,
and was compacted betwene them in England at the sayd
Florence's there late being, and not w^thout the privitie and
great furtheraunce of Sir Owen MacCarthy, who by all meanes
endevoureth to back, and iniuriouslie to raise up the sayd
Florence against his kinsman, Donell Mac Carthy, as well
in ye succession of the Captency of his countrey, as also in all
other causes, that may advauntage him thereunto ; wherein
yt it is very certein that ye Earle alsoe hath ever greatly
favored him.

Besydes yt is here by manie reported (the further proofes
whereof I have not yett had tyme to syfte out) that the sayd
Earle gave to Flor. at his cõming, his secrete l^res to his wife,
to that effect wch now hath happened; to whome pntly after
his arrivall he repayred wth the same, and soone after dispatched his hidden intent. And for more lykelyhode that yt
was then wrought and concluded in England, I am certeinlie
given to understand, that at ye instant of his departure from

thence, Capt. Jaques being then in company wth him, coun-
seled him very earnestly, whatsoever he did, to goe through
wth the mariage out of hand; assuring him that for obteyn-
ing Her Ma'ts consent thereunto, he would so work wth some
of his frends there, that yt should be brought to passe; and
to the end to be more spedily advertized of his proceedings,
he sent a servaunt of his owne ou^r hether in company wth
Flor., who upon conclusion of the matter was presentlie dispatched hence back agayne. The further knowledg and intent whereof may there, I think, best be boulted out of the
sayd Jaques, who thereby seemeth to have beene acquainted
wth the enterprize from ye beginning, and to be privie to any
other purpose that may depend thereupon; for sure yt carrieth great shewe of deepe consequence, considering how
strongly ye sayd Florence is allied to such as evill may be
looked from. 1st. His mother was sister to James Fitz
Morice, the Arch Traytour, whereby he is nephew to the
L. Roche's wife, and to the Lo. of Muscries mother; and
coosen german to the Seneschall of Imokhillies wife; all w^ch
psons doe hang upon one weake thred, and have their
eyes sett all upon hope of forreyne helpes: but namely, the
sayd Lo. Roche, who sheweth himself in all his behaveo^r, and
also in some open speaches, to be discontented with this government, repyning obstinately against all directions of the
State here, and supporting himself wth the vayne conceipt of
his secrete hope, whereof heretofore he hath, and yett dayly
doth give apparent demonstrations: so that now the sayd
Florence, by this his late knott hath given great strength to
that syde, and hath combined all the releques of the House
of James Fitz Morice to the kindred of the Clancarties, w^ch
being the greatest name and nacōn now in Mounster (*all Desmond, all Carbery, all Muscry, all Dowalla, being of that line*),
yt inferreth great importaunce, and matter of neare respect
to be prevented, or at the least well eyed; the rather for that
the sayd Clancarties have heretofore, before the comīng in of
the Geraldines uppon them, had all this province in their sub-
iecčon, *the continuall memory whereof they yett use to nourish
emongst them, and to deliver to their posterities by dew succession;*
and now this new occasion meeting in a man of the same
race, being of his quality and sorte, who by blood is so nigh
allyed to forreyne practizers; by difference of Religion devoted to the contrarie parte; by his owne private disposičon
hath always shewed himself dearly well affected and inclined
to the Spaniard; being also generally favored of all his
countrey, and now in very plausible acceptaunce, the rather

for the late gratious fovours wch he received of Her Ma'tie;
and that by this attempt hath discovered his ambicious desyre
to make himself great.

It is greatlie to be regarded, to what ende the same may
grow. Moreover, now latelie (whether for any further intent,
or that it is through his heedlesse unhappinesse so fallen out),
he hath by all meanes laboured to be interested in the Old
Head of Kinsale, wch is the Lo. Courcies auncient Manor
House, and a place often heretofore eyed and earnestlie mo-
tioned, for opinion of great strength to be fortifyed; the title
whereof he hath (as I understand) compassed, and was, the
same day that he was apprehended, mynded to ryde thether
to take possession of; all wch concurring so daungerously to
the encrease of doubt, I would therefore wish (under refor-
maçon of better advizement) that tho' hereafter he shall,
paps, work himselfe grace or pardon of the present dislyke,
yett that very good assuraunces be taken of him· before his
enlargement, for avoyding of the evills which are depending
uppon the circumstances of person and condiçon. Him now
I have according to Her High. pleasure comitted; as also,
according to y^r later direccion in yor Ho.'s l^res of the 4th of
the last moneth, have caused the Countesse, Mac Finin, Teig
Merrigagh, and such others as I could learne to have bene
privy to the practise, to be apprehended, as I could come by
them; and doe not doubt but very shortly to come by the
rest likewise, of the wch I understand that O'Sullevan More
was the greatest forwarder, and nearest of councell; though
indeed all the chief of that countrey were wrought by
Florence to consent thereunto, who (as I am lett to understand), *before the mariage, gott all their hands to firme that agreement, by a generall confirmaçon of them;* and soone after accomplished the sayd mariage in an old broken church thereby,
not in such solemnity and good sort as behoved, and as order
of Law and Her Mat^s iniunction doe require.

" Thus am I carried by large relaçon of particulares into
a tedious length of lines, wch I besech your Lp. to pardon in
regard of the urgentnes of the matter, and many occasions
meeting in the same. Further, I have thought good to advertize yor Lp. of the psent good quiett of this province, in
wch yt is not unlikely to continew, yf forreyne invasion doe
not occasion the chaunge, &c., &c.

" THO^s NORREYS.

" From Limerick, 1 July, 1588."

" 1588. *July* 1. NOTES *for* HER MA'TIE *to consider of.*

" The strength of the L^{ls} of great countries and theire allyance and followers.

" The Earle of Clankertie that now is, cometh of thelder brother of that House.

" The Lo. of Muskery cometh of the Second House of the Clan Karties. Sir Owen Mc Kertie is, as the countrie saith, a bastard of the House of Clan Kerties, and thereby enioyeth the country of Carbery. Mac Donoghe, Captein of the Countrie of Dowalla, enioyeth, that Countrie as the third Sonne descended of the Howse of the Earle of Clan Kartie.

" Dependers and Followers of the capteins of these Contries :—

" To the Earle of Clan Kertie.—O'Sullyvan Moore, O'Sullyvan Beare, Mac Fynian. These are also of the House of Clan Kertie.

" To the Lo. of Muskery.—Teig Mc Owen of Drishain.

" To the Lord of Carbery.—Sir Fynian O'Driscoe, Connoher Oh Driscoe, the Mahons, and their Septs.

" To the Lord of Dowalla. —The Calahone, the Chieffe [O'Keefes]. The Earle of Clan Kartie doth appoint the Lo. of this countrie.

" Out of the House of Clan Kartie's are now lyving these that followe :—1st. The Earle of Clan Kertie that now is, who is without yssue male ; he hath onely one daughter. After the Earle's decease his countrie is in Her Majestie to dispose. The Captein or Lo. of Muskery, who hath two sonnes ; and a brother called Teig Mc Dermonde, and Charles, sonne of Sir Cormac Teig, last Lo. of Muskery.

" Donell Mc Kerthie, alias Donell Pype, who is the right legetimate heir of the countrey of Carbery, descended of thelder brother of the Lo. of Carbery. He hath two sonnes. ·

" Florence Mac Kartie, descended of Sir Donogh Mc Karthy, second Brother of the Lo. of Carbery, who is maryed to the only daughter of the Earle of Clan Kartie. He hath one brother lyvinge, called Cormac Mac Donoghe. (This Cormac was illegitimate ; Florence's only legitimate brother was Dermod Moyle.)

" Sir Owen Mc Karty, the thirde brother of the Lo. of Carbery, is now Lo. of that contrie, and hath three sonnes.

· " These that followe are allyd, and have matched with the House of Clan Karty :—A Syster of the late Earle of Desmond, married to the Earle of Clan Kartie. A syster of James Fitz Morrice was married to Sir Donoghe McCarty, by whome he

FLORENCE MACCARTHY MOR. 43

had yssue Florence and his brother. Corm^c. Mc Dermode now Lo. of Muskery's Mother was another Syster of the saide James Fitz Morrice, the Traytor.

" The Lo. Roche married a thirde Syster of the said James, by whom he hath a sonne and a daughther; which daughter is married to Mc Donoghe, now Lord of Dowalla.

" The Seneschall is marryed to a daughter of the said James Fitz Morrice.

" To conclude, when these great Lords of Countries, viz., the Earle of Clancarty, the Lords of Muskerrie, Carbery, Dowalla, O'Sullyvan Moore, O'Sullyvan Beare, being all Carties, and the Lo. Roche, and Seneschall allyed by James Fitz Morryce to that howse, yf the match and greatnes of Florence Mc Kartie be not pvented, that Secte will growe greater in Mounster then ever the Earle of Desmonde was, and no lesse daungerous. The streingth of this house being so great there is great care to be taken that they may be kepte in such sorte as not to combyne themselves in stronger manner togither, then they are at this tyme; wherein especially care must be had that the mariage of Florence wth the Earles daughter may be separated, and he cut off by lawe, yf by his demerits he hath deserved it.

" Also, whereas Sir Owen Mc Karty, now Lo. of Carbery, hath enlarged his possessions by getting the Lo. Coorsies Countrey and other lands, it were convenient that Donell Pype's tytle to that countrie of Carbery should be favoured, who hath the best tytle thereunto; so neither of them shalbe half so strong as nowe one of them is. Likewise, where the Lo. of Muskerry hath now that whole Countrey to himself, and hath enlarged the same by other gruants from Her Ma'tie, it were convenient that the tytle of the sonne to Sir Cormac Teig should be favoured, wch Sir Cormac yelded up that Countrey to Her Ma'tie, and tooke it of Her Heghnes to him and his heires;· so, should the greatnes of one be abated, and be made equall, they will be opposite one to the other; and whereas there is Contencon for Doalla betwene two of the Mc Donoghes, it were likewise convenient, for the reasons aforesaid, that the countrey were devyded betwene them.

" The Seneschall, Patricke Condon, Patrick Fitz Morryce, the Whyte Knight, are all suspected to be very dangerous psons, and nearer to be seen unto then others, the most of them having ben principall actors in the last rebellion."

. Such was the result of the inquiry which the Queen had ordered to be made into the matter of this marriage; it was more than enough to fill up the measure of her indigna-

tion against a nephew of the arch-traitor, James Fitz Morrice.
The designs of Florence were now sufficiently unveiled; his
conduct had been looked into by the keenest eyes in Munster,
and the precautions fit to be taken against him suggested by
the plainest-spoken man in the Queen's service. If Florence,
or the O'Sullivans, Patrick Condon, the Seneschal, Donal the
Base, or Sir Owen and his sons, should be left at liberty to
plot mischief henceforth, the fault could not be laid at the
door of Sir Warham St. Leger. The pen of Sir Thomas
Norreys had done its work as industriously as that of his
colleague; it had even written passages more perilous for
Florence; for it had shown that the ambitious designs which
St. Leger had foreshadowed had already commenced their
operation; he had acquired the Spanish language, secured a
harbour suitable for the landing of Spanish forces, and, worst
of all, he was in connexion with a notorious foreigner, then
in a London prison for designs against the Queen's life; yet
that prophetic pen had pointed to a possibility, the belief in
which, probably, no man, except Florence himself, entertained,
that he might " hereafter work himselfe grace or pardon of
the present dislyke."

Sir Robert Cecyll, who had attentively studied the mind
of his royal mistress, has left it on record that the affairs of
Ireland in an especial manner disturbed her composure! and
indeed at times they *were* of a nature to ruffle the serenity of
even a calmer temperament than was possessed by this gentle
Lady, "whose fame—as we read in the Pacata Hibernia—was
eternized with the shrill-sounding trumpet of triumphant
Fame, for the meekest and mildest Prince that ever reigned."
When the despatches of St. Leger and Norreys, touching the
contemptuous marriage of Florence MacCarthy, reached the
English Cabinet, a Tudor hurricane burst with swift and fierce
disaster upon all concerned in it. That the writers of these
vexatious papers should themselves have escaped uninjured
from the lightnings of that ruthless storm, was probably as
much matter of wonder as of joy to themselves; but upon
every member of the bridal party in the old broken church,
the tempest fell with unmitigated fury. That any man
should be found at such a moment to step forward and place
himself between the anger of Elizabeth and the feeblest of its
victims, is even more gratifying than it is surprising. There
was one man in Munster who had the courage and the humanity to do this. It was a man who had long lifted up his
voice against tyranny and iniquity in high places; who had,
for " his own particular, held his even course of justice despite

much obloquy and malice;" a man whose loyalty and honour
were above attaint; who had suffered many private wrongs
from the kinsmen of the prisoners; who had every reason,
save a manly feeling of compassion for the helpless, to hold
his hand from any petition in the behalf of any of them. To
the great honour of Sir William Herbert, he at once applied
to the Vice-President in favour of the aged Countess of
Clancar, took upon himself the responsibility of her safe
custody, made his own house her prison, and wrote to
England the story of the domestic sorrows of that oppressed
lady.

"1588. *July* 12. *To the* R⁴. *Hon.* SIR F. WALSYNGHAM, K⁴, *principal
Secretary to Her Most Excel⁴ Majestie.*

"R⁴ Hon : My most humble dewtie premised.
"Since my last letters unto your Honor touchinge the mariage of the
Earl of Clin Carrs daughter, thear have bean hear apprehended by Mr. Vice
President's direction, beasyde Florence Mak Cartye, whom the Bishop of
Corke tooke, The Countes of Clincarr, Mak Finnin, and others, whoe wear
all comitted to Castlemayne. Mr. Sprenge, whoe apprehended them, had
alsoe warrant from O'Sullivan Moore, whoe then was not in the countrey,
but upon his retorne hearinge of it, repayred unto mea, and submitted himsealf to Her Majestye, whereupon I took order with him for his repayr to
Mr. Vice President ; myself having noe further direction for him : but in
respect that it was mayde apparant unto mea that the Countes had don
nothinge in the matter, but with the priuitea and approbation of the Earl,
and that hea now maketh shew of the contrary, and wishethe the Countess
troble and ruin, that by her deathe hea might aduance him sealf to som
newe mariage, whearbye Her Majestye's right for Remaynder may bea
impeatched, I was mooued both in comiseration of the Countesses poore
and lamentable estate, and to preuent what I might, the euill that mowght
insue of her troble, to beacom a Suiter unto the Vicepresident, for the en-
lardgment of the Countess out of that uile and unhulsome place, and that
shea might remayne with mea tyll Her Majestye's pleasure wear further
known, which it pleased him to grawnt mea, whearof I have thought it
my part to aduertise your Honor ; conceauing, in my poore opinion, that
the Countess, beaynge farr stroken in years, and without hope of childearne,
wear to bea fauoured ; and whereas she liued in · extream misery, hauinge
all this last year but 20 nobles allowed her toe mayntayne her sealf, her
daughter and famelye, a stipend more likely to starue them then to sarue
them, shea by your honorable fauor may haue som portion allowed her of
her husband's liuinge to mayntayne hersealfe in som goode sort, beaynge
the wyfe, sister, and dawghter of an Earl, euer of verye modest and good
demeanure, though matched with one most disorderlye and dissolute.
"Her affirmation touchinge the mariage is this (whitch shea offreth
to proue by threa goode witnesses), that shea receaued a letter from the
Earl toe repayr toe Corke, and thear to geau creadite to that whitch Patrike
Galloway showld from him deliuer unto her, whoe thear gaue her to understande that it was the Earl's pleasure that shea showld send her dawghter
ouer into Englande, or if shea thought not goode to doe soe, shea showld
mary her daughter to Florence Mak Carty, and receau of him a band for

the payment of toe or threa hundred pownde to the Earl of Clinn Karr in
England : to the whitch she answeared that shea was willinge to send her
daughter to Englande if thear had been any moneys sent ouer to furnish,
or any fytt to attend her, or if any Gentlemañ of creadite had written
that, at her cominge ouer, hea woolde haue had care of her ; but to My
Lorde of Clinkarrs care, soe unfurnished, and unprouided, shea durst not
comitt her, and thearfore enclined to the oother cowrs, the Earl puttinge
it to her choyce : she protesteth that shea neuer harde that Her Majestye
had forbidden the mariage, but had only denied to pass to them the lande.
Hearof I thought goode to advertice your Honor, and that since this
mariage I understand of another in hand no less dangerous, betwean
Sir Owen O'Suilevan's daughter, beaynge the Lorde of Bear hauen, and one
Donell Mak Cartye, the Earl of Clincarrs bass soñe, whom the inhabitants
of Desmonde much affect ; hea is the only man in theas toe cowntres that
leadeth a loose, disloyall life, shonninge all officers, and standinge upon his
garde with some few followers, though doynge noe oother harme ; it wear
very requisite hea wear taken ; thear is goode matter to bea objected
agaynst him to cut him off, he will ells in tyme bread some troble ; for in
the first discents Bastardie is no impediment, and hea is a person both willinge and able to doe mischeaf. I haue euer bean of opinion that hea was
to bea apprehended ; the Vice President howldeth another cours.

" It was prouidently layde down in Her Majestye's articles for the in-
habitation of this prouince, that noe undertaker showld haue any bands of
sowldiers in pay : I woolde it wear as well obseaured ! I fear thear are,
that to continew themsealves in pay, can bea content to continew the
province in troble, and I wonder it is soe quiett ; for on the one syde
the Gentlemen beaynge stroken, euill entreated, and abused, outrageous
woordes and violent deads rife and comon towards all sorts of the Irish, on
the oother syde the Vice President's sowldiers suffered to goe up and down
the countrey, taking of mete and drinke and money for themselves, and
theyr woomen and boys, uppon the poore people ; it seameth unto mea the
ready way to make the Irish weary of theyr loyaltie and of their lyues.
Mysealf, according to Her Majesty's directions, and to my most bowndeñ
dewtie, howldinge an upright cours of justice, without respect of persons or
nations, and endeauouring thearby to reduce theas parts to a loue of justice
and government, and to sutch quietnes and perfect obedience as Her
Majestye should noe more nead to keap bands or garrisons hear then in
Surrey or Middlesex,—feal and fynd dayly the mislike and malice that is
borne mea for it ; whitch as I haue toutched in som former letters of myne
unto your Honor, so to acquaynt your Honor more thorowly with the
estate of things, I make bowlde to send to your Honor what of late I haue
written thearof to Mr. Vice President, and to Mr. Chiefe Justice, althowgh
I look theare for little remedye, yeat to discharge my dewtie, and to clear
mysealf of that suspition that myght bea conceaued of mea, I layd the
whole matter before them, which I humbly beseatch your Honor to
voutchsaf the perusall of. Amonge many defects I fynde in theas parts,
I fynde none more then of a goode Bishop, whitch I wish to bea an Irishman, for soe might hea doe most goode. I hear that one Pattinson is a
suiter for it, a most indiscreat, rash, and dissentious man, no way fytt for
any goode function, as hereafter I shall make more clear unto your Honor.
In the mean tyme I most humbly recomend unto your Honor my poor en-
deuors in these partes, wheareof sutch shall the effect bea as the countenance is that is geaven them ; and without your honorable favor they must
and will quayl ; but I despayr not of that whitch I have ever found, and
whitch I shall ever labor by the best meanes I may to demerite. I have

sent your Honor, for a smale token of my most dewtifull goode will, a Goshawke. I wish shea prove as goode as shea is geauen with a goode hart. I cease further to troble your Honor, and comitt the same to the tuition of the most Mightea.

" WILLIAM HERBERT.
" From the Castle of the Iland, 12 July, 1588."

Posterity will award to the writer of this letter the praise due to an upright, fearless, and kind-hearted man; but to posterity it signifies little that " the Countess was far stroken in years and without hope of childearne," or that the Queen's charges would have been diminished by the suppression of the soldiers entertained at her Highness's cost by the under-takers, contrary to the articles providently laid down; to the contemporaries of Herbert these were no matters of indiffer-ence; a child borne to the Earl of Clancar would have extin-guished many Signories, nay, have " empeatched the Queen's *rights;*" and the suppression of the soldiers would have sup-pressed their employers. The reader will presently see how trifling were the mislikes and calumnies to which the writer had hitherto submitted, in comparison with the fierce indig-nation which this letter excited against him.

The storm had gathered over the head of Florence at the beginning of July; an aggravated history of his offence had been sent home by Norreys himself, who had accused him of outwitting and deceiving him, and who might, not unnatu-rally, expect that some portion of the Queen's anger would fall upon himself; and yet an entire month does not elapse before we find Sir Thomas writing home letters to the minister in favour of Florence!

He had, he said, become better acquainted with him; he found he had erred in *simplicity*, not knowing her Highness's pleasure! He was very penitent for his fault, and there was no denying to his good demeanour and carriage of himself, letters recommending him to favour.

Had this been a solitary instance in the life of Florence in which further acquaintance with him converted fierce hos-tility into sudden good-will, we might attribute it, as Browne did, to bribery, as probably Lord Burghley did also, when he underlined Browne's bold assertion; but wilier men, fiercer antagonists than Norreys, were examples of a conversion quite as extraordinary; and we are at a loss to explain the fact, except by attributing it to the blandishments of his personal address, or a simulation of innocence so masterly as to make men look upon their previous conviction of his guilt as an injury, for which reparation was due to him.

"1588.   *July* 28.   SIR THOMAS NORREYS *to* SIR F. WALSYNGHAM.

"R^t. Hon. My humble dutie premised.

"By my form^r l^{res} I did at lardge advertize y^r Honor of the manner and meanes used by Mr. Florence McCartie, in contrivinge the marriadge betweene him and the Erle of Clancarties daughter, and therefore thinke it nedeles to troble your Honor furder therewith ; but beinge now mynded to send over his man, he hath earnestlie entreated me to recommende him by my l^{res} unto your Honor's good favour, wch I have the rather presumed to doe, as well by reason of the good demen^r and carriadge of himself, where- with I have ben longer acquainted, as allso for that havinge sundri tymes sithens his coimtment had conference wth him, I fynde him verry peni- tente for his falt so offensive to her Majestie, protestinge that the ignorance of her Highness' pleasure, and no illmeaninge in himself was the cause of his error, the consideracon of which I leave to your Honor's grave judg- ment, and so comittinge the same to Godes holie tucion, doe most humblie take leave this 28 July 1588.

                                                    "THOMAS NORREYS.
        "Corke."

The inquiry into this marriage, which had led to Sir Warham St. Leger's tracts upon the state of Munster, had brought many names into discredit, besides those actually concerned in it ; amongst others, blackened by the taint of alliance in blood to Florence, was the Lord Roche, his uncle, the same who a few years earlier had attended Sir Henry Sidney at the Christmas meeting in Cork ; the interval had not improved his loyalty, whilst certain encroachments upon his country by the undertakers had much diminished his contentment.   The minister was reminded that he had married a sister of James Fitz Morrice, the arch-traitor— sister also of Florence's mother—but as the Lord Roche set little value upon a character for attachment to the English Government, he submitted to this revival of suspicions against him without a murmur.   Not so another individual, also related to the arch-traitor, who had joined his lot loyally and earnestly with the Queen's cause.   John Fitz Edmond Fitzgerald, of Clone, had not been alluded to in the official reports sent home from Munster ; but it chanced that he was Florence's godfather, and the rumour in the country was, that the Countess of Clancar had asked his advice touching the marriage of her daughter with Florence, and that he had counselled its accomplishment.   Against such an offence, the services of a whole life would have availed him little ; and this loyal gentleman hastened to protest against the accusa- tion as a malicious slander ; this too was made a matter of State, and needed a despatch from the Vice-President to explain it.   This despatch adds something to the details of Florence's marriage, and it is therefore laid before the reader.

"1588.   *September* 30.   Sir Thomas Norreys *to* Sir F. Walsyngam.

" R: Hon: My dutye most humblye pmised.

" Mr. John Fitz Edmond of Cloyne havynge intelligence that some of his adversaryes in England have informed your Honor that he should be a practyser in compassynge ye matche betwene the Earle of Clan Kartye's daughter and Florence Mc Kartye, and therefore requested me to certifye my knoleadge therin to yo᷑ Honor, for the better avoydinge the sayd suggestyon. And for that, upon the fyrst receapt of Her Maj᷑ᵗˢ L᷑ʳᵉˢ, I made verye earnest and diligent enquyrye for all such as were compassers, or anye waye dealers in the sayd matche, it appered that the Countesse of Clankartye hersealfe had bene w᷑ᵗʰ the sayd Mr. Fitz Edmond for advise and councell therein, and that he utterlye refused anye waye to deale in the matter, altogether diswadinge the Countesse, and shewinge what dangers and incommodytyes would thereof ensue to all that dealte in the same, as by the testymonye of Mr. James Roanan and Wylliam Roache, boath mē of Corke, and verye suffytyent men, dyd appeere: in respeacte whereof, and the good caryage of the gentlemā beinge, since I had charge in this pvynce, verye forward, and alwayes readye and well furnyshed to answere anye services as neede requyred, and wythall most wyllinge to discour the bad practyses of lewd psones, I could not refuse to afford him my l᷑ʳᵉ to yo᷑ Hon᷑ˢ, referrynge the consyderatyon thereof to yo᷑ Hon᷑ˢ grave iudgement. So humblye takinge leave, I comytt yo᷑ Hon᷑ʳ to God's most holye Tuytyon.

                                          " Thoˢ Norreys.

" Youghall, the last of Sept᷑ʳ, 1588."

Time was creeping on; nearly six months had elapsed since the marriage, and no decision had yet reached Munster relative to the ultimate fate of the prisoners. Sir Thomas Norreys' letter of recommendation, and Florence's great penitence, might have produced their effect; the heart of the Queen might have relented. Florence and his friends were of good cheer; their restraint had been made as light as was consistent with their safe keeping; and their evil-wishers were in alarm lest the dark cloud should bear its thunders over them, and explode harmlessly in the void—lest the marriage should be submitted to as a mischief past remedy, and the offenders be enlarged: moreover, certain passages in the noble letter of Sir William Herbert had produced an effect which added bitterness to the distasteful draught which Florence had presented to the lips of his enemies. Certain horsemen, who, rather by the connivance of the authorities in Munster, than by consent from home, had been allotted, at the Queen's charge, to the undertakers for their protection, were to be withdrawn, and the custody of each man's lands to be left to himself. This was considered, and scarcely

                                                        E

without reason, as an invitation to every ejected Irishman to deal as he pleased with the men whom the Queen had herself enticed to dispossess him. To Sir Valentine Browne, who had placed himself beyond the barriers of Slievelogher, in the remotest and wildest tracts of Desmond, and had some twelve or more of these horsemen for his guard, this determination sounded like the inevitable doom of all his acquisitions, of all his toil, his outlay, and his hopes for his family. He was not an " importunate suiter, and had patiently borne many thwarts without troubling the minister ;" but this last blow wrung from him a cry of anguish, which, though as just as it was piteous, fell upon hearts hardened—ears deafened against him.

Upon the memorable occasion when Sir Henry Sidney had passed his Christmas holidays in Cork, he thought it not unbecoming the dignity of the Privy Council, and his own, to inform them how that festive season had been spent, namely, " in shows and tokens, the best the citizens had been able to devise to evince their loyalty." Sir Valentine Browne, in like manner, thought it not unseemly that he should inform the Lord Treasurer how Florence and his young bride were spending their honeymoon ; and how, under mournful presage of coming ruin, he was himself making Christmas doleful in Dublin.

" 1588.   *Octob*^r 16.   SIR VALENTINE BROWNE *to* WALSYNGHAM.

" I am not a shameles suitor, and cannot therefore advaunce my longer services w^t importunitie, and therefore have the more neade of such Hon: favours, whereof I had never more nead then nowe, havinge wth manie thwarts beene greatlie burdened by chardge; firste ymployed as an undertaker, and my landes given from me by Her ^Ma^{tie} to the Earle of Clan Car^{re}, and next by dealinge wth the same Earle for the redempçõn thereof from him; and the more to increase the same, the horsemen allowed untoe me, are wth the rest to be presentlie dischardged, and so layde uppon my burden; wherein I crave your healpe to have a contynuance for four or five yeares of twelve onlie, for that I stand in greate doubte that all the Mc Carties will joyne against my three sonnes that are possessed of those lands wch Florence Mc Cartie did chieflie looke to have had uppon the marriadge of the Earle's daughter; and beinge soe (as I am advertised yt is), withoute her Ma^{ts} assistaunce,—lyinge so farre remote from this state, —they shall never be able to holde owte. Donell Mc Carthie, thEarle's bastarde, is gone to the woodes, and lyethe as an owte lawe, resortinge contynually to the Mc Carthies of Carbrye, and is there secretlie supported. Yt were not good that those countreis should be loste in th Erle's tyme, for puttinge Her ^Ma^{tie} to greate chardge in recoveringe the same, except shee will yealde all unto them, as Florence Mc Cartye and his friendes dothe not sticke to reporte she will; and allso allowe of the marriadge, w^ch (as he falslie publishethe) was not forbydden him; and so at Corcke, where he remaynethe w‍ᵗh the resorte of his frends and thEarle's daughter, w‍ᵗh small restraynte, he rather reioyceth w‍ᵗh banquettinge, then that he seemethe sorie for his contempte. And yf he and the rest were removed thence, and broughte to Dublin, it woulde be more securyte to her Highness, and cause them the better to knowe themselves. I am hartelie sorrie to heare of y‍ʳ ofte̅n sicknes, and so praie to the Lord Almightie to restore you to pfecte healthe, and longe contynuance of the same.

"At Dublin this 16th of Octobre, 1588.

"Y‍ʳ Honor's bounden at cõmaundment,
"VALENTYNE BROWNE.

"To the Rᴛ. Hoɴ. Sɪʀ F. WALSYNGHAM, &c."

Smarting under the disappointment attending their over-tures with the Earl of Clancar for the hand and inheritance of his daughter, Nicholas Browne had vented his indignation in threats against the Earl, and Sir Valentine petulantly charged Sir William Herbert with having lent himself to promote the designs of Florence, and with using his official influence to bring this shame and indignity upon their family. Much angry correspondence passed between the parties; and Sir William, conceiving that his official character had been impugned, to the injury of the Queen's service, sent copies of the Brownes' accusations, and his own replies, to the English minister. Were it not for much incidental matter contained in these letters, it must have fallen to the author of this life of Florence, himself to present to the reader such description as he was able of that remarkable body of men, who, under the designation of Undertakers, were destined by the policy of the English Cabinet to introduce civility amongst our rude ancestors, and to form an Elizabethan nobility, which, rein-forced a century later by the distinguished warriors of the Commonwealth, expanded into that brilliant territorial aris-tocracy which has shed so much splendour upon the country of their adoption!

Sir William Herbert (called, by a pleasantry of Nicholas Browne, Sir William hard-beard) was a grave and conscien-tious man, and, by his own testimony, was held in repute by all the bishops, judges, and magistrates of cities, and the gravest and wisest of his province ; his opportunities of acquiring a thorough knowledge of the characters of these enterprising men were unequalled, and therefore his account of them bears with it more authority than the author of these pages could claim for any opinion of his own.

"1588.   October 20.   Sir W. HERBERT to BURGHLEY.

"I have just caus to be agreaud that Her Majestye is abused w‍ᵗʰ sutch undertakers, I associated w‍ᵗʰ sutch com-

E 2

panions, and an honourable accion disgraced wth such lewd, indiscreat, and insufficient men. I thinke mysealf nothinge too hasty in writinge to my Lo: Threasurer, for it is high tyme theas frawds wear met w^{th}al, and tyme doth not alter, but confirm my opinion. Theas horsemen are a superflous chardge unto Her Highnes: soe wrott I to Mr. Secretary som months since, and soe avowed I to Mr. Attorney Generall at his beinge hear in Munster."

"1588. *December* 27. HERBERT *to* BURGHLEY.

"My dislick of the proceedings hear, contrary to the purport of Her Majesty's articles, and the ground plott of this accion [the *undertaking* of the lands of the Irish] hath drawn upon mea the enmitea of Sir Valentine Browne, Sir Edward Denny, and others of that sort, that measur conscience by comodite, and law by lust. They are growne to a combinacion and a resolucion, resemblinge that mentioned in the 2^d chapter of the wisdome of Solomon, &c. &c."

That Nicholas Browne should feel great wrath against the Earl of Clancar, who had made his position at once painful and grotesque, is natural and excusable; and had it not been for the officious interference of Sir W. Herbert, in the matter of the Queen's horsemen, this anger would doubtless have been concentrated on the Earl and his more favoured rival; but the dispute with Herbert for a while drew away his thoughts from the marriage, and all concerned in it.

"1589. *January* 6. NICHOLAS BROWNE *to* WALSYNGHAM.

"My humble duty remembred. R^t Honb^le w^t no les thankes to yor Honor for yor favor and furtherance shewed unto me, wherby I presume thus fur to troble you, by whose good meanes I may be rid of troble iminent unto me. So yt is, R^t Hon: that the mariadge betwene the Erle of Clancarthys daughter and myself breaking of, by contempt againste Her Matie, and contrarye to her consent given therein to me, I was allotted 12 horsemen in pay, for the better defence of myself and my brothren who are the onelie English that ar residint in that remote wilde place of all the west of Ireland; of the wch horsemen we ar discharged, whose services upon the Spaniards, with whose repetition I will not troble you wch is [defaced] so prudiciall to our state, that we shalbe constrained, to our utter undoinge, to leave the contrey, where our expenses have benn greate, and to wery Her Matie wth sute for recompence, whose title tothe whole Erldom after the disseas of this man, if it be not prevented, will not be wthout great chardg recovered or maintained. My humble suite unto your good Honor therefore is this, that as unto a pore follower of your's, you will be a means to Her Highnes eyther to restore me to my former number of horsemen, or in lieu of them 20 fotemen, or els, for my further conntennance, and les chardg to Her Matie to derecte her l^{res} to hir Deputye here, to appoint me hir officer, and Shriffe (wch place I have heretofore executed) over Desmond and Kerry duringe the space of some 4 or five year next ensuinge: wch motion, if your Honor shall first like, and then make in my behalfe unto Her Matie, her title dependinge so much uppon yt, and the preservacion of us, there is verye good hope of Her Highnes allowing therof, and your Honor shall bind us in great dutye devote unto your sarvice. Thus wishinge your Honor long life, good health, and all increase of Honnor, I humbly leave you to the tuityon of th Almightye.

"Your Honor's humble follower,

"NICHOLAS BROWNE.

"From Dublin, 6 January, 1588.'

About the same time Browne wrote to Sir E. Denny "concerning Finin Mc Carty, if occasion be ministred, preach at least how daungerous a subiect he may prove. Sir I am famalier with you like a neighbour, and bold as a fiend, wherefore, I pray, think of Tom Spring [Tom was another undertaker, and a relation of Browne's] and me sometimes even in the Privy Chamber."

To this dispute we are indebted not only for considerable entertainment, but for some further illustration of the men who through life were Florence's bitterest enemies. The entire history of " *the honourable accion* " (the Undertaking), certainly contains nothing more curious, or more ingenuous, than the concluding passages of the following letter, in which the writer points out to Walsyngham the precautions *he meant to take* to prevent such noble Signories from falling into the hands of men that measured conscience by " comodite." These lands had belonged to the MacCarthys in the days when the English first set foot in the country; history gravely informs us that they had *acquired* them in the days of Heremon and Heber (anno Mundi 2737), who were, in their generation, twenty-second in descent from Feniusa Farsa, King of Scythia, and twenty-sixth from Noah! Donal Mac Carthy Mor was in life and health at the time this letter was written, and it may be doubted whether he entertained as clear a perception as the writer, of the nature of English tenure, by which, since he received his Earldom, he held his lands.

" 1588. *Dec.* 27. SIR WILLIAM HERBERT *to* WALSYNGHAM.

" I desire nothinge more then that my whole woords, deads, and demeanure in theas parts may bea called in question. I dowbt not to have the testimonye for mea, of the Bishops, Judges, Magistrates of citeas, and gravest and wisest of this province, the generall voyce of theas toe counties, the judgement of my Lord Deputye, and of the Chief of this Estate; and the very letters and handwrytinges of my greatest adversaryes, whoes accusations shall prove myne ornament, and whoes combinations shall discover theyr shame, if I may have justice. I must confess, I have in hart abhorred many of theyr actions, but never any of themsealves. I have ever wished them well, but could not brooke that whitch I knew evill; they on the other side detract and detest all my doynges; not becaus they are evill, but becaus they are myne. Hearof it is that Sir Edw^{de} Denye mislickes any that affects mea, tells everye body that hea will doe more for them then twenty Sir William Herberts, that hea is your Honor's coosen Germane, and that Ireland shall know him soe to bea before Easter; that I pretend the authoritea I have not, and exercies the Government never committed unto mea, endevor to dischardge a trust never reposed in mea, and delude the people with hope of reformations of iniuries, that lieth not in my power to procure. But having of recitall of woords far woors, and deads many, marvelous, injurious, which for threa especiall causes (beasydes many other), I have endured with great patience. First, for that hea was a Groome of her Majesty's privye chamber; secondly, for that hea was your Honor's kinsman; thirdly, for that whitch I will pass with greafe and scilence, and whitch tyme and his own actions will discover. Whearin he is spurred on by Springe, Constable of Castlemayne, assisted by Mr. Browne, with all oothers in theas parts that measure theyr conscience by theayr comoditie. I cannot omitt what passingly displeased mea. Thoes rare thinges in trewth of goode valew of the Duke of Medina Sidonea's cast into his hands, as I enterpreat, by God's providence (to the end they might bea presented to Her Majestyea), hea beayinge Her Highnes' sworne servant, of Her Privye Chamber, sworne councellor of this province, sworne sheriff of this county, hea shewed ceayrteyn frends of his at his hous of Trally, and declared how hea ment to dispose of every part of them; som to this nobleman, some to that; one thinge thear was whitch coest threa thowsand Duketts in Spayn; that hea sayed hea shoulde, but woolde not, bestowe upon your Honor; for that your Honor was allreadye sufficientlye bent to doe him goode; but hea woolde bestow it upon anoother, that had diswaded Her Majestye from forgeavinge him the rent of his signorye, whome by that gift hea hoped to make his frend.

" For that I mean to take 6000 akers within the countye of Kerry, and am desirous to have oother 6000 akers in the countye of Desmonde, after the Earl of Glincarr's death, I beseatch your Honorable favour and furtherance to Her Majesty, that I may thear have Castle Logh, the Pallace, and Ballicarbry, with 6000 akers of land about them. I write the rather thus tymely, if not out of tyme, least some other shoolde first make means and suit for them."

It was not the fortune of Sir Valentine Browne to see this angry controversy to its end, for he was called away from all his earthly cares on the 8th day of February, 1589; his son Nicholas became the head of that adventurous family, heir to all the anxieties which had haunted his father—and they were neither imaginary nor trifling—and of all the schemes for saving a noble Signory from falling back into the hands of the man from whom he had won it by a shrewd mortgage, the Queen's patent, and the Queen's horsemen. We shall see that he was equal to the occasion. His feud with Herbert long continued to enliven the meetings of the Privy Council; but his fight for the signory of Molahiff dis-

played an energy and perseverance which fill us with admiration. The last mournful autograph of Sir Valentine had not
been without its effect; the banquetings in the Cork prison,
and the festive hours which the young bride was spending
with her husband, were rudely interrupted. Orders came
from England to separate the offenders. Florence was to be
sent to Dublin, the Lady Ellen to be detained in safe keeping, though at large, within the city of Cork. Sir Warham
St. Leger poured more of his prophetic warnings, and timely
remedies, into the chamber of the Privy Council. Had the
advice of this far-seeing man been taken—and it was, after
all, not of a nature to shock the sensibility of the Privy Council by any extreme of severity,—the Queen might perchance
have been spared many years of trouble, and, what was of
equal importance in the opinion of the writer, more than
£100,000 of treasure! The terror of Spanish invasion was
the constant subject of despatches between Ireland and the
English Ministers; and it was with the view to cut off foreign
attempts that this rough statesman now wrote to the Council.

1588. *Dec. 7.* St. LEGER *to the* LORDS.

"To cut of foraine attempts, and the daunger that maie growe to the
disturbance of this Realme, the Seneschall, Patricke Fitzmorris, and Patricke Condone, nowe captyves in the said Castell of Dublin, woulde be made
shorter by the *heades* if they maie be brought within compasse of lawe ; and
if the white Knighte and his sonn in lawe, Donoge Mac Cormack, kept
them companie, they were well rydd out of this comonwealth; and yf they
cannot be brought within compasse of lawe, whereby they maie have their
iuste desertes, then woulde they be comytted to some safe prysone in Englande; for assuredliey yf they remaine where they are, they will, at one
tyme or other, breake pryson, for the wᶜʰ, yf they doe, they will cause the
Queene to spende £100,000! they will never be goode excepte they were to
be made again newe, being periured wretches, some of them having twyce
forsworne themselves before me uppon the Testamente, and therefore yt
were a good sacryfice to God to rydd them out of this worlde, where they
will never do good. We have nowe sente from hence to Doblyn to the
L. Chancellor (by dyrection from the L. Deputie) Florence Mac Cartie,
whoe contemptuously haith marryed the Earle of Clanker's onelie daughter,
to answere that his doinges. It were good for this Goverment yf he were,
for his contempte, keepte a prysoner duringe this daungerous tyme, he
beinge a person that the mailecontentes of this provynce greatlie bende
themselves unto, and the onlie man, in their conceiptes, lykelie againe to
set up the House of the Garaldynes, of which he is dyscended by his
Mother, whoe was daughter to Morrys of Desmonde, unkell to the late
wicked Earle of Desmonde; by which parentage, together with his own,
beinge dyscended out of one of the chiefe of the house of the Clankerties,
he is like to be a person of greate power, yf he be not prevented, and his
ambitious desiers cutt shorte, &c.
"And yf Sir Owen Mac Cartie were also appoynted to remayne in
Englande and his twoe sonnes with him, tyll the worlde be quyeter, yt

were a happie turne for this ende of Irelande; for assuredlie, my L., although
Sir Owen be symple in shewe, yet is he a verey ipocryte, and one that
carrieth as cankerd a mynd towardes English Goverment as anie one of
them, yf he durste shewe it, &c.   And chiefelie yf the marriage of Florence
McCartie maie be undone, and she marryed to some English Gentⁿ by the
Queen's appoyntment; whereby her father maie be (by him that shall marrie
her) dyrected to governe his countrie accordinge to the lawes of this realm,
which is the daungereste countrie for forraine invasyon to attempte, that
appertayneth to this realm.
                                        " WARHAM SAINTLEGER.
"From Corke, 7 Dec^r, 1588."

   Some portion of this prompt policy was adopted. The advice was given in a letter dated the 7th of December; on the
19th of the same month came the order to despatch Florence
to England. The postscript to the following letter will
show how keen had recently become the official scrutiny
into Florence's conduct in matters of more moment than his
marriage.

   1589. *Jan.* 28. THE LO. DEPUTY FITZWILLIAMS *to* WALSYNGHAM.

   "SIR,—Your l^{er} of the 19th of the last, signifyinge your Honour's ex-
pectacon of Florence McCartie's dispatche thetherwards, I receaved not till
the 19th of this instant, whome nowe I have sent by my man Chichester,
this bearer, hauing not before receaved other direction thence, then for
the separatinge of the yonge Lady from him, and the removinge of him
from Corke to Dublin, both which were accomplished, and she delivered
by the Erle her father's appointment to the keping of certaine of his own
servants.
   "P. S. I am credibly informed that one William Hurlye, late of Eng-
land, followinge some causes of Florence McCartie, his M^r., under color of
going into Ireland, slipt into France, where it is said he is : And that one
Allen Martin, of Gallwaie, either is, or the last somer was, with the D. of
Parma, from the said Florence. I have sent to Gallwaie for that Allen
Martyn to be brought unto me, yf he be there to be had; and I have laied
for William Hurley at his retorne, whome yf I gett, I will send over unto
your Honor.
                                        " H. FITZ WILLIAMS.
"From Her Majesty's Castle of Dublin, 28 Jan^y, 1589."

   On the 10th of February, 1589, in the company of Chichester, and with the curious attendance of his *fencing-master*,—a
certain Patrick Cullen, whom, at his last being in England,
he had induced to enter his service, and whom now his evil
fortune took back to London, to finish a strange career upon
the gallows,—Florence arrived safely in London, and was at
once given over into the custody of Sir Owen Hopton, Lieutenant of Her Majesty's Tower of London. The domestic
arrangements of that establishment required certain quarterly
returns to be made to the Privy Council of the expenses in-

curred for its inmates. From these returns, not all of which
have perished, we are enabled to learn more of Florence than
was known beyond those walls for a considerable period.
For a long series of years those Tower bills had been headed
by the name of James Fitz Gerald, the child of the great
rebel. To that mournful roll the name of Florence MacCarthy was now added for the first time. Subsequently it became as unfailing an ornament to those quarterly bills as had
been that of his unfortunate cousin !

"The Demaundes of Sir Owen Hopton, Knight, Lewitennant of her Majestie's Tower of London, for the Diette and other chardges of prisoñrs
in his custodie, from the Nativitie of our Saviour Christe last paste,
1588, till Th' Annunciacõn of our Blessed Ladye the Virgyn then nexte
following, beeinge one quarter of a yeare, as hereafter is particularly
declared.

" Florence Mac Carty.
" For the dyette & other chardges of Florence Mac Carty from the x^h of
Februarye, 1588, till the xxjv^h of March then nexte followinge, beeinge vj
weekes at xxvj^s. viii^d. the weeke.   For himselfe, viij^{li}.
"Item, One Keeper at v^s. the weeke, xxx^s.
"Item, Fewell and Candell at iiij^s. the weeke, xxiiij^s.
"Tota^{lis}, x^{li}. xiiij^s."

A similar bill was sent in for the time intervening between
24th of June, 1589, and 24th of December then next following, with this difference, that two keepers, instead of one,
are charged for; and for fewel and candel, 8s. instead of 4s.
were allowed weekly. Attached to one of these bills is this
brief notice :—" Florence MacCarty, Esquire, prisoner 8
months; the cause best known to your Honours.—Referred
to her Majesty."

CHAPTER III.

FLORENCE was now withdrawn from the country, which his adversaries had declared he alone had kept in trouble and disaffection. What effect his withdrawal had upon the peace and loyalty of Carbery and Desmond we shall shortly see. It is not a little remarkable that, amidst so many arrests, the Earl of Clancar himself should have been excepted. Had there been no head cleverer than his own to guide him through the tortuous ways by which he had advanced to this marriage—the simulated quarrel with Florence; the bargain with Browne; the appeal for the Queen's consent, and his absence from Ireland at the time of its solemnization,— Donal MacCarthy Mor would probably have been in the Tower of London to welcome his son-in-law; but the contingency had been foreseen, and well provided for:—at an opportune moment, five gentlemen stepped forward and deposed that they were themselves witnesses that the Earl had consented to the marriage but "conditionally." So great had been his respect for the will of his sovereign, that he had, on the delivery of the marriage deeds, expressly stipulated, in their hearing, that unless the consent of her Majesty were first obtained, all that he had done should have no effect in law. The evidence of these gentlemen, set forth in the document following, bore the Earl harmless through his share of the offence :—

"1588. *March* 9. A true copie of a condicion made betwixt Maister Florence Mc Carty and the Earl of Clancare.

"To all Xpian people to whome thies pnts may appertayne; knowe ye that we the pties whose names are underwritten thincking it charitable to testifie the truethe, especially being thereunto required, at the request of the Right Hon: the Earle of Clancare, do witnesse as followethe, that wheare the said Earle hath covenaunted and passed writings to Mr. Florence Mc Carty for the injoyning of his daughter, dame Ellen, to wife, and hathe by several deeds contracted wth the said Florence for the same; that upon the deliverye of all the sayd deeds, a condicion was mencioned by the said Earle by worde, and agreed unto by the said Florence, viz: that yf the said Florence might procure Her M^a^ties assent to the same marriage, and procure his patent to his Daughter aforesaid, and to the heyres of her body, then they meant the said deeds should staund in full force, otherwise should be of no effect in lawe.

" In witnes whereof we have hereunto subscribed, and put our seales,
being present at the delivery of the said Deeds, and the said contract between the said Earle and the said Florence.
" Dated the 9th day of the monethe of March, 1587.
                                        " RYCHARD POWER.
                                        " JAMES TRANT.
                                        " DENIS FALVEY.
                                        " PATRICK GALWEY.
                                        " DERMODE LEYNE."

Had nothing further happened to exasperate the mind of
Elizabeth in the matter of Florence's marriage, it is probable
that her womanly heart would have relented, and the storm
have passed away without much damage to any of the parties
concerned in it; but this was not destined to be the termination of the matter. The marriage itself had been sufficiently
romantic; celebrated " in the old broken church, and with a
mass," amidst the magic scenery of the lake country, attended
only by the aged Countess, and O'Sullivan Mor—the first of
the Earl's subordinate chieftains, with whom was the giving
of the rod, the symbol of sovereignty over the half of Munster,—much more romantic was its sequel !
    It has been seen that Sir Warham St. Leger had not con-
tented himself with sending to the Minister a narrative of all
he could discover concerning the time, manner, and contrivers
of the marriage ; but had traced out a dismal series of calamities likely to fall upon the country, unless something effectual
and speedy were done to cut off Florence in this first of his
ambitious designs. The remedies he prescribed were reducible
to two—to weaken his alliances, and to annul his marriage.
The former consisted in prosecuting by course of law, all who
were connected with him, and in excluding him, if possible,
from succession to the Captaincy of Carbery. The present chief
of that country was Sir Owen MacCarthy. The Tanist, or successor to him was Donal-na-Pipy, and the successsor to Donal
was Florence. Donal, as we have mentioned, had bound himself in bonds of £100,000 not to surrender his lands to the
Queen, nor to turn the succession from its due course. The existence of this contract was well known in Munster; for it had
been submitted to Sir John Popham, the English Attorney-
General, when in Ireland. Donal had sons of his own, and
would willingly have evaded this contract, had there been any
possibility of escaping from the bonds : it occurred, or was
suggested to him, that his ancestor, Finin M'Dermod, had,
several generations back, placed his country under English
law and succession, and that, by virtue of letters patent then
granted, he, Donal, ought at that very moment to be Lord

of Carbery ; for his father had been Sir Owen's eldest brother, and he ought to have succeeded to him. The support of this claim, which Donal was thrust forward to assert, was one of the devices proposed by St. Leger. Its success, at best, was very doubtful, and must under any circumstances, be a work of time ; it gave Florence no concern.

The second suggestion—the disallowing of the marriage, and the bestowing the heiress, together with a patent of inheritance of the Earl's country, on some English gentleman who would be answerable for her father's loyalty—was a more serious matter. Florence knew that this was no idle threat ; he knew that overtures had already been made to the Earl to induce him to reclaim the custody of his daughter ; and the lawyers had pronounced that with *him* rested the power to dispose of her hand, for she was under age. Florence knew too well the character of his father-in-law to doubt for an instant what course he would take, if the Queen insisted upon divorcing his wife from him. His resolution was taken at once ; there had been no hesitation in the old broken church —there was none now !

It would appear from Sir Warham St. Leger's letters that the Lady Ellen had been delivered to the custody of the "gentleman porter ;" (an officer attached to the staff of the Presidents of Munster) Sir Thomas Norreys says, " to a merchant of the town," by whom she was allowed all freedom consistent with her safe keeping : the Lord Deputy wrote that she had been entrusted to "certain servants of the Earl," and Florence declared that the Earl had, by Sir Valentine Browne's means, procured letters to the Commissioners of Munster to deliver her into *his* hands. However this may have been, and whoever were her keepers,—and the issue makes it highly probable that the officers of the Earl were really the parties,—it happened that one day early in February, a few days after Florence's arrival in London, and towards dusk, at the closing of the town-gates, two female figures passed outward from the city of Cork without question ; they were joined by a peasant who had been loitering about in the neighbourhood, and in a few minutes the three became dim in the distance —lost in the twilight. That night the gentleman porter, or the merchant, or the servants of the Earl, saw no more of their prisoner ! The Lady Ellen was gone ! and for nearly two years she might have been numbered with the dead for aught that the Vice-President, the Lord Deputy, or Mr. Justice Smythe, could discover to the contrary.

To the lot of Sir Warham St. Leger it fell to announce

this flight, as it had fallen to advertise Her Majesty of the marriage of Florence. Sir Thomas Norreys was absent, as he had been formerly absent; and now, as then, his despatches followed, telling, with trifling variations, and the addition of a few conjectures, the same provoking story. Instant was the pursuit, keen the search, after the fugitive! The authorities of Munster, and the Lord Deputy, were not without their practised espyals and intelligencers; but the prisoner in the Tower was better served than they were. Mr. Justice Smythe, as it appeared, could make a discovery that was sufficiently interesting, but how this girl probably not above sixteen or seventeen years of age, had managed to escape, or what had become of her, it passed his ingenuity to find out.

"1589. *February* 18. Sir Warham St. Leger *to* L^d. Burghleigh.

The Flight of Florence's Wife.

" I judge it my dutie to advertise you what hathe happened since I last wrote. The yonge Ladie (beinge comÿtted in this Towne to the safe keepinge of the Gentleman Porter), on Fridaie wass a sennighte, late towardes nighte, aboute the shuttinge of the gates, stale out of this Towne disguysed, and a maide of hers with her. What is become of her it cannot yet certenlie be learned. I am informed (by a gentleman of good creadyt, of the countrie of Carburie, whence Florence McCartie is) that a man of the saied Florences, called Bryan Carda, in English called Bryan of the Cards (a nickname geven him, because he is cunnynge at the cardes), receyved her without the gates, beinge her guyde. Whither she is gone; and yf that be true, then her departure out of this Towne is not without the consente of the said Florence; and it is greatlie to be presumed that he is acquaynted with her goinge, for that he sent a messinger unto her secretlie from Doblyn, upon whose cominge unto her, and returninge unto him againe, she the morrowe after stale out of this Towne.

"Her conveighance is marvellous secretlie kept, and a greate cunnynge used by her close keepeinge, thinkinge thereby to keape her absent tyll she be of full yeres of consente irrevocable, he doubtinge, that yf she sholde have ben delyvered unto her Father (she beinge under yeres), her father might persuade her to yeld to be devorsed from Florence; the which might very well have ben doñ, had she not ben conveighed awaie as she is.

"She was the slenderlier lookte unto by the gentleman porter, for that the said Florence, before his departure out of this Towne to Doblyn, entered in band of recognisaunce before me of fower hundred poundes to the Quenes Ma^{ts} use, that she sholde remayne in this Towne true prysoner till she were delyvered by order from Her Highnes out of Inglande : the which baude he hath forfeycted to her Matie (a thinge that wolde not be let goe with him) by this (and other) forfietures Her Highnes may take into her handes a castell and lands of great importaunce, called Castell Lough, the which the said Florence haith in mortgage of the Earle of Clancartie for the sum of fower or fyve hundred Poundes he lente to the saide Earle. It is the strongeste scytuacõn of a castell that is in Irelande ; a thinge of that force, as a lytle fortyfycacõn would make yt imprignable, and therefore (not offendinge in this my writinge), a matter not to be forstoude, but Her Highnes to enter thereon. (The Castle stands in a great Lough, where there is great store of orient pearls found.)

                                        " WARHAM SAINTLEGER."

" 1589. *March* 8. NORREYS *to* WALSYNGHAM.

" R^t Hon : my dutie pmised wth all humilitie. At such tyme as I was called by the Lo. Deputie to the service in Ulster, it pleased His Lp. to send direction to Sir Warham St. Leger, and the Justices to whom in my absence the chardge of the Province was comitted for the sendinge upp of the yonge Ladie of Clancartie to Dublin, w^{ch}, as well in respecte of her yong yeares, as for wante of convenient means to convey her thether, they did not greatlie hasten; and moved wth pittie, not suspectinge any gile, were pswaded to allow her the libertye of the Towne, and to comitt her to the chardge of a merchant, onelie takinge bandes of Florence MacCarty that she shold remayne treu prisoner there, who, as I am crediblie informed, hath by secret meanes seduced her to abandon the place, and to convey herself either to England or ellswhere, covertlie to be shrowded, abusinge thereby the lenity that hath ben used towardes her, and practisinge by this meanes to pvnt y^t wch y^r Honors hath determined, wch I have hetherto consealed, beinge still in hope, by some means to have notice of her, whereof beinge now somewhat dowtefull, and having wthall so good opportunity, I thought it my dutie to advertise yor Hono^r thereof, as well in myne owne dischardge as to make him better knowen unto yor Hono^r who hath ben the worker of it, leaving the consideracõn thereof to your Honor's grave judgment, and so forbearing at this tyme furder to troble your Honor, comitt the same to Gode's Holie tuicon.

"Tho⁵. Norreys.

"Shandon, 8 March, 1588."

"1859. *March* 11. Mr. Justice Smythe *to* Walsyngham.

"My dewti to your Honor most humbly remembred. Pleasth the same to be advertised, that wee cannot learne as yett whither Clancarty's daughter hath conveyde herself, although eversithens her departure, nowe a monthe paste, her neareste alies, fosterers, and frinds remayne in durance, to make them thereby declare their knowledges of her. It is thoughte by us here to have happened by the practices of Mr. Florence McCarty. She is nowe knowne not to be wᵗh chylde, as he untreuly made us belive she was. In my late beinge in Dublin, I heard that Florence was apointed by our foreyne enemyes to be Lᵈ President of Mounster by a Spanish comyssion. He hath forfeyted a Recognizans of £400 by her escape and flight, in wᶜh he was bound shea shold remayne trew prysoner, and nott seeke to escape.

"J. Smythe.

"11 March, 1588."

No wonder that the Irish despatches should force from Queen Elizabeth the exclamation that "she was weary of hearing them," and from Cecyll the remark that "he could not blame her!" They had scarcely had time to lay the letter of Sir Thomas Norreys, in favour of Florence, before the Queen, and to consider it in the Privy Council, the assurance of Florence's good carriage and repentance was still sounding in their ears, when the tidings of this fresh contempt reached them. One single crumb of comfort the Munster correspondents could find in this banquet of evil news. The lady's husband *must* have been cognizant of her escape! although their endeavours to prove such knowledge had utterly failed, and although he forfeited a large sum of money by her flight: he *must* have known it, reasoned the Vice-President, and *therefore* his securities were forfeited. And Castle Lough was worth the Queen's notice; for great store of orient pearls were to be found in the lake in which it stood, and a little outlay might make it impregnable. Thrice happy the Englishman who should find himself commanding a garrison there!

In dispensing with the Queen's permission for his marriage, in seducing away his wife from her keepers in Cork, for so Sir Thomas Norreys asserted that he did—Florence had, doubtless, made up his mind to the consequences, and he could not have been taken by surprise at finding himself a prisoner in the Tower. In viewing his position at the worst, there was not in it, after all, anything to cause him very serious alarm : the question of divorce was at an end; and for what remained, a word adroitly spoken by Cecyll or Burghley, Stanhope or Raleigh, might suffice to make his peace with Elizabeth. Browne, Norreys, and St. Leger had their enemies, as well as other men—and all men's enemies were to be found at the Court—and every passage connected with that marriage, from the day when Florence's plausibility induced Sir Thomas Norreys to send him into Desmond with authority to possess himself of the Earl's lands, to that autumn evening when the lady vanished from the custody of St. Leger—from the time when Browne the elder settled to his satisfaction the price for his son's bride, to the day on which, to the great scandal of Sir William Herbert, Browne the younger raved about "an Italian fig" for the lady's father —possessed too many traits of absurdity for the gravity even of the Privy Counsel to resist. That Florence's enemies looked upon his offence as a matter not likely to be attended by any lengthened or severe punishment, may be judged from the alacrity with which they dropped all mention of the marriage as soon as they bethought them of anything more serious with which to charge him.

That any man in Ireland could find aught else of which to accuse him, Florence was ignorant till he reached London. On the day after his arrival he had passed from the hands of Chichester to the custody of Sir Owen Hopton, and nearly six weeks passed away before any further notice was taken of him. This interval was doubtless spent in collecting—not, indeed, evidence against him, for none was eventually produced— but such loose charges as were thrown out by his enemies, with the hope of inducing his judges to make the offence of his marriage a plea for his continued imprisonment. At last, on the 23rd of March, the important examination, which Florence must have been daily expecting since his arrival, took place; whether in the imposing presence of the Privy Council, or of officers deputed by them, we know not; if before the Lords themselves, Florence must have found himself in the presence of old acquaintances, and even friends. There was a certain stern simplicity about the examination

that ensued: the questions were put to him, and his answers
noted down; there was neither pleading nor reproach; no
attempt was made to cross-question him, or object to his replies. It might seem like a formality used by men whose
opinion was already formed. Great must have been the
amazement of the prisoner at discovering that not one single
syllable about his marriage, or his wife's flight, was produced
against him!

Clearly to understand the gravity of the charges about to
burst upon the head of Florence, it will be necessary to introduce to the reader the name of a man who had been long
held in honour, but who had recently become as fatal as a
pestilence to all who had ever been connected with him in
amity or companionship.

Amongst the many brave men who had for years sustained the power of Elizabeth in Ireland, who formed the
barrier between the wild warriors of O'Neill and the counties
of the Pale, who had served through the fierce struggles of
the despair of the Earl of Desmond, there was not a braver,
or an abler, or a more respected soldier than Sir William
Stanley. Nor of the multitude of knights created by Sir
Henry Sidney, and the various deputies who were privileged
to bestow that honour, was there one who more signally than
he did, shed a lustre upon the chivalry of his country. This
gallant man had held posts of high trust in Ireland; he had
been a constant and intimate adviser of the Cabinet of Dublin,
the correspondent and friend of Burghley. Who would have
imagined that there could be danger or disgrace in being the
friend of such a man? Florence had served with Sir William
Stanley through the seven or eight years of the wars in
Desmond, and so long an association in a common enterprise
and peril might justify the claim of friendship. Whilst
Florence had been loitering, apparently without an object,
about the Court of Elizabeth, Sir William Stanley had been
sent, at the head of certain bands of Irish soldiers enlisted by
himself, to serve under the Earl of Leicester, his especial
friend and patron, in the Low Countries. How he had conducted himself there may be judged from that nobleman's
despatch of 28th September, 1586, to Walsyngham :—

"There was not in the field (at the battle of Zutphen) of ours, of horse,
in the whole ij c. whereof these Lords and gentlemen, with their followers,
to the number of iij score at most, did all this feate, with the help onlie of
Sir William Stanley, who had but 300 for their 3,000 foote, and he did
most valiantlye himsealf, and his owen horsse receaued viij shott of the
muskett, and yett himsealf not hurt. He and old Read are worth their
weight in pearle, theie be ij of as rare captens as anie prince living hath."

F

Scarcely more could be written of the gallant Sir Philip Sidney, who fell upon that fatal field. And yet Stanley had seen rougher work than that fight of Zutphen! Who would suppose it possible that the loyalty of such a man could falter? Who that had known him, served and fought at his side for years in the country where˚ he had enlisted that brave band of 300 foot, could imagine, whilst reading that choice sentence of his general, " that he was worth his weight in pearl," that the most hateful charge which an enemy could bring against him was that he had been the friend or associate of such a man ?

Amongst the successes of the Earl of Leicester had been the capture of Deventer on the Isel; mainly by the address and daring of Stanley this prize had been secured, and it was not considered an undue reward that its captor should be appointed the Governor of the city. Great was the dismay, greater the grief of all who had known the long and loyal career of Sir William Stanley, when the following letter from the Privy Council was read by the Lords and the Deputy of Ireland!

"1587. *January* 30. *Draught of a Letter from the* LORDS *to the* LORD DEPUTY OF IRELAND.

"After, &c., &c., we have verie latelie receaved advertisements from the Lowe Countries that Sir William Standleie and Rowland Yorke, the one appointed by my L. of Leicester to the governm^t of the toune of Deuenter, a place of great importaunce upon the Isell, the other to the commaunding of the fort before Zutphen, recovered this Sommer by his L^p, have about the 19th of this ꝑnt most disloially and treacherouslie delieured over the places committed to their severall charges into hands of the enemy, and wth all not onley for there owne persons made a most shamefull and traiterous revolt and defection, but also seduced and drawen after them diverse others of her Ma^ts subjects, and namely those Irish bands serving under the said Stanley to do the like, to the great dishonour and sclaunder of the nation, and detriment of her Ma^ts service, which fact, as we find it straung, in respect of the said Stanley, considering the generall good opinion conceaved of his loialty and fidelity; so, nowe by many circumstances induced to thinke that this treasonable revolt of his hath proceeded of some other grounds then is yet discovered. And because we have receaved many advertisements of some foreine invasion intended this yeare by the Spaniard against that realm, wherin his long trauell and experience may make him a daungerous instrument for the enemy, we have thought it meete to give your L^p knovledge thereof to thintent you maie carry a watchfull eie upon all such as you knowe to have bene his secrett freinds and dependants, and especially one Jacques de Francesco his lieutenaunt; of whom both in respect he is a straunger ill affected in relligion, and noted to have had some intelligences wth Ballard, lately executed here for the conspiracie against her Maties life, we thinke fitt to be removed out of his charge, and sent hither before this fact of his capten be divulged; bestowing such charge and commaundement as the said Stanley

hath yet in enterteinement there upon such other as by yᵣ Lᵖ and the rest
of the Council shall be found most meete and worthie for the same. We
think it also meete that yᵣ Lᵖ, immediatly upon the receipt hereof, do cause
his house to be verie narrowly searched, and his wife and children restrained, and such of his freinds and followers as you shall suspect, to be
very diligently examined.   [The rest is in Burghly's writing].   And for
yᵗ we here yᵗ befor this his treaterross act, he did send sōe of his followars
or servants from hym, as may be supposed to pass by sea into Irlãd, we
thynk it cōvenient that inq'rey be made, what parties are come frō hym, or
may hereafter arryve in yᵗ realm, ether in yᵉ province of Moūster or els-
where, and theruppō to mak stay of any such, and diligently to examȳ
them of the cause of ther cōm̄g, and of yᵉ tyme of ther deptur frō Stanley;
and furdᵣ, to use them as you shall thynk cōvenient, both for discovery of
any ther lewd purposes; and also to stay thē frō any evill attempt yᵗ may
be in ther power, and of your doyngs we reqre to be advŧised."

How surprising and how painful this intelligence must
have been to the Lords of the Council, to whom Stanley had
been known through his whole career, the reader may judge!
They who can believe that *any* human eloquence can find
aught to say in defence of the man who could do such an
action, or that the most exalted charity can excuse it, may
perhaps find cause to feel leniently towards Sir William
Stanley, by the perusal of a little work written by Cardinal
Allen in his defence.

It will be within the reader's recollection that this Jacques
de Franceschi, the Lieutenant of Sir William Stanley, thus
arrested, had been mentioned by Sir Thomas Norreys as a
chief counsellor of Florence in the affair of his marriage, the
man who had advised him, "whatever you do, go through
with the marriage; when all is done, it will be easy for your
friends to skreen you from any serious consequences." Jacques
had served under Stanley, and with Florence, in Desmond, he
had borne a good name too ; for upon an occasion of his
going to England, Adam Loftus, the Chancellor and Archbishop of Dublin, had not hesitated to give him a letter to Lord
Burghley, couched in these strong terms :—

" I crave pardon for my continual boldness in troubling you so often in
the behalf of such as I know to have well deserved, as especially this
gentleman, amongst the worthiest of his sort, is one.   During all the time
of his service here, I have been thoroughly acquainted with him, and do
certainly know he hath spent his time both in Ulster and Munster in her
Majesty's service, as Lieutenant to Sir William Stanley, in as forward and
valiant manner as any gentleman possibly may do; sundry times lost his
blood, and very hardly escaped with life; his behaviour otherwise such as
may beseem a civil, honest gentleman."

With this civil and honest gentleman, as with Stanley,
Florence had been on terms of much intimacy. Here then

F 2

was material 'for his enemies for accusation, far weightier than the contemptuous marriage.

The revolt of Stanley and the arrest of Jacques had taken place some months before the marriage ; and the advice alluded to by Norreys, if ever really given, must have been given from a state prison; the inference was damaging, as it was meant to be, to the loyalty of Florence. There had probably been a little statecraft used in dealing with this foreigner : for so summary an arrest, and committal to the tower, something more like a crime must have been urged against him than the fact of his having served under Stanley in the Queen's army; and an accusation quite sufficient to justify this, or even a greater amount of severity, was not wanting ; he was charged with having been an accomplice with Ballard, who had been executed for attempting the Queen's life. Jacques was kept in prison for a season ; the charge was then discredited, and he was sent out of the country, when his first act, naturally, was to seek Stanley, who made him his lieutenant again. To accuse Florence of high treason, to force him upon the Queen's notice as the friend of a traitor and of an assassin, even if the charges should eventually be unproved, showed more. worldly wisdom in his enemies than to make a matter of state out of the romance of his marriage.

Such, accordingly, were the charges which formed the subject of Florence's first examination—

" 1589.   *March* 23.   *Articles to be mynistred unto* FLORENCE MAC CARTY.

" 1.   What acquaintance he hath had wth Sir Willm Stanley ? How long, and when he laste sawe him ?

" 2.   What l^{res} he hath written to Sir W^m. Stanley, or receaved from him, and by whom the same were convayed ? as also what messages have passed betwene them since their first acquaintance ?

" 3.   What message he hath sent unto the said Stanley, or to any other in the partes beyond the seas, by William Hurley, his late agent ?

" 4.   What was the cause of the said agent's going beyonde the seas ?

" 5.   What l^{res} or messages have passed betwen one Jacques Francischi, sometimes Sir William Stanley's Lieutenant, and one Wayman, Ensigne to the said Stanley, and whither he did not speake with the said Wayman before his departure out of Ireland.

" 6.   Whither he do not knowe one Ed. Bremyngham that hath remayned some good time here in England ?

" 7.   Whither he was not previe unto certaine messages or l^{res} sent by the said Bremingham unto Sir William Stanley, or anie other pson in forraine partes ?

" 8.   Whither he did not knowe one Donough O'Conar, an Ierish man and an artificer dwelling in London, and whither the said Donough O'Conar were not sent about some sp'iall matter wth Edwd Bremyngham to the D. of Parma.

" 9.   What messages or l^res have passed betwen the said examinate and certaine Ierish Busshops, and others of that nation remayning in Spaine, w^thin the space of 2 yeares ?

" Whither he did not knowe one Allen Martin of Galloway, and whither he were not made previe to certaine messages and l^res of his that were sent to the D. of Parma ?"

" 1588.   *March* 23.   *The Exa :   taken of* FLORENCE MC CARTYE *the* 23^d *Mar,* 1588.

" 1.   To the fyrst he saythe that he grew acquaynted wth Sr Wm Stanley at sooche tyme as the sayd Sir W. was Shrive of the C^o of Corke.

" 2.   To the second he sayeth y^t he never had any dealyngs wth the said Sir Wm Stanley sythence his departure from Her Ma^ts servyce.

" 3, 4.   The thirde and 4 he denyeth, sayeing y^t he never heard of Hurley sythince his departur out of this realme.

" 5.   To the fifth he saythe that he receyved a message from Jacques by Wayman, wch was only to requyre the said Exa to pay £20, dewe unto one Mr. Marberry, servaunt to the L. Chaunceler.

" 6, 7, 8, 9.   To the 6, 7, 8, 9, he aunswerethe negative.

" 10.   To the tenth he saythe he knowethe one Allen Martyn, a student of one of the Innes of Coort, and that he was made acquainted with him by one Mr. James Fitz Edmonde's sonne, or by one Garrett, Sir Walter Rayley's servant, but dothe not knowe that the sayd Allen had any dealyngs wth the D. of Parma."

Eight days after this examination, Florence wrote his first letter from the Tower ; the first of a long series from that gloomy residence.   It will be seen that it was written in good heart ; indeed, it took a great deal to wring a murmur from him ; and sharp must have been his trials in later life, when his letters and petitions became peevish and desponding.

" 1589.   *March* 31.

" After hartie com̃endaῖons, and for as much as I am as yett uncerten when I shall retourne into those parts, I have thought good, to desire yõ, that uppõ sight hereoff, yõ do not fayle to deliu^r my blak silk stoquenes (which I left yõ in trust to receive with the three bookes wch I left with you to be kepte) to Mr. Browne, praïinge him, in my behalf, that he do not fayle to deliu^er those to som marchant of Dublinge that is his trusty frend, gevenge him express charge to see those thinges salfely deliu^erd at Mr Clasies at Westmester, in Kinges-streete, to Mrs Catherne Buttler, Attendaunte uppon the La: of Ormond, to be deliu^red to me, writtinge a letter to the sayd Catherne to that effect.   Thus leueinge to troble you further, with my hartie com̃endaῖons to my Frends, I take leue.

" At the Towre, the last of March, 1588.

" Your loueinge Frend,

" ffLOR: M^cCARTHY."

To whom the above letter was written appears not; from its tone, it is evident that the writer desired to produce amongst his friends in Ireland the impression that his restraint would not be of long duration, and that a few books would suffice to keep his mind tranquil until he should have occasion for the " blak silk stoquenes " to complete the adornment of his person for attendance at the court. The autograph of Florence, which has been preserved, would seem to have been rather a rough draught than the letter actually sent into Ireland; for it is written, not upon a sheet, or half sheet of the paper he commonly used, but upon some stray scrap; it bears no superscription, and on the back of it is written a rough draught also of matter foreign to the subject of the letter, namely, a list of the sureties ready to be bound for his remaining true prisoner. The letter and the list force upon us the conviction that, by some member of the august tribunal that had judged him, Florence had been led to believe that his imprisonment would not be of long duration, and that the formal security of a few of his own friends would suffice to restore him to freedom.

" 1589. *March* 31.

" The sureties that are now psently readie to enter into bonds for my true imprisōmet are these whose names are under written.

" Mr. Charles Mac Carthy, son and heire to Donogh Mac Cormack Mac Carthy, als McDonogh, Chefe Lorde of the contrie of Dowalla in Cork.

" Mr. Piers Butler of Knok-in-anama wch is his chefe house. He is son to the Lo: of Caher, and brother to the Lo: of Cahir that now is, his liueing stands in the com: of Tiperary nere the towne of Clounmell.

" Capten Edwarde Fitz Geralde, son to Sir Maurice Fitz Thomas of Laikagh. He is of the House of Kildare, and his Liueinge stands in the com of Kildare in the province of Leinster.

" Mr Ceallaghan Mac Conoghoir, son and heir to O'Ceallaghain, chefe Lorde of O'Ceallaghan's countrie, that stands in the com of Corck by the Towne of Mala.

" They are all knowen to those of the Councell of Ireland that are appointed comissioners to heare Ireish causes, and to diuers other Gentn of this land, such as dwells, or hath to do, in Moūster chefelie."

No sooner was Florence safely shut up in the Tower, than the effect of it was felt in Desmond; and it was found, contrary to the opinion of Carewe, expressed at a later period, that it *was* possible to have a worse man at the head of his restless kindred. As long as he had been at liberty, the froward nature of the Earl of Clancar had been kept under some control : to what extent that reckless man had

allowed himself to be guided by the advice of Florence, how
efficiently that advice had operated upon his timely abandonment of his unfortunate brother-in-law of Desmond, may be
matter of conjecture ; but justice would seem to demand,
that if Florence were denied credit for the tranquil and
orderly behaviour of his father-in-law whilst he was by his
side, he should not have been blamed for the excesses into
which the Earl fell when he was removed from him ; and yet
to the "revengeful feelings of Florence" was attributed
every irregularity that now disturbed the peace of Munster.
Very vague and cloudy seems to have been the comprehension of the Earl of Clancar, of the terms on which he stood
with Browne, in consequence of the so-called mortgage of
his lands; and to assist him in his perplexity, he had but a
strange counsellor to appeal to. The life of this nobleman
had been dissolute and scandalous; a family of bastards, if
if they did not actually live under the same roof with his
Countess and his daughter, certainly were openly acknowledged by him; and the fame of their evil conduct filled the
country in which they resided. Of this base brood, Donal
was his father's favourite : he had certainly one virtue, for he
was brave; but his vices were especial, and past numbering.
It was the pleasure of several of the English authorities to
call Donal "the Munster Robin Hood." Of education, we
have no proofs that he had any, except what he had derived
from his father's servants and soldiers. He had shed blood,
but it had been in anger. He was called a *rebel*, which merely
meant that he had been so fortunate as to break his way out
of Her Majesty's prison, and from that time had lived under
the ban of every ruler in Munster, in woods, and bogs inaccessible, the enemy of all honest men, but most especially
the hater and tormentor of Nicholas Browne, and all that
belonged to him.

That fearless undertaker, with two of his brothers, had
made their home, as we have mentioned, in the wilds of
Desmond; they had imported numerous English labourers,
and by their intelligence, capital, and industry, raised a
thriving settlement in the howling wilderness, in which
Donal, and evil spirits like him, prowled and ravened.
Peace and the Brownes parted, the day they first had dealings with the Earl of Clancar: their cattle were seized, their
horses were maimed or slaughtered, their villages plundered
and burnt, their English followers murdered, and, as the
eldest of the brothers truly said, everything was done to
scare them from the country. But Nicholas Browne was not

a man to be intimidated. He had obtained from Sir Thomas
Norreys a guard of horsemen in the Queen's pay, to protect
his property; and every now and then he sallied forth at
their head, in pursuit of his arch enemy. In these "journies"
Donal lost many of his followers; but they were more easily
replaced than the burned villages, or even than the slaughtered horses. In spite of Browne, Donal kept his head upon
his shoulders; and when the horsemen returned, jaded and
disappointed from their chase, he was again down upon
village and homestead, burning, maiming, murdering, till the
heart of Nicholas Rrowne was frenzied by rage. In the
midst of this exciting domestic warfare, Browne learned to
his dismay—Donal, doubtless, in a transport of exultation—
that the Queen would no longer tolerate the burthen of these
charges of horsemen, quartered through the country where-
ever there was an undertaker to be protected. The former
wrote at once to the Minister, that his ruin was inevitable if
his guard were to be withdrawn; and that without them he
must abandon his Signory, after all the pains and charges he
had been at.

With Donal there was no reasoning; the filmy niceties
of the law lay beyond his intellectual perception; sufficient
was it for him to know that Mr. Browne's stacks of corn were
unguarded; a garran, a cow, or an Englishman astray at
dusk, or early dawn, for him and his forty loose swords to
burst upon them without mercy, to appropriate to himself
what he could remove, and to hang the Englishman if he had
the address to capture him; but from the Earl more moderation might fairly be looked for; and, in fact, not until his son-
in-law had been sent to England did he evince any inclination
to defy the law. Every atrocity committed by Donal
Browne had ascribed to the malice of Florence, who, as he
declared, set him on, by secret advertisement from England.
To Florence certainly could not be attributed the following
" presumptuous dealinge" which, in proof of the accomplishment of his many evil prophecies, St. Leger now reported to
Lord Burleigh:—

"1589. *June* 22. S*t*. LEGER *to* LO: BURGHLEY.

" The Earle of Clanker upon Tuesdaie laste cam̃ wth a hundred men
with him in forceable manner to a peece of grownde founde in offyce for
the Queenes M*a*tie called Clan Donnell Roe, being xxvtie plowe landes, the
which Landes one Alexander Clarke holdeth as an undertaker from Mr.
Attorney geñall of Englande, yt beinge parcell of the Seignyorie that her
highnes dysposed on the said Mr. Attorney, and dyspossessed the said
Clarke, threatning him that yf he wolde not departe the landes he wolde

kyll him and all his, usinge farder prowde contemptuous wordes to the
said Clarke, whoe reproved him for his presumptuous dealinge, in dys-
possessinge him out of the Queenes landes, sainge to him that yt wold not
be well taken of the L: Deputie, and Vicepresydent when he shold complaine to them of these his doinges. The said Earle prowdlie answeringe
him, that nether the L. Deputie nor Vicepresydent sholde have to do with
those landes, for rather he wolde spende his lyfe then anie man shold enioy
those landes but him selfe. Sainge furder to the said Clarke that yf he
and his companie wold not departe those landes, he wold cut them in
peeces. And presentlie willed his men to kyll the said Clarke, which they
had don, he beinge amongste them, had he not ben mounted upon a good
horse, they beinge a foote, and through a pystall he had, which he bent
againste them, and by that meanes and his horse together broke from
amongste them, otherwyse he had not come hither to have declared his
griefe. And not thus contented with his unlawfull acte, he tooke from
the said grounde twoe paier geldinges, and a hackney, caryinge them with
him into his contrie, and will not delyver them. And besydes sent certen
of his men to take such other cattell as there was upon the saide grounde,
but those were rescued by Clarke and his companie. By this his outra-
gious doinge and threatninge wordes the poore gentleman is constrayned
to forsake the grounde, a matter (under correction) not to be let passe over
without severe punyshment; for yf this be suffered to be let goe with him,
unpunyshed, in vayne will it be for anie undertakers to settle in this contrie. I wold to God that the said wicked Earle had ben kepte in Inglande when he was there, for he was never borne to do good to this
contrie. It is greatlie to be feared that his doinges ys but a preparatyve
to a furder myschiefe. The cause that moveth me thus much to wryte is
for that Base sonn of his called Donnell Mac Cartie haith latelie mordered
an honeste subiecte of the Queene dwellinge in Desmonde for reprowinge
him in usinge Irish extorcoñs, who presentlie (upon fyndinge falte with
him therefore) with his skeyne stobd him in thre or fower places in the
bodie, whereof he presentlie dyed. Synce which his detestable morder he
is out with xvj^{eu} or xx^{tie} swordes, playnge the Robyn Hood in takinge
meate, dryncke, and spoyle where he can get yt, not without the consente
of his wicked father, as yt is here generallie geven out; and to confyrme
yt to be true, ho oontynueth and his companio in his fathers contrie within
fower myles of him when he is fardeste of. The which he colde not do,
were yt not by his fathers sufferance, considering how he is prosecuted by
the Vicepresidentes forces, for yf his father had a good will to bannyshe
him, yt were unpossyble for him to nessell in that contrie as he doeth. It
is thought that this detestable morder was coñmytted by the Earles consente,
for that the partie mordered wolde not relyeve him with money, to beare
out his druncken charges at Dublyn."

This raid by the Earl upon his own lands of Clan Donnel
Roe appears to have attracted very little notice, beyond the
report made of it to Lord Burghley ; indeed, it seems exceedingly doubtful whether any offence against the law had been
committed at all; and notwithstanding Sir Warham St. Leger's
talk of severe punishment, this military promenade seems to
have concerned the Privy Council of England very little ; and
had Mr. Alexander Clarke not been so fortunate as to terrify
the hundred followers of the Earl with his pistol bent against

them, had the hasty command to kill the said Clarke, been executed, it would but have cost Sir Warham St. Leger the variation of a phrase in his letter, and Mr. Attorney-General Popham an advertisement for a new undertaker. Such were not the elements out of which quarrels were made in those days between the authorities and the native lords.

The nature of the transaction between the Earl and Browne was worthier of the shrewdness, than of the wisdom, of Sir Valentine, who had not lent his money at a given rate of interest upon security of the Earl's lands, but had received a large tract of country,—33 quarters, nearly double the quantity for which he figures in the list made out by Phyton and Popham,—out of which to indemnify himself for the interest of his loan. How little he ever contemplated the parting with a single acre of these lands, is manifest from his subsequent proceedings. In the contract made with the Earl was a clause empowering him, at any time he pleased, on payment of the moneys advanced to him, to reclaim his lands: that he would never do this, that, if he had the will, he would never have the means, Browne might feel certain; and as by law, this land, with all the Earl's inheritance, would at his death revert to the Queen, it followed that at that time he must lose all security for his money. To guard against this contingency, he applied for letters patent, granting him at the Earl's death, a lease in perpetuity of the said lands at a moderate rent; urging, with great truth, that he had introduced English civility, and obedience to English law, into that wild country, that he had invested a large capital there, and imported many English Protestants, whose loyalty was unquestionable. His petition was granted: a patent prepared under his own eye, and to which no formality, or legal learning was denied, was accorded to him; and from that moment the utmost foresight of Browne could perceive no hindrance, save Donal and his outlaws, to the full enjoyment of his acquisition. He had yet to learn how the most wary may sometimes slip; and how elastic are the ingenuities and evasions of the law. For the present he had overreached a needy and unprincipled man; and appears to have excited little sympathy with his complaints of the acts of violence which troubled his repose. It was not until Florence became his adversary instead of Donal, that the law moved in the matter.

Many months had elapsed since Florence had been withdrawn from the society of his fellow-men, and no more was heard of him than if he had slept the while within the vaults of the Tower Chapel. No murmur against her Highness' decision escaped him, no petition for mercy kept alive his offence in the memory of the Queen: but his Irish chronicles, and his own dreams for the future, sustained him in good courage, whilst the conduct of his relations in Desmond was such as might almost have made Browne himself a suitor for his release. Much that is obscure in the career of Florence would be presently enlightened, if we could give ready faith to that declaration of Nicholas Browne,—" I *know* him to be a great briber to his power." It is certain that from the prison in which his silent life was gliding by, he found means to awaken the interest of some one in his behalf. What had become of his young wife all this time no one seems to have known; all search after her had long ago ceased; the lady was probably of sufficient age by this time, certainly had been too long married, to allow, with any decency, the renewal of the project of a divorce. Florence was not a man to trust anything to hazard; and we may therefore conclude that he knew well beforehand what would be the result of the following petition, which, after fifteen months of imprisonment, was presented to Lord Burghley. If this petition were granted there was an end for ever to all questions concerning his marriage, or the withdrawal of his wife. The tone, also, of the petition plainly shows his conviction that all anger upon the subject had passed away from the mind of the Queen; for he has not denied himself some little triumph in the address with which, in spite of the vigilance of the Munster authorities, the escape of his wife had been conducted, and in the secrecy with which, from that time to the present, the lady had been concealed. Of the formidable charge against him of treasonable complicity with Stanley and Jacques, not a word more was uttered for several years:—

" *May* 14th, 1590.   *To the* RIGHT HON[ble.] THE LO. BOURGHLEY, L. Highe Tresorer of England, 14 May, 1590.

In most humble manner besecheth yo[r] Hon[ble] good Lo: Florence McCarthy; that where ThErle of Clancarty, hath by S[r] Valentine Browne's meanes, and by misinforminge the Lo: Deputie of Ireland, procured his letters to the commissioners in Mounster to deliu[r] yo[r] sup[lts] wife, Ellyn M[c]Carthy, into his hands, who was accordingly deliu[rd] into the hands of such of his men as he apointed to receve her, by whom she beinge somwhat hardly used, she is about a yere and a half ago escaped frõ them, and hath eu[r] since kept herselfe in such sorte as few men knowes what is become of her: And for as much as the sayd Earle doth daily make search for her there, to have her brought into his owne hands, with intent to dispose of her, accordinge to his pleasure, and contrary to her will, and mynd; he therefore most humblie besecheth yor good L^p to direct yor letters to the Vice President of Mounster, that the sayd Earle or anie other be not permitted to offer her anie wronge, or other molestacõn, and that she may be sufferd to liue at his house, or wth his friends, where she shal be always forthcomĩnge at yor Lo^{ps} pleasure; and that none of her friends that hath kept or reliuved her, may be trobled for the same; and he shall pray, &c.

"ffLOR : M^{c}CARTHY."

The signature of Sir Owen Hopton, on a separate slip of paper, is affixed to the foot of this letter, showing that Florence was still in the Tower. He had been prisoner there fifteen months.

Florence had occasion, at a later period, to refer again incidentally to this flight of his wife; but then, as now, prudence withheld him from giving any more details concerning it. His petition was granted; and the fugitive now appeared openly at the Court of Elizabeth as a suitor for her husband's release from the Tower. The Queen could scarcely give this young bride her liberty without being prepared to restore her husband to her; for the wife at Court, and the husband in the Tower for marrying her, was a position so false for all parties concerned in it, that it could scarcely last; seven months more, however, elapsed before she obtained his liberation; but, in the meanwhile, all who were skilled in interpreting the royal mind might unerringly have predicted, not alone the freedom of the prisoner, but his reinstatement in royal favour.

Calculating that the ruin of Florence was complete when they had seen the Tower Gates fairly close upon him, a flight of human vultures had descended upon his lands, the hungriest of whom, and the most audacious, were the son-in-law of Her Majesty's Attorney-General, Rogers, and his agent Worth. The next venture of Florence was to petition the Queen that his property might be protected as long it was her royal pleasure to disallow his return to Ireland. The following order, extracted from the Registers of the Privy Council, will show the progress he was making in the royal favour :—

"1590. *December* 15*th.*

"For as much as Her Majesty's pleasure is that the suppliant shall not during the time of his restraint here receive any prejudice in his right, these are to require you to take present order as well that his servants officers and tenants may be continued in the peaceable possession of the said lands and castles, and that they may not be removed or evicted from the same until he shall be able to answer for the defence and title thereunto. As also that such sureties as have been committed to prison, or otherwise damnified by distresses taken upon their goods for default of the presence of such of the suppliant's servants as could not by reason of their attendance here upon the Lady Ellen Mac Carthy his wife repaire unto that Realm, according to their bondes, may be released and set at liberty, and their goods restored unto them. And likewise that Daniel Roche, Alonse O'Brien, and Edmund Slabagh, or any of the servants of the said Florence Mac Carthy may be permitted at all times to repaire into that province, or any other parte of that Realm, and to return hither again, behaving themselves as dutiful subjects with such commodities and other necessary things as they shall transporte for the use and relief of their said Master, whereof praying you to have such convenient regard that there may be no further occasion of complainte by them made unto us in this business.

· " To the LORDS JUSTICES."

By the preceding official communication the Irish authorities must have been made aware that powerful influence was busy in working for the pardon of Florence. Of all his friends none served him more practically than the Earl of Ormond, who came forward to stand security for him in the sum of a thousand pounds. This security availed to obtain his freedom. On the 19th of January, 1591, an order from the Privy Council was directed to the Lieutenant of the Tower—

" To set Florence Mac Carthy at liberty upon certain notice given him by Mr. Wills and Mr. Wade, Clerks of Her Majesty's Privy Council, that the Earl of Ormond is entered bond for £1000 here to Her Majesty's use, with condition that the said Florence now under his charge shall not depart the realm, nor three miles from the city of London, nor repaire to the court without special license in that behalf first had and obtained from Her Majesty's Privy Council; He likewise having first taken bond of the said Florence himself of £2000 with condition as above said: and touching the charge of his diete &c. during his being there, because of his present inability, the said Lieutenant must staie till the next warrant."

Thus terminated the actual incarceration of Florence, which had lasted two years all but twenty days! but though actually confined all this time within the walls of the Tower, and to that portion of it precisely, called " The Cold Harbert," the nature of his imprisonment was by no means the same during the earlier, and later part of his stay there ; so different indeed was it, that whilst he describes himself, during the first few months, as a *close prisoner*, he alludes to the later period as to his *first liberty*. We have seen that the earliest letter written by him from the Tower was not allowed to go forth without the signature at foot of Sir Owen Hopton ; his later petitions are without this stamp of his captivity.

Florence was now comparatively free ; he was not indeed free to return to Ireland, or to stray beyond three miles from the city of London ; but he was at liberty, for the first time since his marriage, to live in the society of his wife, and to resume, without restraint, the acquaintances he had had at court before his troubles commenced, and thus to take more effective measures to obtain his entire liberty to return to his own country. No murmur is extant in any of his writings during these last two years against the restraint he had suffered ; but how bitter was the impression produced by it in his mind we shall learn a few years later, when he declared to Carewe, that "he had of long time tasted of miseries and wants, and therefore, like the burned child, he feared to run into any inconvenience, and that he would rather fly from his country, or run any fortune, than expose himself to a second imprisonment." No charge is more frequently made against Florence by his enemies than that of *ingratitude*. In the hypocritical language of the day, this liberation from the Tower, after two years' imprisonment, for having made a contemptuous marriage, is described as a great grace and bounty of Her Highness ! That Florence did receive favours from the Queen, his letters frequently and emphatically declare, but it does not seem to have occurred to him that this three miles' liberty was one of them. What he would indeed have considered as an especial favour at this time, would have been the permission to return to Munster ; and to obtain this, he became one of a portentous list of suitors, who wearied the heart of the Minister with petitions. The rigid conditions of his bond were speedily relaxed, for we find him attending the royal progresses with his petitions ; but no entreaty, no influence could for some time longer, obtain for him permission to make a brief visit to Ireland ; and when at last he had recovered so much favour with the Queen as to accomplish this, it was still as one nominally a prisoner, and within the restraint of the penalties of his bail, should it please the Minister to enforce them.

Had Florence been able, from his abode in the Tower, or even from his lodgings in Westminster, to manage his Munster estates, and derive a regular income from them, it would have been by far the most surprising thing that he ever achieved. This he found impossible. Several of the undertakers, and some even of his own family, concluding that he was not

likely ever to pass out from his cell in the Tower, had
scrambled for his lands, confusion had ensued, his money
resources were cut off, and, like other gentlemen in similar
difficulties, he was driven to seek the means of subsistence
by mortgaging and leasing his estates; and it may be remarked, as a little suggestive at the least, that these transactions, ruinous to himself as he represented them, and
consequently beneficial to the other parties concerned in
them, were entered into, not with undertakers, but with Sir
Thomas Norreys, and others in authority in Ireland, and with
gentlemen living, like himself, at the court; but even this
resource began to fail him at last, and he fell into the inevitable misfortune of contracting heavy debts in London. These
debts increased; for at this time his wife was living with
him, and he had no longer Sir Owen Hopton, and Sir Michael
Blount to pay his monthly bills for "diette," "fewell," and
other necessaries; his Munster remittances diminished, and the
tone of his creditors ascended by the usual diapason of hints,
remonstrances, and threats.

Ever since his liberation from the Tower, Florence had
been earnestly pressing his suit for permission to return to
Ireland. He had fairly won the good opinion and friendly
influence of Lo: Burghley, and of his son Sir Robert Cecyll,
the former of whom joined with Lady Ellen to solicit this
grace from Elizabeth. The friendly endeavours of Lord
Burghley are made known to us by Florence's writing; but
for the influence which prevailed with the Queen to render
all solicitations in his favour vain for a considerable time
longer, we must look elsewhere, and the search is neither
long nor difficult. Every enemy of Florence in Ireland,—
Barry, Fenton, Browne, Denny, the Bishop of Cork, and a
host that was countless,—poured their insinuations, auguries,
charges, and warnings into the ear of Sir Francis Walsingham.
The last letter of the Bishop contained, besides the charge of
certain minor treasonable matter against Florence, a discovery
of a very delicate and surprising matter, tending, indeed, to
no less than to impeach Her Majesty's *rights* to the entire
inheritance of the Earl of Clancar, and at the same time to a
more effectual cutting off of the greatness of Florence than
all the remedies of Sir W. St. Leger.

"Rt. Woorshippll. my veree hartie and humble commendacions don to
your self with my good La: Such newes as the other weeke I had intelligence of I thought good to certifie your woorshipp, namely I was certainly let to understand that Florence McCartie, a man whose disposition
is already verie well known to yr Woorpp, had a boy called John Teig, or

John Donovan, the boy I know verie well, and the three maisters he served before he was Florence his boy; this same boy hath he sent on his message into Spayne: let y^r Woor^p judge for what cause; no good you may be suer! Whether he be yet returned I cannot learne. Other newes have I none save that *the Earle of Clancar his wife is with chield!* The remembrance of my self I leave to your Woorshippes consideracion.

" W^m. CORK CLOYNE & ROSS.
" Cork, this 24 Febr^y, 1591."
Endorsed " the Bishop of Cork to Sir Warham St. Leger."

The Attorney-General, Sir John Popham,—defeated in his designs of carving Signories for himself and his son-in-law, Rogers, out of Florence's lands in Carbery,—corroborated every tale of his ambition and disloyalty; and thus, was formed around the Privy Council and the Queen, an united opposition, which effectually resisted the friendly exertions of Burghley, and the entreaties of Florence's wife, until delay had so greatly multiplied his pecuniary difficulties, that he was compelled to abandon his suit to return to his home, and in lieu of it to solicit for " relief and some present means of living." The petition which he sent to Lord Burghley at at this time is, for many reasons, one of peculiar interest. So involved was he in difficulties with his creditors, that he was afraid to venture abroad, even to call on the minister, lest he should be arrested. His wife was now far advanced in pregnancy, unable to travel with him to Ireland, even had permission been granted to him to go, and he had no resources to leave with her for her support in England; hence he writes to Lord Burghley that he no longer desires his return! but prays that Her Majesty may be moved to allow to him, and to his wife some maintenance, as long as it shall please her to keep him in England. This letter is one of the most pleasing of the many extant in Florence's writing. It is valuable, not only as proving that Lord Burghley's conduct to him was really friendly, but as showing that up to this time, at least, the fruits of his marriage were not wholly bitter.

Had Carewe not forced Florence to extremities, he might possibly, in his great prudence, have kept Carbery and Desmond from insurrection; and had the same unscrupulous man forborne to tamper with the vain weak mind of his wife, Florence's matrimonial life might have endured happily to the end. That his disposition was singularly forbearing, and gentle, that he was averse to strife, even with his enemies, is sufficiently proved; and certainly not his bitterest enemy ever reproached him with any failing that could justly forfeit the confidence and affection of his wife :—

" 1592. *June* 17. Mr. Florence M^{ac} Chartie to my Lo. Burghley.

" Right Hon. my most humble dutie remembered. Having heeretofore divers times entreated your Hon. Lo^p to be a meane unto Her Ma^t that I might have leve to go into my countrey seeing I have no meanes to maintain myself here, and perceevinge by Your Lo^p at my last being with your Honor that you moved Her Ma'tie therein whom your Lo^p found unwilling to grant it, I have thereupon caused my wife not to trouble Her Ma'tie any further for the same, and willed her to sue for some maintenance whereby myself and Shee might live until Her Ma'tie granted my libertie which she hath don still since my being with your Lo^p, all which time I could never acquaint your Lo^p withal, because I dare not go before your Lo^p or anywhere else abroad for fear of being arested for myne owne and my wyfes diet; and for as much as she doth now fynd Her Ma'tie well inclined thereunto, and that Her Highness doth daily promise to give order to your Lo^p for her, I am therefore most humblie to beseech your Hon. Lo^p to move Her Ma'tie now for me, and to be a mean that I may be partly releived with some maintenance whereby myself and my wife and folkes may live whyle Her Ma'tie shall think good to kepe me here, beseeching Your Lo^p not to move her Ma'tie for my libertie to go into Ireland, because I am not desirous to go thither, knowing Her Ma'tie to be unwilling, as also that I have no meanes to leave my wife any maintenance, who is great with child, and not able to go any where, thus beseeching your Lop to be myndful of me, herein I humbly take leave this 16th of June 1592.

"Y^r Lo^{ps} most humble to command,
"ffLOR. M^cCARTHYE."

This petition, seconded by the influence of Lord Burghley, was graciously accepted by the Queen. Amongst Her Majesty's virtues, few were so conspicuous as her frugality; her royal grandsire himself had not more reluctantly parted with the smallest coin of the treasure of the commonwealth than she did. Florence's distresses increased daily, and his urgent prayer was for prompt rescue from the pursuit of threatening creditors, and for money for his maintenance. Both suits were graciously acceded to; the one immediately, and the other without unreasonable delay. In the manner in which the Queen administered to his present relief there was an admirable simplicity. Florence obtained, not indeed a sum of money, but what was for the time of equal value to a receipt in full from every money-lender whose bailiffs were on his track; it was a warrant of protection against arrest for debt. The second portion of his suit required a little more deliberation; but we shall see in the sequel that in the means by which this also was accomplished, there was even greater proof of royal ingenuity than in the former.

Florence had been married nearly four years, and was still childless: the circumstance of his wife's pregnancy, which he mentioned to Burghley, to show how urgent was his need of present assistance, it is no exaggeration to say, moved the hearts of men in Munster more than would the birth of a royal child have stirred the feelings of Englishmen. A male child would one day inherit Carbery from his father, Desmond from his mother, and save from extinction the time-honoured, and historic designation of MacCarthy Mor. It pleased Providence that a male child should be born; and, as we should judge from Florence's last letter to Lord Burghley, in humble lodgings in London, and under circumstances of painful pecuniary privations; but no sooner was Lady Ellen restored to health, than she repaired with the young heir to Ireland; and how this child was there welcomed, the keen eyes of the Bishop of Cork were the first to perceive. A year earlier his Lordship had, as the reader has seen, made a discovery somewhat akin to this, viz., that this babe's grandmother, the old Countess of Clan Car, was with child. Sir William Herbert, who looked into these delicate matters with not less gentle sensibility than the Bishop, said at the time that he thought this not likely; and indeed now after thirteen months of patient gestation that venerable lady had not yet produced a male heir to mar the welcome of Florence's child; that welcome scandalized the Bishop, who at once wrote to Sir Geoffry Fenton upon the matter, and Sir Geoffry Fenton, not less affected, passed the tidings on to the Lord Treasurer.

"1593. *March 8th.* *The* BISHOP OF CORK AND CLONE *to* SIR G. FENTON (enclosure in Fenton's letter of 15th March to Wals^m).

"My dewtie remembred to y^r Worship. I thought yt my dutie to certifie you of such thinges as are of importance, and concerne the state. Heare is a yonge childe of Fynnynge McChartyes, who after this countrey manner is used amonge the people as a yonge Prince, caryed abowt the contrey w^th

three nurses, and .six horssmen, when he removeth to anie
place; and happie is he that can have him to foster for a
moneth! and so from moneth to moneth, to the best of the
contrey to be fostred, wth such songes of reioycinge in the
praise of his father Fynnynge, and the yong Impe, that yt
weare good his father at his cominge over shold be looked
unto, wch wilbe very shortlie, as his cousin Donnell McChartye,
wch came latelie owt of England told me; and delyvered
unto me manie other matters, wch I cannot now sett downe
because of the hast of the messenger; but at lardge you
shall haue yt by the next that cometh.   So humblie take my
leaue.

"viij M'cij 1582.

" Yo^r Wo̅'s at Coma̅undm^t

" WILLIAM CORKE & CLONE."

" 1593. *March* 15.   SIR GEOFFRY FENTON *to* LORD
            BURLEIGH.

" My dutie used, uppon pclosinge of the joynt ^lres now
sent to your L. consistinge uppon manie ptes I receaved this
adu'tisement inclosed from the Bushop of Corke wch I am
bold to sende to yor L. wth the privilige of the Ld Deputie
whome I first acquainted wth the contents thereof. This
outward pompe used towardes the childe, beinge far above
the usage of the best and greatest psons in that province,
maketh showe of an inward pretente to raise an extraordinarie greatnes to the parents, and to drawe a multytude of
followers to be readie to serve a torne, when fytte oportu-
nitye shold offer: wch beinge considered wth the father's
former ambic̃on not unknowne to yor L. mynistreth cause
to dowbt further inconveniences by that famyly, and to
pvent them. Fynnyn McArty the father is as yet about
London or the court, who though he be (as I heare) in some
towardnes to retorne hither yet (wth y^r L. favor) yt weare
not amyss to have him still detyned there, either directlie by
authoritie or by device, at least tyll this sommer be passed
over, for yf any attempt be made in Mounster by the forreine
enemye, there is none in all the province so likely to become
the head of a faction, or to move or countenaunce a tumult,
as he, whereof I make bold to adu'tise yor L. onely, and so
to leaue yt to yor L. further will and pleasure. In grett
haste.

" At Dublyn the 15 M^tij 1592. G. FENTON."
                    G 2

An account, thus substantiated, might be very opportune to furnish the Minister with a ready answer to Florence when he should next appear with the story of his pecuniary grievances; but it needed local jealousies, and enemies as bitter as Fenton and the Bishop, to put it forward as a fit reason for prolonging Florence's restraint. Donal Pipy had carried back, from London to Munster, tidings of the approaching birth of Florence's child. He had carried back also news of other matter more alarming. Florence was in favour at court! and especially protected by Burghley and Cecyll! the common enemy would assuredly, before long, be let loose! The amount of Florence's influence with those statesmen was greater than Donal reported, or his enemies would have readily believed.

CHAPTER IV.

THE tidings of Florence MacCarthy's certain return to Ireland, which Donal-na-Pipy had brought with him from the court, and communicated to the Bishop of Cork, sufficed to occasion absolute consternation amongst a large community of undertakers in Munster. Roused by the shrill alarum from the episcopal trumpet, his old enemies, headed by the fiercest of them all, David Barry, the Lord Viscount Buttevant, rushed with renewed fury upon their foe : the first shaft, winged more directly, and with most of malice, at the heart of the common enemy, was shot from the bow of Barry. Florence appears, through life, to have been able to keep his personal dislikes in a wise subordination to his political requirements : in all cases *except* the single one of this Lord Buttevant. His enemies were countless! for they included every man who had a chance of deriving benefit from his ruin, every man injured by a MacCarthy in Munster, every man who hoped to thrive by inventing or discovering anything that would prove him to be dangerous, or disaffected, Spanish in heart, or popular in Desmond, every man who hated his religion, or coveted his possessions. Donal, his wife's base brother, MacCarthy Reagh his cousin, Browne, with his resolute clutch upon Molahiff, and David Barry, were the great captains in this army of evil wishers. Towards none of them, save Barry, does he appear to have entertained any rancour which could not be put aside when occasion required. His contention with the Brownes we shall see conducted with temper and decorum; of Donal he speaks invariably rather with contempt than with acrimony; and with his cousin of Carbery we shall see him before long holding confidential counsel "in the bay window of Kilbrittain Castle," his birth-place ; but Barry was the solitary object of his especial detestation! and in *his* instance alone did he permit himself to use language unbecoming his own high breeding, and the dignity of the Privy Council to whom his letters were addressed.

What had been the original cause of this rancorous feud we know not for certain ; it had, in all probability, arisen out of the Desmond rebellion, in which Florence and his father and Barry and *his* father had taken opposite sides. Whatever may have been the cause, the quarrel itself was longlasting, and bitter. To Florence's secret handling of the bands of desperadoes who found asylum in the Earl's country, Barry attributed the frequent incursions of those robbers upon his lands ; whilst to Barry's "inventions and false suggestions to Sir Thomas Norreys," at the time of his marriage, his adversary ascribed his imprisonment. The rumour of Florence's return set half the pens of Munster into motion : whilst Browne hastened to kindle alarm in the mind of Sir Edward Denny, the old enemy of Herbert, an undertaker like himself—Barry with similar purpose bestowed upon the Lord Chief Justice, Sir John Popham, a spirited chapter of the biography of Donal, which must have forcibly reminded that eminent judge of certain adventures, and companions of his own youth. Popham needed little solicitation to induce him to exert any influence he might possess, to injure Florence. He, and his son-in-law Rogers, as the reader will perceive presently, had been disappointed in their endeavours to place themselves as undertakers in Carbery ; we shall at a later period see them making a fresh, and equally unsuccessful attempt upon Florence's patrimonial estates.

"1589. *March* 4.

" John Popham placed himself at Mallow being but 6000 acres, and at the earnest request of Sir Thomas Norreys, and sundry of the Gent. undertakers, left it unto Sir Tho[s]. Norreys, who expecting to have been placed at Imokilly, and finding no place there, for that it is all claimed as chargeable lands, sent his people to the Bantry, where Edward Rogers, Esq[re]. was to have been placed; and finding there in all not passing 4000 acres, the place being far off and dangerous, and all the rest thereabouts claimed by others of the Irish, is driven, and the same Edw[d]. Rogers also, to return all their people, saving some few that of themselves are contented still to stay there. John Beecher hath the one-half of Kinalmeaky passed unto him by patent; he sold not, nor yet doeth enjoy it quietly, in respect of Mac Carthy Reagh, and the O'Mahons, although the titles were this summer adjudged against Mac Carthy Reagh, and therefore not many people are there as yet. Hugh Worth hath the other moiety of Kinalmeaky, who hath received the like disturbance, and therefore hath had few there.

"J. POPHAM."

The *undertaking* of lands in Ireland, some of which were declared forfeited by royal decree, others by a less ceremonious process of the undertakers themselves, may not have been without its risks, but certainly it must have had also its attractions, to have retained so enduring a hold upon

the mind of this great legal functionary. When filling the
high office of Her Majesty's Attorney-General, he had found
time to visit Ireland, and make a personal survey of the
lands of several of the native chiefs, which, though not
yet forfeited by their owners, nor formally distributable by
royal letters, were looked upon as in effect available to any
one with sufficient capital to occupy them, and sufficient
interest to secure their possession when occupied. Upon
that occasion Popham had contracted friendship and alliance
with men of similar appetite for Irish lands; hence when the
terrors of Donal Pipy, and the Bishop, had spread amongst
the entire body of the undertakers, Barry at once invoked
the influence of Popham for the common cause. Two years
later we shall behold this powerful enemy making himself
the medium of a renewal of every suspicion and accusation
that had been current against Florence for years; at present
he contented himself with laying Barry's letter before the
Privy Council, who were in anxious deliberation how best to
put an end to the troubles of Munster, without sending
thither the man who was seemingly alone qualified to
do it.

"Donal, the natural son of the Earl of Clancar, was
playing the Robinhood worse than ever:" the enemies of
Florence attributed this to "his malicious instigations, very
secretly sent to him." Florence had the address to persuade
Cecyll that no one but himself could put an end to these
disorders; but the distrust of the Queen was not so easily
overcome; she still hesitated to give her consent for his
return to Ireland. Matters got rapidly worse : " the Bastard
was out with some forty swords." " Browne was yet living
in hopes of his head;" but that wicked head was still safe,
and full of evil devices "against all men who wore hose
after the English fashion." " Good Sir Thomas," nearly at
his wit's end, suggested to the Minister the policy of giving
him a free pardon, and taking him and his loose men into
the Queen's pay and employment ; but in the mean time he
assisted Browne with what means he could, to hunt him
further into the wilderness. Sir William Herbert also, forgetful of former quarrels, made common cause with the chief
assailant of the common nuisance. In return " Donell
robbed Herbert's man of seven pound and his weapon !"
The next tidings of this restless spirit that reached the
Privy Council, and quickened their deliberations, was that
" he had spoiled and preyed the Abbey of Bantry !" Other
exploits of his are duly set forth by Barry, who little sus-

pected that his narrative could have brought upon him the very evil that he was striving to avert.

"*Endorsed,* 1593. *March* 22. *The* LORD BUTTEVANT *to the R*ᵗ. *Hon*ᵇˡᵉ *and his good Lord* SIR JOHN POPHAM, *K*ᵗ. *L. Chife Justice of Englande geve this.*

"Rᵗ. Honᵇˡᵉ Having ben bold to troble yʳ Honor wth sundry my former tedious lʳᵉˢ, and having receivid that contynuall favur att yʳ hands as I cannot well tell howe to reqnite the same, yet never the lesse I shall and wilbe to the uttermoste of my power att yʳ comandment, and therefore psuminge the more upon the contynuance of yʳ Honᵇˡᵉ favʳ, I thought good to advertise you of certain rebellious attempts offred here lately by Daniell, the base son of the Earle of Clancarty who, wthin this moneth, by meanes of certein directons and adutisements of Florence Mac Cartyes sent hither very secreatlye unto him, as I understand, The said Daniell hath hanged a man belonginge to Mr. Nicholas Browne, and to his father (father-*in-law.* Browne had recently married Sir Owen's daughter; that is the daughter of O'Sullevan *Beare,* not of O'Sullevan *Mor,* Florence's brother-in-law) Sir Owen O'Sullevan, and hath also murthered one Patricke Garland, both good servitors, and besids geven two onsetts to kill Sir Owen is eldest soñ; and diuers other bad attemptes hath ben by him geven. His company is not great, not above fortie, and therefore the more dangerous, What mischiefes may ensue by him, to avoide tediousnes, I refer to yʳ Lᵖ; but to be briefe with yʳ Honor, I do assure you, yf the said Florence do once escape from thence, and have any scope, considering what practizes the said Florence formerly used wth Daniell Graney, for his rebellions in Kinelmeaky, and delivering him his own weapon to attempt those bad enterprisses that he toke in hand, it cannot be, but that he will nowe run to farr more dangerous dealings, whereby may ensue chardges to Her Maᵗⁱᵉ, and great losse and ruine to this poore comonwealth; to wᶜʰ as I knowe yʳ honor to beare a zealous favʳ, so wth this smale caveat, taking my leave, I humbly betake the care thereof to yʳ Hoʳ, and yʳ Hoʳ to Goddes tuicion

"Barries Coũrte, the 22ᵈ of Marche, 1592.
                                        "DAVID BUTTEVANTE."

Notwithstanding the military promenade of the Earl of Clancar to his off-lying lands of Clandonell Roe, referred to in a previous page, and the excesses of his son, which Barry called "rebellious attempts," the province of Munster was unusually tranquil; discontent indeed there was, and, considering the behaviour of the undertakers, "the indiscreet and lewd men" whose association was so revolting to Sir William Herbert, it was, to use that gentleman's words, "wonderful they were so quiet as they were;" abundant rumours of brooding rebellion there also were; but, except within the unapproachable wilds and bogs of Donal's country, every part of the province was in obedience. The same complaints respecting Donal which Barry had sent to the Lord

Chief Justice, Sir Thomas Norreys wrote to Lord Burghley.
That some remedy was urgent for disorders so scandalous,
practised immediately under the eye of the Vice-President,
became manifest to the Privy Council. The first tidings of
the remedy about to be tried, the first proof which my Lord
Barry received of the effect of his letter to Popham, must
have fallen upon his perception as something utterly fabulous,
and incredible.

Florence continued to urge his suit to be allowed to return
to Ireland; he was now driven, besides, to petition for "some
means for his support, and for money to satisfy his creditors."
Out of the complaints of Barry, and the disorders of Donal,
the ingenuity of Elizabeth, or of her Ministers, or the far more
fertile mind of Florence himself, extracted the motive, and the
resources for the acceding to both of his petitions. Florence
had at last succeeded in persuading the Queen, as he had persuaded her Ministers, that no man but himself was competent
to deal with the turbulent Donal, but to effect such a service
without money was more than even he could undertake; and
to draw money from the Queen's Exchequer for any purpose
merely Irish, was nearly as hopeless an attempt; Florence
was far too prudent to essay it; his ingenuity discovered an
alternative, which he could scarcely have proposed, without a
smile, or Lord Burghley, who was, as Camden informs us, "a
man of reverend presence, and undisturbed countenance,"
have listened to with that gravity for which he was admired
in his generation. It happened that on the death of Barry's
father in prison, for his participation in the Desmond rebellion,
great interest had been needed to save the blood of the son
from attainder, and his estates from forfeiture; these misfortunes had only been averted by the imposition of a fine of
£500. Many years had gone by; and as no measures had
been taken to enforce the payment of this sum, Barry and
his friends had long looked upon it as a mere bond for good
behaviour. That the man whose contemptuous marriage he
had been amongst the first to make known to Sir Thomas
Norreys; whose rebellious practices he had been incessantly
occupied in watching and reporting; whose wife's brother's
enormities he had so recently exhibited in all their black
details; should have found any loyal man to listen to him in
reviving the faded recollection of that fine, may have reasonably surprised him. How much greater amazement was in
store for him let the reader judge! Early in November, 1593,
Florence Mac Carthy landed in Ireland; on the 9th of the
same month was the following extraordinary letter signed

by the hand of Her Majesty, presented by him, together with another by Lord Burghley, to the Lord Deputy.

"FLORENCE M^cCARTY

" *Rot. Mem.* 34-45 *Eliz. Inrolment at request of fflorence Mc Cartie Gent.**

" ELIZABETH.

" Right trustie and welbeloved wee grete youe well Whereas the Viscount Barry havinge in the last rebellion associate himselfe to the late traitor the Earle of Desmonde was afterwardes receved to his submission in the time of the Goveremt. of the Lo. Graie our late Deputie in that Realme uppon condicion of a fine acknowledged by him for his said offences to our said Deputie and Councell of the some of five hundred pounds to our use, the paiement wherof hathe since been respited. Wee let youe understand that knowinge noe cause whie wee should anie longer forbeare the same, and havinge w^thall a disposicion to relieve fflorence McCartie a subeicte of that our Realme who hathe desearved to have some gracious consideracon to be had of him, Wee are pleased to bestowe on him the benefitt of the said fyne of the Viscounte Barries, wherefore wee will and comaunde you that uppon the Receipte herof youe cause the Record of the fine to be sought out and theruppon to pcead by estreate or other pces of our Exchequior to extend and recover the same. And beinge recovered to give Warraunte to the officers of our Exchequior theare to make paiem^t therof to the said fflorence McCartie or his assigns as of our ffree gifte and liberalitie without accompte impreste or other chardge to be sett uppon him for the same, And thease our lr̃es shalbe to youe and to them sufficient Warraunte for the doinge herof.

" Given under our Signett at our Castle of Windesore the viij^th of August 1593 in the xxxv^th yeare of our reigne.

" To our right trustie and welbeloved Sir William fitz Wilℓms Knight our Deputy of our Realme of Ireland, or to anie other Deputie Justice or other Governor of our said Realme that herafter for the time shalbe."

Had a thunderbolt fallen upon the Baronial residence of Barriescourt, or upon the Episcopal palace of the Lord Bishop of Cork and Cloyne; had her sacred Majesty suddenly bestowed the fiercely contested Signory of Molahiff upon Donal the bastard, greater astonishment could not have fallen upon their several owners than was occasioned by this startling letter of the Queen! Her Majesty knew no cause why Barry should not pay his fine! nor why she should not bestow the same upon Mr. Florence Mac Carthy, "who had deserved to have some gracious consideration to be had of him!" Had

* For this inrolment the author is indebted to the kindness of Herbert F. Hore, Esq., whose competency, and readiness, to assist any effort to elucidate the history of Ireland are well known. In Her Majesty's "State Paper Office" is preserved the original letter to the Lord Deputy, the one, probably, which Florence took with him to Ireland. It is characteristic of Florence's extreme wariness that he should have caused it to be thus officially inrolled.

Florence been allowed, himself to prepare the draught of this epistle, he could scarcely have selected language better suited to confirm the opinion entertained by his own people of the influence he possessed at court; nor could he have found phrases more contemptuous towards the man whom, upon all occasions, he emphatically styles "myne adversary." Needy as he was, it is probable that he would not have sold this £500 fine for double the sum counted out of Her Majesty's Exchequer. Barry might—as indeed he seems to have done —have considered the incident a mere spiteful pleasantry; but Browne, and a host of others, could not fail to interpret it as it was plainly meant; the Privy Council was about to attempt a new experiment in the government of Munster; Florence was the author of this novel policy; he was to be conciliated; Barry was to pay this £500 to indemnify him for his long imprisonment, and to remind that importunate correspondent that the earlier passages of his own life were not forgotten; Browne and others might take warning from the fate of Barry.

It may be doubted whether the Lord Deputy himself was less surprised, or better pleased, than the enemies of Florence, when the Queen's letter was handed to him. Barry had of late been ostentatiously loyal; he had been owing this money for ten years to the Queen, and, as he with much ingenuousness acknowledged in one of his letters, " he had always looked upon it rather as a warning to the rebellious people of his own country than as a sum ever seriously intended to be exacted from him. To pay it at all, to pay it to Florence MacCarthy, seems at once to have fixed itself in his mind as a sheer impossibility. When invited by the Lord Deputy to pay the money, his reply was prompt and emphatic :—" He had it not !" The consequence might have been foreseen; Florence claimed, and received security on the lands of his adversary to the full amount of the fine, and the Deputy reported his proceedings to Lord Burghley.

" 1593. *November* 10. *The* LORD DEPUTY SIR W. FITZ WILLIAMS *to The* LO: BURLEIGH.

" It maie please y[r] Lo. I receavid yesterdaie two l[res] from y[r] Lo. by Florence Cartie, the one of the 26th of August in his favor generallie, and the other of the 14th of Septembre pticulerly to expedite unto him her Ma[ts] graunte of the Lo. Barries Fine of £500; besides her Majesty's allowance of him, and remittall of his concealed offence; whereunto I am ever in dutie to apply my likinge. It is, and while I live shalbe a motive sufficient to me to knowe that y[r] Lo. doth favor him, and so will I make it appeare to him and all others, as y[r] Lo. hath by y[r] contynuall favors bound

me: accordinglie I did forthwith uppon the readinge of your l^res touchinge that fine, give direčon to Mr. Chief Baron, a gentleman so earnest,
&c. &c. &c.

WM. FITZ WILLIAMS.

" 1594. *January* 20. FITZWILLIAMS *to* LO: BURLEIGH.

" Havinge receaved by Mr. Florence McCartie y^r hono^rable l^res on his
behalf for the recovery of the some of £500,—due by the Lo. Barry for
the Fyne of his pdon in the goůment of the Lo. Grey, wch yt hath pleased
Her Moste Excellent Maty to bestowe on the said Florence, So yt is that
havinge called the said Lo. Barry to aunswere whie the same shold not be
paied I have so farre proceeded as there is band of recognisance taken for
payment of the said Some at four seůall payments; the first whereof beinge for £125 is payable the 2^d. of Feby. next, and so quarterlie till the
whole be paied within 9 monethes, wch in answere of yor Lps favourable
l^res on his behalf I have humblie thought good to make knowne to your
Lp. And so wth harty prayer for yor prosperous success in all your affayres do take leave from Dublin the 20th of Jany. 1593."

Phrensied with rage and shame at " the disgrace put
upon him," Barry rushed, without licence from the Irish authorities, to court; thereby forfeited his sureties, and Florence,
without delay, was put into possession of about a third of his
lands. The contest for this fine, though in its early stages
sufficiently curious and amusing, trained itself on into a languishing tediousness, in which the vivacity of its commence-
ment is forgotten, and which only now and then sparkles into
fleeting brilliancy by its grotesque intrusion into letters upon
subjects wholly foreign to it. Between the grant and the
payment there was destined to be a long interval, and the
revenge proved in the sequel as costly as it was sweet.
Quickly following Barry in his flight to England sped a letter
from Florence, which is too remarkable to be laid before the
reader without a few words of introduction. In it the writer
pleads earnestly for his fine, as indeed he seldom fails to do in
the multitude of letters, which, from this time forward, he is
constantly writing to one or other of the Ministers, or to the
Privy Council: he alludes with much address to the Minister's
friends, Goring, Norreys, and others, whose pecuniary interests
must suffer damage by the retention from him of the Queen's
gracious gift, and then passes to matters which show at once
the nature of the conditions on which he had obtained permission to return to Ireland.

The severest struggle which England ever had to retain
her hold upon Ireland was preparing: O'Neill and O'Donell
felt their strength, and were already making essay of it by
occasional outbreaks from their unassailable dominions upon
loyal subjects within the Pale. Munster was evincing unmis-

takable evidence of sympathy with the northern chiefs, and
Florence perceived, opening before him, a career worthier of
his influence and abilities than the pursuit of his revenge
upon Barry, or the harassing uncertainties of litigation. He·
seemed on the point of commencing his political life; for "at
the same moment the Vice-President desired his help in
Munster, and the Lord Deputy contemplated using his services in the North." The cloud, however, passed away from
Ulster for the present; Munster, in ominous sympathy, subsided into its usual state of sullen submission, and Florence
fell back upon his law-suit. That Florence MacCarthy was
in truth better able than any man living to secure the peace
of his province, and to ensure to the Queen's Government the
adhesion of the powerful Sept of which he was the most distinguished member, was a fact which the English authorities
had full opportunity of knowing; and could they have safely
trusted him to aid them in subjugating his own people, he
might have named his own price for his services: but they
not unreasonably required "some imprest of previous service,"
before they would wholly relax their hold upon him. That
the Queen's Government could more effectually ensure to
Florence the great prize which his heart coveted—succession
to the inheritance of MacCarthy Mor—than any alliance with
the northern chieftains could do it, he perfectly well knew;
and could he have trusted the men who put so little trust in
him, he might perchance, as his father Sir Donough had done,
have kept for the remainder of his days every member of his
race in obedience; but he, in his turn, naturally required
"some imprest of previous benefit." Of this the only earnest
yet offered to him was, that he had been allowed to return
to Ireland for a prisoner's holiday; subject at any moment to
a ministerial order to repair again to England, and to the
Tower itself, had the Queen so willed it. The result could
scarcely be satisfactory to either party. Crippled loyalty
was rendered in exchange for crippled liberty. ·

It may be well, before proceeding further, frankly to encounter a question which probably the reader has already
desired to ask, and which assuredly, as this life advances, he
will be anxious to have answered. Was Florence MacCarthy
true to the Queen? true to his fellow-countrymen? or true
only to himself? It was the opinion of all men in his generation, both English and Irish, friends and foes, that he was
"a Rebel!" To the reader of the Pacata Hibernia it would
seem that he had failed his party in their extremity, and left
the Sugaun Earl to be crushed when he might have saved

him! Uncertain whether praise or blame may attach to the
first of these charges, the writer will prefer to leave it as it
stood with his contemporaries; the reputation of any mere
Irishman may tolerate the accusation of disloyalty to Queen
Elizabeth, without any fatal injury; at the same time we
may safely assert—for it was asserted by Carewe and Sir
Robert Cecyll at the time—that he had done nothing for
which the law could touch him, nothing but what he had
ministerial warrant for doing, and pardon for having done.
That James Fitz Thomas did repeatedly urge him "boldly
to cease temporizing, and join him in attacking the forces of
the President;" and later, when his followers were falling from
him, piteously call upon him for help, is true—if the letters
published by Carewe were genuine, as doubtless they were;
but he does not appear to have understood that it was precisely the temporizing attitude of Florence which paralyzed
the arm of the President, and was alone between him and
his destruction. In alarm for the safety of his own force,
which he had not the skill to handle with effect, or latterly
even to keep together, the Earl seems to have forgotten
that at that very time Florence had watchmen upon the
mountains of Desmond looking landward for the arrival of
the northern Earls, and seaward from the battlements of the
" Old Head of Kinsale," for the coming of the Spaniards.

    Carewe understood the tactics of Florence better, and
chafed against them as fretfully as Fitz Thomas could do.
To expect to see him rush openly into action the first moment
that a national banner was raised, to proceed as undisguisedly
as did the northern Chieftains, whose persons and possessions
were beyond the reach of the English power, or like men of
the stamp of Donal, or even the younger sons and brothers
of the chiefs in his own country, men of little repute or consequence, and with no lands to lose, were greatly to miscon-
ceive his character. Florence was by nature more wary than
any man of his age; he frequently received hard names from
the various English authorities with whom he came in contact, men who distrusted him, and yet failed to convict him
of any violation of law; and this most prominent feature of
his character was the one that invariably attracted their
notice; by some he was called ambitious, by others dangerous,
by others mere Spanish, but one and all described him as
subtle and cunning. His friends, Ormond and Stanhope,
referred to the same peculiarity in his nature, when they,
with more politeness, termed it "his great prudence and
wisdom." This quality, whether cunning or wisdom, acquired

immense development by his experience of the English character as it was exhibited in Ireland. Had the life of Florence been written by native writers, we should probably have seen the question of his duties to the Queen considered from a point of view different from any taken by the correspondents to whom we are indebted for the uniform decision that he was an ungrateful rebel. It is likely that her Majesty would not have admitted the propriety of any reasoning upon such a subject; nevertheless there were views taken of the duties and rights of an Irish Chieftain different in some important particulars from hers; and it was with these views that the Irish mind was the most familiar. Florence was the son of one of the wealthiest and most powerful of the native Chiefs : his father had been pronounced by Sir Henry Sidney, an altogether " special man and good subject," he had fought for the Queen, and been graciously allowed to marry the lady of his choice, although that lady was the sister of " James Fitz Morrice the Arch Traitor," without bringing upon himself for it eleven years of exile and captivity ; it is, therefore, likely that he trained his son in the prudential principles of loyalty. Unfortunately Sir Donogh died when his son was scarcely fifteen years of age, and thus there may have existed some want of completeness in his discipline as to this, and other matters; but Sir Donogh undoubtedly taught his son the full measure of the *rights* of an Irish Chief, and, as we have seen, encouraged him to enforce them at the early age of twelve years, sending him out against refractory tenants " with a train of horsemen, galloglass, and kerne, to take meat and drink with force and extortion, and to levy sums of money called cowe, not only against the will of the freeholders, but even of the cessor of the county."

In Sir Donogh's days the *undertaking* of Irish lands had not yet been heard of ; needy Englishmen, ravenous for Irish plunder, there were, indeed, in plenty upon the staff of the Vice-President 'of the province, but none of them appear to have trespassed upon the lands of MacCarthy Reagh ; hence Sir Donogh left no precedent to rule the loyalty of his son in his treatment of undertakers when they came. With his education perfect upon the one subject of his rights, Florence had to trust to his own observation for its extension to many others. His experience of English views as to *the use of Ireland*, gained by his visit to the court, and his observation how these views were carried out by the undertakers, " those indiscreet men who measured conscience by commodity, and law by lust," greatly advanced his education in a new direction; and the knowledge he eventually acquired of the worst parts of the English character gave a forced growth to that "subtlety and cunning"—prudence and wisdom—which men discovered to be the most prominent quality of his nature. Whatever other lessons might be wanting to him upon minor points circumstances had gradually supplied. His exile and imprisonment on account of his marriage, and the invasion of his property by a swarm of undertakers and others, must have defined in his conscience with great distinctness how much of loyalty he owed to the Queen. The time came when the English Ministers, rather than allow Munster to set all Ireland in a blaze, chose to make a bargain with Florence Mac Carthy. Her Majesty would make over to him an old claim, upon a man of questionable solvency, for £500; would probably pardon the offence of his marriage; probably give him his entire liberty; and probably otherwise benefit him at the death of his father-in-law; if he would assist in establishing English authority over every Chieftain in Ireland, and enable her to break up, and distribute the estates of the native lords amongst such adventurers as would pledge themselves to introduce English religion and English law into his native country. The reader will scarcely need again to inquire whether Florence MacCarthy was a loyal subject.

It may appear from the letter immediately following, that Florence was playing the part of informer against his countrymen; for he tells the Minister, *confidentially* that several of them were likely to be discontented, and might be dangerous, and that sufficient sureties should be taken from them for their good behaviour; and prays that it may be kept secret that he had given such advice. Let the reader be assured that this was no treachery to the parties named; but a simple demonstration of the writer's great prudence and wisdom: the undertakers and the law were daily provoking these men to rebel, and Norreys and Cecyll knew, as well as Florence could tell them, that they were discontented, and likely to grow desperate; to take sureties from them might keep them from blundering prematurely into rebellion, bringing ruin upon their own heads, and thus rendering them powerless to help in the great struggle that was coming. The facility with which, after an absence of six years from Ireland, Florence could at once raise 400 men of his own people for any cause, even for the Queen's, and that without himself so much as going amongst them, can scarcely have escaped the keen observation of the Secretary. But Florence's services were not required; the northern Chieftains were not yet ready; the danger seemed to have been overrated, and for a time matters became again tranquil. Four years more were to pass by before Florence's political life should begin, and it needed that full period to enable him to overcome the distrust of the English Privy Council, and to obtain the Queen's authority to enter upon the inheritance fallen to him by the demise of his wife's father.

"1594 *March* 16*th*. FLORENCE MAC CARTHY *to* LO: BURGHLEY.

"Right honorable, and my most approved good Lo. My humble and bonden dutie remembered; having deliud the Lo. deputie yor lops: letters, concerning myself, and the fine of v. hundred^li due of the Lo. Barry, wch yor Lop. obtained of her Matie for me, wherupon I found his Lop. very willing to fauor me, And fynding in the rowles of the Chauncery, the fiant of the said Lo. Barry is pardon, wherein he acknowledged the sayd fyne, and also his recognizance, in the councell book for the paime^t. thereof I received theruppon (by order of the Lo. Deputie and councell) sufficient assurance for the paiment of the sayd fyne; yett notw^thstandinge the Lo. Barry hath not onely broken his promess wth the Lo. Deputie and councell, but also forfetted what assurance he made, and is gon ou into England, coutrary to the Lo. Deputie and councells pleasure and to the Vice-president of Mounsters comandemet, wherefore I humblie beseech yor Lo^p (as I have allwayes found you my most hono^rable good Lo. and chefest frend) that it may please yor Lo^p now to be a mean, that the sayd Lo. Barry may not obtaine any thing that may hinder or prejudice me in my sayd suit, nor in the benefitt of the recognizance wch he hath forfetted, and which is myne by an order out of the Excheq^l, the rather that he hath by his going ou in that sorte disobeyed her Ma^ts lawes and pleasure and con-temned the state here, wherein yf he be borne w^thall, it shall be a great example and occasion of disobedience to all this realme, as the Lo. Deputie and councell hath at large enformed now by their letters, he beinge also one that was with the Earle of Desmond in all the last rebellion, whereby he deserves the less fauor: besechinge yor. hon^lable Lo^p therefore that you will as well consider myne imprisomet. and troble these vj. yeres past by the said Barry is malicious meanes and misinformacons. Her Matie havinge bestowed this suite uppon me to help to satisfie my creditors for my charges dureinge my sayd troble; as also what great charges I have bene at for this matter, hauinge folowed Her Matie for it since I was dis-charged at Cicester in the last progress, untill yor L^p got it signed at Her Highnes last being at Windsore, and since my cominge into Ireland (I pro-test unto yor L^p) it coste me aboue £200 in lawe and othewise, and was neu^r able to see my wife and contrey since my coming, being not able to absent myself from Dublinge by reason of this matter.

"After all which charges, trobles, and loss of time I assure yor L^p (on my faythe) yf the sayd Lo. Barry shold obtaine anythinge to hinder or preudice me in this matter, I haue no other meanes to live, or satisfie my creditors (hauing already in my troble morgaged and leased what living I had to Sir Thomas Norreys, Mr. George Goreing and others) but to folow Her Matie againe untill yor Lo^p do obtaine som meanes of Her Highnes for me whereby I may recouer my self, for the wch I wold have repaired now into Engeland, but fearing that I shold have som important occasion to serve Her Matie here by reason of the suspicoons which is conceived uppon

H

the behauiors of the Earle of Tireowen and O'Donell, who although they
have bene lately wth the Councell at Dundalk yet notwithstanding som of
them are holden very varyable; being also edgged forward by all the people
and knaves of those parts, who are growen to be very bold, whereby yf
there be anything to be don against them I do purpose to goe thyther w^th
three or four hundred men of myne owne, for I have divers who knowes
all that contrey very well, hauinge (dureing my troble) served in all those
parts, and are of very great estimaĉon there: Also the Earle of Clancarty
is bastard, having remained in action against Her M^atie since the last yere,
doth still kepe in that contrey, and because his company is so few as he
may not be cutt off by service, because he doth but lurk among som of
his secrett frends, wherby nothing cann hurt him but friendship; by
reason whereof Sir Thomas Norreys requested me to go thyther, where I
am going now at this p'sent to see what I may do in that case, and whatsoever I may do eyther in the North or in Mounster, it shall not cost Her
M^atie anythinge; Her Highness hauing alreadie bene so gracious unto me,
as I shall hardlie be able to deserve it whyle I live, neyther do I desire
any better reward but that Her Highness and yor Lo^p shall fynd that ye
are not deceived in the good opinion wch Her M^atie and yor Lo^p was
pleased to conceave of me, for the wch I will assure yor Lo^p of one thinge
wch is that no inconvenience shall grow in Mounster but that Her M^atie
and yor Lo^p shall understand it in time; and for that I haue bene (as I am
sure yor Lo^p doth remember earnest with yor Lo^p for Dermod McOwen
McCarthy the yong McDonogh, who hauing obtained letters there came
hyther, but the Lo. Deputie and Councell hauing referred him to the law,
wherby I take him, and Sir Owen O'Sullevan to be greatly discontented
and very desperat, therefore I take it very necessary that in the next
letter concerninge matters of state that yor Lo^p and the Councell do write
hyther the Lo. Deputie, or Sir Thomas Norreys be willed to cause those
two aforenamed to fynd sufficient securities, wch they may doe very
easiely, for the Lo. Roche, McCarthy Reogh, the Lo. Barry, and all the
chefest men for the most parte in Mounster are their frends. Lett those
sureties be taken of Sir Owen and his iii. eldest sonnes, for these rumores
in the North wold greatlie stirr discontented and desperat men to evill.
Thus craving pardon for my tediousnes, the rather that I think it necessary to acquaint yor Lo^p at large wth these circumstances wch I leaue to
yor Lo^ps honorable consideraĉon, and do humblie take leaue this xvj. of
March 1593.
" yor Lops most humble and bonden
"fflor: M^cCARTHY.
" I humblie beseche yor Lo^p not to acquaint anie with these thinges that
I wrote to be my doinges."

Poor Sir Owen, the Lord of Carbery, was not going to
occasion any further uneasiness to Minister or Deputy. About
the time this letter was written there passed, with little notice,
from the troubled world of Munster, this man, " so specious
in show, so badly bent, this malicious Papist." As in the case
of his predecessor Sir Donogh, the opinion recorded of him by
the annalists of his own country differs widely from that
entertained of him by his English contemporaries. What
indeed could Sir Warham St. Leger, or the men immortalized
by Sir William Herbert, be likely to know of Sir Owen's *piety*

and *hospitality?* Words certainly have many significations; and St. Leger's words, quoted above, may perhaps have borne a meaning not widely different from that with which his character was sketched by the Four Masters : " Malicious Papist," may have meant "pious and noble-minded man!" And "badly bent" may bear the interpretation of " truly hospitable"—to men out of favour with this rough writer.

Thus is the demise of Sir Owen MacCarthy chronicled by the Four Masters :—

" Mac Carthy Reagh (Owen son of Donell, son of Finin), Lord of Carbry died. He was a sensible, pious, and truly hospitable, and noble-minded man. Donell, the son of Cormac-na-Hoine, took his place."

We have extant a letter written by this Irish Chieftain to Lord Burghley; this letter has a postscript, and both are now presented to the reader. The style of the letter may perhaps have been suggested to Sir Owen by "his agent, the bearer," as suited to the dignity of the great Minister for whom it was intended ; but no agent, surely, assisted in the composition of that irresistible postscript! The document bears pleasing proof of the flourishing state of Sir Owen's finances ; it shows also the peculiar signification which the writer attached to the office of the " Lorde High *Treasurer* of the Realme of Englande ;" but what is of most consequence, both portions of the epistle tend to prove the justice of the character given to him by the Four Masters, that "he was a sensible man! and truly hospitable."

" 1587. *December* 23. *From* SIR OWEN MAC CARTHY (REAGH) *to the* RT. HON: *and his singular good Lorde the* LORDE BURLEIGH, *Lorde High Treasurer of the Realme of England.*

" Rt. Hon: and my veray goode Lorde, my humble duetie don to yor good Lp. It may please yor Honor to understand, that havinge spent so much money as I thought would suffice duringe myne aboade here, and remayning neverthelesse in debt of one hundreth pounds) I have been emboldened by your Lps favourable inclynacōn towards me, to direct the bearer myne agent, humblie praing yor Honor to deliuer unto him, in Loane for me, 2 or 3 hundred li. for which I will passe a bande from me, to see it repaied either to the Deputie or to the President of Mounster, within two moneths after my landing in Ireland. And so (acknowledging myself bonde unto yr Lp during life) I humbly take leave.

" From my Lodgings at Westmystre this 23d of December 1587.

" I humbly besech your Hon : Lp : to respect my p'nt extremytie, and to suply my want with the Loane of one fortie ponds to refresh me theis holydayes.

" Your Honorable Lps obedient at Commaundment,
" OWEN CARTY.

Sir Owen had been true to the family agreement; he had not

H 2

turned aside the Captaincy of Carbery from the Tanist, in
favour of his own sons ; and Donal Pipy, when he " took his
place," took it under assurances of £10,000 to leave the usage
of Tanistry as he found it. How this engagement was eventually kept the reader will see later. By the death of Sir
Owen MacCarthy, Florence became Tanist, or heir apparent
of Carbery ; and thus seemed approaching the fearful day,
foreshadowed by Sir Warham St. Leger, when he would
become MacCarthy Reagh, and MacCarthy Mor, and thus re-
unite in his own person the vast inheritance which had been
divided since the days of Donal Mor-na-Currah.

Barry in the meantime had repaired to court, where he
complained loudly of injustice done to him by the Lord Deputy
and the Vice-President, whom he accused of having made over
" all his lands" into the hands of Florence. He then fell
fiercely upon his adversary, whom he openly charged with
treason against the State, and declared that he could bring
witnesses to *prove* his assertions. In spite of Florence's prayer
to Lord Burghley not to listen to anything that Barry might
say against him, charges so grave, and made so openly, had
their effect, and the Minister obtained from the Queen a new
order to the authorities in Ireland, to suspend for the present
any further proceedings in the matter of the fine, and to call
Florence before them, and examine him upon the charges which
the Lord Barry would make against him.

CHAPTER V.

FROM the significant terms in which Sir William Fitzwilliams
had replied to Lord Burghley's first letter in favour of Florence,
it is plain that he had a previous distrust to put aside before
he could make her Majesty's pleasure entirely his own; but
with his usual address Florence had used the opportunities of
his intercourse with the Deputy to such purpose, that he dissipated much previous prejudice, gained his good-will, and
convinced him, as he had previously convinced Cecyll himself, that Barry was, as his father had been before him, a
traitor in heart and action : but far more than anything that
Florence could say, did the intemperance of Barry, in charging
the Deputy with partiality and injustice in the extending of
his lands, provoke that high functionary against him. He
was in the active pursuit of this fine, and in contemplation of
using Florence's services with O'Neill, when the order reached
him to summon Florence before him to give answer to fresh
accusations, emanating from the man whose charge against
himself had prepared him to put little trust in any accusation
he might make against an enemy. Sir Thomas Norreys was
called away from his government in Munster to take part in
this examination, and it appears that Fitzwilliams expected to
receive from him some elucidation of this sudden change in
court feeling, and some explanation of the new charges. Sir
Thomas declared that *he* had no accusations to make against
Florence, nor did he know of anything new that could be
brought against him. Barry had arrived from England, and
notice was sent to him to repair without delay to Dublin. He
lingered by the way; and the Lord Deputy and the Vice-
President found themselves in the undignified position of
having summoned a supposed criminal before them upon
charges of the nature of which they were themselves ignorant;
and without an accuser. Some little ill-temper under the circumstances may be excused; some was certainly felt; for, after
consultation, the Deputy resolved to wait till the morrow, and
if Barry did not then make his appearance, to send a government pursuivant to fetch him. Happily for his own dignity,
Barry appeared within the time, with his charges and his

witnesses. What his judges thought of the entire transaction the reader will have little difficulty in discovering.

"1594. *June* 12. *The* LORD DEPUTY FITZWILLIAMS *to* BURGHLEY:

"I wrote unto your Lordship in my last that I had receaved Her Majestys l^res for the examination of Florence Mac Carty upon something there informed against him by the Lo. Barry, and that there were no articles or instructions sent whereupon to examine him, but onlie reference to Sir Thomas Norreys who is to ioyne wth me in thexaminačon. I have since receaved another l^re from Her Matie muche to the same effect, wch geveth me to conceave that somewhat is looked for to fall out. Sir Thomas hathe bene here nowe these four daies, and hathe broughte Florence wth him, as I wrote to him he shold, but knoweth no matter whereupon to examine him. In his way hithurward through Waterford he found the Lo. Barry there nuely landed, and willed him to hasten aftre, wch he promised to do. He mighte easely haue bene heare two daies since though he made a step home for some occasion he said he had so to do. If he come not this daie I purpose tomorrowe to send a pursewant to hasten him awaie and then soone after Her ^Matie shall, according to her pleasure signified, be advertised from me and Sir Thomas what we find."

"1594. *June* 17. *The* LORD DEPUTY *and* SIS THOS. NORREYS *to my* LO.

"It maie please y^r Lo. before the winde did serve to carrie the other dispach that comes herewth from me the Deputie, the Lo Barry made his repaire unto us, and neith^r I the Deputie, having receaved instrucõns thence, as I haue in my oth^r l^res written to y^r Lo. nor I the Vice-p'sident knowing anie thing wherupon Florence Mc Cartie was to be examined, according to the reference mentioned in Her Ma^ts l^res, wee willed him to deli^ur us in writing the matters he had to charge Florence wth. The same containing 8 articles, wch are twoo more then he saith he p'ferred there, togeth^r wth Florence's answers, and thexaminacõns of 4 of the witnesses, named by the Lo. Barry wch are nowe here, whereof 2 his *owne men*, y^r Lo. shall receave herewith to be imparted to her ^Matie according to Her pleasure signified lately to me the Deputie by 2 severall l^res of the 3^d & 13th of the last monethe. A numbre of witnesses more are to be examined, whereof 18 in Mounster, besides the 2 already examined here, and 5 aboute the court there, as by the schedule inclosed shall appere to y^r Lo. But these 4 examinacõns taken here seme not to us so forciblie to import, as that wee think it mete to put Her ^Matie to the charge of fetching so manie so farr of, by purseuants, to be exãied here; wee haue therefore determined, for the best and spedeist waie, that I the Vice-p'sident, who am to depart wthin twoo daies, shall upon my coming home send for them, and examin them, taking the assistance of Mr. Atturney Gen^rall and Provost Marshall of that pvince or eith^r of them; and so wth all expedicõn send their examinacõns hither to be dispatched over by me the Deputie, if mine abode here be so long. In the meane time wee are to noate to y^r Lo. one suggestion of the Lo. Barries (whitch of forgetfullness or otherwise) *that toucheth him in honour*, concerning the seazure of *all* his lands, to answere the £500 fine given to Florence, where indede all that was extended for that cause excedeth not the third of his lands. And so we humblie take leave 17 June 1594.

                                        "W. FITZWILLIAMS.
                                        "THO: NORREYS."

(Schedule enclosed in the above letter):

" To be examined. All these are of Carbery, of Florence his countrie, his followers, cosens, and kinsmen:—
" Donell McCarty, al^s. McCarty Reogh; Donogh Oge O'Cullen; Reynold Oge O'Hurley th' elder; Teigh-en-orsie McCarty; Kryrone McMoragho McSwynie; Teig Oreigan; Moroghoe McDermod Oreigan, Dermod, John, and Donell, sonnes to the said Morgho. Teig McDonell Icrooly, al^s. Brannagh; Owen McDermodie McDonell Cartie."

Before a tribunal the judges of which he had grievously offended by an accusation of partiality, Barry produced the charges which had made sufficient impression on the Lords of the Privy Council of England to .cause them to suspend further proceedings in Florence's favour relative to the fine : that he should have presented such accusations, and that the Ministers should have entertained them as something new, is incomprehensible ; they were but a repetition of the articles laid to Florence's charge soon after his marriage, and respecting which, by order of the same Ministers, he had been examined then, nearly six years before. Upon the former occasion no witnesses had openly appeared against him ; the charges had then evidently been hastily made up out of the rumours hovering around the residences of the Vice-President of Munster and the Lord Deputy: but since those days, indeed, very recently, Cullen the fencing-master, had been judged guilty of designing the murder of the Queen, and had been executed. It was doubtless Florence's former connexion with this man, and the offer of Barry *to prove* the truth of his accusations that obtained a re-opening of the investigation. So heinous had been the treachery of Stanley, so savage the persistence of Jacques in search of some one to assassinate the Queen, that, could the enemies of Florence have proved against him any intercourse with those persons of late years, his ruin would have been certain. We shall shortly see a far abler, and a less scrupulous man than Barry—no less a personage than the Lord Chief Justice of England—lending himself to collect and lay before the Queen a similar catalogue of charges ; and even that wily and skilled intriguer could conceive nothing more damaging to the character of the man whom he wished to ruin, than these baneful traditions, still floating about the uneasy homes of the undertakers. The answers of Florence upon the former occasion had been little more than denials of the truth of the accusations made against him—a simple pleading of not guilty. In nothing do his eminent " prudence and wisdom" appear so conspicuous as in the difference between his previous cautious

silence, and his present gratuitous, and circumstantial explanation of all that had appeared equivocal in his conduct
through his whole career. Before judges whom he had accused of injustice, and who had already detected, and laid
before the Privy Council, an instance of his want of veracity
that "*touched him in honor*," the Lord Barry produced "the
Articles," and Florence MacCarthy the "Answers" following:—

"1594. *June* 27. *Copy of Articles preferred against* FLORENCE
MAC CARTY *by the* LORD BARRY.

1st. "Allen Marten Gent, borne in Galwaye, Student of Her Ma^ts
comon lawes, beinge mainteined and kept by Florence Cartie, bothe in
England and Ireland for a time, till he was sent by the said Florence over
to Sir William Stanly and Jaques, wch Sir William and Jaques hathe
p'ferred the said Marten to the Prince of Parma where he was appointed
one of his secretaries.

2d. "William Hurley born in com̄: of Lym̄erick, broughte up in Oxen-
ford, professor of the Civill Lawe, was at the time of the apprehension of
the said Florence his retainer in this realme imployed by the said Florence
to the said Sir William Stanley and Jaques, furnished wth money and
horse, undre collōr to p'cure a discharge from England for the said Florence,
wch Hurley remaines there as yet by his direction.

3. "Cormock McDonell McFynin Cartie Gent, coosen and servaunt
tothe said Florence, being the man that broughte the said Florenceis wife
into England, being accompanied wth a brother of his called Callaghan,
wch twoo being p'ferred by the said Florence to Jaques, where the said
Cormock as yet remaines, and his brother Callaghan died there in the
enemie's service.

4th. "Donogh McCartie base brother to the said Florence who went
out of this realme into England, in the companie of Donell Grame
O'Mahonie, and being sent for by Florence and was imployed by the said
Florence to the said Jaques; where he is as yet, and obtained penc̄ion from
the king of Spaine either for his brother, or himself.

5th. "Fynin McCormack McFinnin Cartie of Glanencroem wthin the
contry of Carbrie in the Countie of Cork, cozen and retainer tothe said
Florence, wch Finin p'tended title to Glanencroem aforesaid, was sent over
by the said Florence to Sir William Stanley and Jaques aforesaid, where
he serves and remaines as yet.

6. "Gullepatrick O'Cullen (fencer by p'fession) executed of late in
England *for treason against Her Matie was the only servant and follower of
the said Florence, as well long time before his imprisonment or restraint, as
also long time in his restraint;* and after sent him over unto Jaques where
he continued, till of late he returned where he received according his deserts.

7. "Owen McCartie als Owen Gamsagh, who was likewise in service
against Her Matie wth Jaques aforesaid, and came from thence at the
time that Cullen above written came into England before XXmas last past,
and from thence came over upon Christmas Holidaies to this realme to
the said Florence, who knowing him to be as aforesaid hath ever sithence
kept him in his service, wch Owen was borne in Carberie in the com̄ of
Corke.

8. "It is to be considered beside the rest, that the said Florence and
Jaques were sworne brothers &c. &c.
"17 *June* 1594.   "DAVID BUTTEUANTE."

" 1594.   *June* 17.   *The Answers of* FLORENCE MAC CARTHY *to the*
Articles preferred against him by the LORD BARRY.

1st. " As for Allen Martyne myne acquaintance with him was laide to
my charge by Mr. Secretarie Walsyngham and others of the Councill wch
were appointed to examine me within six or seven weeks after my comming tothe Tower, for the wch I have sattisfied them then: Having noe
acquaintance wth him nor never seene him but in the Innes of courte,
where I became acquainted wth him, and where I left him at my coming
into Ireland, of whome I never hearde other newes but that at my first
litty in the tower about four years past, I heard he died in Fraunce or
Flaunders, Before God I knowe not wch: His father and freinds can tell
best, but at the tyme I heard that, Jaques was then in the Fleete, whereby I could not send him to him, nor never did send him to him or to anie
other, as God judg me; neither doe I knowe when he went, nor whether,
but that I left him in the Innes of courte where I found or knewe him
first, when I came into Ireland.
2. " William Hurley of the County of Lymerick havinge studied at
Oxford a longe while came into Ireland a litle after my first cominge out
of England, aboute the tyme that I was committed by Sir Thomas Norreys
at Cork; at wch time I being desyrous to send som agent into England to
procure my litty, dealt wth Mich Skiddy of Cork (whoe was Sir Frauncis
Walsynham's man) wth whome I did not agree, for want of money, and
the said William Hurley being then com to Cork, I dealt wth him, unto
whome I mortgaged or made over some land for goinge thither; whoe
being gon and having followed my cause for three or four moneths, as I
understood, he was hardlie used by the Erle of Clancartyes man Donoghe
Offaylve, whoe made Sir Valentyne Browne to use him hardlie, and to
threaten him, and also as I understoode they among them procured
Mr. Secretarie to give him verie hard speeches, whereby he was soe feared
and terrified that he depted the realme and went into som forraine country
to followe his studies, of whome I never heard sinĉe, but that he followed
his studie beyond the seas in France or Germany, for whome I have also
aunswered Mr. Secretarie and the rest in my last impsonm*, Jaques being
then in the fleete, when I was examined for him.
3. " As touchinge Cormack M*c*Donell M*c*Fynine and Callaghan his
brother, indeede I must confesse him to be of my countie and name, and
somwhat akyn to me afarre off: p'haps, he hathe, as I understoode served
Sir William Mohowne in Cornewall, and beinge com to London, when I
had my first littie in the Towre, he desired to be admitted to see me,
whoe being brought by my keeper Michell Siblie, he used afterwardes for
a sevenight or a fortnight to com to me at my request to carie my l*res* to
my friends at Courte that sued for my littie, and having psuaded myself
at that tyme that my wyfe would be the fittest suter to obtaine Her Ma*ts*
favr for myne enlargem* I entreated him to goe into this countrie for her;
having pcured him som money and a passporte, and having written to her
to com; whereuppon she came into England, and one David Roche, a man
of mine being com to the Courte he waited uppon my wife; and I being
still in the Towre and not able to keepe anye, the said Cormuck told me
he would goe into Cornewall; and whether he be gone thither or into
Fraunce I knowe not, but that I heard, as I remember, that he was in
Fraunce, by an Irish souldier whoe is now at Moyalloe, whose name I will
learne: his father dwelles at Moyalloe, I sawe him wth Mr. M*c*Donoghoe,
Dermod M*c*Owen, And as for Callaghane his brother I never knewe none
such, nor never sawe any; but my wyfe, & he alsoe told me that he brought

over from hence wth him a boy of the adge of twelve yeres or thereabouts, of that name, whoe was his brother by the father; what is becom of him I knowe not, having never seene him as aforesaid.

4. " Donogh McCarty whoe is, and hath bene still in the countrey taken for my Father's base sonne, came into England in the companie of som of my men, as namely one Edmond Slabagh, whoe is wth me nowe, and whoe broght me som Hawkes, and who alsoe broght the same boy wth him to help him, in whose companie alsoe Donell Gram went over to sue for his lands of Kinallmeky, and the said boy having remained wth me in England afterwards until I came into Ireland, he staied in England against my will, at my coming away, being promyst by litle Teige McCarthy my Lord of Ormonds man, to be preferred to som gent there of whom I heard no other newes but that he went wth some English souldiers into Fraunce and Flaunders, and being com from one of those countryes, back while I was in Ireland, I heard he was sick a long time in England, and when I was sent over by Mr. Chichester I did not see him, being by Mr. Chichester by direction from the Councill delivered the next daie to the Lyvtenant of of the Towere, but afterwards about a yere or more after my commitment to the Towre, Jaques being then in the fleete for hurting Michell Apsley, he found the said boy and kept him wth him, and being enlarged and dispatched out of the Realme by Mr. Secretarie he broght him wth him, as I understoode, and where he is, whether he be wth him or wth some other, or what is becom of him, I knowe not since that tyme.

5. " Fynine McCormucke McFinin of Gleancruym beinge gone over by reason of his adversarie Teigenorsy, whoe went over with Sir Walter Raliegh to surrendre the said Gleanecruym, and his father being my father's follower and foster brother, the boy came to me to the Towre and told me he had noe frinds nor meanes to followe his cause, whereuppon for Pittie, and contrie's sake, I gave my worde to one Robert Foster of Towre Streete for his diett, and having putt upp his severall petitions to the Councill, Sir Owen Hopton being removed from the Towre and Sir Michell Blount placed, the said Sir Michell would lett noe prisoner have anie libtie uppon anie warrt directed to his pdecessore; whereuppon the aforesaid Foster, seing me restrained, would not credit the poore yong man for his diet, whereby he was constrained through extreame misery to goe wth som souldiers into Brittayne, where he was about four or five yeres past killed aboute Gingam, as I heard of everybodie that came from Sir John Merreys, since.

6. " As for Patrick Cullen the Fencer, none of all these have ever beene my man, nor never woare my cloth, but this Patrick onelie, wth whome I became acquainted in a fencing schoole, seven or eight yeres ago, or perhaps somewhat more. He could play well, wch made me desire him to com wth me into Ireland, wch he promist to doe; but I being at the courte, he, for some fray, or som cause or other wch I doe not knowe, went to keepe schoole at Westchester; and I beinge com to London from the courte, I enquired for the said Patrick at the fencing schoole where I understood that he and one Joffrey another man, an Englishman, whoe is here nowe at Dublin keeping a fencing schoole, went to keepe schoole at Westchester, I being wthin a while after determined to goe into Ireland, I desired one Mr. Lucas a ñchant of Waterford to lend me som money, wch I would cause one of my freinds to place in Ireland uppon sight of my lre. He told me he would go for som money into Westchester, where his father being an Englishman was born, and that he woulde lend me soe much money as I desired, wch was £55. Whereuppon I, understandinge that he was to goe to Chester for it, and remembring the said litle fencinge

youth or boy, I desired him to enquire at the fencinge schoole for such a one, and to desire him to com wth me into Ireland, accordinge to his promisse; whereupon he came to me wth Mr. Lucas, and came wth me hither, and was wth me while I was restrained at Corke, and here, and went over wth me when I was sent by Mr. Chichester, and being the next day comitted to the Towre, he went awaie and served som other, or as I hearde he kepte a fencing schoole in London, and being comitted for a robbery, or for some suspicion of som such matter, he went and fledd awaie somwhere, I know not whither. All this while after my committment for a yere or more I was still a close prisoner in cold harbert,* and this much as aforesaid I heard at my first libtie; he being gon before my first libtie, and **Jaques** being in the Fleet a good while after: Alsoe the said Culone whoe was never a whole yere wth me, is now hanged, and executed, and examined, whereby it cannot be unknowne to the Councill if he could saye aniething of me.

7. "As for Owen McCarthy or Owen Gamsagh, I knowe him not by that name, but in troth one Owen McTeige MacDonell Oge mett me in the countre where I dwell. nowe of late since my cominge, and told me that he came from Sir John Merehe'sis Regiment out of Brittaine, and being assembled amongst the rest of the countre, when the Sherrif extended som land from me. he went at my request wth som of mine owne men, namelie Molrony O'Croly, and Edward Slabagh to keepe the castle of Tymolaigge for me, for his hire; and since I left him in the countrey, and is there, I am sure, to be had if my Lo. or his uncle McCarthy Reough or som other of my Lo. Barries freinds hath not by som meanes put him out of the way, of purpose to accuse me for him: neither was he ever my man, nor doe I knowe that he was ever wth Jaques, or aniewhere ells beyond seas, but under Her Maᵗˢ Generall in Brittaine as he telleth me.

8th. "As for the last article, I avowe it to be merelie false, neither had I ever, or did I ever, by anie signe, or otherwise shewe that I had anie freindshipp wth Jaques but while he served Her Maᵗⁱᵉ. Having never wisht him noe better looke than to loose his Lyfe since I heard that he went to the enemyes.

"The Aunswers of me Florence Mᶜ Carthy to the Articles preferred by the Lo. Barry to the Lo. Deputy and Sir Thomas Norreys against me the 17 of June 1594.

" By me ffLORENCE MᶜCARTHY.

" A true Copie.

" August 31.

    " W. FITZ WILLIAMS,
    " THO. NORREYS."

This defence of Florence is one of the most interesting of the many documents he has left us. It will be noticed that the two first articles in his reply are concerning law students. It is impossible to peruse his numberless petitions, to see the supreme address with which was carried on a struggle of half a century about his property, the care with which every legal document concerning it was preserved, the readiness with which, upon occasion, they were invariably forthcoming, and,

---

* Part of the Tower of London, so called.

above all, the consummate skill with which, at the most
critical moments of his career, his correspondence was conducted, and not at once conclude that he must, through life,
have retained in his employment very wary and learned legal
advisers; doubtless the Brehons of Munster were equally
made use of in his intercourse with his own followers. That
he employed the rhymers, or bards, and knew them to be
most efficient instruments in the hands of any one who could
influence them, we shall have incidental proof at a later, and
very critical period of his life; but we should still remain
puzzled to conjecture the origin of this extreme wariness,
were it not for the presentments made to Sir William Drury,
already laid before the reader, and confirmed by his answers
to Barry. To his legal friends he owed, not indeed this
triumph over his adversary—for these charges had been
answered years before, and a mere repetition of his previous
replies would have been at least as credible as such testimony
as Barry had produced—but the means of pointing every
petition in after life with the declaration that "nothing had
ever been proved against him;" and the acknowledgment of
Carewe to the Council at Dublin, and of Cecyll himself to
Carewe, "that all he had done he had brought within the
reach of his protections and pardons." There exists amongst
Her Majesty's State Papers an official return of "the names
of Irish Gentlemen Students of Law in Gray's Inn." This
document is undated, and therefore placed provisionally
amongst other papers also undated; but it is conjectured to
belong to the end of the reign of James I. In this list
occurs the name of Hurley; and the call for this return
would seem to arise so naturally from the charges of Barry,
that it is difficult not to entertain the supposition that the
date suited to it would be that of this renewed attack upon
Florence. The list may possess an interest of its own, and
it is therefore offered to the reader's notice:—

"NAMES OF THE IRISH GENTLEMEN OF GRAY'S INN."

1. " Bradey, who lodgeth in a low chamber at the East end of
Mr. William Ellis his building in Gray's Inn, but not in Co^ens.
2. " Barnewall G^o. who lodgeth at the E: end of Gray's in Chappel,
but not in Co^ens.
3. " Byse: who when he is in Towne lodgeth at one Jacksonne's a
Victualler in Holborne.
4. " Hurley who lodgeth in Mr. Fullwood's new buildings.
5. " Ball, who lodgeth at one Stanley's a joiner hard by Staple Inne.
6. " Seagrave James; and, 7, Seagrave Richard, who lodge at Jacksonne's afores^d. but one not in Co^ens.
8. Morris John; and 9 FitzWilliam, which are not in Towne.

" Staple Inn.   To the Worshipful the Readers of Gray's Inn.

" There hath not been in Commons in Staple· Inn, which are as yet of that house, any more Irishmen at any time within these 3 years, but those who are hereunder named:—

1. " Char⁵. Ryan Gent: went into Irel^d. (as far as I can learne) about 5 weeks now last past.

2. " Christopher Rerdon Gent: lyeth in this Citie, and eats, as I hear, at Bull's Ordinary, in Fleete Street, most commonly.

3. " Edwd. Tafe of Cookestown, in Ireland, Gent. I cannot learne whether he be in Eng^d. or Irel^d.

4. " Thomas Roache, Gent. he lyeth in High Holborne, but hath not been in Commons these six weekes.

" Thos. Frese, *Principal.*"

Florence was evidently well pleased to seize this opportunity of a feeble accusation, to make a powerful, and as he might hope, a final reply; and he purposely went beyond the range of those charges to give explanation upon matters which, he must have known, had not escaped the quick eyes of the authorities, although Barry had not the sagacity to lay them to his charge. The allusion to the story of young Finin of Gleanachrime invites a few words of explanation relative to a dark episode in our family history.

The MacCarthys Duna descended, as did the more historic branch of MacCarthy Reagh, from Donal God, third in descent from St. Cormac, Bishop and King of Munster, and fifth from Carthach, from whom the Sept name was derived. From Donal Caomh (Donal the Handsome) grandson of Donal God, proceeded Donal Glas I., and Cormac Don; from the former sprung the MacCarthys Reagh, and from the latter the Mac-Carthys Duna, or of Dunmanway. These had their home in the pleasant lands of Gleanachrime, where, from about the year 1300, their chieftains lived in contented submission to their more turbulent cousins, who early assumed the supremacy of the whole of Carbery. In Sir William Drury's time a shocking crime, and an ignominious punishment had brought disgrace upon this family. Cormac Don, a namesake of the first Lord of Gleanachrime, who stood by Tanist law next in succession to the chieftainship, had murdered his uncle and chieftain, the murderer was apprehended, tried by a jury, and hanged in chains at Cork! Had this been the end of the matter, no voice could have impugned the justice of the verdict, or the propriety of the punishment; but this was by no means the end of it, nor indeed was it, except incidentally, any part of the purpose of Sir William Drury to trouble the Queen's officers with any domestic irregularities amongst the Irish Septs. " The fixed principle" of Sir Henry Sidney " to dissipate the Estates of the rebel Irish" had quickened the ingenuity of all subsequent presidents, and deputies, and eminently of the Parliaments held at Dublin. At the first of these Parliaments that met after the execution of Cormac Don, this criminal, who had been hanged for the *Murder* of his uncle, was declared to have been guilty of *Treason!* and "Atteynted, so as his lands of Glan-y-crime came to Her Majestie."

The history of the transaction is curious in all its phases. The elected life-occupant of large Sept domains is murdered; the right of succession is, by Irish law, in his nephew, the murderer; the Queen's authorities in Munster, instead of declaring the estates of the murdered man to descend, as by English law they would, to his son, for once acknowledge "the vile and lewd usage of Tanistry," recognise the murderer as the just heir, try him for *Murder,* execute him for *Treason,* and by Act of Parliament declare him attainted, and the estates of the MacCarthys of Gleanachrime to belong, not any longer to them, as by law of Tanistry (now for this once recognised), they did, nor to the son of the murdered chieftain as they would by English law, but to the Queen! Even more curious was the sequel of this effort for the fixed principle; for, whilst "the twelve men at Corke" were, according to their lights, finding it "Murder" in Cormac Don to have killed his uncle, and Cormac Don was in consequence of his sentence expiating his offence on the gibbet; whilst the Dublin Parliament was loyally finding it "High Treason" to have slain this descendant of King Dermod, and was tracing the rights of succession to his property through the mazes of rival laws, and conflicting claims, Teig O'Norsie—Teig of the Forces—a name sufficiently suggestive of the validity of Teig's claim, whether against his cousin, or the Queen,—who by Tanistry was justly the successor to his brother, the murderer, quietly entered into the possession of the contested lands, and the Queen, as complacently, submitted without a word of protest to this annulling of so much parliamentary acuteness, and the disloyal invasion of her rights! It was not until after ten or twelve years' enjoyment of the fruits of his brother's crime that there occurred to the mind of Teig O'Norsie any doubt of the sufficiency of his title; but when the forlorn son of the murdered chieftain, then growing up to manhood, had made his way—probably begged it—to London, and found there a friend, in a man whose energies might seem sufficiently absorbed by his own misfortunes, Teig, with full reliance upon the benignity of the Queen, bethought him of the expedient, always pleasing to Elizabeth, of offering the surrender of his lands to Her Majesty, that he might receive them back, subject to some trifling rent, to be held, for all time to come, by English tenure. He had powerful friends, and repaired with his suit to court. The poor disinherited lad, who had wandered to the banks of the Thames in search of a patron, found there a friendly hand to pen his petition for him, and interest sufficient to bring it under the notice of the Privy Council.

The petition of Teig O'Norsie was a discreet and diplomatic document: had it not been for the incidents of the murder, the sentence of the Cork jury, and the declaration of attainder by the Dublin Parliament, the petitioner would doubtless have premised his right to the lands of Gleanachrime by Tanist usage immemorial, as did other petitioners in similar circumstances, and have gracefully laid all such claim at the Queen's feet; but these were not recollections to be rashly revived; Teig, therefore, in making his petition, reserved within his own breast so much of the preamble as would have recapitulated the Tanist rights which he sought to surrender. The petition of Finin McCormac is a far more interesting and curious document; the hand that wrote it is traceable in every paragraph. The petition contains not a word of any rights accruing to the suppliant by Irish law; by Tanistry Teig O'Norsie was justly chieftain of the MacCarthys of Gleanachrime; and this Finin knew. The petitioner might, unaided, have thought of accusing Teig of a share, by evil counsel, in the death of his, the petitioner's father, and of the subsequent murder of a cousin who had assumed the protection of Finin; but that Teig O'Norsie had by certain ways other than those leading through the grand antechambers " procured speech of Her Majesty, and was in hopes of procuring a grant of his lands without knowledge of the Lords of the Privy Council; nay, to steal away Her Majesty's letters unknown to their Lordships," was an assertion which it was much safer for this simple suppliant, than for his prompter, to make ; as, assuredly, it was a discovery that needed more experience of Court proceedings than it was likely Finin could have picked up during his short abode under the roof of Foster, the victualler, in Tower-street.

"1587·   *The humble petition of* FININ M^cCORMUCK *to the Right Honble. the Lords and others of her Majesty's most honorable Privy Council.*

"In most humble manner, sheweth unto your Lordships, your poor suppliant Fynin McCormuck of Glaincruim in Carbry, within the county of Corke gent. That whereas your said suppliant his father Cormuck

McFynin being as is known to the Right Honble. Sir John Parrott, lawfully possessed of the lands of Glaincrim in the country of Carbry aforesaid, was at the instigation of one Teig in Orssy murdered by Cormuck Downe, the said Teig in Orssy his eldest brother, for the which his said brother was by S^r. W^m. Drury, being then Lord President of Monster, hanged in chains at Cork; and afterwards a cousin of your suppliant, named Felíme McOwen pretending to possess the said land, of Glainncrim for, and in the name of your suppliant, was by the said Teig in Orssy in like sort murdered, since which time he doth, as well by reason of his wealth, as by cause of your suppliants tender age, being constrained for the safety of his life to forsake his country since his fathers death, contrary to all equity and justice, possess your said suppliant's father's lands as tenant to Sr Owen Mc Carty, being therein maintained by the said Sr Owen, by reason that he hath fostered his eldest son, and the better to entitle himself thereunto is now come hither with intent to surrender the said land unto Her Majesty, and for as much as those lands doth of right belong to your suppliant, and that the said Teig in Orssy hath already procured means whereby he hath spoken unto Her Majesty, and preferred his supplications to Her Highness touching the said lands, and being here these six months, ever since S^r. Walter Raleigh came out of Ireland, a suitor unto Her Majesty for these lands, he hath never all that while acquainted any of your Lordships with the matter; whereby it appears that he had no right thereunto, and that his intent is to steal away Her Majesty's letters unknown to your Lordships, which he had done already but that M^r. Secretary Walsingham, according to your Lordship's former resolution, did hinder it; wherefore he humbly beseecheth your Lordships for God's sake and for the equity of his cause, to be a means unto Her Majesty that his said surrender may not be received, and that there may be a stay made thereof before your suppliants title be tried, which, being found right, that he may be put in possession of the said lands according to equity and justice, and he shall pray, &c.

"The humble Petition of Fynin Mc Cormuck to the Lords of the Council."

Royal letters were sent to Ireland, ordering inquiry to be made into the justice of these rival suits. An inquiry was made, not indeed into the grounds of the dispute between Teig O'Norsie and the pauper Finin M'Cormack, but simply for the record of the sentence passed upon the murderer ten years before, and its bearing upon the succession to the lands of Gleanachrime. Record of the transaction was readily found, and it was conclusive:—

"1587. 28 *Eliz., Cap.* 7.

"Cormac Don Mac Carty was executed for Treason by verdict of XII men at Corke in Sir William Drurys time; and after, he was, at the last parliament at Dublyn, atteynted, so as his lands of Glan-y-cryme came to Her M_a^{tie}.

"Teig O'Norsey Mac Carty, a younger brother to the said Cormac, who hathe occupied the said lands unjustlie ever since his brother's deathe, is nowe a suyter to surrender the said lands, and to retake them agayne of Her M_a^{tie}.

"A cousin of his, named Finin Mac Cormac Mac Cartie, does crosse the

said Teig in his sute, for that he pretendethe title to the said lands, but
the Right thereof is in Her Matie as aforesaid."

Letters Patent were passed; the country was vested in
Teig O'Norsie and his heirs male for ever, and no more would
ever have been heard of Finin McCormac, but for this reply of
Florence MacCarthy to the charges of Barry. Of the assertions of Barry that "Cormac McFinin had been sent by
Florence to Sir William Stanley," and of Florence that "the
unfortunate youth, constrained by extreme misery, had joined
himself with certain soldiers, and gone with them into
Brittayne," the reader may select that which he thinks the
more credible, for no proof is offered of either; but that "the
youth had lost his life some four or five years previous to the
date of these charges" was, fortunately for him, not exact.
In the year 1642,—forty-eight years later than the date of
these articles, fifty-two or fifty-three after his rumoured death
—Finin McCormac gave such evidence of his existence as
Barry would have expected. A portentous list of MacCarthys
accused of rebellion was produced at the Assizes held at
Youghal, in the month of August of that year: the third
name upon this list was that of Finin McCormac, of Gleanachrime! the twenty-eighth was Teige O'Downy (the son of
Teige O'Norsey, to whom Her Gracious Majesty had given
her Letters Patent for the lands of Gleanachrime); the twenty-
ninth was Teig O'Norsey (II.) of Togher, grandson of Teig
O'Norsie the first; and the thirtieth Dermot McTeig of Dunmanway, another grandson of the grantee. *Eighty-two* more
names followed, of gentlemen of the Sept, called to account
on that day of solemn reckoning!

Of all the charges which the malignity of Barry had collected against his adversary, the sixth was by far the most
dangerous. Respecting this Cullen Camden writes :—

"The next day was also Patrick Cullen condemned, an Irish Fencing
Master, who had been laden with great promises by the fugitives in the
Low Countries, and some time since sent privily over, with money to bear
his charges, on purpose to kill the Queen. Who as good as confessing
his crime, and the same being also proved against him by sufficient evidence, he was taken and executed, when he was otherways ready to die of
a languishing sickness."

Florence met this accusation with the candour of a man
who felt that he had no motive for concealment, and no objection that the entire truth of his connection with this Cullen
should be known to the whole world; for he readily acknowledges the curious fact that he had been at some pains to
secure his services, that he had taken him with him to Ireland,

kept him about his person at the time of his marriage, *during his imprisonment* at Cork, and took him with him to Dublin; that whilst he was under the custody of Chichester he was allowed to retain him, and that it was only when the Tower gates closed between them that they separated. His having had this Patrick Cullen at one time (four years previously) in his service was no greater proof of his conspiracy to murder the Queen, than his acquaintance with Stanley and Jacques (in the times of the old Earl of Desmond) had been of his complicity in the surrender of Deventer, on the Issell, to the Spaniards. If Queen Elizabeth could have believed these charges, her subsequent conduct towards Florence would have added, to the many claims which this Royal Lady has upon the admiration of posterity, that of a Christian forgiveness of her worst enemies. Had the accusation been made against her principal Secretary Cecyll, or her Deputy Mountjoy, or her President Carewe, Her Majesty might have believed it! for each of these noblemen has left it to posterity in his own handwriting that he had hired men to do murder—the third had himself, with his own hand, done it! Such a man as Jacques de Franceschi might use the weapons of these great statesmen, but the poor Irish fencing master, Cullen, did *not!* Nor—be it said without disrespect to Camden—"did he as good as confess his crime," but he denied it on his oath; nor was he "convicted of it by sufficient evidence," though he was sufficiently hanged for it, but he "scrupled in his conscience at doing such a deed." Her Majesty *could not*, even had she been disposed, believe this accusation of Barry; for the Lords of the Privy Council had already in their possession a more satisfactory refutation of this atrocious slander than it was in the power of Florence to produce. It will be within the recollection of the reader that the principal charge against him in his previous examination had been his intimacy with Sir William Stanley and Jacques de Franceschi. Since those days the evil fame of both these men had increased a hundredfold; the sole object of the life of Stanley had become the invasion of Ireland, and the sole pursuit of Jacques the discovery of some able desperado to murder the Queen. Patrick Cullen, as we have mentioned, was apprehended on suspicion of having undertaken to do it. He confessed that Jacques had proposed it to him, but he declared "that he had had scruples as to the lawfulness of the deed, and that whilst in communication with Jacques he had received a warning from one of his countrymen to be careful, for that Jacques was a cunning fellow, and that as he (Cullen) was known to M^r. Florence

Mac Carthy, he would surely forfeit his esteem if he joined in any such practice." This was the deposition of a dying man, made before the Privy Council, and of which Florence could not by any possibility have cognizance.

No sooner had Florence made his reply to Barry's charges than he hurried away to England to plead his cause in person with Lord Burghley and Sir Robert Cecyll, "whom he had always found his very good Lord, and best friends." His earliest welcome in London was from his creditors, who doubtless had watched every phase of that long enduring contest with interest scarcely less vivid than his own. With the same coin with which he had managed to silence them before he now endeavoured to hush them again. His first suit to his friends was for a renewal of the old warrant of immunity from arrest for debt. This was a species of paper money in great repute, and abundant circulation amongst gentlemen, who, like himself, were " in attendance upon the Court with suits." The Queen's gift of the fine, far from improving his circumstances, or enabling him to pay off his former debts, had greatly added to his embarrassments; for "in pursuit of it he had already expended £200 in law and otherwise." Before long we shall find this sum rapidly growing into three, and finally into five, hundred pounds—the full and precise amount of the fine itself—and had not his succession to the inheritance of his father-in-law, and his political troubles intervened, it certainly would have amounted to as many thousands before my Lord Barry ceased to petition for its remittal, or Florence for its payment. It was the Queen's own change of purpose that stood between the creditors of Florence and their money, it was but reasonable that her warrant should interpose also between him and their impatience.

"1594. *Sept.* 29. FLORENCE MAC CARTHY *to* SIR ROBT. CECILL KT.

"It may please yor Hono^r to understand; where, at my beinge here, by reason of the longe continuance of my restraint and troble for the space of five yeres, havinge both wife and children here at my charges, I was constrayned not onely to morgadge and lease what livinge I had, but also to runn very farr indebted here, whereuppon it hath pleased my very good Lo. the Lord Trerrer and the rest of the councill to grant me a warrant that I might not be arrested or trobled untill I had receaved som benefitt of the suite wch Her Matie bestowed uppon me for the satisfieinge of my creditors, wch beinge since hindered by myne adversaryeis last beinge here, wherby I could nev^r since receiv any benefitt by the same, wherefore I humblie besech yor Hono^r to be a mean that the sayd warrant (which I have sent here enclosed to yor Hono^r to peruse) may be now renewed againe, for the wch I shall think myselfe most bound to pray for yor Hono^r

I 2

and even so wth the remebrance of my most bounden duetie I humblie take
leue this 29th Sept. 1594.

"ffLOR McCARTHY."

With his mind at ease, at least upon the subject of his
personal freedom, Florence was ready to resume his legal
combat. The time occupied in the business of procuring the
warrant, and restoring the temper of his creditors, afforded no
interval of rest to the mind of the Secretary from this wearisome contest; for the Irish despatches bore their usual burden
of accusations against Florence, and Barry's customary wailing
over his poverty and his fine. Sir Robert Cecyll may have
been pleasantly surprised for once at learning that his correspondent had generously accompanied his letter with "a
present of three Hawck and a coupell of hobbies;" but he
could not fail to perceive that, in commenting upon the issue
of his recent charges against Florence, Barry was scarcely
mending his previous indiscretion, by which he had so greatly
offended his judges; his present accusation glanced aside from
his adversary, and struck straight at the honour and loyalty
of the Lord Deputy and the Vice-President; for he charged
them, in as temperate phrase as he had at his command, with
refusing to entertain his evidence, and with partiality to a
man accused of treason:—

"1594. *Oct.* 1. BARRY *to* CECYLL. *Written from Ireland.*

"R⁺ Hon. Sir my dutie wth moost hartie thancks remembered for your
manyfold curtesies and great frendly favors by me ther lately receved,
wherof sithence I have enjoied the benefitt. Florence McCartie hath
lately repaired thither, wholy bent yf by false suggestions and practices
he may worck my hurt: whath proceedings have bene used against him
touching the articels I preferd againest him, and the directions made in
that behalf to the late deputie, I am not acquainted wthal; butt that I
doo know there was no stricte course observed be tacking examinations
upon presumptions and surcumstance againest him, and yf I have felt any
favor extraordinary don to the said Florence, I do in regard of dutifull
reverence for so highe authorities omitt to charg any; but I dare affirme
and assure your Honⁿᵒʳ that yf Florence be dealt wth in sort as his dissembling and cunning requires, he shall be found, upon tharticles that I
have ministered against him, a practiser and a conspirator wth the rebells
and enemies, of Spain, and also a puocker and sturrer of rebellion here
in Ireland by Donell McCartie base son to thErle of Clancare, whose
rebellious accions have trubled this quiet state chiefly of the English in-
habitances in Kerrye, and have brought many subjects to ther end with
loss of ther blood, of the said Florencis Conspiracie wth the said Donell;
and sturing this rebellion, manifest is extant by examinacions takn by
Justice Smythes late chife Justice of this pvence of Mounster, wch ex-
aminacons ether returned to the late L. Deputie, or elsh remaineth wth the
said Justice Smythe's widow, himself being dead; and for as moch as the

said Florencis bad practises in this traitorous actions do touch ore Soveraigne in the highest d'gree I humbly and hartly beseche yor hon^{nor} so to
mannage the course of pceeding wth him as Her Ma^{ts} service being
circumspectly pvided for, my true informaĉons may take soch place as
my zealous affection hath deservid and expected, and that for my duetifull
good meaninge I be not hardly spocken nor thought of; I also besech
yor Honnor to p'vent such suts as the said Florence may p'ferr againest
me, for my fyne, the which Her ^{M}a^{tie} granted unto him; and after by
yor honorable meanes was revokd by Hir Highnes, for I am not able
through many losses susteyned by me, to paye the same at this time; and
as Hir Highnes hath forboren the paiment therof hitherto that yor Hoñor
so work Hir Highness pleasor, to contynue for tollerating the same till
ether my habilitye may afourd the paiment, or Hir Matie be further
inclined to remett the same by my good service here. I could not by so
well furnyshed for my abscence in England that I myght visite yor Honor
wth soch tokens as my good will coulde wishe or y^r honourable favor
deserve, onely at this tyme I pray your Honor to accept of these thrie
Hawck and a coupell of hobbies, wch as a poor rememberance of bounden
dutie I do send yor Hoñor by this berer my servant. I could have sent
yor Hoñor som more hawck, but that Florence, before I came into Erland
tock an eary of my hawck, and coñytted many other spoils upon my
tenants. So altogether leaving to your honourable favor and frendshipp
I humbly take my leave.

   " Barrye Courte this 1st of October 1594.

                                     " DAVID BUTTEVANTE."

Few things more curious are on record than the confidential correspondence between Sir R. Cecyll and Sir G. Carewe;
plain dealing phrases that meant but one thing were of so
much more importance to these men than any safer diplomatic ambiguity of words, that we are left in no obscurity
as to the opinion of these writers respecting the men who,
like Barry now, and the Earl of Thomond a little later, poured
out their confidence to the Minister or the Privy Council. What
Sir R. Cecyll thought of Lord Buttevant's effusions, and of
Lord Buttevant himself, we shall eventually see in his own
words.

CHAPTER VI.

WHILST Sir Robert Cecyll was pondering over the last favour of the Lord Barry, Florence was occupied in composing one of his most elaborate and successful letters to Lord Burghley, in which, after a spirited recital of his father's services and his own, and a fearless appeal to a multitude of great names in evidence of his veracity, he turns upon Barry and his father a torrent of invective, which, if its truth but equalled its burning and its bitterness, should have sufficed at once to settle the value of any charges which such an accuser could make, and to mark the Lord Buttevant as the one of Her Majesty's subjects fitter than all others to be made to pay any amount of fine that could be extracted from him.

The Lord Deputy Fitzwilliams was now in England, and at hand, to give explanation of the conduct of Barry, past and present. Florence had brought with him letters of recommendation from the Vice-President of Munster, *one* of his recent judges; and from the confidence with which he appeals again and again to the testimony of the Lord Deputy, it is sufficiently manifest that he was well assured of the good offices of *the other.* With unerring instinct both Florence and his adversary endeavoured to account for the rancour with which each thought himself persecuted, by attributing it to revelations which, in their conscientious loyalty, they had felt compelled to make against each other, of rebellious practices against the State. This argument was, no doubt, intended for the musings of Her Majesty; but Florence, with ready address, seized upon the unhappy slip of the Lord Barry relative to the seizure " of *all his means of living* as security for the payment of his fine," which evidently was but a sudden explosion of petulance, but which implied a grave charge against his judges. Fitzwilliams as well as Norreys had stigmatised that assertion as " touching him in honour ;" and now that the former of these great functionaries was to be questioned on the matter, Florence assisted his remembrance of the circumstance by renewing Barry's charge, and appealing to his judge to satisfy the Minister with respect to it.

But the following letter contains matter of greater interest than any that can be derived from the writer's enmity to Barry. The reader has long since been informed that Sir Donogh MacCarthy, the father of Florence, had taken an active part with the Queen's forces against the rebel Earl of Desmond, and that Sir Henry Sidney had thereupon pronounced him "an especial man, and good subject, and desired that he might be nobilitated;" this letter assures us that Florence continued in the same loyal track as his father; that during several years he had led his own followers against the earl, and received many marks of Her Majesty's approbation of his services; these seemingly plain proofs of his cordial support of English rule in his native country he used with vigour and effect to overthrow the accusations of Barry; they might be used by his biographer now for the assertion that Florence was, at least at one period of his life, a model of loyalty! Alas for the sagacity of Sir Henry Sydney! for the claims of Florence, or his father, to the gratitude of the Lord Deputy, or the Queen! the Annals of Ireland for 400 years furnish us with far other motive for the hostility of the Mac-Carthys to the Fitzgeralds than loyalty to their English rulers. The great family feuds and alliances of the Irish and their Norman neighbours would explain many an apparent inconsistency in the conduct of individual chieftains. If a Butler or a Fitzgerald quarrelled with the Queen's Deputy, certain Irish chiefs would assuredly share their blame as rebels, and others for a while acquire the fame of devoted and loyal subjects; their rebellion and their loyalty consisted but in their fidelity to their alliances, and to their rivalries; bearing this in mind, the reader will find less inconsistency in the conduct of Florence in the earlier and later periods of his career.

" 1594. *Nov.* 29.   FLORENCE MAC CARTHY *to* LO. BURLEIGH.

" My very approved good Lo: my humble and most bonden dutie remẽbered: having allways since my cõming hyther expected onely yoᵣ Loᴾˢ leasure to peruse what hath bene advertised out of Ireland concern- inge me, to the end that yoᵣ Loᴾ might thereafter take such order for me as you thought mete: and perceiving now that Barry myne adversary hath sent one of his men hyther, and hath, (as he is accustomed) written sundrye lies of me, as well to yoᵣ Loᴾ as to others, onely to delay my dis- patch, whereby I might be here consumed wth longe attendance, as I was already utterly undon wth the long continuance of my troble, whereunto I was brought by his lieinge devices and fals informaĉons. In regard whereof I humblie besech yoᵣ honorable Loᴾ to consider how farr he hath

abused and misinformed yor Lo^p and the rest òf the Councell at his beinge
here, as Sir William Fitzwilliams can tell, and as apeares by such infor-
maçõns as yor Lo^p received from Sir Thomas Norreys; for where he hath
affirmed here that the best parte of his livinge was extended unto me, it is
manifest (as I am sure Sir Thomas hath advertised yor Lo^p) that I received
scarce 14 or 15 ploughlands, valued at £42 Ireish a yere, wch is not the
10th parte of that livinge wch he doth uniustly holde! Also he hath
accused me of divers haynous matters, wch he did constantly affirme here,
that he wold *prove in Ireland*, where he could neù prove none; myself
having remained there untill I answered all those matters before Sir
William Fitzwilliams (unto whose reporte I referr myself) and Sir Thomas
Norreys at Dublinge, and afterwards sufficiently satisfied Sir Thomas in
Mounster for them all, w^{t}hout wch I coulde hardly obtaine (since Sir
Thomas informed yor Lo^p of these matters) not onely his pasporte to com
hyther, but also his letters hyther, testifieinge how earnest and carefull I
was to do Her ^{M}a^{tie} service while I was in Ireland, wch he knowes I had
performed yf I had not bene hyndered by these matters.

" Neyther do I think yf my former life be justly considered, but that
I deserve well Her Ma^{ts} gyft, and he deserved very ill to live or enjoye
anythinge under her Highnes; for his father who was a man of no regardé
untill he attained to Barry Roe's Countrey by murderinge the heyres
thereof, and also gott Barrymore's countrey by deceit and trechery, being
not of Barrymore of Buttevant's countrey nor kindred, nor having nothing
to do with him, nor never recoùed anything by law, nor was never established by any prince; and being Sir John of Desmond's onely confederat
to breede the last rebellion, he was therefore comtted by the Lo: Justice
and Lo: Generall to the Castell of Dublinge where he was kept untill he
died, wch is no good monument of his loyaltie: his son also, this Barry,
having folowed the Earle of Desmond in all the last rebellion, burning
and spoyleing Her Mat^{ts} subiects, and killinge and murderinge her English
souldiers, both in Bantrye and other places, who being afterwards pardoned,
he hath a great while after kept secretly wth him one Walter Bregin, a
preiste, who being still a chefe person wth him and with Doctor
Sanders in all the last rebellion, was a great while after sent by the sayd
Barry into Spaine, about som practices of treason, where he is still resident
for him at Lisbune, yf he be alive; besides also that now of late, when I
was here a prisonner, the sayd Barry, wth other accomplices of his, mett
in a certen place, where they were swerne to a rebellious combinaçõn, and
drank wine out of a chalice, uppon that condiçõn; and attempted in vayne
one Owen M'Murty, agent, by whom Mr. Cormuk Mac Dermod is much
ledd, in hope to bring Mr. Cormuk to enter therein: yee and had don
worss yf Sir Thomas Norreys had not bene wise and vigilant inough to
prevent his treason and vilainey, wch when I understood at my being there
now, I inquired of Sir Thomas Norreys whether he understood of the
matter, and he told me that he heard an inklinge therof at the same time,
and told me the manner of it.

" And as for myself I doubt not but here are som that have served
under Sir Henry Sidney in Mounster, to whose report (*and to Her Ma^{ts}
owne letters to my Father*) I referr how faithfull and forward my father was
at all times to serve Her Highnes, who having bene wth the Lo: Deputye
aforesaid at the sige of Balimarter at Glann-Moyr, and in all other places
where he had occasion to use anyforces for Her ^{M}a^{tie}, where he brought
him more mẽ then any two in Mounster; and in Sir William Fitzwilliams
is time when the Earle of Desmond escaped out of Dublinge, I am sure
Sir William (who wrote to him then against the sayd Earle, and received

answer to his contentaĉon from him) doth very well remˉber his constancie
and faythfullnes to Her Maᵗⁱᵉ: and not onely Sir William, but also Sir
Walter Rawleigh (by the reporte of his brother Sir Humfrey Gilbert), and
divers others here, who remeˉbers what pains he hath taken, and charges he
hath bene at, in Her Maᵗˢ service, both in the time of Sir Humfrey
Gilbert, Sir John Perrott, and all such as gouˉned there. Myself also,
beinge at the beginninge of the Earle of Desmond's rebellion but of the
adge of 16 or 17 yeres, hauinge a litle before (uppon the death of my
father) taken charge of his folowers, and his owne lands, since wch time I
have euˉr assisted in person in almost all the jorneys that were don in Her
Maᵗˢ service, both under Sir William Pelham, the Lo: Gray, the Earl of
Ormond, Mr. John Zouch, Sir George Bourchier, and all such as gouˉned,
or coˉmaunded there; as is well knoweˉ to Sir Walter Rawleigh, Sir Georg
Bourchier, Capten Francis Bartly, and a great number of captens, officers,
and Gent', which I do see here now dayly, who knowes when they wanted
forces I brought them still readily 300 of myne owne men; and when the
Earl of Desmond liued uppon the spoyl of the Earle of Clancartyes
contrey, I wth above 300 of myne owne meˉ joined wth Sir Edward Bartly
and his companie, and kilde his receiver Morice Roe, and others, and
chased him out of that countrey, into his owne waste countrey, where all
his men were constrained to forsake him; and being kept and maintained
a good while by Gory Mᶜ Swiney, a companie of my men wch I sent to
serve uppon the rebells kilde the sayd Gory, wherby the Earle was kilde
wthin a weke or ten dayes after, being not able to kepe himself without
him any time. Of all wch matters both Her Maᵗⁱᵉ and yoʳ Loᵖ was sufficiently informed at my first coˉminge hyther, for which Her Hignes hath
rewarded me; the remembrance whereof, as well as of my fathers service
and myne, as also of Her Maᵗˢ bountifull rewards and fauˉ towards me
(myne aˉncesters, contrey, and kinred, hauinge also remained euˉ good subiects, wherby none of my Contry or name was neuˉ stained) did at all times,
and doth still, woork more in me, and is (as any man in reason may judge)
esteemed more by me, then any frendship or familiari͜ies that euˉ I had
wth so light a felow as Jaques was, whom I neuˉ knew to be three dayes of
one mynd, and wth whom I neuˉ had very much to do at all, being but a
device of myne adversary, for want of any matter to be found against me,
as appeared when the matter was heard both in Dublinge and Mounster.

   " Wherefore I most humbly besech yoʳ Honorable Loᵖ (whom I have
always found my very good Lo: and best frend) to consider as well my
father's service and myne, and his father's wiked murders and rebellious
intencˉons, for the wch he died, together wth his owne trayterous inclinacˉon
and oppon rebellion, as also myne imprisonment and troble these five yers
past, wherunto I was brought by his lieing deuices and fals informatcˉons,
during wch time I was constrained to lease, and sell, what living I had,
having both wife and children here at my charges; besids also that this
suite cost me in Ireland about £300, both in provinge the same due, in
getting his assurance for the paiment therof, and in extending a small
parcell of his land when he forfetted his assurance, and came hyther; in
regard whereof, I most humblie besech yoʳ honourable Loᵖ (for that I am
not able to live or maintaˉin myself here any longer) to be a mean that I
may haue som spedier order wherby I may receiv the benefitt of Her Maᵗˢ
gift, wth consideracˉon for my charges aforesayd, which (I protest) I wold
not desire yf it might in any sort preiudice Her Maᵗⁱᵉ or the State, as yoʳ
Loᵖ may at large perceve, and be therin throughly satisfied by Sir Wilham
Fitzwilliams, who, with Sir Thomas Norreys, had the hearing and determ-.
ineinge of the matter, and who knowes what the oppinion of Sir Thomas

and the councell is, as well of this matter as of me, and the said Barry; being rather an example to encoradge both himself and the rest of Mounster and Ireland to rebellious attempts, wthout regarde or fear of any punishment for the same, then otherwise, yf this fine were remitted; and being also a favour wch he neü deserved, nor was neñ thought mete to be remitted in Ireland nor here; for himself beinge here about 7 yeres past to sue for a remittall thereof, he was denied; whereby Her Highnes may not remitt, nor respitt the same now, having alrady bestowed it. Thus refferring both myself and the whole state of my cause to yor Lop's honourable consideraĉon, praing God to preserve and kepe you in health I humblie take leue this 29th of Novr. 1594.   Yo^r. Lops allways most humble and bonden

                                    " fflor M^c CARTHY."

Barry, though his wits were not bright, nor his invention very fertile, was not yet at the end of his resources ; moreover, " the disgrace put upon him" had given new energy to the turbulent spirits of Munster, who, by their excesses, furnished him with new grievances, all of which, as his wont was, he laid to the charge of Florence.   Donal the bastard was again upon the prowl !   He and his loose swords had broken out anew from their bogs and fastnesses, and were behaving in the most " unjust and unchristianlike manner to Nicholas Browne, spitefully killing his horses and cattle, taking preys of his Town, and making his life miserable ;" and Browne, again at the head of his Hogesden chivalry, was daily sallying forth in pursuit of the fierce destroyer !   When the Brownes took a lease of the lands of MacCarthy Mor, they should have leased together with them the services of the hereditary Bard of the Sept, for this feud was worthy of the inspiration of Fyn O'Daly ; nay, not an unbecoming theme for the harp of Oisin of the Fians.   In default of professional song, Nicholas Browne was compelled himself to chaunt the incidents of that rural contest, and the reader will admit that he has done so in language highly creditable to his feeling and genius.   But vain were all attempts against Donal! he was neither to be starved nor caught :—" The ordinary food of these rebel Irish," the Minister was informed by one of his English correspondents, " is a kind of grass ; neither clothes nor houses do they care for ; hounds can scarcely follow them, much less men."   The man was not yet in Munster who was to capture or tame that fleet-footed outlaw.

In a fit of despondency, opportunely timed with Barry's renewed attack upon Florence, Browne betook himself to write the record of his wrongs to Lord Burghley.   Nothing more spirited has been penned by any of that Minister's correspondents than the description of the chase, " through woods, boggs, rocks, mountains, and glains," after Donal;

nor more touching than the tremulous cadence in which that high spirit declares that "now at last tidings of a worse matter have reached him! A new adversary had sprung up —one Finin, calling himself Florence—a man who, by great promises, had induced all the MacCarthys in Cork and Kerry to make a common purse to aid him in his projects." If the writer felt for a moment the despondency he so pathetically described—if he at that time of writing contemplated waiting but for a gentle *caveat* to realize what stock Donal had left him, and to be gone—he greatly wronged his own chivalrous spirit. He had inherited his Signory, he had fought many a spirited fight to hold it, he would yet stand many an onslaught from the freebooters, who surrounded him, he would transmit that Signory unimpaired to his son, Valentine II.; and by sword and pike, the means by which he had held it, would it continue to be held to the fourth generation. This noted family feud lasted nearly half a century; many of its vicissitudes were happily veiled from the vision of Nicholas Browne, who, when his letter was sealed and sent, and his heart unburthened, took fresh courage, and was reconciled to his lot. And now for the misdeeds of Donal, whose fortune it was to have as many biographers as there were English functionaries, and English letter-writers in his native land!

"1594. *December* 4. NICHOLAS BROWNE *to* LO: BURGHLEY.

" It may pleas yor good Lordship to understand the uniust practizes, and unchristianlike y^t hath bein used against me by the Clancarties, since first my father had. his signorye allotted him in those lands of O'Donogho Moor, and Coshmainy; the wch lands uppon the Earl of Clancartyes surmises (after my fathor had drawne many menne over to his great charge) we were disposest by derection of Hir ^{M}a^{tie}, notwithstanding his title was as good thereunto, as to any other of the escheted lands throughout all Mounster, wch since, I have found to my cost and hinderaunce: for wheras the Earle produced wittnes here to prouve the freholders of those lands to be his tenants at will, wch bare proff being accepted of him, we thereupon, by way of morgage, agreed wth him for those lands, and Hir ^{M}a^{tie} graunted us Hir gratious pattent for the reversion of them after his deceas; wch morgage, when I thought quietly to enioy, I found many parcells of those lands possest by divers gentlemen, by vertue of estates made unto them by the freholders, and by law cannot be recovered from them; the triall whereof hath cost me very much; yea, and the Earl himself doeth detain som part of them by device of former conveyaunce from the freholders to other men, yet he continuing in the possession of the same; whereby yor Honnor may perceive how hard an estate I rest in. Hir Matie's title, wch was iust, she hath not defended; and the Earl's title, wch was none but fals suggestions, being brought to the true triall, falls out to be of no validity, to my undoing.
" Besides these crosses his bastard sonn continuing still in rebellion, hath cruelly murdered my men, spitefully killed my horses and cattel,

tooke praye of my Towne, and laid divers malitious plottes for mine own
life, wᶜh other men thinks to be donn by the procurement of his father, to
drive me, by the terror of such dealings, to forsake my lands; I iudg
more charitably; yet may not trust him, for the like outrages have not
benñ used to any of the English inhabitaunts and undertakers that are his
neighbors; but those courses, and God will! shall not serve his tourne
(though my life be miserable in the mean time), for I have followed him
through woods, boggs, rocks, mountains, and glains, wᵗʰ companyes of men,
to my great charge and pains (as all the Inglish and Irish in the province
can testify); I have drawen his followers from him; divers have I killed;
and brought some to the triall of the lawe; and lastly, though my fortune.
hath not extended to the getting of his head (whereof I do not despaire);
yet I have reduced him (being principally assisted by the good countenance
of worthy Sir Thomas Norreys) from three score, to himself and two
others, comfortles and frendles.

" All these devices and wrongs, my good Lord, since I have borne their
chefest heat, I am the better armed, and animated to oppose myself against
any second attempt, if the like shold happen; but now I am enformed,
and certainly knowe, of another course, wᶜh terrifies me very much, as
tending to my overthrow, and may prouve no less daungerous to the rest
of the undertakers, wᶜh is one Finin MᵒCarty, who calls himself Florence,
who by reason of the late trobles, and disgrace he procured to the Lord
Barry, hath drawne such an opinion amongst the Irish of him, that the
Barron Coursy hath, at his last being there, givin him possession of his
chefe House of Down MᶜPatrick, an auncient Fort against the Irishry; and
as many as are his frends in the countrys of Desmond, Carbry, Muskry,
Dowalla, have, as yt were, erected a coṁon purse to further him to those
great matters wᶜh he promises them, and assures himself. The Lord
Coursy's land he enioys as much as was in the old Baron to give him. To
be Lord of Carbry he doubts not of, as belonging to him by custom of
Tanistry. But his great matter is to be MᶜCarty More, wᶜh by one of two
means he will seak to procure; the one is by his wife's right, wᶜh can be
no more in hir then was in hir uncle's daughter and heir; this Earl's eldest
brother, who never had any part of the contry allowed hir; nor indede
had any woman before hir amongst the Irishry; the other (if he dares not
seu for so great a matter as the Earldom), yet sute must be made eyther
by his Father in law, his wife, or himself, for thre of MᶜCarty Mores
houses, the wᶜh if any of the Clancartyes be in possession of, they will
ever be in hope to recover the whole jurisdiction that MᶜCarty More hath
had in times past; and if it were but in right of those mannors, to whom
the cheif rents and sarvices (wᶜh are MᶜCarty's greatest living) were
alwayse due.

The said Florence hath also brought over, upon his charges, one of the
O'Mahownes, a pore man, and of no rekoning in the country, to serve for
Kinalmeaky (the signory allotted to Mr. Beecher and others,) and upon
recouery thereof is to have the one half, as is generally reported, and thereupon divers of Clan Donell Ro, Rosbrin, Clan Dermond, wᵗh many others
from all parts, will deal wᵗh him in like case ; to the great disturbance of
such undertakers, and the Quenes fermours, as are planted upon those
places. I protest to yoʳ Honor that the great reports that the Irish makes
of him in Desmond hath kept Inglish away from planting themselves under
me, and those that ar alredy wᵗh me are in fear that all there former
endevors haue bein in vain, and the rather for that the said Florence and
his wife having benn at variaunce, and seperated almost all the last year;
the cause of there falling out, as she hath reported, was whither his followers,

.or hirs, shold inhabit my lands, wch makes me somewhat jealous of the man; for I *knowe* him to be ambicious and subtle, *a great briber to his power*, frended by som great menn *of Irland*, who have procured him favourable countenance wth som of *great calling* in England, an importunate sutor, and indede the onely daungerous man in Mounster, having benn brought up, and *in league wth James Fitz Morrice*, Docter Saunders, Sir William Stanley, and Jaques; wherefore I most humblie entreat' yor Honnor (upon whose help I onely relye) to tender my case but this much, that eyther you will prevent his rising, whose present Estate can never preiudice anie of Hir Mat^ies loyal subiects, nor be able to better yt, w^thout speciall favor to countenaunce him from hence, or else, if there be anie intention to rayse him, and the House of McCarty More (wch by God's handywork is now utterlie extinkt) in the hart of whose countrie, most daungerously, I dwell; that you wold in compassion give me an honourable caveat whereby I may in som good time, recall me and mine, wth our lest damages, from a place so perilous; and we (who ar a great many) shall be bound daly to pray for long continuance of Yo^r Honors life. Thus most humbly craving pardon for my tedious boldness, I leave Yo^r Hon^r to the tuition of Th.Almighty.

"Your Honor's most humble and daly Orator,

"Nich^s Browne."

Nicholas Browne pleaded earnestly, but not ingenuously. He knew that the condition of Florence's wife was utterly unlike that of her uncle's daughter, to which in his letter, he had compared it; the latter had not succeeded to the lands of MacCarthy Mor because her father had left a brother, to whom, by Tanistry, the Chieftaincy and the lands belonged; nor would Lady Ellen have succeeded, had the Earl her father left brother, nephew, or cousin male, to survive him, and had it not pleased the Sept to elect her husband as their chief, in default of heirs male of the elder branch of the MacCarthys. The reader will shortly have an opportunity of seeing how differently Florence, or his legal advisers, handled the question thus incidentally opened. However, this spirited production was not without its effect upon the mind of the Lord Treasurer; certain passages, as the reader will have noticed, are in *italics*, in the original they are underlined, and, doubtless, by the pen of Lord Burghley himself It is interesting to remark to which of the sentences of his correspondent he attached the most importance. All the able exposition of Browne's wrongs and rights, all his lamentation over the evil treatment he had experienced in Desmond passed without eliciting any mark of Ministerial sympathy; even the spiteful conduct of Donal, and the wonderful chase of that evil spirit through the wild scenery so suitable for the abiding place of outlaws and murderers, appears to have possessed little interest for the Lord Treasurer. But the passages concerning Florence evidently sank deeper into his mind; they were of a nature sufficiently suggestive to revive all the suspicions of which he had been the object for the last ten years; they were made, also, with as much assurance as the accusations of Barry. The writer declares that he *knew* that Florence was "ambitious and subtle;" this, doubtless, Lord Burghley knew also; it needed no underline to impress it upon his memory; but Browne *knew* furthermore, that he was " a great briber to his power! that he was friended by some great men in Ireland, and by some of great calling in England!" These were daring assertions; and had the writer possessed the "prudence and wisdom" of Florence, he would scarcely have ventured to make them; they might one day require great courage—a quality in which, to say truth, Nicholas Browne was not deficient—in case those marks of the English Minister's admiration were meant to keep these passages in his recollection as well for Browne's elucidation as for his own guidance.

It is difficult to avoid believing what the writer declares that he *knew!* And certainly, Florence's repeated extrication of himself from situations full of danger, is more easily explained by this assertion of Browne than by any other means. Effusive and refreshing as this letter was, the mind of the writer was not yet sufficiently unburthened; the "expected greatness of" Florence MacCarthy towered over his imagination, and appeared to him to cast a lurid shadow of coming peril over the State, of which the English authorities seemed fatally unobservant. The following letter was a fresh attempt to awaken the alarm of Lord Burghley. The map alluded to in it, is said to be "wanting" amongst the State Papers; but in a collection of maps of the time there exists one, probably more correct than any which Browne could have got up at short notice, of the Earl of Clan Car's Country: if to this had been appended a map of MacCarthy Reagh's country, the fertile and far-spreading plains of Carbery, and to both a list of the "rights of chiefry," and especially the number of fighting men due as *rising out* from these countries to their chiefs, the alarm-cry of Browne, at seeing all this greatness about to fall to a man whom he declared to be in heart a rebel, might justly seem to the Privy Council a warning not to be neglected.

"1594. *Dec*. 21. NICHOLAS BROWNE *to the* LORD TREASURER.

"My very good Lord. I was bold, the last day, to troble yor Hon^r wth the relation of the trobles I haue endured amongst the Clancartys; and now that those being past, newe fears ariseth of the endevors of

Florence McCarty, and by his expected greatnes, wherefor that Y^r Ho^l might the better concieve of the quantyty of the countreys wch are like to be, as y^t were, subiect to him, if he may enioy all that he promises himself, I haue drawne a mapp wch I humbly desire yor Hon^r to accept of the rudeness thereof; and thus, wth my humble duty remembered, I ceas to troble you.

"*Hogesden.*"

"NICH^s BROWNE.

In spite of all, Florence had recovered the confidence of both the Cecylls, and continued to urge, with increasing vehemence, his attack upon his adversary, with an occasional blow, and a severe one, at Browne, who, since his disappointment with the Earl of Clancar's daughter, had given himself consolation by marrying Barry's niece. Quickly following upon Browne's able summary of his own grievances, and the misdeeds of Donal, was despatched another petition from Florence to the Lord Treasurer, which happily contained one passage which the Minister judged deserving of consideration. He underlined it, and it is probable that it went far to neutralise the accusations of Browne, and to turn back his suspicions upon the head of the accuser.

"1595. *Jan^y*. 11. *To* Lo: BURGHLEY.

"My very approved good Lord, my humble and most bonden dutie remembered. I can hardlie judge whether mine imprisonment and troble for five or six yeares, to the losse of my living, which I was constrayned to lease and sell them (whereuntoe I was brought by such false and malicious informations of mine adversarie Barry, as he procured Sir Warham Salinger to prefer hither for him against me), was more hurtfull, chargeable, troblesome, and domageable untoe me, or this Fyne of the said Barry's, which Her Majestie bestowed uppon me; who, onlie to delay the payment of the said Fyne, (which is all his intent and purpose) he hathe, for want of anie matter against me, forged, and alledged that all such Irishmen as went from hence beyond seas in seven or eight years (whose names he learned amongst his countrymen here) were sent by me to one Jacques, with whom I was onlie acquainted in Her Majestie's service, as I was with every other capten here, being contented to lose my life if ever I have seen him, or received one letter from him in 'two yeares, or thereabouts, before he went out of England; for all which matters having satisfied the Lord Deputie, and Vice-President of Mounster, untoe whom they were referred, I came hither before Michælmas last to satisfie your Lordship, and the rest of the council alsoe, in person for them; since which time I have alwaies waited here about your Lordship, and am readie to satisfie your Lordship and the rest, either for these, or anie other matters, that are delivered since by his nephew, Nicholas Browne, Sir Valentine Browne's son, who married his niece, and who is here for him, to prefer such devices as he sent by himselfe, and to him, to be preferred. Browne himselfe alsoe bing one who doeth not a little malice me, *by reason of my wife's father's lands, which he holdeth ;* Wherefore I most humblie beseeche your Hon: Lordship to be a mean that I may be speedilie brought before

·the council for these matters, as soon as time serves, whereby I may not perish here for want of maintenance, having spent all that I got amongst my frends to bring this sute to an end in Ireland, and to come hither about it.

"Thus beseeching God to preserve your Lordship's health, I humblie take leve this xj Jany 1594.   ¡

'"Your Lordship's most humble and bonden
"fflor McCarthy."

In the printed catalogue of the MSS. preserved at Lambeth, it is asserted that Tome 626, a thick folio of pedigrees, is "in the handwriting of Lord Burghley ;" this is erroneous; the writing is Sir George Carewe's;* but scattered through the Irish State Papers there exists a multitude of genealogical scraps, written by Lord Burghley on the margins of letters, sufficient to prove that the Lord Treasurer, if not a lover of pedigrees for their own sake, was by no means insensible to the importance which might at any moment attach to them. The correspondents of the English Minister were constantly sending to him lists of "the descentes of the meere Irish," and "pedigrees of the Lords and Gentlemen of the Irish nation."† It is not then surprising that an assertion,

* Entertaining no doubt himself whose was the handwriting of this volume, the author of these pages is able to present to his reader the more trustworthy opinion of a gentleman probably more familiar than anyone living with the writing of Carewe, and who has had numberless occasions of perusing also the writings of Lord Burghley. The authority in whom so much confidence is expressed is John Maclean, Esq., of the War Office, editor of "The Life and Times of Sir Peter Carew," and of the "Letters from Sir Robert Cecil to Sir George Carew." It may be remarked that Mr. Maclean has appended to each of these volumes copious genealogical notes, evincing very great research, and written in a style singularly condensed and clear, which are admirable models of genealogical annotation. Mr. Maclean's opinion is sufficiently explicit and positive:—

"I remember," he writes, "having had some conversation with you respecting the handwriting attributed (by the 'Lambeth Calendar') to Lord Burghley; and I have no hesitation in stating now, as I did then, that it is that of Carew. The handwriting of the latter is very familiar to me. I know also that of the former, and I cannot be mistaken. Whilst there is some general resemblance between the writing of the two, in detail there is a considerable difference. I am glad to be able to establish this fact; for Carew was a higher genealogical authority than Burghley, especially as relating to Irish families. Volume 635 of the same collection I am equally well acquainted with; the pedigrees therein are also in the handwriting of Carew."

† In the year 1601, a certain Richard Ha [dsor?], a lawyer, wrote to Sir Robert Cecyll:—" . . . I drew a discourse wc^h was presented by Captn fitz gerald this last winter unto yor ho: importing the genealogie of all the greate howses, and gentlemē of the meere Irish, comonly called the Wyld Irish, wherein there lynage and discent frō the auncient Irish kings, and ther kyndred, and allyaunce one to another is sett forth." This dis-

however true, yet probably thrown out by Florence at random in one of his recent letters, " that Barry had no claim to the title and lands he held," and " that his birth was obscure," should have caught the attention of the Lord Treasurer, and that he should call upon the writer for proof of its truth.

By no man living, except perhaps Fyn O'Daly, the great bard of Munster himself, could such explanation have been so promptly furnished. Florence had cast this slur on the birth of Barry on the 11th of January; on the 15th, the pedigree of Barry Roe, of Barry Mor, of all the Barrys, was ready, showing how " James of the Rath in Ibawne (who not long before, in murdering of his cousin Redmund Barry, and his brothers, had made himself Lord of Ibawne, otherwise called Barry Roe's country), did by Treason get into possession of Barryscourt, which is the Lord Barry's chief house, and by strong hand dispossessed the Lady Catherine, wife to the now L^d. Power; which castle and country he possessed during his life, calling himself Viscount of Buttevaunt, which title and possession David his son at this present doth enjoy, in pre-judice of the right heirs of James Barry, the true and lawful Viscount Buttevaunt." Florence writes that "he sends en-closed" the information which Lord Burghley had required. The inclosure referred to is not to be found with the letter, nor is any trace of it discoverable at Lambeth; but in Carewe's collection of pedigrees, in fol. 635 of his MSS., there is a copy of the Barry pedigree in Carewe's handwriting, introduced with these notable words :—" This Pedigree with the notes was given me by Florence MacCarthy;" the one in Florence's handwriting is, as far as we know, lost; it was sent to Burghley, not given to Carewe. Surprising as it may appear that at the period those words of Carewe were penned —when Carewe's Presidency was over, and his victim was in the Tower—any literary courtesies could have passed between men circumstanced relatively as these men were, there is yet no doubting the truth of so positive an assertion; nor, indeed, is it the only instance in which Sir George Carewe availed himself of the unrivalled stores of national lore of the man whose fortunes he had so ruthlessly and so basely ruined; for in the pedigree of his own family he quotes matter derived

course has, unfortunately, been lost sight of; it can scarcely be that a volume of so much value should have been allowed to perish. Attention is invited to the fact that this work of Ha [dsor?] is not known to exist in any public library. If it be in any private collection, its owner would afford a gratification to very many of the descendants of these "meere or Wyld Irish," if he would make known at least its existence.

K

from "a chronicle belonging to Florence." Certain it is,
however, that Florence sent his account of Barry's family to
Lord Burghley, and a fresh and bitter attack along with it;
letter upon letter to the same effect followed; and it is astonishing that the Minister should not long since, were it only
to withdraw himself from such a tempest of angry correspondence, have referred the matter to some tribunal for
inquiry.

"1595. Jany. 15. *To* Lo: BURGHLEY.

" My humble and most bonden dutie remembered. I have according
to yor Lo^ps pleasure sent here inclosed the names of the last Viscounts of
Buttiavañt, wth' such issue as remaines of them, wherein I have alsoe made
menčon of the Barry Roes of Ibawne, otherwise called Barry-Roe's contre,
and of James Barry, this supsosed Lo: Barryes father, who descended of a
bastard of Barry Roe's house, and cõntry; as also by what meanes the
sayd James did attaine, first to Barry Roe's contry, and afterwards to the
Lo: Viscount Barrymore of Buttiavaunt's contry, by whose son this Barry
is fals and malicious informačons (wch about the time of my marriadge he
procured Sir Warham Salinger to preferr against me) I haue suffered
aboue fiue yeres imprisonment, to myne utter undoeing and the loss of my
liuinge wch I was constrayned to lease and sell, to maintaine myself and
my wife here in my sayd troble; after the which having by yor Lo^ps honor-·
able meanes and furtherañces obtained of her ^Ma^tie to satisfie my creditors
here, a Fine due unto Her Highnes of the sayd Barry, for the paiment
whereof, the Lo: Deputie and councell took sufficient assurance of him,
wch notwthstanding he hath forfetted, and came hyther contrary tothe
Vice President of Mounsters cõmaundment and theirs; who sayd (to delay
paiment) all the Irishmen who had left Ireland were sent by me to Jacques,
who being Sir Willeam Stanleyes Lieutenant in Ireland, I fell acquainted
with him there in the last warres, having then (wth four or five hundred
of myne owne men that folowed me) served against the Earle of Desmond,
and Barry, who was with him; at which time I not onlie purchased the
said Barry's illwill, but made acquaintance not with Jacques onlie, but
with all the captens in the same service, which is all that I had to do with
Jacques, having (I protest) never seen him in a year and a half or two years
before he went from hence.   ·

" All which matters, as the said Barry preferred here against me (where-·
· upon he obtained letters for the possession of a small parcel of lands which
the sheriff, by due course of law, and by the Lord Deputy and council and
Vice President of Munster's several commandments, did extend, and deliver unto me, for the said fine), being by your Lordship and the rest of
the council referred to the Lord Deputy Sir William Fitzwilliams, and to
Sir Thomas Norreys, before whom I appeared, the said Barry being also
come thither from his country, where he staid a good while after his arrival
to seek proofs and witnesses, of all which matters (notwithstanding he was
there in person to urge and prefer them), I have cleared myself, and
satisfied for them all, both Sir Thomas Norreys, and the Lord Deputy who·
is here now, and to whose report I refer myself; whereupon the said Barry,
having then no other way to delay payment (which is all his intent and desire), he promised to produce more witnesses in Munster, where he brought
sometimes one mean ignorant knave or other of his own, other whiles he
procured some of the country gentlemen to be sent for, who knew nothing

of the matter; whereupon Sir Thomas (finding by them nothing worthy to bring me in question for it) wrote hither of all their proceedings; and afterwards, I being desirous to satisfy in person for all those matters, your Lordship and the rest of the council, to whom they were first preferred, I came hither before Michelmas last, with Sir Thomas' favourable letters and passports; since which time I waited here for that purpose, and am ready to satisfy your Lordship and the rest, either for those or any other matters that are delivered since by his nephew Mr. Nicholas Browne. Wherefore I most humbly beseech your Honorable Lordship, whom I have always found my most approved good Lord and best freind (seeing I have no means to maintain myself after so many trobles (this fine having causet me above £300), to be a mean that I may be brought before the council for these matters, where I desire no other favour but what your Lordship shall judge my desert to be worthy of it. So beseeching God both to send, and preserve your Lordship health, I humbly take my leave this 15 Jany 1594.

"fflor McCarthy."

The scruples of Barry touching his present obedience to the Queen's order for the payment of his fine had been based simply upon his knowledge of Florence's unworthiness to have it; he had sent in his charges, and they had been replied to; but the matter was kept open for further charges, and further explanations. We are indebted to this dispute, tedious as the main subject of it had become, for more knowledge of the private life of Florence MacCarthy than to any other incident of his career. Matters were looking unpromising for Barry and Browne, when the genius, apparently of the latter —for Barry had scarcely the resources of his nephew—opened a new subject of attack of a sufficiently hopeful appearance, but destined to a termination more disastrous for them than the old story of Jacques and Stanley. They had seen the necessity of strengthening and extending their alliance against their able and vigilant opponent. It was not difficult to find men to join with them in any attempt to damage the character of a man whose prosperity must be their ruin. Amongst the many who, during Florence's imprisonment, had found means—they were never difficult to find, a body of the Queen's soldiers allowed for the protection of undertakers— to help themselves to his lands, was a Mr. Rogers, who had with great liberality bestowed upon himself no less than twenty-nine ploughlands. Florence was not likely to be long at liberty without seeking the recovery of 3,190 acres of his patrimony, the precise amount appropriated by Rogers, hence was this gentleman ready for the alliance of Browne and his uncle. Since the death of Sir Owen MacCarthy, Donal Pipy, now MacCarthy Reagh, had groaned under the burden of the bonds which a dozen years before he had signed to trans-

mit Carbery after him intact to Florence; Donal, then, was
also ready for any association that promised him relief. Out
of these bonds arose the strategy of a new and loud-sounding
assault. What influence Barry and Browne possessed with
the Minister they had fully discovered; that Donal Pipy and
Mr. Rogers were likely to possess more, might be fairly
doubted; but it so was that the last-named gentleman had
espoused the daughter of a (so-called) *English highwayman*,
who—by one of those wonderful strokes of luck which leave
it beyond doubt that the son of Maia, " furax, et furum.
magister," can at times get access to the wheel of fortune,
and give it such a whirl as to dazzle the sight of mortals—
had become the Lord Chief Justice of England! and before
this great legal and influential functionary was laid the family
compact which was the great grief, and temptation of Donal.
Sir John Popham readily consented to come to the rescue of
the fair estate of his daughter's husband. All these gentlemen, it may be remarked, accustomed themselves to call the
lands they occupied *their* lands! Browne called the lands of
Balecarbry and Molahiff *his Signory!* Mr. Rogers, with as
good reason, called the pleasant slice he had taken off the
lands of Carbery *his estate!* A document bearing an alarming
indorsement, and which is a pleasant specimen of the Lord
Chief Justice's legal skill, but which was void of all entertainment to Florence at the time, resulted from this combination of many interests against him. It needed, indeed,
much cunning and subtility to be always on his guard against
attacks so incessant, and so various! Florence's vigilance
rarely failed him; before the legal document was ready, he
had himself related, and explained, to Lord Burghley the
entire matter of the bonds, as well as the motive of the
Lord Chief Justice in assailing him.

The explanation given in the ensuing letter by Florence
of the matter of these bonds, and of the custom followed
by the Government of indemnifying the Tanist in cases
where the actual chief chose to avail himself of the Queen's
invitation to surrender the Sept lands, and resume them
to be held by English tenure, and with lineal succession, is interesting and instructive. The object never
lost sight of by the Government of Elizabeth was " *the
dissipation of the great Irish estates.*" It was the policy
most clearly enunciated by Sir Henry Sidney, and continued to be the policy of the English Privy Council till
every chieftain's estate was in fact *dissipated.* By no
means could this dismemberment of Irish territories be more

equitably effected than by the plan followed in some instances, and to which Florence offered contentedly to submit himself; this was by " dividing the countries amongst such individuals of the Sept as stood within the range of succession to the Captaincy by usage of Tanistry." What effect resulted from the attempts of Donal Pipy to repudiate his bond, and how Florence fared as to his rights both to the Captaincy and to the lands of Carbery, the reader will see in the sequel!

" 1595. *March* 21. FLORENCE *to* LO: BURGHLEY.

"My humble and most bonden dutie remembered: Your Lo^{ps} honourable and continuall fauors alwayes towards me, aswell in obtaininge Her Ma^{ts} bountifull reward for my service, and Her Highnes gracious acceptacōn thereof, myne enlargement out of the Towre where I was (to the loss of all my livinge wchich I was constrained to morgdage, and sell) brought into six yers imprisonment and troble, by such fals and malicious accusacōns as myne adversary Dauid Barry, whom I offended in Her Ma^{ts} service when he was a traytor wth the Earle of Desmond, procured Sir Warham Salinger to preferr against me; as also yor Lo^{ps} honorable oppinion lately delivered to the Councell of such malicious informacōns as the sayd Barry hath deuised against me, doth move me now in myne extreme miserie and greatest distress, being otherwise hopeless of any relife or comfort, to betake myself onely unto yor Lo^p as my most honorable patron and best frend; and perceiving lately that myne adversary being out of hope to hurt me wth his last deuices (som of those knaves for whom he accused me, being kild under Sir John Norreys in Brittaine, and another retourned from thence hom into his contrey, as his Capten Petter Cripps and Sir John Norreys is soldiers can testifie), wch moved my sayd adversarys Barry and Donell Mc Carthy, alias Mac Carthy Reogh, havinge at the Lo: Chefe Justice of Englands beinge in Ireland, procured his frendshipp against me, by meanes of his son in law Mr Rogers, and Mr Woorth, agent of his, who in myne absence dispossest me, and one of my men, wrongfully of 29 ploughlands, unto whom the sayd Barry and Mac Carthy, for want of other matters against me sent a Bond wherein Sir Owen Mc Carthy and I are bound not to hinder Donell Mc Carthy (who is now Mac Carthy Reough), by surrender or otherwise, of the seignorie of that countrey after Sir Owen's death. The sayd Donell himself being also bound to me and to Sir Owen's heires in like sorte, he being also the occasion of all that agrement, who when Sir Owen Mc Carthy, about 12 or 13 yeres past was determined to com hyther, the sayd Donell gott him to enter into those covenants fearing lesst that Sir Owen wolde surrender the Contrey wch he possest then, and convert the same to the use of him and his heires, of wch bond my Lo: Chefe Justice (by their instructions and at their request) made now a great matter to Her Ma^{tye} against me, who was never the auctor thereof, wherein I know not who I have offended, Her Ma^{tye} the law, nor any body els; the sayd custome being not generally abolished by statute, nor forbidden any of my name in particuler; but a power onely geven to him that is in possession to surrender, and my father who succeded his elder brother, and Sir Owen, and this man, having enioyed the sayd contrey, all in Her Ma^{ts} raigne by that custome: But yf Her Matie or yor Lo^p, and the rest of the Councell will at any time think fitt to suppress that custome, and to make a division of the countrey betwine us who are lawfully interested therein, as was don wth the Brenhy for the O'Reyllies, the Analy for the O'Farrells, Beare and Bantrie, and divers other countreyes, I shalbe contented to surrender my right, and putt in sufficient sureties to hold myself for ever satisfied wth such a porcõn as shalbe by yor Lo^p and the rest allotted unto me, so as myne adversary will do the like; and for that I rest here in a most extreme state having not (I protest) 3 ploughlands nor £3 rent any where. The fyne wch Her Ma^{tye} bestowed uppon me having also cost me £500, whereby my wife (being great with childe) is constrained to go from place to place among my frends for want of meanes to live, wherefor I humbly besech yõr Honorable Lo^p, as I have allwayes found you my most approved good Lo: and best frind, to extend your accustomed faour towards me now, in acquainting Her Ma^{tye} wth the state of this matter, and the former matters wherby Her Highnes may be as well satisfied in them as yor Lo^p. Thus beseching God to preserve yor Lo^{ps} health I humblie take leaue this 21 March, 1594.

" Yo^r Lops most humble, bondẽ
" and thankfull
"fflor M^c CARTHY."

" 1595. April 1. To the Right Hon: my very approved good Lo: the LORD BURGHLEY, Lord High Tre^r of England, &c.

" My very approved good Lo : My humble and most bondẽ dutie remẽbered, I have according to yor Lo^{ps} pleasure sent hereinclosed the copie of the bond wherin Donell Pypy is bound to me, wch as I told yor Lo^p was don about 12 yeres past [1583], and neũ don, I protest by any compulsion of Sir Owẽ, but onely by the sayd Donell's meanes, who when Sir Owen was about to com hyther at that time the sayd Donell got him to enter into those couenants, fearing less that Sir Owẽ wold surrender the contry wch hé possesst then; and where yor Lo^p hath enquired who was heir of the said contrey; as for my parte I know not a more lawfull heir then myself, seeing Law doth allow custome as well in Englande as in Ireland, and that custome hath bene ever inviolablie kept there, wch yf yor Lo^p and the rest of the Councell do think fitt to take any indifrent order for the contrey, yor Lo^p shall fynd me more comfortable then Donell Pypy himselfe or Dearmed Mc Carthy, or Donogh Oge Mc Carthy, or Donogh Mc Owen, McCarthy or Florence Mc Owen, or any other of the Cept: assuring yor Lo^p that neyther they, nor the Councell of Ireland, nor Governor of Mounster doth not think it to be any parte of yor Lo^{ps} meaning to disherit the whole Cept, because Donell Pypy is the eldest brother's heir, being a thing that was never don in Ireland hytherto, For in Beare and Bantrye although Donell O'Sulivan was the eldest brothers heir, yet Sir Owen O'Sulivan's heir, being but the second brothers son hath the best parte of the contrie. In the Brenhy also wher custome was lately supprest, although Sir John O'Reylly was, in possession, O'Reylly, and theldest brother, yet his owne second brother, Philip, and also Edmonde O'Reylly and Cahir O'Reylly have almost as good a porcõn to every of them as the sayd Sir John. Fergus Mc Bryen O'Farell being the eldest brother's heir having not so good a porcõn of the Analie as others of the Cept. Wherefore seeing this is but a device of myne adversaries to hurte me being a thing don manie yeres past by the whole Cept, and the sayd Donell Pypy himselfe being aucthor thereof, and that I am ready to abyde the tryall of Law in Ireland for the whole matter, or els to surrender my right into yor Lo^{ps} hands, and to submitt myself to yor Lo^{ps} and the rest of the Councell's order, I humblie besech your Hon. Lo^p, as I have allwayes found you my most approved

good Lo: and frend, to satisfie Her ᴹaᵗⁱᵉ both in this, and in the rest of
their deuices, for the wch I shall (as I have ever had cause) rest most
bound to pray for yoʳ Loᵖ.
"And even soe I humblie take leve this 1st April 1595.
                                "Yoʳ Loᵖˢ most humble and bonden,
                                        "fflor: Mᶜ Carthy."

With the last two letters before him Lord Burghley was
well prepared for the reception of the formidable "Report"
which the allies, Barry, Browne, Donal Pipy, Rogers, and
Worth, and the Lord Chief Justice of England, had at last
launched against the owner or heir of so many Signories
and lands which these men coveted:—

"1595. July 8. *Report on* Florence, *supposed by* Popham.

"Touching Florence Mᶜ Carthy, wherby he is deemed the dangerousest
man of all the Irish nation.

"——— ——— he hathe bene holden to be a most connyng and subtil
pson, and at my being in Ireland was estemed to be mere Spanyshe. *He was
combyned wth Desmond in hys* rebellion, and hadd *prepared forces to have
joyned with that party in accion,* but was stayed by the meanes off Donell
Mc Carty (now Mc Carthy Rewe of Carbery) and off one Randall Oge as
the same Donell and others affirmed to me in Ireland. *Imediatly before
the Spanysh ptended Invasyon this Florence depted into Ireland* wth yoʳ
Maᵗˢ gude grace & Favour, but psentlie upon hys comying thyther, he
marryed the Daughter and heire to the Earle off Clancarre beinge Mc Carty
More, and the Cheiff of all the Mc Cartyes, and then gote from that Earle
one of *the cheiff places of strengthe in all Desmond,* and at that very tyme
alsoe gote from Sir Owen Mc Carty the old Hedd off Kynsale, being holden
a *place of the gretyst strength in all Mōnster,* and *both these places most tending upon Spayne. At that very tyme also ther passed curryers and messengers betwene thys Florence and Jaques that notable Traytor,* as both the
Lo: Barry and Donell Mc Carty then informed me; and as yt might
appear by my Lord Treasurer's speches, Patryck Collene that was sent
over by Jaques to have kylled yoʳ Majestie had heretofore served Florens
Mᶜ Carty; and yt may welbe supposed that this Patryck Collene was the
man that was the curryer betwene Florens Mᶜ Carty and Jaques. When
Donell Mc Carthy (who onely ought to enioy Carbery by Letters Pattents
from King Henry VII) was put out thereoff by Sir Owen Mᶜ Carthy, the
same man, durying the nō age of the said Donell, the said Sir Owen
through hys greatness forced Donell at hys full age to enter into great
bands (I saw a copy of that band) to pmytt Carbry to goe in Tanestrye
acording to the Irish costome, and not according to the Letters Pattents,
wherby Florens Mᶜ Carty expecteth certenlie to be Mc Carty Rewe next
after the death of this Donell : So by these meanes the said Florens
mytbe both *Mc Carty more and* Mc Carty *Rewe,* and therby *become farre
greater* in Munster then ever was Desmond, and *greater then* any man in
all Ireland, *that hath ben in this age,* for O'Sulyvan More and O'Sulyvan
Bere they do depend on Mac Carthy More; The O'Driscoes do depend
upon Mac Carthy Rewe: The Lords of Muskry and Duallow being both

great territories are off the Mac Cartyes, and depend upon that cheiff
house, and so do diuers other pettie Lords of smaller terrytories all wch do
lye, the one upon the other from Cork above sixty myles together westward
upon the very uttermost pts next towards Spayne, The more he ptendeth
to pvent the greatnes off others in Ireland the more (in respect off the
pmisses) yt may be doubted that yt ys but an ambicious plott in tyme to
mak his own advancement the more certen and the gretter. Yt ys to be
noted that the Mc Cartyes do ptend to come lynyally from that King off
Munster that was expelled uppon the conquest of Ireland."

How so shrewd a man as Sir John Popham should have
lent himself to the adoption of accusations and assertions so
nonsensical, on the mere information of Barry and Donal
Pipy, both of whom perfectly knew their untruth and their
absurdity, is surprising! Fortunately for Florence, either by
the power of his friends at Court, or his position in his own
country, he was lifted beyond the reach even of the Lord
Chief Justice! Popham, in the days of his prosperity, had
by some admirer of himself, or his luck, been styled "a
réformed highwayman." Alas! that the exactness of historic
truth should be conjured away from notice by the magic of
this friendly epigram! As well might it be said of a certain
Lord President of Munster, a contemporary of Popham, that
he was "a réformed murderer." In the long career of these
men, traces of reform are no where discoverable!

Knowing the character of Popham, even as a reformed
man, and the great motive he had for the ruin of Florence,
we may be surprised that the charges which he had been so
long preparing should be so tame, and contain so little of
novelty! To assert that Florence had been "an abettor of
Desmond's rebellion, and only prevented from openly joining
him by the loyal persuasions of Donal Pipy!" was to betray an
amount of ignorance of the public transactions of his time
sufficient to cast discredit upon any statement he might make.
Florence "had served for eight years, *with the Queen's commission, against the Earl,* and received Her Majesty's approbation, and many favours, for his zeal and loyalty," as was
well known to the veteran Ormond, who had commanded
Her Majesty's forces through the many years the rebellion
lasted. The story of the bonds entered into between Donal,
Florence, and Sir Owen MacCarthy, was already explained; a
copy of the document was in the hands of Lord Burghley,
and Popham's malignant misrepresentation of the transaction
harmless! The remainder of his charges were but the faded
calumnies of Florence's intimacy with Cullen, Stanley, and
Jacques; and his warnings were but the perils foreseen in the

vision of St. Leger, many years before, and recorded in his tracts. Such, however, as they were, the Lord Chief Justice laid them before the Privy Council; and Her Majesty had thus a fresh witness that Florence was "a most cunnyng and subtil man;" and a fresh warning to look well into what hands had fallen "The old Hedd of Kynsale."

CHAPTER VII.

SHORTLY after Florence had written his last letter on the subject of his cousin, the bonds and the succession to Carbery, another glimpse of political life, fleeting as all former ones, excited his hope for an occupation more dignified than his long pursuit of Barry's fine. O'Neill, Maguire, O'Donell, and others were in arms; there was much moving of troops, and a few skirmishes; but O'Neill was not yet prepared to push matters to extremity with the Queen's Government, nor were the authorities anxious to take extreme measures against him, and thus cut off all hope of reconciliation. Hence, though the Lord Deputy had an army on O'Neill's borders, proposals were constantly under consideration between both parties for his submission. The reader has seen that upon a former occasion Florence had been desirous to be employed as a mediator between the Northern Chieftains and the Government; he seized the present opportunity to renew the offer of his services; and to make one more trial upon the patience of the Minister relative to the matter of "the said fyne."

"1595. *July* 8. FLORENCE MAC CARTHY *to* SIR ROBERT CECYLL.

————" And now understanding that not onelie the rest of the Gent' of Mounster, but also by reason of myne absence, my young⌐ brother is, wᵗh som forces prepared by the countrey, to accompanie the Lo: President to this service; For that I have had som experience heretofore in Her Maᵗˢ seruice, hauinge allwayes ledd three or four hundred folowers out of that countrey to serue Her Highnes, and don better seruice than anie Gent' of Mounster, for the wᶜh I was, at my comynge hyther, not onely fauorablie used by Her Maᵗⁱᵉ and the councell; and hauing now diuers folowers there who haue serued long in the North, and doth know that countrey best of any other, hauing comaunded manie, and attained to great reputacōn there, by whose meanes, and knowledge of that countrey, and by other wayes wᶜh I wold willingly acquaint yoⁱ honoⁱ wᵗhall, I doubt not but that I wold quiklie do hir Maᵗⁱᵉ good seruice yf I were there; and forasmuch as I am by the loss of liuing in my troble, and the sute of this fyne, wᶜh cost me aboue £500, destitute of meanes to live, I humblie besech yoⁱ Hon̄ that I may haue yoⁱ furtherance, eyther to obtain the benefit of the sayd fyne, according to Her Maᵗˢ graunt, wᶜh by Her Highnes letters in the behalf of myne aduersarie was onely stayd untill such matters as he deliūed against me had bene heard, or els that I, and my wife may enioie to us, and our heirees males, two parcells of my father in law is lands, wᶜh he morgadged, the one to his said daughter my wife, for her marriadge goodes, and thother parcell to others there, of whom she will redeme it, or otherwise, to obtaine that Her Maᵗⁱᵉ will allow Sir Thomas Norreys two hundred Pounds of the composicōn of Mounster, and graunt Mr. Harbert Pelham, and George Goreinge som consideracōn here for those two parcells of myne owne liuinge wᶜh I was constrayned to morgadge, and lease; the one to Sir Thomas and thother to them, in the time of my troble. Thus humblie besechinge yoᴵ Honⁿable fauour, and furtherance, especially in dealeing wᵗh my Lo: yoᴵ Father for me, and conferringe wᵗh him hereof: and wᶜh of these things yoᴵ Honⁿ shall think metest, I will uppon knowledge of yoᴵ Honⁿs pleasure, procure Her Maᵗⁱᵉ to be moued therein; So wᵗh the remembraunce of my most bonden dutie, beseching God to preserue yoᴵ Honⁿ; I humblie take leue this 8ᵗʰ July 1595.   Yoᴵ Honⁿs most humble and bondē to comaund.

" fflOR MᶜCARTHY."

The attention of the Minister was called away from these contentions, but not from the chief party concerned in them —for it was to be his lot to have the affairs of Florence before him to the last day of his life—by the voice of a man almost as open an enemy of Florence as Barry himself. A despatch from Sir Geoffrey Fenton brought tidings full of import to the destiny of Florence: his father-in-law was near his end, and the first note of warning of a fresh storm was sounded! The man whose story of his poverty filled so many letters had but lately " drawn to himself the old Head of Kinsale."

" 1595·   Oct. 17.   Endorsed:—SIR GEOFFRY FENTON to LORD BURGHLEY: delivered at Kinsale to a bark, 17 Oct. 1595.

"In my journey from Kinsale to Baltimore along the sea coste, I find that the old Head of Kinsale is latelie drawn into possession of Florence Mᶜ Cartie, now about the Courte in London; and as I learne from his neighbours, he hathe morgaged most parte of his owne patremonie in the inland countrie to this end: and in truth I find that in all these partes there is not one soe fitt to be made the head of a faccion. There is no other cause for alarme here; for the Geralines are all under foote; and the Lord Barry, and the Mᶜ Carthies, are so addicted to the plough, and husbandry, &c., &c. The Earle of Clancar, who is Mᶜ·Carty More, is so poore, and sicklie as there is noe reckoning to be made of him, or his name.

" GEOFFRY FENTON."

During the whole reign of Elizabeth it was the custom— encouraged by her successive Ministers—for every petty functionary in Ireland to write frequent, long, unofficial letters to their particular patrons in the Privy Council; the consequence of which was, that there poured daily into England a vast flood of loose, contradictory, and malignant charges against men whom the writers, for whatever motive, desired to injure. From these charges no man who had anything which his neighbour coveted could escape ; hence is the voluminous correspondence, preserved in the " State Paper Office," a vast *repertorium* of the gossip and private history of the time. This letter of Fenton is a fair specimen of the official correspondence of his day ; of such rumours and such suspicions, were the despatches from Ireland full. As long back as May, 1589, Sir Thomas Norreys had written home that " Florence had compassed the title of the Old Head of Kinsale, and was the same day that he was apprehended mynded to ryde thether to take possession of it." If Florence had mortgaged his lands to effect this purchase, he must have mortgaged them six years before Fenton wrote. It has been mentioned that he had inherited great wealth ; he certainly needed not to mortgage the greater part of his property to possess himself of Kinsale ! Another correspondent had written that the old Lord de Coursie had *given* this old fort to Florence, and with it as much of his lands as it was in his power to give.

We are informed by the " Carbriæ Notitia"—a MS. often quoted by the late learned Dr. O'Donovan, and a copy of which is in the possession of the writer of these pages—that " Sir Donogh McCarthy gave to his son Florence no less than 27 ploughlands, as I think, worth £1,500 per annum; so that 'twas said this Florence his estate in Carbry was better than his estate by his Wife, Heiress of McCarthy Mor." Certain it is that as long as he was a freeman, that is, up to the time of his marriage, Florence appears rather as a lender than a borrower. The reader will recollect his appearance before Sir Thomas Norreys, and his obtaining that gentleman's letters into Desmond to authorize him to enter into possession of portions of the Earl of Clancar's lands, because that nobleman had failed in the performance of certain conditions on which he had advanced money to the Earl. It was not until the time of his trouble, when the gates of the Tower were between him and his resources, and the host of men who had invaded his lands, that he was compelled to enter into the traffic of lease and mortgage with money-lenders in London, with his friends about the Court, and with the Vice-President of Munster, Norreys himself. Fenton possessed the keen eye of a detective, and had the credit of being a spy upon every Lord Deputy who came to Ireland ; hence a saying that " he was a moth in the garments of every Lord Deputy of his time :" his passing glance was relied upon by Lord Burghley as seldom erring, and his opinion as a safe guide mostly ; he was now able correctly to report what his own eyes beheld; that "the followers of the Lord Barry, and the McCarthies were all addicted to the plough and husbandry;" but wonderfully erroneous were the conclusions he drew from it, and from what he learned from their neighbours! Before long, every man in Munster, where "there was no cause for alarm," was in arms! The Geraldines, that "were all underfoot," mustered eight thousand weaponed men, and shut up all the Queen's forces within a circle of a mile or two of the city of Cork! and notwithstanding the many warnings of Norreys, St. Leger, Browne, Barry, Popham, and Fenton, Kinsale and its old Head, "a fortress erected against the Irishry in times past," was left undefended, to welcome the Spanish fleet when it came.

This letter of Fenton had no ill effect upon the fortunes of Florence; happily for him, he was in London at the time, and at hand to give to Lord Burghley any explanation that he might think requisite. Sir Geoffry Fenton had returned from Kinsale to Dublin, and been sent thence, with Sir Robert Gardiner, to Dundalk, to conduct one of the various negotiations with the Northern Chiefs for a truce. Shortly previous to his leaving Dublin Florence arrived there. He had brought with him letters from the Lord Treasurer, not only to the Deputy, Sir William Russel, and to the Council, but also to the Vice-President of Munster, about his suit; from which it would appear that the English Minister had at length handed over that wearisome matter to the local legal authorities. The opinion expressed by Florence in the following letter, of the little knowledge that his countrymen had of the great power of the Government which they so recklessly defied, gives the reader a clue to the after-conduct of the writer, which neither Carewe nor his own countrymen seem to have understood. Florence perfectly well knew, not only the number and the character of the Queen's forces in Ireland, but the matchless resources of the English nation, and the fierce resolution of Elizabeth to empty the whole treasure of her kingdom, and to send every British soldier into Ireland, rather than that her pride should be made to bend before the pride of O'Neill, and that rebellious subjects should bring discredit upon her reputation, in the face of those Continental powers which she most hated. The opinion of Florence has been repeated by Cox, in the very words in which Florence wrote it:—"The Irish chiefs were grown into such extreme pride and folly, that they were standing upon great terms." The first of these terms was *a general liberty of conscience.*

The sequel showed that the interpretation by these foolish Irish of the motive of the Queen's " strong desire of a Peace" was the true one. All that resulted from the diplomatic ability of Gardiner and Fenton was a truce for three months. How much respect was shown by Fenton to the bearer of the Lord Treasurer's letters Florence did not fail to make known to the writer.

"1596. *April* 13.   *To* Sir Robert Cecil.

"It may please yoʳ Honⁿ, hauing about the time that Sir Robart Gardner came hyther, deliued my letters to the Lo: Deputie, by whom, and the rest of the Councell (onely Sir Geffrey Fenton excepted) I was honourablie used, and told by his Loᵖ that I shalbe well imployed yf there by an occasion, but I was denied of a protection, because the Judges who are of the Councell, wold grant none.   The Lord Genⁿall hath on Freday laste, being the Freeday before Easter, taken his jorney towards Dundalk to parle wth the Earle of Tireowen, who as I do heare comonly reported is (yf, as it be suspected, he doth not dissemble) desireous to accept any condicⁿons of peace that her Matie wilbe pleased to grant him; but O'Donnel, and the rest of those fooles, are growen into such extreme pride and folie, by reason they have neyther witt, knowledge, nor experience to judg or weigh her Mats power, that they stand uppon greate tearmes, as it is sayd; but I pray God the Earle himself have witt or grace to show now his thankfullnes for the great advauncements that he hath received at her Maᵗˢ hands.   Before the Lo: Genⁿall departed I had conference with his Loᵖ concerning those of the North, and wold have gon wth him, but that I haue no credit, nor acquaintance wth the Earle of Tireowen, but before his Loᵖ departed I told him what creditt and acquaintance I had with O'Donnell, and what good hope I had, uppon conference wth him, to bring him to som good conformitie, as also that I was very willing to venter my life, or bestow any paines or travayle that lay in me to benefit her Maᵗⁱᵉ in what sorte soever his Loᵖ wold direct me; whereuppon his Loᵖ, accepting well of myne offer, willed me to stay here at Doubling for the space of ten dayes, and that he wold parle wth the Earle; and yf ODonnel be there his Loᵖ will send for me; or yf he find the Earle conformable to any reason he will send for me and send me to O'Donnell.   In regard thereof I haue omitted to go into Mounster wth my Lo: Trᷗer's letters about my suite, or about any other busines, untill I know whether my service here now, may in any sorte avayle or benefitt her Matie; but I wrote thyther that som souldiers may be in areadines for me, yf the warres be not now at an end, and so hauing thought fitt to acquaint yoʳ Honor herewthal, what myne endeū may do herein The Lo: Generall will aquaint your honor withall,
    " 1596.   I humblie take leue this 13ᵗʰ day of April yoʳ Honoʳˡ. most humble and bondē.
                                        " fflor MᶜCarthy."

Were there not such undeniable evidence of reality in the animosity of Florence towards Barry, we might be tempted to suspect that all the long noisy contest for the £500, and the reiterated story of the ruin to his finances occasioned by.

it, was but the present of a little dust—"*pulveris exigui parva munera*"—for the eyes of the authorities, both in Ireland and England, whilst he purchased a harbour in which to receive the Spanish fleet, and a fortress which in other hands might dispute its entry. What his enemies represented as a "common purse made up for him to enable him to do the great things he had promised them" was, with much apparent ingenuousness, avowed by Florence as means supplied by his friends to enable him to bring this vexatious suit to an end, and to bear up against the ruinous legal charges occasioned by it. But a great crisis was at hand in the fortunes, both pecuniary and political, of Florence! The Earl of Clancar, who had been sickening when Fenton last wrote, died towards the close of the year 1596. It is in vain that we turn to the " Annals of the Four Masters" for some few passages of eulogy upon this great Irish Lord. Sir Donogh, and Sir Owen MacCarthy, the father and the uncle of Florence, as the reader has seen, both received their tribute of commendation from the chroniclers of their country; MacCarthy Mor was a greater chieftain than they; could these writers have conscientiously recorded one word of veneration or regret for him, they would have surely written it! All that they record is that "MacCarthy Mor died; namely, Donnell, the son of Donnell, son of Cormac Ladhrach, son of Teige; and, although he was usually styled MacCarthy Mor, he had been honourably created Earl by order of the Sovereign of England. There was no male heir who could be installed in his place (nor any heir), except one daughter (Ellen), who was the wife of the son of MacCarthy Reagh, *i.e.*, Fineen; and all thought that *he* was the heir of the deceased MacCarthy, *i.e.*, Donell."

It would be well for the fame of this English Earl if the enumeration of his illustrious ancestors could stand with sufficiency in the stead of personal virtues; if the names of Finin of Ringroan, of Donal Mor-ne-Curra, of St. Cormac of Cashel, could reflect so much of their patriotism, their gallantry, and their piety upon this last male heir of their elder line, as to turn away the mind of the reader from seeking other merit from their descendant! Can nothing, then, be discovered, absolutely nothing, decently to cover the memory of this last on the list of so many Chieftains? Must the final name of an illustrious roll pass out of sight into ignominy with that pitiful letter of Herbert as the sole just *epitaphium* of MacCarthy Mor? Alas! little can be said over the dust one would so willingly hold in honour! but yet not

absolutely nothing! The reader has but too often had occasion to see that the Earl's private life had not been edifying;
he may be surprised to learn that out of this infirmity of his
nature has proceeded what remains best to be said of his
memory!

"Donald MacCarthy," we are informed by the very learned
Edward O'Reilly, in his "Transactions of the Iberno-Celtic
Society," created first Earl of Clan-Carthy this year (1565),
was author of some poems, two only of which have reached
us—1. A small poem, of sixteen verses, beginning, Aisling-
thruagh do mhear meisi, 'A sorrowful vision has deceived
me;' 2. A poem of forty-four verses, beginning 'Uch an
uch! a Mhuire bu de.' 'Alas! Alas! O benign Mary,' a
pious address to the Blessed Virgin Mary."

MacCarthy Mor had rather *consented* to be made an Earl,
than solicited the honour. He was removed from the usual
inducement of surrendering his lands, and resuming them
from the Queen; for he had an only son, and neither brother
nor nephew, who might, by usage of Tanistry, delay his son's
succession; but it was the fate of this unwise nobleman to
be in constant oscillation between rebellion and submission.
In one of his periods of disgrace he found himself compelled
to secure the pardon of Elizabeth by relinquishing the title
of King of Munster, which he had assumed—and which the
Earl of Thomond, without assuming, was fiercely disputing
with him—and accepting this Earldom, which brought upon
him the jealousy and scorn of Shane O'Neill. Had the acceptance of this title been unattended by the exaction of any
equivalent, the English reader might, perhaps, think that the
Earl had been rather rewarded than punished for his disloyalty; but this Earldom carried with it conditions which no
just sovereign could impose, no honest man accept. Mac-
Carthy Mor was called upon to resign into the hands of the
Queen lands which were not his own! and to resume them
as her free gift, with succession to his son! and in failure of
heirs male, supposing his son to die without issue male, the
reversion of the said lands to be in the Queen! Thus were
the parties to this iniquitous bargain committing three
grievous violations of the rights of other men; for, first, the
lands were Sept lands, not the property of the life occupant,
to make subject of traffic and conditions; to the Sept alone,
from whom he had received them, could MacCarthy Mor
resign them, and from them alone could he hold them. Secondly, the succession to the high trust of Headship over no
less than "14 Lords of countries" depended, not upon the

accident of Donal MacCarthy's leaving issue, male or female
or no issue, but upon the free *Election* of those Lords, as
much as the succession to an Earldom depended upon such
arrangement as the Queen might choose to make! And,
thirdly, the reversion of the lands was the undoubted right
of any one qualified to hold, and regularly endowed with them
by the free election of the Sept.

With no care on the part of the Earl but to avert a present danger, and no consideration on that of the Queen but
to abolish the rights of chiefry and of Sept election, and, as
opportunity might offer, to "dissipate" the largest remaining
Irish estates in the South of Ireland, this bargain was made.
The supposed case occurred; the Earl died, and his son died,
and no male issue survived them. The reader has been
already informed that the young Baron Valentia had been
seized in his childhood as a hostage for his father's good behaviour; and that shortly after the death of the Earl of Desmond, his uncle, the authorities in Dublin, anxious to be rid
of so great responsibility, had sent him to London; from
London he was sent back to Dublin, destined to receive his
education in the Castle there. " Within four months the boy
undutifully escaped to France." His cousin Fitzgerald, the
son of the great rebel of Desmond—a child like himself—was
shut up in the Tower of London. It was not likely that as
long as this imprisonment lasted young Valentia would desire,
or be allowed, to return to Ireland : before long the follower
of his father, "who had enticed and conveyed him away,"
was found begging in Desmond "for some relief for the
young Lord." From France this boyish exile never returned.
We learn, incidentally, by a statement from Florence Mac-
Carthy, that he died in that country. His death must have
taken place before the Christmas of 1588; for at that time
was written by Sir W. Herbert to Walsingham, the notable
letter in which he says that, "besides the 6,000 Acres which
he meant to take, he was desirous to have other 6,000
Acres after the Earl of Glincar's death." ' Browne, too, was
at that same period bickering with Herbert over the lands of
Bally M'Daniel and Smerwick. It was not till the latter days
of the Earl's life, when Florence was evidently rising in
favour at Court, as was shown by the matter of Barry's fine,
that any of the Undertakers had the least doubt but that,
at the Earl's death, the whole of his possessions would be
seized by the Queen, and distributed amongst such of them
as might be so fortunate as to stand well with one or other
of the great Lords of the Privy Council. How many attempts

to blacken the reputation of Florence these men made the reader has seen; how successfully he had been able to discredit or explain away all their charges was hidden from their eyes till the Earl's death, when his great possessions were to be distributed.

No sooner was the breath out of the body of MacCarthy Mor, than began such a scramble for the lands of Desmond as had not been seen since the great forfeiture of the Fitzgeralds; but it was presently discovered that the political condition of Ireland had made Florence MacCarthy a person of importance, and the Undertakers not only of no account, but a source of weakness to the Government, on which fell the discredit of their evil actions; and it was at once perceived that the only claimants to the Earl's inheritance likely to meet with any consideration, were his widow, Florence in right of his wife the Earl's only legitimate child, and Donal the base son. Each of these separate claims was referred to lawyers and functionaries of the Irish Government, in order that upon their recommendation the Queen's decision might be made. In the meanwhile a tremour passed through every English home in Munster, and "the poor English Gentlemen" made a final attempt to communicate their terrors to the Privy Council. No more was heard about the thousands of acres which these men "meant to take," but their prayer was to be "protected from the revenge of Florence MacCarthy, who was not likely to forget the loss of so many of his near kinsmen and friends." Had the common dread of Florence's ambition been less deep-rooted than it was, some at least of his adversaries might have seen rather a gain than a loss in his succession to the inheritance of his father-in-law; for, were he once in possession of the vast Lordship of Desmond, the succession to Carbery would be of less importance; and the fine so clamourously contested would not be worth the time and vexation spent in the pursuit of it. But Barry probably knew that he had offended his adversary too grievously to be forgiven; MacCarthy Reagh may have considered the acquisition of Desmond as but a more certain means of securing the succession to Carbery; but for the Brownes, who appear to have thrown the bulk of their fortune into the Irish land scheme, who for many years had dedicated their skill and industry to the amelioration of *their* Signory, the prospect was one of utter ruin. It is true that Browne was in possession of his patent, which purported to secure to him, on payment of a moderate yearly rent to the Queen, the enjoyment of his lands in perpetuity; it was surely too late

now for Florence, or any one else, to tender payment of the
sums lent to the Earl, and so to clear off the mortgage?
Alas for the inexperience of Nicholas Browne! He was a
model farmer; he might be a match for Oisin in song, and his
son Oscar in valour! the deathless echoes of the tramp and
splash of his Hogesden horsemen through the glens and bogs of
Desmond may scare the peasantry of those weird solitudes to
this day; but in the niceties of legal dialectics what chance
had he with a man who from his cradle had been associated
with lawyers—whose father, uncles, and other lords "had,"
as the Cork jurors complained, "wrought such a policy to
entertain all the lawyers of the province, whereby no freeholder nor poor man could have a lawyer to speak in his cause,
be it never so just"—whose pathway through life had been a
network of legal springes—whose feet as instinctively gave
tidings of their ambush, as the antennæ of insects of the
meshes spread by *their* attorneys for *them*—and who had made
the succession to the estates of the Earl his especial study for
years past?

A flight of suits and suitors was presently winged across
the Irish Channel; and in lodgings in Westminster, in chambers of the Inns of Court, was to be fought a fiercer and more
effective fight for the lands of Desmond than had been fought
in the contested country itself by Raymond le Gros and the
ancestors of Florence. Browne with his patent, Barry with
his charges, their allies episcopal and political, turned their
faces to the decisive battle ground where the Lords of the
Privy Council were to decide the matter. If anything could
add to the displeasure with which Browne contemplated his
position, it must have been that the man who had been the
plague of his existence for so many years was to meet him
where neither good Sir Thomas's warrant nor the Queen's
horsemen could avail him. Donal, the Munster Robin Hood,
as it was the pleasure of his English biographers to call him
—that flitting, fiery light of the Swamps of Desmond—would
be already awaiting his arrival in London. This man—nurtured in woods and bogs, knowing no pursuit save the pursuit of Browne's cattle, no pastime but the worrying of his
English peasantry, and the wanton destruction of everything
that was his, knowing, and desiring to know, nothing of
patents or mortgages. law or lawyers—this man, whose
plunderings were countless, whose murders were not a few,
who had "preyed a Church," and would gladly have burned
an Archbishop, if Miler M'Grath, the Pope's ex-Capuchin, Her
Majesty's Southern Metropolitan, had fallen within his clutch

L 2

—was now metamorphosed, as if by magic, into an ordinary civilized subject; and, putting aside the raiment of his country, and attired in decent hose like Browne or the Archbishop himself, was actually repairing with his parchments and papers, like any common suitor, to the lawyers, and Ministers in London! Donal, with his name in whole volumes of English correspondence, who could walk over pitfalls, for he saw them not, fearlessly presented himself before the Vice-President of Munster, and requested letters of recommendation to the Lo: Treasurer; and Sir Thomas Norreys, with his usual urbanity, furnished the letters, and Donal departed.

There is, doubtless, something remarkable in the readiness with which Sir Thomas Norreys afforded his letters of recommendation to Florence upon all occasions when it was of urgent importance to him to have them. We have seen instances of this already, and we shall see more of them hereafter. Some little exercise of compression upon his conscience may have been requisite upon these emergencies; but, if so, how great a violence must he have done to its susceptibility in wording as he now did a letter in favour of Donal! An anonymous writer, towards the end of the year 1598, gives a commentary of his own on the conduct of the Vice-President towards Donal, and all who, like him, lived after a law of their own.

The following document, written shortly *after* the death of Sir Thomas Norreys, furnishes a true type of *the loose swords*, such as Donal had so long commanded, and a description of the treatment such men met with when captured; it expresses also, in as open language as the writer dared to make use of, his opinion of the little resistance Donal and men like him met with from the authorities of his province:—

" 1598.

" Murtagh Oge Mac Shee, aud his brothers Rorie and Edmund from the cradle inclined to mischief, as all that Sept hath been, being oft apprehended, and imprisoned, and having broken prisons (Murtagh at Limerick, Rory at Kilkenny), after many favors went into open accion and in thend were cutt off. Murtagh was greeved (as he said) that he was oft protected, but cold never get his pardon; that when the date of his protection was expired he must pay money for the continuance of it to Sir Thomas Norreys from time to time, and that he was no longer able to feed him. This rebel was marked by nature: he had a strong arm, a desperate villanie, and a skilful targeteer. He was taken in a wood killing of porkes, and. making provision to entertain the rebels of Leinster Tyrell the Traitor his company. Being brought to Cork and arraigned, evidence was given against him that he had prayed spoiled and murdered about four score

English families. Small resistance to the Rebell, and small aid to the subject, did the President give! When any came to complain that he had lost his cows, Why (saieth he) must I keep thy cows? In the end sentence was given upon this traitor that he shold have his arms and his thies broken with a sledge, and hang in chaines, So was he executed without the north gate of Cork, an° 1597. Rory was killed by an Irish kerne, and Edmund was killed by an Englishman at the spoil of Kilkolman. At this time Davie Lacie with his brotheren Pierce, Ulick, and William played the rebels, being once pardoned. Davie was after killed in service, Pierce was hanged at Limerick, Ulick and William were hanged at Kilkenny by the commandment of the Earl of Ormond. Fair riddance of Such rebells."

Had Lord Burghley invited Nicholas Browne to explain to him his meaning of that passage of his letter which he had underlined, doubtless with the intent of seeking such explanation. "I know him (Florence) to be a great Briber to his power," we should have escaped the danger of guessing, upon occasions like this, whom he had in his hidden thought when he wrote. But Donal now intended to tread in the steps of the Lo^rd Chief Justice of England, to reform his life, and to hold his possessions—those he had in prospective—according to English tenure, by submission, that is, to statute law, in so far as it related to his accepting the protection of English authority against Browne and the Queen's horsemen. Hence Sir Thomas Norreys may have had the less reluctance to furnish him with the character which he intended to deserve. From the letters of Browne, of Norreys, Herbert, St. Leger, and a multitude of others, the reader has had plentiful opportunity of forming an opinion of the character of Donal; with this present to his mind, he will more easily appreciate the social value of Donal's brethren, the other base sons, three in number, whom the Earl left behind him, when he is informed that the Vice-President of Munster was able to assure the Lord Treasurer that Donal was, " of all this base brood, the one of beste reputacion." He had been "reclaymed to duetifull offycess;" and Sir Thomas was of opinion, as were also the other gentlemen charged with him to report upon Donal's claims, that it would contribute to the quiet of the country of Desmond to allow him to inherit the lands left to him by his father's will.

" 1597. 14 *January*. Norreys *and others to the Privy Council in favour of* Donell M'Carthy, *base Son of the* Earl *of* Clancarr.

" It may pleaze your moste Honourable good Ll: to be advertized that this. bearer Donell Mc Cartye, base Sonne to the late Earl of Clancare deceased, myndinge to repayre into Englande desyred our l^res of testymonye of his carriadge sithence he was by us reclaymed to duetifull offyces, and also in commendaĉon of his suyte wᶜh he meaneth to make to Her Maᵗⁱᵉ. Truely he hath verye coȷ̃endablie, cyvylle, and duetyfullie behaved hymselfe sithence his coȷ̃ynge in uppon Her Maᵗˢ protectyon. In regarde whereof we haue byn the rather moued for his better mayntenance to contynue his possession in the pcels of landes wᶜh he can shewe to have byn conveyed unto him by the said Earle in his liefe tyme (althoughe some ceremonyes wanted wᶜh the extremitye of the lawe in transmutation of possessions requyrythe) And nowe that wee understande the said Earle to have ben but tenant in Tayle of the said landes, the revertion in Her Maᵗʸ, and therefore uppon his deathe wthout yssue inherytable to the same, his intereste in the said lande verye weake, we humblye commende his suyte (wᶜh he meanythe to make to Her Highnes for the said landes) to your Honour's favourable consideratyon. And likewyes that yt will stande wth yʳ Ll: good pleasure to grant lʳᵉˢ for the passinge Her Highnes pardon unto him (yf it shall so seme good to yoʳ Hoˢ.) wᶜh suyts beinge to him graunted wee thinck shalbe a verye good occasion to settle great quiett in the contrey of Desmonde. The consideraĉon whereof wee most humblye leave to yoʳ honourable regarde.

" From Mallow 14 Janʸ 1596.
" Thos. Norreys.   G. Golde.   F. Barkley."

No time was lost in furnishing the Loʳᵈ Treasurer with the opinions which he had demanded respecting the more important claims of Florence to the estates of the late Earl. The very next day after the Vice-President had despatched Donal, he and Robinson sent the following opinion of the expediency of " allowing to Florence some favour and relief, and thus avoiding the grief and discontent that it would breed in all the Clancarties to see the Earl's daughter utterly disinherited." Most important was it that Sir Thomas had not allowed any delay between his last and his present despatch! for the manifesto of " the poore English Gentlemen" was preparing; and, judging from the remarkable absence of the signature of the Lord Barry, we are led to surmise that that document was at last hurried away in the hope of its reaching London before the decision of the Privy Council should be pronounced.

" 1597. *January* 15.   Norreys & Robinson *to the* Lᵈ. Treasurer.

" Rᵗ Hon. we receiued yoˡ Loᵖˢ lʳᵉ dated the 2ᵈ of November 1595, wth a note inclosed, conteininge the names of certein pcells of lande in Desmonde, and have accordinge to yoˡ hoȷ̃s direction caused a jurie of the best and sufficientest Gent' of that contrie to enquyre of the nature, condicion and value of them, and allso of the truthe of a pretendede mortegadge to the late Earle of Clancare's daughter for her advancement in mariadge, and whether they be of the landes intayled to the Crowne, all wᶜh maye appear by the psentmentes of the jurie, wᶜh herewith we send unto yoˡ Ho: not signede by the chief Justice by reason of his absence. And whereas your Hoʳˢ pleasure is that wee signifie our oppinions whether wee thinke fitte those landes to be graunted unto Florence Mᶜ Cartye; and to certifie any other thinge meete for your Hoʳˢ knowledge touchinge his

suite for those landes, wee humblye recomende unto yor Ho^{rs} grave iudgm^t
the longe and troublesome suits and imprisonement wch the Gent' hath
sustayned by reasone of his matche wth the Earle's daughter, wch together wth his good careadge, and endevors in Her Ma^{ts} service inforceth
us to deme hime worthye of fauo^{1} and releefe, assurringe ourselves that
if he were setteled, and some wayes inhabled, he would applye himself
wholye to aduance Her Highnes service and the good of that contrye of
Desmonde; wch for that it is remote, barrene, and of verie litle value,
and allso for that the late Earle hath lefte behinde him three base sonnes
suche as are verie likelie to watche all opportunitie to disturbbe anye
that shall possesse it; wch Florence by reasone of his alyance is best hable
to prevente, wee thinke fittere to be bestowede on him then anye other.
Soe as he hould from Her Matie at reasonable reservaçon the landes onely,
wthout the tytle of Mac Cartye More, or the signory over the rest of the
Clancarties of Muskrye and Dowally, and that some litle porcion be leafte
unto Donoghe Mc Cartye, and Donelle Mc Carthy, base uncle, and base
sonne of beste reputaçon, to the late Earle. The consideraçon whereof,
togethere wth the grife and discontentm^t that it may breede in all the
Clancarties to see the Earl's heire uppon occation of hir father's surrender,
and his unthriftie mortgadges, utterlie disinheritted, Wee most humblie
submitte to yo^{1} Ho^{rs} grave iudgem^t, and rest ever pra'ing for the longe
continuance of yo^{1} Ho estate.
    " Killmallocke the 15 of Jany. 1596.
                                        " THOS. NORREYS.
                                        " —— ROBINSON."

This official opinion was in the hands of the Lord Treasurer
before the remonstrance of the poor English Gentlemen could
be sent from Ireland; he had thus time to ponder well which
of the two evils were the weightier, to grieve and discontent
the whole race of the MacCarthys and their allies, or the
Bishop of Ardfert and the five Undertakers whose respectable
signatures adorn as remarkable a document as is to be found
amongst Her Majesty's " State Papers."

" 1597. *February* 12. BP. *of* ARDFERT, *the* BROWNES, *and*
        others to the Privy Council.

" R^t. Hon : & our Singler good Lords, most humblie cravinge
pardon we have presumed, understandinge that Florence
Mc Cartie prepareth himself to be a suiter under Her M$_a$^{tie} and
your Honors for the landes and honor of the late deceasede
Earle of Clancartie, to sett downe unto your Honors the state
of the Countrie, as allso the condition of the partie, wth the
nature of the people, the trobles maie ensue unto Her M^{tie} and
State, wth the miseries lieke to fale uppon us poore English
Gentlemen, and all Englishe inhabitants heere dwellinge. The
Countrie, a great continent of greate fastnes and strenghes,
and the saied Florence alreadie Taniste of Carberie, a countrie
allmoste as great as the Earle's, and all these whose names

are heere inclosed being Lordes of Countries, and great commanders, his allies or followers : The Gentleman himselfe a
moste notable papiste, and a favorer of all superstitious maner
of livinge, broughte upp wth his uncle James Fitz Morris, and
his conversation hath bene much wth men not well affected
unto Her M^{a}a^{tie}, as wth Jacques, and such lieke : Himselfe and
all his Howse come out of Spaine.   The natures of the people
and his followers, are only to followe their Lo : not respectinge
anie alleagens unto ther prince, as good prooffe hath bine made
by a follower of O'Sullevant Moores who deliuered in open
sessions ' He knewe no prince but O'Sullevant More'—for w^{c}h
he loste his ears.   The danger wee poore Englishemen stande
in cannot be but great, for a man of his greatnes if he obtaine
his suite, cannot forgeat in his own nature the losse of so
manie his neer kinsemen and frinds ; if he woulde, his followers and kinsemen who have ever beene bluddie and
desierous of revenge, woulde never forgeat ; wherefore our
humble sute unto your Honors is that it maie be divided
amongste Gentlemen of good sorte and condition, and such
as alwaies have byne, and are lieke to continew good subiects
and moste to the benefite of Her Ma^{tye}, and not to be a
strenghe in one man's handes, in whome their is great psump-
tion of troble unto Her M^{a}a^{tie} and State, and so an utter sub-
vertion and overthrowe unto us Her Ma^{ts} most trew and
obediente poore subiectes.   And thus humblie submittinge
ourselves and our cause unto your Honourable consideration
we humbly take leave this.   Yo^{r}. Lps to be comaunded.
      " 12 of Febr^{y} 1596.

> " NICHO. ARTFERTE.
> " EDW^{d}. GRAYE.
> " CHA. HERBERT.
> " THO. SPRINGE.
> " NIC. BROWNE.
> " THO. BROWNE."

(Enclosure)—" A not of such as are Lordes of Cuntries being
   Finnin Mac Cartis kinsmen, and followers of the Earls of
   Clancarte wthin Desmond and the County of Cork adioin-
   ing uppon Desmond.

> " CORMOK M^{ac} DERMONDE, ⎫
> " TEG ^{ac} DDERMOND,   ⎬ Finnin's Aunt's Sonns.
> " O'SULLEVAN MOOAR, married unto Finnin's Sister.
> ' O'SULLEVANT BEAR.
> " O'DONNAOGH-GLAN.
> " M^{ac} GILLO CUDDIE.

" M^{ac} CREHON.
" M^{ac} GILLO NEWLAN.
" M^c DONNELL.
" HUGH CORMOK of Dungwill.
" CLAN DERMOND.
" CLAN LAWRAS.
" HUGH DONILL BRIK.
" M^c FINNIN.
" M^c FINNIN DUFF.
" CLAN TEIGE KETTAS.
" M^c DONNOGH BARRET.
" M^{ac} CAWLEF.
" O'KIFFE.
" O'KELAHAN.
" O'DALE.

" With many others, and alied by himselfe and his wife unto most of the noblemen in Iereland.'

Two days after the date of this petition followed a despatch from Sir Geoffry Fenton. His collusion with the men whose names followed that of the Bishop of Ardfert is so glaring, that he might as well have signed their paper, and embodied in it his own advice for the issue of letters to the Vice-President " to lay hold of Florence." It was evidently considered more effective strategy to send the official letter separately. It reached the hands of Sir Robert Cecyll, doubtless by the same post that carried its counterpart to the Privy Council.

" 1597. *Feb^{ry}*. 14. *To* SIR ROBERT CECYLL.

" The Earle of Clancar a great Lord in Munster being now dead, and Florence Mac Carthy, by marrying with his heir general, having an apparent pretence to the Earledom, I fear some alteration will grow in those partes by Florence, who is more Spanish than English; and I received this day advice from Munster that Florence alreadie begins to stir coales, in which respect I wish your Honour to advise with my Lord Treasurer out of hand, to have him either sent for thither, or some special letter written to the Lord President of Munster to lay hold of him, to make stay of him in his person, or to see him assured upon good pledges; for without the one of these two preventions I look that he will be a dangerous Robin Hood in Munster.
" 14 Feby. 1596.
                                                 " GEOFFRY FENTON."

Florence needed no warrant from the Lo: Treasurer to compel his repair to London; within ten days of the date of this letter of Fenton he applied to the Vice-President for his passport, and received, as usual, Sir Thomas's certificate of his good and dutiful carriage.

" 1597. *Feb^y*. 23. NORREYS *to* CECYLL.
" R^t. Hon.
" I haue ben earnestlie entreated by M^r. Florence Mc Cartye to recomende him to yor good fauor in these feowe, w^{ch}, for that his good and dutifulle carriadge towardes Her Matie hath meritted noe lesse, I coulde not but grante him. His suite is at this tyme to be inhabelede to live a setteled course of life on somewhat that his late dicesed father in lawe hath lefte behynde him; the pticuleareties I leave to his owne relacõn, humbly craveinge that you will be pleased to continewe your fauorable regarde of him wch he acknowlegeth alreadye to have tastede of in lardge measure. Thus leavinge him to yor Ho^{rs} regarde, and yor. Ho: to Godes divine ptection, I rest moste dutifullie affected to doe you service.
" Moyallo 23 Feby 1596.
"THO^s NORREYS."

It is impossible not to recognise, in the simple and speedy settlement of the minor claims on this inheritance, the prompt and prudent management of Florence himself. The claim of the Countess met with no opposition from him; that of Donal was admitted—not indeed as of right, but of favour—there remained the pretensions of Browne, and, after them, the rights of the Queen. How he proceeded to deal with the former, we shall presently see. Between him and the effect of his eloquence with Her Majesty there interposed another of those terrible documents which, at various critical periods of his life, pursued him even into the Privy Council, with denunciations of his birth, his alliances, his religion, and his cunning! The first claim to be despatched was that of Donal, in whose behalf the will of his father was allowed to take effect; Her Majesty's gracious Warrant in favour of the aged Countess next followed.

" 1598 *May* 25. ROGER WILBRAHAM *to* SIR ROB^r. CECYLL.

" According as you require I have considered all the state of Donell Mac Carthy.
" First I find by pap^rs only (and as it seemeth signed by the Earle his Fathers hand) all the parcells mentioned in the Survey, were assigned to the Petitioner Donell and his heirs, by the said Earle, and so the verditt and Survey true, saving that a parcell called Cannasamad specified in 5th Article in the Survey, is not so called in the Earle's writing, but is called Killegen, which he sayeth is all one thing besides names, and I think his suggestion true because it agreeeth in quantitie.
" The contents of said lands are seven Quarters, some Quarters containing four ploughlands, some three, some five, as the country manner is variable. I think mete, if it please Her Majestie, that he have an Estate to him and his heires males of his body, of the said seven quarters, lying

in the remote partes of Kerry and Desmond: And when the Jury in the Survey value each Quarter to be four shillings Irish per Annum I wish the Rent to be encreased to xx shillings Irish per An^m. each quarter of land, with these condicions

" 1st. That there be a saving of all strangers' rights.

" 2^d. The Estate to be forfeited if he or his heirs commit treason.

" 3^d. That if hereafter upon survey it appears to exceed 7 q^rs he shall pay for the surplusage 20^s p^r. an^m. for each quarter.

" 4. It will be convenient letters be written to keep him in possession of such as he or his tenants at will hath had quiet possession of for one or two years last past; and of the rest not to disturb the possessioners, till he have recovered by order of law, or before the gouernor or Lord President. And so returning herein all the papers touching that cause which Your Honor sent me, and submitting the cause to your Honor's good consideration I most humbly take leave.

" From Gray's Inn this 25 May 1598.

" ROGER WILBRAHAM."

"1598· Augs^t 13. Warrant to the Government in Ireland to allott a sufficient Dower to HONORA COUNTESS of CLANCARTY.

" Trusty, &c. We greet you well. Whereas we have by our late letters required you to authorize by our commission our President of Munster and others to enquire out and survey all the lands, rents, services and duties which ought to come to us by the death of the late Earl of Clancarie without heirs males of his body, and that the surveyors of those lands should without further warrant allott to Onora Countess of Clancary a reasonable portion for her dower. Now that the said survey may not (as is doubted) be speedily effected, we think mete, if none of our Council of Dublin can be spared for that service, that then other mete persons may proceed herein without delay: and further to express our princely favour for the relief of the said Countess, we do hereby require you that if the said survey of the late Earl's lands may not be effected within two months after the Countesses repair into our realm of Ireland, that then you give direction to our said President of Munster to possess the said Countess of a full third part of all the late Earl's castles, lands, rents, services, customs, and duties belonging to us, and whereof by our laws she is dowable, to hold the same as her dower during her life; and if any other profits and hereditaments of the said Earl may hereafter be found out and discovered for us by survey or other lawful means, whereof she is dowable, you shall by this our authority establish her in the quiet possession of the third part in full satisfaction of her dower, in which designment, as we mean of our especial grace that the said Countess shall have a full third part in certainty for her dower of all the said Earl's late inheritance as may be most convenient for her estate and maintenance, so likewise we expect the other two parts thereof to be reserved so entire to us as may be convenient for our service, and for the best satisfaction of such as shall be humbly suitors to us for those lands. Lastly if it appears to the commissioners of the said survey that the said Countess hath not received a third part of the mean profits of the premises sithens the death of her husband, then we require you after it shall be found out by jury or otherwise what the mean profits are, and who have received the same, then the Commissioners assign to the said Countess so much as belongs to her for her dower, reserving the residue to us, and for such uses as are expressed in our former letter therein," &c.

Cleared of the claims of Donal and the Countess, the question of the inheritance was much simplified. There still remained a vast possession, which, if the surrender of the Earl was to be held effective, lapsed to the Queen. Of a large portion of these lands Her Majesty had granted, during the Earl's lifetime, a prospective lease in perpetuity to the Brownes; but the Earl, ignoring altogether any rights either present or prospective, in the Queen consequent upon his surrender of his country to her, and recognising, as far as Browne was concerned, only his claim to hold certain portions of his lands as long as he held certain sums of Browne's money, had executed other mortgages of these and other lands, on a grand scale, to Florence, as dower with his daughter. Florence adopted the Earl's views of his rights, and proceeded to lay before the Queen his "Reasons" why the Earl's lands ought to descend to Ellen his wife, and to his heirs. Shortly afterwards he petitioned Her Majesty graciously to waive her claims in his favour; to allow him to repay the trifling sums lent by Browne, and to resume all the lands which Browne, by some singular mental process, had evidently convinced himself he was justified in calling *his Signory*. The political condition of Ireland quickened the decision of the Irish lawyers to whom the matter had been referred for investigation, and of the Privy Council, to whose final award the Queen had left it. It had become of importance to conciliate the numerous and powerful sept of the MacCarthys—none any longer to gratify the Brownes and their allies.

Nicholas Browne held Her Majesty's patent for a lease in perpetuity of the lands of the late Earl of Clancar : mountains, rocks, bogs, and glens, as he described them; castles, lakes, mines, fisheries, as they were enumerated by old Sir Warham St. Leger ; the fairy shores, the matchless waters of Killarney, spread away in endless variety and beauty through the fastnesses of Desmond, and formed a Signory probably not inferior to the patrimonial Signory of Hogsden. All this was accurately set forth in Browne's patent, and it was not easy to perceive how, consistently with honourable regard to the sign manual, that could be set aside. It had been prepared by his father's lawyers : if it contained a flaw, "any ceremonyes wanted which the extremety of the law in transmutation of propertie requyrythe"—certainly the hand of Florence had not been in it. A flaw, glaring and fatal, it did contain ! A single word had been left out; a single word too many had been introduced; and, when the finger of Florence pointed to the fatal passage, Browne's patent became a

weapon pointed against his own breast. " Should the Earl
die without *heirs*," said this delusive document, "*then*" (and of
course, by implication, not otherwise), " did the Queen assign
the Seignory to Browne for ever!" Alas for the reliance upon
legal shrewdness! Ten or more years had elapsed since this
patent had contented the acute Sir Valentine, and his martial
son; and it occurred to neither of them that an *heir* was all
this while living and moving amongst them, and that since
those days several more young heirs had come trooping into
the world as fast as the years came round. This very patent,
it was now discovered, by insertion of the word *heirs*, and
omission of the word *male*, itself plainly showed that, as the
contingency on which the grant was to take effect had not
occurred, no claim could be pretended for Browne! whilst the
mention of *heirs* at all made it manifest that Her Majesty's
gracious intention had been, that, if the Earl *should* leave
any, the conditional grant to Browne should be null, *because*
the lands would be theirs. Such was the legal interpretation
of what Her Majesty's gracious meaning had been, when she
promised those lands to Browne for ever! Such was the
pitiless answer to the Memorial of the poor English Gentlemen!

> " Suspensi Euripylum scitatum oracula Phœbi
> Mittimus, isque adytis hæc tristia dicta reportat."

Thus was at last given that gentle caveat for which
Browne had once plaintively solicited, "in case it were intended to give all to Florence, as he pretended." Had this
model Undertaker possessed only the usual enterprise and
tenacity of his class, he would have secured his retreat into
the flourishing English County from which his father had set
out upon his pilgrimage of contradiction, before Donal should
be back, with his short lesson of civilization forgotten; but
Nicholas Browne was unaccustomed to defeat; the lands of
Clan Donal-Roe, of Bally M'Daniel, and Malahiff were trophies
of twenty years of successful warfare; they had not been
easily come by, and they were not to be easily snatched from
the grasp that had held them so firmly and so long! Whilst
Florence was preparing his " Reasons," and Norreys and
Robinson their report, and friendly recommendation of him
to the Lord Treasurer, Browne and others, as the reader has
seen, were in conclave, inditing that famous Memorial to the
Privy Council, in which a last and solemn warning was put
on record, gravely attested by signature and seal, of Florence's
friendship of old with Jacques and Stanley, of his ambition

and great alliances, and of " the coming of himself and all his house out of Spain." The outcry against this last scandal to the feelings of the petitioners affords, at least, gratifying proof of the firm faith of these learned men in the antiquity and truth of our traditions.

Doubtless the ancestors of Florence *did* " come out of Spain ;" but it was scarcely ingenuous, whilst communicating so grave a circumstance, to pass over the fact that their sojourn there had been but a brief incident in the history of their race ; for they stayed there but 170 years. Florence's ancestors were the descendants of Magog the Scythian, not of Thubal the Spaniard. It is an undeniable *genealogical* fact that Milesius was born in Spain, A.M. 2690 ; but Baath was born to Magog, in Scythia, A.M. 1708 ; between these two ancestors of Florence intervened twenty generations, and a period of 980 years. Nenual, the eldest son of Feniusa Farsa, retained the inheritance of his father, and ruled in Scythia ; the descendants of his brother, Niul the Linguist, from whom Florence was 103rd in descent, wandered widely, backwards and forwards across the earth ; their steps are traceable over the plains of Shinar, into Egypt, to Lybia ; back to Scythia, to " Golgotha the stormy ;" to Cappadocia ; to Galatia, where they abode 300 years ; thence to Spain ; again to Scythia, thence to Egypt, and finally, once more to Spain. Such was the paternal ancestry of Florence, and such their migrations ! Furthermore, it was well known that in the female line Florence was descended from Pharaoh Cingris, whose daughter Scota was the wife of Niul the Linguist. Had these archæological gentlemen more carefully read the hieroglyphic inscription upon the obelisk erected at Zan or Goshen by Florence's maternal ancestor, they might have better informed themselves of the prosapia of their great adversary, and have discovered in him, to the great furtherance of their petition, even more dangerous hereditary tendencies than their Memorial proclaimed ; for Niul was the intimate friend of the leaders of the great revolutionary movement which resulted in the drowning of his father-in-law, with all his army, in the waters of the Red Sea. It was to ponder well upon the perils of these facts to the English nation, and upon the necessity of distributing Florence's property amongst Springe, Browne, and the rest, to avert them, that the poor English Gentlemen solicited a meeting of the Privy Council in the fortieth year of Queen Elizabeth ! A less venerable signature than that of the Bishop of Ardfert (although the prelate is presumably the person whom Sir

Robert Cec ll calls " Sir Walter Rawleig's last silly priest")
. would have better served the purpose of these poor English
Gentlemen. Unfortunately for them, Robinson, Wilbraham,
and Norreys were names more in repute with the Privy
Council ; and the document which *they* attested was not in
accord with the logic of the Memorial.

" *Reasons that* FLORENCE MAC CARTHY *alleged to prove that the* EARL *of*
CLANCAR'S *Lands ought to descend to* ELLEN *his Wife, and to his Heirs.*

" Donell Mac Carthy Mor Earle of Clancar sonne to Donell Mac Cormac Leirie was by the old Lord Roche, called David Roche, taken prisoner,
and Sir Henry Sidney, then Deputie, mistrusting the rebellious intentions
of Gerald the last Earle of Desmond, sent the aforesaid Donell Mac Carthy
Mor into England, to the intent that by Her Majesties good usage of him
he might be made an instrument against the said Desmond. The Queene
of her bountie both bestowed money upon him to defray his charges, and
made him Earle of Clancar. And in the patent of his Earldom did grant
unto him both the said title and all his lands, to him and to the heirs
males lawfully begotten; whose son and heir [Teige] the Baron of Valentia
being dead, he went again to England, as well to recover some of his lands
that the English undertakers of Munster challenged, as to get his lands to
be confirmed by Her Majestie unto his daughter, who at that time by his
consent was to be married to Florence Mac Carthy, for the performance
whereof bonds of £6000 did passe betwixt the said Earle and Florence.
His lands he obtained, but no grant to his daughter, because no surrender
of his was extant or formalie made, yet neverthelesse Her Majestie agreed
to pass him a grant of his lands, on the condition that his daughter would
marry an Englishman, which the Earle adopted, and accordinglie made his
surrender; which condition and surrender in Law is Void, because his
daughter was formerlie married to Florence aforesaid; as alsoe that the
said surrender was never duly perfected. Moreover Donell Mac Cormac
Leirie, Father to the said Earle, in his lifetime entayled all these lands to
his onlie sonne the aforenamed Earle of Clancar and his heirs; and for
want of such issue in him, to the heirs of James Earle of Desmond by
Ellen his daughter, wife to the said Desmond, and sister to the aforenamed
Earle of Clancar, and the remainder to the right heirs of the aforesaid
Ellen for ever, which [right heir] is Ellen daughter to the Earle her brother,
and wife to Florence aforesaid, considering that the said Earle of Clancar
survived Sir James of Desmond her sonne, and Eleanore, wife to Edward
Butler, her daughter, who both died witout issue. This Entayle made by
Donell Mac Cormac Leirie was perfected, and diverse of the witnesses yet
living that were at the perfecting thereof, in the first and second yeare of
Phillip and Mary, and now readie to be produced."

The suit of Donal had been decided some time since in
his favour, and he had hurried back to his native country; for
he judged wisely that the bogs and wilds of Desmond were
safer for him than too continuous proximity to Her Majesty's
Tower of London. But the suit of Florence made tardier
progress. Notwithstanding the favourable report sent home

by the legal authorities in Munster, no satisfactory intelligence reached him from England. He had never yet visited the saloons of Cecyll but to his advantage; and, although he had but recently left London, and his presence in Munster was of the utmost importance to him, he yet determined to return thither; for the state of Ireland now left the English Ministers but a choice between him and some chieftain like Donal, perhaps Donal himself. There was a dark cloud over Ireland! The day that Carewe had foreseen, and foretold four years before, was at hand; and the English authorities were already counting in dismay their friends and their enemies, their soldiers, their warlike stores, and their money. The result appalled even the stout heart of Ormond himself, who wrote home that "at no time had England been so ill prepared for a great struggle as at that moment;" and yet that a great struggle was at hand was apparent to all men. As usual, the rumours of coming Spaniards were revived, and universally credited. At this critical moment Florence waited upon the Vice-President of Munster, and requested his customary letters of recommendation to Cecyll; Sir Thomas, with his usual courtesy, bore willing testimony to his good and dutiful carriage towards Her Majesty. Florence in this interview casually adverted to the uneasiness caused by the rumours of a Spanish invasion, and informed the Vice-President confidentially that, when last in England, he had offered, upon emergency, to procure, by agents of his own, reliable information out of Spain of what might be destined against Ireland; that Sir Robert Cecyll had gladly accepted of his offer, and that he now proposed sending a trustworthy person thither for that purpose. Norreys was sufficient of a statesman to manifest no surprise at such an arrangement; but the matter had not been mentioned in the Minister's despatches to him, and he, with more than his usual prudence, reported this interview to his Government.

" 1598· *May* 30.   Sir Thomas Norreys *to* Sir Robert Cecyll.

" Rt. Honble,

" This gentleman Mr. Florence Mac Cartye being (as he sayeth) directed from Her Majestie to learn such Spanish intelligences as from tyme to tyme he could, hath by the examinacion of some latelie come thence, understood that there are now remayning in great credit and estimacion two of his kinsmen, who are such as being accordingly dealt with may doe Her Majestie verie acceptable service, and now he, intending presentlie to send unto them a frend of his owne, and a verye trustie messenger, with his effectual letters to persuade them thereunto, hath entreated me to advertize your Honor hereof, and withal to recommend his poore and weake estate altogether decayed, to your Honors good regard, whereunto humblie submitting himself, and doubting not but your Honor in your wonted favour towards him, and for the better encouraging him to continue his good affection to Her Majesties service, will be a mean for the repairing thereof in such sort, as your Honor shall think meete. Whom now leaving to your gracious consideracion I doe rest, readie at your Honors commandment.

" Tho⁸. Norreys.

" *May* 30, 1598."

No mischief came of this suspicion of Sir Thomas Norreys; indeed, no official notice appears to have been taken of it. It is certainly surprising that Florence, with the full knowledge of the charge so frequently made against him of his Spanish tendencies, should thus ingenuously inform the Minister of his having two near relations in great repute at the Spanish Court; but, like the matter of the bonds, and the common purse to enable him to do great things in Munster, it was a formidable accusation on the lips of Barry, Browne, and the Lord Chief Justice, but a harmless, nay a prepossessing admission, when made thus incidentally by Florence himself.

Florence took his departure, not directly to England, but in the first instance to Dublin, that he might procure additional letters from Ormond, then Lord General of Her Majesty's Forces in Ireland. His application was made at a moment when the presence of every man on whom the authorities thought they could place reliance was a matter of urgent importance, and Ormond consented to his departure with evident reluctance; the brief letter which the impatient old man wrote to Sir Robert Cecyll is characteristic :—

" 1598.   *June* 18.   Ormond *to* Cecyll."

" This bearer Florence Mᶜ Carthy is now to make repair into England about some suit of his own, which in regard to this dangerous time, he may be hardly spared from hence, I am heartily to pray you to favour him in his lawful suits, and that he may be despatched from thence; whom I leave to your favourable regard, and so I commit you to Gods most blessed guiding.
" From Dublin this 18th June 1598.
" Your fast assured Friend,
" Tho⁸. Ormond & Oss."

It would be desirable to avoid, if possible, further reference to the political condition of Ireland until the matter of the inheritance to the Earl's estates were conducted to its close; one or two more letters of Florence will suffice for this purpose; but in those letters are allusions which necessitate some mention of the state of Munster. Donal, so

M

recently graced by Her Majesty's permission to inherit the estate left to him by the will of his father—whose energies hitherto had found but insufficient scope in the obscure adventures of an outlaw, whose celebrity was yet but in its dawn—had waited for no authority from Queen or Council, but immediately on his return from England, had put himself into communication with O'Neill and the Geraldines, had taken into his pay 500 bonaghts or hired soldiers, and, to the amazement of Munster, had proclaimed himself, under favour of O'Neill, MacCarthy Mor! From the merely incidental notice of this occurrence, in a despatch to the Privy Council, it would appear that the Vice-President of Munster attached no great importance to the assumption, nor saw in it anything that greatly concerned the Queen's Government. Had there been no authority but his to oppose to the ambition of Donal, it is probable that all the Clan Carthy must have submitted to him, for O'Neill was looked upon as little less than King of Ireland at the time; he had called into being a new Earl of Desmond, who had been immediately accepted by all the Fitz Geralds, and he now secured to Donal the support of every man who was in action, and of every *bonaght* who was under arms; for these hired soldiers, although in the pay of a multitude of minor chieftains, all acknowledged a supremacy in O'Neill; but there was something between Donal and the great prize, which not even O'Neill could remove.

Endorsed—" SIR THOMAS NORREYS *to the Privy Council, by the hands of Spencer.*

" In Desmond Donall Mc Carthy, base sonne to the Earle of Clancar, opposeth himself against Darby Mc Owen Mc Carthy for the Earldom: but they agree both to be Traytors to Her M^{atie}. O'Sullivan Mor doeth as yet refuse to give the Rod (according to ancient custom) to either of them."

This despatch removed an illusion under which the Queen and her Chief Secretary had been conducting their policy with regard to the Irish Septs in Munster, and which had influenced them hitherto in their treatment of Florence. They had too hastily concluded that the Earl's surrender of his country and rights of chiefry would have put an end for ever to all sept titles, sept election, and, in short, to Tanist law amongst his followers. The only hesitation in the Royal mind, since the death of the Earl, had been whether his lands should be " undertaken," and his title left extinct, or lands and Earldom bestowed upon Florence. Whilst the Queen

hesitated, Donal decided! and his decision quickened that of
Her Majesty. The Earldom not even Donal cared for, or he
would assuredly have assumed it as readily as he did the
chieftainship; but he had no wish to meddle with Her Majesty's titles of honour; he remembered that "in the first
degree bastardy is no bar to succession amongst the Irish,"
and he saw no invasion of Royal rights, in his assuming the
title borne by his ancestors for centuries. Donal, therefore,
proclaimed himself chieftain of South Munster; and during
the short period that he bore the time-honoured title of Mac-
Carthy Mor he proved that, in valour at least, no member of
his race since the days of King Dermod—not Finin of Ringroan, nor Donal-Mor-ne Currah himself—had surpassed him!
Fortune, too, which had so long preserved him from Browne's
pursuit, and the perils of the Queen's horsemen, had in reserve
for him a triumph such as had been rarely accorded to any
mere Irishman since the days of Henry the Second. Donal
had the honour of meeting in fair fight the Queen's "Lo:
L^t. Genl.," and the exquisite enjoyment of chasing that illustrious functionary before him, not only out of his own domains,
but far on his way to the confines of Munster! Donal Mac
Carthy has not received from the writers of his country that
eulogy which his warlike exploits deserved. Florence saw,
and cannot have failed to admire, the audacity with which,
in defiance of all authority, his base brother-in-law assumed
a title beyond all others coveted by himself, "præ quo, vel
Cæsaris titulus in Hiberniâ sordet," and hateful to the Queen;
the following petitions show how adroitly he could turn the
circumstance to his advantage:—

"1597. *Feby.* 12. Flo. *to* [Cecyll].

"May it please Your Honour to understand your suppliant Florence
M'Carthy's humble suit unto Her ^{Ma}tie is for the demaine lands of his
father in law the Earle of Clancarthy, and specially for two parcells
thereof, thone morgadged by his sayd Father in law about 12 or 13 yeres
past to his daughter, your suppliant's wife, for her mariadge goods, as
appeares by the presentments of the office, signed and sent over hither by
Sir Thomas Norreys, and the Queenes Attorney of Mounster, wch Your
Honour hath, and by the sayd Earles deade of mortgadge, ready to be
shewed, wch parcell of land called Castell logh, the Palice, and Balcarbry,
doth containe 14 or 15 quarters of lands; the other parcell, called both the
Coishmainges, and Onaght, doth containe 31 quarters of lands, and was
also morgadged by his sayd father in law to Sir Valentine Browne, and
his son Nicolas Browne jointly, for five hundred and three score pounds:
there is also another parcell of the sayd Earles, holden by Nicolas Browne,
called Clan Donelle-Roe, wch containeth 7 or 8 quarters of land. Your
suppliants humble suit unto Her M^{tie} is, that he may obtaine those demain
lands, onely to hold of Her ^{Ma}tie, to him and his heires males, together

M 2

wth such prouision as was due to the sayd Earle of certen Septs of people of his folowers, wch in that contrey and lands being but a certen quantitie of otthen meale, barell- butter, porck, and beafe, which he had yerely of certen Scepts of his folowers for his provision, And your supplicant will not onely yeld Her $^{M}a^{tie}$ a reasonable reservaçõn out of the lands, and remitt unto Her Highnes all such rents, chiefries, duties, creaçõns, and comaunds, as was, and is, still due to that House, of the Lords of Muskry, Dowalla, Clan Mc Donell, and all other lords of that House, but will allso venter his life, and all his people, frends and followers, to recover the same of his enemies, who have now entered therunto wth intent to defeate him thereof, and are becom traytors to Her $^{M}a^{tie}$; and will also, whensoever he doth recover those lands, submitt himself to Her $^{M}a^{ties}$ pleasure for the payment of the sayd Brownes Morgadge, wherin not doubting of Yo$^?$. hono$^?$s furtherance, wherof he doth holde himself moste assured, he will allways pray for yo$^?$. hono$^?$, and rest eü readie to do yo$^?$ hono$^?$ any service that lies in him."

" 1597. *Feb^y*. 12.   FLORENCE'S *Petition to recover the mortgaged lands of his late Father in law.*

" My humble suit unto Her most sacred and Excellent Ma^{tye} is, for that parcell morgadged by my father in law to Browne, and a small pece of land wch he also made oü unto my wife for her preferrment, together wth som litle prouision of meale, butter, and flessh, wch is due of certen Septs of his folowers wthin that contrey, for the maintenance of his House; wch land I will holde of Her $^{M}a^{tie}$, and not only yelde Her High-nes a reasonable reservaçõn, but also procure Browne sufficient securities, or mortgadge unto him a sufficient quantitie of land for his money, although he got about £2000 thereby already, these 10 yeres past, wherby Browne shalbe satisfied of more then his due, and Her $^{M}a^{tie}$ shall haue, in cer-tentie, not onely all the comaunds, creaçõns, rents, duties and cheferies, due unto that House, of other Lords and contreyes, wch was ever the chefest parte of thErls greatnes, and liuinge, but also a reasonable reser-vaçõn out of so much demaines as aforsayd, wch in that wilde craggy, barren, and unprofitable contrey, is the beste thing that may benefit my-self, or enhable me to do Her $^{M}a^{tie}$ servise, considering the p'ent state of that countrey, and all the people thereof, who have joined wth the Earle of Desmond, and the rest of his adherents, and haue geven the bastard that was here, a kind of supereoritie over them, maintaining 500 of Tireowens souldiers for him, wherunto they were moved only because Browne (when my father in law mortgaged it unto him) thrust them out of those lands, wch they and their añcestors eü held of my father in law, and his añcestors, in wch action they will allwayes persist to the last man, and not onely kepe themselfes salfe, but also bak and maintaine all the rebells of Mounster with that strong countrey, yf I be not able to assure them, by Her Ma^{ts} speciall grant, that they shall holde those lands of me, as formerly they held them of my father in law; for they are but folowers, whose living is to hoolde, and inhabit their Lords lands, as their manner is in all Ireland; of wch land yf I be able to assure them, I do not doubt (wth some litle meanes) to reduce that contrey very shortly into good quietnes, and con-formitie; and wth that contrey and people (wch stands at the bak of all the rebells of Monster so comodiously to annoy them) to do Her $^{M}a^{tie}$ that service that a thousand men in pay cannot do; and that (in reducing Mõnster to obedience) will salue Her Highnes above three score thousand pounds: for the performance of which service I will ever rest readie to venter, and spend myne owne life, and the lifes of all such as will followe me."

CHAPTER VIII.

THE year 1598 opened with gloomy indications of what would assuredly come upon Ireland before its close. Distasteful as the topic of Irish troubles had become to Elizabeth, and unwilling as was the Council of Dublin to force so unwelcome a subject upon the attention of Her Highness, mischief was too swiftly coming, and the unprepared state of the Government much too alarming, to allow of any further silence or inaction. It is indeed surprising that events so long foreseen, so frequently foretold by the many persons in Ireland in active correspondence with Cecyll, so earnestly occupying the thoughts of that Minister himself, that he had employed Sir George Carewe, so far back as 1594, to reduce to writing his reasoned opinion, not only on the probability, but on the likely details, of a great rebellion, should have come at last and found no sufficient resources to encounter them; but so, unquestionably it was. "Now," says Camden, "was the condition of Ireland in a manner desperate, for almost the whole nation was broke out into rebellion." Early in January the Lords Justices write from Dublin that "they find cause of great distrust in Tirone!" "the King of Spain beareth a great sting of mind against Her Majesty." "Tirone receiveth letters from the King of Scots." "Scotland beareth up this rebellion." Before the end of the same month Sir H. Brounker wrote to Cecyll his opinion of "the lamentable state of this accursed country; the enemy is grown insolent, and intractable; in discipline, and weapons, he is little inferior to us; the men of most spirit follow the rebels, and leave the rascals to the Queen's service."

The Lords Justices, entrusted with the government of Ireland, on the death of Lord Borrough, the late Deputy, were not men from whom a calm opinion upon the condition of the country could be expected, or whose proceedings needed to cause much alarm in the minds of the Lords of the Privy Council; but Ormond, whom no man could accuse of timidity, or hastiness to take fright, whose every word should have been a word of guidance to his Government, for no one

knew the Irish character better than he did, and no man was
more truthful, and plain spoken, wrote to the same effect,
" the times are more miserable than ever before! the rebels
are getting all the armour and weapon into their hands. If
the wants of the army be not speedily supplied the whole
kingdom will be overthrown " " there are only three barrels
of powder in Her Majesty's store " and—by far the most distasteful of all his complaints!—" no means to withstand
O'Neill." " The English gentlemen in Leinster do not dare
to look out of their castles."

As the months crept on, these complaints, and melancholy
forebodings became louder, and gloomier—there were of
rebels in arms :—

In Leinster	3,048 Foot.	182 Horse.
In Ulster	7,220 Do.	1,702 Do.
In Munster	5,030 Do.	242 Do.
In Connaught	3,070 Do.	220 Do.

Eighteen thousand, three hundred and sixty-eight Foot,
Two thousand, three hundred and forty-six Horse!

To meet this formidable force Her Majesty had in Ireland,
at the end of April, but 8,282 soldiers !

The effect produced on the minds of the Lords Justices by
the comparison of the Queen's forces with those of the rebels,
it would be to little purpose to describe; their equanimity
wholly abandoned them, the council table creaked under the
trembling hands that wrote upon it. Even the strong nerves
of the Lord General Ormond quivered, and his impatient
temper flashed into wrathful remonstrance when he comtem-
plated the scanty, ill-appointed, cowardly force to which was
intrusted his own reputation, and the defence of Ireland ; he
wrote incessantly, and with ever-increasing urgency to the
Privy Council for reinforcements, declaring that " the country
would be overrun, for he had no means of resistance ! his
army could not be trusted, for it was filled with Irish soldiers,
and they ran away, whenever occasion offered, to the rebels."

Ralf Lane wrote to Lord Burghley, " the army is filled
with Connors, Moores, and bastard Geraldines." The Queen
was informed that " her soldiers were more like prisoners,
worn out with hard afflictions than soldiers," that " poverty
and nakedness made the soldiers run to the rebels " and by
Fenton, that " O'Neill had procured means to cess the three
furies, penury, sickness, and famine, on the Queen's troops."
It was too late now for the Minister to derive any benefit
from the discovery of " a stratagem of O'Neill, who having

had six companies under his command, at the Queen's pay, he altered and changed the men so often, that thereby his whole force became disciplined soldiers." The only stratagem attending the formation of the Queen's Irish army was the stratagem by which the men had been forced or inveigled from their ploughs and rural homes, which they encountered by a simple stratagem, in their turn, that, namely, of running back to them with as much speed as opportunity allowed, and which was met by the Lord General, fertile in resources, by another even simpler—he hanged them as surely as he caught them! Their officers in tranquil times little regretted their disappearance, but filled their places with mere Irish, who were willing to keep Her Majesty's fortresses, and to receive Her Majesty's pay and food—about clothing they were no wise particular; indeed Cecyll at last, in a suspicious mood, refused to allow any change under the head of "apparel," for, as he said "they wear none," and considering that the regulation-apparel of the Queen's English soldiers was "a cassock, a dublet, a pair of veneecians, shirts, stockings, shoes, caps, and bands," it must be admitted that these Irish warriors were a great economy. But the gaps in the Royal Army occasioned by these escapes, were as nothing, compared to the chasms speedily caused by "the nature of the service, and the want of all things, but chiefly of clothing." The Government of Ireland was smitten by intense panic; and assuredly, since the day—the darkest in her annals—when the Normans first set foot in the country, never had their conquest been in equal jeopardy.

The province of Munster had for many months remained in ominous calm, watching eagerly the proceedings of the Northern chieftains; Sir Thomas Norreys was not ignorant of the impatience with which the native lords of his own province were awaiting O'Neill's signal for action, and he called as incessantly and urgently for aid, as did the authorities at Dublin! With the exceptions of the Lord Barry, Fitz Edmund of Clone, MacCarthy Reagh, and MacCarthy of Muskerry, there was not one of the gentlemen of Munster, but was prepared for instant outbreak; and though the great Lords just named might themselves remain passive; their brothers, or nearest of kin, and their followers, to a man, would assuredly before long be in action. He declared that less than a reinforcement of 2,000 men, and a body of horse, would not suffice to maintain the Queen's authority in the province. Cecyll replied that "he grieved to hear such ill tidings; but that 2,000 men should be forthwith sent, with treasure, clothing, arms, and victuals; for the Queen was determined to make war like a princess that, at the greatest Monarch's hand, would not take any bravado. And he added that "though he doubted not the Irish were as fastly bound together as rebels could be, yet they were an inconstant, and quarrelsome people." "Two of the MacCarthy's of Muskerry were at strife for the Lordship of that country: let the Queen's support be promised to the weaker of them! Two of the chiefs of Dowally were in similar contention: let there be division made wider between them, by promises of a like nature." "Certain undertakers were clamouring for the lands of Condon, and of the White Knight: let these chiefs be told that their lands should be safe to them; their adversaries satisfied some other way."

Politic and wise, but all too late were these state expedients: the rival claimants of these lands preferred awaiting the arbitrament of O'Neill, or the chance of arms, to listening to the tardy promises of a functionary whose hold upon Munster was as precarious as theirs upon such portions of the disputed lands as they had seized. During the months of June and July O'Neill had been engaged in one of his local conflicts with the authorities. These conflicts were but the normal condition of the debatable land about his boundaries, and as long as they did not pass beyond the accustomed limits, or very far within the marches of the pale, they were not considered rebellion; they were hereditary encroachments and resistances, which it was known would not spread, and they did not prevent frequent communication between the great northern chieftain and the Lord Deputy, or even his occasional repair to Dublin. Upon O'Neill's border stood the strong fort of the Blackwater; it was the key to his wild country, and the object of incessant strife between him and the authorities; the struggle for the possession of this fort had of late assumed a more than usual importance, owing to the known revolutionary sentiments of the country; and the despatches from Ireland had been wholly taken up with the recital of the preparations of Ormond to revictual the fortress, and make ready a force sufficient to drive O'Neill from its walls. Such a force was at last in readiness; it consisted of 4,000 foot and 350 horse, and was commanded by Marshal Bagnal, one of the most experienced of the Queen's officers. The Lords Justices learned with dismay that the only army they possessed was to be divided into two nearly equal portions; one-half to be sent upon this expedition against O'Neill, and the other to be led away by Ormond himself, "to prosecute the matters of Leinster." Piteously,"they entreated that his Lordship would stay with them to protect the city." The stern man, regardless of their tremours and entreaties, hurried away to the service on which he had resolved, and left Dublin without a soldier.

About the middle of August a despatch, abrupt, fragmentary, without details or explanation, startled the Lords of the Privy Council; it was entitled "The ill news out of Ireland." Evil news was it, indeed, for those who wrote, and for those who received it! What it was to every living creature of the Irish race, let the reader judge! The " Jorney of the Blackwater" had been fought between the Queen's forces under Marshal Bagnal, and the Kerns and Galloglass of O'Neill. "Tirowen triumphed (says Camden) according to his heart's desire over his adversary, and obtained a remarkable victory over the English; and doubtless, since they first set foot in Ireland, they never received a greater overthrow! 13 stout captains being slain, and 1,500 of the common soldiers, who, being scattered by a shameful flight, all the fields over, were slain, and vanquished by the enemy; they that remained alive laid the blame of the miscarriage, not upon their own cowardice, but the unskilfulness of their leaders, which was now grown a common custom." On the evening of that 14th day of August, 1,500 dejected fugitives were all that was left of the English army! their colours, cannon, and—what was beyond price to O'Neill's ill-furnished multitudes—the arms which the slain had dropped, and the fugitives had flung from them, remained with the victor; whilst the survivors, flying before the face of O'Neill, rushed for refuge back into Armagh, where there was provision for only eight or nine days, no possibility of succour, no means of further retreat, except through the masses of the victorious army, and "having to pass through a dangerous straight between the Newry and Dundalk." The Lo: General was away in Kilkenny, or its neighbourhood, and the Lords Justices "most greeved that this wicked land would not yield better matter to advertise their Lo³ :"

Had the next despatch reached the Privy Council, dated from "Beaumorris or Westchester," their Lordships could have felt no astonishment equal to that with which they learned " that the fugitives had been allowed by O'Neill to retire unmolested," and the Irish capital left undisturbed. O'Neill was not ignorant that Ormond, in full confidence of the success of Bagnall, had quitted Dublin, and taken with him every remaining soldier that the Queen possessed in Ireland. He must have known that had he chosen to lead his victorious followers against that defenceless city, there was no force to oppose him; all that he was ignorant of was the disgraceful terror of the Lords Justices, and their hourly expectation of seeing him at their gates. Why did he not leave the garrison of the Blackwater to die of hunger, as it must soon have done, and the runaway troops to starve in Armagh, or perish in the attempt to force a passage through " the dangerous straight between the Newry and Dundalk," and march his elated troops to the capital? The only explanation of this historical enigma which the writer of these pages can venture to propose to the consideration of his reader, is the following :—

Situated on the confines of O'Neill's country, effectually barring all admission, or keeping the pathway into it at all times clear and open, accordingly as it might be in possession of O'Neill, or of the Royal forces—stood, as we have said, the Fort of the Blackwater. Upon the temporary occupancy of this stronghold depended the submission or the independence of O'Neill; hence was the possession of it a constant source of contest between the Irish Chieftain and the Lord Deputy. For the last four years it had been the scene of repeated and determined conflict. So important was the possession of it considered to the maintenance of the Queen's authority, that the Lord Deputy Russel, and after him the Deputy Lord Borrough, twice, in person, marched from Dublin to secure it. Each time it has re-victualled, its defences augmented, and its garrison increased; and each time, as soon as the Royal army returned to Dublin, it was again beleaguered by O'Neill, its communications and supplies cut off, and the garrison reduced to the verge of starvation. Upon occasion of the last relief by Lord Borrough, the command of the fort had been entrusted to a picked officer of the name of Williams; it had been well garrisoned and well stored, and then of necessity left to its own resources. As usual, no sooner had the Lo: Deputy turned his columns towards Dublin than O'Neill again closed around the fort. He at first assaulted it with his best troops, and lost many valuable lives beneath its walls; he then sat down before it, " swearing by his barbarous hand, as Fenton wrote, that he would no more withdraw from it till the garrison was starved into surrender !" Williams, as it proved, took a great deal to starve him, for he, in the first instance, rigidly economised the food that had been left with him, and when that was consumed, made occasional sallies from his walls for the double

purpose of assailing his besiegers, and of capturing their
horses. These four-hooted enemies assisted in keeping
famine at bay for a while.

Sir R. Cecyll had been informed by one of the more intelligent of his correspondents that "grass was a common food
of the rebel Irish." The gallant Williams and his soldiers
were reduced, when their last horse was eaten, to make trial
of this Irish diet. In the meantime the sufferings and the
gallantry of this brave garrison afflicted the hearts of the
Lords Justices, who, to rescue them from famine, wished to
surrender the fort; but they excited the choler and admiration of Ormond and Marshal Bagnal, and *they* determined
to relieve it. The result of the ill-fated expedition made for
this purpose the reader has seen.

Bagnal and half the Queen's Irish army perished almost
within sight of the fatal fortress; but even then the Royal
banner floated as defiantly as before, above its battlements.
Williams and his men continued to roam about their ram-
parts in search of pasture, and in reply to some whispering
amongst his men about surrender, this brave soldier fiercely
swore that he would "with his own hand sooner blow the
place and its defenders up into the skies, than those miscreants should enjoy that charge of his."

It was now for O'Neill to make his election, whether to
leave under the walls of that obstinate fortress a force sufficient to keep shut up the starving garrison, and in like
manner close-in the scarcely better provided fugitives in
Armagh, and march upon Dublin, with the chance of en-
countering Ormond hastening back to defend the capital, or
open negociations with the two imprisoned forces. Had he,
during the last three or four years, been in a position to
aspire to more than the expulsion of the Queen's forces from
his own country, had it ever occurred to him to rouse the
native Irish beyond his own province, and attempt a general
rising throughout Ireland, he would not have been a moment
in doubt how to choose! but till that unexpected victory he
had been so oppressed by his habitual awe of the might and
majesty of the Queen's government, and so unaware of his
own strength, that he scarcely took a single step in advance
of his customary hesitating insubordination, without at once
pausing, explaining, and excusing himself, and negociating
for a formal reconciliation; the suddenness and completeness
of his success over Bagnal took him by surprise, he had con-
quered Ireland without knowing it: the country, which it
had been the tradition of his ancestors for 400 years to re-

conquer, was won! it was his, if he had but stretched out his hand and taken it! It was lost to the Queen before he had bestowed a thought upon any general scheme for its liberation! it was lost to *him* before it even occurred to him, as a thing possible, that the power of England could have fallen so prostrate before the Kerns and Galloglass of his wild country. Had he taken any course but the one he did, he might have awakened in time to the consciousness of his great fortune; but, with fatal precipitation, he put away from him the possibility of profiting by such a chance as had never been given to any Irishman before him. The possession of Dublin, with the possibility of an encounter with Ormond, with the knowledge that a reinforcement of 2,000 men was on its way to Ireland, and a certainty of eventually bringing the whole power of England upon him, may have seemed a less desirable prize than a lone fort on the edge of the bogs, which protected his own country! With inconceivable infatuation he allowed many of his followers to return to their homes, and contented himself with encamping under the walls of Armagh, and opening negociations with the fugitives within. He offered a safe passage to the force to retire to Dublin, on the simple condition of the surrender of the fort of the Blackwater. The officers of the famishing and terrified rabble demanded permission to refer the matter to the Lords Justices, for to *their* orders alone was it likely Williams would yield the fortress; this also, involving the loss of much time that would have been precious, had not O'Neill rendered all time, and all opportunities alike useless to him henceforth—he accorded, and agreed to leave the fugitives unmolested till the return of their messenger.. How readily such terms were accepted by the craven Council in Dublin, who on the first tidings of the disaster had armed 600 citizens, lured them outside their walls, and at once bricked up all their city gates behind them, and wrote to implore the Victor " to be contented with his victory, and to spare the Queen's soldiers," the reader need scarcely be told. Never was knighthood better merited than by Thomas Williams, the Hero of the Blackwater! for he alone rescued the remnants of the Queen's army, and saved her Irish capital! Within a month, reinforcements of horse and foot had arrived; Ormond had led back his division of the original army to Dublin: and a muster of the royal forces was made, with the result following :—

A Conjectural Estimate of Her Mat⁹ Armye in Ireland
20 Septr. 1598.

In the end of April last the Armye in Ireland was certified to be in heads—

Of English	....	....	....	2,319		
Of Palemen	....	....	....	1,785	6,582	
Meere Irishe	....	....	....	2,478		
In July last there were sent out	....	....	2,000			10,082
which considering the dead pays and the deficiencies may be accounted					1,700	
More sent in August with Sir Samuel Bagnal, accounted 2,000, which in head may be			....	....	1,800	
At this time 100 horse were sent.						

Whereof by estimate there might be lost at the defeat of the Marshall, and Runaway 1,300

And so remain about   8,782

How many of them English, or Irish, is uncertain : if all English, then so many the fewer remaining

Of those, English by estimate	....	5,319	
Pale men, and Meer Irish	....	....	3,263

It is to be remembered that since the certificate sent in, the end of April, many are like to be decayed, which will abate their total.

In April aforesaid there were certified to be of Horse in Bands

viz., Of English	....	....	....	100		
Pale men	....	....	....	292	521	
Mere Irish	....	....	...	129		671
And sent with Sir Samuel Bagnall	....	....	100			
And with Sir Richard Bingham....	....	....	50			

Whereof English, 250.

Although with their confidence in the superiority of the soldiers of their own country much shaken, and with a just terror of the numbers, and valour of their Irish enemies, the Lords Justices derived much consolation from the unexpected recovery of so many of the runaways from Armagh, and from the unaccountable inaction of O'Neill, who was in no respect, save the possession of a fort which he had bought dearly by surrendering to the authorities, in their hour of greatest need, the most valiant captain, and three hundred of the bravest men in Ireland, in a better condition than he was on the day when Bagnal marched out from Armagh to meet him. How bitter were the tidings of this disaster to Elizabeth, and how excited her indignation by the unworthy conduct of the Lords Justices may be perceived from a passage in a despatch from Sir Robert Cecyll. "Her Majesty's sense of dishonour doeth greatly touch her to receive such a blow by so vile a rebel." Her Majesty was greatly touched also by the conduct of her Lords Justices, on whom she

poured all that remained in the royal mind of the anger
which had been so abundantly shed upon the head of O'Neill.
Those pusillanimous functionaries, relieved from the apprehension of seeing "the vile rebel" at the gates of Dublin,
had taken courage to throw the whole blame of the disaster
upon Ormond, who had rejected their counsel, and staked
the safety of the capital, nay the possession of Ireland itself,
upon the success of Bagnal. O'Neill, in the mean time was
slowly acquiring the perception of his own strength, and of
the weakness of the Irish government.

It was not until October—precisely three months too late
—that he manifested any design of extending his views
beyond a provincial revolt, and of rousing the whole Irish
people to an united effort to free themselves from their long
bondage. How ripe the country was for this great effort
may be judged from the effect of his summons on the southern
Septs. His first proceeding was to send a large force, under
Tirell, and John Fitz Gerald, into Munster; and Cecyll was
informed "that the very day they set foot within the Province, Munster, to a man, was in arms before noon."

And now was the great Desmond injustice, which had
sprung from Sir H. Sidney's *fixed principle*, about to bring a
pitiless retribution upon the undertakers who had been the
instruments of the *dissipation* of the inheritance of the Geraldines. When the bonies of O'Neill burst into Munster, they
bore with them the mandate of that "arch rebel" to the
two sons of Sir Thomas of Desmond. It was the will of
O'Neill that James Fitz Thomas the elder brother should immediately assume the title that belonged to him, and swear
to hold it, and the patrimony of the Geraldines, of *him!* but
if he had not the courage to do so, let him live as he had
lived hitherto, despoiled of his birthright, and let his younger
brother, John, if he had the manhood to join in his country's
cause, be at once proclaimed the head of his race. James
Fitz Thomas required no time for deliberation; he assumed
the title which had been snatched from his father by his imperious brother the great rebel, and was at once greeted by
every member and dependent of his race as their chief.

James Fitz Thomas received from his cotemporaries a
designation which would seem to indicate an usurpation by
him of a title, and position to which he had no right, and for
which he was wholly unfitted. Whatever might be his
qualifications for the conduct of a rebellion, and the command of followers and bonies equally unaccustomed to dis-
scipline, there can at least be no doubt as to what his exact

position was by birth. James the 15th Earl of Desmond had
married four wives. The *First* was Joan, daughter of Maurice Lord Fermoy, by whom he had a son *Thomas*. His
second wife was More, Mourny, or Maud, only daughter of
Sir Moelrony Mac Shane O'Carroll, and by her had two sons,
and four daughters. The eldest of these sons was Gerald the
great rebel "Ingens rebellibus Exemplar," and this son it
pleased his father to declare, by will and other settlements,
his heir, thus setting aside his son Thomas by his first wife.
James Fitz Thomas, called the Sougaun Earl, was the son of
this Thomas! He had a brother John, and a sister, married
to Donal Pipi Mac Carthy Reagh. Had this Earldom been
an Irish Chieftainship held under usage of Tanistry, no objection could have been offered to the election of Gerald by
his father, approved as it was by all his followers; but
English Sovereigns, and English lawyers had declared
Tanistry to be "a vile and lewd usage." And it was as essentially a part of the law of England that the eldest legitimate son of a nobleman was as absolutely heir to his father's
rank, as was the Prince of Wales to the crown of England.
As soon as the tidings of the decision of James Fitz Thomas
reached the ears of the Earl of Ormond, that determined
man, though despatching daily to the Queen and the Privy
Council, letters of mingled wrath, shame, and despondency,
wrote a grand letter to him, to which personal respect for
the writer obtained from the young man a temperate, and
modest answer.

THE EARL OF ORMOND *to* JAMES FITZ THOMAS.

" James Fitz Thomas. Hit seemed to us most strange when wee hard
you were combined, and ioyned wth theis Leinster Traytors, lately repayred into Munster, considering how your father Sir Thomas alwaies
contynued a dutifull subject, and did manie good offices to further Her
Mat's service, from wch course if you should degresse, and now ioyn w^th
those unnaturall Traytors, we maie think you very unwise, and that you
bring uppon yoursealf your own confusion wch is thende of all Traytors;
as by daylye experience you have seene: wherefore wee will that you doe
pntly make your repaire unto us, wheresoever you shall hear of our beinge,
to lay down your griefes, and complaints, if you have anie; and if you
stand in anie doubt of yoursealf, theis our l^res shall be for you, and such as
shall accompanie you in your cominge, and retorneng from us, your safe-
tyes; and further, in your drauinge neere the place where wee shalle be,
wee will send safe conduct for you.
                            " THOMAS ORMOND AND OSSERY.
" Geven at the Campe of Cowlin, 8 Oct., 1598.
" Wee need not put you in mind of the late overthrowe of the Earle
your uncle, who was plaged, wth his ptakers by fier, sworde, and famine;

and be assured, if you pceede in anie traiterous actions, you will have the like ende. What Her Mat's forces have done against the King of Spaine, and is hable to doe against anie other enemie, the world hath seene, to Her Highnes immortall fame: by which you maie iudge what she is hable to doe against you, or anie other that shall become traytors.
"To James Fitz Geralde.
Geve theis in Hast."

JAMES FITZ THOMAS *to the* EARL OF ORMOND.

" Rᵗ. Hon: I receaued your Los: lʳᵉˢ wherin yoʳ Lo: dothe specifie that you think it verie straunge that I shoalde ioyn in acon wᵗʰ theis gentⁿ of Leinster. It is soe that I have euer at all times behaved myself dutifullie, and as a true subiect to Her Matie as ever laie in me, and as it is well known to yoʳ Lo: I have showed my willingness in seruice against my uncle, and his adherents, wherebie I haue bin partelie a meane of his distruction. Before my uncle's deseace it maie be remenbered by yor Lo: that I haue bin in England from my Father, cleamienge title to his inherit-ance of the House of Desmonde, wᶜʰ is manifestlie known to be his righte; whereupon Her Matye hath pmissed of her gratious favour to doe me iustice, uppon the deseace of my uncle, who then was in acon, and haue allowed me a marke sterling pʳ diem towards my maintenance, untill Her Matts further pleasure were knowne, of wᶜʰ I neuer receaued but one yeare's paie, and euer since my uncle's deseace I could gett no hearinge concerning my inheritance of the Earldome of Desmond; but haue bestowed the same uppon diuers undertakers, to disinherite me for euer; haueing all this while staied myself, in hope to be gratiouslie delt withall by Her Matie: seeinge no other remedie and that I could gett noe indifferencie, I will followe by all the meanes I can to maintaine my right, trustinge in thAl-mightie to further the same.
" My verie good Lord, I haue seene so manie bad exsamples, in seek-ing of diuerse manie Gents, bluddely false and sinister accusations, cutt off and executed to deathe, that the noblemen and chief gentlěn of this pro-vince cannot thinck themselves assured of their lyves if they were contented to loose their lands and liuings; as for example Redmond Fitz Geralde uppon the false informacon of a scurfey boy for safeguard of his leif, was putt to death, being a Gentⁿ of good callinge, being 3 score years of age, and innocent of the crime chardged wᵗʰall. Donogh Mᶜ Craghe alsoe was executed uppon the false informacon of a villainous Kerne, who wᵗʰin a sevennight was putt to death, wᵗʰin your Loᵖˢ Libertie at Clonmell, who tooke uppon his salvacon all that he said against the said Donogh was un-true, that he was subborned by others. Of late a poore cosen of ours, James Fitz Morrys of Mochollopa is soe abbominablie dealt wᵗʰall, uppon the false informacon of an Englisheman, accusinge him of murder, who neuer drewe sworde in anger all the daies of his leife, and is manifestlie knowne that he neuer gave cause to be suspected of the like: Pierce Lacie, who was an earnest servitor, and had the killinge of Rory Mᶜ Mor-rogho, and the apprehension of Morrogho Oge, till he left him in the Geoale of Limerick, and after all his services, was driuen, for the sauegarde of his leif, to be a fugitive. To be briefe wᵗʰ yo: Lo: Englishemen were not contented to haue our landes and liuings, but unmercifullie to seeke our leives by false, and sinister meanes, under cullor of Lawe; and as for my pte, I will prevent it the best I maie.
"Committinge yo: Lo: to God, I am yo. Lo.'s Loveinge Cosen,
"Ja: DESMONDE.

" From the Camp at Carrigrone, 12 October, 1598."
" To the Right Hono : my verie good Lo: and Cosen, thEarle of
Ormond and Ossery, Lo. Lieu^t. General of Her Mat's forces wthin the
realme of Ireland, theis to be delieuered."

Whilst Ormond was penning his remonstrance, and his
superb will to the rebel at the head of several thousands of
his followers, he was also writing, not in serene temper, a letter
of complaint to the Queen, in which he described the conduct
of Her Majesty's undertakers, the men on whose support he
should have been able to rely; for to enrich *them* all this
trouble had been brought upon the land.

" 1598. *Oct*^{r}. 12. *The* EARL OF ORMOND *to the* QUEEN.

" At my coming to this province (Munster) I found that all the undertakers, three or four excepted, under your Highness correction, had most
shamefullye, forsaken all their Castells, and dwelling plases, before anie
rebell cam in sight of them, and left their Castells with their municons,
stuff, and cattell to the traytors, and no maner of resistance made, &c."

A piteous cry from the Chief Justice of Munster was the
first announcement to the English Government of the rush-
ing of the Northern rebels into his province, the unwelcome
apparition in arms of the injured Desmond, and the first consequences to the loyal men who had been dwelling till then
in tranquillity on the lands forfeited by the attainted usurper.
What details of the proceedings of James Fitz Thomas
escaped the knowledge of the Chief Justice, were supplied
by a letter from William Weever, to whom we are indebted
for sufficient of the manifesto of the northern chieftain to
account for the promptitude of the Munster movement.
" O'Neale," he wrote, " would haue euerie man established in
his owne lande, as it was before the English Governmente."
We must presume that the meaning of the writer was before
the English Government of Queen Elizabeth ! not that of
Hen. II., otherwise James Fitz Thomas and his Earldom
would have fared no better than did the Lo : Barry, whose
peculiar ill-fortune the reader will presently learn. Had the
writer added that O'Neill would have every man at liberty to
resume the *religion*, as well as the *lands* of his forefathers, he
would have put on record the entire motive which induced
every mere Irishman to take a share in that great struggle.

" 1598. *Oct*^{r}. 26.

" In lamentable wise advertiseth yor Hon^{rs} Los: humble orato^r Willm̃
Saxey Chief Justice of Mounster in Yrland, of the most barbarous, and

N

fearfull rebellion now raginge in the said province: About the vth of this pnt moneth of October there came into the said province, by Arlough, and so into the com̃ of Lymerick, about 3000 rebells, sent from the arch Trait^r, Tirone, under the leading of John Fitzthom^s, second sonne to Sir Thom^s of Desmond Knight deceassed, elder brother tothe last attainted Earle of Dessmond, and of one Tirrell, as is reported; and psently upon their coming into the said province, the said John was proclaimed Earle of Dessmond; who (as is said) toke yt upon him, yf his elder brother James wold not ioyne wth them, and assent tobe proclaymed Earle him self. This donne this rebellious rowte entred further into the said com̃ of Lymerick, and have burnt and spoiled the most part of the countrey townes, and villages, wthin that county. On Saturday morning the vij of this psent James Fitz Thomas of Dessmond, elder sonne of the said S^r. Thom^s came tothe traitors with 16 horse and 20 foote; and the ppose of the traitors then was to create him Earle of Dessmond at the hill of Ballioghly; about wch time the Vice President had assembled the forces of the province, wth full ppose to encounter wth the traitors, finding the said forces so assembled, to be in shewe able to equall the strength of the enemy; but, albeit, divers of the noblemen and chief gent^n of the province weare then and there ready (as yt seemed) to assist and accompany the governo^r in this conflict to be taken in hand, yet at the very instant the most part of the folowers of the said noblemen, and gent^n. went to the enemy, &c."

" 1598.   Octob^r.   WILLIAM WEEVER to SIR R. CECYLL.

" The same daie, the 8th Oct^r, in the eveninge there came to Ballingarrie, out of Rannallaghe, Cahir Mc Hughe, brother to the late Feagh Mc Hughe, Thomas Butler, and others, with some 160 men, and encamped there, wheare the rebells expected the cominge of James Fitz Thomas Desmond, to whome they had formerlie sent, that yf he woulde not come and take the title of Earle of Desmond, and houlde of O'Neale (for so they tearme the Earle of Teirone) that then they woulde create his youngest brother Earle: whereuppon, the 10th of October he came to them accompanied with some 20 horsemen, the rebells beinge then unitinge their forces betwixt Rathkeale, and Ballingarrie, and accepted to houlde the Earledome of Desmond, because O'Neale woulde have eurie man established in his owne lande as it was before the Englishe Government.

" W. WEEVER."

Sir Thomas Norreys had reported truly the state of his province; it now remained for him to narrate the fulfilment of his predictions. The greater chiefs had learned cunning, if not wisdom; they remained faithful in their professions of loyalty, were earnest in expressions of sympathy with the Vice-President, afforded him the comfort of their patronage, for they attended him personally in Cork; but the times were evil! they would brave the menaces of O'Neill, withhold all encouragement from the new Earl of Desmond; but their brothers, cousins, sons, and followers had forgotten their allegiance to their chiefs, as well as to their sovereign; their power was gone, their country open.

Foremost amongst the Irish to break from an ungenial idleness was, as might be expected, Donal—self-styled

MacCarth Mor. We have seen that to pacify him Her Majesty had ygraciously consented to allow him to inherit the lands left him by his father, notwithstanding that certain ploughlands were designated in the Earl's will by so fanciful a spelling that the discovery of them upon the face of the earth was at the last, rather matter of conjecture than of certainty; and but for this clash of arms which roused his martial nature, he might have roamed through a spacious, and the most picturesque, domain in Ireland, where no vestige of civilized life, no English footprint could anger him; but with the revival of the Earldom of Desmond, Donal, as we have related, startled his countrymen with the ominous sound of a new MacCarthy Mor, and with the aid of his friends the Connaught bonies, and certain loose men who as instinctively sought Donal, as Donal sought strife and bloodshed, he speedily possessed himself of the whole country of his ancestors. With no small sagacity, and a condescending respect for the privileges of his great feudatories, the new chieftain applied to O'Sullevan Mor for the Rod of inauguration; but O'Sullevan was the fast friend of Florence, whose sister he had married; he refused to the bastard that symbol of sovereignty, and Donal had to content himself with the election of O'Neill.

Florence was at this time in England busy with his *suits*, an occupation in which he had spent many years of his life; indeed so familiar was Sir Robert Cecyll with the purport of his visits to the court, that when, at a subsequent period, he desired to entice him away from Ireland, he wrote to Carewe " to allure him to London with the plea of prosecuting some suit." The matter, however, which had been so tediously training, and which had caused so much correspondence, was wonderfully accelerated by the late intelligence from Munster. Whilst the Privy Council was hesitating to trust the professions of Florence, a worse thing had happened; Desmond had acknowledged Donal! and Donal had acknowledged O'Neill. As soon as the tidings of Tirell's entry into Munster reached Sir Robert Cecyll, that Minister signed an order for the payment of £100 to Florence.

The receipt for this sum signed, sealed also by Florence, is preserved: it is the most sunny, contented, and compact piece of his composition extant. This gratuity was evidently intended to enable its accipient to return to Ireland; but the tidings which had quickened the decision of the English Minister had strangely calmed the impatience of Florence to be gone. Up to this period the reader may have taken the word of his enemies for his "great cunning and subtlety." He has appeared rather, as Browne described him, "an importunate suitor," a successful courtier; but we have had no proof of any cunning, or great subtlety. From this moment the circumstances of his position underwent an entire change. The acquisition, not only of the immense estates of his father-in-law, but the rights, chiefries, and preeminence of the head of his race, required and developed a diplomatic address, coolness, and wariness equal to that of Cecyll himself. He had urged his suit for permission to return to Ireland, with as much earnestness as if every hour's absence from Munster were an aggravation of the wrongs he had endured, and of which he had complained so often that it would seem even the Lords of the Privy Council had come to view his restraint as a cruelty; he knew that his reckless relative Donal had possessed himself of Desmond, and that only the consent of O'Sullivan, and a few more of his friends was needed to make him, in the estimation of the country, legitimately their Lord, and to place beyond his own reach, as long as the rebellion should last, all chance of the recovery of the lands which he had been so long in pursuit of; yet he made no sign of leaving London. The question of his succession to the estates of his father-in-law had not yet been decided; he was still nominally a prisoner, and it required less sagacity than was possessed both by him and Cecyll, to perceive that the terms which would have been gladly accepted a few months earlier, were no longer commensurate with the service now within his power to perform. In reply to the permission offered him to return to Ireland he answered that he had no wish to mingle in the strife raging there, nor any desire again to incur the suspicions of Her Majesty, for that ruined as he was by his long restraint, he had no power to serve her. This display of reluctance to quit England, if not very genuine, must have been a piece of skilful acting; for he was able in later life to appeal to Cecyll himself, and to Sir John Stanhope, a mutual friend, whether he had not declared his unwillingness to meddle at this time in Irish troubles, and whether he had not been overruled by them.

Letters gloomier than any that had ever come from Ireland since the conquest poured daily into the office of the Secretary, and *sour answers* went back to the complaining correspondents. To Sir Henry Wallop, Cecyll wrote that "he must pardon those who were public ministers if they wrote sourly, being daily partakers of Her Majesty's dislike of all things that belong to Ireland, and he could not blame her." But not the less did the Lords Justices write, that "the rebellion had grown into an Irish war," that the rebels pretended to shake off all English Government; that the Irish aspired to their ancient liberty and nobility! that no doubt the Lord Ormond did his best, but the sores of Ireland had festered above all the remedies he had applied."

Sir Thomas Norreys declared that "disobedience had spread from the rural districts to the walled cities and post towns; that the gentlemen who had promised the most had fallen from their allegiance; that Condon, the White Knight and McDonogh were out with the rebels; that 200 of Ormond's soldiers had deserted to the enemy, who were an insufferable, disdainful, insolent people." Nor could Ormond infuse one word of comfort into this melancholy correspondence: "The rebellion," he said, "was most violent, universal, and dangerous! the Queen was leaving him without the means to repress it; his poor soldiers were in that bitter time (fast adopting the Irish war-dress) they were *without hose or shoes.*"

It was in vain for Cecyll to turn from letter to letter of his numerous correspondents, whether the despatches were from Dublin or from Cork, the tone was the same: Fenton, from the former city, wrote that "the fortune of the time had made the rebels all soldiers." Nicholas Walshe, from the latter, "that there was no county in Munster but was impassable for any faithful subject, especially for all who wore hose or breeches, after the English manner." Wallop grew from day to day even more desponding, "unless," he wrote, "Her Majesty shall royally undertake the prosecution of the rebels the kingdom will be lost, *there is nothing now left but Dublin and part of Wexford.*" Upon Ormond, with whom lay the heaviest responsibility, and whose complaints were the angriest and most outspoken, Her Majesty turned with much asperity. "The Queen takes it much to heart," the Secretary was desired to write to him, "that with 10,000 men she is in no part able to defend herself."

Serenely the while, amidst all this moil and turmoil, proceeded the deliberations of the law. The undertakers and their signories had been long since scattered to the winds; their mortgages and patents were of an order of things that had passed away, yet the stately movements of the Privy Council permitted no precipitation. The legal functionaries to whom had been referred the many adverse claims upon the estates of the deceased Earl of Clancar, calmly ignored the change that had come over the country respecting which they were so leisurely deliberating. An agreement between Cecyll and Florence at last brought their procrastinations to an abrupt issue, and Sir Nicholas Browne might console himself in that, though legal wisdom had discovered that his patent was worthless, it could not place him in a worse condition than had the less learned conclusion of Donal. On the 16th day of March, 1599, in a solemn assembly of grave counsellors and learned lawyers the claims to the inheritance of the late Earl were considered, and following in the track broadly beaten by Donal and his bonies, these venerable men swept legally before them all the pretensions of Browne to the 32 quarters of the Earl's land, and assigned to him—which Donal had omitted to do —the just repayment of the moneys which he had in times past lent to the Earl. All the rest of that vast inheritance, it was recommended should be bestowed upon Florence and his wife, "in hope of his loyalty and service."

"1599.   March 16.

" The state of the seuerall petitions and clayms by Florence McCarthy and Nicholas Browne, to all the inheritance of the late Erle of Clancare.

The Erle's Patent.—It appeareth the Erle in 7 Reginæ, accepted all his Erledome of Her Masty by lres patents to him and the heires masles of his bodie, and died wthout heire masle, having one daughter and heire maried to the said Florence.

" Browne's Mortgage.—The Erle about x yeares past mortgaged for the some of 1000 markes or thereabouts 32 quarters of his lands to Nicholas Browne and his heires, and because that mortgage was not good longer then the Erle had heirs masles, the Queen's Maty in favour granted lres patents to the said Browne of those 32 quarters at cxx li annuall rente or thereabouts, to beginne after the death of the Erle wthout heires of his bodie, where it should have bene wthout heirs *masles* by wᶜh imprisions Browne's lres patents are voied, till the Erles daughter shall die wthout heirs of her bodie.

" The Erle died seised of xvi quarters of land more (besids his said lands mortgaged) and likewise of the Signories, rents, and duties, belonging to his Earldom, all wᶜh are reverted to Her Maty, and in her disposition, as the Lls do conceave by·relation of the Mʳ of the Rolles, and Her Mat's Solicitor in Ireland, albeit Florence shewed forth a deed of entaile of all the Erledom, in the tyme of Queene Marie, wch deed having slept so long, and for some respects is not of credit in their Lps opinion.

" Florence and his wyf to have the lands in fee farme.

" So as all the Erle's lands being now in Her Mats disposition, their Lo:^s thinke convenient for Her Mats service, in hope of Florence, his loyaltie, and service, being best hable to recover those lands out of the rebells hands, to moove Her Mty to grant all the 32 quarters wch Browne held; and th other xvj whereof the Erle died siesed, to Florence, and his wyfe, and his heires, being doughter and sole heire to the late Erle for £cxx li per annum, because the rent wch Browne paid is conceaved to be somewhat at too high a rate, for those barren lands, in so remote a place.

" Browne to have assurance for his mortgage.

" And for Browne's satisfaction of his mortgage money, that Florence do make an estate presentlie upon the ensealing of his lres patents, to Browne and his heires, of the said 32 quarters formerelie mortgaged to him, paying Her Maty the Queen's rent, ratably till the mortgage shall be satisfied, as Browne's counsell learned shall devise.

" The Erle's cheefreis to be reserved to Her Maty.

" And touching the Erle's Signories, Rents, and superiorities, these to be reserved to the Queen's Maty's disposition, and to be collected by some officer to be appointed, till Her Maty shall otherwise dispose of them.

" This cause was hard at the Court the xvjth day of March, 1598 before.

" Lo : Lieutenant.
" Lo : Chamberlain.
" Lo : Buckhurst.
" Mr. Secretary.

" Anth. Sentleger.
" Roger Wilbraham."

It would seem that now Florence was not only free to return to Ireland, but that further loitering in London would manifest an unwillingness to perform the conditions on which this concession had been made to him. Raised by the Queen's great grace from penury and captivity to freedom, and the prospect of a princely estate, it would appear difficult to imagine that there remained anything which, in reason, he could further desire, yet he moved not! Ostensibly he was still scrupulous lest the resources granted to him might not be adequate to the performance of the great services expected from him. What, in truth he wanted was what he could scarcely venture to state in explicit terms, for he knew that by express design, and at the particular command of the Queen, it had been withheld in the patent preparing for him. This was " the possession of the rights and chiefries in as ample manner as his predecessor had enjoyed them." The Queen knew nothing of the details of these chiefries; to her they were of importance only as they affected the dignity of her royal prerogative; Florence knew that the reverence and authority of the chieftainship depended mainly on them, hence his delay about the Court, and the circuitous phrases of his petitions. There was something more which he coveted as much, and which the Queen as purposely withheld, as these rights and chiefries, but this he did not at present dare, in any terms however insinuating, to ask for—the title of MacCarthy Mor. For two months longer he continued to employ himself in the composition of letters and petitions for which he had a singular facility, and of which he never wearied.

" 1599. *March* 16.   *The humble Peticon of* FLORENCE MACARTHY.

" Maye yt please yoᴿ Honᵒʳ I cannot imagine howe I maie ever (by that course wᶜʰ I perceived latelie by yoʳ Honor and the rest) either paie so much rent as is spoken of, or reduce the countrey people to conformitie, because they will streight, uppon knowledge of that rent, judge that neither I, nor themselves, shall never be able to live thereby; wᶜʰ will move them to mainteyne myne enemies the rebells stronger in the countrey then my selfe; this rent of vi score li a yeare, being but promist by Sʳ Valentine, and never paide; no Irishman being ever heretofore taxed, nor none there would take any land att that rate; the undertakers (whoe for want of experience or knowledge of that countrey promist it) being never able to paie yt; but because yoʳ Honor shall not think me desirous either to hinder Her Maty's proffitt, or to refuse yoʳ Honor's offer, I shalbe contented to take every quarter thereof either as yt was surveyed, and valued by an office of inquirie before Sir Thomas Norreys, and the counsell there, and certified by hym, and the Queene's Attorney hither, or as Her Matie graunted vij quarters thereof tothe Earle's bastard; or yf this will not suffice, lett the Solicitor of Ireland that sawe those lands, consider of Sir Thomas 'Norreys' Surrey; what *he* thinkes I maye paie out of every quarter over and above the same, I will paie yt; and where I have heretofore made mention unto your Honor of a little provision of meale, butter, and flesh, due unto my father in law, of certeine Scepts of his followers, within that countrey, I humblie beseech yoʳ honʳ, att the reporting of my cause to Her Matye, as well to remember the same, as to consider that all the countrey whereunto I goe, are out in action, and able to make above xii hundred men in armes; that all the meanes lyving or abilitye that I had is consumed in 12 yeares imprisonmt, and sute, and all myne owne father's countrey spoyled through my staie here; whereby althoug I can gett men to recover my countrey, and to doe Her Matie service, yet I am not able discharge my self herehence, whereby I shalbe hardlie able to doe my self much good, or Her Matie that service that I purpose, except yor Hon^r be a meane that I maye have a *convenient charge*, and be well furnished, and enabled by Her Highness, for the wh^{ch} yor. sup^t. will ever praye for yor Hon^r, &c.

"fflor. M^{c}CARTHY.

A *convenient charge* meant a commission in Her Majesty's army, suitable in pay, clothing, appointments, arms and rank to the number of men he should bring to serve Her Majesty. In his extreme youth, when barely fifteen years of age, and when commanding his own followers—four men to every man of the Queen's placed under him—he held Her Majesty's commission, with the rank of Captain ; and when at a later period he was again pleading for a convenient charge, he stated plainly that the rank of a Captain would not suffice.

"1599. *April.   The humble Petiĉon of* FLORENCE MCCARTHY

"Yo^r suppl^t Florence McCarthy humblye beseecheth yor Hon^r to be a mean that Her Matie may consider the number of armed rebells that hath taken the possession of his countrey, through his long stay here; that all his meanes and liuinge is consumed in tuelf yeres imprisomēt and suites, whereby he is unable to erect, arme or furnish his people, or to horss any of them wthout Her Mats help; his brother, cousens and people, being kild, taken, and spoyled of their goods, for want of weapon and furniture; and the recovering of his countrey, wch is the strength, bak, and fastnes of the rebels of Monster, being the necessariest that can be don for Her Mats service there; besids that himself hath lived here this half yere wth-out exhibiĉon (an allowance of £3 p^r. week which the Queen had for a con-siderable time allowed him for his maintenance) wch brought him greatly indebted; and that it will please yor Hon^r also to be ameā that som men-ĉon may be made in Her Ma^{ts} letter to the Lo Liftenānt of iij quarters of those lands that stands in the cõm of Cork, and of those litle duties or pro-vision due unto his father in law within his countrey, siguifieing onely in the sayd letter that Her Ma^{ts} pleasure is that his Lo^p (uppon knowledge, and informaĉon of the qualitie therof), may yf he think it good, grant the same; and that where yor sup^{lt} hath (to enhable him to recoũ his countrey) sued for a charge, that Her Highnes hath referred unto his Lo^p to grant him what charge he thinkes fit for him, and beneficiall for Her Ma^{ts} ser-vice, and yor sup^t, as he is boñd shall ever pray for yor Hon^r, &c.

It might seem to the reader, from the frequency of Florence's visits to Ireland, and his voluntary returns to England in pursuance of his interests at the Court, as well as from the letters furnished to him from time to time by Sir Robert Cecyll, suggesting to the Lord Deputy, or the Lord General, to employ him in the Queen's service, and by the Vice-President of Munster in testimony of his loyal con-duct, and excellent intentions, that he could scarcely be considered a prisoner any time during the last eight years. Florence spent 1 year 11 months and 9 days actually shut up within the Tower of London, and some part of the time " *Close* Prisoner," without the power of seeing any one belonging to him. He was then let out, as the reader has seen, on the security, and under heavy bail of his friends : then began his petitions to be allowed to return to Ireland. In August, 1593, this favour was conceded to him, and with it the gift of the famous fine of the Lord Barry; given, as Her Majesty was pleased to say, " because she had a disposition to relieve Mr. Florence McCarthy, who had deserved to have some gracious consideration to be had of him." But notwithstanding his deserts, he continued to train his chain from England to Ireland, backwards and forwards, year by year, each one duly and mournfully calendered. "My troble these five years past," these 6, 10, 11, and now "these 12 years of imprisonment," his country "invaded or lying waste the while, and all his means of living consumed." How real this captivity was, and how grievous, we shall later have an opportunity of judging from his own expressions to Carewe.

The reader unaccustomed to the perusal of State papers of the period of Elizabeth may have noticed a discrepancy between the dates of various documents, and the events recorded in them: he may have noticed, for example, that whereas Florence was not taken prisoner in Cork till January, 1589, a charge was made by Sir Owen Hopton, the Lieutenant of the Tower, for diet, &c., from the 10th of February, 1588 ! This seeming discordance proceeded, not from error, but from the difference between the mode of computing the historical, and the civil, or legal year. The former commenced as at present, on the first of January, whilst the latter did not begin till the 25th of March ! all letters written between the first of January and the 25th of March continued to bear the date of the year past. In the above letter Florence represents the entire period of his imprisonment as twelve years; it was in fact but ten, of which for two years he was actually incarcerated in the Tower, but by dating it from 1588, instead of 1589, as Sir Owen Hopton had done, it becomes eleven; and, as he had been apprehended in January, and was not liberated till April, he was advanced three months into a new year, the twelfth !

" 1599. *April* 20.   *To the Right Hono'able his most approved frend* S^r.
ROBART CECILL, *Knight, Principall Secretary to the Queenes most Excellent Matie, and one of her Highnes most hono'able Priuie Councell, &c.*

" It may please your Hon^r I am very sory that I was driven to troble
yor Hon^r so often, considering yor owne desire to help me; neyther do I
now troble yor Hon^r wth intent to stay, or sue any more, for I will away
pntly as yor hon^r shall think good, wth any thing that yor Hon^r can obtaine
for me. At my last being wth yor Honor, I told you how doutfull I was
of my wife's resignaĉon; for she is so froward, and foolish, as she will
streight think that it is a device of myne to make away her Inheritance,
as I did myn owne, in all my trobles past; w^{c}h yf she had consented to do
(as I protest I am sure she will not) I cannott imagine how to bring her;
and I know my Lo will not stay at Dublin untill she com; neyther can a
Fine be leauied bnt there; whereunto Sir Robart Gardner, and those of
the councell that are learned (unto whom the Earle of Essex will put it
over) will look so narrowly, as I am sure I shall not get a Pattent if therebe
any menĉon of a Fine, or any thing of my wifes; And yf Her Matie shold
write in generall termes to the Lo Liftenãant, to take order wth me that
Her Highnes be not further trobled wth any claime, or chaleng, for those
lands, I know it will hinder it, yf his Lo^p do not take myne owne assurance,
or som reasonable course that lies in me to do; Also it is menĉoned that
all the Earle's Rents and cheferies shalbe reserved for Her Majestie, and
yf Her Highnes have his rents and cheferies that he had out of those
lands that is granted me, it cannott be woorth me nothing; therefore it is
necessary to specifie there that all the sayd Earl's rents and cheferies may
be reserved for Her Highnes but such as is due out of those lands, or
countrey of Desmond, that is granted me; out of the which I must pay
about vi score £ a yere, as Browne was to pay. The consideraĉon wherof
I referr unto yor Hon^r whom I beseech God long to continue, and prosper.
" I humblie take leaue this xxth day of April 1599.
" Yo^r Hon^{rs} most humble and thankful,
" fflor: M^{c}CARTHY."

No wonder that Florence was troubled by the sound of
the word Fine! or that he expected his foolish froward wife
to be alarmed when she should recollect the history of the
only fine with which she had any acquaintance, that, namely,
which Her Majesty, of "*her gracious consideration,*" had
bestowed upon her husband; in pursuit of which he had
already spent its precise nominal value, and £500 over its
real worth. Florence might understand, as no doubt he did,
that this fine might be a mere acknowledgment to the Queen
of his receiving his succession from her, and not from any
right accruing from sept election, or as a tribute from his
generosity—more or less voluntary—in reciprocation of Her
Majesty's handsome order upon the exchequer of the Lo:
Barry; or, possibly, like the memorable fine itself, a security
for his good behaviour; but it is not surprising that he
should expect his wife to be obstinately deaf to all explanation . of the matter, and foolishly resist every attempt to
make her estates chargeable with expenses connected with

any future fine, whether to be paid to the Queen, or to be recovered, should Her Majesty be pleased to bestow any more such gifts upon Florence.

Cecyll freed himself from further importunity upon this point by referring it to the decision of the Earl of Essex, recently appointed Lord Lieutenant of Ireland, who had been a strenuous adviser of the sending of Florence into Ireland, and had even declared his intention of "giving him some charge" in the Queen's service.

In these letters of Florence to Cecyll, written on the eve of his departure for Ireland, we find no mention of a subject out of which arose the first and loudest of the charges made against him on his landing in Munster. Nothing is said in them of any permission, sought or ceded, for his *holding inter-course with rebels!* To do so, without warrant, was high treason! and yet we shall perceive that the earliest of his proceedings, when he landed in Ireland, was to repair to the camp of the Earl of Desmond, and to treat with him, and with the other chiefs in arms, for the recovery of his country. He did this *with the authority in writing of the Commissioners in Munster;* and, without loss of time, wrote to Cecyll a detailed account of his doing so, and of his curious entertainment in the rebel camp. Later he repaired to the camp of O'Neill himself for the same purpose (amongst others); this, indeed, he did not think it necessary to report at the time, either to the Commissioners or to the Minister; but eventually, when he had to give a rigid account of all his conduct when in Ireland, and when this was well known to Cecyll, and also to the President of Munster, neither made it a charge against him; but Cecyll in a letter to Carewe, and Carewe in a despatch to the Lords of the Council in Dublin, declared that "he had brought all his actions—treasons rather—within the limit of his pardons;" hence we are led to conclude that the necessity of his parting with rebels was foreseen, and admitted as a self-evident requirement, to be settled, as in fact it was settled, by Florence with the authorities in Munster. It must have been as evident to Sir Robert Cecyll as to himself, that, as he was to go into a country actually in rebellion, and as his hopes of recovering Desmond depended wholly on the good will of the inhabitants, he could not effect anything without direct communication with men, with whom, without the Queen's warrant, it would be treason to treat or parley.

But whilst Florence had been still petitioning, the lawyers still consulting, and Cecyll still wavering between trust and distrust of the petitioner, the "inheritance of the late Earl," and the inheritance of Her Majesty, had alike slipped, for the time, through the hands of all these undecided personages. The days were gone by when the Queen's soldiers could hunt Donal through the mountains and glens of Desmond. Within a brief year, fortune had reversed all things. Donal was now "a great Lord in Desmond;" and was become the huntsman in his turn, and his horsemen were far more numerous than the companies formerly allotted for the defence of the Under-takers. To such purpose did he and others hunt down "the poor people," who had been enticed into that wild country, that we are informed no fewer than 1,800 fled to Waterford, and were so fortunate as to find their way back to their English homes.

Although the reputation of Donal might not unreasonably claim some space for its development in this biography of his relative, and the Munster campaign, of which he was a distin-guished leader, some room for its details, we must reluctantly leave this portion of our history in the obscurity in which both English and Irish writers have left it; but not before bestowing a few words upon his two great achievements, "The Assault of the Castle of Molahiff," and "The Fight of the Gap of Feathers."

Though not an English yeoman was to be seen in the fields of Desmond, and though all the Undertakers, according to the angry testimony of the Earl of Ormond, "did, with two or three exceptions, most shamefully abandon their dwellings and castles before any rebel came in sight of them," there was at least one stronghold, and one Under-taker, who deserved not that reproach—Nicholas Browne spurned the thought of surrendering his castle. He relin-quished certainly the temptation of affording to its defence the advantage of his personal presence—and of all the inci-dents of his chequered life, this was for him the most fortu-nate!—but his orders to his lieutenant were to defend it to the uttermost.

ASSAULT OF THE CASTLE OF MOLAHIFF.

By a manifest grace of fortune, the assault of the castle of Molahiff has been related for posterity in the language of Livy, by Philip O'Sullevan Beare :—

"As many English," says that historian, "as resided within the countries of those who had taken up arms against the Queen were despoiled of their property, and driven away. Some castles belonging to these men were taken by assault;

they were little worthy of notice, with the exception of the Molathibian Fortress (Molathibh) which was defended by thirty royalist soldiers, placed there by Nicholas Browne. Three hundred foot, led by William Burke, Thomas Fitz-Gerald, called Juvenis (*i.e.*, Thomas Oge FitzGerald), and some horse of the MacCarthys, who dwelt on the river Mang, were sent to assail this stronghold." Then follow all the fierce details of the assault. Tempests of shot swept over windows and battlements, so that no defenders could stand against them ; but from loophole and cranny, cleft and chink, shot hailed back with more fatal effect upon the assailants. It is related that so wonderful was the aim of one of the soldiers (tam mire collineabat), that with his leaden bullets—plumbeis' glandibus—he killed or wounded sixteen of the assailants ! From this deadly aim the attacking party shrunk ; engines called sows were moved up against the building, under shelter of which the wall was breeched; but the assailants were met as they entered, and a furious fight raged amidst the ruins. The defenders turned to retreat, and their foe followed, but it was to meet death from flagstones and torn-up floors—pavimentum et tabula diruta—which were hurled down upon their heads ; the survivors fell back to give place to the crashing ruin, they were pushed again forward by fresh multitudes, and then, with a fierce rush of over-whelming numbers, the defenders were overpowered, the castle taken, and its defenders slaughtered. Customary Euthanasia of the minor heroes of these Irish wars ! Thus fell the citadel of this English Signory ! thus perished thirty brave soldiers ! The story of the chase of Donal through the woods, rocks, bogs, mountains and glens of Desmond reads pleasantly in the State papers of England ; it may entertain the reader now, as it may have entertained Lord Burghley three centuries ago ! Alas ! that this sprightly narrative should not have been left as those letters left it ! that it should have come into the mind of O'Sullevan Beare to relate so circumstantially its wholly unamusing sequel ! Alas for the barbarity of the unchristian, spiteful people amongst whom the lot of so many enterprising English gentlemen had cast them ! Thirty lives of loyal soldiers, civilizing, well-to-do, jolly English yeomen taken for a few loose kerns, a few savages left upon the trees along the track of the Queen's horsemen, by the shores of Logh Lene !

Amidst the ruins of the fallen fortress of Molahiff arose a sudden and angry contest for the title of MacCarthy Mor ; for " Dermot, of the MacCarthys of Alla (the Darby of Sir

William Norreys), a competitor for the chieftainship, deeming
that there was no one living more worthy than himself of the
pre-eminence and name of MacCarthy Mor; strove, with his
hired Connaught men and his own friends, to secure that
dignity. But Daniel the Bastard, encompassed by a multitude of his friends, and of followers whom he also had hired
out of Connaught, disputed the prize with Dermot ; asserting
that the pre-eminence and name (partis ! patris ?) of his
father belonged of right to him, and to no other." But a competitor more fatal to the ambition of Donal than the powerful
chieftain of Dowalla, was awaiting but the removal of some
final scruples from the mind of the English Minister, to enter
upon the troubled scene of these Irish rivalries, and this last
act of Donal quickened his arrival. In the midst of the deliberations of Sir Robert Cecyll, relative to the policy of
sending Florence back to Ireland, was placed in his hands a
despatch from the Vice-President of Munster. It was fortunate for Florence that he was at hand to declare to the
Minister that he was better pleased to remain in England,
than to go on so perilous a service, under suspicions so
hastily conceived, and so readily entertained.

1599. *March* 26. SIR THOMAS NORREYS *to the* PRIVY COUNCIL.

"It may please yor Hoñ : Lds. since my last written in Ross I contynued in that countrey untill the xvj of this present, *but cold not heare
any confirmation of the arryval of the Spaniards*, mentioned in a lre, the
copie whereof I then sent. I compelled those traytors that invaded that
countrey to withdrawe themselves from thence, and have taken pledges
and assuraunce of all the Gent: and inhabitants, saving O'Donouan Fininen
M[c] Ouen, M[c] Charty, and Dermot Moyle M[c] Chartye, Mr. Florence
M[c] Charties brother, who before my cominge had given their pledges and
oths to those traytors, and therefore refused to come at me ; whereupon I
caused their castles, and *howses to be taken and razed*, and their people and
landes to be spoyled, and have taken order that M[c]Chartye and the rest of
· that countrey shall menteyne of their owne people, at their owne chardges,
300 men contynually in armes, wth w[c]h, and wth such assistaunce as upon
any extraordinary occasion I shall give them I hope they wilbe hable to
defend themselves, and annoyc the traytors. It is there spoken *that this
Dermod Moyle doeth nothinge without his Brother Florence's his counsell;* but
I cold not get any pticuler prooffe thereof, nevertheles (under fav[r]), I
thinke yt very convenient that he remayne there.

This was the last warning respecting Florence which Sir
Robert Cecyll was destined to receive—and to neglect ! The
insult offered to royal authority by the assumption of Donal,
which had been immensely aggravated by its ratification by
O'Neill, put an end at once to all further irresolution in the
mind of the Queen with respect to the late Earl's inheritance.

At a Cabinet Council, attended by the Earl of Essex, the
newly appointed Lord-Lieutenant of Ireland, Sir Robert
Cecyll, the Solicitor, and the Master of the Rolls, a final
deliberation took place on the state of Munster, and the
expediency of sending Florence to attempt its pacification.
Few arguments were needed to convince these statesmen
that unless *something* were done speedily, the whole Province
would be lost to the Queen; that no chieftain could possibly
be worse than Donal; and that no man, except Florence,
could put forward any hopeful claim to the chieftainship and
country of MacCarthy Mor, or expel the bold rebel who had
usurped both.   Whatever misgivings may have been excited
by the last despatch of Sir Thomas Norreys, as to the loyalty
of Florence, it was resolved to act towards him as if unlimited trust were reposed in his professions, and to send
him to Ireland supported by the Queen's authority.   At the
date of this decision, and not earlier, terminated Florence's
imprisonment!   In the month of April, in the 12th year of
his captivity, he was liberated, as he had been arrested, by
the Queen's sole order, and without the interference of law,
or the formality of a trial.

   Sir Robert Cecyl has received from posterity the reputation of a sagacious, and prudent statesman; he is supposed
to have possessed in an eminent degree that quality which, in
Florence, was designated by so many names—subtlety, cunning, hypocricy, prudence, wisdom; but it has escaped the
notice of his admirers that, in combination with this quality
of the serpent, he possessed a credulity exceeding that of
Eve: and a simplicity worthy of early childhood.   With a
full knowledge of all the accusations made against Florence,
from the earliest warnings of St. Leger to the most recent
by the Bishop of Ardfert, and Fenton; with a perfect consciousness of all the injustice, and cruelty, committed against
him—eleven years of imprisonment and exile, without trial,
for his marriage! the open endeavour to prevent his succession to the chieftaincy of Carbery, his birthright! the permitted invasion of his private estates by any unprincipled
relative or neighbour who might consider them as intended
by the Queen for open scramble! and now, lastly, the with-
holding of his wife's patrimony, as if he had been engaged
in as flagrant rebellion as the great Earl of Desmond himself,
and thus enabling the bastard to usurp that supremacy of
his sept which the gentlemen of Desmond had destined for
him!   With all this present to his mind, and with full knowledge of the abilities, the ambition, and the subtlety of Flo-

rence, Sir Robert Cecyll, when at the end of his expedients, had sent for this man of evil repute, and made with him a bargain which affords pleasing proof that a generous reliance on the integrity of his fellow-creatures was the basis of the policy of this estimable statesman. Unfortunately this quality has been considered by distrustful men an amiable *weakness!* Florence has been judged to have abused the confidence placed in him, and no sooner to have set foot in Ireland than to have plunged at once into treason!

For nearly 300 years the vapouring, and loose charges scattered through the pages of the Pacata Hibernia have been received as true history; and the character drawn by Carewe of Florence has met with no contradiction: happily Carewe wrote many things not printed in that famous volume! and what has not been printed hitherto will serve better than what has, to enable us to judge between Florence, Cecyll, and Carewe. It is important on entering upon the political life of Florence, to state with the utmost distinctness the conditions upon which he was sent back into his native country ; the services which he undertook to render; and the means by which he was to effect them. The first charges that we shall find made against Florence by his enemies were that "he had filled his country with Bonaghts!" and that "he had parled with rebels!" They omit to add that he had warrant for doing both! nay, that the very nature of the service on which he was sent required that he should do so! Cecyll was not ignorant of the state of Munster! He knew that the Earl of Desmond, Tyrell, Dermod O'Connor, Burke, Pierce Lacy, and other minor chieftains, each with several hundreds of hired soldiers, occupied the province; that Donal, with O'Neill's authority, and with many of O'Neill's forces, kept the gentlemen of Desmond in subjection, and that to send Florence amongst them to recover his country, without permission to raise an armed force to expel them, or to secure it when recovered, would have been purely childish. As the reader has seen, and will again see, Florence repeatedly wróte to Sir Robert Cecyll stating that "he could at all times raise any number of *men!* That followers were plenty; weapon and munition alone, scarce." Cecyll himself had written on one occasion a recommendation to the Lord Deputy to make use of Florence's services, as "he understood from him that he could raise some hundreds of men if required!" In fact it was the knowledge that Florence *would* "fill his country with Bonaghts," and with them expel the Bastard from Desmond, that was

O

one principal cause of his sending him to Ireland! *A second* was the knowledge that "he *would* parle with rebels" and thus rid Munster of Donal, and the Geraldines! Cecyll knew that the gentlemen of Desmond desired Florence for their chief; that O'Sullevan Mor was reserving the white rod of Investiture for him; that his authority could withdraw every clansman from rebellion; and that it was mainly on his relationship, and influence, with the Fitz Geralds that his power to serve the Queen depended! To turn these advantages to account it would require *free* and *frequent intercourse* with men in rebellion. To parle, without licence, with rebels, was judged treasonable; but to hold such intercourse, with the knowledge, and permission of the Government, was so common that authority to do so usually formed a clause in the commission given by the Lord Deputy to the governors of Provinces, and by them, as occasion required, to officers whom they employed on special service. Upon a previous occasion Florence had written to Sir Robert Cecyll that the Lord Deputy Fitzwilliams had it in contemplation to send him to parle with O'Neill, and O'Donnel, both, at the time, in insurrection! And we shall presently see that the earliest proceedings of Florence, after presenting his letters to the Commissioners, were to repair to the camp of the rebels, and to parle with their assembled chiefs "with the express authority, in writing" of the veteran St. Leger and Sir H. Power! and on his return, to write to Cecyll of his having done so!

Without authority to raise forces, and without permitted intercourse with his relatives, and followers in arms, Florence might as well have remained in England! With such authority it is difficult to imagine what, short of waging war against the Queen, he could do that would expose him to censure! Could Sir Robert Cecyll have devised any plan more promising than the one agreed upon with Florence, it may be fairly doubted whether he would, with the latest warning of the Vice-President before him, have persevered in his intention of sending a person so suspected, into Ireland; but time pressed, and his lengthened deliberation had not resulted in the discovery of any alternative other than that of Florence, or Donal! In this choice of evils it was decided to trust to Florence, and to fate! Without more delay the bargain between the Minister and the man whom he so reluctantly trusted, was concluded; it was then agreed in the first place, that Florence should receive Her Majesty's gracious pardon for all past misdeeds; that is, for the marriage he had contracted eleven or twelve years previously! for his friendship with Stanley! his acquaintance with Jacques, Cullen the fencer, Hurley the student-at-law, and others! for the coming of his house out of Spain! his descent, that is, from Milesius—his relationship to James, Fitz Maurice, the arch Traitor, his mother's brother! his "being to succeed by Tanistry to the Lordship of Carbery! and his being allied, by himself and his wife, unto most of the noblemen of Ireland!" all this was to be forgiven, and he was to repair at once to Ireland, to receive a patent for the country of his late father-in-law; for the present the Earldom was withheld, and the title of "MacCarthy" forbidden! And, that he might be able to expel Donal from Desmond, and induce the Geraldines, and all others to withdraw thence, he was authorized to arm his followers "at his own charges," and to hire Bonaghts. In return Florence undertook to withdraw every member and dependent of his Sept from "the action" and to hold his country in obedience to Her Majesty! This was the sum of his engagement! and it was no slight undertaking! it was certainly what no man but Florence could do, and what no other Irishman would have consented to do!

Let it not, however, be supposed that the writer of these pages acknowledges any disingenuous intention in Florence; and that he smiles at the credulity of the Minister, as if he were *outwitted* in this transaction! or as if, using the Queen's permission to return to Ireland, under promise of recovering the country of Desmond for her, it was his intention to recover it for himself, and not to acknowledge the authority of her Government within it!

Florence recovered his country with troops hired at his own cost, and with the "rising out" of his own followers, and with no aid from the Queen, but her permission to do it, and one barrel of powder, and he held it no otherwise than the late Earl had held it, and as every MacCarthy Mor had held it, from the days of Donal-Mor-ne-Curra! that is, in compliance with the usage of Tanistry, as far as related to the privileges and rights of his gentlemen and freeholders; and, relatively to the Queen, with the same submission—whatever that may have been—as the Earl, and his ancestors had yielded to the various Presidents and Vice-Presidents sent from England into Munster since the Conquest.

Under the very tree of knowledge the serpent slumbered! No trait in the character of Florence was unknown to Cecyll; no action of his life had escaped the keen eyes, and instant reporting of the officials of Munster; and yet *such* were the conditions with which he sent back Florence into Ireland, at a time when every native Irishman was in arms for the expulsion of his rulers. Alas! human nature is frail and inconstant! no man is secure at all times in his wisdom. Even Sir Valentine Browne erred in the matter of his patent, although *his* Signory of Molahiff depended upon it. Nay, Florence himself, with all his reputed subtlety and cunning, *once*, as we shall see, stumbled! *once only*, as far as we know —he trusted his liberty to the word of honour of "an English Gentleman!" as indeed who might not have done? his person to a pledge "solemnly and advisedly given" by the Queen's President, in the Queen's name! Forty years of exile and prison life was the penalty of this mistake! But for this weakness of Florence, the error of Cecyll might have been of more importance.

CHAPTER IX.

It had finally been decided by the Privy Council that Florence should¦ repair to Ireland, there to receive his patent of inheritance, and be appointed to some charge by the Lord-Lieutenant, the Earl of Essex, who was himself on the point of leaving England to take possession of his Government. Towards the end of the month of March, Florence, who was still in London, had the opportunity of witnessing the pageantry of the Earl's departure, the popularity of his person, and of the expedition with which he was sent. From the magnitude of the force which had preceded the Earl, he had been able to judge of the determination of the Queen to subdue his country, and of the zeal with which this determination was supported by the English people. "An army was appointed for him (for Essex)," says Camden, "as great as he could require, and such a one as Ireland had never seen before, to wit, 16,000 foot, and 2,000 horse!" A proclamation was sent before him, declaring that the Irish rebels had so long abused the Queen's clemency and patience, that she was now constrained to make use of her power to bridle and restrain them.

"Towards the end of March, the Earl was accompanied out of London with a gallant train of the flower of the nobility, and followed by the people with joyful acclamations!" but it was remarked, as of evil omen, that it happened to thunder in the clear day, and a violent storm of rain followed soon after; and that in his passing to Ireland, "in sailing over, he was tossed to and fro with a contrary wind." The policy of his government had been debated in the Privy Council, and mainly resolved upon in consequence of his own opinion. "He had twitted former Deputies that the war had been protracted by frequent parleys with the enemy," hence it was decided that "he should pass by all other rebels whatsoever, and bend his whole force against Tir Oen, the arch-rebel." As soon as the Earl reached Dublin, and had taken the sword, his very first proceeding was precisely to reverse the instructions he had received: to pass by the arch-rebel,

and bend his whole force against all other rebels whatsoever!
He distributed numerous small bodies of troops amongst the
towns and fortresses on the borders of the disturbed districts, sent a force under Sir Harry Harrington into the
mountains of Wicklow to *punish Feaugh M'Hughue Sonnes,*
and then himself advanced, says Camden, *with all his forces,*
against certain petty rebels in Munster. We are informed
by O'Sullevan Beare that he took only 7,000 foot and 900
horse upon this expedition; and Dymok, his Lordship's
secretary, writes that "after resting certen daies at Dublin,
for establishinge the state of that kingdome, he departed
thence towards the champion feildes between the villages of
Killrush and Castlemartine, in which place he appointed to
meet him 27 ensignes of foot and 300 horse." It eventually
became matter of angry inquiry why the Earl's instructions,
to which his full consent had been given before leaving
London, had been, in contempt of the Queen and the Privy
Council, so suddenly and entirely reversed! The Lords of
the Council at Dublin, as their wont was, threw the blame
from themselves. Essex declared that he had acted in compliance with the wish of the Lords of his Council at Dublin,
to whom, in regard of their great and long experience in
Irish matters, he could not but yield and assent! This the
Lords, with all respect, absolutely denied! Between the
assertions of parties so eminent, and so worthy of credence,
we can scarcely err in according our belief to either; or in
suggesting that, with the disaster of Marshal Bagnal fresh
in their memory, the Council might more willingly see the
army led anywhere than towards the ill-omened fort of the
Blackwater, and rather within the jurisdiction of the Vice-
President of Munster than their's. Camden has a brief commentary of his own upon this question. The Earl did it, he
says, by the persuasion of some of the Queen's Council at
Dublin, whose minds were too much bent on their own
private respects.

Whatever may have been his motive, he had scarely been
a month in Ireland when these military measures were taken,
and Essex hurried into Munster. Very few lines suffice to
record the result of the eight weeks that ensued. "He
took," says Camden, "Cahir Castle, environed with the river
Swire; he spread a great terror of himself far and near,
driving away great numbers of cattle, and dispersing the
rebels round about into the woods and thickets." Although
the Irish were thus scared and scattered, the Earl, with the
keen observation of an experienced commander, readily per-

ceived, and appreciated, the qualities of the men who fled
before him; and not having any matter of opposition, or absolute conquest, to form the subject of a despatch, he wrote
to Her Majesty a description of the Irish rebels, their tactics,
and the chief cause of their recent successes. " The people
in general," he said, "have able bodies by nature, and have
gotten by custom ready use of arms, and by their late successes, boldness to fight your Majesty's troops!" He had
previously complained that his Carmarthenshire soldiers were
mostly taken out of prison, and boys; he now added, "these
rebels have (though I do unwillingly confess it) better bodies
and perfecter use of their arms than these men which your
Majesty sends over. Your Majesty's commanders being advised and exercised, know all advantages, and by the
strength of their order *will, in great fights, beat the rebels;* for
they neither march, nor lodge, nor fight in order, but *only by
the benefit of footmanship can come on and go off at their pleasure.*"
The sole touch yet wanting to this picture of the Irish soldier
is supplied by Camden, who adds, " *They* (the Irish) *trust more
to the nimbleness of their heels than to the valour of their hands
in the open field.*"

Having successfully driven away a multitude of cows, and
garrisoned the Castle of Cahir, the Earl turned his steps
homewards.

It may be presumed that he began this return with an
undiminished force; for of the rebels he had as yet seen no
more than was last visible of such dress as they wore as
they plunged into the woods and thickets. Ireland had
never seen such a force as that now under the Earl's command! It is asserted that, in its equipment, "nothing which
he had desired had been denied to him." He had been accompanied out of London by a gallant train of the flower of the
nobility, and we have certain evidence that a great portion
of this gallant train accompanied him to Dublin, and shared
with him the glories of his Munster campaign. What greatly
dazzled the imagination of the wild Irish rebels was the
splendour of the plumed hats worn by these gallant soldiers.
Without so much of contest as could have tarnished the
equipments of his army, Essex began his homeward march.
Between English and Irish writers no difference occurs in
their recital of the incidents of the campaign hitherto; but
now at once commences a strange discrepancy. Of what happened to the army of Essex, between his beginning his march
and his arrival in Dublin, not a single passage has been recorded, either by any despatches of the Earl, or by the English

historians who have written of his previous and subsequent fortunes.

Our native writers have not left the incidents of that homeward march in such absolute obscurity. We might believe with O'Sullevan Bear—were we not put on our guard by Sir Richard Cox, not to credit many words he says—that the path of the Earl lay through those woods and thickets into which he had frightened the rebels; particularly through a certain narrow pass, about a mile long, hemmed in on all sides by a thick wood. What name this pass bore up to that time we know not; it had perhaps none; but it has in all time since been known by the chivalrous appellation of "The Gap of Feathers," or "The Pass of Plumes," *Transitus plumarum*, on account of the *multas plumeas apices* brought thither by the flower of the nobility. In this pass Donal and his terrified followers, who, as the Earl said, "by the benefit of footmanship could come on and go off as they pleased," now rallied, and came on. He, and others of the O'Mores, and the Geraldines, plotted a famous ambuscade along this pass through wood and bog, and into it the Earl and his soldiers plunged headlong! What slaughter, and what panic, what going off, and what feats of footmanship ensued, our imagination has little difficulty in suggesting, from the name given to this pass; and from the description, *by English historians*, of the condition in which the Earl and his companions at last reached Dublin. Successful as this ambuscade had been, it did not satisfy the expectation of the Irish leaders: there had been some want of coolness, or of intelligence, in the companies employed, and a suspected officer, mainly through the stern urgency of Donal, was put to death.

For six days continued the retreat of Essex, and they were days of incessant battle; of the incidents of these days, of the "bloody fight near Crome," as of the defile of Plumes, the only information we have is from the pen of O'Sullevan, to whom, says Cox, there is little credit to be given; and yet some things that he says must be allowed to be true."

Once beyond the confines of the countries of Donal and of the Geraldines, Essex experienced little more molestation. He arrived in Dublin, says Camden, " with *his men wearied out, distressed, and their companies incredibly wasted !*" The Queen was very much troubled at this expedition, whereby *so great loss had been sustained*, &c., &c. " He found *his army so wasted* that he was forced to demand a new supply of men," for the expedition he was *now* ready to make against Tir Oen! Her

Majesty, he wrote, must not think Ireland a summer's work, nor an easy task! The Irish have able bodies, good use of the arms they carry, and boldness to attempt. Our common sort of men have neither bodies, spirits, nor practice of arms," which completes a remarkable picture, for they had before, as the reader has seen, neither shoes nor hose, nor apparel of any sort! and nothing to eat! And now souls and bodies also gone! leaving it a wonder what remained of them.

On his arrival in Dublin, Essex was made acquainted with the issue of the expedition which had been punishing Feagh McHughue's sons! It is wonderful how by that national quality which Camden calls *" the nimbleness of their heels,"* and the Earl of Essex, *"mere footmanship,"* the Irish managed to escape destruction from the powerful force which had accompanied the Lord Lieutenant into Ireland! Their escape in Munster we have seen; how this quality served them in the Mountains of Wicklow we have now to see. A force of about six hundred foot, and three score and eight horse, under Sir Henry Harrington, left Dublin a little before Essex set out on his campaign against the Munster rebels; they were met by an equal number of the men whom they were sent to punish. Ample accounts, both by Harrington and his officers, exist of what immediately ensued.

"No sooner had our soldiers discovered the enemy (and noticed the nimbleness of their heels) but they were presently possessed by such a feare that they caste away their arms, and would not strike one blow for their lives! Yet the enemy no more in number than they were!" "All that I could ever do, wrote Sir Henry Harrington, could never make one of them once to turn his face towards the rebels! And notwithstanding that our horse, that were in the reare, charged twice between both battailes, whereby they won our men breathe, and ground enough to have better resolved, they rather (that they might be on equal terms with their enemy, and that in other respects their imitation of them might be as near as possible perfect) took that as an opportunity to stripp themselves not only of their weapones, but of their clothes!"

Having written home urgently for supplies, the Lord Lieutenant, in continuation of the reversed policy, occupied himself with the preparation of an expedition on a larger scale, which was to act in combination with a design which he had formed of himself proceeding against O'Neill. The reader will pardon a few paragraphs of retrospective history; they will give additional interest to the narrative of the proceedings of the Lord Lieutenant, and help to enliven, and illustrate the history of the pacification of Ireland.

In the year 1591 a pleasant spectacle entertained the citizens of London. Brian O'Rork, "a great Lord of Brenny," after some controversy with the Lord Deputy of Ireland, had taken refuge in Scotland, and been delivered up by King James to Queen Elizabeth. The peculiarity of this Irish Chieftain's offence had excited amongst the loyal populace of London a lively impatience to witness the last scene of his career; humorous anecdotes were also passed abroad respecting him which had greatly quickened the public curiosity to see him.

As far back as the year 1563 " Her* Gracious Majesty had, by a Proclamation,—embellished by the courtly pen of Sir William Cecyll,—announced to her people that "none of the portraits which had hitherto been taken of her person did justice to the original; that, at the request of her Council, she had resolved to procure an exact likeness, from the pencil of some able artist; that it should soon be published, for the gratification of her loving subjects; and that, on this account, she strictly forbade all persons whomsoever, to paint, or engrave, any new portraits of her features without licence, or to show, or publish, any of the old portraits till they had been reformed according to the copy to be set forth by authority."

Of the peculiar and incredible malice of this Irish Chieftain, and of his traitorous contempt of the Queen's sacred person, and authority, let the reader now judge! Brian O'Rorke had, besides " entertaining† in his house certain shipwrecked Spaniards," commanded the Queen's picture, painted on a table, to be tied to a horse's tail, and hurried about the streets in scorn, and at last disgracefully to be cut in pieces!" Alas! for the chivalry of this great Lord of Brenny! Her Majesty was, at the time, but in the 56th year of her virginity, and radiant in the bloom of that beauty, which even 14 years later, when she had reached her climacterical year, to wit, the 70th year of her age, " adorned the world, as her wisdom was the miracle of the age." Sir George Carewe, "when he compared the felicities which other men enjoyed, with his unfortunate destiny to bee deprived from the sight of Her Majesty's Royall person, &c., lived like one lost to himselfe! and withered out his days in torment of mind!" And when his torment wrung from him this cry of despondency, he knew that "his lines were unworthy of her divine eyes," his consolation was " to kiss the shadowes of her Royall feet!" Beauty and wisdom, the Queen's feet and their shadows, were alike lost upon the Prince of Brenny! Nor did his evil behaviour fail to find imitators ; and thus, for their insolence, as for his own, was O'Rorke justly responsible.

In the 65th year of Her Majesty's life, another portrait, in flagrant contempt of her Proclamation, and divine person, was given to the world. "An *intelligent 'foreigner"* wrote to his friends abroad, that "Her Majesty wore false hair, of a red colour, surmounted with a crown of gold; the wrinkles of age were imprinted on her face ; her eyes were small ; her teeth black ; her nose prominent." "It was commonly observed that Her Majesty, when she came to be seen, was continually painted ; not only all over her face but her very necke and breaste also." How treasonable and how scandalous were these unlikenesses of the Queen of England is apparent from the veracious record of Sir George Carewe ! We are forced to the opinion that Herr Hentzner, when he wrote them, had never seen Her Majesty at all! but had received these malignant accounts from the family of O'Rorke, when he was travelling through the picturesque scenery of the Brenny. That the loyal feelings of the citizens of London were outraged by the conduct of this barbarous Irishman is not surprising ; furthermore, all the circumstances attending his conduct since his capture were in keeping with the insolence, and incivility of his offence ! "Being, as we are informed by Camden, made to understand these accusations by an interpreter (for he understood not English), out of a barbarous insolency, he refused to submit himself to a trial by 12 men, unless he might have longer time given, the accusations sent out of Ireland might be delivered into his hands, and the Queen herself sit as his judge upon the Bench!" But, in addition to his barbarous insolency, two pleasant stories were abroad concerning him, the second of which excited the mirth of Lord Bacon. "He gravely petitioned the Queen, not for his life, or pardon, but that he might be hanged with a gad, or withy, after his own country fashion." The scenes customary on these festive occasions, the multitudinous assemblage of the citizens of London—attracted by a strong veneration for retributive justice—and the hilarity usual amongst the youth of both sexes, is known to the world! but upon this occasion not only was an insolent barbarian to be disposed of, and a laughable instrument to be used for his despatch, but a scene of especial divertisement was looked

forward to. "The criminal understood not English," and
therefore the humanity of his judges had provided for him
an ecclesiastic of his own country to encourage him in his
last moments; but it chanced that the condemned man was
a Roman Catholic; the spiritual attendant appointed for him
had also once been of the same religion, nay a Capuchine friar,
and a bishop thereof, but of late days had conformed to the
religion of the state! He was a notable personage in his
age, and the reader will again meet with him in the after
pages of this work. It was the Archbishop of Cashel, Miler
McGrath. As was expected, the spiritual ministry of this
prelate was not acceptable to the criminal, who turned from
him with much impatience, but the archbishop persevered
till O'Rork put an end to his exhorations by an observation
which was, fortunately, not so intelligible to the multitude
as to his Grace. He offered himself to the executioner, and
then, amidst bursts of acclamation, and numberless pleasant
and witty remarks the ludicrous gad was produced, the
great Lord of Brenny strangled, and the entertainment terminated! Fortunate would it have been for some of the
countrymen of that merry multitude if every son of that
barbarous chieftain, and every wild follower of his name and
race could have been, that same day, carted to Tyburn, and
strangled with him!

Fourteen years passed away, and this entertaining spectacle was growing faint in the memory of those citizens of
London, when men's attention was suddenly called to a scene
acting far away in the wilds of Connaught. Stung by the
reproaches of the Queen, and of the Privy Council, Essex had
resolved to act in the spirit, though not absolutely according
to the letter, of his instructions; "he sent orders to Sir Coniers
Clifford, the Governor of Connaught, to march against Belick,
that the rebel forces might be distracted whilst he himself
should set upon them in another part." Clifford accordingly
set forth, as we are informed by Dymok, with 1,900 men,
under 25 ensigns, and 200 English and Irish horse. He
arrived about four o'clock in the afternoon of the 15th of
August, at the entrance of the Corlews, the most dangerous
pass in Connaught. Clifford was informed that the pass was
undefended; and he resolved to hurry through it that same
evening. When fairly entangled betwixt wood and bog, he
found himself suddenly in face of O'Rork (not the ghost of
the O'Rork of Tyburn, but his son), with 400 rebels, and "our
men being tired, and wanting powder (O'Rork not having
offered them any refreshment, nor having provided any

ammunition for them) were utterly routed. Clifford and Sir Alexander Radcliffe fell—for they refused to fly—and "they were accompanied to the gates of death by dyvers worthy, both lieutenants and ensigns, who were followed by 200 base and cowardly rascals; the rest, which els had all perished, were saved by the horse. The Governor's (Clifford's) head was sent that night for a present to O'Rork."

Two hundred men slain! as many wounded! Nineteen hundred *old soldiers* scattered and disgraced! for they fled " in a general rowte, throwing away not only their arms, but their very clothes," and the head of Her Majesty's Governor of Connaught to be spiked upon the battlements of O'Rork's Castle—as the head of his father had been upon London Bridge—should that barbarous chieftain have the sense to take a lesson of civility from his English neighbours, was the Eric taken by the son for the blood of his parent!

Irish history abounds in tales of bloody requital like this, for cruelty and insult inflicted by her English conquerors. Savage practical jokes between nations are the costliest of all entertainments! It was in an evil hour that Bryan O'Rork dragged the Queen's portrait,—the effigies of that beauty which adorned the world—in the mud! It was in a worse when the Londoners, amused with their pleasant jest of the gad, thronged to witness the ignominious death of an inso- lent barbarian (an Irish Prince)! but it was in the worst of all when the tragedy in the Corlews, washed out with the blood of several distinguished English officers, and several hundred old soldiers, the shame of that ghastly revel around the Tyburn gibbet!

After this disaster of Clifford, Essex wrote again to the Privy Council the result of his further acquaintance with the condition of the enemy's and the Queen's armies! He de- scribed the pitiful charactér of the Royal troops, and their want of all things! With them he contrasted the bravery, the training, the endurance, the soldierly qualities of the Irish, and the abundance of all things, which their possession of the country afforded them. In all these particulars his assertions were borne out by Fenton, Wallop, and indeed by every man who wrote letters to Cecyll. " All things," they said, " daily decline, and wax worse and worse ! The soldiers decay, and come to nothing, *for want of apparel!* The sol- diers fall dead in marching, with very poverty, and want of victuals ! They lodge on the ground, without covering, and *clothes they have none!*"

· The reader may have felt some surprise at the incessant

appeal of all the Queen's Generals for *apparel* for the troops ;
and the repeated complaint that in the bitterest weather
they were left without clothes! This surprise, and much
suspicion also, was evidently felt by Sir Ro. Cecyll, who,
finding that notwithstanding all the supplies that he sent to
Ireland, his despatches contained ever the same complaint,
that Her Majesty's forces were still campaigning without
any clothing, he at last became convinced that, from some
motive that was undiscoverable by him, the men preferred
to wear none! He was before long informed that in the
recent expeditions of Harrington and Clifford, their men no
sooner came in sight of the enemy, than they turned about,
and instantly began to *stripp themselves!* In the case of Sir
Coniers Clifford . there were 1,500 men thus occupied! in
that of Sir Henry Harrington, about seven or eight hundred!
Struck by the singularity of this proceeding on a field of
battle, his enquiries led to the discovery that this casting
away of their clothes by the Queen's soldiers arose from the
two-fold motive of a desire to imitate their Irish enemy, who
wore none, and the hope of being thus the better able to
equal them in the *nimbleness*, and *footmanship* to which they
owed their successes in all the recent encounters.

"Neither clothes, nor houses do they (the Irish) care for,"
wrote the English intelligencer from Munster. "I will pay
for no apparel for the Queen's mere Irish soldiers, exclaimed
the Minister, for they wear none!" Her Majesty may have
smiled at this simple equipment of her Carmarthenshire warriors, and admired the acuteness of her Principal Secretary,
who proposed to make this national peculiarity a means of considerable saving to her exchequer. It was soon found that
there was room for even further economy ; though, alas! for
no further smile! "the ordinary food of these rebel Irish—
wrote the same accurate observer of Irish manners—is a
kind of grass!" The reader may remember that the gallant
Williams, at the Blackwater, had been reduced to make trial
of this diet, and certainly his valour throve well upon it;
this, too, the flower of the nobility was about to try; for it
was not long before Ormond informed Her Majesty that "*her
poor soldiers were perishing from cold, nakedness, and rotten, unserviceable food*," whilst, in mournful contrast with these
shameful details, O'Niell, he wrote, wanted for nothing; he
was supplied with arms and treasure from Spain ; he could
command the resources of the whole realm.

These unwelcome truths greatly exasperated the Queen,
she wrote back to urge above all things, "the necessity of

holding up her greatness against a wretch whom she had
raised from the dust, and who could never prosper if the
charges she had been at, were orderly employed." Cecyll
wrote that "something must be done to pull down the
Traitor's pride, who braggeth much in foreign parts, to the
disquiet of Her Majesty's mind." This something that was
requisite it appeared that Essex was at last resolved to perform; for he now marched to the confines of Ulster with only
1,300 men; a force which must have placed him entirely in
the power of the Arch Rebel. A scene worthy of the palmy
days of knight-errantry ensued. "Tirone rode towards him
at the head of a few horsemen, and craved a parley. They
adjourned accordingly, having dismissed their attendants, to
a ford of the river called Ballaclinch; O'Neill riding his
horse into the water up to the belly, saluted with great
.respect the Lord Lieutenant, who paused on the river's brink;
and near an hour was spent in the interchanging of words
betwixt the two, without any by to hear them." The result
was that it was agreed that " there should be a truce from six
weeks to six weeks, to begin that very day, till the first of
May, yet so as it should be free for both sides to renew acts
of hostility after fourteen days' notice given."

The embarrassment occasioned by the conduct of the
Earl of Essex, who immediately after this interview hurried
away, without licence, to England; and the consequent
change in the royal estimate of the Irish war, was soon
apparent in the language both of the Queen, and her Principal Secretary. Cecyll had in the beginning of the great
struggle declared, that " the Queen would wage war like a
Princess who would take no insult from the hands of the
most powerful monarch." He now wrote that " the worst
peace was better than the best war." And Elizabeth, forgetful of the haughty language with which, until now, she
had ever spoken of Tirone, instructed the Lords of the Irish
Council " to strive to mature this truce into a settled peace."
She sent word to O'Neill that " she would make known her
pleasure to him by some so confident personage, as when he
should look down into the centre of his faults, and up to the
height of her mercy, he should see that he was the creature
of a gracious Sovereign more content to save than to
destroy." Negotiations for a settled peace were entered
upon: the Irish authorities endeavoured to conduct their
diplomatic encounter to more prosperous issue than had
attended their military operations; but the demands of
O'Neill were too distasteful to be sent home. In the mean

time the first six weeks of truce expired, and O'Neill, not even yet thoroughly consious of his power, permitted a second to commence. The Queen had once more appointed the veteran Earl of Ormond Lieutenant-General of her Forces; and this determined man used the most rigorous measures for the reorganization of his wretched army, and to enforce some sort of obedience in the provinces where he had any strength. Many scores of miserable fugitives were caught in the port towns, whither they had fled hoping to obtain passage back to their English homes, and were instantly hanged! He continued to write urgently to England for all things; clothing, swords, powder, but most of all for men who had seen some service.

Although history is silent respecting the victories gained by the Earl of Essex during his brief stay in Ireland, an idea may be formed of the cost at which he gained them, from the fact that he had brought 16,000 foot and 2,000 horse with him into Ireland, and that as soon as he had returned to England the Earl of Ormond resumed his appeals for reinforcements of men, for clothes, and food, with the same urgency as if the Earl had taken back his army with him. To the nimbleness of Irish heels may be solely attributable "the Baffle in the Glens," and "the Disaster in the Corlieues," but not so the *incredible diminution* in the army of Essex; for the nimbleness of his Lordship had excelled that of Donal; rather must we attribute it, to the thunder and rain and the stormy passage which the Earl encountered at the beginning of his Irish Government.

The survivors of the fugitives from the expedition to punish Feaugh McHughe's sons were, by the severity of Essex, *decimated!* From the expedition of Clifford, considering the treatment of O'Rork's father, and the scenes at Tyburn, it might be needless to look for many survivors; and from those whom, from defective footmanship, the Earl was compelled to leave behind on his retirement from Munster, it is to be hoped that the humanity of Donal led him to take their parole not to serve again in McC. Mor's country, and that so he spared them; but it may be apprehended that they did not rejoin their colours! The failure of these various small strategic experiments is far insufficient to account for the *incredible waste* of the Earl's great army; the reader must be content to accept the accounts of O'Sullevan Beare as true history, and thus believe that "Essex *was* chased, with incredible losses, by Donal and the Geraldines out of Munster," or, with Cox, disbelieve him, and leave the disappearance of the better part of 16,000 foot and 2,000 horse, within so few months, as an enigma into which no man cared to make enquiry! Certain it is that when the wrecks of this fine force were handed over to the Earl of Ormond, his complaints of the want of men, weapons, clothes, and food, were as clamorous as before Essex and his army set foot in Ireland.

Although the letter from Sir Robert Cecyll to the Lord Lieutenant concerning Florence and his patent, bears date in April, that is immediately after the Earl's departure from London, it would appear that Florence did not himself land in Cork before the autumn! His desire to see the result of Essex's expedition into Munster was doubtless the cause of this delay; for, had the Earl succeeded, his country would have been won for him without any expense or effort of his own. When he at last landed in Cork he found the Government in other hands than he had known it almost since his boyhood! Sir Thomas Norreys was no more!

Very shortly after his last letter to Sir R. Cecyll he had endeavoured to assemble in arms those Irish gentlemen who had not yet renounced their allegiance to the Queen. Some of them attended him, but without followers; the Septs had found other leaders, and were in arms for another cause.

It was the fate of that "Noble Knight of great name and honour" to finish a distinguished career in an obscure skirmish!

As soon as the tidings of his death had reached Dublin the Lords had appointed to the government of Munster, with the title of Commissioners, Sir H. Power and Sir Warham St. Leger! and thus, in place of the man who, for so many years had been alternately his enemy and his friend, he found the author of those tracts to which he owed eleven years of captivity.

To these Commissioners, in the absence of the Earl of Essex, Florence presented himself with the letter of Her Majesty's Chief Secretary. That important document is now laid before the reader; it had cost Sir R. Cecyll much study, and it may be permitted to us to hope, for the satisfactory guidance of all who were concerned in the perfect comprehension of it, that the document was considerably more intelligible than the draught of it which was put aside for posterity! This draught is in his own handwriting, but so blotted by alterations, and interlined with corrections as to be extremely difficult to decipher.

P

1599. *April.* SIR ROBERT CECYLL *to the* LO: LIEUTENANT, *the* EARL
OF ESSEX.

" May it please yor Lo, you shall receave by the hands of Florence
MacCarthy a lre, whereby Her Ma^y hath geven you authority, to passe
unto him, a grant of such lands of the Erle of Clancarthy his father-in-
law, and wth such reservations as were thought convenient upon the conference had me when Her Maty directed me the Secretary, to attend your Lo:
in the consideration of that cause, assisted by two of Her Ma^ts learned
Counsell, the Master of the Roles, and the Sollicitor; since this tyme ther
hath ben something written out of Munster, in gñrall terms frõ the President (though not alleadging any pticuler cause, safe that his brother, and
others, are out) tending rather to wish his stay, then his sending thether;
Her Maty, notwithstanding, finding the contrey so farr out as it is aledly,
and the lands wch he claymed, possessed by rebells, hath a gratious disposition *rather* to commit some trust to this man,—who hath long endured
lack and want, and who undertaketh, or at the least offereth, to assiste her
service wth all the meanes he, and his frends can make,—then to make him
desperate; having ben so long kept in confinement; she hath therfore ben
pleased (according to yor former opinion) to resolve to geve him an estate
in those lands, according to the note subscribed by their hands, whereof
yor Lo. allowed before yor going; nevertheles she hath commanded us, in
private, to say thus much unto you, that if you shall, now that you are
arrived in that kingdome, understand by further conference wth our
counsell, or any other, that this grant of ours may be likely tobe dangerous
to our service, and that, in respect of that he shalde heire to Mac Carthy
lykewise, may geve him too great a greatness hereafter, and that these ex-
emptions, and reservations of all those matters of rule and chiefryes, together with the imposition of rent and prohibition, and such other circumstances wh^ch doe abridge ye superiority over other Lords, wh^ch theEarle
hath, do not now make a sufficient alteration in this man's state, and his
father's that then, in this case Her Majestie is pleased yor Lo^p doe proceede
with him to passe unto him ether more or lesse, so it be of these things
limited in Her Matie's letter; and where yor Lo: shall receaue lykewise his
petition, whereby it appeareth to Her Matie yor Lo^p meant to make some
use of his seruice Her Matie hath thus despatched him; in y^t respect
leaveth him in all things to be used by you, and to receaue that benefyt by
Her l^re wch you in y^r wisdome shall thinke good.

Had Florence decided to follow the Lord Lieutenant to
Dublin, or to present himself, with the Queen's letters to the
Lords of the Council, and occupy himself with the legal
arrangement of his patent, fine, chiefries, and other matters
referred by Cecyll to the Earl of Essex, he must have left
Donal triumphant in Munster, and his best friend O'Sullevan
Mor exposed to a renewed application for the rod; possibly
under some pressure from the victorious Bonaghts in Donal's
pay. His first care was to exhibit the Queen's letter to the
Commissioners; plainly, not with any view to their undertaking the final arrangement which had been referred to the
decision of the Lord Lieutenant, but as an undeniable proof

of the trust reposed in him by Her Majesty. He explained
to St. Leger and Power that the purpose for which he was
sent into Ireland was "to recover Desmond for the Queen,
out of the hands of Donal; to rid the province of O'Neill's
mercenaries; and to withdraw every member of his own
numerous and powerful Sept. from 'the action' into which
their usurping chieftain had forced them." To effect this, it
was urgent that he should, without delay, levy from amongst
his own people a force able to secure them from the pre-
dominance of the soldiers in Donal's pay. In this he
expected little difficulty; men were plenty; all were well
disposed to him; all loyal; but he was without weapon to
arm them! this too, he suggested might be remedied if the
Commissioners would permit Her Majesty's stores to be
applied to the purpose; but scarcely less important than
these other preliminaries was the matter of "the title."

Carewe had written that "Tirone thirsted to be called
O'Neill—which in his estimation was more gratifying than
to be entituled Cæsar." Florence thirsted to be called Mac
Carthy Mor.

In his petitions and letters to Cecyll he made no demand,
indeed it is manifest that he had no desire for the English
title of Earl of Clancar; for it was only when, at a later
period, the appellation so much coveted was denied to him,
that he petitioned, "if that ancient designation must be
extinguished, that then it be extinguished in the Earldom."
Cecyll would have done better to keep him in England than
to send him back with a limited reliance on his loyalty.
The title was sure to be an early difficulty for all parties:
Florence knew it, Cecyll might have foreseen it. The gentlemen of Desmond were well inclined to receive Forence as
their Chief, but they were not prepared to renounce their
right to elect him, or to diminish their own dignity by submitting themselves to a man who feared to receive the title
with which the Rights of Chieftainship were connected.
Florence knew that the earlier he should recover his country
the earlier would he be in collision with the Government,
unless this preliminary were satisfactorily settled; but he
knew also, and evidently much better than it was known to
the Commissioners, that the Queen abhorred this title! that
she looked upon it as an invasion of her sovereignty. She
had once already merged it in the English style of Clancar,
and subsequently Cecyll declared there would be little difficulty in reviving for Florence the extinct Earldom; but even
that she was not prepared to confer upon him till he had

P 2

effected, without it, the only purpose for which it could be useful. At the risk of thus early awakening the suspicions of the Queen, Florence saw the necessity of calling her attention to the matter, and he had the address to lead the Commissioners, even the wary St. Leger, to write to the Secretary that " *they* thought it agreeable to policy to grace him with the title."

1599. *Dec.* 10*th.* St. Leger *and* Power *to* Cecyll.

" Right Honorable: May it please yoʳ Honʳ to understande that wheare (at the request of Mr. Florence Mac Cartye) we presume to write to yoʳ Honʳ on his behalf, beinge lately arrived here oute of Englande, with Hir Matie's lres tothe Lord Lieuteñant, both for his father-in-lawes landes, and also for som convenient chardge to serve Hir Highnes, which (by reason of the Lord Lieuteñant's absence) took not effect, answerable to his loial meañg, wherupon he was enforced to crave oʳ ayd and advise in that behalf; determining with all expediĉon to employ him self for the recovery of that countrey, and for that, his owne people and followers (whereof he hath a greate nomber), are altogether destitut of weapon, and muniĉon, he became supplᵗ unto us for the same; which (altho we knewe it verye beneficiall for the furderance of Her Highnes' said service) we could not graunt, by reason of the smale store here, being neverthelesse persuaded that the recovery of that countrey would be verye availeable for Her Matie, and so much the more preiudiciall unto the Traitors, they having placed their chiefest aboade in that countrey, as their greatest strengt and fastnes, we therefore hold opinion that it were requisit he shoulde be asisted by all goode meanes, considering that he is (at this psent,) driven to entertaigne some fyve or sixe hundreth Conaght men, which he doth not altogether trust. And so for the Tytle of Mac Carthy (which the Bastard Donell Mac Carty doth nowe usurpe, withholdinge thereby the countrey) we also think it agreeable to policy, to th' end he might the rather induce the countrey people to forsak the rebells (which no doubt by this meanes they will) to graze him with the title of Mac Carty, wherby he shalbe the better en-abled both to obtayne and defend that countrey; in which we desire to knowe yoʳ Honor's pleasur, and even so recomending him to yoʳ honᵇˡᵉ and grave consideraĉon, with remembrance of our dueties we humblie take leaue.

" At Cork this x day of Decʳ, 1599, yoʳ Honʳˢ humblie to be comanded.

" War. St. Leger."
" H. Power."

A far more interesting, curious, and spirited despatch than that of the Commissioners, went by the same courier as theirs to England. To most men a position like that of Florence at this period would have been critical and perilous : a single false step would have ruined his hopes at the outset. The ease and gaiety with which he now wrote to Sir R. Cecyll, shows how steadily he could walk between the suspicions of his old enemies, and the doubts of men who

naturally expected to engage him at once in the same open
action in which they had themselves staked land and life.
Florence had no intention of compromising himself so
hastily. To withdraw himself from the reach of the authorities of the Province, to break into rebellion, and proclaim
himself MacCarthy Mor, would be to walk in the steps of
his brother-in-law; he had no such design; his purpose was
to obtain the territory and lordship of his Sept by the usual
election, and with the Queen's consent; something more
than the audacity of Donal was needed to accomplish this.
The sketch of life in the Irish camp may have afforded some
amusement to Cecyll, amidst the cares that were thickening
around him; but to many who lived within reach of Dowally,
there was left little cause to smile at the narrative of the
two beds, or the plans, that night, settled between the bed-
fellows.

"1599. *Dec.* 12. FLORENE M. C. *to* SIR ROB^t. CECILL.

" My moste honden dutie remēbered: Although my fortune doth still
continue in one hard moode, for want of meanes to recou'l and defend me
my countrey, and to serv Her Matie against a sight of weake and senseles
traytors, wherby I was not, since my cominge, able to doe aniething woorth
the writieng unto yor Hon^r; yet notwithstanding, because yor Hon^r shall
not think me unthankfull of yor great fau'l towards me, nor unmindfull to
do yor Hon^r any service that lies in me, as also lest any matter had bene
inferred over against me, as is don here alreadie, I thought fit to aquaint
yor Hon^r wth the state of this province, wch is now comaunded for Her
Matie by Sir Warham Sent Leger and Sir Henry Power, whom I met at
Cork, at my landing there ; at wch time James McThomas, wch they call
Earle of Desmond, stoode about Castellmainge wth all his forces, to
suffer nobody to goe in nor out; but while his Conaught Buonies were
there, and his Mounster mé, my wife, that defends such another Castell
thereby, called Castell Logh, against her base brother; and my brother-
in-law O'Sulevan that dwelles there by, could wth frendshipp send in a
messeng^r; but after the Buonies were changed, and that Desmond himself,
wth his cheefest, and faythfullest folowers, and wth Capten Terell and his
companie of four or v hundred, came about it, those poore English and
Ireishmen that were in the Castell almost famished, were constrained to
deliu'l it a litle after my landing; wch all Mounster could not have taken
from Her Matie yf I were possesst of my countrey, wch comes to that
castell gate on the south side. Sir Warham and Sir Henry Power were
very carefull to relive it, but their forces were so weake, and the weather
so foule and so reinie, that no English forces could go ou'l Slieav Luochra:
besids that I perceiv all the Lords and Gent of these parts unwillinge to
serv, and hazard them selfes and their mē, the Queene's pay being given
to those young felows, and Captens of small skill, and abilitie, that are
preferred there, although most of those Lords and Gent do beare the rebells
noe affection; whereby I could wish that Her Matie had entertained those
that are able to bring good meanes tothe warr, and that manifested their
evill will tothe Traytors by killing and spoyling them, or by being killed

or spoyled by them, whereof there are a great number: for the Rebells doth nothing but kill, and spoyle, ev'lywhere dayly, as I know of late by experience, for after Castellmaing was had, Desmond came wth his forces to Drishane in Muskrey: His forces consisted of Twelf hundred foote, wthout anie horsmẽ to be spoken of. I had Sʳ Warham and Sir Henry Power's warrant to parle, or send to anye rebells, and was then in Dowall, wthin four miles of them, and sent to them for assurañce to parle wth them: they all swer to do me no hurte, and sent Captẽ Terell and Piers Lacie for me; where when I came, it passes how joyfull they were all of my coñiing; onelie they misliked that night myne Englis attire; but much more my piercing speches in Her Maᵗˢ behalfe, and against their foolish senceless, damned, actõn, to the undoing of themselfes, and all men els nere them. That night I sayd nothing; but the next morninge I entreated them that they wold not fauo'l myne adversarie, my base brother in law, nor help him wth anye of their men, nor defend my countrey for him against me: whereuppon they sent me aside, and they, and the Bishopp Mᶜ Cragh consulted concerning me, and they sent me woord by Piers Lacie that yf I wold promese to take their parte, and to frend them, they wold wthin foure dayes settle me in my countrey. I told them that my kinred to them, and alsoe my frendshipp in times past, was well know to themselfes; and craued the Bishoppes ayd in regarde of my religion; but, ⸺ ⸺ all wold not avayle ; for ⸺ ⸺ they promest me no fauo'l; their answer being that my countrey was the bak and strengthe of all Moñster, and that yf I possest it I shold destroy them all in a momẽt for Her Matie, wᶜʰ they wold wth all their endeauoʳ hinder me of, except I were swerne at the least to do them no hurte; wᶜʰ, ⸺ ⸺, I refused to do: wheruppon I departed wth as litle fauoʳ as they could afford me; but as I was wth them that night, after their supper of Beefe and watter, wᶜʰ is all the meales they make in a day, they had not for their xij hundred men but ij bedds; thone for the Bishopp and another divine of great acompt among them, his name is Dermod; and thother for Desmond, where he wolde neds haue me to lie alsoe; wherby one of Her Maᵗˢ, and another of Tireowens, lay together that night. Wherof, and of my being there, my Lo Barry made upp great matters every where here; but Sir Warham, and Sir Henry Power told him that I went by their advise and warrant; but he never thought to tell them how himselfe promest his doughter in mariadg to Desmond, wᶜʰ Sir Warham and Sir Henry doth well know. At my departing from the Rebells I took one of their best Captens with ij hundred men from them, and so went to Cork to aquaint the councell there with their intentõns; wheruppon Sir Henry Power caused all the forces hereabouts to be gathered; they being gon through Muskery into my Father's countrey of Carbry, where, thay spoyled the three best, and welthiest folowers that I had, hauing lodged all their forces in their vilages, and consumed all their coone and cattell. I went to them againe uppon assurance, at their coñiing out of Carbrie, thinking to bring them and the Queene's forces to mete; but all the witt in the world could not persuade them to be one houre out of their bogges and wodds, wherby they could not be fought wthall. After their departure, I tooke Sir Warham and Sir Henrie's advise for my jorney into my countrie, to recouʳ it. I tolde them what forces of Conaght mẽ I entertained, wᶜʰ are about v or vi hundred, and how I could not make up any number to be spoken of of myne owne men for want of weapon, whereuppon, (because Her Matie's storehouse here is not well stored of municõn now, as my self hath seene), they thought fitt to write unto yoʳ Honʳ in my behalf, and to signifie how beneficiall the recou'ling of my countrie wold be unto Her Matie, and, what service I am able to do her yf I might haue meanes; wherefore I humblie beseech yor Honor, as I have allwayes found you a most hon^{ble} and carefull frend, to be a mean (by acquainting Her Highnes, and the councell, with what is certified in my behalf, and by furthering it) that I maye obtaine som hon^{ble} chardge, and that I may haue weapon and municõn, for iij C, all in pikes and calivers, wch I will answer out of myne entertainemen^t or otherwise, as Her Maty's pleasure may be signified to the councell of Ireland both herein, and concerning the Title of Mc Carthy, wch the Bastard hathe taken uppon him, and wch is a great motiue to the foolish contrey people to follow him; for they will hardly folow such a mã as I am, that will not suffer him self to be called Mc Carthy, where they may find one that is publikly so called ; wch matter is one of the chefest causes what detains me out of the countrey; for yf I oûcom the the sayd bastard and Buonies that be wth him, the people of the countrey, wch are almost altogether for me, will, against my will, call me Mc Carthy: wch will, for fear of imprisõment yf I came in, and for feare of being reputed, and acompted a Rebell, yf I stayed out, make me leaue Her Ma^{ts} service, and runn bak into England, or into France, or to som other place of Her Ma^{ts} frends, being long since wearie of imprisõment, in wch calamitie I spent a dozen yers already; And so humblie beseching Yo^r Hono^{rs} spedie comfort in these matteres, beseching God long to kepe and prosper y^r, I humblie take leaue.

"Yo^r honor's most humble, faythfull, and thankfull to be cõmaunded,

"fflOR M^{c}CARTHY."

"Kinsale, 12 Decr. 1599.

Cecyll might be diverted from his doubts of the loyalty of Florence by the frank and mirthful tone of his letter; the Commissioners of Munster might be deluded by the solicitude of Florence to take no step without their cognizance and advice; but there were keener and more distrustful eyes than theirs watching every move he made. As usual the Lord Barry discovered disloyalty in all his proceedings, and now loudly proclaimed his visit to the rebel camp, as an overt act of treason. Had this man of dull perception, and sharp temper, been able to learn wisdom, the vicissitudes of the times in which he lived might long since have taught it to him. Had he watched the signs of coming mischief that were obvious to all eyes but his, he would have hastened to pay that long disputed fine—with interest, if he had it— and make quick amends for the calumnies of the last twelve years.

Florence came back from the camp of the Sougaun Earl, and reported to the Commissioners the temptations which had been offered to his loyalty, the grave advice he had given to his misguided relatives, and generally, the little success of his visit. Up to that period the rebel force had been indulging in free quarters in the fertile plains of Carbery, Florence's hereditary property. After that unsatisfactory interview, their leaders, touched by his rebukes, put

their force into movement, and marched every soldier beyond
the limits of his country. Whither this multitude of hungry
buonies next betook themselves was not long a matter of
uncertainty! Suddenly there burst from the lips of Barry
three loud, sharp cries, whose reverberations startled the
Commissioners in Cork, the Lords of the Council at Dublin,
and reached, though more faintly, the ears of Sir Robert
Cecyll himself.

> Do léigemair trj gartha goil
> Do chuirfeadh brojc as gach gleann.
> We gave three shouts of lamentation
> Enough to drive badgers out of every glen.
> FEN[n] POEMS, "The chase of Sliabh Guillean."

The Sougaun Earl,Tyrell,with the soldiers of O'Neill, Donal,
with his own followers, and his hired Connaught men, "700
cabbage-soldiers," as Barry contemptuously but bitterly styled
them, had burst like a flood over his Barony of Ibawne! The
first of those piercing cries was of pain at the loss of "the chief
stay of his living;" the second swelled into a fierce charge
against Florence for directing "that graceless company against
him;" and the third died away in sobs of lamentation over the
ever mournful memory of his Eyne! The Commissioners and
the Lords at Dublin warmly sympathized with the sufferer;
scarcely so Her Majesty's Principal Secretary, for he wrote a
letter, which doubtless never met, as it was never intended to
meet, the eye of the Lo: Barry, in which he says, "I would
be verie glad to be certified whether one thing be true, that
I have heard, and which is so commonly spoken: that the
Lo: Barry was *not* spoyled so much by the Erle of Tyrone as
was sayde." This inquiry, though made at a later period,
and after a second and far more terrible visit of the rebels to
the country of Barry, proves that not every one who heard
that nobleman's cries pitied him as tenderly as he pitied himself. That he had, however, reason for one shout of lamentation is unquestionable; for the discipline of the rebels was
not exemplary; and it pleased them to prolong their stay in his
domains for six weeks; but with what justice he attributed
the infliction of this great injury to the malice of his old
enemy, must be left to the reader's judgment, and his estimate of the magnanimity of Florence. The Barony of
Ibawne "was but a small cantred;" and 700 men but a small
detachment of the force at the command of Florence's kinsmen: Barry had more cantreds, and Desmond more bonies,
Donal, even, more cabbage-soldiers; and had not indignation

made desperate the heart of Barry, he would, even in his first grief, have hastened to pay, rather than to seek " the re- myttal of his old Fyne."

" 1599· Feby. 12. BARRY to CECYLL.

"My dutie always remembered. I am driven upon occasions to trouble yor Hon^r, ꝑsuming uppon yor great curtesy, I hope you will accept in good ꝑte thèreof. I am nowe to complaine to yor Hon^r of Florence Mac Cartie howe by his affinitye wth the traytor James Fitz Thomas, and his accesse unto him, hath of late assemled together seven houndereth of the Traytors bonies, otherwise called here amonge us cabbage Soldiors. The *first service* he attempted wth that graceles company was to directe them to a small cantred or Barony of mine *called Ibawne*, linge on a remote corner towards the sea, nyre Carribrie, and ther for the space of six wyeks remayned, takinge forceably meate, drinke, and monye, besides the spoyell of all my poore tenãnts ther; so as they are in manner quite undon. That small Baronye was one of the best stayes of liveing that I had; and nowe, by the said Florences meanes, my said teñants threof are scarse able to sus- tayne them se]ves. I was able tohave wthstoode those inyories, *but that yor honable l^{re}* on Florence's behalf I respected, and therfore have not mynestered any empedim^t tothe said Florence's ꝑcedinges; yett the said abusses I reffer to yor hon^r to by considered of, I wold by glad, if it seemed good to yor Hon^r that Her Matie wold graunt the *remyttall of my old fyne that I might not hereafter be trobled* for the same which I pray your Honour to procure, &c. &c.

" DAVID BUTTEVANT."

In the previous Desmond rebellion, when Ormond was charged by the Queen to uphold the Royal cause in Munster, most of the Irish Chieftains rallied to his support. Since those days the rapacity of the undertakers had left the English Government without a friend. " Forthwith, writes Camden, almost all Munster revolted; and that not so much upon the fortunate success of the rebels as out of hatred of the inhabitants against the English undertakers, and planters, who had been settled in the lands confiscate, after the Earl of Desmond's rebellion." No sooner did James Fitz Thomas accept his Earldom from O'Neill than every follower of his house joined him; every castle, with one exception, Castle- maing, was surrendered to him, and he became the absolute ruler of Munster without a contest, or the loss of a man. It has been mentioned that the sole achievement of Essex in his excursion into Munster (exclusive of the capture of the cows) had been the capture of the Castle of Cahir; and this, as soon as he retired, surrendered again to the Geraldines!

The truce had been declared binding upon all O'Neill's friends in arms, whether in Munster, or in his own province. It found the Earl of Desmond vigorously besieging the Fort of·Castlemaing. He consented to withhold his forces from any fresh assault upon its walls, and from any depredations beyond his own country; but firmly refused to move a single soldier away from before the devoted castle, or to allow victuals into it; and when, at last, " Famine, which had made no truce with any man who bore the Queen's weapon," starved the garrison into surrender, he gave them their lives, as he said, " in consideration of O'Neills truce."

The visit of Florence to the Commissioners, to report to them the result of his interview with the rebel leaders, was the last intercourse that he had with those functionaries; from that moment he no longer sought their advice, or considered it necessary to report to them any steps he might take in pursuit of the object for which he had been sent back to Ireland. Requiring more freedom of action than he could possess immediately under the eyes, and within the control of the authorities, he quitted Cork, and fixed his residence, in the first instance, at Kinsale, which, with its famous fort of " the old head most tending towards Spain," he was now allowed to occupy, in defiance of all the suspicions, and evil auguries of Norreys, Fenton, and St. Leger himself.

The reader may remember that two or three years earlier, when Florence was in expectation of being employed by the Lord Deputy Fitz Williams against the Northern chieftains, he had written to Cecyll to inform him that he had within reach certain followers of his own, who, during his imprisonment had employed themselves in the contests ever obtaining in the countries of O'Donnell and O'Neill, and who had acquired great skill in arms, and knowledge of the country. It has been mentioned also that the chieftains of Carbery, the MacCarthys Reagh, had for several generations entertained in their service two small Septs, who were exclusively warriors, namely the O'Shyies and McSwynies. These men possessed no tract of country of their own; they had been invited into Munster by Dermod-an-Duna, Florence's great grandfather, to maintain him and his sons in the captaincy, against the sons of his elder brothers, and they received lands in Carbery, which they and their descendants held on condition of their military service; by degrees they usurped to themselves, or were burdened with the main portion of the fighting required by the chiefs of that branch of the Mac Carthys.

Notwithstanding the jealousy with which Donal Pipy regarded his cousin, all these men, with or without his consent, attached themselves to the fortunes of Florence. They were of themselves more than sufficient to dispose of Donal and

his Connaught men; and had Florence had no object in view
beyond his expulsion, he would have needed no additional
force; but in truth, his brother-in-law, unsupported by a single
chieftain of any note or influence, caused him no concern;
but an army of several thousand Geraldines, the hereditary
rivals of his race, whom his address had indeed removed for
the present beyond his boundaries, but who might at any
time return, required far other forces to bar their way than
those needed to deal with the handful of mercenaries who
followed Donal.   The great national market of fighting men
that was open to James FitzThomas was open also to him,
and to every man who could afford to offer Bonnaght.
There were numerous bodies of these Connaught soldiers
seeking service at the time, and as it chanced, some of them
commanded by the O'Connor-Kerry, a near relative—a nephew
—of Florence.   Many hundreds of them passed noiselessly
into his service, and Donal, without a contest, but with many
threats and extreme ill-humour, followed the main force of
the rebels out of Carbery into Barry's Barony of Ibawne.

All the approaches inio Florence's country, which was
" the bak and strength of all Mounster," were instantly
closed!   What took place from that time forward within the
vast and populous territories of MacCarthy Mor, the English
Government had no means of knowing, except by the letters
which Florence might himself choose to write to Sir Robert
Cecyll.   From his own account we learn that his thoughts
and his time were wholly occupied in restoring order and
friendly intercouse between the gentlemen of his Sept.   He
found the country in such state as Donal and his father could
alone have left it.   " His best gentlemen were at feud one
with another, and ready to tear each other to pieces;" the
land had been preyed and spoiled; all was in confusion, and
it needed all his energies and resources to withdraw his
followers from the action into which the authority and evil
example of his usurping brother-in-law had led them.   Accounts
materially differing from this, filled all the letters which were
written from Munster to the English Secretary.   Cecyll was
informed that " Florence was in daily intercourse with rebels,"
that "he had so strengthened his country that none could
enter into it;" that all his Castles were filled with Bonnaghts,"
that " he was a more dangerous enemy than the Sugaun Earl
himself."

Respecting these mercenaries whose name will be so often
before the reader, it may be well to introduce, before proceeding further, the brief account which Sir George Carewe has

left us of them, and of the name which was applied to them, though it, in reality, signified the payment or appointments for which they served. In ordinary times Bonnaghts, or Bonies, were retained in the pay of the native chiefs, partly for their own protection, and partly for the performance of such military service as they owed to the Sovereign, in proportion to the magnitude of their respective countries.

" Bonnaght is of two sorts, Bonnaght Bonny, and Bonnaght Beg; Bonnaght bonny being, or at least I take it, is a certain payment or allowance made unto Her Majesty's Galloglas or Kerne, of the Irishry only, who are severally bound to yield a yearly proportion both of money and victuals for their finding, every one according to their ability, so that the Kerne and galloglass are kept all the year by the Irishry, and divided at times amongst them. Bonnaght beg, or little Bonnaght, is a proportion of money rateably charged upon every ploughland towards the finding of the Galloglas. Sorren is also a kind of allowance over, and besides the Bonnaght, which the Galloglas expect upon the poor people by way of spending-money, viz., 2s. 8d. for a day and night; to be divided between 3 spears, for their meat, drink, and lodgings. And as this Bonnaght is found by the Lords for the King's service, so also every particular lord hath a certain number for their own defence; some more, some less, and are maintained upon their tenants.

How great the dignity, and how real the power of the officer whose hereditary function it was to inaugurate the greater Irish Chieftains, may be judged from the present conduct of O'Sullevan Mor, and from the effect of his decision. The late MacCarthy Mor had died without legitimate male issue ; but, as has been observed, bastardy in the first degree was not considered by the Irish as a bar to succession ; and of illegal offspring to the Earl there was no deficiency. Donal, his eldest son, aided by his friends, had at once claimed the vacant dignity ; but the White Rod, without which no election could be valid, was refused to him. The man for whom O'Sullevan reserved it was at the time a prisoner in England. Donal was on the spot ; he was in arms in the national cause ; he was fearlessly perilling the estates which he had so recently acquired, nay, he had filled Munster with the fame of his encounters with Essex, and was moreover abetted by O'Neill himself in his pretensions ; but neither by the authority of O'Neill, nor by the rival claims, and even greater power of the MacCarthy of Alla, was O'Sullevan to be moved from the exercise of his hereditary right. Had it chanced that his choice had differed from that of the Queen, the only consequence would have been three rejected candidates in the place of two.
Without a word of contention, or any show of opposition,

except from Donal—who had for the present retired from
Desmond, and betaken himself to O'Neill, to complain that
the dignty and preeminence conferred by O'Neill himself
upon him, had been denied to him by theyfollowers of his
father, and bestowed by them upon a chieftain of their own
("a treacherous deceitful Englishman")—Florence entered
into possession of the demesne lands, and various castles of
the head of his Sept, and to supreme rule within the vast
districts known as M. C. Mors country.

There is preserved at Lambeth, amongst the Carewe
MSS. vol. 625:—

"A general survey of all such lands as are conteyned
within the country of Desmond, as well of such as were the
Earl of Clan-Carty's own demesne land, as of all lands belonging to the Lords, and others, the freeholders of the said
country'; with what duties, rents, and chiefries are custome-
ably to be paid to the said Earl out of the same; taken upon
the report of the seargeantes, and officers of the said
country."

This interesting survey was made by order of the Lords
at Dublin, to enable Her Majesty to understand the extent
and nature of the inheritance which had fallen to her in consequence of the failure of heirs male to the Earl of Clancar.
It specifies the exact lands bequeathed by the Earl—who
never clearly understood Her Majesty's rights of succession
to his country—to his base brother and son; and also those
mortgaged to Florence, Browne, Denny, and others; all his
fisheries, and revenues arising from payments in kind and
money, from each of his Lords and freeholders, whose territories are exactly defined, and of which maps or plots were
made at the time, and are still preserved. This valuable
survey is far too voluminous to be laid before the reader in
these pages; the rights and chiefries, which are very numerous, and were in themselves valuable as constituting the
greater portion of the Earl's revenue, are most curious as
remains of a civilization dating before the period of acknowledged history. The boundaries of this territory, and a few
of the Earl's military chiefries are presented to the reader,
for the purpose of showing to what inheritance, through the
grace of Her Majesty, and the election of his Sept, Florence
had succeeded.

"Desmond is a parcel of the countrie of Kerry, and is
divided into three baronies and a-half, viz., Magonny, Juragha,
Dunkerran, and the half barony of Glanaroghto. In the
north side it is bounded by the river Mang, which doeth

divide Desmond from the rest of Kerry. The south part doeth bound with certain mountains of Bear and Bantry, beginning from Kilmallockoshista, and continuing to O'Leary and O'Donovan's lands in the C⁰. of Corke, in the mountain of Sleughlogher, and are divided by the head of the river of the Blackwater; the rest of Desmond is bounded by the main ocean sea."

Then follow the names of the castles and demesne lands attached to each of them. The chief of these castles were the Palace, Bally Carbry, and Castle Logh.

Amongst the military chiefries of the lord, the principal were—

Garemsloeg, or a rising, upon a warning given, of all the able men of the country; every man to be furnished with sufficient weapon, and three days victuals; and for every default to be fined at a choice cowe, or xx^li. old money.

Gallogologh were a certain company of foot soldiers bearing axes, with whom the Earl would charge the country whensoever he would make war, against the Prince, the Earl of Desmond, or any other strong lord his neighbour, and

Kearnty was a company of light footmen that, upon like occasion, the Earl would charge the country with.

Mousteroon was a charge of workmen put in upon the Earl's own tenants, both for their wages and victuals, for any work or building he would undertake.

Of similar kind, and endless variety, were the remainder of these chiefries; and all of them the Queen was desirous to abolish. It must be borne in mind that these duties and services were *all* that, under Tanist law, the tenant paid for the lands he enjoyed! *He paid no rent!*

The object of Her Majesty, in the abolition of these rights, was not by any means to relieve the freeholder, but to transfer his dependence from his lord to herself; hence, though she would abolish these chiefries, she wished to impose a *yearly money rent* in the place of them. This was a novelty so displeasing to the Irish that, as we shall presently see, Florence was unwilling to accept his country on such conditions. He informed Sir R. Cecyll that *the Irish had never paid rent for land! would not pay any, and would not acknowledge any chieftain who undertook to impose it on them!* He added that Browne and the undertakers, though they promised, never did, and never could pay such rents.

In addition to this noble and powerful lordship, Florence was actually in possession of his own patrimony in Carbery, which is declared to have been of more value than that

which he received with his wife ; furthermore he was Tanist,
or heir apparent to MacCarthy Reagh. A list of the ploughlands of all the minor Carbery chiefs dependent on MacCarthy
Reagh, and of the demesne lands of the lord,—298 of the
former, (of which the MacCarthys of Gleann-a-Chroim had 52,)
and 70½ of the latter, has been preserved for us by Carewe;
and the extent, boundaries, castles, and towns of Carbery, by
the anonymous author of the Carbriæ Notitia.

The latter author thus writes of the noble tract of country
under his notice :—

Carbery, the largest and most famous barony in Ireland
hath, with the other territories of that island, often altered its
dimensions and bounds, as the power and fortunes of its lords
was more or less prevalent. It is not improbable that it did
extend as far north as the river Lea; or (as the old verse has
it) from Carrig-o-Glaveen, or Misen-head, to Cork ; but however that be, I shall describe its more certain extent from the
Harbour of Kinsale to the Bay of Bantry; containing all that
great tract of land which at this day makes the baronies of
East and West Carbery, Ibawne, Barry Roe, Kinalmeeky, and
Courcys.

In an early chapter in this volume was given by Sir
Warham St. Leger, a list of the dependents of MacCarthy
Mor; those subject to the chieftainship of MacCarthy Reagh
were chiefly the O'Mahons, the O'Driscolls, O'Donovans,
O'Dalys, O'Crowlys, and the O'Muirrihys ; the MacCarthys of
Gleann-a-Chroim, who branched not off from the stem of Mac
Carthy Reagh, but descended as they did from Donal Caomh,
were, although subjected by their more powerful cousins, in
the centre of whose country they were seated, legally inde-
pendent chiefs, as was plainly acknowledged in the dispute
between Teig O'Norsie and Finin MacCormac, mentioned in a
previous chapter of this volume, for the possession of that
lordship and its lands. Appeal was made, not to Donal Pipi,
then MacCarthy Reagh—with whom alone would have rested
the arbitrament of such contest, had the claimants been his
dependents—but to the Queen. This was well known to
Florence, who wrote Finin's petition for him; it received
further, and more conclusive proof from the circumstance of
the country of Gleann-a-Chroim being surrendered to Elizabeth
by Teig O'Norsie ; this could not have been done had those
lands formed any portion of the lordship of MacCarthy
Reagh.

It is frequently mentioned by Florence in his letters to
Sir Robert Cecyll, that his country was *the back and strength of*

all Munster; in confirmation of this is a passage from one of Carew's despatches, written at a time when Florence had so effectually closed his country against all the spies of the President, that it was not known to him even whether he was in Ireland at all, or gone, as was rumoured, to Spain, to hasten the coming of Don Juan D'Aquila.

" If Florence be gone, it were necessary to place the Earl of Desmond (the Tower Earl) presently in his country, and that he be master of the castles there, especially the Pallice, Castle Logh, Ross-o-Donogho, and Killorgan ; but above all, of Bally Carbry ! for although these four before be upon the edge of Logh Lene, and the river of Lawne, and may stop all the passages of Desmond, yet Bally Carbry is of far more import-ance, for it is upon the ocean sea joining the island of Valen-tia, which is a very good harbour for shipping; and thither will Florence come if he bring any· Spaniards with him ; besides that the castle will command all the country on that side, which is between the fastness and the sea. The fastness of that country is incredible, for no one will believe it but he that sees it," &c., &c.

It is not surprising that the authorities in Munster, well acquainted with all these matters, and distrustful of the loyalty of Florence, should be so repeatedly urging it upon the Ministers to "cutt off his pretentions !" Nor is it to be wondered at that men striving to form for themselves Signories in the midst of these great native possessions, should tremble at seeing so much greatness falling to the ablest of their adversaries, and should be ever in combination for his ruin. The prerogatives attached to the chieftainship had been recognised, and the tributes paid for hundreds of years ; they were paid willingly, for many privileges were enjoyed by the freeholders as compensation for them; and although Her Majesty was vehemently desirous of abolishing every such token of preeminence in the chief, and although she had expressly declared, in the patent destined for Florence, that most of such rights and chiefries should cease, we are not made aware of any attempt or disposition on the part of the gentlemen of Desmond to restrain his authority and revenue within limits narrower than had been for ages claimed and recognised by the Lord and his principal followers.

All things might have prospered with Florence, and pro-found tranquillity might have reigned throughout his do-mains, if his countrymen, who had staked all things upon the success of their insurrection, could have appreciated the prudence and wisdom which had withdrawn all his clansmen from their ranks, and contrived by gentle pressure the extrusion of their too free-disciplined multitudes beyond his borders; or if they had had the wit to perceive what speedily became apparent to the Queen's Commissioners, that as long as his unassailable country was full of fighting men, no force which Ormond could spare, could venture to pass a night without the walls of Cork; and consequently that the whole open country was at their disposal. This James Fitz Thomas never fully understood, even to the end, although during the latter part of his career his existence depended mainly upon it. But there were other causes than the impatience of his immediate neighbours which threatened to disturb the quiet that Florence had established about him. Her Majesty expected "some imprest of service in return for her great bounties to him," and, what was of far greater moment, the Victor of Armagh had declared that he would, before long, pass into Munster, "that he would hold as an enemy every man who did not join him, and he would do him all the hurt in his power." In the meanwhile O'Neill's truces still continued, but, like fragile ice, dangerous to trust, and with incessant recurrence of ominous and alarming rumblings below their surface.

O'Neill levied tribute upon his foes—the Queen's friends —whenever he had the power; and this was complained of as a violation of the Truce! Ormond, on the other hand, "had the reasonable slaying of some seven score of loose men," against which O'Neill, in his turn, angrily protested, declaring that the men slain were "*his* men!" In truth all men were his men; and the only people Ormond could reasonably slay, without violating his enemy's interpretation of the conditions of the truce, were the English soldiers striving to desert. Winter was at hand, and these poor dispirited men were strewn about the country like dead leaves, "whilst the Mayor of Limerick could send out wine to the camp of the Sugaun Earl, *the Queen's soldiers were perishing from cold, nakedness, and rotten unserviceable food.*" The value of the soldiers furnished by the Lords of the Pale for the Queen's service, may be judged of by the contribution of the Lord Howth, who sent 200 ill-appointed vagabonds to Ormond, and wrote, "that he dared not adventure his life to lead them." Nothing seemed more hopeless for the Queen than an honourable and safe issue from this obstinate struggle, although a very different result had been predicted by Sir Geoffry Fenton, "unless—to use his own uncivil phrase— some power very different from the beggarly chieftains of

Ireland took it in hand." Well might Sir Robert Cecyll ex-
claim, that "they were vexed with a world of difficulties,
how to pour out water enough from England to quench the
fire in Ireland." " I speak it with grief," he said, in a letter
to Carewe, " (whatsoever you thinke, that there are sub-
sidies, and Prises, and such perquisites which doe accrew to
Her Majesty,) that all the receipts are so short of the issue,
as my hairs stande vpright to thinke of it: wherof I neede
geue no other particular instance but this, that this fower
yeares daye, Ireland hath cost £300,000 li a yeare, the least
yeares."

CHAPTER X.

WHILST these truces afforded time to the Lieutenant-General and the Lords of the Council, only the better to discover, and the more vehemently to proclaim their want of all things, O'Neill busied himself with preparations for a personal excursion into Munster. He sent before him his letters —little less than regal in style and pretension—to Mac-Carthy of Muskerry, to Lord Roche, the Lord Barry, the White Knight, to the Earl of Desmond, and finally to Florence MacCarthy; the purport of all was the same. "He would come to learn the intentions of the Gentlemen of Munster with regard to the great question of the nation's liberty, and religion." At the moment that suited his own convenience, much better than it did that of the Lords at Dublin, the Northern Chieftain gave formal notice of his intention to renew the truce no more, and that he would resume hostilities at the expiration of the present term. He even wrote to Ormond that "it was his intention presently to journey into Munster to know the minds of the people of that province; and that he had appointed the Holy Cross in Tiperary as the place at which he would meet his friends." He added this notable lesson of politeness to the Lieutenant-General, who was a person of impetuous temper, and unused to place much restraint upon his phrases, "When you next write desire your secretary to use the word *Rebel* as seldom as may be."

Early in January, 1600, O'Neill was in motion, and the heart of every man in Munster beat exultingly when tidings of his first day's march reached them; but there were especially two men whom, for very different reasons, these tidings plunged into perplexity and alarm. The Lord, Barry the son of a rebel, born and trained in actual rebellion, had for once, as it at first seemed, inauspiciously, but as the event proved —though not till after a long and painful interval—felicitously for himself, cast his lot, for good or for evil, with the Queen's Government. The coming of O'Neill was to him a sentence of swift destruction! but to his great adversary, to

Q 2

Florence, the declaration of the Northern Chieftain that he would consider as enemies all who did not join him, and that he would do them all the hurt in his power, must have been cause of no less alarm. The hurt that O'Neill could do, Barry at least already knew in some slight degree, by experience; and Florence also knew, at Barry's cost.

Nothing could be more inopportune to him than this imperious call to make his election between the cause of the Queen and " the question of the nation's liberty." Two years of close restraint within the Tower of London, eleven of banishment, and the consequent confusion of his affairs, had given him more practical knowledge of the power of Elizabeth than was possessed by any of the men who had plunged so impetuously into this national contest. O'Neill was not tarrying on his way; and what Florence meant to do he must do quickly. The choice before him was threefold. He might join O'Neill, as he was invited to do, and thus declare himself in open rebellion; or the Queen, and keep aloof from the rebels, as he had till now done from the Commissioners, and open a communication with Ormond, who was hastening with an army into Munster; or, finally, he might declare himself neutral, and trust to his bonies to defend his frontiers!

There was little comfort in any of these courses; the first would be to stake his life, or at least his liberty, and his newly-acquired position, upon the issue of a struggle, which, however mildly it might affect O'Neill, could not fail to bring the Southern Septs again under royal authority; for their country was not like the inaccessible domains of the Northern Chief, but open at all times to the force at the command of the Vice-President of Munster. The second would have made him the reproach of the whole Irish people, and far more than Barry himself, the object of O'Neill's hatred and revenge. The third course might possibly be permitted by O'Neill to whom he might offer such explanations as would obtain his forbearance for a time; but how was it likely to be accepted by the local authorities, whom all men would be urging to proceed against him? by the Queen? by the Secretary, who would probably expect to hear that he had not even waited for the coming of Ormond, but had at once assailed the rebels, and driven them out of Munster, as he had repeatedly declared that he alone could do? To most men the example of Barry would seem the simplest, and in the long run, the safest; to make up his mind and ally himself in time, with one or other of the great parties in the coming conflict! that at the worst, he might save himself at last by

the indemnity, with which a struggle of parties so evenly
matched, would most probably terminate.

No sooner had Ormond received the defiant letter from
O'Neill, of his intention to meet his friends at the Holy Cross,
or in politic official language, "To confirm the determination
of all the Traitors of Munster with new oathes, before that
Idol, whom the Irish nation more superstitiously reverence
than all the other idolatries in Ireland," than, to the great
dismay of the Lords of the Council, he determined to march
with 5,000 men to give him meeting. In vain did these discreet men call to his remembrance the last meeting of the
Queen's forces with that formidable rebel, and their advice,
which he had then despised, the neglect of which had been
the source of all their misfortunes. In vain did they plainly
inform him that "they desired not such another Jorney as
that of the Blackwater." It was the lot of these timid
counsellors a second time to waste their warnings upon a
man too wilful to hearken to prudent counsel, and again to
tremble within the walls of Dublin for the existence of the
Queen's army. Ormond with a straightforward reliance upon
the punctuality of O'Neill, hurried towards the Holy Cross.
But the Lords Justices had no real cause for their alarm;
the speed of the royal troops had of late days usually been
in such direction as left safe distance between them and the
arch rebel. O'Neill was punctual to his trysting place; "he
led his force to the gate of the monastery of the Holy Cross,
paused there for the contentment of his devotion," and at his
pleasure moved thence to Cashel, where he was joined by
James Fitz Thomas, "who had been previously appointed,
by his own command, and on his own authority, contrary to
the Statute of the Sovereign, Earl of Desmond."

Florence had been pronounced in the saloons of Cecyll
"wise and prudent." Could his prudence and his wisdom but
extricate him safely from his present entanglement, those
qualities might be his boast for all time! From the moment
that O'Neill left the province of Ulster he began, in accord-
ance with the notice he had fairly given, to do all the hurt in
his power to all who did not join him.

His army marched in a column of flame; the track of
earth behind him was bare and black; and the heavens over
it black also, with smoke and ashes. If such was the doom
of cold friends, or men who dreaded more the danger of the
future than of the present, what might the undertaker, and
the open enemy expect?

This terrible force paused only to destroy; Barry watched

it as it drew daily nearer to his home, he had ample time to make his election between the cause of his countrymen, and of the Queen, and his resolution was taken! whatever might be the doom of Barryscourt, to the Queen, who had embittered the last ten years of his existence by "the affronts put upon him in the matter of the Fyne," his fidelity should remain unshaken, and he would abide the consequences!

Florence's turn must come next! "O'Neill—say the annals of the four masters—proceeded southward across the river Lea, and pitched his camp between that river and Bandon, on the confines of Muskerry and Carbery. To this camp all the MacCartheys, both southern and northern, came into the house of O'Neill, in this camp (i. e. submitted to him), thither repaired two who were at strife with each other concerning the Lordship of Desmond, namely, the son of MacCarthy Reagh, i. e. Fineen (Florence) son of Donogh, son of Donell, son of Fineen, and MacCarthy Mor, i. e. Donell, &c."

There can be no reason to doubt the truth of the account given by Florence of his reception in the camp of O'Neill: the northern chieftain had undoubtedly, at the outbreak of the insurrection, and when he could have had no expectation of the liberation of Florence, acknowledged Donell as "MacCarthy Mor," but when Florence landed in Ireland, and the Gentlemen of Desmond united to oppose Donal, and to choose him for their Lord, he must have felt much embarrassment; and it is likely, as Florence has related the matter, that all decision was for awhile postponed, and referred to certain indifferent arbitrators, in union with the parties of whom it was the hereditary right to decide such election; but whether the election took place at this time, in the camp of O'Neill— as the spies of the' Government reported—or later, in the camp of the Earl of Desmond, there can be no doubt but that in either case the election was unanimous, and the inauguration solemn and ceremonious. " Tyrone—writes the author of the Pacata Hibernia—finding that Florence was not only forward in his own person, but also a fartherer of others, making new proselytes, the children of perdition as well as himself, by the consent of all the Popish Bishops, Fryers, and Jesuits, and all the Irish Nobilitie there assembled, created him MacCarthy More; using in this creation, all the rites and ceremonies accustomed amongst the ancient Irish." Notwithstanding the sneers of this passage it would be impossible to imagine an election, and inauguration of an Irish chieftain more solemn, or more authoritative than this of Florence, the last recorded, and doubtless the last practised in the Sept of the MacCarthys. In the camp of O'Neill,—as later, in the camp of Fitz-Thomas,—were, as this author says, assembled every man of note of the clergy, and nobility of the National party in Ireland. Circumstances seldom furnished an attendance so numerous, or so influential. In ordinary and quiet times, O'Sullevan Mor, and certain other hereditary functionaries, holding offices quite as dignified, and by services more manly than those of the nobles attending an English coronation, would with the assistance of the local Episcopacy and clergy, have sufficed for the instalment of the head of an Irish Sept : but this was an occasion of greater solemnity than had ever occurred within the period during which Ireland had had relation with England. The National camps held assembled all men of birth, position, or territorial influence, in arms for the recovery of the nation's liberty and religion. With the exception of O'Neill, there was not within that great assembly an individual, by birth, inheritance, and marriage, of equal power with the elected Chief; nor, without excepting the Northern Chieftain himself, was there one his equal in ability, in the knowledge of his own country's strength and weakness, and of the resources of the Government with which they were to contend, and of the character of the Queen and Ministers of England; nor one so competent to guide their undertaking to a successful issue. The officer who presented a white wand, or he who offered " wheat and salt in prediction of future peace and plenty," as effectually and really bore symbol of Sovereignty to the Chief elect, as did those nobles who had carried silver and gold sticks before Elizabeth on the day of her coronation; the solemn rite which accompanied the inauguration of Florence was, as to its Christian portion, the same that had been used by the Provincial Kings, his ancestors, from the age of St. Patrick, centuries before the Norman had set foot in England; and as to its less sacred symbolical ceremonies, they had been practised by the Pagan Monarchs of the race of Heber, from the earliest period of historic time, in his native country.

Of the exact nature of Florence's interview with Desmond and O'Neill, nothing could be known with certainty, at the time, to the Commissioners ; but we are informed by national writers that Donal, who had previously declared himself MacCarthy Mor, with the consent of O'Neill, was *deposed* from that dignity, and that Florence having sworn to be true to the cause for which the nation was in arms, was elected in his place, " with the consent of the church, and the nobility." What it was difficult to know, it was easy to conjecture, and

to assert; tidings of this repair of Florence to the camp of
O'Neill, were instantly carried to Power and St. Leger; and
by them, and by a host of others, as instantly reported to
England. Grave men in high stations did not hesitate to
pass from one to another every invention current at Cork
and Kinsale; the Commissioners alone spoke at first with
some decent reservation.

The track of the Northern Chieftain as he advanced into
the country of lukewarm friends, and open adversaries, was,
as he had led men to expect it would be, of wider and more
complete desolation. Such English agricultural capital as
the undertakers had imported into the lands which they
pleasantly called *theirs*, *their* comfortable homes, and model
homesteads, blazed along his pathway; and, to the disgust
of Ormond, not an undertaker stayed to show his title to the
Signories which the Queen's Letters Patent had conferred
upon him! but chiefly upon the doomed country of the Lord
Barry was directed the accumulated anger of the followers
both of Desmond and O'Neill. Barry watched from the hills
of Ibawne as these whirlwinds of ashes were borne each hour
nearer to his devoted country; there poured at last a torrent
of fire and destruction over "all his towns and villages;"
"O'Neill remained in his territory—say the Irish annals of
the four masters—until he traversed, plundered, and burned
it, from one extremity to the other, both plain and wood,
both level and rugged, so that no one hoped, or expected
that it could be inhabited for a long time afterwards."
This sweeping ruin was however not inflicted without repeated efforts made to overcome his loyalty. Desmond,
O'Neill, and O'Donnell each wrote to him, and finally
McCragh, the Pope's Bishop of Cork conjured him to make
common cause with them for his religion and his country, and
threatened him with excommunication—for he was a Catholic
—unless he joined them. Barry's loyalty, and his indignation
were proof equally against exhortations, and threats temporal
and spiritual. When not a rick of corn, nor a hovel, of *all
his towns*, was left unburnt, fresh letters of like tenour were
written to him: to these his reply was desperate, and not
undignified. "Restore to me, he said, my 4,000 kine, my
3,000 mares and garrans! I require restitution of my spoyle,
and prisoners! I doubt not, with the helpe of God and my
Prince, to be quitt with some of you hereafter, though now
not able to use resistance." Deep-rooted in the heart of
Barry must have been his hatred of Florence, when in this
savage destruction of his property he could see no hand but

that of his ancient adversary! The relation of Florence's visit
to the camp of O'Neill was coupled, in all the letters
that reached England, with this cruel spoliation of the
country of Barry: but an incident even more tragical
than the plunder of the herds of Ibawne, occurred at the
same time, and more deeply crimsoned the pages which
poured daily into the Council Chamber of England, and which
also cast its baleful reflection upon the rumours respecting
Florence; it was nothing less than the death of Sir Warham
St. Leger, which took place in an encounter with McGuire,
who commanded O'Neill's horse, in which the combatants
wounded each other to the death: the tale of this tragical
occurrence was more vividly told by a churchman, the Bishop
of Cork, than by any of the martial correspondents who
hastened to impart the tidings to Cecyll.

On the first of March the Commissioners of Munster
wrote to Ormond that the Lo: Barry's country was all
burned by O'Neill. "On Saturday, they add, Florence
McCarthy came unto Tirone, whereuppon they are now with
their whole forces gon towards Kinsale; to what ende wee
cannot yet certeinly learne. Sithence the wrytinge hereof
it hath pleased Godd to call unto his mercy Sr Warham
Sentleger."

Beyond the fact that Florence had visited the camp of
O'Neill nothing was yet known with certainty respecting
him: his enemies readily supplied the intelligence for which
they were anxiously waiting. The Lord Power passed the
rumours on to Ormond as they reached him. "The intelligencers inform me, he wrote, that Fynin is made McCarty
More by the followers of th'Earle of Clancartie's countrey,
as in right of his wife; and the bastard, Donell, is com to
Tyron's camp. Darby McCormocke is com from Fynen to
Tyron wth som 200 men, and his brother Carbry remaynes
with Fynen still."

On the 4th of March Sir Henry Power made up his
despatches for the Privy Council, in which he detailed the
progress of O'Neill, the spoiling of Barry's country, the
encounter between St. Leger and McGuire, and the repair of
Florence to the camp of the rebels.

"1600. *March* 4. Sir H. Power *to the* Lords of the Privy Council.

"May yt please yor Lo^s: to be advertised. Since the last letters from
us, wherein yor Lordships were given to understand of Tyrones coming
into this province I have heerein according to my promyse, sett down his
proceadings; At hys first drawing into the country, he lodged some six

dayes in ye L. Rooche his country, doing very little harme, the common report being y^t he had temporizd wth him, the wch as yet I beleaue, because he will not repayer hether to cleare himselfe of some obiections layde against him by certayne ofthe country, tending to y^t purpose.

"The 18th of Febr^y. he passed the black water, not being able before to doo yt by reason of ye hight theereof; and marcht presently towardes Corke, about w^{ch}, sometymes wthin 2 myles, and sometymes 3 or 4 myles of he hath lodged untill this present day; in wch tyme he hath by letters and menaces, sought all the meanes he could, to draue the gentlemen wch arr subiects into his faction, especially ye Lo: Barry, whom finding resolutely bent to contynew his alleageaunce towardes Hir ^{M}a^{tie}, he burnt and spoyled all his country, and kild or caryed away all such cattle as he could come by, and by an unknowen passage, past men into his Iland, and burnt yt, he not knowing, but y^t yf a foord weere defended they could not have come in, the wch I put men upon, and secured yt. Yt is thought y^t some haue given their pledges to him, of whome as yet we have no notice, and I am the rather pswaded thereunto, because he hath not used y^t violent course towardes them, wch he hath towardes the Lord Barry, and to Charles Mc Carty, and some other. In these troubles the L. Barry hath caryed himselfe very honorably and shewed himselfe a very loyall subiect towardes Hir ^{M}a^{tie}.

"After he had used most extreame tyranny towardes him he marcht by this towne, and lodged at Cariggrohan, one myle distaunt from hence, wher McGuire passing wth the horsemen to spoyle and burnn the country, he himselfe afterwardes past, and encampt fast by y^e river syde, the country burning; wth such horse as I had, I went to see what countenaunce the rebells bore, thinking to gett up some straglers, to whose second McGuire stood wth a grose of 45 horse, and 16 shott, upon whom my fortunn was to happen. Wth me was Sr Warra$^?$ S^t. Ledger whom hardly I drew to consent to ye charging of them; but in ye end I put towardes them, and then the resydue followed me, wch McGuire perceauing prepared himselfe for the encounter; at the first, his shott did us some harme, and amongst the rest kiled one of my best horses wth a bullett in ye head: they being disperst, I ioined wth the horse, and after some conflict ouerthrew them: there weere 32 of his horsemen slayne, amongst whom McGuire made one, his foster father, his priest, all the commaunders of his regiment, and fiue or six of Tyrones principall gentlemen dyed wth him; I had one blow at his eldest soonn wth my staffe, leauing the head of yt buried in him, and him for dead, but sence brought into their camp aliue, but not likely to be recouered; and the better to make the overthrow manifest, I gayned his cornet, a very faire one, and sett yt on the topp of my castle, somewhat distant from ye townn in the view of their camp. I left to persew y^m any farther, the approching of ye night, and the nearenes of their camp forbidding me: of us they hurt not many; onely Sr Warram St Ledger wth a blow of staffe daùgerously throughe the skull, myselfe a blowe on the head wth a sword, and a pushe into the arme wth a staffe, but both of y^m faintly giuen, and not much hurtfull. Thus this auncient Traytor to Hir Matie ended his dayes, hauing prosperously contynewed theise xvj yeares, and being the meanes of drawing ye rest into action, who ever before vaùted of his giuing blowes. This day they are passing further up into ye country. Florence McCarty ys come unto Tyrone, but by his letter assureth us of his loyalty. Yf he prove false they will endaunger Kinsale, all the town being for ye most part of his allyaunce; but he hath protested much, and as yet hath given us no cause to think him dishonest.

"H. POWER."

What Sir Henry Power hesitated to assert the less scrupulous pen of the Bishop of Cork fearlessly detailed to Sir Robert Cecyll : his letter was dated four days later than the Commissioner's despatch ; the contemptuous conduct which he ascribes to Florence, took place, he affirms, in the interval.

" 1600. *March* 5. BP. *of* CORK *to* CECYLL.

"On Saterday last, beinge the 1st of this moneth, MᶜGuyre wth others were sent by Tirone into Kirriwbirry (the Signorie of old Sir Warrham Sᵗ Leger), to burne and spoile: In his retourne a litell before night he was encountred withall by Sʳ. Warrham Sᵗ. Leger and Sʳ. Henrie Power, who issued forth with certen horse out of Cork; and about the sunne set, MᶜGuyre was slayne by Sir Warrhame himself, and he again wounded by MᵃᶜGwyre, in the head, wth an horse man's staffe, to death (as it is thought), the same tyme were slaine MᵃᶜGwyre's sonne, his priest, his foster brother, wth divers others of accoumpt amongst the traitors: some of theire horsemen's staues and MᵃᶜGuyre's coollors were brought away. He left his staf in Sir Warrhames head, and flead wounded; and, by reason of the fall of the evening, after he had ridden about a mile, not being further pursued, fell downe from his horse, died that night under a bush, and is gone to his place, the next morning was carried tothe rebells camp dead. Florence MᶜCarthie is ioined wth O'Neyle, surrendered his patent, and all his right unto O'Neyle, hath yielded to hould the countery of him, and ioineth with him in the action. This was done at his camp on Monday last, the 3ᵈ of this moneth, and since confurmed to the councill heere by a gentleman of good accoumpt and credit."

Two days later than the letter of the Bishop, were despatched further tidings from the Government of Munster to Cecyll. "Tyrone hastneth homewards—they inform him —havinge before his departure, made Florence MᶜCarthy Governor of this our province, and given him the title of MacCarthy More, who is now also parted from Tirone."

Fenton also was ready with evidence of like kind. He wrote, on the information of the Provost-Marshal of Munster, "the Lords of Carbry and Muskry have given their pledges to Tirone ; and Florence MᶜCarty hath thrown away his English patent, and is created MᶜCarty More·by Tirone, and is now with Tirone "

The Lords Justices though they had no intelligence to add to these details, could at least record their readiness to believe them. To the Privy Council they wrote "touching the revoltinge of Florence MᶜCarthy we, that haue known him longest, did never look for other fruits out of such a Spanish heart."

And finally, that the list of Florence's old enemies might not·be incomplete, Mr. Justice Saxey, who with a tender regard for his personal safety had fled away to England on the first tidings of the march of O'Neill, passed on from Poole to the Minister, the information that was sent to him from Munster.

1600. *March 28th.* Mr. Justice Saxey *to* Sir Ro: Cecyll. *From Poole.*

"S^r,—Florence McCarty having rec^d gracious favours from Her Matye, and ptending title tothe countrey of Dessmond under Her Highnes graunt, hath lately (as Mc Carty More) taken a rodd according to the Yrish custome, and holdeth the possession of that countrey by that abolished custome, and not by Her Mat's Lawes. The banishm^t of that country of Donald Mc Carty (backt by the Traytor Dessmond before Florence's coming over), did argue that Florence was greatly graced, yf not supported, by Tyrone; and Florence him self being charged both therewth, and with private conference wth Dessmond, hath lately confessed, that synce his late coming into Yrland he lay wth the Traytor Dessmond two nights, and gave out that yt is Hir Ma^{ts} pleasure that he should converse wth him.

"About the 4th of March Florence came to Tyrone, then being in the com. of Cork, and there toke his oath to be true to him, and to serve him ag^t the English, and gave him his brother for pledge, untill he might send unto him his sonne and heire, and thereupon Tirone appointed him Governor of Monster, and pferreth him, for that he is Mere Yrish, before Dessmond because he is of English race. Mc Carty Reugh Lo: of Carbury is brother in law to James Fitz Thomas the supposed Earle of Dessmond.

" Carbury can make 1,000 men armed ag^t Her Ma^t, but to serve Her Ma^t there are not 30.

" Muskery can make 1,000 armed men to do service against Her Majesty, but for her skant 60. The lyke of Barry's countrey: the lyke of Roche's countrey."

Whilst Mr. Justice Saxey was writing to Sir Robert Cecyll such tidings of Irish disasters as reached him in his retreat, a multitude of complaints were following him from Ireland. Sir Henry Power wrote, "Mr. Justice Saxey's fear urges him to leave for England; the like he did before at Youghal." " S^{t}Leger had described him as obstinate, and overcome with choler and passion." " Thornton had prayed the Lord Lieutenant Essex not to suffer him to be overtopped by one who never could agree long with any one." But severest of all was the complaint of the Lords of the Council at Dublin, who "prayed the Privy Council that Mr. Saxey, Chief Justice of Munster, might receive some publique reproof for his contemptuous manner in departing without licence! that he may be staid in England, and no more returned to fill so high an office!"

To all which Mr. Chief Justice replied by a touching appeal to the feelings of Sir Robert Cecyll, that "he had formerly made £500 p^r an^m by private practice! that he was three score years of age! and had a wife and seven children unprovided!"

The Earl of Ormond, who had hastened with all the disposable forces at his command, to give O'Neill meeting at the Holy Cross, followed on his track, and was within six miles of the great rebel, when, by the simple stratagem of leaving his camp fires lighted, the Northern Chieftain, by a night march, evaded him. "His retreat—wrote Fenton—was considered a masterly performance, and gained him more estimation in the minds of his countrymen than any thing he had yet done." "On going into Munster he was thirteen days, and three in returning." Although he quitted his friends in Munster with abruptness, and seemingly in flight from the royal forces, he by no means left them an easy prey to their enemies. Dermod O'Connor, with a thousand Connaught men was left behind, as rumour said, at the command of Florence. From the inaccessible fastnesses of Desmond, whither he had retired on the departure of O'Neill, Florence now wrote to Sir Henry Power. He informed him that his loyalty was unshaken; that availing himself of Sir Henry's previous warrant he had not scrupled to visit the camp of O'Neill, and *had thereby rendered a great service to the Queen's Majesty!* and so, in truth, he had; for not a torch blazed in Carbery, not a hostile bony had set foot in Desmond, which he avowed he continued to hold in perfect tranquillity in obedience to Her Majesty. But not all he could do, as he afterwards gravely wrote to Sir Robert Cecyll, could make Power comprehend the service he had thus rendered to the Government! To the pen of the Bishop of Cork, who was a more plain spoken and, it may be added, a more lively correspondent than the generalty of the functionaries of the Irish Government, we are indebted for the discovery of the next movements of Florence, who, well aware of the equivocal nature of his position, no longer stirred except with the attendance of a large body of his followers; and from this time forward to the end of his career never placed himself within reach of the authorities except after receiving from them an *absolute and unconditional pardon for all possible past offences! and a safe conduct to go and return!* with as many attendants as he thought proper to take with him.

"1600· *April* 2. BISHOP OF CORK *to* MY LORD.

*With a note what conference passed between Florence M*c*Carty and Donnell*
*M*c*Carty.*

" My duty most humbly remembered unto your Honor,
" May it please the same; since conference had with M^r. Watson, I have
presumed to advertise your Honor of the success of things here, hoping of
your Honor's favorable acceptance thereof, only done in discharge of my
duty in my place.   After that the traitor O'Neyll had taken a full view of
the harbours of Cork and Kensall (which are ten myles asunder) and had
don his will upon the inhabitants in the borders, he retourned the way he
came, into Muskry, into the Lord Roche's countrey, and so into Arlo
Woodds, where he was the eighth day of the last moneth, at which tyme
my Lord of Ormond passed with his forces that way toward Limerick,
about some six myles of.   Tirone getting knowledge of his being passed
by, raised his camp at midnight, leaft his fyres burning, went on his journey northward, and that peece of the night, and the next day, marched 23
miles at least.   Tirone, amongst other establishments of his for our
southren rebells hath deputed his Cosin Florence Mc Carthy, his Mac
Cartȳ Moore, the chief commander over the Irishry; and James Fitz
Thomas his Earle of Desmond, over the English-Irish rebells, that is, those
Irish of ancient English stock, now Irished altogether.   Since that,
Florence Mc Carthie, the traitor, is so stronge upon all this coast, viz.,
from the old head of Kensall untill Dingle-Cush, and within the river of
Limerick in Kerry-side; it is needefull (under correction) that his coast be
well garded, and kept from foreign forces, wch doubtlesse Florence will by
all meanes seek to drawe to him.   Florence gave two^e pleadges unto Tirone
for his loyalty, and fidelity, and to bringe in to him his eldest sonne; viz.,
his own brother Dermode, that traitor, and one Finin Mc Donell Carthy,
his foster brother, a freeholder; the said pleadge, his eldest sonne was to
be given to Dermode O'Conohor, O'Neyll's deputie, for that purpose, about
the 12th of the last moneth, the delivery is yet uncertain.   O'Neyll hath
taken one of the said twoe pleadges with him unto the north; the other—
y^t is Florence's brother—is retourned home.   The said Dermode O'Conohor
is leaft·behind wth O'Neylls other forces to attend on Florence; having a
thousand of O'Neylles Northern rebells under his commaund, to be at
Florence's direction.   The case thus standing, Florence Mc Carthy, yet, for
all this, pollitikely and impudently gives it forth by l^{res} and messages to
his friends in the townes, where he is well favoured, especially in Kinsall,
that he continueth loyall to Her Majestie; and did what is done in deape
pollicie to coossen Tirone, by warr^t out of England, for the better safety
of himself and his countries.   The Irish do beleeve this, and hold him for
a good subject; yea, and of the English also, not knowing that this was the
verie practise of O'Neyll himself at his first entrance into action of rebellion, to dally with the State, and the worlde, untill he had fitted himself,
as your Honor best knoweth.   Florence being in camp besides Kinsall
with O'Neyll, had thereout, upon his l^{res}, from his friends bottells of wyne,
and better relief.   I cannot but deliver this unto your Honor, wishing it
might be looked into, with other of the Towne's doings.
  " The 27th of the last, Florence wrote unto Sir Henry Power, for *protection* to parley with him; the council did agree, and gave him ward. The
day following comes Florence within twoe miles of Cork, with 300 Connaught Bonewes, by a woodside, (for he would not come into Cork).
Theether went Sir Henrie, and Sir George Thornton, and Sir Charles

Willmott; and Florence comes out of the wood all armed with a pistoll at his gerdell, verie timorous. First conferred with him Sir Henrie and Sir George, and after Sir Charles with them. His speeches in defence of his doings are so frivolous, as that I will trouble you Honor therewith, as, if Her Matie would have him to leave all, and beg in England, he wold do it; with other vaine words. But no likelihood of any hope that he is, or will be, a thankfull subject for so many great favours, and graces, received of Her Highnes. The generall opinion of him heere is that he will shew an Irish trick, ingratitude, for a good turne, and whatsoever he allegeth, sure it is his joining with O'Neil was voluntary; he might have kept him from him, but he aimeth to be as great in the south as the other in the north. *The Lord of Hosts confound them both! I pray in charity.*

" At the old head of Kensall, there is a strong fort, lately in Florence's keeping, but now taken by direction, and a ward there placed. O'Neyll hath equally divided betwixt his cosin Florence, and his Earle of Desmond, all pfits gotten in the province, or coming from beyond the seayes. Pardon me, Right Honble, I beseech you: to yield a poor opinion, it were very requisite that some of Her Majesty's pinnaces be appointed for this coast, and the river of the Shannon. The consideration I humbly leave to your Honour's grave and deep judgment, craving pardon for my boldness.

" Cork this 2nd of April, 1600.

" Your Honor's humbly to be commanded,

" WILLIAM CORK & ROSS."

" The Lord President is not yet come into the province, but looked for daily.

" To the Right Honble Sir Robert Cecil, Knight, Principal Secretary to the Queen's Most excellent Majesty."

Inclosure in April 2, 1600.

"*Certn conference past betwixt* FLORENCE M^{c}CARTHIE *and* DONELL M^{c}CARTY, *alias* M^{c}CARTY REAUGH; *delivered by the said* DONELL M^{c}CARTHIE, *to me, the* BISHOP *of* CORK.

" The said M^{ac}Carty and Florence being together at Kilbrittan, at what tyme James Fitz Thomas the traitor was in Coursey's countrey or 4 or 5 myles of from that place, The said Florence asked of Mc Carthie Reaugh (they twaine standing in the. window in Kilbrittaine castell next to the sea) what course he would take ? Mc Carty made answere that he purposed to houlde, as he had done, on Her Ma^{ts} side. Florence made answeare and said, ' take heede what you do! the Queene is not able to overcome us; trust not in the English, for *they are not sound among themselves, and the Councill is devided, and no man knoweth it better than I do;* and be suer that the Irish will prevaile; and if I obteyne Mc Carty More's countrey (as I have no doubt but I shall), it is a fast and safe countrey, and full of rocks and mountains, and great fastnesse, and there we shalbe safe if we cannot keepe this countrey : there we shalbe strong enough for the English.' These and other despitefull and traiterous words Florence uttered to Mc Carty, as Mc Carthie enformed me. Charles Mc Carthie, now in England, and Owen O'Swillivan told unto me the 4th of the last moneth, that O'Downin a Rimer of Muskrie being in the north with O'Neyll, O'Neyll shewed him divers l^{res} sent to him from Florence Mc Carthie; some, three yeares ago, some later.

" WM. CORK & ROSS."

" Since the writing of this note it is certainely signified that Florence Mc Carty sent one Richard Burk, a Capt^{en} of some of the northern rebels, to spoile the Barony of Ybawne, belonging to the Lord Barry; where the said Burk was slaine by the nephew of the Lo: Barrie's; in this conflict was slaine also the said nephew, who had the charge of Ybawne, under the Lord Barry. On Burk's side wth himself were slaine 9 of the best gentlemen he had, and 40 other."

The rule of Sir Henry Power was drawing rapidly to a close. The arrival of a newly-appointed President of Munster was expected daily, and Power himself was under orders to repair to Dublin, and enter upon such charge as had been appointed for him; yet even under these circumstances, when any man of ordinary discretion would have abstained from all action tending to impair the freedom of his successor, his impatience, and the same phantom which had haunted the authorities of Munster for so many years, urged him to an act of needless barbarity, which had not even the poor plea of expedience. " The *doubt*, as he expressed it, which he conceived of Florence caused him to lay a plot upon a castle which he possessed, called the Old Head of Kinsale, which took effect." For this he had no warrant but his own will, and no motive but his *doubt*. It was in direct violation of the rights conferred upon Florence by the Queen, and was not a whit more justifiable than if Florence had laid a plot against Shandon Castle. But not for this great provocation did Florence permit a single bony to join Fitz Thomas, much less a follower of his own to resist the Queen's authority. The next step of Sir H. Power is so extraordinary, so abhorrent to every feeling of humanity, that it would seem incredible had he not with inconceivable and stupid frankness himself avowed it to the Queen's Government, "Florence was plausible, and in spite of appearances, had not given him any cause to believe him other than an honest man, but he *doubted* him," and *therefore* " sent the Queen's soldiers into Carbery—Florence's chiefest place—either to waste it, or to take assurances of the freeholders !' How this sanguinary order was understood by the person employed to execute it shall be told in his own words. Power was about to surrender his trust, and he thought fit on doing so, to write to Cecyll an account of his government; how he found the province, and how he left it, namely " in far better terms than he received it." His successor also wrote an account of the condition in which Munster was left, and *he* asserted, " the confusion and distemper thereof hath never been greater than now it is." The history of the encounter of the Queen's troops with the bonies of O'Neill, left at the command of Florence, reached the Minister from no less than six different sources: the first was Captain Flower, who conducted it, and who, like many greater captains knew as well what to conceal, as what to exaggerate; the next was Sir Henry Power, who improved even upon the sagacity of Flower, from whom he received his information; then followed Cuffe and Aylmer, both eye-witnesses, indeed actors in the engagement, and whose narratives reflect unwilling praise upon Florence, who, in a manner especially characteristic of his usual wariness, had planned, and led in person the attack of that day.

Florence's bitterest enemy, upon many occasions, called him a *coward!* He called him also a *fool!* Cowardice and folly were both shown that day, by whom let the reader judge!

From the age of 15 to 23 Florence had held a commission in the Queen's service, and with Ormond, Stanley, and every English officer in repute in Ireland in those days, had served through the wars in Desmond! Nothing heroic is recorded of him, but evidently his cowardice had not been discovered, for he had received for his services, besides other proofs of Her Majesty's favour, a present of a thousand marks and a pension of two hundred marks; but of what he may have been, and probably was, afraid in later days, we shall have occasion to show shortly, and with what reason the reader shall form his own opinion. The fifth account of this day's adventure was written in full detail by the Lord President elect of Munster, in a letter from Dublin to Sir Walter Raleigh, then in England. What is become of that letter is unknown to the author of these pages. The last chronicler of this single feat of generalship of Florence was Florence himself; and if his account of the previous conduct of Flower and Bostock, and their soldiers, be true, it is impossible not to admire his moderation and magnanimity in declaring that "could he have had his own desire he would have sent the latter—the soldiers—safe back to Cork!" equally impossible to accuse him of misconceiving the deserts of the former— Flower and Bostock—in declaring that "he would have hanged them both."

The orders given by Power to Flower, were "to burn and spoil all such as would not come in." Flower has omitted to inform us in what way he made known to the wretched peasantry the option, which had been humanely left them! one such excursion as this of Flower through

R

Carbery was enough to make savages of a whole nation; "he killed—he says with shameless boasting—many of their churles and poor people, and left not a grain of corn within ten miles of his way of march."

" 1600. April 1. *A brief note of* CAPT. FLOWER'S *Journey into Roskarbry, the first of April,* 1600.

" First beinge appoynted by Sir Henry Power, chief comaunder of the forces here, to marche into Carbry; (ther to borne and spoyl all suche as were revolted from their loialty, yf they would not come in) and put in sufficient pleges for their subiection.

" The first daye that I marched from Kynsale in our passage over the ryver of the Bandon we were enterteigned wth a light skermishe by some of Florence Mᶜ Carties men, where we slew 12 of them, wherof ther was three gent; and toke iiij cowes, borned Carregnase, wherin Florences ward was, and all that borders, wth great store of corne belonginge to Dermond Moyle M'Cartie (Florence's brother) now a rebbell.

" The third dayes march in our waye to Ross we borned a castell called the Muntan, belonginge to a foster father of Florence MᶜCartie's, wᶜh was then as pledge wth Tyrone for Florence's brother to him; wth mayny townes belonging to the said castell, where was borned much corne; and our soldiers had great store of armes, and other spoyls.

" From thence wee marched to Rosse, where we rested two dayes.

" From Rosse we marched over the Leape into O'Donovan's country, where we borned all those ptes, and had the kylling of mayny of *there churles and poore people, leavinge not therein any one grayne of corne wthin ten myles of our waye wherever we marched ;* and toke a praye of 500 cowes, wᶜh I caused to be drowned, and kylled, for that we would not trouble ourselves to dryve them in that jorney. Beyond the Leape we stayd three dayes; in wᶜh tyme we borned and spoyled all the Sept of the Clan Dermondes (Mac Carthys) then in accõn and upon our marche into O'Mahon feins (Fin's) countrey, I had sertayne intelligence that Florence MᶜCartie was prepared wth 1,800 men to entercepte my passage backe to Rosse; upõ wᶜh newes I retorned to Rosse; and the same night Florence came and camped wthin two myles of me, wth parte of his forces; and Dermond O'Connor comaunder of the Conought men wth 1,000 Connaughe souldiers camped one the other side of me, wthin iij myles of us, to entercept our passage to Corke (as they saied) but we were so troublesome neighbours to those Conought men, that we enforced them to draw their forces together, wher they remayned before us tene dayes, in wᶜh tyme Sir Henry Power sent me espetiall order to draw to Corke wth all speed I coulde; upõ wᶜh receipt I marched towards Kynsayle. The enemie understanding of my rysinge, followed us wth all their force all that daye, but by reasone we gott the playnes, and a myle before them, I would never suffer them to brenge up their strength to fyght, but still kept them in wth our horse; in that dayes marche we killed xlij wherof were fyfe gent.

" When we came to Kynsayle, I received direction to marche to Corke, and leavinge 250 of th army behinde to gard that towne (in my jorney to Cork unexpected) wee were enterteigned wth ther whole force, wher the inforced us, by reason of a bridge that they had gayned of us, *to fight upon a retreate, for half a myle, and better,* but afterwardes, finding my advauntage, both of tyme and grounde I charged there first battelle wth some horse and brok them; and had the executõn of them a myle. In that chardge we slewe dead 137, wherof 8 were capt⁸, besides 37 sore wounded. Of them ther died the first night, wᶜh were hurt, sixtene. My self beinge at that time and in the begiñge hurt, uppō the first chardge, wth a picke, nine inches into the thighe (by their generall). At that chardge I had one horse killed under me with three picks in his body, and tow bulletts. When we bracke them I fought hand to hand wth their geñall where I received my second hurt in my head, by one that carried their collors (I having one ꝑte of them in my hand, aud he th other). Her I had my second horse slayne wth picke, under me. So I thank God we were masters of· the feild, and in all that jorney we lost but one lyveteñant and nine soldiers being slayne, and myself wth fiftene others hurt."

" 1600· *April* 21. JOSHUA AYLMER *to* CECYLL.

" And least yoʳ Honʳ should think me carelesse of my endeavours, I, in discharge of my duetie ꝑsent unto yoʳ Honʳ what hath happened here sence my arrivall, and in especiallie this daies service, wherin I was an actor, and eie witness. Please it yoʳ Honʳ therefore to understand that Florence Mc Carta entertayned one Dermond O'Knowhoer wth 600 others of Conaght, and levied theforce of his owne countie wᶜh he ioyned tothem, and in all they were 1,200, wth wᶜh force he oppenlie opposed him self as a Traitʳ against Her Matie, wheruppon Her Highnes forces tothe number of 1,000 fotte and 80 horse, entered his countrie, burned prayed, and spoyled a great ꝑte thereof, and killed about 60 of his men. On Sundaie the 20ᵗʰ of this instant they returned to Kinsale, and ther rested all night. Mondaie the 21ˢᵗ in the morninge leavinge behinde them Sir Richarde Percie and Captaine Bostocke companies contayning 250 fotte, Captaine Flower wth 500 fotte and 60 horse, beinge Serjeant Major, and sole comander ofthat armie, marched towards Cork; and havinge no intelligence ofthe enemie that morning, did little suspecte ther beinge in that ꝑte of the countrye; but Florence MacCartta accompanied as aforesaid, seckinge all meanes he might to defeate Her Mats forces, privelie conveied himselfe, and in the mid waie to Corke, at a little narrowe bridge, the forde deppe and daungerous. envirowned wth wood and bogge, ther he imbattled all his companie, deviding them into two severall battales: Dermond O'Knowhoer coāmanded the first, and him self the seconde; ther they laie flatt on the grounde, attendinge our cominge, and suffered our scotts to passe the bridge, and to returne againe, wᶜh the did wthout any discovered; Till our horse goinge downe the hill to passe the bridge, made a halte, and stayinge to vewe the place, discried them as the laie, by the sonne shyninge on their murions; *wee retyred to put ourselves in order,* but the toke ther ꝑnte advantage, and ther vangarde wth the winges of shotts charged us before we could recover the hill, so as the horse was faine to bide the fury of their force, till the fotte were in order to fight; and then expectinge they wolde have discharged ther duties, and made good ther ground, *they all retired* most shamefullie with little lesse then runninge awaye, till the came to a little castell more then a quarter of a myle of; wher some toke the castell in hoppe to save them selves; the rest stod to defende the Bawne, the bankes wherof were briste high, uppon the wᶜh were placed 60 shotte wᶜh discharged so luckelie as they killed many of the enemie, the rest for the must ꝑte let fall their armes, and ranne awaie; the horse followinge the chase killed 200 of them wᶜh laie ther in the felde, wherof Dermond O'Knowhore, his second brother was one, and quatuor more ofther best leaders wth 10 gent of accompt ther were hurt, bie report from them, as may more of them. Dermond O'Knowhore and Florence were both shotte

R 2

wth pistols, but the had no hurt: on our part there was slain lieutenant Grime, and some 8 other horsemen, and 15 hurt; whereof Captain Flower was hurt in the thighs with a pike. We lost in this fight 30 horses. In the end we had the field and made the enemy flee; but by the faint courage of the foot was lost the benefit of the 2 day's service, which being duely executed, had ended the war of that part, and cut off Florence and all his rebellious company; but if the castle had been one quarter of a mile further, all her Majesty's forces had been cut off! and scarce any had come away to tell who had hurt them."

"1600. *April* 23. *To the Right Hon*^ble SIR ROBERT CECIL, K^t., *Principal Secretary to Her Majesty and one of Her Highness' most Hon*^ble *Privy Council.*

" Right Honble,
" Myselfe amongst many others beinge tyed by your great favors, acknowledge it a dutie to give you advertisem^t of the accidents wch happen in these partes; of one fortune made me ptaker uppon my first landinge at Kensale, wher pte of our forces, to the number of, 600 foote & 80, horse, under the comande of Captn Flower, wear newly retorned from Karribry, beinge followed by Florence Mc Carty, who had drawen in Dermond O'Connoher wth 2,000 to resist Her Mats forces; of wch companyes, the day before my arivall, our horse had cutt of 50 foote y^t laye in ambushe to discover wch way we tooke; we being to martch unto Corke, and the enemy determininge to fight wth us, had placed uppon a fourde in the waye, a regiment of 700, who beinge discovered, *Captn Flower retired* to a place of better advauntaidge, himselfe wth the horse keeping the reare, wch they charged very hotlye, owt of an assured hope to have gotten the daye, havinge two other regiments near at hande; but ther expectation was made voyde by some 80 shott that wear ambushed uppon our retiringe, who discharginge killed some and stroake such an amasemente in ye rest y^t many castinge away ther armes betooke them to their heeles, but the horse pursewinge the occasion, beat them into their battaile; killed 200, five commanders, and divers gentlemen; we lost aboute 70 men & of horses kilde, and hurte above twentye. I cannott informe you of the strenth of the companyes having not yett vewed them, &c. &c. In the meane time I recomend my service & myselfe to your honorable regard, and so take humble leave.
" Corke the 23rd of Aprill 1600.
" Your Honor's most asseured and redy to be comanded
" HN: CUFFE."

It is worthy of remark how closely the Queen's army was copying the light equipments, and rivalling the more obvious accomplishments of their enemy! It is the boast of the highly civilized soldier that he can readily discover, and quickly adopt any advantage which a keener sense of self-defence may have taught to a savage adversary. The royal troops accustomed to fighting in the low countries had found little to learn from their Spanish enemy, but when they came against the mere or wild Irish, they found all things different! They saw before them an enemy who " *wore no apparel, and*

*who trusted rather to the nimbleness of their heels, than to their
hands in time of battle!"* These peculiarities could not fail to
attract their admiration, and as the reader has seen, in the
fights under Harrington in the Glynns, and Clifford, in the
Corlews, they owed their success chiefly to their prompt
adoption of these Irish tactics! But it admits of doubt, after
all, whether these imitations by the Royal troops were, except
in an Irish sense, improvements! The amount of *clothing* in
the two armies was speedily equalised, for in addition to the
usual consumption of cassocks, dublets, veneccians, shirts,
caps, and bands, inseparable from a campaign, their new mode
of fighting was inevitably attended with much waste. The
propriety of this return in the winter season, and the Irish
climate, to the primeval dignity of the human creature may
be fairly questioned! it is certain that the abruptness of the
change had not a beneficial effect upon the health of the
English farm-servant, the Bristol recruit, or even of the hardier
soldiers trained in the Carmarthenshire jails.

But worse than change of attire was the alteration of *diet*
in the Queen's army! *"The Irish soldier fed upon grass,"* and
this was certainly pleasanter and wholesomer feeding than
" rotten unserviceable food," as was seen in the case of Williams
and his men, who used it for a considerable time, and of the
Munster rebels, of whom Essex testified that they had able
bodies, ready use of their arms, and boldness to fight Her
Majesty's troops ; whereas Ormond wrote to the Queen that
"her poor soldiers dropped dead on the march, owing to the
victuals dealt out to them." But if, at the cost of such heavy
losses as were reported by Ormond, Bagnal, Fenton, and
others, her Majesty was resolved upon assimilating her
soldiers to the Irish in diet and apparel, the troops themselves
were apt imitators of another accomplishment of their adversaries! Cecyll had been informed that " hounds could scarcely
follow them" (the Irish), much less men." This comparison
was significant, as Cecyll probably perceived. From the
time of Fin McCool Ireland had always been celebrated
for the fleetness of her hounds. " The Fenian force let loose
3,000 matchless hounds of pure blood at the chase of Sliabh-
na-mban, and they killed 6,000 deer," but what was the speed
of Sgeolan, or Bran, or Ciar-throil, which outstripped every
hound, or Iosgad-ur swifter than a blackbird, in comparison
with the fleet-footed soldiers of Harrington, when once freed
from their incumbrances? Rejectis exuviis?

After brief experience the Queen's officers learned to com-
bine speed with method, and reduced that extreme nimble-

ness of heels, which to Sir Henry Harrington had appeared too nearly to resemble "cowardice and flight," to a more systematic process of footmanship, which was recognised under the expression of "fighting in retreat." The tactics were not absolutely new; in fact, they were rather the revival of a mode of warfare practised by an ancient nation of renowned warriors; when Flower marked the aptitude of the Queen's soldiers for such surprising celerity in what the Earl of Essex had called "*going off*," his classical re-membrances enabled him at once to recognise their resem-blance to "the ferocious Parthians." He was the first to turn this accomplishment to account in his engagement with the bonies of O'Conor, and the followers of Florence. Aylmer, who was himself present at this victory of the Queen's troops, thus described to Cecyll the first experiment of the new tactics :—" As soon as they (Flower and his Parthians) de-tected the forces of the rebels lying down in ambush to await their coming, "*they retired* to put themselves in order, expecting the foot to discharge their duty; but *they retired* most shamefully, little else than running away, till they came to a castle, more than a quarter of a mile off; but if the castle had been one quarter of a mile further, all Her Majesty's forces had been cut off, and scarce any one had come away to tell who had hurt them." The shameful running away was a hasty and petulant judgment of Aylmer, for he admits that "his men in the end had the field, and *made the enemy flee*," and Captain Flower, who commanded the Queen's troops on the occasion, knew nothing more of this running away, except that "he was at one time *obliged to fight in a retreat*."

"1600. *April* 30. SIR H. POWER *to the* LORDS OF H.M.'s PRIVY COUNCIL.

"The Lord President ys come to this Province the 24th of this instant to whom I have delyvered the charge, which was committed unto me. And for that I maye the better yeald yr Lls: accompt thereof, &c. &c. How Tyrone came into the country and of his attemptes I have formerly adver-tised yr Lls. as also of Florence Mc Cartyes coming to him, and having setled the State, making Florence cheefe, in regard he was of ye race of ye meere Irishe: With much more hast than he came into the province he de-parted, and the first night marchinge to the broad-water, although by reason of the hight thereof, it was not passable, yet he attempted yt, notwthstand-ing so doing he lost many of his men. There Florence McCarty parted from him, and went into his own country &c. &c. The doubt which I then con-ceaved of Florence caused me to lay a plott upon a castle which he possessed called ye Old Head, standing very offensive to the harbors of this Towne, and Kinsale wh: tooke effecte; and I assure yr Lordships there is no place in this province of greater import than yt, &c. &c.

" I sent a 1,000 men into Carbury (Florence his cheifest place to mayne-
tayne his hierlinges in, and to offend most out), wth derection, eyther to
wast yt, or to take assuraunce of ye freeholders at their first entrye they
tooke a great pray, and kild divers of ye Mahoans, ye principall men of y^t
part; and afterwardes passed ye Leape, *wasting, burnıng, and killing ye
cattle of all y^t country;* and so retourned to Rosse, to effect y^t charge w^ch
was comitted to them; wheer they lay 14 dayes taking in of pledges.
Florence in the mean tyme gathering together of his followers and hierlings
1,800 men, came and lay by them.   Upon the news of ye Earle of Ormond,
I sent for them to draw hether: at their rysing ye rebells made profer to
fight, but came not on, although they lost their forlornn hoope, consisting
of 40 of their best men, wch was defeated by ye horse, and ye reare of
Florence's own battle broken, and 10 of them kild; and so they came to
Kinsale wthout losse; whear leauinge the guarysonns of that townn behind
them, they came towardes Corke wth 100 horse and 600 foott.   In their
way, Florence wth all of his force was layd in an ambushe, and did it so
secreatly y^t they weere ready to ioin before they weare discouered.   Y^t
ground not serving our men to fight on, they retrayted towardes a playne,
and in ye way layd aboue 100 shott in ambushe; wch retrayte bread a
boldnes in the rebells, and moved them to follow them; in wch doing they
fell into the ambuscade of shott, and receaved the vollye, in wch their weere
many of the rebells commaunders, and gentlemen slayne: The resydew
neglected their attempt, and our horse charged, and put them all to flight;
their weere slayne six captaines, 10 gentlemen, and 140 that carryed armes,
of ye rebells; of ours theer weere onely eight slayne, and Cap. Flower and
some others lightly hurt: The rebells begann to make heade againe, but my
coming in wth 40 freshe horse, wch I had gathered, altered their determination; and so I brought them to Corke to entertayne ye L Presydent, to
whom I layve the province, in farr better termes then I found yt, for
wheereas before thear was no passage in any part of ye country, now two
men may passe between this and Waterford, wch ys 50 myles, and in like
manner to Kilmalock; neyther has theer beein any man intercepted sence
Tyrone's departure; theise partes being now very quiett, and populous.   I
doubt not but that I should have rendred yor Ll^s a larger accoumpt of
theise warrs, yf I had had 200 horse; but I never saw aboue thirty sence
my coming, wch were of companyes, for although Sir Anth Cookes, Captn
Whytes, and Captn Taffe's horse weere sett down for this province yet my
L of Ormond sent capt. Taffe's horse into Meath, and kept Sir Anthony
Cookes, till they weere so spent wth travell y^t they could not endure any
longer.   I am now going to Dublyn to receave y^t charge, wch yor Ll^s in yor
Ho: care towardes me, have assigned for me; from whence, how yor Ll^s
order shall take effect, I wilbe carefull to acquaynt yor Ll^s; as also, con-
tynually of my proceedinges, and thus wth my most humble duty to yor
Ll^s, humbly submitting myselfe to yor Ll^s most ^hoble censures, I take my
leaue.

" Cork ye 30th of Apr^ill 1600."

" Yo^r Ll^s most bounden,
" H. POWER.

It would seem that now at last Florence was fairly compromised! to use the words of the President of Munster, "he
had with colours displayed, encountered the Queen's forces
in the field!" But such had been the unprovoked and inhuman attack commanded by Sir H. Power upon a peaceful
peasantry, that there at once ensued on all. sides, an almost

total silence respecting it. Sir Robert Cecyll *never* alluded
to it; Carewe but once, and then only to say he exceedingly
regretted that the expedition had ever taken place; and the
many enemies of Florence but feebly used it amongst their
other accusations. We shall presently see that when
Florence found it necessary to explain to Cecyll much of his
recent conduct, he entered fearlessly into all the circumstances concerning that shameful excursion into his native
district, openly declared that Flower and Bostock had been
bribed by his evil-wishers to commit the outrages they did,
and far from evading the share he had had in opposing
them, he indignantly repelled a suspicion of his own followers "that he had been unwilling to allow them to fight
the spoilers of their country," and only regretted that "it
had not been his fortune to capture the two leaders, that he
might have hanged them both."

Could Florence have entertained any doubt of Cecyll's
disapprobation of the conduct of Sir H. Power, his defence
would have been a reckless defiance of the Queen's authority.
His letter produced no word of reproof, and when, shortly
after, in obedience to the wish of the President, he waited
upon him in Cork, he stipulated for, and received, before
doing so, an absolute pardon, not for this seemingly audacious act of rebellion in particular, but for each and every
offence he might have given to Her Majesty; and this barbarous act of the Munster authorities, and Florence's
rebellious opposition to it, like a thousand similar acts and
oppositions, fell into forgetfulness.

The time was now come for the removal of Sir H. Power
from Munster, and he thought it not unnecessary to give
some account of his government. If Queen Elizabeth
perused the document which he sent to the Privy Council
upon that occasion, to see upon what grounds he had employed her soldiers to "enter a peaceful country, to lay all
waste within ten miles of their line of march! to burn the
habitations! drown the cattle! and slaughter, *not fighting
men, but churles, and poor people!*" the only cause she would
find there alleged was the *doubt which he conceived of Florence!*
Bearing the same date as this despatch of Power, was written
another, of very different tenor, by the able man who replaced him, and from this we shall learn something more
than Power chose to write, probably more than he really
knew. Of the force—followers and bonies—that Florence
had noiselessly taken into his service, of the surprising
strength of his country, and the position and army of the

Earl of Desmond, and of the disgraceful limits within which
the royal authority had been restricted during the whole
period of his government Sir Robert Cecyll could have conjectured little from the report of the retiring Commissioner.
How startling, after the declaration that "he was leaving
the province in far better terms than he had received it, that
whereas, on his arrival there was no passage through any
part of the country, now two men could pass between Cork
and Waterford, which is fifty miles, and in like manner to
Kilmallock," must have been the tale that followed it! "the
provincial rebels are no less than 7,000 able, weaponed men!
Florence McCarty, by his friends and followers, will be the
strongest, and of greatest force of any Traitor in Munster;
in so much that 1,500 of Her Majesty's forces must of necessity be employed against him!"

CHAPTER XI.

SIR GEORGE CAREWE.

IN the month of June, 1583, in the streets of Dublin, in broad daylight, in the presence of the Mayor and magistrates of the city, and of hundreds of spectators was committed " *a ʼfoul, and heinous crime !* "
Deeds of violence, unhappily, crimson many pages of the annals which trace the progress of our race—·a race of quick passions and proud impulses—from rude beginnings to a self-subduing civilization. The frequency of homicide amongst the Irish, and their apparent indifference to human life, has at all times shocked the calmer minds of English writers, who, with greater control over their emotions, have recorded with perfect justice, and impressive repetition, their horror of such fierce and ruthless passions ; but in the *ʼfoul and heinous crime* alluded to, were circumstances of such unusual baseness and barbarity, that magistrates and people were alike struck with astonishment and disgust.

Apart from the consideration that a man's life had been taken in cold blood, under the very eyes of the civic authorities, were other circumstances attending this murder which fixed upon it a deeper guilt than usually attaches to such a crime. Dublin was not in those days open to every roving swordsman who might take a fancy to visit. it, a free pass was necessary for the admission of a mere Irishman within its gates, and none would venture thither without a written protection from the Government, and the certainty of free exit. There had come into the city only three days previously, with protection and official pass from the Lords Justices, two men of the mere Irish, one of them a chief of the Kavanaghs, and the other his follower. They had recently rendered a service to the Government, such service as was rarely rendered by any of the Irish—captured a man on whose head a price had been set—had received their payment, according to covenant, and were remaining for their own pleasure within the city, under the special licence and protection of the Government which they had served. It chanced that one of these men had been engaged, *three years previously*, in an action in which an English force had endeavoured to penetrate a wild country called the Glins, and became entangled in a pathless defile amongst woods and bogs, in which two-thirds of their men were slain. It was a gallant action, "the hottest, wrote a brave man who was in it, the hottest piece of service, for the time it lasted, that ever I saw in any place;" the invading force had no cause to look back upon it with any shame, except for the rashness which had led them to entangle themselves in a country from which extrication was nearly hopeless ; the officers and men who fell, fell with honor! and the survivors could, with no justice, entertain any feelings of rancour against the brave men who had, in defence of their own wild homes, slain them.

Whilst strolling through the city, on Midsummer-eve, these men—fighting-men from their cradles—were naturally attracted by "an assembly of the youth of the city in some show of arms, according to an ancient custom ;" they had entered a booth or building, and were seated together, when an English gentleman, who had lost a brother in the action of the Glins, walked up to the two Irishmen, asked which of them was Owen O'Nassie, and upon receiving an answer "*plunged a dagger into the bosom of the man, and presentlie one of his men shot him with a pistol and two bullets, and gave him many wounds, whereof he presently died! and immediately upon the act the English gentleman fled away!*" What reasons induced the Lord Justices to consider this murder as more than usually deserving of their displeasure the reader will presently see in their own words. With every allowance "for what flesh and blood will work in young men to revenge the killinge of their brothers and allies," they yet judged it expedient to call a jury of the citizens to examine into this deed, and the jury thought it expedient to pronounce a sentence of "*Wilful Murder against the English gentleman, two English friends who had stood by whilst the murder was done, and two servants who had finished the affair with the pistol and two bullets,*" all but one of whom had fled away, no one knew whither.

In the month of April, 1599, sixteen years after this foul and heinous action, a new Lord President arrived in Munster, a man of great repute, high in favour with the Queen, and an especial friend of Sir Robert Cecyll ; it was *the English gentleman of the Lords Justices! the Wilful Murderer of the Dublin Jury! the Convict of* 1583 ! Sir George Carewe, who had given a lesson to those mere Irish how it was becoming to avenge the death of a brother officer slain in battle!

The account of the skirmish in the Glins, in which the brother of this gentleman had fallen, has reached. us from the pen of an English officer, whose gallantry and coolness mainly contributed to the extrication of the few of his countrymen who survived.

The writer was Sir William Stanley, whose name the reader has so often met with in these pages associated with Jacques de Franceschi; and alas! the friend also of Florence ; the most fatal of all friends! whose friendship had cost him eleven years of captivity, volumes of evil repute, and finally the sum of £500, which, but for this fatal friendship, would assuredly have been squeezed out of the Lo : Barry, or his lands.

It is now laid before the reader that he may search it through for such provocation as may extenuate the conduct of the man who, after a lapse of three years, committed a foul and heinous murder to avenge the fall of his relative. The details of the murder itself, with the apology of the Lords Justices for venturing to take proceedings against the English gentleman, are also exhibited in the words of the Lords Justices ; for no less an authority could suffice to render such a crime credible of a man chosen by the Queen to govern an Irish province.

" THE EXPLOIT INTO THE, GLEN."

" 1580· Augt. 31. SIR WILLIAM STANLEY to ———

" Rt Hon: I rec'l your hon. letter dated the 12th day of Augst, which maketh me confess myself still further bound unto you. I am lothe to write at this time because I have no acceptable news to write, but such as I am lothe to remember; yet duty bindeth me, so often as I have any convenient messenger, to trouble your honor with my letters. I know your honor is certified of our unhappy exploit made into the Glen the 25th day of August. I am the bolder to write the discourse thereof unto your Honor, because I knew no man can say truly he saw more of it than myself. There was of us a Colonel, four captains, and one lieutenant, appointed to go through the aforesaid Glen with half our*   company, Mr. George More, was our and our leader; with him in the vanward was Lt. Peter Carewe, Captain Audley, and the lieutenant of Captn Furr's. The leading of the rearward was committed to Mr. Harry Bagnall and myself; the place was such as the enemy had all the advantage that might be; when we entered the foresaid Glen we were forced to slide sometimes 3 or 4 fedoms or we could stay or feet; it was in depth where we entered, at the least a mile full of stones, rocks and bogs, and wood; in the bottom thereof a river full of loose stones, which we were driven to cross divers times; so long as our leaders kept the bottom, the odds of the skermish was on our side; but our colonel being a corpulent man, not able to endure travail, before we were half through the glen, which was 4 miles in length, led us

* Illegible.

up the hill that was a long mile in height; it was so steep that we were
forced to use our hands, as well to climb, as our feet, and the vanward
being gone up the hill we must of necessity folloue; and the enemy charged
us very hotly; divers of them had served amongst English men under the
leading of Cap^{tn} Green that had served in Connaught, and was carried by
one Garrett a Cap^{tn} to the rebels. It was the hottest piece of service for
the time, that ever I saw in any place. I was in the rearward, and with
me 28 soldiers of mine, whereof were slaine 8, and hurt 10. I had with me
my drum, whom I caused to sound many alarms, which was well answered
by them that was in the rearwards, which staid them from pulling us down
by the heels; but I lost divers of my dear friends. They were laid along
the woods as we should pass behind their rocks, crags, bogs, and in covert;
yet so long as we kept the bottom I lost never a man, till we were drawn
up the hill by our leader, when we could observe no orders; we could have
no sight of them, but were fain only to beat the place where we saw the
smoke of their pieces; but the hazard of myself, and the loss of my company was the safeguard of many others. I know and confess that it was
the hand of Almighty God that preserved me; the place was so very ill
that were a man never so slightly hurt he was lost; because no man was
able to help him up the hill. Some died being so out of breath that they
were able to go no further, being not hurt at all. Thus having troubled
your honor further than willingly I would, I do here most humbly take my
leave, commending myself and my service to your honor.

" Dublin the laste of Augst, 1580.

" Your Honor's most humbly to command,

" W. STANLEY."

" The names of such as were lost.

" Sir Peter Carewe.
" Cap^{tn}. Audley and his Lieutenant.
" Mr. Cosbie, Mr. George More.
" George Staffard

" My own Company.

" Hastinges, Wise, John Shawe a nephew of Capt. Rauf Salusbrie, that
was born in Spain, my page, with 5 others.
" There was not in all above 30 Englishmen slain."

" THE KILLING OF A MERE IRISHMAN.

" 1583. *June 23. The Lords Justices to the Privy Council.*

" It may please your Lordships. In our letters of the
14th of this month we declared to your Lordships of the
apprehension of Walter Cusack, brother to the late Viscount
of Baltinglas, and certain of his followers; and how the
instruments which were used in that service were two Irishmen, the principal whereof was Bryen oge Cavenaghe, and
the other a follower of his, Owen O'Nasye; to whom, according the covenant made with them, we delivered their reward
immediately upon the presenting of the prisoner. Since
which time the said Bryen and Owen remained in this city,
well and courteously entreated, till within these three days.

A sudden rumour was raised in this town that Owen O'Nasye should give forth in public speeches that he was an actor in the killing of Sir Peter Carewe; which rumour came to the ears of his brother George Carewe, being in this town ready to embark into England; but how proved or testified by sufficient witnesses, we cannot yet learn; upon this occasion only, as it should seem, a heinous act is here committed in the street of Dublin, upon Midsummer-eve last, where Brian oge and the said Owen beholding the assembly of the youth of this city in some show of arms, according to an ancient custom here, Mr. Carewe, accompanied with two other gentlemen, George Harvye and John Hill, and certain of his own servants, walking down by the quai where the shewes were presented, found the said Bryen and Owen sitting together; and taking Owen by the garments, and demanding of his name, immediately upon the naming of it, thrust his dagger into his bosom, and presently one of his men shot him with a pistol and two bullets, and gave him many wounds, whereof he presently died! Immediately upon the act Carewe and Harvey, with their men fled, we know not whither. But Mr. Hill remained, alleging for himself that he was utterly ignorant of the matter, and did but only accompany the others in walking, without knowledge of any such pretence; whom, notwithstanding, we have committed to the Castle here to abide Her Majesty's pleasure, or his further trial by law. By all examinations hitherto taken we do not hear of any violence used to Bryen Cavenaghe; but the execution only meant upon the other before-named; and whether purposely as seeking him, we cannot yet discover. Thus much for the manner of the fact; which as it was very foul and heinous in itself, done also in a public place, and at a most inconvenient time, even in the view of the Mayor and the Citizens, and while some Irish be here that be not altogether clear, in their own consciences; so, for as much as these parties were such as had newly done very good service, procured to themselves thereby great enmity of the evil affected Irish, and, that which is most to be regarded, had our protection in writing for their safety, we cannot but note that the estate is hereby dishonoured, and our credit so much impaired as hardly we shall be able to work the Irish to trust to our words or writings hereafter, much less to attempt any service against the rebels. For better manifesting of our dislike of this fact we have assembled such of the Council as were here, in the Castle of this town, where the Coroner's quest presented a verdict of wilful murder against the three gentlemen and two of Carewe's servants. We have, before the Mayor and his brethren, declared our opinion and have encouraged them to deal in it by the ordinary course of Justice, and offered our assistance every way that law may take place; which we neither did then, nor say now, to aggravate the offence in the gentlemen, knowing how much flesh and blood will work in young men to revenge the killing of their brethren and allies: but rather in equity and justice to report a truth; and complainingly in this, that Mr. Carewe had no more regard to the time and place, the occasion of the man's coming hither, his late good deserts, and finally to our protection, which is in treaty shamefully violated, and that our nacion may hereby be thought faithless; whereof may spring many inconveniences, in this broken state, where protections must be used; otherwise, for the man slain, we cannot say anything of him, but that he was base, a mean follower of the Cavanaghes, and in continual rebellion, till now that he was in action in this tragedy of Walter Eustace. For the better satisfaction of Brian oge, upon whom the other depended, we have entered with him in new treaty of further service, and have given him two months' respite to accomplish it; and in the mean season have assigned him a pay of 2s. hire, and 12 kerne in wages, wherewith he departed very well persuaded, and not so drowned in sorrow but that we think he would be content to lose another of his followers, of the same price. We humbly desire your Lordships to write unto us your opinions, and how we are further to proceed in this cause, and so do commit you to God. At Dublin the 25th June, 1583."

If in the course of these pages it shall appear that the murderer of Owen O'Nassy be found hiring assassins to murder other men, the reader will have no cause left for astonishment! That he be found deliberately relating to a Secretary of State the minutest details of such attempts may indeed be a little more unexpected; but if by his own words it shall be shown that Sir George Carewe could solemnly put in pledge the word of his Sovereign, and by a deliberate treachery make the word of that Royal lady a lie, it must be allowed that he has found means to add to the infamy with which the verdict of the Dublin jury had already branded him. Men have committed murders upon slighter provocation; and in those dark cruel times many men in authority hired assassins to murder for them; but not in those days, or in any days, have there been English gentlemen so reckless of truth and honour as to violate a safe conduct given in their Sovereign's name, under their solemn pledge and writing! All these things did Sir George Carewe, to his lasting shame and dishonour! The patent of King James created him an Earl, but the verdict of that Irish jury, when they declared him to be a "FELON," gave him a title which he deserved better, and which will last as long. It is expedient to know beforehand the character of the man who was to be Florence's great antagonist. Never were two men so ill-matched for a contest as the bland, the astute, the "wise and prudent" chieftain of the wild Irish, and the arrogant, envious, faithless courtier of Queen Elizabeth! The address of Florence at the outset of this encounter decided on the weapons with which it was to be fought—weapons of which he was an accomplished, indeed an unrivalled master. His adversary, with an overweening confidence, accepted, nay, thought that he had himself selected them. He used them to his utter discomfiture, and when the combat, fought in the face of the country, with Queen and Ministers anxious spectators, was going against him, and the man whom he had called "a fool and an idiot" had proved himself wiser, or more skilful at least than he was, he burst through the restraints of honourable contest, and finished by outrage what he had undertaken to decide by fair encounter. Every pass and parry in this great "show of arms" is made before us; and nothing in the life of Florence proves the surprising versatility of his mind so clearly as the ready and various expedients with which he encountered and foiled each capricious variation in the designs of Carewe, and the cunning of a host of spies, traitors, secret and open enemies, until the hour when he trusted—what had hitherto been held sacred—the pledged word of the Queen's representative! The letters which will be laid before the reader will exhibit every shift and evasion practised in this interesting contest. It will be seen how, whilst time was passing, and every day rendered more embarrassing the position of the President, who saw his danger, but not the means by which to extricate himself from it, he was forced to confess to the Minister who watched this strife of address, that "What to make of his adversary he protested he knew not! he was fairly perplexed."

Late in March, and after the account of Florence's visit to the camp of O'Neill, and the rumours of his treachery had reached England from so many correspondents, a letter was delivered to him, which, though it bore the signature of Sir John Stanhope, was the joint production of him and

Cecyll. The rough draft of it is preserved, and shows how much study its composition had cost the Minister, for he first elaborately corrected the original, and then as thoughtfully varied his own corrections. The confidence which Cecyll had forced himself, after so lengthened a deliberation, and with so many misgivings, to place in Florence, was wavering under the pressure of other men's suspicions; but he dared scarcely more openly acknowledge to himself than he did to his reader the amount of distrust which was already forcing itself upon him. The passages in italics are his own corrections.

"1600· *March* 20*th.* SIR JOHN STANHOPE *to* FLORENCE MAC CARTHY.

" Although it be true that many reportes from Mounster of yor proceedinges synce Tyrone came thither, do give an occasion to those who wish you ill there, to number you amongst the ill affected subjects, yet tyll it be heard from yo^rself, and seene by more infaylable proofes, yor frends y^t *know you, cannot but* retayne that assured opynion wch they have ever conceaved of yor unseparable duty towards your gracyous soveraigne. For first it is as well knowen to me as to any man lyving that Hir Maty in her owne nature hath ever ben so farre from condemning you *heretofore*, and when dyvers of her counsell have urged circumstances against you, she dyd ever conclude you inwardly faithfull toher.   Next methinks, when I remember you Mr. Florence a wyse and cyvill gent. generally beloved of their sort, and ptyculerly *esteemed* by dyverse of extraordynary place and credytt, I am so farre from beliefe that you have incorporated yo^rselfe with the combynaĉon of savag traytours, as I doe assure myselfe that the manner of your formall assocyating, or temporysing wth them *in this confusion* hath no other end then thereby to *inable you* to shewe yor resolucyon and affectyon to doe Hir Maty service.   In doeing whereof (even now when greatest tryall may be made of valour and duty) you are assured to gayne yourself hono^r quyet, and happynes.   Thus have I now playnly shewed you my beliefe, from wch I protest nothing can remove me but yourselfe, wherein, yf I be deceaved, (wch yet I hold impossyble,) let me in requytall of all former good will heare from you what is true, or false; *and then shall I conclude there is no fayth in Israell.   If otherwise it be, and y^t you haue any secret purpose; and honest desires to make knowen, let me be informed of them;* and I will impt it to Her Maty, who styll laugheth at ye folly of any of those *flying* bruets which do but tend to suspyĉon of any resolved defectyon *in you;* and I assure myselfe would be more pleased with any *good* servyces that you shold do her then with ten tymes so much of others, whom she knoweth not, nor values not.   You may be nowe assured of all ye favour which ye Presydent ćan shewe you, for the Q. dyd pryncypally recomend you to hym, and of myselfe you may expect all ye offices which your good carryag can deserve from *him that hath ever* ben yor loving freend."

Endorsed, " *Copie from* SIR JOHN STANHOPE *to* FLORENCE MAC CARTHY. *March* 20."

Four days after the date of the above letter, but doubtless before it reached him, Florence wrote to the Earl of Ormond,

S

complaining of the ill-usage he was experiencing from the
Commissioners and others in authority. The Earl was at the
time at Kilkenny, expecting a visit from the Lord President,
who was on his way from Dublin to the seat of his government.
The strange incident of the capture of this powerful nobleman, so long Her Majesty's Commander-in-chief, and who
but a month earlier had driven the army of O'Neill out of
Munster, and the narrow escape from capture, by the same
daring swoop of the Sept of the O'Mores, of the Lord President and the Earl of Thomond, is familiar to the reader.
Had O'Neill, or the wild warriors who captured this great
personage, been as ready with the gibbet as the stern man
who had fallen into their hands had been all through his life,
there was nothing to prevent their dealing with him as he
had dealt with so many of the noble blood of the Fitzgeralds.
The captivity of the Earl was not of long duration. On the
recovery of his liberty he wrote his answer to Florence—a
friendly, straightforward, loyal answer. Of this letter he
thought it prudent to send a copy for the perusal of
Sir Robert Cecyll.

"1600. *July* 18. ORMOND *to* CECYLL.

"Sone before my unfortunate comynge into the Traytor's hands I receaved a lre from Florence Mc Cartie, wherein he seemed to justifie himself
upon hard opynion conceaved of him by some, by reason of sondry extremities, wherein he stood; and what my answere is unto him (noue after
my delyùie, havinge found an opportunitie to sende unto him) I thought
good to make knowne to yo\] by th enclosed copie; so leavige, comytt you
to the blessed guydance of the Almightie.
"From Kilkenny the 18th of Juelie, 1600.   Your veray assured Frend,
"THOˢ. ORMOND & OSS."

Copy of letter from ORMOND *to* FLORENCE.

" I receaued a lre from yo\] of the 24th of Marche laste, wch I would
have answered longe since, if my unfortunate myshapp had not byne in
lightinge, into the hands of the wicked traitoʳ Ownye Mᶜ Rorie. Before
wᶜh tyme I wrote on yo\] behalf, to my Lo Deputy; and made yoʳ greffs
knowen to his Lᵖ, in sort as yo wrote them to me. But how hardlie
soever you were dealt wth by any man, I did hold you too wise, to be
drawne by any meane, from the remembrance of your bounden duetie to
her sacred Matie, to whom you owe allegiance; and besids you knowe
what most gracious and manifold favoʳ Her Highnes hath don unto you,
in setinge you at libertie, when you were in the Towre, in gevinge you
lardge sumes of money when you were in wante, and many other thinges
of great benefitt; soe as nothinge ought eù to cause you to forgett the
same. I have had some conference touchinge you wth my Lo President,
who is an honoˡable and worthy Gent, and I doubt notwill deale favoʳably
and frendlie wth you—you deservinge the same by yoʳ service doinge, to

her Highnes. And if contrarywise you shold proue the man, that will
beare armes againste yor naturall Prince; You amongest all, or moste men
of this kingdom that are in accōn would be accompted the most odious;
and myself become your greatest enemye, in regard of that wch in kindness I had heretofore don for you; wherefore as to one, to whome I shold
not nede to use this discourse, but that yt proceedeth of my affecōn to
wishe yor good in yor Prince's and countrey's cause, I aduise you to
submytt yo^rself in all humble sorte, wthout standinge upon high condiōns
unfitt for a duetifull subiect; and whilest there is hope of grace and mercye
to take the benefitt thereof, settinge aside the vain expectaōn of foraine
ayde, beinge that whereby the traitors are deluded; and if you stand duetifull I shalbe contented to be a meane for you: No more can I write to the
dearest frend or kinseman I have; Hopinge that this sufficeth to one of
your witt and iudgement, and wishinge to heare from you howe thinges
stand wth you from tyme to tyme, I end.
      " From Kilkenny the 16th of Juely, 1600.
                    " Your assured Frend while you be duetifull,
                              "THOMAS ORMOND & OSSORY."

On the 24th of April, 1600, Sir George Carewe entered
upon his charge as Lord President of Munster. Six days
elapsed before he considered himself possessed of information
sufficiently trustworthy to communicate to the Lords of Her
Majesty's Privy Council. Very different was the document
which then he forwarded from the smooth and comfortable
despatch of Sir H. Power! It bore the signatures of the
Earl of Thomond, who had accompanied him to Cork, and of
the members of his Council, and contained only such general
facts as he could learn from them. His second letter, which
was composed without their assistance, contains a picture
far gloomier, and more alarming! "The entire province
was disaffected; with sufficient worldly wisdom the great
Lords continued subjects in show, but their followers were in
action with FitzThomas; the walled towns were corrupted;
and the open country was wholly in the possession of the
Geraldines, and shut against the Queen's loyal subjects."

" 1600. *April* 30. *From the* LORD PRESIDENT, *the* EARL OF THOMOND,
    and COUNCIL OF MUNSTER, *For Her Mat's speciall Affaires, To the R^t.
    Honble. the* LORDS *of Her Mats* PRIVIE COUNCELL.

" It may please yor Ll^s. The 24th of this instant I the President arryved heare, where since my cominge (havinge been employed wth the
councell for the most pte to understande in some pfect sort the state of this
province) I do fynde that the confusion and distemper therof hath not bin
greater then now yt is, since the first beginninge of theis trobles; neither
may wee expect any suddin reformation therof, other then such as wee can
worke by Her Mat's forces against so stronge an enemy, who (by a generall
computacion of the Ll^s of the countreys here, and of the vulgar sort) of
Provinciall rebells and Bonnoughtes, are no less then 7,000 hable, weaponed
men; and their annoyaunce to the poore subiects wilbe the greater, in re-
                                    S 2

garde wee can neither looke, nor hope , for any assistaunce from the L^ls of
the countreys, who are onely in psonall shewes subiects, as the Lo: Power,
the Lo: of Dunboyne, Lo: Roche, the Lo: of Cahir, Cormock Mc Dermot,
chief of Muskery, McCharty Reough, chief of Carrebry, Garrald Fitz
James chief of the Deasyes, Patrick Condon, O'Calloughan, and all others
(except the Lo Barry, who of late hath don good service) being assured
from the rest to recaive no ayde for Her Matie wth their forces, the most
of them hauinge either their brothers, or next kinsmen in actuall rebellion.

" Florence McCartie (if he contynue in this disloyall course, wch he
hath begonn, (wherof as yet we have no other hope) by his frends *namely*,
both the O'Sulyvans, Mc Fynnen, the Carties of Desmond, O'Donnevan,
O'Crowly, O'Mahon-Carbrey, O'Mahon-Fin, sundry of the Septes of the
Carthys of Carbery, the Mc Swynes, most of the Carties of Muskery, all
the Carties of Dowallo, O'Keefe, Mc Awlye, and many of the O'Callanghans,
with his and their followers, and kinsmen, who before weare better disposed by their outward affections, wilbe the strongest, and of greatest
force of any traytor in Mounster; insomuch as wee are of opinion (under
reformation of yor Ll^s more grave judgments) that 1,500 of Her Mats
forces (a chardge heretofore not expected) must of necessitie be employed
against him, which might otherwise have been disposed towardes the prosecution of James Fitz Thomas and his adherents, wherby the reducinge
of the province is much more difficult then before; besides the preestes
haue in their divellysh doctrine so much prevayled amongstthe people in
generall in this province, as for feare of excommunication very few dare
serve against the rebells, or any way ayde Her Maty: and this infection
has so farr crept into the hartes of the inhabitants of the cities, and cor-
pat townes, as the chief magistrates and maiors therof do now refuse to
come to the church, wch at no tyme heretofore hath bin seene, that yt is to
be feared (yf the Spanierdes do make any invasion, wch many of them,
and the rebells do expect) the citties and townes are in daunger to be lost
by revolt, &c. &c.

" And lastly as wee have manifested to yor Lls the staggering and
uncertein humours wch the insolent traytors of this province are possessed wth (being apt to forsake their dutie and obedience, upon any
triflinge occasion) so, give us leave wee most humbly besech yor Ll^s, to recommend unto yor favourable regarde the desertes of such as have constantly endeuored by all their meanes, to approve their affeccions in loyall
sort to Her Maty: of whome fynding the Lo: Barry to be most forward,
as a nobleman willing enough to contynue in welldoinge, but that his
pouertie is now such, chiefly growen through the spoyles wch the traytor
Tyrone did upon him, by wasting his landes, that he is not hable to keepe
his men together as heretofore he hath don, either to attend Her Mats.
army into the field wth any company, or to preserve his countrey from any
further spoyle; and onless he may be releeved wth some enterteynemt
of chardge from Her High^s, he wilbe of less hability to do service; wch wee
humbly leave to yor Ll^s graue wisdome to consider of. In wch like respect
wee are moved to become sutors to yor Ll^s for Charles McCarthy sonne to
Sir Cormock McTeige, who being of the best blodde, and allyaunce in this
countrey, and in his owne pson valliaunt, hath don, and is willing to do,
acceptable service to Her Maty, weare yt not that the like povertie doth
dishable him. Of the ennemy (yf he wold have bin wonne away from his
obedience) he had lardge offers, and is dayly much importuned to ptake
wth them; but the yonge gent^me, of his naturall inclynation to remayne a
subiect, and hoping to be considered *of wth a company of foote of his owne
countrey birth*, will not harken to their perswasions; but yf the Lo: Barry

and he be left to themselves unprovided for, and not some way comforted with releefe from Her Maty, wee dare not promise a pseveraunce in them; wch wee likewise refer to yor honourable censures. And so do humbly take o^l leave.

" At Corke ultimo Aprill^s 1600.

" Yo^r L^ls most humbley ever to be comaunded,

" GEORGE CAREWE.

" Thomond; W^m. Cork & Ross &c. Henry Cuffe. Rich^d. Walshe."

Such was the first despatch which emanated from the new President and Council of Munster. It contained much more than was known to the late Governor, much less than became very speedily known to Carewe himself. Accordingly three days later he wrote again to Sir Ro. Cecyl, the first of a series of letters, which will leave the reader as they left the English Secretary, nothing to conjecture, nothing to desire, of the mind of the writer. Between these two correspondents there existed a perfect and shameless freedom ; no cloudy ambiguity of phrase was needed between the man who, with his own hand committed a murder in Dublin, and the man in London who deliberately wrote that " to take a rebel alive, or to take his head, he was contented to hear the promise of an assassin," and none existed. We find Carewe's opinion of Florence, and his own designs with regard to him, pictured as clearly as they existed in his own mind. It is incomprehensible that having at the very outset of his dealings with Florence declared that it was important to temporize with him, he should immediately have proceeded to exhibit the greatest distrust of him, to seek his humiliation, and to endeavour to entangle him in overt opposition to authority. He had no sooner taken possession of his Government than he desired Florence to wait upon him in Cork, for no purpose but to make open profession thereby of his entire devotion to the English Government. It was in vain that Florence pointed out to him the impolicy of such a step at that moment; that he pictured to him in the clearest manner the delicate nature of his own position, requiring the utmost wariness and prudence ; that he showed him the detriment to the Queen's service that must ensue if he should bring upon himself the distrust of all Munster by so manifest a declaration against the national cause. It was in vain that he prayed to be allowed at least to defer his visit till he should have time to take precautions against the revolt of his followers during his absence from his own country ! Carewe would listen to no such arguments, but insisted upon his instant repair to Cork ; and Florence, rather than bring matters to a rupture, obeyed him. Had Sir George Carewe had but six months' experience of Donal's mode of ruling Desmond, Florence's letter might have found him more ready to admit its truth.

, It is not the purpose of these writings to relate in what way Carewe proceeded to recover for Her Majesty the province over which she had appointed him President. When he arrived at the seat of his Government, the walled towns were all that remained in obedience, and they but of very lukewarm loyalty. The Irish—to use the words of Cecyll— were no doubt " as well compacted together as such rebels could be." Every castle was in the hands of FitzThomas, or the Bonies, or the Irish Chieftains, to whom they belonged, and who, if they were not in open action, certainly were not in obedience to the Queen, or her Governor. The Pacata Hibernia has sufficiently shown how this rope of sand fell to pieces ; how the captains of the Bonies sold themselves, and each other ; and how, by a skilful admixture of bribery, bravery, teachery, and conciliation, the overthrow of all, and the reconquest of Munster was accomplished. With these proceedings, only as far as they relate to the fortunes of Florence are we concerned ! the first difficulty of Carewe was precisely with Florence. Carbery was an open country, and a second visit of Flower and Bostock could have laid it desolate a second time, by an expedition similar to the last, namely, by slaughtering the churls and poor people; but not so the country of MacCarthy Mor in Desmond, which was " a remote, strong, inaccessible country, far from the help of Her Majesty's forces, and incommodious for them to serve in." The number of weaponed men in Florence's pay was uncertain, but it was known that they were considerable ; and to venture another excursion into Carbery, or to proceed against FitzThomas, and O'Neill's Bonies under Dermod O'Connor, in the open country, with the possibility of Florence's closing upon his rear, was what the President did not venture ; hence the embarrassment, impatience, and wavering of purpose betrayed in the following letters :—

" 1600. *May* 2. PRESIDENT CAREWE *to* CECYLL.

Shandon.
" Sir,
" Although there is no man that more mislikes that companies should be bestowed upon Irishe Captens then myselfe, yett when I find it to be expedient for the Queen's service I am bound in dutie to signifie my opinion; and therefore to encouradge my Lo: Barry, who is now in blood with the traytors, since his losses when Tyrone was in these parts, I thinke it were meet that a companye of foote were bestowed uppon him; he is

exceedinge poor, and stronge in followers: When I came into the province he mett me betwene Yonghall and Corke with 500 foote, and 100 horse of his owne; he is mightelye discontented, and thinkes that the state neglects him, that he is nott in the Queen's pay ; there is no doubt but he is able to do great service; but yf he be not relieved, allthough himsellfe will remayne a subiect, yett then he will underhand niggle wth the enemye, and lett his men be loose amongst them, yf he do nott worse, whereof I have some doubt. In like manner Charles McCartie were fitt to be considered of, who is of a sturringe spirit, muche esteemed of in Mounster, exceedinge willinge to do service, vehe-mentlye importuned by the traytors with lardge intysinge proffers to ioin wth them, valliant in his person; and yf he would be a rebell, there is no doubt but he were able to carrye all the force of Muskrye wth him, in despite of Cormock MacDermond his adversarye, wch is 1000 men at the least: his discontentments are equall to Barries, and, Sir, believe me I feare his courses will be naught except he be pleased: he is able to do the Queen more service with a companye than three of the best Englishe Captens in Mounster; for the pay of one band he will evermore serve the Queen with treble the number, &c. &c.

" Your Honnour (by the opinion of all the Counsil here) understands that the rebells be 7000 good able men; the Queen's forces but 3000 in list, whereof dead pays deducts about 700, so as upon the reckoninge I have but 2700; of the wch allowinge sicke and hurt men, together with willful defallts of Captens, and those that by deathe will be wantinge, if I shall be 2400 by the pole stronge, I shall thinke myself happie; of the wch number I must be enforced, when I draw into the felld, to leave at Yoghall 100, at Kinsale 100, at Killmallocke 156, at Mallo 100, at Dungarvan 50, at the Castell of Caer 30, besides in other pettye wards, wch must not be lost, as Lisfinin, Strankallye, the Old head of Kinsale, Wallstowne, and other places, above 50 more, and of the whole number wch should be turned over to me, wch should be 3000 foote, I do want 80; beinge employed by my Lo Deputie in Leinster, who as yett I cannot gett to be removed from the places they are in; all which deductions being added together there is nott remayninge to go into the felld wth me by the pole but 1740 foote; wch is but a weake army to sustain the force of the traytors, except my strenght in horse did overtoppe them, wherein allso I do assure your honnour the troopes are weake, &c. &c. &c.

" James Mc Thomas with all the forces that he can make are drawne to a head to impeache my goinge to Limericke, and have amassed as muche victualls as he can make to tarry my cominge, which he should not long expecte yf that ydeott Florence did not necessarilye holld me to attend his pleasure, whether he will turne subiect or persever traytor, as he now is; yf the man hadd faythe or honestie in him he woulld have bene wth me ere this tyme, as by his lettre to mysellfe, wch I receved in my cominge from Dublin, and his messadges, may appeare; and the lyke may be judged by other lettres written by him, the copies whereof wth these I do send unto your honnour; but my hopes are dead, and I thinke he will never be honest; att his owne request I have sent John Fits Edmonds twice unto him, not six myles from this towne; but his retornes are nothinge butt oathes, and protestations of loyalttie, and thatt he loves honnours and res-pects me as muche as any man lyvinge; and yt he will come unto me, but his feares do so muche prevayle in him, as he dares not for feare of deten-tion trust me; to assure him, tomorrow, at his request, my Lo: of Tomond dothe parlye wth him, wth whome he promises to come unto me, whereof I am doubtfull, expecting but delayes; for to say my opinion directlye as I thinke, I do beleeve that before he lefte England these treasons were hatched ! wᶜh yf they were, then- is he past recoverye; but yf it be no more then he pretends, wᶜh is parlyinge and patchinge wth Tyrone to save his countrye from spoyle, and fighting against Her Matie's forces betwene Kinsale and Corke, there is no doubt but he will be reduced.

"The maner of that fight I have at lardge discoursed in Sir Wallter Raleghe's letre, wᶜh I have sent unsealed unto you ; the enemye lost 98, and we but 8 persons : yet notwthstandinge I am exceedinge sorrye that Sir Henry Poore did command the jorney, for now he *cañ alleadge nothinge else to cause him to feare to come att me* but because he was in the filld wth his collors flyinge against Her Maties forces.

" Florence himsellfe is in nature a coward, and as muche addicted to his ease as any man lyvinge, and therefore unmeet to be a rebell, wᶜh makes me glad, yᵗ he is the chiefe com̃ander of Carbrye and Desmond forces, for yf he were gone his wyfe's bastard brother woulld be farre worse then he. He hathe required my oathe that he may come, and go safe from me, wᶜh my L. of Tomond, in my behallfe, will sweare unto him ; when he required John Fits Edmonds to aske the same of me I do thinke att that tyme he did purpose to see me ; but his feares do so abound as I have no hope of his comĩnge. Yf by no meanes he may be assured to the state, yett I thinke itt nott amysse to temporise wth him, and to permitt him to be newtrall wᶜh I suppose he chieflye desires ; beinge att all tymes readye to ioin wth Spaniards, yf they come, or to retourne to be a subiect yf the rebells prevayle nott ; by this temporizinge course, I shall spare 1500 men of my 3000, towards the prosecution of James MᶜThomas, for lesse than 1500 is to little to prosecute Florence ; to undertake bothe together I cannott ; and therefore, unlesse I be otherwise commanded out of England, I will temporize wth Florence, and prosecute the other, whose kingdome I hope, in a reasonable tyme, will be dissolved. Florence since my cominge into this province did never write unto me, wᶜh makes me to mistrust him the more.

" The white knight hathe sent sundrye messendgers unto me promisinge to be an honest man: A more faythlesse man never lyved upon the earthe, &c. &c. If anythinge do move him to keepe his promise, and to come unto me, it is the internall malice between James McThomas and him, which is irreconciliable, &c. The Bushopp of Cashell is busilye workinge. Within a few days that stratagem will either take effect or fayle ; but I have two more as good or better then that ; I hope att last, yf the divell be not his good Mr., but one will hitt, &c. &c.

" GEORGE CAREWE."

In the tactics of Carewe, so circumstantially developed in the last and the following letters, it is difficult to perceive what end he had in view, except the mere personal ruin of Florence ; or what possible good he could propose to himself if he succeeded. He knew that before Florence returned into Munster all his country had been in the possession of Donal, and in open rebellion ; and that if Florence were driven out of Desmond, the country must fall back again into the hands of, Donal, and relapse into revolt. He knew that it was expressly to put an end to this that the Queen had sent Florence into Ireland, with permission to recover Desmond as best he might, either by arms or by treaty. He found Desmond, nay Carbery and Muskerry also, tranquillized by the able conduct of Florence. He might have been contented, for that Florence could by any possibility force or persuade his followers to bear arms against FitzThomas, in aid of the Queen, was what no sane man could expect. To insist upon Florence's delivering up to him his son as a pledge of his fidelity to the Government could but lead, as a matter of course, to his abandonment by all the Bonies in his pay, and to Donal, and raging rebellion. All this Florence clearly and earnestly pointed out to him; but Carewe was as obtuse as Sir Henry Power had been; he chose to ignore the fact that Florence was as much sent by Queen Elizabeth to do the very thing he was doing, as he was himself sent to be Lord President of Munster! and regardless of all consequences, he determined to compromise him in the estimation of his followers, and thus imperil the very neutrality which he declared to be of so much importance to him.

The earliest professed wish of Carewe after his arrival at Cork, was *to reclaim Florence*, that he might, without apprehension of any hostility from him, employ the few troops he had—about 1,700, after supplying the garrisons—in prosecution of James FitzThomas. To effect this reclamation he used the good offices of FitzEdmond, of Clone, the foster father of Florence, of the Earl of Thomond, and Sir Nicholas Walshe. Florence had meeting with these mutual friends, and the result of a long conference was that he wrote to the President an explanation of much of his late conduct; and Carewe, in reply, pressed him again to visit him in Cork, and sent him a safe conduct for his free coming and departing. Florence with much reluctance yielded himself at last to this invitation. Carewe's account of what took place at their interview, and Florence's previous letter of explanation, were sent to Cecyll. These letters are now laid before the reader, as also one written under the President's roof, by Florence, containing a circumstantial narrative of his encounter with Flower, and of his repair to the camp of O'Neill. There was no attempt at concealment; the former act he justified, as he might have done resistance to a highway robber, and the latter as warranted by his permission in writing from the Commissioners of Munster, to parle with rebels for the Queen's service.

" 1600· *May 6.· From* SIR GEORGE CAREWE, *President of Munster*,
6 *May*, 1600.

" Sir,

" When I despatched all .my lettres, and the lettre 'from me and the Counsell here unto the L^ls, bearinge date the last of Aprill, I reserved the writinge of my lettre unto your Honnour untill the wynd served to embarque, wch bare date the 2nd of May, since wch tyme the wind nott serving. In these I thought good to relate unto whatt hath passed betwene Florence McCartie and me. In the former lettre of the 2nd of May I wrote that Florence McCartie desired me to send my L. of Tomond to speake wth him, wch att my request his L. was contented to do, the same morninge Florence wrote a lettre to me wch I iṁediattlye answered. The copies of them, wth these I send unto your honnour. After the Erle and he mett, and more then two hours spent uppon the oathes of him and Sir Nicolas Wellshe, thatt I had promised to permitt him to retourne safe, he came to my house, and as sone as he came unto me, kneelinge he humbled hymsellfe wth many protestations of the sinceritie of his hart, and the treu loyalltie wch he bare toward Her Matie, desiringe me to receve him unto Her Matie's favour, and thatt he woulld do her more service then any man in Mounster. After I had reproved him for his trayterous behaviours, and layd before him the fowlnesse of his faullt, and the monstrous ingratitude towards Her Matie from whom he had receved so many great favours and benefitts, all wch he coulld not deny, I tooke him by the hand, and ledd him aside, preachinge obedience unto him, and usinge all the arguments I colld to reduce him to conformitie ; the Erle of Tomond, Sir Nicolas Wellshe, and John FitzEdmond, did the lyke ; and unto us, in generall termes, he seemed as reasonable and dutifull as we coulld desire : the same night he supt wth me, and the Erle of Tomond conducted him to his lodginge ; for so fearefull a creature I did never see, mistrustinge to be killed by every man he saw.

" The next day, wch was the 4th of this present, he dyned wth me : after dynner the Erle of Tomond, Sir Nycolas Wellshe, the Byshoppe of Corke, M^r. Cuffe, John FitzEdmonds, and my sellfe called him before us ; and, as at his first cominge, I layd his faulltes before him, challendged performance of his promises, wch was not onely to desist from doinge yll, but to do some suche service as might meritt reward, wch was expected att his handes, beinge so muche bound unto Her Matie as he was ; and because thatt my sellfe might nott be thought to deal slacklye for the queene, and partiallye, I did require from him his eldest sonne for a pledge of his good behaviour, and assurance of the services wch he pretended to do, wch he refused ; alleadginge many reasons to the contrarye, pretendinge thatt the puttinge in of his sonne in pledge woulld cause the bonies to forsake him, and to erect his wyfe's base brother, and so dryve him out of his countrye to his utter ruyne ; that he had of longe tyme tasted of myseries and wants, thatt he had recovered his countrye of Desmond wth greatt travayle, danger, and chardges ; thatt when he shoulld be a begger he knewe the queene woulld not regard him, and then he shoulld be unable to serve her, and therefore desired thatt his pledge might nott be exacted, beinge needlesse to be required att his hands, for thatt he was in his soule addicted to serve Her Matie by all the meanes he might ; whereunto all the reasons thatt we coulld make was used to incite him to delyver his pledge ; when reasons coulld nott prevayle, frendly persuasions for his good was delyvered unto him ; and att last, when nothinge coulld move him, I the president (wherein the Erle of Tomond was also very vehement) threatened him wth sharpe prosecution, protestinge to neglect all other services, untill his countrye were spoyled, and him sellfe banished ; wch did muche amase him ; and then he sayd he was content to put his sonne pledge for him, uppon condition, that Her Matie woulld be pleased to passe the countrye of Desmond unto him as she had done unto his father in law, to give him the name of McCartie More, or Erle of Clancare, and to give him 300 men in wadges ! wch exorbitant demands was so muche misliked by us all, as we bad him be gone, beinge weary to heare a man so farre out of reason ; and immediatelye we brake of, and the counsell departed, leavinge the Earle of Tomond, Florence and my sellfe in the chamber.

"After long speeche debatinge the matter very seriouslye, he swore that the onlye cause why he was loathe to delyver his sonne, was as he before alleadged, the present losse of his countrye, wch he knew woulld be taken out of his possession, yf he were reconciled to the state, and not want of dutie to Her Matie; thatt he woulld write by this dispatche into England unto your Honnour, humblye to pray you to be a meane for the passinge of Desmond unto him, wth the title of Mc Cartie More, or Erle; as for a chardge he woulld not require itt before he did deserve the same, by some service that might merritt so great a favour; wch yf he might obtayne, he woulld nott doubt but in a shorte tyme to be the best instrument for the finishinge of the warre in Mounster; I tolld him his courses were nought; and thatt I woulld nott give him any assistance in the same, being more meet for him to entreat mercye for his offences, then to be so insolent in demandinge of reward; and did beat downe his pride (wch is incredible) as muche as I coulld; in the end I demaunded of him whatt his purposes were yf he did nott prevayle in his desires? he sware unto me, uppon a booke, thatt he woulld never beare armes agaynst Her Maties forces, except he were assallted in Desmond! and thatt all his followers shoulld likewyse abstayne from actuall rebellion; but his bonies were more att the comandment of Dermond O'Connor than of himsellfe, and therefore whensoever Dermond woulld send for them he coulld not restrayne them; he likewyse did swere unto me thatt whensover I did send for him, uppon my word, thatt he woulld come unto me; and in the meane tyme he woulld evermore send me intellygence of the rebells' proceedings, and do me the best underhand service he coulld, and for testimonye of his obedience, he would att any tyme when your Honnour pleasethe to send for him (uppon your faythfull promyse thatt he shall nott be a prisoner, for he sayethe thatt he will rather runne any fortune then to be detayned), go into England, to make knowne unto you his sincere meaninge.

"This is all y^t passed between us ; and more then to be a neutrall he would nott promise! or could be exacted from him! Of his goinge into England I woulld be glad that your Honnour would make tryall; wch I do nott beleeve that he will performe, for the wch he sware uppon a Pius Quintus, for uppon no other booke the Erle woulld believe him. He protests thatt for his particular he dothe nott expect the ayde of Spaniards, althoughe Tyrone in a lettre very latelye did assure him thatt they woulld be here presentlye; he confessethe thatt he knowes thatt att the last the Queene must, and will prevayle in Ireland; but yett he had rather dye then to be a beggar agayne, to feele the wants he hathe done, wch he is sure to do yf he be reconcyled; but these excuses are but devices to draw the queene to yelld to his demands; thinkinge thatt the tyme serves, for rebels to obtayne whattsoever they aske; but herein I hope his pollycye shall fayle him; for I have as muche from him as I desire, wch is to have no cause to employe any part of Her Maties forces against him; for by his oathe he is bound nott to serve agaynst us, or annoy any of Her Matie's good subiects; but to lyve pryvatlye, in Desmond, and to keepe his countrye, wch if he performe I shall be att the bettre leasure to prosecute James Mc Thomas; and when thatt worke is fynished, a few dayes will serve to humble Florence, and teache him submissive entreaties, and forgett to capitulatt ether for land, titles, or chardge. I never rackt my witts more to beat reason into a man's head then I did to him; but pride dothe so muche possesse him in beinge called McCartimore, that his understandinge is lost, and not capable of any reasons but his owne.

" John Fits Edmonds is his godfather, and when he saw his foolishe obstinacye, beleevinge before thatt his credditt had bene able to have prevayled wth him, in a great furye after many revylinges, cursed him to his face; in reasoning, persuadinge, and threateninge, a whole afternoone was spent; all the benefitts thatt the Queene hathe formerlye bestowed uppon him are meerlye lost; for the remembrance of his imprisonments onely remaynethe; whatt he will prove I knowe nott, beinge exceedinge doubtfull of him, thatt att the last he will brake his faythe; nothinge gives me hope that he will be neutrall but his-extreeme cowardysse, and the small accompt wch he makes of the Romishe priestes, raylinge att them openlye in the hearinge of all men. Yf this temporisinge course, wch for a tyme I thinke good to be helld wth him, be misliked, then I pray your Honnour to lett me understand itt; thatt I may beginne the warre uppon him; but as the world yett framethe, in my opinion, itt is good counsell to lett him holld a neutrall course, wch att the last, will confound him, althoughe your purposes be to deny his petitions, yett for awhile itt were nott amysse (as I thinke) to holld him in some colld hope to wynne tyme uppon him; and to drawe the same to more lenght, itt were good counsell for your Honnour to send for him into England; and in his absence I doubt not but to erect his wyve's base brother, who before his retourne will be stronge yenoughe to yoke him; but before I deale therein, I do pray to be advised from you least I may offend; yf the Queene be so gratious unto him as to graunt him his desires, surelye I thinke for the present, he will requite her favours wth his best services; but itt will in after tymes make him to great, for he is heyre to Carbrye, wch is a greater countrye then Desmond; and his foolishe ambition is boundlesse.

" When I was thus farre proceeded in my lettre I stayed fynishinge of the same, expectinge these lettres of Florence's unto yoursellfe, Sir Walter Raleghe, and Sir John Stanhoppe; but he havinge not drunke wyne in many dayes before, to put care awaye, so filled his skynne wth sacke as the whole daye was loste in sleepe; this day better remembring himsellfe he brought me these three letters unsealed, and gave them unto me to read; wch varyes nothinge from his former lettres to me and others; but I do nott geve credditt unto them, or to any thinge he sayes; for my intelligences assures me thatt underhand he combynes wth the rebells as firmely as he may; and yett his oathes are to the contrarye. The report of the fight betwene Her Maties forces and him is fallse; lett your Honnour beleeve whatt I have wrotten to Sir Walter Raleghe, wch is a true narration of thatt daye's service, testified under a discreet Irishemans hand, who did view the bodies. This day I find him more tractable then before, gevinge me some good hope thatt he will delyver his sonne, presentlye, pleadge into my handes; but such is his inconsistancie as I dare nott trust him, for his feares on ether side do so besiedge him as he cannot well resolve whether it were good for him to be a subiect or a rebell; and to say my opinion of him he is good for nether of them bothe. Yf I were assured thatt he woulld keepe his promise wth me, and do me underhand service as he protests, I coulld then be more gladd of his wallkinge in the woodes then in the citye of Corke; but cowards are faythlesse and so I think I shall find him. But howsoever he deale wth me I doubt not but to make some advantadge of him, and fight wth him att his owne weapon, so as he shall nott overreache me. The White Knight hathe sent this day a messendger unto me wth faythfull promise to submit himsellfe, so as he may be pardoned for his lyfe, and goodes restored in blood, have his lands by a new graunt from Her Matie, and forgeven the arrearadge of his rents due uppon him since the rebellion; all w^ch, because they are nott unreasonable demands, and suche as are nether unprofitable, or dishonourable to the Queene, and suche as I am sure att the last, when he hathe done more harme, Her Majesty will graunt unto him, I will be so adventurous as to promise them unto him, hopeinge that the queene will nott mislyke itt. The stay of Florence from aydinge James Mc Thomas, and the drawinge in of the White Knight, dothe in a manner free the countye of Corke; then my taske lyes onelye in Lymericke and Kerrye, in wch counties, I doubt nott but to rayse uppe factions agaynstt Desmond and his brother, wch willgeve a fayre hope towards the fynishinge of this warre. This bearer Capten Browne, sonne to Sir Valentyne, and a cashiered capten, I may nott forget to recomend unto your Honnour's good favour, besechinge you to give him your ayde and assistance, yf he shall have cause to be a suter for the same. He is an honest man, very valiant, and thatt wch I like best, one that loves me. So humblye rest at your Honnours service.

"Your Honnours most humblye to serve you,

"GEORGE CAREWE.

"Shanden This 6th of May, 1600."

"Lett my censuringe of Florence, I beseche you^r honnour be kept as secretlye as you may, for otherwise my credditt will be crackt wth him; for nowe he trusts muche in my frendship, wch I did unfaynedlye afford him before I sawe his follye."

"The Lord President of munster to my M^r."

The feelings of the Irish towards Elizabeth are exhibited in an unexpected manner by the passage in the President's despatch, relative to the *Pius Quintus!* it exposes one of those unobtrusive, yet most impressive means by which nations, under pressure of great tyranny, give expression to the bitterness of their hatred of their rulers. The main purpose of that famous Bull had been to excommunicate the Queen, and so precious was that Papal sentence to the whole Irish race, that the document which proclaimed it came presently into common use as the most sacred witness of truth which could be invoked between man and man.

Amidst the multitude of depreciating and loose observations which Carewe from time to time made upon Florence, was one now written to Cecyll, that he "incessantly railed against the Priests." The reader has already seen the declaration of Sir W. St. Leger, that "*Florence was fervently attached to the old religion*" (the religion of the priests), and the statement that the pious Countess of Clancar would never have consented to the marriage of her daughter with him, had she not known that he was conscientiously devout and Catholic. Had the Earl of Thomond considered that Florence held the most solemn oaths as Carewe held them, he would have been less particular on what book he made him swear: he could have perjured himself as readily on a Pius Quintus as on a Testament.

"1600.   May 3.   (*Inclosure in 6 May*, 1600.)

"*Copy.   From* FLORENCE Mᶜ CARTHY *unto me*.

"*Household.*

"*To the Right Honᵇˡᵉ his very approved friend* SIR GEORGE CAREWE, Kᵗ., *Lord President of Munster give these with all speed.*

"It may please yoʳ Lo., at the Erle of Tyrone's beinge here I did assuredly beleve that the best service that I could pforme, and the best course that I could take for Her Maty, was to confer with him, consideringe the psent state that I stood in, *first I had a warrant wᶜh I have here now extant, to conferr wth any rebell and to entertayne any rebells*, which, with one barrell of powder, was all the helpe and meanes that I got of those that commanded Mounster for Her Maty, and all the charges that Her Highnes was at for the recovery of the countrey of Desmond from the rebells, wch I recovered wth great paynes and chardges, wth the helpe of other rebells, who were more faythfull to the Erle of Tyrone then to my self, who if I had not come to Tyrone would have lefte me to my enemies, to be used at ther will, or ledd me prysoner to Tyrone, if I had not runne away to some towne wher I had no means to lyve, or repayred into England, ther to tell a foolyshe cowardly tale, wᶜh is, that I durst not for feare of the rebells that helde my country, go in sight thereof, and to put Her Maty to more chardges to small profit, whereof I knewe her to be wearie before. Therfore I assure your Lo that if I had not come to conferr wth Tyrone, he had wth his force, in psone, spoyled, preyed and burned all Carbrie, and starved and killed all the people there, and had sent Redmond Bourke, and Dermod O'Conor wth all the Connaght people and bonies in Munster, and thereabouts, to dispossesse me of Desmond, and to settle Donell MᶜCarthy there; destroyinge, prayeinge and burninge both the O'Sulyuanes, and all my frends there; all wch was the cause of my goinge to conferr wth Tyrone, who, as Mr. John Fitz Edmonds, and all Munster doth knowe, could presently worke all these mischeffs against me, if I had not come to conferr wth him; wch course, consyderinge myself to be sure of my owne faythfulnes to Her Maty, I tooke the best for Her Highnes, and for my-self; for yf I had taken banishment, and lost my country, people, and frends, I should but ether charge Her Maty to maintayne myself, or ells lyve and dye miserably, wthout meanes to helpe myself; wheras by mainteyninge myself in the possession of my country, I doubt not but to do Her Maty, and your Lo, more service then any other in these ptes of Mounster; wᶜh, besydes that I am bound to do for Her Maty all that is in me, I protest, I am for yoʳ owne sake, and Mr. Secretary, and Sir Walter's sakes (for whose pleasures I would not, so God helpe me, refuse to do any thinge that any of them comaunded) willinge to do yoʳ Lo any service I maye.

"In regard whereof I am moved to open unto yoʳ Lo my present estate, quest, wch is reasonable, and benefyciall for Her Matye's service, and my mainteyninge in the possession of my country; for at this present tyme ther are 300 of O'Neiles bonies, as they terme themselves, in Carbrie, and as many in Desmond; 200 in Muskery, and 150 in Dowalla; and now wthin these 4 or 5 dayes, James Mc Thomas of Desmond wrote to Dermod O'Conor for 500 or 600 to be entertayned by him; whereof Dermod brought him now the most pte, and will now presently get him the rest; all wch bonies, wth the saide Dermod O'Conor, will laye hands upon all my people and followers, and dispossesse me of my country of Desmond, wch is a remote, stronge, inaccessable country, farr from the helpe of Her Maties forces, and incomodious for them to serve in; and the said Dermod O'Conor, and all those bonies, will psently acknowledg Donell McCarthy, and take his pte, and they, together wth the Geraldines, and Redmond Bourke, who hath as many bonies as Dermod O'Conor or more, will altogether banish me, and maintayne Donell Mc Carthy, or Dermod Mc Owen, in the possession of my country, if now upon the sodayne I had gone to yor Lo; and these bonies that are wth me will straight goe to Donell, thinkinge that I have abandoned and betrayed them; whereby my state will hardly wth great tyme, and charges be recovered.

" My humble request therefore unto yor Lo is to accept me as a subjecte, and to respytt me for some such tyme as you shall thinke meete, wherby I may be as farr out of ther danger as I may; and they may not be able to dispossesse me so sodaynely as they may do nowe; as also that I maye wryte into England, to Mr. Secretary, Sir Walter, and Sir John Stanhope, whose l^{re} I sent yor Lo to puse, and wch I must answere; and besechinge yor Lo to sende me his letter agayne. In wch l^{res} I must acquaint them wth the spoyles, and burninges, and kyllings of my people exercysed by Flowor, and Bostoke, against me, wherunto they were hyred by myne adversaries; And if it please yor Lo to do me this favour, I wilbe sworne to my Lo of Thomond, and to Mr. Justice Welshe, and Mr. John Fitz Edmonds, or to any of them, to come to yor Lo, and to do anythinge that they and yor Lo will comand me: And so referringe unto yor Lo the consideracon of my presente estate, and inward intencion, w^{ch}, God let me not lyve yf I have not wthout dissimulation opened to yor Lo! I humbly take leave, this 3rd of May, 1600.

" Your Lo: moste humble to comaund to his power.

" ffor. Mc Carthy."

CHAPTER XII.

WHILST the Lord President had Florence under his roof, and between the intervals of the various attacks made upon him by each of the members of the Council in turn, and occasionally by the imposing union of them all, and not improbably whilst, in Carewe's opinion, sleeping off the effects of a skinful of sack, Florence wrote one of the most explicit, able, and interesting of all his extant letters. In writing to Carewe he had justified his visit to O'Neill, not only by the necessity of it for his own safety, and its expediency for the Queen's service, but by reference to the warrant in his possession authorizing him to parle with rebels. His letter to Sir Robert Cecyll was an able and logical apology for all his conduct since his return to Ireland! And Cecyll must in his conscience have acknowledged that Florence had effected precisely the purpose for which he had been sent back to Ireland, and that he had used the very means which it had been foreseen he would require to use, and which he had the Queen's authority for using. He had driven Donal and his Bonies out of Desmond, had pushed all rebellion beyond his boundaries, and had done it at his own charges, minus one barrel of powder, which had been furnished to him out of Her Majesty's stores. He had accomplished it by arming his own people and hiring Bonnaghts, but mainly by his parling with rebels, as by his warrant ("ready to be shown," and no doubt really shown to the Lord President), he was authorized to do. But Cecyll now learned that Carewe, owing to his great distrust of Florence, felt his hands fettered, and his purpose to act openly against FitzThomas paralyzed by the very condition of things which Florence had been sent to effect, and had effected.

What Carewe required of Florence would have thrown Desmond back into the hands of Donal, and would have undone all that Florence had been sent to do; this he himself saw, and it was this that forced from him the admission that "he was fairly bewildered, and knew not what to think." He had written that "Donal would be a far worse, because braver opponent than Florence, and that therefore he *rejoiced that Florence was the commander of the forces of his country;*" and presently, in the contortions of his bewilderment, we see him desirous to remove Florence, under any pretext, and to raise Donal up to wrest his country from him! Under the many accusations against Florence of "parling with rebels," Cecyll kept a profound silence; it was now manifest that Carewe intended to reverse, on his own authority, the policy of the Privy Council, which had sent Florence to Ireland; and Cecyll, either distrustful of his own opinion, or well pleased that on another should fall the responsibility which had weighed so painfully on himself, left it to the ability and unscrupulous energy of Carewe to deal with him, with Donal, and with Desmond, as his difficulties should suggest.

Carewe had professed "his contentment to fight Florence with his own weapons;" he had declared him to be "a fool, an idiot, and a coward!" the contest then must have been all in his own favour; and so he really believed it to be. Had the Lord President fought this famous duel of wits *fairly* to the end, the result of it might have left the question of Florence's cowardice in doubt, but would have left us no hesitation in declaring which of the combatants best merited those other uncivil epithets. Florence went to Cork, " kneeled very humbly before the President," was cajoled, preached to, and finally threatened and sworn at; he had promised to deliver his son as a pledge, and taken oath on a Pius Quintus not to oppose the Queen's forces *"unless* they attacked him, or his people!" Such was the result of Sir George Carewe's first moves in the great diplomatic encounter; he had had many promises of Florence before! he had now several additional ones! "and the consolation of pronouncing him a perjurer if he broke them; and of soon teaching him submissive entreaties if he kept them!" Great must have been the prudence and wisdom requisite to keep Florence from a rupture with such a man, and to ward off the distrust of his followers, which the perverse requirements of Carewe exposed him to! It is a remarkable instance of the partial blindness so often the result of terror, that Carewe could see no danger to be apprehended but that of Florence joining his forces with those of the Earl of Desmond! to prevent this he was willing to throw the whole resources of Carbery and Desmond into the hands of a man who knew no restraints of prudence, who had no scruples, who neither hoped nor feared anything from the Queen, who had been all his life in arms, who was in rebellion at the time, and

whose earliest proceeding would have been to direct every
bony and follower that he had, towards the great rebel camp
at Arlow. The President of Munster, and the Queen's army
—" 1,740 *fotte by the pole*"—were saved from ruin, in his
own despite, by the superlative prudence of the man whom
in his peevish perversity he called an idiot.

" 1600. *May 6ᵗʰ*. FLORENCE Mᶜ CARTIE *to the Right Honble his most
approved friend* SIR RO: CECIL, Kᵗ. &c. &c. -

" It may please yoʳ Honorr, Before I was entangled in the warres of
Desmond I wrote one letter unto your Honour; but since I went thyther I
neü had so much time, leasure or meanes, as to write, untill I drew Donell
Mᶜ Cartie, and his 700 Connaght buonies out of that countrey, although he
was baked, assisted and faüed by all the rebels of Moñster, unto whom th
Erle of Tireowen wrote dayely, aleadging that I, with English policie went
about to recoü that countrey, wᶜh was the bak and strength of all Mounster,
wth the wᶜh I wold undo all the rebells there; yet notwthstanding all their
endeoüs I scattered asonder, and drew out of the countrey, the sayd Donell
and all his buonies, and acomplices, and was no soner retourned unto the
countrey, but wthin ij dayes I received Tireowen's letter, signifieing that he
was com into Mounster, and intreating me earnestly to come to him pntly;
and writeing also to Carbrie O'Conoⁱ and the rest of the captaines of my
buonies or souldiers, and to all th other captaines of his adherents in those
parts, that, uppon paine of death (yf I came not to him pntly,) they shold
all forsake me, and bring me a prisoner unto him, yf they could; wch (I
protest) I am perswaded they had don yf it had not bene for Carbrie
O'Conor's frendshipp towards, me; but yet for all that he could do, the captaines and souldiers, uppon knowledge of Tireowen's coñandmẽt, grew
into an uprore, mutinge against me, and alleadging me to be an infidell,
and a betrayer of themselfes, and all the rest of Ireland to Englishmen;
wheruppon they all departed in a vengible, furious, humour, leauing myself, and both the O'Swlivans, and all the rest of the gent of the countrey
there, alone to the mercie of Donell Mᶜ Carthy and his buonies, yf they had
the witt or valour to retourne; or to the mercie of any other men of warr
whatsoever.
" Wᶜh when I saw, and that there was no other meanes of saeftie, I
followed them; and by swering that I wold then write pntly to Tireowen,
and (uppon sufficient assurance for myselfe returninge), that I wold go
speake to him whensoever he came into the coñ of Cork, I pacified them,
and thereuppon wrote to Tireowen; and within three days after, Dermod
O'Conor, a great commander of Connaught buonies, came with vj or vii
hundred footmẽ into the edge of my countrey, and sent unto me eyther to
com speake wth him, or els that he wold com into the countrey to speake
wth me; wᶜh moved me to ride unto him, from whom I could hardly departe, or escape, by swering that I wolde folow him to Tireowen; whom in
the end I folowed very slowly, for I made Tireowen stay a fortnight in the
coñ of Cork for me before I came to him, wᶜh afterwards made him say
still that I onely spoyled his jorney, and starved his people: before I came
to Tireowen I had his protection, and got himself, and all the captaines and
genᵗ wth him, swerne to send me, and such as came wth me salfe bak againe;
wᶜh protection I do send here inclosed: at the first ij dayes, both he, and
James Mᶜ Thomas of Desmond, whom they call Earle of Desmond, wth
bishopp Mᶜ Cragh, and Archer, were all very earnestly in hand wth me to

enter into their actōn of rebellion with them; whom, I protest, I utterly refused; for I renounce God if ever, at any times, I promest him to do anything against Her Matie, or the State of England and Ireland, but that I wold eū continue for Her Matie, as I have allwayes don; wch when they saw, then Bishopp Mc Cragh curssed me, and they all concluded to take my countrey of Desmond from me, and to settle Donell Mc Carthy there, and pntly to distroy all the countrey of Carbrie.

" To wch purpose they removed the next morninge toward Carbrie, and stayd that night uppon the river of Kinsale, where I made meanes to all Tireowen's gent, and people, to intreat for me unto him ; whose fau^l they obtaine'd in som sorte, so as I might satisfie him for Donell McCarthy, whom (as himself told me) he created McCarthy More by his meanes ; whereby it stoode him uppon in hono^l, to maintain his right, and that I shold nedes geue him thaward of the said Tireowen himself, and Bishopp McCragh, wch I utterly refused ; for eu^l when I shold speak for myself before them the sayd bastardly rascall Donell McCarthy, came and abused me wth vilanous words, calling me allwayes a trecherous deceitfull Englishma^l, wherein Oneyll did still beare wth him, and doth still fauo^l him, and write unto him by the name of McCarthy, wch made me refuse him as an arbitrato^l ; whereuppon he asked me to whose arbitrement I wold stand wth the said Donell for the Signorie of Desmond ? I told him that I wolde stand to thaward of both the Oswlivans, and all the rest of the gent, freeholders, and folowers of that countrey, who ever elected him, that was McCarthy, or lord of that countrey; of wch arbitremēt he wold have the umpireship to be to himself, and to Bishopp McCragh, or to one of them both ; wch I also refused ; at last wee agreed that the Oswlivans, and the gent of the countrey shold agree the matter, and that Bishopp McCragh, as one of the arbitrators, shold be joined wth them, and that the sayd bishopp shold go into Desmond by May-day, and agree the matter, he and the Oswlivans, and gent of the countrey; and to the end they shold be sure of my performance when Tireown were gon, they wold have my son as an ostadge; whom I promest; but because my promese wold not serv, they wold nedes haue the best ostadges that I had, untill I brought my son; whereuppon I gave them my brother, wth whom they wold neds haue a gent of good estimacon of my name, that was wth me; wch I was also constrained to deliū; and therewthall retourned their forces from Carbrie, and consulted together how to take Kinsale; wch when I understood, I wrote to Capten Bostok that was there, and to the townesmen, to stand well uppon their kepinge, and afterwards went to Tireowen, and tolde him that it was a most foolish oppinion of them that persuaded him to attempt anything against the towne of Kinsale, wch himself, and all the Ireish forces in Ireland, could neyther force, nor surprise; whereuppon he removed, and went towards Kinsale, to view the towne.

" I was wth him still; and all the Mounster men that were there persuaded him earnestly to assault the towne, wch in deade was reasonable weake, yet I prevayled against all their wills, and got him to go towards Cork; and next day he went a very great jorney, and the day after; and complained of me that I deceved him, and delivered him not my son, but my brother, who ever tooke his parte; and therewthall enlarged my brother, and commanded my gent to be kept fast by Dermod O'Conor. Dureing my being wth him I dealth for Her Matie wth the best gent of Mounster that were there; among whom I won the White Knight, and the Knight of Kierry, and M^r McDonogh, the White Knight's son-in-law, and O'Conor Kierry, who were all contented, at my request and entreatie, to

becom Her Mat's subiects; but the same night that I departed, O'Conor
Kierries horsses being tired stayd him behind; but M^r McDonogh, wth
the White Knight, and the Knight of Kierry, were all aprehended, and
caried away: at my departure he understood of my lo. of Ormond's being
afore him, wch made him desire me to go further wth him, wch I refused;
having told him that I wold carie no armes against Her Matie, nor feight
against my lo. of Ormond for any other of Ireland, but wold feight wth
any other of Ireland for him; he desired me then to send ij hundred
buonies, wch accompanied me, wth him; I told him yf he could send unto
them, (for they were coming after me,) and persuade them to com wth
him, I wold geve them leave; but when his messeng¹ came' with me, I
perswaded the souldiers secretly to retourne wth myself; assureing them
that they shold have nothing wth Tireowen but blows, hunger, and
travayle; wch made them refuse to go to him.

"And so I retourned, and pntly I understood that I was taken at
Cork, and everywhere els, for a rebell! wch made me afeaid to go in, lest
I shold be restrained; whereuppon I wrote to Sir Henry Power, unto
whom I made knowen the necessities that constrained me to com speake
to Tireowen; for God let me not live an howre, yf I had not com to him
he wolde, and might as easiely as I can write one line, by comaunding my
buonies to bring me unto him, and by comaunding Dermod O'Conor, and
Redmond Bourk, or any of them, wth his regiment of a thousand or
twelf or fourtene hundred foote men, to go wth Donell McCarthy and
establish him in my countrey; w^{ch}, as God judge me, they might, and
wold do pntly, and wold burne, kill, and spoyll, all my frends and folowers
there; and yf I rann away from ther buonies myself, I had no other
meanes to live but to starv in som towne, or to repair into England to put
Her Matie to more charges; wherof I knew her to be wearie alreadie;
wch moved me to elect the best course that I could take for Her Matie,
for I knew yf I had not com to Tireowen I shold lose the countrey of
Desmond, w^{ch}, wth great paines, charges, and dangers I recovered, without
any charges of Her Matie; and wch wold go nere to maintaine the rebellion of Mounster for ever; whereas, by kepeing myself in possession
thereof, and speaking not one woord against the rebells, and buonies of
Mounster, I shalbe able, whensoever yt shall please Her Matie to set me
to work, to do Her Highnes more service then any three in these parts of
Ireland; wch the councill of Mounster wolde not, nor could not, understand! for all that I could write to Sir Henry Power could do me no good.

W^{ch} moved me, wthin a weeke after my retourning, to com speake to
Sir Henry Power; and within a mile or two of Cork, I came alone from
my people, and conferred with him, and wth Sir Charles Willmott, and the
Marshall Sir George Torinton; unto whom I told that I wrote to the Lo.
Deputie, and to the Lo. President, and wold go to Dubling yf I were so
directed by them; whereuppon they sayd they wold expect their Lops
resolucon, and that my people shold take no hurt in the mean time, so as
they did not anoy none of Her Mat's subiects; and yf I undertook for the
whole countrey of Carbrie, that they shold take no hurt by them, which
I refused to do before I had conferred wth the countrey, because som of
them were in acton, and others that were none of my people; wheruppon
I departed, and willed som of my people, that duelt hard by Kinsale, to
draw home their cattaylls, and go duell in their houses; whereuppon
Bostok first went to a castell of myne called Downe McPatrik, and finding there but two or three, went in and kept the place to himself, and all
the goods and cattaylls there; and retourning to Corck, himself and Capten
Flowre were sent, wth Her Matie's forces, into Carbrie, where they did

nothing but burne two castells of myne, and kill as manie men, women,
and children as they found in them, and burned as manie villadges, houses,
and corne, as appertained to any of my people; takinge away all their
cattayll, and so overrunn the countrey to Ross-Carbrie, and over the
Leap.

" At wch time I was uppon my way into Desmond, having before dismissed ij or three companies of footmē before me thyther; and having
stayd wth me but one hundred footmen, I retourned, and met one hundred
more of that countrey, wch two hundred I sent to geve Flowre and Bostok
som impedimēt, and divert them from going any further into the countrey;
wch when they understood of my being there, they retourned in haste
to Ross, havinge not the witt, nor the conduct, to kepe the higheway;
although the forces that they had, consisted of one thousand men, with two
troopes of horsemen: Uppon the reporte of these forces going from Cork
to spoyle Carbrie, Dermod O'Conor, who understood thereof, and had
Tireowen's warrant to take som part of his pay, or buonaght, of that
countrey, came thyther, wth vj or vij hundred men, and encamped himself
ij or iij miles east of Ross, in their way to Cork and Kinsale; he sent me
divers letters, and messengers, to desire me to com and take charge of all
the forces, and to revenge the wronges and losses wch I received at the
hands of Flowre and Bostok; wch I refused still to do, and wrote unto
him that I wold seeke my revenge otherwise; whereuppon he removed,
and toke his way directly towards Desmond, protesting, in a great rage,
that he wold, wth all the buonies in Mounster, spoyle Desmond, and dis-
posses me thereof for Donell McCarthy; wth wch hard messadge he dispatched my brother, with som of that countrey genť unto me, and sent
som of his owne people wth them.

" W^ch moved me ṗntly that night to ride to him; whereuppon he
retourned towards Ross, where he was before; where wee stayd a sene-
night; the Captaines remaining still at Ross, and coming foorth dayly, as
yf they were marching away; at last I desired to speak with Sir Henry
Power's liutenant, to know whether those forces were aucthorished, or
appointed by the Councell to burne, and spoyll those lands of myne? or
whether they did it of their owne heads? for I imagined because McCarthy
Reogh gave Flowre a couple of horss, and another to Bostok, and that I
understood that Flowre receeved som reward of my Lo. Barry, that they
were hiered to annoy me, w^h I understood afterwards to be so: the
liuetenant told me he knew nothing of the matter; and so went away.
The next morninge, betimes, the captaines drew out their forces, and
marched, in all haste, towards Kinsale ; at wch time, all the buonies
almost were gon for victualls, whereby there was not above four hundred
there together, who took armes, and folowed them in their tayle, untill the
passadge, or fery of Kinsale, and then retourned iiij or v miles bakward, where
they met the rest of their people ; and then they accused me, alleadging
that my parley wth thEnglish liutenant the day before, sent away the
Captens salfe; whereof, I protest unto yor Hon^r, I was inocent; for God
is my judge, my mynd concerning those forces, unto whom the Queenes
Matie gave pay, was that yf they all were at my disposicon, I wold send
all the horssmen, and footemen, with their furniture and coolors, salfe to
Cork; and wold hang Flowre and Bostok!

" Yet was I, by my souldiers, wrongfully accused and exclaimed uppon
by every body of them, wch moved me to rayle at them all, accuseing
them uniustly of cowardlyness, and disobedience, and protesting that
ṗntly I wold bring them to feight wth those captens; and wth that, dismissed them to go to supper, and to arm: ṗntly after supper, wch being

don, I traveyled that night over the river of Kinsale, and so through the
countrey, untill I came uppon the way betwen Cork and Kinsale, where
those Captaines came; at whose sight, they ran, in order, very desperatly
uppon them, and overthrew them; their horssmen stood still betwene both,
and were sore distressed by the Ireish shott; untill they forsook the place,
and then they ran uppon their battayle of footmẽ, and made them runn
away, out of order, killing a number of them, untill they came to a little
castell, where, uppon a trench that was thereby, they discharged their shott
at the Ireishmen, wᶜh did somwhat annoy them; and, supposeing som
strength or impedimẽt to be in that trench tourned bak; all the credit that
I had being unable to make them retourne; and striving to constrain them
I was myself shott in the arme, wᶜh made me retire wth them; none
folowing but vij or viij horssmen, wᶜh did them litle hurt, but retourned
shortly; the Ireishmen being stayd uppon the hill where they begun the
feight.

" Of the Ireishmen there were xvij kild; whereof four were captens,
and xv wounded; of the capten's side I am not certen what number were
kild; for I told them not; but I *saw above one hundred bodies* of all sorts,
besids such as died by the way, and at Cork afterwards.   Within three or
four dayes after, the Lo. President Sir George Carew, and the Earle of
Thomond came to Cork; at wᶜh time I was gon after Dermod O'Conor, to
have the genƫ, that Tireowen held as an hostadge untill May, for the per-
formeing of the arbitremẽt wth Donell McCarthy; wᶜh genƫ was delivered
me by Dermod O'Conor, at May-day; from whom I departed pntly to the
Lo. President and thEarle of Thomond; and uppon their words I came to
them to Corck, wᶜh I beleve wilbe myne undoing! for I feare me all the
buonies, rebells and Ireish forces wilbe uppon my bak; for my being here
will persuade them that I am their enemie.   My Lo President wolld have
me deliver my son as an hostadge ; wᶜh yf I had don, I shold not dare go
out of this towne; for my chefe strength being my buonies, they wold be
the first that wold lay hands uppon me; neyther have I any of myne owne
men armed able to wthstand them; besids that, wthout doubt, all the
buonies, and rebells of Mounster wold runn uppon me, and kill, spoyle,
and distroy all my people, and countrey, and send me a prisoner to Tireowen; or yf I escaped their hands, I shold [be] constrained to starv, or live
like a begger in this towne, where Flowre or Bostok, or any of these
universal Captens, or damned drunken felowes, for a nagg of my Lo.
Barrie's, or McCarthyes, wold knock me in the head, or murther me.

" Wᶜh makes me that I cannott lose my countrey wilfully; for by God,
yf I do refuse, my buonies—(I) having no meanes, nor charge of Her
Matie, to arme, and maintayne myne owne people,—all the buonies of
Mounster, wth the rebells, will set uppon me, and establish Donell McCarthy in my place; a thing that neyther myself, nor all Her Maᵗˢ forces in
Mounster, cannott defend; because the rebells are so great in number all
aboutt my countrey ; having hole countreys of rebells betwene me and
every towne and garison; therefore I humblie besech yoʳ Honoʳ to be a
mean unto Her ᴹatie that I may obtaine my countrey of Desmond, of
Her Highnes, in as ample a manner as my father-in-law, and ancestors,
enioyed the same, and that it will please her Highnes, wth som sufficient
charge to enhable me to defend myself, and serv Her Highnes against all
the rebells of Ireland, as forwardly, and as faythfully, as any other, and yf
yoʳ Honoʳ do not pntly find my service to be more avayleable then any
others in these parts, and heare all the rebells of Mounster or Ireland
exclaime and complaine of me, I am contented to lose my liveing, charge,
and creditt wth yoʳ Honoʳ !   I told my Lo. President that so sone as I had

yor Hono^{rs} resolucõn hereof, he shold have my son, and any ostadges he pleased; in the mean time I will the best I can, prepare myself, and my people, to be out of the danger of the buonies, and rebells, and take such order, as the Lo President shall understand any practice of theirs against, and shalbe advertised of anything that may advaunce, Her Ma^{ts} service in these parts; but, I feare me most of all things, that because of my coming hyther now, all the bonies and rebells will sett uppon me, and drive me away, and that the foolish malicious Captens here will not suffer me to do Her Matie service; for, as I understand, they wold now here go about to kill me, but for feare of the Lo. President; and yf I be once driven out of Desmond, it will ever hardly be recovered; for it is so wild, strong, and unaccessable, all, almost, consisting of woods, steepe moun-taines, bogges, lakes, and rivers, as no English forces are able to sustaine the paines of service there; yf through any former imputacõn by myne adversaries, sent against me, for my parley wth Tireowen, or renued now, any body there will suspect me, or beleve not what I write, I will uppon yor Hono^{rs} letter, and uppon yor fayth that I shall have no hurt, nor stay, repair unto you myself, to affirme what I write; therefore let yor Hon^r rest assured that whatsoever y^rself, Sir Walter Raleigh, and Sir John Stanop doth say, I will beleve it; and whatsoever you will have me do I will do it; so as I may live in good sorte, out of restraint. And so refer-ring my whole state to yor Hono^{rs} pleasure, and disposicõn; for whatsoever you say or promise I will beleve it, sooner, as God judge me, then the Pope's Holines. I humblie take leave, Cork, this 6th of May, 1600.

" Yo^r Hono^{rs} most humble
" and bonden ever to be comãunded,
" ffloᴿ. MᶜCᴀʀᴛʜʏ."

The fate which one, at least, of the men who had been sent by Sir Henry Power to lay waste the country, and destroy the churles and poor people of Carbery, escaped at the hands of Florence, he more narrowly missed from the Government in whose name that barbarity had been perpe-trated. Shortly after his return, Captain Bostock fell under the same suspicion which had for so many years pursued Florence himself, namely, of treasonable dealings with that contagious traitor Jacques de Franceschi. This suspicion reached Carewe not from his own intelligencers, but in a despatch from the English Secretary, who was better served by his spies in Munster, than was the Lord President him-self. On the 29th June, 1601, Cecyll wrote to Carewe :—

" You shall nowe therefore understand that I am credybly advertysed that Jacques contynually holdeth correspondencey with Captaine Bos-tocke, who, as my informer tells me, resydeth still in Youghall; the carryer between them is a Frenchman who, they saye, doeth ordynarily passe up and down : because you do best understand the quallity of the man, and can compare the circumstances of his actions with this infor-mation, I must referre much to your judgement herein ; being, for my own opinion, thus perswaded that yf you could suddenly cause his papers to be seysed and serched, and then his person to be stayed, and well examyned, there will somethinge be founde in his papers, or somethinge pycked out by your examinacion, which may laye open the matter : all

which, if it might be done upon some other grounde, it were the better ;
though rather then not to be don, let it be quacunq via."

It was done; the man's coffers were searched by Carewe,
as desired "upon some other ground," but the phantom
of Jacques' treachery, as usual, evaded them! there was
found nothing! but not the less did the Lord Deputy of
Ireland, to whom Cecyll had also written, promise to "keep
very good spial upon Bostock, awaiting more particular and
certain ground to charge him with; which we must receive
from thence (England); yet, in the meantime, he shall be so
narrowly looked unto, as if he have the will (*which we doubt
not*) he shall not have means to hurt much."

Notwithstanding the President's opinion that "Florence
was a fool," the prudence and ability with which he extricated himself from a position of rare difficulty, contrasts
creditably with the blundering barbarity of Power, and the
reckless impolicy of Carewe. The President however
declared himself not ill pleased with the result of his encounter with Florence, as these last letters had left it. "He
doubted not so to deal with him as to derive his advantage
from him; and had no fear of being over-reached." Accordingly Florence was allowed for this time to depart freely to
Cork; he at once made his repair to Iniskeane, in Carbery,
where, far beyond the reach of the Queen's forces, and surrounded by his own armed followers, and hired bonies, he
resumed his diplomatic contest. He had promised to deliver
his son into the hands of Carewe, but the child was ill; and
this was impossible for the present! he had promised to
diminish the number of the bonies in his pay, "the senseless
behaviour of Carewe's own Captains" prevented this, in some
measure, but, to a certain extent, it was done! He had
promised to furnish the President with all intelligence that
he judged might be of interest to him, and he accordingly
wrote that the Gentlemen of Desmond, and O'Sullevan, had
laid upon him the title of MacCarthy Mor! which, *as it much
conduced to Her Majesty's advantage,* he had accepted! He
added that a Friar, and an Archbishop had come from Spain
into Ireland, bringing with them treasure, weapon, and
munition. This last piece of intelligence was, if not a great
secret, accepted as a proof of his veracity, and went some
little way towards neutralizing less welcome information
which accompanied it; and Carewe begins to show symptoms
of wavering in his harsh opinion of him. Still the sick child
was withheld from him! and until he got *him* he could have
no trust in Florence's loyalty.

"1600· *May* 14. FLORENCE MacCARTHY *to* SIR G. CAREWE.

" It may please yor Honorable Lo:. At my deptinge from you (God is my Judge) myne intention and full purpose was, and is styll, (yf yor vaine wickéd foolishe Capteins do suffer me) to quytt myself ofthe Connagh Buonies, and of all these wicked roagues, and rebells, wth so much speede as I may for my lyf; I mean those that I entertayne, who as sone as I have dischardged myself of them, yf I do not by service utterly overthrowe them, or dryve them out of all Munster,. let me lose all my frends, and credyte wth Her Maty, and wth all honest men ! in the meane tyme I will not fayle to praye and spoyle the reste of them, and to kyll as many of them, especially of the O'Mayllies, (who wth three foystes [boats] are now in my country,) as I can; therefore seeinge they ar ther, hasten Sir Fynen O'Driscoll's sonne to me; and wryte unto me by Capten Harvey; for I will not trust him, nor nobodye in this adge and country, but such as I will trust upon yor Lo^s: word, and fayth; whether he be subiect or rebell; and wthout trusting him I can hardly succour him, nor do the Queen's sacred Maty any service by his helpe or meanes!

" It may be some of my mallitious adversaries may alledge many matters against me, wch may happly be furthered by some odd councillor or other, as was done before yor Lo: came, by such as doeth not know, nor understand my intention, or what may best avayle her Matie, and further . Her Highnes' service. My humble sute therfore unto yor Lo, (unto whome I have made knowne all my mynde and intention,) is that my temporisinge wth the rebells, untyll I maye effecte my purpose, may not be mysconstrued ; wch course I assure yor Lo I do take, onely because the assuringe and maintayninge of myself in the possession of Desmond, is the only waye that is to overthrow all the rebells of Munster, and dryve awaye quickely, or utterly overthrowe, all the Bonies there; for the compassinge of wch my humble sute unto Her Sacred Maty is that it will please her Highenes to graunt me my country of Desmond on the same manner that my father in laue and grandfather held it; and as Her Highenes graunted it (would have granted it ?) to any other of the byrth of England that should marry my wyf; (wch graunt I have ready to be seene under the clerke of the signet, M^r. Wyndebankes hand,) tolleratinge wth me to beare the nam of Mc Carty More, wch both the O'Sullevans, and the rest of the Gent freeholders and followers of the country layde upon me, and constrayned me to accepte, thereby to procure the countrie to yelde unto me, and to come in, and forsake that bastard Donell Mac Carthy, and the reste of the rebells; for before·I tooke the name upon me, I protest I could not gett 20 of the country men of warr, or comõn people, to come at me, as was knowne to Sir Warham S^t. Leger, and Sir Henry Power, who wrate to M^r. Secretary then to that effecte; assuringe yor Lo that I would never, by any meanes, accepte it, yf the recoveringe of that countrie (wch of all other here is most avayleable for Her Mat's service) stood not upon it; wch notwthstandinge, yf it please her Maty to abolishe, I humbly beseche that it may be abolyshed in me, by that meanes of creation that it was abolyshed in my father in lawe !

" I beseche yor Lo also to consyder how remote my country stands from all succour, havinge all the rebells of Mounster, and ther countries, betwene it, and not any towne of garryson, or any place or country that ar her Maty's subiects; wch ar as well knowne to yor Lo as to myself; wherby it is moste certayne that the rebells and bonies will waste, and destroye my country, whensoever I goe to worke for Her Mats paye: whereupon·I humbly beseche that I may have a sufficient chardge to serve her

Majesty wthal; nether will a capten's chardge serve for him that must
keepe many companies; nor I do not meane to charge Her Maty wth half
so many as I will bringe to her service; all which I humbly refer to her
Mat's divine consideracon; besechinge yo᷄ʳ Lo to be an humble sute in my
behalf; the rather that what, whatsoever it shall please her Maty to•deale
wth me, my full purpose and intention was, and shalbe allwayes, to rest
her Hignes faythfull, true servant, to pforme wth my lyf any service that
may benefyte her moste Sacred Maty; assuring yo᷄ʳ Lo in proof thereof,
that I will not fayle, from tyme to tyme, to advertyse and advyse yo᷄ʳ Lo
by my lʳᵉˢ, the beste I maye, to further her Maty's service; and so, hopinge
that yo᷄ʳ Lo will not omyt to further my sute, I humbly take leave.
    " Iniskayne this 14ᵗʰ of May 1600.
                    " Yo᷄ʳ moste humble and assured,
                                        " fflor M ᶜCARTHY.

    " The younge man of my wyf's country that I tolde yo᷄ʳ Lordship of, that
came now out of Spayne, is called Teage O'Faylue, a foster brother of my
wyfe; he hath bene these 9 years in Spayne a student, and hath this laste
yere remayned wth the Byshop of Kyerie, one Michaell Walter, borne at
Limericke, who beinge deade about half a yere paste, he hath synce remayned wth Friar Peter-de-los-Angelos, provinciall of the Franciskans of
Andelozia, and guardian of Sivilla, who affyrmed and assured some of his
frends there that Fryer Mathias de Oviedo, who was commissarye generall of the Fryers of North Spayne, and now is Byshop of Dublyn, is
come over wth a greate deale of treasure, weapon, and munition; and that
a greate nomber of men ar ready to be sent to the Irishmen hyther, if
they will have them.   Synce the wrytinge of this lʳᵉ ther ar some of my
men come from the countre of Lymericke and Kyrrie, who brought me
dyvers newes that concernes you; wherby I must wryte you now another
lʳᵉ, and so requestinge yo᷄ʳ Lo in any wyse to sende me Morryce Moore, I
humbly take leave.
                        " Yo᷄ʳ Lo to comãnd,
                                        " fflo MᶜCARTHY."

    To this letter, Carewe, when he enclosed it to Cecyll,
added the following remarks :—

    " In this lettre he speakes nothinge of his sonne, whome he promysed
faythfully to send unto me to Limericke; and in another lettre unto me he
doeth omitt the same ; and allso excuses his owne cominge to me to
Limericke, wᶜh he likewyse promised; pretendinge that itt woulld turne to
his great hinderance; wᶜh omission, and excuse, I nothinge like; In my
answere unto him I urge him to performme his promises in those pointes ;
but in them I feare he will breake.   This newes of Spayne I thinke to be
very trew.
                                " GEORGE CAREWE."

    Almost sufficiently convinced at last, that he might rely
upon Florence's professions of loyalty—certainly upon his
neutrality—and having conducted to a point of good promise
certain negotiations with various Captains of the Bonaghts,
Sir George Carewe decided that the time was come when he
might venture to break out beyond the circuit of a mile or

two of the City of Cork, within which the Queen's forces had
long suffered themselves to be most shamefully enclosed. He
accordingly began to give out speeches that he would by the
6th of May, set forth on his way to Limerick; "that he
would batter every castle, and lay desolate the country
along his route, of every man who was in action!" But he
had on his hands at the time, transactions of a delicate, and
rather uncertain character, as the reader will presently see,
which might cause some delay in his setting forth. James
FitzThomas took the President at his word, and made instant preparations to give him meeting: when he came to
assemble the various bands of Bonaghts left to him by O'Neill,
he became aware of certain results of the President's diplomacy; he found that Redmund Burke, with 500 men had
suddenly drawn himself off, and had settled within the confines of Ormond, and by no persuasion could be induced
to join him. With the force however of Dermod O'Connor,
he contrived to muster sixteen or seventeen hundred men,
and with them placed himself in the great wood called Kil-
more, between Moyallow and Kilmallock; the President
tarried, the patience of FitzThomas' unruly stipendiaries
held out for ten days, they then dispersed. Sir Richard
Piercy, the Governor of Kinsale, at once burst out from his
garrison, and poured what horse he had into Kinalmeaky.
He succeeded in surprising, and slaying 10 bonaghts, and
wrote indignantly to Carewe that he would have killed
many more, but that Florence MacCarthy had got tidings of
his intent, and given warning to the Queen's enemies.

The expedition of Carewe, which FitzThomas had been
expecting from the 10th to the 16th of the month was
rumoured to be in readiness, and about to set forth, and it
was then that the Earl wrote to Florence the first of the
letters which are printed in the Pacata Hibernia. "He hoped
to be able to muster sixteen or seventeen hundred men, sufficient to meet the President in front, if Florence would
prosecute him freshly from the rearward." This letter contained nothing but what was known to Carewe, and to all
the world. FitzThomas openly barred the President's way
to Limerick, and hoped effectually to stop him. Florence
may have sent this letter to Carewe to prove *his readiness to
do him underhand service,*—proceedings of this kind were the
weapons with which these two great combatants were contented to fight each other, they were called *Florence's own
weapons.* Having sent the letter to the President, with such
explanations and professions as he thought proper, Florence

bore in person his answer to the camp of FitzThomas; but it chanced that there was another gentleman at the time in action, who for a purpose equally diplomatic, found it expedient also, to make known to the President the purport of this personal answer of Florence.

" 1600. Augt. 25.

" Gerote Lyston of Skehanaghe in the countie of Limericke, Gentⁿ, beinge in actuall rebellion wth James Fitz Thomas attended him into the countie of Kerry to a village (possessed before the rebellion by James Hussye) called Bellaghafenan, beinge neare 2 miles distant from Castlemayne, whither about 5 weekes since Florence McCarty, garded with 100 foote under Morroghe-ne-Moe came, where, after they had saluted eche other Florence tooke upon him to excuse himself to James Fitz Thomas for nott havinge mett the said James wth his forces to joyne both their forces together, accordinge to some former agreement concluded upon betwene them to fight with the Lo: President and her Mat's armies, and alleadged for the reason of his absence, that it would have bene a greate weakeninge to that opeynion which the country conceeved of their strengthe, and an utter overthroue to their credytts if they two (with their joint forces) beinge the chefe actores and supporters of the action, should be together, and not able to put the Lo: President to the worst, which Florence seemed much to mystrust, and after his excuses had pacefied James Fitz Thomas, in the hearinge and presence of McAwlyffe, Thomas Oge Moriertagh McShihie, John Ulick and me the said Gerot Lyston that he would contynue with James Fitz Thomas in this action, and take such parte therein as he dyd; and although James Fitz Thomas would geve over this rebellion (which Florence termed a Just Warre) yet he himselfe would kepe lyff in it so long as he could get anye one to followe him, if O'Neill himselfe would holde out with him, with whome he was sworne, and resolved to sincke or swymme: and hereupon James and his Chefe Gentlemen being satysfied, they departed; James to the Castle of the Currans, where he laye that night, and Florence lodged at Molaghhiff, which was the house wherein M^r. Nicholas Browne dwelt."

The business of Carewe, which has been dimly alluded to as delaying his march to Limerick, was not yet in a state of sufficient forwardness to allow of his leaving Cork. He had on hand certainly two, and not improbably three negotiations which, if successful, would open his way without let, to Limerick or whithersoever else. But it will naturally occur to the reader—reminiscent of certain passages of the President's past life—to ask why all this painful endurance of suspense? this long submission to the fear of two or three individuals, open enemies, or at best but lukewarm friends of Her Majesty? Could this be the English Gentleman of 1583? this, the fearless man who at midday, in the face of the Mayor, and thousands of the citizens of Dublin, had so bravely stabbed the poor swordsman of the Kava-

naghs? or, if years and dignities had tempered the daring of
other days, was there no one to be found who from motives
of loyalty, and some reasonable remuneration, would rid the
Queen of these rebels? There were plenty! the instruments
for a fresh foul and heinous crime abounded! and by that
unerring instinct which teaches the assassin and the traitor
to scent out his employer, every murderer and traitor in Munster could smell the blood of O'Nassie on the hand of the
President! Whilst Carewe was vainly tormenting himself
with a longing to obtain possession of Florence's son, he
found his position each day less satisfactory! Tidings
reached him that FitzThomas was hiring more bonies, that
he was ostentatiously barring the road which he must travel
on his way to Limerick; and still did his fear of that idiot
Florence prevent him from venturing beyond the walls of
Cork; the 1,740 men-by-the-poll saw a larger force of as well
weaponed men as themselves in their front, and a multitude
of many thousands threatening to close upon their rear. Six
weeks of diplomacy had scarcely improved the President's
position, his temporizing with Florence had been a triumph;
it had retained all the Clan Carthy and their hired bonies in
strict neutrality; it was all that he desired; but wishing
now to profit by his triumph, and to proceed against Fitz-
Thomas, he discovered that a neutral force many times
larger than the Queen's army, in a position to intercept, if it
were willing, his return to the city he was leaving, was a
force little less rebellious than that which he was desirous to
attack.

In his perplexity, the genius of his youth returned to his
relief.

CHAPTER XIII.

THE reader must have been struck by a mysterious passage in one of the Lord President's recent letters to his friend Sir Robert Cecyll. It savours so much of the achievement of 1583 that the meaning of the writer already gleams confidentially through its disguise. "The Bushopp of Cashell is busilye workinge! within a feu days that stratageme will either take effect or fayle; but howsoever it do succeed, I have two more as good or better then that: I hope att last yf the divell be not his good Mr. but one will hitt!"

Between Carewe and his three agents, and his three stratagems, one as good or better than another, even the good Master himself might be embarrassed in his choice.

THE THREE DRAUGHTS.

There were at this crisis four personages, living far asunder, and not all known to each other, on the combination of whose rare characters and acquirements mainly depended the hopes of the Lord President for the prosperous administration of his province—that is, for the success of three stratagems, as good one as another, nay, each succeeding one, far better than the one that went before it. These stratagems, in the usual diplomatic language of the day, were called "*draughts!*" and the employing of them against any one much in the way, and not otherwise accessible, was termed *drawing!* hence "*to draw a draught*" against any one of the Queen's enemies—O'Neill, for example—meant to stab him, or shoot him, or take his head! it might even have the milder meaning of *enticing the approach of an enemy, under solemn parole, for his freedom to come and go, and then dexterously laying hands on him, and thrusting him into prison for the rest of his days;* the usual signification, however, was the severer one. The Act of 1583, which the Lords Justices, in the first moments of their anger, had called a *foul and heinous crime*, and the Dublin jury a *wilful murder*, was a *draught!* In fact, Sir George Carewe had *drawn a draught upon Owen*

O'Nassie! who was supposed to have slain his brother in
action; he had now three several such draughts on hand,
and an invocation of "the Good Master" was not inap-
propriate.

Of the four personages engaged in these transactions,
the first in station and authority was the Lo : President himself! the first in determination and action was John Nugent!
the first in cunning was Miler M'Grath, the Archbishop of
Cashell! and incomparably the first in genius was John
Annyas, called in the State Papers of the time Annyas the
Irishman!

Nature had leashed these men in couples according to
their genius, and destined their careers to much incidence of
resemblance: the two former were of Norman descent, the
latter pure or mere Milesians. Under the direction of the
Lord President, Three Draughts were to be drawn by the
united abilities of these men, upon the three chief disturbers
of the peace of Munster.

DRAUGHT THE FIRST.

JOHN NUGENT.

Of the share of Nugent and Carewe in one of the great
efforts made to deliver the President from his perplexity, the
account is given with admirable candour by Carewe himself.
No pen better than his could have traced for posterity the
narrative of the single historic adventure in the life of John
Nugent, or have more justly adjudged to that unskilful
draughtsman the sentence which accompanied the recital of
its miscarriage ; as assuredly no one so worthily or so well
as Nugent could—had the fates spared him—have testified
to the resources and serene determination of mind of his
employer! Unfortunately the reward followed so quickly
upon the capture of Nugent, that this chapter in the life of
the Lord President remains unwritten. The reader must be
contented with the narrative as it passed in undisguised
confidence, in letters, from Carewe to Cecyll. These letters
are so long that the story of the draughts is much interrupted; but Sir George Carewe had so many anxieties on
his mind at the time, and gave himself so little concern about
the after flight of an arrow that had missed its mark, that
when the failure of Nugent had been related, his thoughts
naturally turned to the business of nearest urgency, and this
was, as it had long been, his encounter with Florence, with

his own weapons. The failure of Nugent disturbed also for a while the arrangements of the Archbishop ; and although he was, as Carewe wrote, working busily, a certain delay between the first and second draught became unavoidable.

" 1600. *August* 17th. CAREWE *to* CECYLL. *From Limerick.*

" Florence Mc Cartie, once since I came from Corke wrote unto me a lettre of good intellygence, and sent me allso a lettre of James Mc Thomas wrotten unto him, to pray his assistance agaynst Her Majesty's armye, wch Florence directlye refused to do; but now since my coming into these parts, he hath ben wth James, and Dermond O'Connor, in Conologhe, not 12 myles from Limericke, and within 2 myles of Her Majesty's garryson att Askeiton. He brought wth him O'Sullevan More, and lefte him prisoner wth Dermond O'Connor (agaynst O'Sullevan's will) as a pledge for the Bonnaghts wch he is to receve in Desmond; and is now departed home agayne, wth intent to retourne wthin fourtene dayes wth all his force, as it is reported; but to say treulye I do not believe that he will enter into rebellion before that he heares from you an answere of his demaundes; but uppon deniall of them then I feare I shall have cause to chandge my opinion: the greatest suspicion that I holld of him, is that at his beinge here so neare as he was, I receved no lettres from him; nor yett do I hear any thinge of his sonne, whome he promised to send unto me. James Mc Thomas' direction of his lettre is " To the Right Honnourable his very good cosin the Lord Mac Carty More! wch title, before he leave itt, will cost the Queene more crownes then Desmond is worthe, and therefore it is worthye of consideration!

" 2049 (Sir George Carewe) found out one called Nugent, who promysed him to do Her Matie service uppon the person of John Mc Thomas; he was imprested by 2049 (Sir George Carewe) wth a horse, a pistoll, some munition, and £10 in money. Nugent, wth a resolved intent, did purpose to kill him with his pistoll; and the same day that I had viewed Loghgier, Nugent and John Mc Thomas came thether ; there was allso one Coppinger sometime a footman to Sir Walter Raleghe, unto whome Nugent did reveale his purpose, and promised him faythefullye to assist him in the enterprize : not longe after, John Mc Thomas departinge thence towards Arlow woods, havinge but onlye these tow above named on horsebacke, and 2 footmen wth him, Nugent tooke his pistoll in his hand, tellinge Coppinger that now he woulld kill him ; and as he was readye to shoote, Coppinger snatcht his pistoll out of his hand, and cryed Treason! Nugent spurringe his horse to have escaped, by misfortune his horse stumbled, and so he was taken ; and wthin 2 days (after he had by Coppinger's accusations, bene enforced to confesse that he did acquaynt 2049 (Sir G. Carewe) with his enterprise) he was fayrelye hanged; of whose deathe ther is no great losse; for he was but a protected traytor; and, I do thinke, he woulld, uppon the least occasion, haved relapsed.

" 2049 (Carewe) denies his knowledge of the pretence, and for my owne parte I was ignorant of it.

" 129 (Dermond O'Connoghor) hath sworne to perform the service. 1070 (Archbishop of Cashel) dothe follow it vehementlie. 2049 (Carewe) wolld willinglie impart the circumstances unto you, but I do forbid him, for feare of interceptinge of his lettres; for, albeitt the passage betwene Limericke and Corke is open, and free from any great force, yett the countrye swarmes wth straglinge rebells, and neutrall companions, that robbe all the messendgers they meet wthall to get intelligences. Ere it be longe you shall here more; for wthin a few dayes the event will appeare, beinge now brought to a periode, and I do verrilye thinke that itt will be effected. In the lettre wch I have written to the L^ls, I do more then doubtfullye speake of Florence; and in this, allmost directlye, that I thinke he purposes to be a rebell; but now I do in some sorte recall that censure, by the receipt of these enclosed lettres, wch I receved as I was writinge of these; and for your bettre understandinge I must paraphrase uppon his owne lettre unto me. The first place underlyned by me is Captain Gawen Harvye, who serves in one of the crompsters (a kind of vessel having a crooked prow—Dutch) and brought money and munitions to this towne from Corke; when he came to Baltimore Florence woulld have had him to come on shoare unto him, wch he refused, and to go aboard Florence refused; and so they never spake. For refusinge to come unto him, Florence calls him foole. The second underlyned he meanes Sir Fynin O'Drischoll; the third place Baltimore; the 4th the Erle of Tomond; the 5th the rebells; the 6th O'Sulevan More; the 7th Oviedo the Spanishe priest that came latelye to Tirone; the 8th the Queene; the 9th James Mc Morris, the famous rebell; the 10th the buonies: the longe Spanishe lettre your Honnour can bettre iudge of that then I; and, for O'Neale's, to ease you from trans-latinge of Irishe, I do send you the originall, and the copie unto you, Englished. What to iudge of Florence I proteste I knowe nott! for as he deales playnelye wth me, so on the other side I know that he doth nott forbeare to do anythinge or to sweare a million of oathes, to secure them of him. Yf his sonne were in my possession I shoulld be confident of him; but untill then I holld him doubtfull."

"Limericke this 17 of August 1600.

"Your Honnours in all bands of love and service,
"GEORGE CAREWE."

"1600.   August 5.   CAREWE to the PRIVY COUNCIL.

"Florence McCartie I do no less dowte then heretofore; for I knowe he is sworne to James FitzThomas; and yet protests the contrary unto me. As soon as I came into Kerry I sent for him to come unto me, at that tyme he being not 10 myles from Carrigfoyle (where I then was) parleyinge wth James FitzThomas. His answere is here enclosed; whereuppon I wrote the second tyme unto him, and according his desire (to leave him without excuse) sent him a safeguarde, the copie of wch lre with these, I present unto yor L^ps; wherein I appointted him a tyme, and place of meetinge, unto wch as yet I never receaved answer. Yf he be a rebell, as otherwayes for anythinge I can judge, I cannot accompt of him, then are the services of this province more difficult then is supposed. For I do assure yor L^ls the Cartyes of Mounster, whome he hopes to drawe into his faction, together with their dependaunts, and followers, are of themselves hable to make above 3000 stronge, w^ch, together with the remaynes of the other dispsed rebells yet in accion, do amount to no less then 7000, at the least. To strengthen this rebellion in a firmer combynacon, Florence McCarty (as I am credibly adũtised, and am constantly psuaded to be true) hath prac-tised a mariadge betweene the sister of Cormock McDermot, L of the countrey of Muskery, and James FitzThomas; which I was adũtised was consummated; but I fynd the contrary, and dowt not but to worke the meanes to frustrate the same. Yf his plott shold holde, then the cittie of Corke (untill by force I do dispse them) in this county wilbe my frontyer;

U

for Muskerry adioins unto the walls of that cittie, and I assure myself
that many that are now subiects, (yf this mariadge take effect,) will ronne
into rebellion.   The Carties countreys wch are lardge and spacius, compre-
hendinge the countreys of Muskerry, Carebry, Dowallie, and Desmond (by
reason of the multytude of huge mountaynes in the same) are in nature
exceeding stronge, and yet full of corne and cattle, hauing felt little of the
warr, unto the w^ch, for the present, all the other rebells of the counties of
Corke, Limericke, and Kerry (whome I have beaten out of their countreys)
do flie for refuge.

" Florence of late had his messenger with Tyrone, (as he pretends) for
the release of O'Sulyvan More his brother in law, who was carryed prisoner by Dermot O'Connor out of this Province; but my intelligencers
assure me that it was onely to procure forces to support this rebellion, for
the hartening whereof Tirone hath sent lres of comfort to all his freinds,
and confiderats in this countrey assuring them that before Michælmas-day
the Spanish forces will lande in Mounster; which is confidently beleeuved
by James FitzThomas; for, notwithstanding his forces are verie weake yet
he vauntes er that tyme, to be the greatest Erle of Desmond that euer was
in Ireland.   Wthin the Province ytself there is no man that can guide
that service but Florence McCartie, who like a dark clowde hanges over
my heade threateninge a storm ouer my heade; but yet (wthout
forreiyne aydes) wth the forces I haue, *together wth other meanes wch I will
procure*, I dowt not but in a short tyme, to make him humble himself,
and to sue for Her Ma^ts mercye.   Notwithstanding I know all that to be
true, yet I think it meete, for a tyme, to hold that temporising course wth
him wch hitherto I have don, being loathe to add so powerful a traitor
unto the other traitors, till the rest be more depressed."

" Enclosure.   FLORENCE *to the* Lo: PRESIDENT.

" My very good Lo: Y^r l^res were safely delyvered unto me, wch had
assuredly cost the messenger his lyff yf he had ben taken by the way: and
as for Yo^r Lo:^s doubt therein whether I stand fyrmely your frend or no,
because it is so longe synce yor Lo. hard from me, I am, I assuere yor Lo.
and shalbe euer found a true subiect to the Queen's most sacred Maty, and
a poore, true, olde, frende of yor Lo: & as faythfull to yor Lo^s. cheifest
frends in England, nether should yor Honor misse to heàre at all tymes
from me if I had meanes to have any lres safely convayed or delyuered, as
Yo^l Lo may iudge by my last severall l^res, wch I sent hyd or stytched up,
in women's apparel; the one of wch women went safe to yor Lo. to Lymerick, by Mr. Marshall's meanes; and thother went safe to my Lo of
Thomond, by whome she sent her Ire; by the contents of wch l^res yor Lo
pceved my mynde and intention towards Her Ma^ts service and thadvancem^t
of yor Lo^s reputation; for I am sure yor Lo. found no greater resistance
then I tolde you.

" Nether did myself, nor any of my people, or of all my country, assist
or relieve any rebells, or others against y^r Lo, as I promysed, mor then
that my brother went downe to Castle Lyshin wth the Kellyes, who promysed him, upon any good opportunity, to take away my brother in lawe
O'Sulyvan More from Dermod O'Connor; for the wch he stayed when the
Geraldines wth their Erle, were taken by Dermod O'Connor; and dyd his
best against Dermod for the recoueringe of the prysoners, in hope to
recouer O'Sulyvan; and after the Gerald men were gott out he stayde ther
styll, untill for want of victualls ther remayned not above 6 wth him.   At

w^{c}h tyme, I protest, I had ben ther with 700 or 800, and had recouered my brother-in-lawe but that I was sure you would be pswaded that I had gon thyther to assist rebells; but yf I had then recovered my brother-in-lawe O'Sulyvan, I assure yor Lop both he and I, or at the leaste myself, had byn at the Glyñ with you, or at Carrygofoyle, at yor fyrst cominge thyther. At the recevinge of yor Lo's l^{res} now, I was (thinkinge lyttle thereof) ner the mountaines of Mangirtagh, to pacefy a mortall contraversie for land betweene the best and chefest Gent here, therby to keepe them from kyllinge one another. At the fyrst I endevoured to prepare myself to ryde unto yor Lo, and had, I assure yor Lo, ventured it upon the soddayne, yf I had any good company of horsemen; for want whereof I sent to gather my people, for I cannot for my lyfe keepe many companies of footemen here a longe tyme together, in one place, for want of victualls; but must dysperse them into dyvers cantreds of the country; and before they came, I understoode that yor Lo's forces were come to Clan Morryce, and that the Geraldines forces were come over the mountaynes, the rest beinge gathered here in Kerry, and Clan Morrice.

" Wherby I could not see how I might goe wth any safety for my country or pson; for yf I had gone I should go headlonge, wthout any assurans for my safe returne from yor Lo, and the Erle of Thomond; and should go into a countrey far off, wher I had no knowledge, or frendship, nor place of retrayte, untyll I had spoken wth yor Lo, or the Erle of Thomond; beinge also ignorant of the intention of the forces w^{c}h yor Lo, sent to Clanmorrice towards me, who stood in my waye; and assured that the Geraldmen would cut me, and all my people in peces, yf they found me going to yor Lo; and yf they had myssed me, that they would spoyle all my country, and place Dermod Mc Owen, or some one of my name there, and wrytt, and blase such matters of me as I should never have my brother in law O'Sulyvan, who is at Tirone's dysposition ; this also beinge a very comõodious tyme for the rebells of Munster to alter and undoe this country, both by reason of O'Sulyvan More's absence, and the dyssention, and contraversie that is betwixt the rest of the chiefest men here. Yf it please yor Lo to sende for me at any tyme, when these forces of the Geraldines are dyspersed, I will not fayle, yf I have any safe waye to go to yor Lo, and to my Lo of Thomond, upon good assurance; for I will not trust myself into any other's hands, havinge alredy past 12 yeres in severall prysons. The nomber of forces that James Mc Thomas brought wth him over the Mountaynes now is aboue 300 foote, (beinge 400, or well neere), and somwhat lesse then 20 horsemen. Thomas Oge ioined wth him wth aboue 200 foote, and 5 or 6 horsèmen. Thus much I learned certynely of one of this country that was there amongethem. The freeholders, or followers of Kerry, I cannot certaynely tell what nomber they will make.

" The Lo Fitz Morrice hath some 200 foote, or very lytle more. The Knight of Kerry hath 300, and abour a dozen horsemen upon the sodayne, and 100 footemen more wthin 3 or 4 dayes warninge; He is my cousene, and one that is allyed to me, and that I have wonne to followe my counsell; but the hard usage of my nephewe O'Connor of Kerry, and the takinge of his castle from him,—myself havinge *pursuaded him to go to yor Lo*, and havinge dealt wth yor Lo, and the Erle of Thomond for him at Corke,— doth make a greate nomber loath to be pswaded by me; yet notwth-standinge, I have pswaded the Knight of Kerry, and he is sworne to followe mine advyse, upon cominge of some of yor Lo forces to Clanmorrice. I wyshed him to send all his cattle over the Maing, for he hath lands of his owne there, by my country; and yf his cattle were there I would be surer of his beinge ruled by me. He hath wryten unto me,

U 2

whose lʳᵉ, together wth James Mᶜ Thomas his lʳᵉ I do sende to yoʳ Lo; besechinge yoʳ Lo: yf you have lʳᵉˢ out of England for me, from Sʳ Robert, and Sʳ Walter, and Sir John Stanhope, to delyver them to my nephewe O'Connor; for upon Mr. Secretary and Sir Walter, I dare put myself, or venter myself any where. I beleve I might better come to yoʳ Lo at Tomond or Lymerick then here; for I would (whensoever you would have me) have you to geav me some tyme to provyde for the safetye of my country, whyles I were absent wth yoʳ Lo; for yf I had any good convenient place to meete my Lo. of Tomond, I would go,—upon yoʳ Loˢ word in wrytinge, and my Lord's fayth for my sendinge safe into my country,—wth him to Tomond or Lymerick; or ells if yoʳ Lo, and my Lo of Tomond can dyrect any surer coursē for my safetie untill I had mett yoʳ selffs, I will be ready to do it. At Corke I might go in my owne strengthe wthin 8 miles thereof, and within fowre or fyve myles of Kinsale. Thus besechinge yoʳ Lo that that I may heare from you shortly, with my moste humble and harty comendačons to yoʳ Lo, and to my very good Lo the Erle of Tomond, I humbly take leave.

　　　　　　　　　　　　" Yoʳ Lo. moste humble and faythfull,
　　　　　　　　　　　　　　　" fflor Mᶜ Carthy.
　　The Palice this 2 of Auguᵗ 1600."
　　If Sr Charles Willmott do contynue in any place here, he shall never, I assure you, receive no hurte by me, nor by any of my countrey; nether will I omytt to afford him any succour that I may convenyently, if he be nere me, in any extremite.—To the Right honorable my very good Lo: Sʳ George Carewe, Knight Lo: Presydent of Munster, Geve these wᵗh speede.

　　Marginal note by Carewe—

　　" O'Connor did never send, or come unto me, untill the Glan was taken, and the cannon in a bark readye to sayle to his castell of Carrgefoyle."
　　It may please yoʳ Honourable Lo synce the wrytinge of my other lʳᵉ, ther is the chefest follower that followed Donell Mc Carty, taken by some of my people, and brought to me; He wae goinge from Donell Mc Carthy tothe Erle of Desmond, or rather to James Mᶜ Thomas; he had a lʳᵉ in Irishe, wᶜh I interpreted; the contents whereof, is that yf the Erle do send for him sufficient Gentlemen to assure him that he shall come and go safe, he will come to him, and will take any indifferent portion at my hands before the Erle; wᶜh yf I will not, and the Erle will not take his pte, he takes God to witnes that it isˆnot his fault to go against the holy action. At the wrytinge hereof ther came a thyrd lʳᵉ to me from Desmond; because, that at the fyrst I wroate tohim, and tolde him playnely that I would not goe to him to meete him, nor to parle with (torn! him, but that I was ?) determined to ryde to yoʳ Lo :, wᶜh, as I heere, made (torn ! him mightely angry ?), and hereupon (he) wrote this lʳᵉ wᶜh I do sende yoʳ Lo. here inclosed. Thus beinge not resolved what to do before I heare from yoʳ Lo. and the Greate Boare of Thomond, I humbly take leave this 2ᵈ Augsᵗ 1600.

　　　　　　　　　　　　" Yoʳ Lo. moste humble and bounden,
　　　　　　　　　　　　　　　" fflor Mᶜ Carthy."

　　" If yoʳ Lo do fynde any salfe way for me to come unto you, send my nephewe O'Connor to me; but he cannot come to salfe; I was parlyenge wth James Mᶜ Thomas at his last beinge here, and went wth him tothe Iland, in hope to get his lʳᵉˢ for the delyvery of O'Sulyvan; but could not: and where it was blazed through the countrey then that I should ioyne wth him, or promyse tohelpe or assist him, I renownce God, and my Christianitie, if ever I promyst to joyne with him, or ever ment it; wch doth make me marvayle what nowe he speakes of."

Under all the anxieties of his dealings with Florence, the President kept steadily in view the two remaining "draughts," preparing for the disturbers of the public peace. His first had failed, and yet that one might have been judged the surest and easiest. The undertaking of Nugent was of extreme simplicity of detail. He had been furnished with a pistol out of the Queen's store, and an experienced hand had loaded it—like the pistol of the English gentleman of 1583 —*with two bullets;* all that was needed was a fitting opportunity and a steady aim. A desperate ruffian like John Nugent might have been judged fully competent to the deed, but it failed! Nugent essayed, like the murderer of O'Nassie, "to flee away, no one knew whither;" but the brother of an Earl of Desmond, though under official disfavour, was not like the poor swordsman of the Kavanaghs; nor had Nugent the luck of the English gentleman! Had that English gentleman, by the same "misfortune," when he hoped to have escaped, stumbled, and so been taken," a felon the less had cumbered the world for 17 years; and John Nugent escaped his temptation and his fate! As it was, he got fairly hanged. "Of whose death," quoth his employer, "there was no great losse, for he was but a protected traytor!"—a man of no ingenuity, or address! upon whom no reliance could thenceforth have been placed!

But before Nugent was hanged, "he confessed (as is customary with great criminals of tender conscience) freely his whole intent, which was to despatch John Fitz Thomas, and immediately to have posted to the Sougaun Earl, to call him aside, in secret manner to relate the particulars of his brother's murder, and then to execute as much upon him also; and," he added, "*there were many others who had solemnly sworn unto the President as much as he intended!*"

These lessons of civility were utterly thrown away upon these wild Irish; they could neither understand the benignity of the rule of their conquerors, nor learn to copy the methods by which it was upheld.

DRAUGHT THE SECOND.

MILER McGRATH, ARCHBISHOP OF CASHEL.

The second draught was, as the reader must have perceived by a passage in Carewe's last letter to Sir Ro. Cecyll, maturing; and from the sentence in his recent despatch to the Privy Council, " I doubt not, with the forces I have, *together with other means which I will procure,* to make him (Florence) humble himself," that the essay of draught the third would not be far behind. The second of these stratagems was of a far more delicate and difficult nature than the former. To capture the Earl in the midst of many hundreds of attached followers would need abler agency than that of Nugent. The ingenuity of the oldest and craftiest of Carewe's political allies was engaged in it, and hence—*chiefly with aid from the good Mr. !*—the great hope of its success. "1070 (Miler Mc Grath, his Grace of Cashel) doethe followe it vehementlye." The third draught also would require skilful agency ; and, what may surprise the reader, Carewe was unwilling to take upon himself the entire responsibility of its attempt and possible failure, and sought, before adventuring far into it, the approbation of Sir R. Cecyll. Well would it be if each of the two remarkable Irishmen whose names have been already mentioned in connexion with these political draughts, had reciprocally recorded for us the biography of his countryman ! but failing this, we are compelled to search through their letters for such notices as they have been pleased to leave us, each one of his own previous life, and to gather from the State archives their respective shares in the second and third adventures to which Carewe trusted for the " pacification of Ireland." The writer of these pages will endeavour, with all brevity, to place the more interesting portions of these sketches before his reader.

" Miler McGrath was born in Ulster, and was therefore a natural follower to the arch-traitor Tirone." He had been from infancy trained up in the religion of his forefathers; his early inclinations had been for the church, and indeed towards the more ascetic retirements of the ecclesiastical life. His presentation of himself to his countrymen in early manhood, was as a Capuchin friar, shaven, frocked, corded, and sandalled: with his wallet upon his back, brother Miler trudged stoutly on through the first stages of his earthly pilgrimage, battling as best he could in the warfare of the flesh, till the

storms and lightnings of the Reformation burst upon him.
After long agony of conscience, cowl and cord, frock and
sandals—the vanities of his monastic life—all but the wallet,
were laid aside; certain vows, needless minutely to describe,
taken with too much precipitation, were renounced, and
Miler, when the tumult in his breast was stilled, like the
stout ship that bore Ilioneus and the brave Achates, was
lifted by the fair Cimothoë from the rocks of celibacy, and
glided into the pleasant waters of matrimony.

> " Cimothoë simul, et Triton adnixus, acuto
> Detrudunt naves scopulo."

He was blessed in course of time with a numerous offspring, sons and daughters, who by prudent marriages
enlarged the circle of his domestic felicity. The devotional
feelings of the convert were by no means cooled: he had
renounced the religion of Rome, but not his vocation to the
ecclesiastical state; he clung still with determined grasp to
the maternal skirts, and followed with willing steps whither
the church of his affections led him. He carried with him
into the community which he joined, many useful qualities,
and much valuable knowledge of the secret policy of the
one which he abandoned. To Walsyngham and Cecyll the
services of such a man were beyond price, and their remuneration of them, though below their value, was not incon-
siderable.

Entirely separate from the attempt upon the life of
John FitzThomas, was the plan arranged between the President and the Archbishop, for the capture of his brother the
Sougaun Earl. Dermod O'Connor, of whom Florence's
letters make so frequent mention, Captain of the Bonaghts
left by O'Neill, at one time in the service of Florence, at
another in that of the Earl himself, undertook, nay, " was
sworne to perform the service," for the sum of £1,000, to
capture and deliver over James FitzThomas into the hands of
Carewe! How this was to be accomplished, and what refine-
ment of artifice was to make plausible the conduct of O'Connor,
is already in print; but what the reader may not perhaps so
clearly perceive is what the Archbishop could have to do in
the matter! It was this: Dermod O'Connor, in an early
stage of the negotiation, observed that *the President was not
known to him!* in plainer words, this meant that Dermod set
no assignable value on the word of honour of the Lord
President: that it would need something more than a pledge
of official veracity to guarantee to him punctual payment of

the price of his captive when entrapped. It would need hostages, the sons of influential men, who in case of accidents, or tardy fulfilment of conditions, could redeem them with money; or, who could be reached in penalty through the imprisonment, or if need be, the death of the pledges. With this distrustful Irish usage Carewe was well acquainted, as the reader has seen, by his eagerness to possess himself of the son and heir of Florence, as pledge for his father's loyalty; but where was the parent to be looked for, of adequate condition, with sufficient reliance upon the good faith of the parties in this traffic of treachery, to trust his children as hostages for the *honesty of Carewe*, to the *humanity of Dermod*? In the emergency a man *was* found to do it! This man was Miler MacGrath, the Archbishop! With that loyal attachment to the interests of the Queen, which had kept him incessantly climbing the ecclesiastical ladder, he now obliged two of his sons, Redmond and Bryan, to fall, with what grace they might, into an ambuscade arranged for them by O'Connor. The first experience of these young men in the contingencies of statecraft was doubtless rougher than they or their father contemplated; for O'Connor's bonies, who seized them, and were unacquainted with the device of their captain, "stripped, and left them almost naked!"

This notable draught is circumstantially related in the Pacata Hibernia: it miscarried, like the former, as the world knows; but it approached sufficiently near to success, painfully to affect the parental feelings of the Archbishop. The Earl was really captured by O'Connor, and delivered over by him to the custody of his wife, Lady Margaret FitzGerald, the cousin of the captive, to be given to the President! Dermod then quitted the Castle of Lishin, for a remoter fortress, where his personal security, a little imperilled by his recent proceeding, might be beyond reach of present casualty: he took with him Carewe's hostages, two Powers, and the two McGraths, and wrote to the President to·send and receive the prisoner from Lady Margaret, and deliver over to her the thousand pounds as agreed. In the mean time great was the commotion caused through the country by the tidings of the Earl's capture, and the story of his treachery, provable as it was rumoured, by an intercepted letter, written to him by the President, bargaining for the betrayal of O'Connor into his hands.

The ingenious contrivance of the letter was worthy of its contrivers! we have seen it repeatedly asserted by Carewe, that Florence was a "*Fool!*" and it has been at times a

painful doubt with this author whether possibly he, and his
benevolent reader, may have been so long engaged upon the
biography of a man passing with the world for wise and prudent, and yet discovered by the Lord President to be in
reality an "*Idiot.*" And yet fool and idiot he must surely
have been to believe that the head of all the National party
in Munster, the man whose brother's life had been so recently
attempted by an assassin, would write letters to the employer of that assassin, offering to deliver up into his hands
the captain of the forces sent to him by O'Neill for his protection, and on whose support his very existence depended!
And yet no sooner did the tidings of the Earl's capture
reach Florence than he hurried away his brother with all
the force he could readily collect, to Castle Lishin, to con-
gratulate O'Connor on his escape from the Earl's treachery!
And Dermod Moyle—as if idiocy and folly was common in
the family—influenced by like infatuation, misunderstood his
brother's meaning, and no sooner arrived in the camp of
the Geraldines, than *he joined with them in the rescue of the
Earl!* and insisted upon the reference of the whole matter to
Florence!

To this pleasant folly of Florence and his brother is attributable the vexatious discomfiture of draught the second! The
position of the Archbishop became, by this failure of his own
scheme, at once both humourous and pathetic; for the President refused to pay the thousand pounds, and Dermod refused
to part with his hostages! nay, he placed them in handlocks,
and thus held the heart of poor Miler M'Grath in as pitiless
custody! Long after the ingenuity of his *plott* had ceased
to excite the admiration of the bonies, we find the afflicted
Prelate writing to Sir Robert Cecyll that "he had been compelled to pay £300 for the ransom of his sons, a sum that he
was reduced to borrow, and to pay £30 p^r an^m for the loan
of it!" All his Grace's draughts were, happily, not of issue
so unsatisfactory as this.

When the Earl of Desmond had been rescued from the
bonies of O'Connor, Dermod Moyle MacCarthy led back his
brother's men into Desmond, and Florence then wrote an
account of the matter to the President. One passage in his
letter is singularly characteristic and pleasant, and reminds
us of the early days of Barry's fine, when the gratification of
exacting it was worth all the money. He informs Carewe
that, understanding the occurrence at Castle Lishin, he had
thought it a good opportunity for effecting the freedom of
his brother-in-law O'Sullevan, whom O'Connor held in cap-

tivity, and *therefore* had sent his brother Dermod to rescue *him !* He would have gone himself for that purpose, but he feared the Lord President *might have thought that he had it in view to aid in the rescue of the Earl !* This thought might indeed have occurred to Carewe, as it chanced that Sir Owen O'Sullevan was not at Castle Lishin at the time !

Without any exception, the incident which it has been *most painful* to the writer of this volume to record is the escape of the English gentleman from Dublin in 1583 ! It admits of some doubt in his mind which is the *most pleasing passage* of the many hundred pages of the Pacata Hibernia ! whether the apotheosis of John Nugent, or the following simple supplement to the narrative of this second draught of the Lo : President upon the Queen's enemies !

" Hee (Dermod O'Connor) being now past Clanrickard, and coming to O'Shaffnesses Countrey, within 17 or 18 miles of Limerick, Theobald-ne-long-Bourke, who had a Company of an hundred foot *in Her Majesty's pay*, notwithstanding all his (O'Connor's) safegards (sent to him by the Lo: President) assaulted him, who for his safetie retired into an olde church, burned it over his head, and on coming foorth of the same, he killed about foortie of his men, and took him prisoner, and the morning following cut off his head ! *tothe great dishonour of Her Majestie, in violating her word solemnly and advisedly given. The Lo : President was exceedingly incensed !*"

This draught had been a surprising succession of errors. There was indeed a capture, a very handsome payment for the captive, and a retribution for the sin of somebody ; but it fell to the lot of the able artificer of the stratagem to capture his own sons ! and to have to pay the money for their ransom ; and to the lot of the Lo: President to see Her Majesty's soldiers mistake Dermod O'Connor for the Earl of Desmond, and (notwithstanding all his *safegards*) cut off his head !

DRAUGHT THE THIRD.

JOHN ANNYAS THE IRISHMAN.

Similar in many of its vicissitudes to the career of Miler M'Grath, had been the career of John Annyas, whom we must now present to the reader as the instrument in the third draught of the Lord President. The learned editor of the Rotulus Pipæ Clonensis—Bishop Swafham's Diocesan Roll of Cloyne—has, with evident unconsciousness of the importance of his discovery, found for us reliable traces of the ancestry

of this remarkable Irishman. At an Inquisition held in the
39th year of Edward III., it was deposed on oath that " John
Anyas tenet 1 Messuagium, 1 carucatam terræ, per homagium,
fidelitatem, et communem Sectam curiæ Domini, et reddendo
Domino per annum, XIIIˢ. iiijd.. 1. lib: ceræ! And, also,
Johannes Anyas de Brewhy fecit Domino homogium, &c., &c.,
per Servitia pertinentia ad Dominum et curiam de Caul-
Colings!" Others of his ancestry are also discoverable,
evincing the respectability of the family, and its connexion
with the church.

Like his countryman the Archbishop, John Annyas had been
reared in the religion of Bishop Swafham, and like him, after
adhering through good and evil repute, through the earlier
years of his life, to the faith of his baptism. had begun at last
" to entertain a scruple in his conscience of the grounds of his
religion." These two men, by a series of unlikely circumstances,
were drawn for a time into some community of action; but
after a brief while their lots fell again far asunder. M'Grath
excelled his countryman in the scope and character of his
education; but this was not to say much; Annyas far outshone the friar in originality of mind and fertility of resource;
in respectability they were nicely equalled! At the time
when the Archbishop placed the liberty of his sons in
jeopardy for the Queen's service, John Annyas was in
trouble! indeed he lay in Her Majesty's Tower of London
under sentence of death for high treason. One companion,
and the chief cause of his misfortune. had been the unfailing
Jacques de Franceschi; another. Cullen the fencer; both of
whom had brought so much suspicion upon Florence. Jacques,
whose consolation it might have been that he was ever cause
of less ill to himself than to others, had been allowed to depart the realm ; but Cullen, who had neither genius nor
daring to render any services for which his life was worth
preserving, was put out of all men's way. There remained
Annyas; but in what forlorn plight! Marked marginally in
the Tower bills as "to be dealt with according to justice!"
waiting only for a certain warrant of Mr. Secretary, to
pass out, some misty morning, to Tyburn or the Tower-
ditch.

The prison accounts. sent quarterly to the Treasury for
payment, enable us mentally, even at this distance of time,
to see him, as Sir Owen Hopton fed. clothed. and converted
him ! His usual attire was fustian ; he was dieted at the cost
of XIIIˢ a week, and in no respect stinted in allowance for
the comforts of light, fewel, and washing; but his mind was

ill at ease; his remorse, his religious anxieties, and certain personal privations (which he seems to have exaggerated) wrung from him a pathetic letter to the Privy Council, in which he unfolds a scheme of matchless ingenuity for the discovery of the secrets of the King of Spain! and the names of all the Queen's subjects who were plotting against Her Majesty. No more remarkable letter than this is extant in the national archives, and assuredly Sir Robèrt Cecyll had no correspondent of equal genius, or so suitable for the accomplishment of the most delicate of State draughts. The discovery of the King of Spain's secrets was not of urgency at the time; but a certain project of the Lord President of Munster needed precisely the state of mind and the qualifications of the writer. And his offer of placing his family in pledge—if they were living, and he could find them—must have been to Her Majesty's Secretary pleasing proof of his zeal and sincerity.

" Domestic Eliz. 1594.

" To the LORDES *of Her Maties Most Honnorable Pryvie Consell.*

" My verry good Lords, may yt please the same. John Annyas Irysman, and a prysoner towe yeres at the Tower, in great myserie, noe clodes at all excepte towe shurtes Mr. Lyftenant gave me, neverthelesse, I have a gyfte, even pacience yn afflyxion: the cause of my faultes (a conspiracy with Jacques to murder the Queen,) was a cartaing opinyon yn Relygion; and be perusinge the Beble howe a yere, I ame fully satysfied, and reformed. To mack amendes for me faultes paste, beholde my Lordes, I am content to venter my lyffe to doe her Majestie great sarvice, and worthie to be comended. Which is to dyscover playnly all those in England which shoulde tack parte wᵗh the Spanysse Kinge againste her Majestie.
" Yf it shall please your honnours to have bannysse me publicklye out of thes realme wᵗh dysgrace, so that yt may be knowen ther manyfestly, then I writ a letter to the Conde de Fontis that yn all hast his Excellencie should send me a warant that I might saffly, wᵗhouth anny let, stay or molestation to me parson, for anny cause whatsomever, but to come and goe saff, to confer secreatlye wᵗh hes Excellencie, for great sarvyce for the Kynge: then I would showe howe I hawe sarved the Kynge along tyme, and howe I hawe bene prysoner towe yeres, and howe I hawe *brocken outh*, and nowe banyssed for the Catholick cause, and howe I hawe proveded, of my one frendes and contremen yᵗ I dare trust as myself, six marriners, talle fellowes, sarwyng yn the Queene's shyppes, and howe I hawe good experience yn mackyng of firewoorckes; myself yn marryner is apparell, wᵗh these sixe wᵗh a smal pennas would fire and burne towentie of the Queene's best shyppes be night, escape oureselves easlye, &c. &c.; and for the great zeale toher Magᵗⁱᵉˢ sarvice, and fervent desyr to mack mendes for my faultes past, to get credit, I wyll assure thes my offer; and for securitie, an please yoᵘ honnours, I hawe to brederen, of one father and mother, the one maryed—yf they be alyve I knowe not! thes eight yeres I never harde

from them—the unmaryed I wyll put hem hostadge: that yn ma ther
shalbe noe fault. Beholde my Lordes, not for lowe to hawe lybertie I
mack thes offer, but for to mack amendes for my faultes! *I hawe dys-
covered to Mr. Lyftenant howe I myght escape, and goe unknowen to my
keper, verye easlye;* and please yo⁾ honnors thes sarvice must be done yn the
longe nightes, for manny resons and ynconvenyences should happen. Yf
thes sarvice please yor honnors not, my humble request is to hawe clodes
to put of the wenter; and yf yor honnors wyll showe ma favoure, that I
may goe to church, I shall mack meanes to relyve my vantes myself. The
wyll of God be done! for to her magestie and to yor honnors it is geven to
comand, and to me to be pacient and obedient, and I shall pray &cc
" JOHN ANNYAS."

This letter was, according to the usage of the Tower,
placed open in the hands of the Lieutenant. It will have
been noticed that a portion of the scheme therein developed,
involved the projector's "breaking out from his prison, and
going away unknown to his keeper very easily!" This part of his
plan was not lost upon the professional mind of Mr. Lieutenant; and, accordingly, we find that, pending the Ministerial meditation on the design of Annyas, that functionary
thought it not amiss to take certain precautions for the safety
of his charge, plainly indicated by the outlay as occurring in
his next quarterly bills, of

" A payre of manacles, and for mending the shackles   ijˢ. vjᵈ.
" Item for ij staples, iiij hinges, and bowlt for a prison
   dore   ..   ..   ijˢ. !"

For a quarter of a year longer Annyas was still an
"Irishman to be proceeded with by justice." At the end of
the year 1599 he and the whole Tower family were handed
over by Sir Michael Blount to the care of Sir Drew Drury;
and successively to Sir Richard Barclay and Sir John Peyton.
And then took place a surprising change in the fortunes of
Annyas! The note against his name, as one condemned,
disappeared; and we next perceive the remarkable charge of
" *Five pounds* for apparel, and other necessaries for him." So
munificent an outlay diminishes our surprise that at our
next meeting with him he is no longer " John Annyas an
Irishman," but " Mr. Annyas, a gentleman travelling from
Cork to the Court of London for purposes of his own."

Restored to a condition more becoming a descendant of
the Annyasses of Brewhy and Coul-Colings, Mr. Annyas paid
his respects to the Lo: President at Shandon Castle, precisely when " Florence MacCarthy was hanging like a dark
cloud over his head, threatening a storm to impeach his

actions." Within a few days he was once more on his way
back to London; but in what altered guise! He was the
bearer now of a letter of friendly introduction from Sir Geo:
Carewe to Her Majesty's Principal Secretary of State.

"1600. *April* 30. SIR GEO: CAREWE *to* SIR R. CECYLL.

" Sir,
    " This bearer M^r. Anias is retourned into England to furnishe himselfe
with some necessaries wch he wants. I have conferred with him, and do
like of his projects: he promises to retourne presentlye, wch I beseeche you
to expedite; and so referringe my lardge discourses to the despatche w^ch
now I haue in hand do humblye reste
                                    " Your honnour's most bounden.
                                                    " GEORGE CAREWE.
    " Shandon Castle this 30 April 1600."

    On the 30th of April, Mr. Annyas started with Carewe's
letter, and his project; and then followed, on the 24th of
May, the attempt and failure of Nugent: and on the 20th of
June, the capture and rescue of the Earl of Desmond! Upon
Annyas seemed now to rest the sole hope of the last of the
President's draughts. These were dangerous practices, and
upon a person of the observation and prudence of Annyas,
the deaths of Nugent and O'Connor, and the bondage and
very uncertain fate of the sons of the Archbishop, were unlikely to be lost. He continued his journey, notwithstanding,
to London, and saw the Minister : the project of Carewe was
laid before Cecyll, and then appears to have ensued a most
singular, nay, unaccountable misunderstanding between these
gentlemen. According to Annyas, they parted perfectly
agreed ; he made what purchases were needful, and returned
to Ireland. The despatches of the President to the Privy
Council contained ominous paragraphs ! " Florence hangs
like a stormy cloud over my head ; what to think I protest I
know not ! I am fairly perplexed !"
    It would seem that Annyas partook of this perplexity ;
instead of repairing at once to the President, he withdrew for
a while from public notice ! What verbal messages he may
have been charged with reached not the ears of Carewe ;
but in place of them a hateful rumour, an odious imputation,
which had passed first through every house and hovel in
Carbery and Desmond, and had been listened to with horror
by every follower of Florence, and every bony in arms in
Munster. " The President and Sir R. Cecyll had found a
man to poison Florence!" " It was no idle Irish camp-fire

story, but a terrible undeniable truth; for the man who had been found to do it, a certain Annyas, had himself confessed it!"

Had this odious imputation made no more impression upon the mind of the English Minister than it did upon Carewe, it would, in all probability, have been denied, or have never reached us. Carewe seems not to have thought more of the matter, after its failure, than he did of the ill success of the two previous draughts: the letter in which he informed Cecyll of the faithless behaviour of Annyas is not discoverable; but the indignant replies of Sir Robert Cecyll are preserved.

"1600. *October* 15.   CECYLL *to* CAREWE.

" Sir, &c. &c.

" It remayneth now that I say something to you concerning Anyas, who hath neuer deceaued me, for I haue held him a villain.   First, the Lord God doth know it, that my soul neuer had the thought to consent to the poysonning of a dogg, much less a Christian.   True it is that, to take a Rebell alyue, or to bring their head, I was contented to heare his promise, though, for myne own parte, I neuer beleeued him; I do therefore pray you, and conjure you by all the love you beare me, to find the meanes to take him, and, seeing he hath otherwayes offended the Law, be assured of this from me that it must be his hanging, and publicq confession that must cleare us from this odious imputation.

" Remember, Sir, what I write, I pray you, and think of it; for there is no other way to cleare it; and, know this from me that, when you haue him, yf you keep him long alyve, he will escape from you by one meanes or other.   Send him not over therefore, nor spare not his lyfe, for then it wilbe thought, whatsoever he sayeth to cleare vs, that it is to safe his necke, &c."

"1600.   *Novr.* 8.   CECYLL *to* CAREWE.

" Sir, &c. &c.,

" In this point, therefore, I will hold you no longer, but onely to remember you that I exspect dayly to vnderstand what you haue done with that wicked and horrible wretch Annias, who hath geuen out (as it seemeth) so vile an vntruth of you and me concerning Florence, of which I protest to the Lord I neuer intertayned the thought.   I trust, therefore you will come by him by one meanes or other, that he may paye the randsome of such a villainy."

No wonder that the soul of Cecyll abhorred so odious an imputation.   He had known Florence for probably 20 years; and during that time circumstances had established considerable intimacy between them!   He was contented to hear the promise of Annyas for his head, but his conscience retched with loathing at this proposal to poison him!   The mistake, if it was one—so material in political ethics—was the mistake of Annyas, not of Cecyll! Annyas had been employed to cut off Florence's head; not to poison him! The distinction, could Florence but have known it, would have reassured him; and the President would have been less shocked by his cowardice when eating his food at the President's table.

But *was* it a mistake? Was this crime really so revolting? *Did* Sir Robert Cecyll ever listen to a proposal for committing so foul a crime? did he know a man of the name of William Atkinson? in short, did he receive and endorse the following letter?, did Atkinson go to Ireland? and did Sir R. Cecyll write to Sir Robert Gardener to find him out, and see what he was doing? His answer is most solemn and sacramental—

" *The Lord God doth know it! that my soul never had the thought to consent to the poysoning of a dog! much less a Christian ! !* "

Preserved amongst Her Majesty's Irish State Papers—those archives of the ineffable wickedness of our English rulers, and of the unfathomable baseness of the men—undertakers and others—who went to teach civilitie to the mere or wild Irish; preserved with the care due to evidences destined to stand as witnesses through all time, and in the face of all nations, between the Irish people and their oppressors, is a letter:—

To the Right honorable S^r. ROBERT CICILL: *one of here Mati. most honorable privie Councell give thes.*

Endorsed in Cecyl's writing.

" Atkinson's lr̃e, the Priest y^t discovered Tychburn, and was broght me by Mr. Fowler.

" Right honorable. Sithence I haue framed the primisses of a loyal myndd, I meane unfeinedlie, in verbo sacerdotis, to make a pfect periode, and to ioyne issue and a compleet conclusion to noe lesse effect, and albeit my creditt before your honour was called in question howe that I should haue abusedd your honour in ployinge theire goods, under pretence of search, by sayinge I was your man; with many other adiects, all which weare false, having as far as I doe remember when they would not search in such places, as I willed, I might use your honours nayme, by saying I would complain to Sir Robert Cicill, or the like, which I only uttered as I ame a

Christian, and noe other, to my remembrance, and albeit
having bereaved my selfe of million of frindds, in regard of
the service I pformed, bring odible to all Catholiques, of
whome before I receyved verie large maintenance, and nowe
onlie reliinge upon your honourable disposition, and gratious
favour, I thought good to present unto your honour some
platforme which I planted, vz., howe that I have obtained
divers letters for Irlandd, one frome Mr. Blackwell, and another
from father Walle (Whalley was Provincial of the Jesuits in
England), *alias* Garnett, and from diverse others of the best
creditt, in my commendations, for I haue made theme for to beleeve howe I intend for to be a religious man, and of the order
of S^t. Francis and in regarde I ame of good acquaintance in
Irland I make choise for toe be under Bishoppe Macraith, by the
which letters, Right Honourable, I assure myself (so that theire
be verie greate sacresie used) for to pFORME SHORTLIE SERVICE
WORTHIE OF A GOOD REWARDD, FOR IT IS MOST EASIE FOR TO
POYSINE TIRONE THROUGH SOME POYSINED HOASTES, the which
in regard I shall be theire where he haith continuall resorte, I
make noe doubte at all, as I shall be saved but to abbreviate,
the Traitors dayes, by that or other meanes, for the Bishoppe
being a Franciscan frier, and all that entreth into that order
in Irland, entreth under him, who is almost daylie with Tirone,
and Father Nangle and Father Archer are his ghostlie fathers,
unto whome I have letters in my behalfe, and beinge verie
well acquainted with them boithe, I shall without difficultie
pforme my desyre, and for a reward I will onelie requier it,
when the service is efected, saving your honourable woord, I
would not seeme to come my selfe to your honour, least some
should by fortune see mee, and therfor I sent my letter by
Mr. Fowler, thus with my daylie praier, for your honours
most psperous and longe life, I rest ever duringe breath to
be commanded by your honour, before any man livinge, I
protest.

" Youre Honnours Continuall Orator,
" WYLLIAM ATKINSONNE, pr."

The penalty of failure in great crimes is usually speedy!
It had followed swiftly upon the ill success both of O'Connor
and of Nugent, and it lingered reluctantly in the instance of
Coppinger, the cause of the failure of the attempt on the life
of John Fitz Thomas. Annyas had need to be wary! It is
true that he could not know that Sir Robert Cecyll had so
urgently desired the President to catch and hang him; but
he probably did know that he had provoked the anger of both

X

those great men by spreading so vile a rumour, and that if he
should fall into the hands of either he would have little
chance of escape from them. How so experienced a man
could, under the circumstances, have ventured within the
walls of Cork, or what new project may have rendered his
presence there indispensable, we have no means of knowing;
but it is certain that his evil luck led him across the very
path of the mayor of the city, who, seeing through his disguise of rags, recognised him, not any longer as the President's friend, Mr. Annyas, but as the Annyas of old—Annyas
the Irishman—who had escaped from Her Majesty's Tower of
London. He was delivered over to Sir George Carewe, who
left to the Mayor himself the pleasure of writing to Cecyll
the story of his capture:

" 1600. *March* 6. JOHN MEADE, *Mayor of Cork, to* SIR ROBERT
CECYLL.

" I am alsoe bold to aduertize y'' hon'' that one John Anias latelie
here restrayned in the Towre, was found uppon the walls of this cittie,
poorlie arraied, barefooted, and altogether disguized from his wonted attire;
vhou being brought before me, I examyned his name, and he said his
name was John Magnes, whom I did know by eing him narrowlie, and
comytted him to the gaole, where he is to remayne till he have his tryall
by law, wth whose aprehension I haue acquaynted the L President, for
wch he was verie thankfull, Yo'' honour hath received notice heretofore of
his behaviour since his last depture from thence, wherefore I thinke yt
unnecessarie to repeate the pticulers."

Carewe had been warned, if he caught Annyas *to hang
him at once!* for if he kept him he would, surely by some
means or other, effect his escape. Whether the Lo. President
neglected this warning, and Annyas did escape, or whether
some new project made his life more useful than his hanging,
we know not: he ceased any longer to be the subject of
ministerial correspondence; but he was not hanged—then,
it is painful to dwell upon the misfortunes of a man of
genius; painful to watch the struggles of an enterprising
mind destined to unvarying failure! The Pacata Hibernia,
and the Domestic State Papers, contain other passages in
the biography of Annyas, and to them the reader is referred.
It will suffice to say that for this time he managed, or was
allowed, another run for his life. When he next, and for the
last time, fell into trouble it was on a new score, and by a
fresh capture.
With the letter of Atkinson in his memory the reader will
not now feel so much surprise, when Carewe and Cecyll pass

from one to another the charge of cowardice against Florence! Florence was not ignorant of the murder of O'Nassy! He perfectly well knew, that " 2049 had found a man to practise upon the person of John FitzThomas," and that the Queen's stores had equipped the assassin! No man ever whispered aught against the courage of Carewe, but it may be doubted whether he would have walked with as much composure through Donal's country as he did in the streets of Cork!*

---

* In most of the following documents the spelling has been partially modernized by the gentleman employed to transcribe them.

CHAPTER XIV.

FOILED in his attempts to capture the Earl of Desmond, to shoot his brother, and to poison Florence, the Lo: President was compelled to fall back upon the more tedious process of fighting Florence with his own weapon, and upon the hopeful endeavour to set up Donal against him. His first attempt was to entice Donal away from the declining fortunes of the Geraldines by offering him the Queen's pardon, and the restitution of the lands left him by his father—which by his rebellion had become fair subject of confiscation—if by some signal act of service he would deserve them. Donal, it must be admitted, had not met with handsome treatment at the hands of O'Neill. He had at the outset of the insurrection been by him created MacCarthy Mor; had fearlessly staked life, and his recent inheritance upon the venture; nay had honourably distinguished himself in repeated encounters with Essex; yet upon the first appearance of Florence in his camp he had consented to depose him! To Florence he owed nothing; and in accepting Carewe's proposal to drive him out of Desmond he may have had no more intention than Florence had, to promote the cause of the Queen, or to fight against his countrymen: but, to the great honour of Donal, what, before accepting Carewe's offers he did do, may not be concealed: "He sent a messenger to the Sougaun Earl, and offered to go to him, and take any indifferent portion at Florence's hands; and that if Florence would not consent to this, and the Earl would not take his part, he took God to witness it would not be *his* fault if he went against the holy action."

Repulsed by Florence and FitzThomas, Donal made alliance with the President, and thus finally was the policy, which had been adopted by the Privy Council, under guidance of Her Majesty's Principal Secretary, the Lord Lieutenant the Earl of Essex, the Master of the Rolls, and the Solicitor, and approved by the Queen, "to authorize Florence to recover his country from Donal," wholly reversed at the sole pleasure of Carewe, who had shortly before written to Sir Robert

Cecyll that he rejoiced that Florence was in command of Desmond, for the Bastard would be far worse, in that he was braver! But between the pardoning of Donal, and Donal's recovery of Desmond, there was an important difference! More would be needed than a diplomatic encounter of letter writing with the man who had filled every castle in it with fighting men; and who, by Carewe's computation, would require 1,500 of the Queen's soldiers to prosecute him.

" 1600. *Aug^{st}*. 30. CAREWE *to the* PRIVY COUNCIL.

" Donell Mc Carthie base brother to Florence's wife (who in the beginning of this rebellion was by the countrey ellected to be Mᶜ Carty More, that is to be chief L of the countrey of Desmond; and displaced by Tyrone at his being in Mounster to erect Florence) hath made his humble submission, and accordingly beseecheth Her Maty's gracious pdon, requiring no rewarde but such as his service shall merritt, promising faithfully that when I shall intend the proseqution of Florence, wth the help of Her Majesty's forces, he hath good hope in a short tyme to banish him the countrey; his proffers I enterteine, and according the quallitie of his service have promised him to a meane to Her Maty that she wilbe pleased to bestowe some porcion of that land upon him.

" Divers reportes are made of Florence's son; some thatt he is gon into Spayne, others thatt he will go shortlie, and tothat effect I have a lʳᵉ of the White Knight, dated the 27ᵗʰ of the month that yf he be not gon alreadie yett he is resolved to go thether wᶜʰ makes me to hope (yf it be trew) thatt they begin to dispayre of Spaniards."

Carewe now resumed his correspondence with Florence; it commenced with expressions of politeness, and friendship, but finished otherwise. He assured him that he had no doubt of his honesty, but that his enemies were saying many things to his prejudice; it was now time for him to declare himself openly, and do for Her Majesty some such manifest service as should put an end to all suspicions, and gratify his English friends; he desired to see him without further delay at Limerick!

The reader will be able to perceive by Carewe's letters how great at this time had become his embarrassment how to proceed with Florence! To Cecyll and to the Privy Council he wrote that he was resolved to prosecute him, and then immediately, that the charge to Her Majesty would be too great, he must still temporize with him!

To his threats of prosecuting Florence the answer was to do so, unless reasonable satisfaction would content him. When he spoke of conciliation Cecyll replied:—

" For Florence if he could be made an honest man it weare pitty to loose him; and I assure you to make him an Erle of the Queene's gifte, I doe not thinke but she would easylye be induced if he seeke it upon any good imprest of loyalltye. It weare verrie good that you did discover him as well as you can what may be lookfor of him, for I see that you take him to be one of the strongest rebelles."

Before this reply reached him he had changed his mind, and wrote again to the Privy Council a gloomy letter about the difficulty of his position and the strength of Florence.

"1600, Septr 17. CAREWE *to* CECYLL.

" I have nottyet heard from Florence; yf he do not presentlye come and submitt himselfe, I have sent him word thatt I will prosecute him as a traytor: for I am resolved nott to beare wth his temporisinge any longer, beinge now bettre enabled then I was, to follow him, wch I was not able to do whyle James Mc Thomas was stronge. I have gotten good blood houndes of his owne countrye birthe to hunt him, out of naturall mallice they beare him, and make no doubt but to send the Queene his head for a token, except he do presentlye submytt himselfe."

"1600. Septr 23rd.

" This eveninge I receved a longe tedious humble lettre from Florence, and prayes to be admitted to speáke wth me; he now stands uppon no titles of Erle or Mc Cartie More, renouncinge his desires to have them; but humblye prayes to be assured of his lyfe, libertie, and lyvinge, wth infynite protestations to be evermore a trew servant to the Queene, and to demonstrate his loyalltie by his service. The first of October I purpose to be in Carbrye, at wch tyme or before, ether Florence shall yelld unto me suche assurance for his loyalltie as I shall thinke is meet to be receved, or ells I will presentlye fall to the prosecution of him: The pride of his hart is abated, and protests that yf your honnour, or Sir Wallter Raleghe woulld have vouchsafed (as in his lettres unto you bothe he promysed and prayed,) to have wrotten unto him, to have gone into England; thatt long since he had bene there, but receivinge no answere from ether of you, and Sir John Stanhope's lettre did but admonyshe him onely to subiection, wthout promise of life, libertie, or lyvinge, for these considerations he helld himsellfe neutrall; but yf he may be assured thatt his offences shall be remitted, he will then endeavour by his services, to recover his lost reputation; by the next I shall be able to certifie your honnour more of him, assuringe you thatt yf he be reduced by my next, the greatest part of the Queen's chardges for Munster may be well spared; but nott before, for feare of a relapse. James Mc Thomas is now no better then a wood kerne, and gone I know not whether, for since his last overthrow, no man can tell me whatt is become of him.
" Cork 23 Septr. 1600."

"1600. Ocb^r. 22. CAREWE *to* CECYLL.

" Florence I daylye expect; yf he com not he is a periured rebell, as his letters can testyfye which Mr. Price hath seene, and I am resolued to prosecute him presentlye, which ere this I would have don yf his protestations of loyalltye had not prevayled with me: but to saye my opynion trewlye of him yt were fitt for the service he should be reduced by force, but then I should geve a longer contynuance of a chardge to Her Matie, the diminucion whereof is chefely expected."

Circumstances, over which the wisdom of Carewe had little influence, began at length to befriend him. The necessities of O'Neill, who was hard pressed by the Lord Deputy, compelled him to recall from Munster great bodies of the bonies in the service of FitzThomas: in a few weeks the force with which he had hitherto defied the President, so rapidly melted away that there remained scarcely 600 men in his camp: with this small force he was one day seeking to make his retreat to Arlow, to wait for better times, when a fortunate sortie of the garrison of Kilmallock under Captain Græme, "the best Captain of horse in the Kingdom," surprised and utterly routed him; his baggage, stores, and munition, all fell a prize to the gallant man who, with a mere handful of horse, had ventured this bold assault. The Earl secured his retreat, but his followers, about 400, who escaped the swords of Græme's horsemen, fled from him dispersed in all directions. The style of Carewe's letters instantly showed that in the first elation at this success he considered the overthrow of FitzThomas to be the overthrow of Florence.

Whilst James FitzThomas with only about four or five followers, " sons of perdition," was lurking for his life now in the woods of Arlow, now in the remoter parts of Tipperary and Ormond, and with his nightly lodging tracked from cabin to cabin, by the keenest of his enemies, and when, in fact, he was reduced, as Carewe described him, to be of little more importance than a wood kern, matters were improving with the Northern Chieftains; letters were written both by O'Neill, and O'Donnel, to Florence, announcing succours of munition, and money from Spain; with promise before long of a force from O'Neill, and the early arrival of a Spanish army in Ireland. Florence in the meanwhile had been urgently pressed by Carewe to repair to him in person, and bring his son with him.

It chanced that certain recent letters from the Lord President had remained unanswered; neither did Florence come! nor was his son sent! It had not occurred to Carewe, till it was pointed out to him by Florence, that, owing to the extreme vigilance of the Queen's officers, and the multitude of roving and loose rogues about, the roads were perilous not less for him than for his messengers. So entirely barred against the subtlest of the President's intelligencers was the whole of Florence's country that Carewe about this time wrote home to Cecyll that the rumour was that he was gone into Spain to hasten the sailing of the fleet for Ireland. Florence at last put an end to much of the anxiety of Carewe by appearing before him at Moyallo.

THE TWO PORTRAITS OF FLORENCE.

PORTRAIT THE FIRST.

We are indebted to the observation of the author of the Pacata Hibernia, Mr. Thomas Stafford, for a description of the personal appearance of Florence upon this occasion. Although something may be allowed for the figurative, and the picturesque, in the following sketch, it is interesting, as the only contemporary portrait that has reached us of this remarkable Irish Chieftain. It is in the manner rather of Hogarth than of Titian ; but a genuine picture none the less, by a domestic artist of the Lord President ; and though, may be, deficient in grace, and accessory, it abounds in vigour, and is valuable, in default of any other, from its undisputed resemblance. Pac. Hib. :—

" But to return again to Florence McCartie ; after all the tergiversations before mentioned, and many others too tedious to be inserted, finding all his neighbours to have submitted themselves, and his own followers so impoverished by the warres, desirous to do the like was contented (tandem aliquando) to repair to the President, lying at Moyallo ; bringing some forty horse in his company, and himselfe in the middest of his troope (like the Great Turke amongst his Janizaries) drew towards the house (the nine and twentiest of October) like Saul, higher by the head and shoulders than any of his followers. Upon his submission, the President, as having forgotten all former matters, gave him kind entertainment, being indeed heartily glad of his presence, as hoping thereby that these warres of Mounster were brought to a finall end."

To this homely sketch a few touches were added by Carewe himself. " Florence is as much addicted to his ease as any man living, and therefore unmeet to be a rebel !" " His pride is incredible." ," Pride doth so much possess him in being called MacCarthy Mor that his understanding is lost, and not capable of any reasons but his own." " His foolish ambition is boundless." " Such is his inconstancy I dare not trust him !"

The last touch of all, and of all the most spirited, was added by the rough hand of his base brother-in-law. It was thrown off in a moment of great anger, and its expression was Donal's sole solace for the loss of Desmond.

" He is a d——d counterfeit Englishman, whose only study, and practice it is to deceive, and betray all the Irish in Ireland."

This rude yet vigorous portrait of the person of their chief contented the relatives of Florence for nearly a century and a half. At that time a descendant of Donal Pipi, flying from a hotter tempest than that of the Glins, or the Corlieus, took refuge in France. He bore with him a master-piece of heraldic literature, compiled by the united learning of Ralph Bighand (Clarencieux) and Isaac Heard (Norroy), enriched with copies of all such documents as were contained in the College of Heralds in London! This authentic history was in two sumptuous folio volumes of *parchemin-vélin*, and was entitled " *Généalogie de la Royale, et Sérénissime Maison de Mac Carthy.*" The first volume was *consecrated* to historic, and the second to genealogical evidences; each page paraphed, attested, and signed by these two kings-at-arms, and sealed with their official seals. Previous to the year 1776, the g^t g^t grandson of Donal Pipi had established himself at Thoulouse ; he had exhibited his two wonderful volumes of genealogy (*proving his " Royal origin"*) to the searching eyes of Monsieur Chérin Pére, Généalogiste des Ordres du Roi, and had at once been " admis aux honneurs de la Cour," (*nobilitated*, that is), created Comte MacCarthy Reagh!

PORTRAIT THE SECOND.

Together with his two heraldic volumes Monsr. le Comte had carried with him out of Ireland the rude effigies which the reader has seen, of the relative whom his ancestor had so greatly esteemed, and so adroitly circumvented. It was hung with honour upon the walls of the château at Thoulouse, and was pointed out with pride as the portrait of *the Lord of Kinsale, and second Earl of Clancar*, and there it remained till about half a century ago. But the rude style of the artist had always been a source of chagrin to the " most serene" descendants of Donal Pipi, and they at last decided to place the picture in the hands of the most eminent artist of this century, in order that it might be *restored*, and receive such embellishments as, without prejudice to the resemblance, would render it more worthy of the merits of the Earl, and more congenial to the taste of the polite people, to whose admiration it was to be exhibited. The reader will admit that the genius of Monsr. Laine has done justice to the great trust reposed in him. The portrait of Florence, thus restored, now forms a chief ornament of the noble city of Thoulouse!

" Florence MacCarthy Mor 2ᵉ Comte de Clancare, avant son marriage était connu sous le titre de Lord de Kinsale. Une taille gigantesque, et des formes herculéennes, unies à la beauté, et à la majesté des traits ; aux jours de combats, le courage du Lion, et le coup d'œil de l'Aigle ; dans le commandement, une bienveillance, et une urbanité naturelles qui ne se démentirent jamais, et qui le firent chérir de tous ceux qui servaient sous ses drapeaux, tel est le portrait que l'histoire a tracé de Florence MacCarthy !"

How impertinent must have appeared to the earnest mind of Monsʳ. Laine the caricature of the Irish painter! How inanimate and mesquin the colouring with which Smith, the English artist, afterwards endeavoured to make amends for the affront offered to the person of the Earl, when " *extraordinary stature*" was all the expression he could find to represent " une taille gigantesque, et des formes herculéennes !" and *competent courage*, " Le courage du Lion, et le coup d'œil de l'Aigle !"

" Of all the MacCartys of Carberry, says Smith, in his History of Cork, the above-mentioned Florence MacDonogh was the most famous. He was a man of extraordinary stature, and as great policy ; he had competent courage, and as much zeal as anybody, for what he imagined to be true religion, and the liberty of his country. He married Ilen, daughter and heiress of the Earl of Clancare ; and purely by his merit dispossessed her base brother Donal of the name and title of MacCarthy Mor."

In far other than the roseate colouring of Monsʳ. Laine, darker even than the dim tints of Smith, did the Lord President describe to Sir Robert Cecyll the appearance of Florence, when he repaired to him at Moyallo.

" 1600. *Novʳ* 2. CAREWE *to* ——

" Florence MᶜCarthie, after many delayes and protracčons (in hope of present succor to subsist in a longer warr) the 29ᵗʰ of the last, made his repaire unto me, submitting himself to hir Matˢ grace, and mrcye, protesting (whose ptestačons I do not much creditt, for his submissions are onely out of feare to be presently ruined by her Matˢ forces) for ever hereafter to remayne a true and faithfull servant unto hir Maty, and to meritt by his future suices the redemption of his late errors. To abate his greatnes I haue taken from him his chiefe dependaunts (namely) the towe O'Sullyvans, the towe O'Donoughoes, MᶜFynnen, O'Crowly and O'Mahowne Carrebry; every of wh are to put in pledges for their owne loyalties, and not to depend upon him: so as his pledges lyes onely for himself, and his brother (who is a most wickid traytor) and those of the Clancarties dwelling upon the landes wᶜh hir Maty hath graunted unto him. The pledge I demaunded was his eldest sonne wch (by reason of his indisposition of

health) he cold not bringe wth him, but in the meantyme hath left wth
me his base brother, who is dearly esteemed by him, hauing for these tenn
yeares past spent his tyme in the warrs of the Lowe Contries, Fraunce
and Hungary, and a foster brother of his, no less by him respected.
Wthin these 20 dayes he assures me to retorne againe, and then bringe his
sonne wth him: *All that I haue promissed to confirme unto him is but his
pdon and liberty*, not condicioninge any further assuraunce for his landes
then such as now he hath; and for the titles wch he so much affectes, w^ch
is either to be called Mc Carty More, or to be created Earle of Clancare, I
have left him hopeles in ether of them. He is now gon to prove his
credytt wth Thomas Oge (Constable of Castlemange for James Fitz
Thomas,) to render the same into hir Mats handes; but I thincke the Erle
of Desmond will prevayle before him, who hath sent to that purpose, but
yf they both fayle I doubt not, by another stratagemme to regaine the
same. The reducton of Florence (although I cannot iudge his hart less
corrupt then before,) giues an assured hope of a present establishm^t of this
province; for upon him the rebells did builde their last refuge; and now
that he is defected from them, straungers wilbe less willinge (hauing no
backe in the country) to venture themselves therein.

                                                    GEORGE CAREWE.
" From Moyallow, 2 Novr 1600."

This submission of Florence was followed by a new experiment of Carewe. He had written home that "since March
he could justly report that he had slain above 1200 weaponed
men, *besides husbandmen, women, and children*, of whom he
made no account: he now proclaimed a general pardon for
all the weaponed men, husbandmen, *women, and children*,
who had survived his butcheries; 10,706 rebels were thus
pardoned. The following list will enable the reader to appreciate the force which the word of Florence could at any
moment call to arms of his own name and dependants
alone :—

Cormac McDermot (Lord of Muskery)	..	480 men.
Florence McCarthy	..	201 „
Donal O'Donovan '	..	596 „
O'Sullevan Mor	..	481 „
Donal McCarthy, *alias* McCarthy Reagh	..	210 „
Dermod Moyle McCarthy (Florence's brother)		221 „
Other O'Sullevan's	..	383 „

When Carewe's alarms were in some measure calmed by
the obedience of Florence in waiting upon him, as he had at
last absolutely commanded him to do, arrived from Cecyll the
reply to his late wavering despatches, and to an assertion
which he had made to a certain Captain Price, that "he
would long since have prosecuted Florence, but for the fear
of displeasing the Minister who befriended him!" This remark

had been communicated by Price to Cecyll, and it brought upon Carewe the only letter of rebuke written to him during his government of Munster.

It was doubtless this letter which induced him, before much longer, to end all his difficulties by the act of perfidy which we shall presently have to relate.

"1600. *Nov^r* 8. Sir R. CECYLL *to* CAREWE, *Lambeth MSS.*

"In the matter of Florence, wee hope by the next to receave some certainty, seeing in manie lettres of late you have used speeches that you would dryve it to some conclusion, in which point it seemeth something strang to me that Capten Pryse reporteth that you should say you would have prosecuted him yf I had not restrayned you, wherein I must needs professe that you haue ether mistaken me, or he hath mistaken you, for, yf you observe all the lettres that I haue written, you shall fynde that I made jugement of nothing which commeth not from you, nor euer send you directions without leving them to the latitude of your owne discretion; And for this matter you must remember, when you wrott of your going into Kerry, you professed you would temporise with him tyll you came back ; and when you were there you wrott that you found nothing in him but perfidious delayes, besydes so extreame ambicion as you became doubtfull whether it were not convenient in some kind for Her Majestie to yeald thereunto; uppon which lettres it was written to you again that you should prosecute him when you saw your tyme, except some convenient satisfaction should contente him. Within few daies after you wrott that such a day you would begin to draw head uppon him, and then to prosecute him, yf new matter from him proceeded not to your liking. Since which tyme you know what is written, and therefore yf wee doe but mooue as you do mooue, and change uppon your grounds, then must your owne reasons be accoumpted the author of your owne resolutions, wherein you neede not be doubtfull more then weé are of you, seeing all that you haue hetherto undertaken hath sped so well, and is so well taken. In this point, therefore, I will hold you no longer, &c. &c."

THE TOWER—EARL OF DESMOND.

In compliance with a fanciful scheme of Carewe for the overthrow of FitzThomas, and the effectual extinction of the troubles of Munster, Sir Robert Cecyll had consented, though with great reluctance, to solicit the Queen to restore in blood, and to the honours of his house, the son of the arch-traitor, the last Earl of Desmond—who had from his childhood been brought up a prisoner in the Tower of London. Elizabeth well remembering the eight years of struggle with his father, at first angrily refused, and when she at last yielded to the importunity of Cecyll, threw the entire responsibility of the risk upon him. Jealously guarded by a certain Captain Price, Patrick Crosby, and Miler McGrath, the youth arrived in Ireland, and Carewe was in full expectation that his mere presence would suffice to lure away every Geraldine from the camp of FitzThomas. This illusion is one of the most singular that ever ruled the mind of this able statesman, for he himself acknowledged that the Sougaun Earl "was more beloved by all the men of Munster than he had ever known any man to be."

A sickly, enervated, passionless shadow of a Geraldine, propped up between Price and Crosby, with "plaisters for his backe, linyment for his syde, aqua cœlestis, comfortable oyntment for the stomack, and electuaries to take in the morning" passed from the Tower of London, to Youghal, and from Youghal to Cork. The reception which this young FitzGerald met with in Ireland is detailed in the Pacata Hibernia; indeed that large volume contains few paragraphs of equal interest.

There has been occasional mention made in these pages of the quarterly bills sent by the Lieutenants of the Tower of London to the Treasury, for diet and other charges of all kinds, including clothes, fuel, lights, and physic, due for their prisoners. These bills furnish a complete diary of the whole prison life of this young Earl. They enable us to trace his struggles through the petty maladies of childhood, his lessons with his schoolmaster, and the treatment of a sickly boyhood. By means of these bills, and by them only, we are enabled to perceive what training was thought necessary for the taming of this young eagle of Desmond, this heir to the insubordination and pride of the mightiest of the Norman houses, which had accumulated during four centuries. And after the painful perusal of these bills we are prepared to see precisely such a phantom as Carewe invoked with the purpose of controlling the fiercest Geraldine tempest that had ever swept over Ireland. The fierce wild followers of his house, who had fought for eight years under his father against the Queen's forces, looked upon the apparition with amazement, until their national superstition suggested to them the only possible meaning of what they saw—*He was a changeling!* not even of human generation, but the *child of Fairies!*

But whatever else he was, he no sooner set foot in Ireland, than he became an object of absolute terror to Sir Robert Cecyll. "I do professe unto you, he wrote to Carewe, that I do neuer shutt myne eyes but with feare at my waking to heare some ill newes of him," and "I must now speake to you my opinion, that you and I haue made a great adventure, to presse and importune for a thinge, soe subject to ill

successe! and I praie you, therefore, when you have him,
take this counsell of me; whenever you fynde any cause to
doubt him, never feare to lay hold of him, for therein we will
never blame you, but we will take it for a thinge that was
necessarie, quoniam ipse dixit."

And again; "I praie you lettus be wise as serpents,
though *we be* as symple as doves, if you fynde no great taske
to be don bye him, rather take a true and wise wai, and mak
suer of him that he cannot escape; &c.—for take this from
me, upon my life, that *whatever you doe to abridge him*, which
you shall saie to be don out of providense, shall never be
ymputed to you as a fault, but exceedinglie commended bye
the Queene; for God doeth knoue that the Queene hath been
the most hardlie drawen unto yt that cold be, and hath
layde yt in my dysh a duson tymes.   Besydes, Sir, yt shalbe
an easie matter for you to cullor whatsoever you shall doe in
that kind, by this course; you maie ether apostate some to
seek to withdraw him, who may betray him to you, or,
rather than fayle, there may be som founde out ther to accuse him, and that may be sufficient reason for you to
remande him, or too restrayne him.   I confesse every perill
noue objects ytself to my sence; still remember what I say
unto you.   Blame shall never betyde you for any caution,
(howe curyous so ever) in the managinge this *puer male
cinctus.*"

Puer male cinctus! "Ut male præcinctum puerum caverent"
(Suetonius), the warning of Sulla, to beware of Cæsar!!

Blame? far otherwise! *how curious soever!* Whether like
that *curious* proceeding that had *abridged* Owen O'Nassie,
or the curious attempt of Nugent and Annyas, to abridge
the FitzThomases and Florence! Had it pleased the Lord
President, in order to calm the terrors of his patron, to essay
any curious experiments whatever on this youthful Cæsar,
had he tried the two leaden bullets, or the drugs of Annyas,
upon a body which had been nurtured from infancy upon the
poisons of the Tower Apothecary, or sought to abridge him
by any ingenious process whatsoever, all would have been
alike powerless upon this phantom changeling! But there
was no cause for any of this alarm! "the young Earl not
agreeing with the manners and customs of Ireland, petitioned
to be allowed to return to England!" "Scorned by all the
Gentlemen of Desmond," he took his departure: and no
trace of his steps was to be thenceforward discoverable upon
the soil which had trembled as with an earthquake under
every tread of his great father! It is true that a traitor

availed himself of the shallow pretext of fidelity to the head
of his house, to surrender to Carewe the fortress of Castlemaing, which James FitzThomas had entrusted to his keeping; but his presence in Ireland was a standing reproach to
every one who had been concerned in his coming. "From
Ireland he repaired to the Court, where after a few months
he died!" returned, that is, to the ethereal parents who had
begotten him by the Lawne, or the Carra's side, and there
sung they his dirge.

> Strew the bed, and strew the bier
> (Who rests upon it, was never man !)
> With all that a little child holds dear
> With violets blue, and violets wan.*

So constantly present to men's minds was the rumour of the
attempt of Cecyll and Carewe to poison Florence, that when
this poor harmless Tower-Earl faded out of life, it went
abroad that *he* had been poisoned ! Cecyll had no motive to
poison him, and he was not at the time of his death within
reach of Carewe !

One after another all the more ingenious schemes of the
President failed; but he was not discouraged : He did not
discontinue his fencing with Florence, although he still
sought on all sides for means more expeditious to deliver
him from his perplexities.

One success would repay him for many failures, and his
good fortune had in store for him a compensation for all his
previous disappointments. Before the last letter of Cecyll
reached him, he was delivered, as we have mentioned, from
much of his anxiety, by the repair of Florence to him at
Moyallo. Florence had renewed his promise to deliver to
him his eldest son, the object he had so long coveted, as
soon as the boy's health would permit him to travel. And
the President had *promised to confirm to him his pardon and
liberty, and such lands as he then had.* With these mutual
promises the parties separated; and Carewe, after communicating to Cecyll a satisfactory incident relative to Copinger,
turned his whole attention to a matter more important than
any further negotiation with Florence, in fact to the drawing
of a new draught by an entirely new hand.

" 1601. *Jan^y*. 25. CAREWE *from Moyallo to the* PRIVY COUNCIL.

" Florence Mc Carthy is now wth me, and to cleare himself of all his
transgressions, doth promise me ymmediatly to sue out his pdon, and to

* Inisfail by Aubrey de Vere, Esq.

send me his eldest sonne, upon receipt of whome I must returne unto him the pledges that now I have; but such was his feares accompanied wth knowen guiltyness of his breech of protecčons since he was receaved into her Mats grace, as he plainely confessed unto me that the same was broken, and therefore did before his cominge humbly pray unto me the renewinge of yt, wth promise hereafter religiously to keepe the same; unto wᶜh request (albeyt I was farr unwillinge) yet least the denyall thereof shold have made diversion in the harts of others in Desmond, inclyned to peace, who then wth him were repayring unto me to give assurance for their future loyalties, as namely O'Sulyvan More, Mᶜ Fynen, and the Twoe O'Donnoughoes, I thought it meete in discretion to remitt the errors past, and to beginn a new accompt, wth whome generally I have now taken sufficient order."

" *Feb'*. 11.   CAREWE *to* CECYLL.

" My Lo. of Upper Osserye of late hathe done good service, havinge slayne of the rebellˢ dead uppon the place 157 and among them Coppinger, Sir Wallter Raleghe's man that savéd John Fitz Thomas from killinge, this last sommer by Nugent, as your Honnour hath bene formerlye enformed.

" G. CAREWE."

DRAUGHT   THE   FOURTH.

THE WHITE KNIGHT.

Since the day of his total overthrow by the charge of Captain Græme, James FitzThomas, mostly with a single companion, Dermod McCragh, the Pope's Bishop of Cork, was reduced to lurk about, as his uncle the great rebel had done some years before, in caves and woods, distrusting all men, yet not a whit wavering in his conviction of the complete re-establishment of his fortunes if he could but manage to escape such men as Dermod O'Connor, and John Nugent, till the spring or summer should bring the Spaniards, or the Northern Chieftains into Munster. The weapon of Nugent, the snare of O'Connor, the poison of Annyas had all failed; but the list of Carewe's agents was not exhausted. As he had formerly found a man for £10 to practise upon John FitzThomas, so now found he a man for £400 to sell into his hands the fugitive, who had caused all this disturbance in Munster : this man was Edward FitzGibbon, the White Knight, of whom Carewe had previously written "*A more faithless man never lived upon the earth!*" he had been till now in rebellion, but was seized by sudden remorse for his past faults. He was himself a Geraldine! a born follower of the Earl! and FitzThomas had been married to his sister! Could he have been content to do the crime he did, and to leave Carewe alone to chronicle it, he might have found in suc-

ceeding generations some, as assuredly in his own he would
have found many, to refuse utterly any credence to his
accuser; but like his employer he could not let his evil deeds
pass into oblivion, or shroud themselves in any ambiguity
either as to the motive, or the mode of his proceedings; but
with his own hand has recorded, with minute detail for
posterity, both the one and the other. The capture of James
FitzThomas in the obscure cave, many fathoms underground,
in the mountain of Slewgrott, is to the full as picturesque,
and dramatic as that of his uncle the 16th Earl, the arch-
rebel, in the cabin of Glaneguinty.

So eagerly did FitzGibbon covet the price for which he
had sold his brother-in-law that he wrote to his employer
" he could not sleep at night for the fear lest any other should
anticipate him in this service."

On the 29th of May, 1601, the gallant and unfortunate
FitzThomas was run down by his relative in person, in the
Cavern described by Carewe. And then was the truth told
of the resources and character of this man, who had been so
much vilified, " He was, writes the President, I can assure
your Lordships, the most potent Geraldine that ever was of
any of the Earles of Desmond his ancestors; and not this
only, but it would be very dangerous to continue him prisoner
in Ireland being so exceedingly beloved as he is."

" 1601. May 29. From the WHITE KNIGHT to CAREWE.

" My dutie most humblie remembreth to yor good Lo. being not un-
myndfull of the great chardge yor Lo. gave me divers tymes, for the
serchinge out of James Fitz Thomas, and especially when nowe last I was
at Cork, I have both to satisfie yor Lo as alsoe to manifest my willingness
to doe my Prince service, all this while endeavored my selfe to enquier after
the saide Ja, for compassinge of wch purposse, I protest to yor L. I could
tak noe rest, for I thinck if any other should take him but my selfe, my
harte would burste. I came in conference wth the harper Dermod O'Doan,
John Shannyghane the priest, and the Baldons, whome yor Lo. knoweth to
be ther last releavers and company, privatly offeringe euie of them ptecu-
lerlie to have her Ma^{ts} mercy and favor extended to them, their wiffes and
children, wth other great rewards, about wch matter I spent a long tyme,
yet euie one of them dyd put me of, taking ther ots they kneewe not whear
the saide James was at all, Yet I founde them piured therein because nowe
I knowe the priest & Doan was that very day wth him. Well, when that
wey failed me I brought before me all those of my countrey that I moste
trusted & that I kneewe to have loved my most. I fell into private conference wth euie of them pticulerly, shewinge them what great danger was
lik to ensue to me & my contrey unless I had don some seurice upon James
Fitz Tho. whoe alwaies was founde to be borderinge upon my contrey.
Wherfore they weare to be suspected for him. And the more to procure
them to ventur themselves for me in my extremitie I published amongst

them that S^r. George Thorneton was bounde for me body for body to appeare at the next cessions. Wherupon I eftsones praied them as they loved
me & my contrey, & to avoyde such great inconvenience, that they would
wourck all the meanes they could to learne me newes of the said James, to
wch eüie one answered that they knewe nothinge of him at all. At last
seing me in that pplexitie one whome I protest I least suspected of all my
countrey, came to me a litle before supper, and tolde me that the said Ja:
and one Thomas Roe Offeighie lay at such a cave or denn be Slevgrott. I
unwillinge to looss my opportunitie, seeing it pleassed God to send me such
good newes, repaired thether pntly wth a very few company, and being
right oü the saide cave or děn, sent downe 3 or 4 men whoe fyndinge them
their James retourned me one fourth putinge me in mynde of his kyndred,
and prainge me, not to remember him at that tyme for any harme he dyd
me before, promissinge to make great amends thereof, and that he was sure
to be well hable to pforme it w^thin two monethes, for that he should haue,
or that tyme 6000 men well prouidèd wth munition and other necessaries
in Mounster, wth many other unreassonable offers wch should be to my
greate profficte. When I would not accept any thinge at his hands, but
told him that he was nowe her Ma^{ts} prison⟩ then began he to raile at me &
laboured my followers & servants to foasake me & take his pte, and that he
would rewarde them lardglie wth lands for their posteritie for ever & other
gifts of great value, whereof he failed, as of the rest. This is the maner
of his takinge, having him and the saide Feighie in my safe keeping w^thin
my castell to be presented to her Matie, and as I haue pformed this w^th
manie other principall services heretofore for her Highnes, even soe doe I
hopp that this shall not be the last. I sent to S^r. George Thorneton to
Kilmallock pntly to bring me a good guarde of horsse and foote to leade
him to yo⟩ L. to Corck tomorrowe.

" Even soe humbly tak my leave, resting yo⟩ Honno^{rs} ever to doe yo⟩
service.

" Kilmeheny this evenynge being the 29th of May 1601.
" EDD GYBBON."

THE APPREHENSION OF JAMES FITZ THOMAS.

" 1601. *June* 3. CAREWE *to the* LORDS OF THE PRIVY COUNCIL.

It may please yor L^{ls}. The 29th of May (being the next day after the
date of my last to yor L^{ls} herewth) the White Knight (by me employed,
and earnestly spourred on to repaye his former errors) did his best endeavors
(wch I thanke God) had the successes desired. For the day aforesaid
(havinge notice by his espyalls wheare James Fitz Thomas (the usurping
Erle of Desmond) laye hidden wthin his countrye in the mountaynes of
Slewgrott in an obscuer cave many fathoms under the grounde, upon
intelligence wth such companies as then weare in his house wth him, not
being of weaponed men above 8 in nomber, repaired to the place, discovered
and there tooke him, and one horseman more who attended him, and
brought them to one of his own castles, from whence Sir George Thornton
wth a good guarde convayed them safe to my house, where in irons he remayneth, out of the wch I dare not els trust him to be kept, being (as he
is) a man the most generally beloved by all sortes (as well in this towne
as in the country), that iu my life I have knowen.

" I cannot sufficiently comm̃ende unto yor L^{ls} this dutifull act of the
White Knightes, who pformed the same more in respect of his dutie to
Her Maty then for the benefitt of the £400 head money proclaymed, and

presently to be paide, for The doinge whereof he was not ignorant to purchase to himself the generall malice of the Province, wherby his desert is made the greater, and (*but by himself*) *I protest unto yor L^ls I do not know any man in Mounster by whome I might have gotten him.* Neither may I leave unrecomended unto yor L^ls the dilligent and painefull endeuor^r of Sir George Thornton, who next unto the Knight himself, hath best deserved, being the chiefest and most effectuall instrument by me employed herein, and therefore (as wel for their incoradgmets to psevere in doinge her Maty service as to move others to forward the same) I most humbly besech yor L^ls that in her Mats name yor wolde take pticuler notice of yt, and by yor l^res to give them the thankes they deserve. For this treator's hope (notwthstandinge all the miseryes wch in this tyme of his distress he hath sustayned) was nothing abated; every day expecting either by Irish or Spanishe ayde (wch ayde from Spaine (as he tells me) he was confident to receave before harvest) to be no lesse hable to mentayne the warrs then in former tymes; assuringe yor L^ls that he was the most potent Geraldyne that ever was of any of the Erles of Desmond his auncestors, as may well appear by the nombers of Provincialls pdoned and cutt short since my cominge hither, as also by the nombers of the Bonnoughtes by me from time to time banished. The manner of his apprehension, (for yor L^ls more pticuler satisfaccon) is expressed in a l^re of the White Knightes unto me wch herewth I send yor L^ls.

" I once purposed to have sente the arch treator by this passadge into England; but upon better consideracon (whereof I hope yor L^ls will give good allowaunce) I do staye him for a tyme, and by the same do hope to avoyde all inconveniences that may happen : for, yf he shold dye before he come to his tryall (as the judges heare inform me) the Queen (but by Act of Parliament) can not be interested in his lands; and also his brother John (by the same reason) is not by the lawe debarred from the title wch this pretender holdes to be good, to the Erledome of Desmond : for theis reasons (by their opinions) I have resolved to have him arraigned, and adiudged, heare, and then do thincke yt meete he be sent into England, and left as yor L^ls shall please to dispose of him. And because yt is likewise by the lawyers told me, that a man condemned in this realme cannot, by the ordinary course of lawe, upon the same Indictment be executed in England, I purpose to send wth him 2 or 3 indictments readye drawne wth sufficient matter, by the wch he may be there at all tymes arraigned. The reasones that induceth me to send him lyvinge into Englande are grounded upon an apparent doubt conceaved that as soone as this arch treator shalbe executed, his brother John will ymmediatly assume the title he did, and prchaunce therby prove no less powerfull than this traitor hath ben; whereas (whilest he lyves) he cannot make any pretence to move ther naturall followers, and dependants of ther howse of Desmond to assist him; likewise I hold yt (under reformacon of yor grave iudgements) to be very daungerous to contynue him any longe tyme prisoner in Ireland, beinge (as aforesaid) so exceedingly beloved as he is, not daringe to comit him into any hands, out of myne owne.

" G. Carewe.

" Cork 3^d June 1601."

In the early hours of his captivity, and when apprehensive of the extreme vengeance of Carewe, and the Privy Council, the unfortunate Earl of Desmond wrote to the President " *The Relation*," which the reader may find in the Pacata

Hibernia. He will notice that the Earl styles himself "Mr. James of Desmond." At the end of the document he had previously written "*James of Desmond!*" To this Carewe had objected! Upon several occasions Sir George Carewe, in his letters to Cecyll, had spoken with a sneer both of Florence and of the Earl, as if the one in assuming the style of MacCarthy Mor, and the other that of Earl of Desmond, were mere impostors! The one was elected, as every head of his race had ever been ; and the other was as we have already stated, the eldest legitimate son of the eldest legitimate son of James, 15th Earl of Desmond, and neither one nor other may have been able to see any thing treasonable, or the necessity of any special authority from the Queen for assuming, the one his birthright, the other the right his by the free election of his Sept. It is impossible to attribute the unmeaning sneers of Carewe to any feeling but jealousy at seeing them reputed, by all men in Munster, rich and poor, English and Irish, as superior in birth and worship to himself. To the original "*Relation*" preserved amongst "the State Papers!" is affixed the following marginal note, which has not been copied into the Pacata Hibernia :—

" 1601. *Marginal note by* CAREWE *to the Relation of* JAMES FITZ THOMAS.

" He first signed his name James Desmond; wch I sent backe unto him, and then he blotted itt out, and hath written his name, in a hand nott accustomed, nor yett wth the ortographie w^ch,—before he assumed the name of Erle,—he wrote, wch was Fitz Geralld, wherby it appeares hou loathe he is to leave the name of Desmond.

" GEORGE CAREWE."

" 1601. *June* 4. CAREWE *to* CECYLL.

" It may please your Honor, yesterday, being the 3^d of June, Patricke Crosbye departed hence wth some packets from me directed unto you, &c. &c.

" The titularye Erle my prisoner is very confident of there cominge, (the Spaniards) wch made him to lead the miserable poore lyfe he did, in hope to be of greater abillitie to continew the warre then at the first; yett he is muche reserved in his speache, and will hardlye discourse anythinge that may advance her Matie's service; but after a few dayes I doubt not but to make him speake more freelye."

Four hundred pounds was the price promised, and in the first instance paid by Carewe for the capture of the Earl of Desmond; the author of the Pacata Hibernia, who no doubt knew all the details of the transaction, informs us that £1,000 was eventually given to the White Knight for it. A gratuity of £600 is the measure of an immense acknowledgment of gratitude, when the frugality of Her Majesty is considered. Five thousand angels had been once offered by Cecyll for the murder of O'Neill!

The heads of these two men would have been cheap to the Queen at two millions, could she have had them but three years earlier.

The emotion caused by the treachery of the White Knight in selling his chieftain! the head of his race! his relative in blood! and the husband of his own sister! has not subsided after the lapse of nearly three centuries, nor will it, as long as history shall last, and ingenuous minds exist to read it! The emotion is not indeed the same as that with which Carewe wrote, and Cecyll read, the account of it, but it is expressed in words that are pleasing to read! like the verdict of the Dublin Jury of 1583.

> " The name of the White Knight shall cease, and his race ;
> His castle down fall, roof and rafter!
> This day is a day of rebuke, but the base
> Shall meet what he merits hereafter!
> > "AUBREY DE VERE.
> > "Inisfail."

" There is no anger but abates (exclaimed a fierce Irish bard at the time of this treachery), except the anger of Christ with Clan Gibbon !"

As it will sometimes happen that one crime will rob another of some portion of its malignity, it may be added, in extenuation, as far as it will stretch, of the perfidy of the White Knight, that he had long hated his relation with a deadly hatred: that in this instance his malice was greater than his covetousness, and his revenge sweeter than the wages of his perfidy. ·

In the month of November, Carewe had vehemently desired that Florence should repair to him. After many attempts to evade this visit, Florence did at last wait upon him, but with much reluctance, and not until he had received the usual promise of "*pardon, and liberty, and the possession of the lands he then had.*" Carewe then exacted from him a fresh promise to deliver up his son.

Early in the March following Florence sent notice to the President that he was ready to come, and himself deliver the boy into his hands, as he had promised to do; but, with his customary precaution, before trusting himself within reach, "he did humbly pray for the renewing of his protection;

unto which request (albeit I (the President) was far unwilling)
I thought it meet, in discretion, to remit the errors past, and
to begin a new account."

·Florence had received many warnings to beware how he
trusted himself within the power of any English authorities
whatever. Amongst others he had received a remarkable
caution from Spain. A relative of his own, a certain Don
Dermutio Carty, a priest—one of those, doubtless, to whom
he alluded when he spoke to Sir Thomas Norreys of his relations in good repute at the Spanish Court—wrote him a long
letter in the Spanish language (which afterwards fell into the
hands of Carewe), in which, after expressing "his joy at
hearing of his landing in Cork, after 11 years of captivity in
England, of which three had been passed in the Tower," he
proceeded to inform him that he had himself seen a letter
written from "the Treasurer of Ireland to the Queen, which
had been intercepted at sea by a Spanish vessel, in which the
real cause of his imprisonment was explained : that it was by
no means, as was pretended, for having married the Earl of
Clancar's daughter without royal permission, but because—"
And here follow all the reasonings contained in Sir W. St.
Leger's Tracts; leaving no room for doubt that the letter
intercepted was the famous despatch of St. Leger, which had,
in effect, caused his long imprisonment. The letter then continues—" It will be very necessary to be on your guard, and
not trust yourself to the English! *for if ever again they get
you into their hands, never more will you escape from them!*"
Happy would it have been for the writer if he could have
taken this good counsel to himself!

Florence by no means neglected these warnings ; the
precautions he took each time he went near the President
bespoke his utter distrust of him; and Carewe again and
again mentioned to Cecyll with vexation the *protections* and
pardons he was compelled to renew before Florence would
approach any place in which he was.

The reader will presently see, in the President's own
words, the remarkable conditions he had been obliged to consent to, upon the occasion of Florence's going to him with
his son. The Sougaun Earl was now in irons ; but not the
less was the mind of Carewe full of embarrassment and
anxiety with regard to Florence. He was daily receiving intelligence of Florence's intercourse with O'Neill and
with Spain ; letters from the Northern Chiefs, intercepted or
reported, announced the actual arrival of treasure and munition, and assurance of the early coming of a Spanish force

into Ireland. The confidential adviser and friend of Cormac
M'Dermod (Lord of Muskerry) made discovery of many past
acts of Florence's disloyalty, but essentially of a recent
attempt to seduce Cormac from his loyalty by inducing him
to give his sister in marriage to Fitz Thomas, to effect which
Florence had offered to give to him vast possessions in Carbery.
All this while Florence continued to reside in Cork, under the
President's eye, under safeguard of his official protection and
pardon. How solemn and inviolable this promise, made in
the Queen's name, was considered, even by Carewe himself
—until he felt how great could be the temptation to break it
—we may judge from the passage, already quoted, when
Dermod O'Connor met with his deserts, in spite of the safeguard given him in the Queen's name. "It was to the great
dishonour of Her Majesty, in violating her word solemnly
and advisedly given: the Lo: President was exceedingly
incensed!"

   This was the position of these two men after a year of
diplomatic contest, when the reproachful letter from Cecyll,
and the capture of Fitz Thomas, suggested to Carewe the
desperate resolve to lay hands upon Florence in defiance of
his protection, and to finish with him at once and for ever!
How wonderful that this easy exit from so much embarrassment should have been delayed so long! that the President
should only now discover that it was a less matter to violate
the Queen's parole than to poison Florence!

THE ARREST OF FLORENCE.

"1601. *June* 18. CAREWE *to* CECYLL."

   "Your Honnour by Patricke Crosbye was fully advertised of all the
affayres of this province untill the date of the lettres he carried, since wᶜʰ
tyme more then the restrayninge of Florence MᶜCarthie, who is now her
Matieˢ prisoner, nothinge hath happened. The treasons wᶜʰ in his breast
he hathe of longe tyme caried agaynst her Matie and the state, was sufficientlye discovered by his entringe into action of rebellion, havinge latelye
before receved extraordinarie favours, att his last beinge in England, and
the continuance of his treasons doth evidentlye appeare by his practisinge
wth Tirone, and Mounster men, when he was uppon protection ; in all
wᶜʰ tyme he never left sollicitinge as well to bringe northern aydes to rayse
new tumults, as to stirre and provoke the provincialls to relapse, wᶜʰ may
appeare manifestlye to be trew by the coppies of sundry lettres and examinations wᶜʰ I have sent unto you, and more fullye by further proofe wᶜʰ I
am able to produce agaynst him.
   "The reasons wᶜʰ persuaded me all this longe tyme to smoother his
faullts, was because he was uppon protection, and yett still woulld have
lett them runne on, yf necessitie had not urdged me to lay holld of him.
To·wynne tyme uppon me he pretended to goe into England, and tothatt

end I did procure him lardge benevolences bothe in Carbrie and Desmond; but perceved no suche intention in him, allso whereas his pardon hath bene under the seale ever since the 7th of Aprill last, by the wch he was enioyned by a tyme prefixed to put in assurance for his further loyallty, at the tyme that I comitted him *there was but* 14 *dayes to come, unexpired;* and that very day of his comitment he was takinge his iorney into Desmond, so as allmost there was no possibillitie for him to retourn to put in his suerties by the limitation of the proviso in his pardon, wch tyme beinge elapsed then he must be newlye protected, and so live unsecured. Upon this quarrell of not puttinge in of suerties according tothe proviso, and proovinge unto him that the tyme must of necessity elapse, and makinge knowne unto him that he hathe dealt falselye and trayterouslye since, and in the tyme of his protections, I did comitt him; att the iustnes whereof himsellfe hathe nothinge to replie, and all men are sufficientlye satisfied wth his restraynt; havinge caused the generallitie of his treasons wth Spayne, Tirone, and att home, to be divulged. The next day after his restraynt he was a petitioner unto me that he might have the benefitt of Her Maties pardon, unto the w^{ch}, *because the tyme in the Proviso was nott fullye expired* I did condyscend, beinge in iustice nott to be denied unto him. His faullt he acknowledges in nott putting in suerties wth more celeritie, and patientlye endures his restraynt, because he finds his guilltinesse of his offences to lie open unto me, and yett is not debarred from the saftie of his life.

" Wth James Fitz Thomas I do purpose to send him into England; and then have I sent you two Erles of there owne makinge, and the most powerfull rebells that ever lyved in Mounster. By the takinge of them I do thinke that Mounster wth a reasonable garrison will be assured from revollt wthin itsellfe, and allso freed from Ullster Bonnaughts to molest itt; and am allso of opinion thatt when itt shall be bruited in Spayne thatt these grandes are her Maties prisoners, thatt itt will devert there purposes, yf they had any, to invade Mounster, for uppon them two, and in especiall uppon Florence, the Spaniards did gronde there hopes in the rest of Irland. Least itt may be thought thatt I did neglect part of my dutie in not soner apprehendinge Florence, having intelligence of his practices in the tymes of his protections, I besehe your Honnour to call to mynd thatt in my former lettres I have acquaynted you thatt *his fashion was, evermore before he woulld come unto me to send for a new protection, wthout any proviso inserted in itt to be answerable for any breache of his former protection, so as every protection was a sufficient savvegard to free him from any offence of an ellder date;* for except unto him onelye I never renewed any man's protection since my cominge into Munster, but thatt the partie stood allwayes answereable for all offences comitted from the date of his first protection; a course never helld in Irland but by mysellfe; and by that course I am sure a hundred rebells have bene hanged within this six moneths, by takinge the advantadge of the breache of those protections. Unto some others itt will be thought I have dealt to soone wth him; because *untill he hathe pleaded his pardon he is nott subiect to restraynt, not havinge broaken his last protection:* I coulld have bene content to have forborne him a little longer, but I was sure yf he had gone out of the towne, and the dayes of his puttinge in of sureties expired, thatt he woulld by neu protections, tryfle out the tyme untill the cominge of Spaniards, and yf they came nott, thatt then himselfe would go into Spayne, so as I was enforced ether to loase him, or ells to take the advantadge of the quarrell I did, wch I am sure nether discontents, nor dislikes any man here; the worlld beinge fullye possessed thatt his trayterlye practices in the tyme of

his protections dothe merritt no favour, and therefore they holld my proceedinge wth him tobe *very just!* and *favourable beyond his merrit!* in
gevinge him the benefitt of her Maties pardon, whereby his life is secured.
James Fitz Thomas is arraygned, and adiudged; I woulld have sent him
and Florence this passadge, but I hope every day to heare out of England
to know Her Matie's pleasure; but yf the winde do settle in the west, I
will send them presentlye unto Her Matie; beinge the best presents thatt
Mounster affordes. James Mᶜ Thomas, to redeeme his owne lyfe, promises,
by his brother John and Pierce Lacye, to gett me Tirone alyve or dead. I
have putt him in confident hope thatt uppon thatt service done, thatt the
Queene will be gratious unto him; and that I may have the bettre ground
to move them to performe the same, I do beseche you thatt I may have a
lettre from her Matie unto me to assure them thatt uppon accomplishinge
the service uppon Tirone thatt James Mᶜ Thomas shall be sure to lyve,
and be sett at libertie! and thatt his brother John, and Pierce Laceye
shall be likewise pardoned. I am promised for £100 to gett Bishoppe
Craghe; and for the like sum the Knight of the Valley : ere itt be longe I
hope to send you the one or bothe: likewise I am profered, for money, to
have Mᶜ William's head in Connaught; but being out of my government
I know nott hou to deale in itt. Here is no money; I beseche your Honnour to mediatt for it; So humblye rest, &c.

"Now will be a good time for Nicholas Browne to come into Desmond ;
and he will be a good stay in that wyllde country whether he have a chardge
or no; for those parts are very quiet. I have payed the White Knight
£400, wᶜh uppon my credditt I procured.

" G. CAREWE.

"Cork this 18ᵗʰ of June 1601."

It was once, during the great Desmond rebellion, proposed
to the veteran Earl of Ormond to do what Carewe had now
done, "to put persons protected into suer hold." The answer
of the Earl was this—and it was written direct to the man
from whom the proposal had reached him—to the Lo:
Burghley :—

"*My Lord I wol never use trechery to any,* for it wol both
toche her highness honor to moch, and myne owne credit,
and who so ever gave the Queene advise thus to write, is
fitter to execute such base sarvice than I am. *Saving my
duetye to her Majestie, I wold I weare to have revenge by my
sword of any man that thus persuadeth the Queene to wryte
to me.*"

Had Carewe resisted the temptation to capture Florence
when the chance offered, posterity might not, considering the
sacred pledge—"the Queen's word solemnly and advisedly
given"—on which Florence had placed himself within his power,
have considered that he had done anything for which to extol
him as a hero of truth; but we must have respected his word,
and have thenceforth believed without questioning, however
unwillingly, all and everything that he gravely affirmed; but
when by his own writing we see that he held as nothing the

most sacred pledge that can pass between the weak and the strong, we know that he thereby forfeited all claim for ever after to be believed upon his oath, whether he swore upon his honour or his life, or his hopes of salvation hereafter! Men will do much to save life, more perhaps to escape the ignominy of the gibbet, but there are things—though Carewe would never have believed it—which a Christian, nay, a commonly honourable man, will *not* do even for these motives! It will need a great deal more than an assertion passing between such moralists as Carewe and Cecyll, to win our belief that "*James M'Thomas, to redeem his life, promised to get him Tirone alive. or dead!*" That Carewe offered life and liberty to the Earl, and pardon for his friends also, if he would accomplish this service, and that therefore he fully believed the Earl would accept such terms, we can have no reason to doubt! but that James Fitz Thomas *did promise* it, the author of these pages, for one, utterly refuses to believe it! What he was willing to do he himself offered in the "Relation" which he wrote, and which the reader may see in the Pacata Hibernia.

By the last paragraph of the preceding letter, the reader may perceive that Sir George Carewe had adopted the traditions of his predecessors, and that, wholly forgetful of Donal, whom he had so lately desired to establish in lieu of Florence, in Desmond, he had fallen back upon the old policy of Browne and the undertakers. Great stir had ensued in Munster and at the Court, as soon as it was known that Florence was restrained; for it was instantly supposed that there was at hand a confiscation scarcely less than that of the Geraldines, at the fall of the arch rebel the 16th Earl. The Lo: Barry might now, at least, fairly count upon the remittal of his fine; and he thought it not unreasonable to apply for a grant of some small portion of Florence's country to indemnify him for the ruin of his own. Many others there were who dispensed altogether with the uncertain process of supplication, and at once seized upon the lands they coveted.

It is a relief to exchange the stifling atmosphere of man-sellers and poisoners for the serener air of mere undertakers, and above all it is gratifying to know that if the inheritance of the Clan Carthy was to be dissipated, Nicholas Browne should get a share of it. Of all the suitors who at once assailed the English Minister for grants of land, Browne met with the readiest favour. He was the first to be recommended by Carewe, and not only did he receive instant promise of a fresh patent, but, with a view to the standing crops, a letter was written authorizing the President to put him at once in possession of his old quarters at Molahiff. It must be admitted that Browne had met with neither fair play nor common honesty from the English Government in the matters of his Signory and Patent. As long as he had been wanted to keep Donal in check, his patent had been held as a thing sacred; and with full reliance upon its unimpeachable validity, he had introduced labourers from England, built villages and castles, and, at great cost, done all those other things which he had in former days vainly enumerated to Lord Burghley. It certainly was not the act of Sir Robert Cecyll that dispossessed him of his lands, but, as the reader may remember, the violence of Donal and his friends, on occasion of the memorable siege of the Molathibian Fortress. How it had fared with his previous patent it is needless to repeat; the time was come for restitution, and although it might be feared that Molahiff would, for a long time to come, be but an uneasy possession, he was well pleased to take his chance, and cast his lot rather in the spacious wilds of Desmond than in his home at Hogsden. Knowing on whose patrimony fortune had spread a tent for him, he would do well to take a lesson from him, from whom he took the land, and see that this time, at least, he understands the language of the learned men whom he may employ to prepare his new patent. Let him bear in mind that the law uses phrases of signification occult at the time of composing such muniments, which are of very surprising meaning when they come to be interpreted. The incautious use of one word, the word "heirs," had wholly vitiated his last patent; let him beware this time! or, best of all counsels, let his next patent be by Act of Parliament, rather than by royal benevolence!

" Sir Robert Cecyll to Carewe.

" After my very hearty commendations to you, Although Her Majesty is now pleased to grant to M^r. Nicholas Brown new letters patents of his lands, and to that end hath written her letters to the Lo: Deputy, yet by reason of the Deputy's absence in Ulster, and other the employment of Brown having the conduction of some men to your Lo: his business cannot be so speedily effected at Dublin as need would require, whereby he is like to incur some prejudice if he should lose the fruits of this harvest, and Her Majesty's service receive great hindrance if his castles were possessed by any other, and for that it is known as well to us here, as to your Lo: there, what detriment the poor Gent: hath already sustained through the defects of his former patent, and the purpose meant for Florence Mc Carty (which now by his manifest misdemeanours is altogether disappointed) I pray

your Lo: therefore to take order that he be presently repossessed of all
such lands as he was possessed of before this last rebellion, notwithstanding any course taken by Florence against him, and to shew him all other
lawful favours for his encouragement to do Her Majesty service, as I know,
of yourself you are willing to do, and to hold me
                "Your very loving and assured friend,
                                        "Robt. Cecyll.
    "This seemeth reasonable to me; but if you know any cause to the
contrary you may use it at your discretion.
    "August 1601."

With the tidings of the arrest of Florence went to England
many documents, the depositions of spies and traitors, and
intercepted letters, all proving what needed no proof; and
without which Carewe would have acted precisely as he did
with them !

Long ago the writer of these pages disclaimed all intention of striving to clear the memory of Florence from the
charge of high treason; sufficient for him is the endeavour
to remove from his fame the suspicion of dishonest dealing
towards his countrymen. Florence desired to obtain what
was his by inheritance, by marriage, and by election. The
Queen desired to drive out of Desmond Donal and the
Geraldines, then in open rebellion. A bargain was made;
Florence undertook to withdraw his Sept from rebellion ; to
recover his country at his own charges, and to hold it from
the Queen, in contradistinction to the tenure of Donal, which
was from O'Neill.

If Cecyll overlooked the natural consequences of this
bargain the fault, or the folly, was his. Carewe felt them
from the first day he set foot in Munster ; he fancied that the
loss of the province was resulting quickly from them ; and,
when he found no other means of freeing himself from his
perplexities, he did it, as he has himself plainly acknowledged,
simply by an act of violence and bad faith ; and all the documents collected at Cecyll's desire to prove Florence's treason,
were but the *appearances* necessary decently to cover the
act he had done. When Florence was arrested, then saw the
world proof of his great prudence and wisdom ! The Pacata
Hibernia says that "there was found in his various residences
a whole sea of traitorous papers."

Some few letters from FitzThomas, from the Northern
Chiefs, and from a Spanish prelate and his secretary, are,
indeed, printed in that volume ; but most, if not all of them,
were *given* by Florence to Carewe, during the days of their
political fencing. That he had a continuous intercourse with

agents of his own, that is, with relations sent and maintained
by him in Spain, seems certain ; and that much correspondence, carried on in some disguised fashion in his name, may
be to this day extant in Spanish archives is likely ; but in his
own handwriting not one single letter (save a few unintelli-
gible allusive lines, written to the White Knight) was discoverable ! But even if a whole ocean of treasonable documents *had been* discovered, they would have afforded no justi-
fication of his arrest. " It was Florence's fashion," wrote
Carewe, " *evermore before he would come unto me, to send for a
new protection, without any proviso inserted in it, to be answerable
for any breache of 'former protection, so as every protection was a
sufficient safeguard to free him 'from any offence of an older date !*"
At the time he was seized "his pardon was under the seal ;
by which he was enjoined, by a time prefixed, to put in assurance for his further loyalty." Had Florence neglected to do
this before the expiration of that time, his neglect would have
been at his own risk ; he would have been unprotected, and
liable to arrest, " but at the time I committed him," wrote
Carewe, " *there were but* 14 *days to come unexpired !*" In
few words, Florence was residing in Cork, by Carewe's wish,
under safeguard of the Queen's pardon and protection ! Had
the President not given him such " protection," he would
have protected himself, by abiding within the fastnesses of
his own country ; and Carewe would have no more ventured
into the neighbourhood of the Palace, or Castle Logh, in the
wilds of Killarney, than he would into the Glynns, amongst
the O'Byrnes, the Kavanaghs, and the relations of Owen
O'Nassie. How far beyond the reach of Carewe he would
have been within his own country the reader may judge from
the results of the only two attempts that were made to penetrate within it. We read in the Pacata Hibernia, that—

" When the Lo: President sent the Sheriff J. Barry into some of
Florence's lands, no sooner did he enter his country, but he was presently
resisted ; and before he could make his retreat, some of his men were
murthered ! The like measure was also offered to some of the garrison of
Kerry, who had no sooner set foot beyond the Mang, a river that parteth
Kerry from Desmond, but they were instantly assaulted by Florence's followers, and two of the soldiers slain."

Carewe had written to Cecyll that Florence was an idiot !
Cecyll replied that he was a fool !

Carewe wrote when Florence, trusting to the Queen's
protection, came to him in Cork ! Cecyll answered when
Florence was in the Tower, and offered to show him the
Queen's *pardons !*

Happily Carewe's thorough knowledge of the conscience of his correspondent, the Queen's Principal Secretary, removed all inducement from his mind to endeavour to disguise the nature of the act he had done. It was a simple act of perfidy! he did it, and acknowledged it as ingenuously as he had narrated his dealings with Nugent for the service upon John FitzThomas, and his bargains with Dermod O'Connor, and the false FitzGibbon, for the betrayal of his brother. Had any one but Carewe recorded the capture of Florence we should doubtless be believing to this day, that the Lo: President had religiously waited for the expiration of the fourteen days—the full period yet to run of the Protection —that Florence had refused to sue out his pardon, and that there were no means left to deal with so contumacious a rebel but by his arrest, to which with great difficulty, and much persuasion of the Earl of Thomond, FitzEdmond of Clone, and the others of the Council, the Lo: President was brought to consent.

In honest accord with the narrative sent by Carewe to the Privy Council on the 18th of June, was the despatch which followed, four days later to the Lo: Deputy, and Council at Dublin, " his cunning carriage hath been such in the management thereof (of his treasons, &c.) as I find him screened by Her Majesty's pardon, assuring the same unto him without touch!"

" 1601. *June* 22. CAREWE *to the* Lo. DEPUTIE *and* COUNCIL.

" It may please your Lo: and the rest, I haue latelie proceeded to the triall of the Arch Traitor James Fitz Thomas, by the ordinarye course of law ; who now remayneth a prisoner condemned, and readie from me, to answer Her Matie's discrecion, as she shall please further to determine of him. But sinse, upon such good causes as shall appeare sufficientlye war-rantable, I haue alsoe commytted to prison Florence MᶜCartye; againstt whom I am well able to proove, as well bye manye examinacions of re-duced Traitors, as by letters sent unto him by Tirone, and O'Donnell, and the Spanish Bishopp, that was in Ulster, (all with myself) and by other particular good circumstances approoving the former, that since his coming in uppon protection he desysted not from conspyring again rebellion with Spaine, Ulster Traitors, and to raise new nocions of turmoyles in the harts of these provincials. *Yett hath his cunning carriage been such in the management thereof, as I find him screened in his having Her Majesty's pardon, assuring the same unto him without touch !* " But in respect of the damage his libertie would work to these Pro-vinces, knowing him, besides, to be the onlie evill instrument now within this province, I do propose to keep him restrayned, and to look no lesse carefullie, and narrowlie to him than unto James Mᵒ Thomas, having re-solved to reserve them both in the condicion they be, until I receive Her Majesty's pleasure, to whom, and the Lords I have alreadie particularly related my proceedings with them. And now that I have these two potent Earls (of their own making) both in Her Matie's hands, although John Mc Thomas should, (taking upon him the title his brother did, and thereuppon endeavour to get new ayds to infest Munster). I doubt the lesse of any accident to work alteracion : And besides him I do not know anie one man of the province that is now able with power to raise head against Her Matie.

" &c.   &c.,
" GEORGE CAREWE.

" At Cork."

The reader may remember that not many months before this last letter was written, Cecyll had, in a moment of great indignation, urged upon Carewe the hurried execution of John Annyas, and that the policy of the President had suspended that severe sentence; the same thing shortly occurred with regard to the captive Earl of Desmond.

" 1602.   Jany. 14.   CAREWE to CECYLL.

" In a letter of yours to my Lo: Deputy you write that your fingers in England tickle to hang James Fitz Thomas : for a little while it were not, in my opinion, unwise to spare him. His brother is now in the province not followed by many, which I think grows out of a respect which the followers have in harming him in the Tower ; but when this petty rebellion in Munster is extinguished, to make him there a fair example were no errour, &c. &c.

" GEO. CAREWE.'

CHAPTER XV.

IN the winter of 1589, Florence crossed the Irish Channel for the first time as a State prisoner, in custody of Chichester, on his way to the Tower of London. His first captivity in that, and other prisons and on bail within three miles of London, lasted for eleven years and some months : the reader will presently see him, in this summer of 1601, start a second time on the same melancholy voyage, in custody of Sir Anthony Cooke, to begin a series of imprisonments, first in the Tower, and subsequently in every jail, without exception, in the British metropolis; not this time for a little more than eleven years, but for a little less than forty!

His first captivity was for a crime difficult accurately to specify,—for "his marriage!" this second for "Treason," but for treason "*in the management of which he was screened*, said the man who had kidnapped him, *in having Her Majesty's pardons assured unto him without touch*," then he was prisoner "for reasons known to your Lordships," at present "Prisoner by discretion."

And now, might we, with him, fairly turn our backs for ever upon his native land, the country of which it may be said, in defiance of all contradiction, that *no land, of which history has trustworthy record, ever existed which has been the victim of conquerors so rapacious! rulers so base! laws so cruel! and misery of every kind so long lasting! A country which had a convicted Felon for the Governor of a great Province*, Captains like Flower and Bostock who *slaughtered churles and poor people, and drowned the cattle, and burned the corn of whole districts!* Where it was not an uncommon political proceeding for an official of the Government at Dublin—Sir Geoffery Fenton, for example—to suggest to the Queen's Principal Secretary, or Her Lord High Treasurer "to move Her Majesty to write to the Lord Deputy, or the General Commanding her Forces, to '*Draw a Draught*' upon any Irish chieftain that was troublesome, and out of easy reach!" And where, to teach civility, were sent, by the evidence of

Sir William Herbert, "lewd indiscreet men who measured conscience by commoditie, and law by lust."

But though Florence was removed there remained many behind, of his Sept and relatives, whose names have been long before the reader, and in the sequel of whose fortunes he may continue to take interest. The following letters will exhibit in clear and straightforward language the efforts of Carewe to justify his conduct towards Florence—the feeble plaint of some lingering feeling of shame! the first and only utterance of a soon-stifled remorse—the condition of the national struggle after Florence was removed from all share in it; the influence upon it, in Carewe's opinion, of Florence's withdrawal; the landing, and failure, of the Spaniards; the last convulsions of the rebellion in Munster; the submission of the Sept; the fate of many of Florence's relatives and friends; the hope of a fresh expedition from Spain; the uneasiness of Carewe, and the Privy Council! and, based upon all these circumstances, the hope of Florence, by the exercise of the same ingenuity which had so well served him before, to persuade the English Government again, that he alone could tranquillize Munster, drive Donal again out of Desmond, reconcile his people to their rulers, and render void for ever all attempts of Spain upon Ireland.

" 1601. Augst 6. CAREWE to the PRIVY COUNCIL.

" . . . ´ As I am informed, Florence Mc Carty did advise their (the Spaniards) cominge to Corke, as the meetest place unto the wch all the Provinciall rebels might best assemble. The consideračon whereof, albeyt my care is equall to all the citties indifferently, yet the defence of this town (for the reasons aforesaid) I do most specially regarde.

" Dermot Moyle McCarty brother to Florence (whome likewise I wold have restrayned,) fynding his owne guilt upon the detenčon of his brother, is fledd this province, and (as I understand) is gone into Ulster, where as he can do little harme, so when he retorns, I dowt not but to make him to repent his relaps. The stayinge heare thus longe of James Fitz Thomas and Florence McCarty from thence, hath ben occasioned by the employm^t of the Queenes shipp this moneth already at Limericke, unlading there the munitions aboard her; for that I purpose to employ her for the waftinge of them over, I do now daily expect her retorne, and then will forthwth send them to yor L^{l_s}, &c. &c.

" GEO. CAREWE.

" At Cork 6th Augs^t 1601."

" 1601. August 6. CAREWE to CECYLL.

" Sir,

" Dermod Moyle McCarty Florence his brother, ever since his restraynt hathe refrayned to come att me; and, as I heare, is gone into Ulster, but in Munster I am sure he is nott. His mallice to the State and our nacion

Z

is no lesse than his brother's, but his abilitie to do harme is very little, and yett he is much vallianter, and wiser then Florence. Yff he were in hand there is nott a man more in this province that I wolde desire to restrayne, &c. &c.

" After I had broken James Mᶜ Thomas forces, and banished his bonies I had my sword over them, (the men of Munster) and might have bene a Tamerlane amongst them ; but then Her Maties chardges coulld nott have bene eased, nor untoe this hower woulld the same heve ended. But yf by Her Matie and the Lˡˢ a sharper course shall be thought more convenient I can att all tymes finde just causes of quarrell to prosecute any one thatt I list to plage, and noe better tyme then now, havinge in my possession all the men's pledges thatt are of quallitie, so as I shall nott need to feare any generall revolt, &c.

" If they Spaniardes do nott come into Irland, I do verelye beleeve thatt the apprehension of James Fitz Thomas and Florence makes the diversion, for but into Mounster I am perswaded they cannot be drawne, and now thatt there assistance fayles them, I knowe nott whatt reason they have to come, or what aydes they can hope of.

" Geo. Carewe.
" Cork 6ᵗʰ Augᵗ. 1601."

In due time, when the Queen's ship made her way from Limerick to Cork, and the wind served, and when FitzThomas had been tried for High Treason by Irish Law, and condemned,—the motive for which proceeding Carewe lucidly explained, and Her Majesty perfectly understood and approved of,—the prisoners, the two potent Earls of their own making, were wafted across the Irish Channel, landed at Bristol, thence conveyed to London, and by order of the Privy Council made over by Sir Anthony Cooke to Sir John Peyton, the Lieutenant of the Tower.

" Carewe to Cecyll.

" Corke this 13ᵗʰ of August 1601.

" It may please your Honnour, the 6ᵗʰ of this monethe I dispatched a packett unto you, but the wynde served nott to deliver att sea untill the nynthe. In thatt I wrote thatt by the nexte James Fitz Thomas, and Florence Mᶜ Cartie shoulld be sent prisoners into England, wᶜʰ now is done by this bearer Sir Anthonye Cooke, your kinsman, &c. Dermond Moyle Mᶜ Cartie, as I did write in my former lettres, is gone into Ullster; but since am advertised thatt his brother Florence did advise him unto it, to drawe Ullster men into Mounster; to rayse a new rebellion, hopinge thatt to appease the rebellion begonne by Dermond his brother, he shall be enlardged. Tyrrell the old rebell is come out of Ullster into Connaught, with 500 Rogues, wᵗʰ a purpose to come for Mounster, as Sʳ Francis Barkley writes; unto whome Dermond Moyle is resorted to persuade his speedier cominge, &c. The three gentlemen which I lately restrayned, viz Dermond Mᶜ Owen, Teig Mᶜ Cormocke, and O'Mahon ; the first is a gentleman of great land, of Florence's surname, his cousin german in blood, and maried to his cousin german; the second, likewise of his surname and maried to his sister, and the third his aunt's sonne: by their restraynts his brother Dermond will want the helpe he expected.

" I have formerlye sent unto you, from tyme to tyme, such things as concerned Florence Mᶜ Cartie; but because these papers may chaunce to be missinge, wth these I send unto your Honnour the originalls of sundry lettres directed unto him, and a great many of examinations; the examinatt's names, except itt be uppon necessitie, I wishe might be concealed, for ells there lyves may perhappes be taken in revendge, wᶜh would discouradge others to reveale the like hearafter; but yf itt be needfull to make them knowne, it were bettre thatt they did undergoe his mallice then the matter shoulld want proofe. Those letters written from James Mᶜ Thomas unto him were sent unto me by himsellfe, to disguise his treasons, for att the same tyme, and evermore, (as James Mᶜ Thomas confesses unto me, he did, in like sorte, show my lettres written unto himself) unto him: he will sware damnablye thatt he was ever in hart a subject, and thatt wᶜh he did was but to temporize wth the enemye to save his people, (as he terms them) from ruininge; and likewise ascribes unto himsellfe thatt he did banishe the buonies out of Mounster; but these particular examinations now sent, iustified by divers nott knowinge one of another, and the lettres directed unto him approves his treasonable hart; and as for the banishing of the buonies, he was the last man in Mounster thatt did continew buonies in pay; yf there be any scruple thatt may seeme doubtfull in the examinations, lett me understand of itt, and I will make itt evident. I do likewise send you the examinations of James Fitz Thomas; he can say little of any worthe, being but a dull spirited traytor, and understandinge no more of his owne business then by his counsyle was put into him, &c. &c.

" Before Sʳ Anthony wᵗʰ his chardge do com to London I humblye pray you to send a direction whither he shall carry them, thatt they may be disposed of to their Lordships' likinge. So humbly rest

"Yours Honor's humbly to serve you,

"GEORGE CAREWE.

" Corke this 13 Aug. 1601."

The President was not left long in suspense as to the effect produced in the minds of the Queen and her Secretary by the apprehension of Fitz Thomas, and the sagacious mode of his treatment of him, by which the scruples of law had been satisfied, and the prisoner's life and estates placed at the Queen's disposal.

" CECYLL to CAREWE.

" June 29, 1601. SIR GEORGE.

" The dispatche which Patricke Crosbie brought hath not a little raysed your reputacyon, for I know not how by force or counsell more could have ben performed, which are Her Majesty's own words. Where you have 'determined to send him over alive Her Majestie allowethe well of your judgement, but especyally in that you ingaged the Provynce in his condemnacion before. Synce I haue receved a lettre from you of your apprehendinge of Florence, in whose case I pray you spare not sending over of any proofes you can, for although Her Majestie is not lykelie to proceed vygorouslie, yet she accounts yt an excellent pledge to haue him safelie sent hither, &c. &c.

Z 2

" I have sent you herewithall a lettre to'the White Knight from my Lords, and Her Majestie hath taken notyce of his sonne, that is here with my Lo of Thomond, and hath lette him kisse her handes with very gracious vsage, &c."

Sir George Carewe would need all the encouragement that the gracious words of the Queen could give him, for the great storm was gathering over his province, the coming of the Spaniards was looked for daily, and it was well known that their expedition was destined for Cork or Limerick. English reinforcements had been promised, but were not yet arrived, and Carewe's alarm was lest the Spanish fleet should come before them. From this apprehension he was also speedily freed.

" 1601. *Sept*. 12. CAREWE *to* CECYLL *from Cork.*

" Now thatt the supplies are come, my hart is eased of a great burthen; and yf the Don Diegos do make an attempt uppon any of the citties in Mounster, my hope is to make them know their errour; assuringe myselfe to holld the same untill I be releeved wth more force, and then I cannot accompt them to be bettre then enfans perdus. As for the provincials I doubt nott of there good natures, beinge naturallye apt to villainie, and therefore am provided, as Tirone's man sayd of his m^r "to be craftie for craftie!" nott purposinge to put myselfe sillilie into their hands to be overtaken as many of my countryemen have beene.

" Cormocke Oge, sonne and heyre to Cormocke Mc Dermond L of Muskrye, is now in Oxford att Schoole, by me recom̃ended to the Deane of Christchurche; by his father he is extreemlye beloved; to keepe him on assured terms of obedience (allbeitt he hathe another sonne, for his pledge in the Queen's hands) itt were good thatt underhand there shoulld be a good eye kept uppon him, thatt he shoulld nott unknowne retourne for Irland: the boy is very forward, of a great witt and spiritt, and att the least 16 yeres olld; hereof I pray your Honour to geve notice to the Deane to be carefull. Ever since Pierce Lacies sonnes were put into my hands, they have bene prisoners att the Queen's chardge; now thatt there father is dead, I thinke itt meet thatt the Queene shoulld be eased of itt, and the chilldren, uppon sureties, tobe enlardged; but yett because hereafter I am assured thatt wthin a few yeres they will be rebells, wthout direction from England, I dare nott lett suche whelpes loose. Florence his sonne thatt is likewise a pledge, now thatt his father is prisoner, yf he be nott enlardged he must be kept at the Queen's chardge. I understand his mother att her goinge into England meanes to be a suter unto me to permitt her to carry him over, whereunto I do purpose to assent, to ease Her Matie of an needlesse chardge; and his beinge in England is as muche saftie for her as yf he were remayninge in Cork. Touchinge Captein Bostocke I have done all thatt I may to discover and find the papers you wrote of, and have searched his coffers, but can find nothinge: the pretext I made was for certayne com̃issions graunted unto him and others about the title of O'Mahon's lands, whereof he had a portion, wch for Her Matie's especiall service was required.

" GEO. CAREWE

" Cork this 12 of Sepr 1601."

Whilst the Ministers were in daily expectation of hearing of the arrival of the Spaniards in Munster, Florence and Fitz Thomas were awaiting their examination before the Privy Council. There was not indeed any need of questioning the Earl, for he was already under sentence of death, except to obtain from him any testimony that could incriminate his fellow-prisoner; and in effect, when he was summoned to the presence of Sir Robert Cecyll, the chief questions put to him had reference to Florence! Then again in a marked manner was apparent the great prudence which ruled the conduct of Florence under all circumstances. He then, and upon every available occasion afterwards, defied any man living to convict him of any overt act of disloyalty, except the single irregularity into which he had been forced, in self-defence, by Flower and Bostock, and which had been included in the unlimited pardons which he had received at various times since. The incessant complaint, running through all his petitions, to the Privy Council, and to Cecyll himself, for years to come, will be found to be that *he had never been called to account for any action during his brief period of rule in Desmond!* It might be supposed that if the revelations of any man could compromise him, they would be those of Fitz Thomas, with whom he had been, to say the least, on terms of the strictest intimacy during the insurrection, and of whom he was believed to be a guide and adviser throughout! And yet from Fitz Thomas nothing to his prejudice could be elicited that was capable of proof. Of the " whole sea of traitorous correspondence found in his houses," no single document bearing his signature had been discovered; but there was in the hands of the authorities a copy of a certain letter written to the Pope, which bore the signatures, genuine or otherwise, of " O'Neill, James Desmond, MacCartie Mor, and Dermod MacCartie, *alias* McDonogh." This letter had caused immense anger in the bosom of Elizabeth; not that it contained any passages personally offensive, but because it prayed for a renewal of the Bull of Excommunication issued against her by Pius Quintus of happy memory. It was the desire of Cecyll to ascertain whether Florence had in reality placed his signature to this letter !

Fitz Thomas acknowledged that his own signature was genuine, and said that Florence had signed it ! Florence denied it, and the prisoners were confronted. The following letter will explain the mistake into which the Earl had fallen, and inform Carewe what the Secretary concluded from his interview with his captives.

"1601.   *Sept^r.* 10.   CECYLL *to* CAREWE.

"Nowe I must touche what happened synce my last of our newes of
Spain, and the examynacion of Desmonde and Florence.
   "For Desmonde I fynd him more dyscreet then I haue hard of hym,
and for Florence the same which I ever expected, which is a malycious
vayne ffoole.   When he came to be examyned he pryncipally and absolutely
denyed that he had don anything in the begynning, but that which he had
warrant to doe from the Commissioners in Munster tyll he had recovered
his countrye; and that for the combynacyon with Spanyards it should
never be proved, especially that particular concerning his writing to the
Pope, when Tyrone was in Munster, or at any tyme.   In which poynt
James Mc Thomas being confronted with him dyd not directly mayntayne
it that he had seen his hande, but that he was privy totheir consultatyons;
and that O'Kegan, when he came for his hand, told him Florence shold
joyne to; mayntayning it there resolutely that whether he wrytt or no, he
was present at all the counsells, and gave his full consent.   He likewise
contesteth agaynst the report that anie message he should send by the
White Knight's daughter ; and for the dissuading of Thomas Oge, (to surrender the Castle of Castle Maing) pretendeth that you were not discontented with it, because you could have been content it should have ben
his act.
   "To be short, he makes it verye merytorious to have delyvered Tyrone's
packetts to you, and I perceaue will draw in all his crymes so farre within
the reache of his pardon, as we must only make him a prysoner by discrecion, and prayse you for your dyscrecion to put it within our power.
And so hathe the Queene willed me to wryte unto you.   Of the Spaniards
purposes I interrogated them; Desmonde affirmes that they meant to come
for Lymericke; but Florence would needes have it that they intended
rather for Gallaway, wherein I assure you I join with hym, being a place
nearer to receaue correspondency from the Rebells then to come into
Munster, where their party was broken, and where the Northern Traytors
are so farre removed from them, &c.

   " From the Court at Aldermeston,
        Sir Humphrey Foster's House,
        10 Septr. 1601."

   We are informed by the author of the Pacata Hibernia
that the sole service rendered to the Queen for the sake of
the young Fitzgerald, the Tower Earl of Desmond, was the
surrender of the fortress of Castle Maing.   So doubtful was
Carewe whether even this much would be accomplished for
his sake, that " fighting Florence with his own weapons, and
having no fear of being overreached by him," he accepted his
offer to go and persuade Thomas Oge FitzGerald, to whose
custody it had been entrusted by the Sugaun Earl, to surrender it to *him,* of course to be held for Her Majesty !   Fitz-
Gerald chose rather to deliver it up, for young FitzGerald's
sake, to Carewe !   Cecyll, not clearly understanding the use
Carewe was making of Florence's weapons, interpreted this

attempt of Florence as an act of treason! Had Carewe
made any charge against Florence in this matter, it would
have been for striving to persuade Thomas Oge not to surrender it at all! but to hold it, as in common honour he was
bound to do, for him who had gained it by his own sword,
and who had entrusted it to him! If Thomas Oge was justified in surrendering Castle Maing to the President, why not
Sir W. Stanley in surrendering Deventer to the Spaniards?
If Stanley was a traitor, what was Thomas Oge Fitz-
Gerald?

Such was the result of the examination of Florence! the
sea of traitorous correspondence, the confessions of rebels
who sold their evidence for their pardon, all that his enemies
could suggest, or the President collect, amounted to this, that
"Carewe's discretion was worthy of praise; that all his
crymes Florence had drawn so far within the reache of his
pardons as he must be made *a prisoner at discretion!*" Whatever other designation Florence may have merited from these
correspondents, they would have done well to seek for it;
assuredly neither of the men so signally outwitted was wise
if he were foolish.

From the presence of Cecyll the captives were taken back
to their separate cells; and from that moment all trace of
their Tower life would be lost, were it not for the Governor's
quarterly bills, many of which have perished, but some, and
happily those relating to the early, if not the earliest, period
of their imprisonment, are preserved. Very few items in
these financial records suffice to reveal the effect produced
on minds of unequal strength, by the memories and regrets of
the last two years, and, by the prospect before them. On
Florence's account charge is made for "a nurse during his
sickness and a surgeon;" but in the case of " *The Titular
Earl of Desmond,*" is the mournful item of " Watchers with
him in his lunacy."

The more vigorous mind of Florence stood firm, nay, as
was speedily shewn, acquired resolution and strength from the
hopeless nature of his position, and from the gladness—as
suggested by Carewe—that he felt at his brother's death.
The mind of Fitz Thomas, we may hope, soon rallied; for
this charge appeared but once.

The demands of Sir John Peyton, Lieutenant of Her Majesty's Tower of London, for one quarter, from St. Michael's
Day, 1602, till the feast of the Birth of our Lord God,
next :—

" Florence McCarthy,

" For the diett and charges of Florence
McCarthy for the foresaid 12 weeks and 8
days, at 53s. 4d. per week. £33 6 8
" For his washing, and to the Barber, for
Apparel, and other necessaries. 7 13 6
" Item for Physicke, Surgeon, and one to
attend him in his sicknesse............   8 17 3

" For James Mc Thomas,

" Sayd tyme at £3 per week, Physicke,
Sourgeon, and Watcher with him in his
lunacy. "

These Tower bills continue till Lady Day, 1604, at which
time both prisoners were removed, one to the gatehouse, and
thence to the Fleet, and the other to the Marshalsea.

THE SUGAUN EARL OF DESMOND.

We shall have no need to make further mention of the
unfortunate Earl of Desmond; it may therefore be permitted
—amongst these sketches of traitors, and arch-traitors, and
vile ungrateful rebels—to add a few compassionate paragraphs to the memory even of James FitzThomas. The
motives which led him to join in the great insurrection of
O'Neill, were doubtless chiefly the great injustice of distributing amongst the English undertakers, the estates of the Geraldines, which were in reality his, and denying him the
Earldom; but in addition were his religion, and the traditional alliances in policy and blood, of his race for four
centuries, with the mere Irish Chieftains around him.

But he was, to use Carewe's words, "unmeet to be a
rebel," for he was of gentler nature and nurture than was
suited to the times, and to the fortunes forced upon him.
He could say with truth that during his day of prosperity,
"he at all times spared life, and befriended the English who
fell into his hands!" As a leader of men, he was the feeblest
that could have been found of all that were in action. Morrough-ny-mart, the great Commander of Sir Donogh
McCarthy's foot-forces, had he had 8,000 well-weaponed men
under his sole command, with an undefended city—Cork—
before him, containing barely 1,700 soldiers, and with a
friendly force, scarcely inferior to his own, in threatening
demonstration, all but in acknowledged alliance, in possession of every place of available retreat, would surely have

made other issue than *he* did of the contest on which land and life, and the honour of his race were staked! James Fitz-Thomas survived his fall a few years, all of which were spent in one or other of the London prisons.

The designation of the "*Sougaun Earl*" or "the Earl of Straw" appears to have been fixed upon him by the mild contempt of the bonies, and fighting men of Desmond.

But there was an Earl living who deserved this slighting epithet better than he did!

In FitzThomas there was at least nothing Sugaun or Sham; in his title to the Earldom, as we have repeatedly shown; nor, as long as his liberty lasted, was there in the position he occupied. "He was, said Carewe, the most powerful Geraldine that had ever been of his race." But he who *was*, in every respect, a Sugaun Earl, was the phantom Earl of Elizabeth. By birth he possessed *no title!* for his father had been an usurper of the rights of his elder brother, Sir Thomas of Desmond, the father of FitzThomas! the very patent of the title that was intended for him by the Queen, was a sham! it was stopped by her own orders, in the hands of Carewe, until it should be seen whether the followers of his house acknowledged him as their Lord. Sugaun or Sham was he as a chieftain! Sugaun as an Irishman at all! Sugaun even as a man! Of these two Geraldines, the younger died about three months after his cousin arrived to take his place in that dreary Tower, in which he had spent the whole of his life, with the exception of a few years of infancy, and one of his wretched manhood! The elder languished, some say for eight, others for twelve years. The epitaphs of each have reached us, and few more touching are upon record! That of FitzGerald was written by himself to Cecyll very soon after his landing in Ireland.

"I find my honourale good Lord kind unto me; but *I am contemptible unto the country.*" ·

Carewe himself wrote for FitzThomas, the less unfortunate of these Earls, a few sufficient words of pleasant remembrance, in substance the same as were afterwards written for Florence.

"He was more beloved than any man of his day!"

Other inscriptions, and widely unlike these, were prepared for the tablets more publicly designed in their memory.

"I must confess, says the Pacata Hibernia, that he (the young Fitz Gerald) was *too good to live among such traitorly followers!* and no man living had a more willing desire to serve Her Majesty than himself, but in all the time of his being in Ireland, not one rebel did, for his sake, submit himself to Her Majesty! He embarked on the 22ᵈ of March, (1601,) and landed at Miniarde, in Somersetshire, and so to the Court, where after a few months he died. The Letters Patents which Her Majesty had granted for his restoration the President never delivered unto him."

"I may well term him (FitzThomas) a notorious traytour," says the same author, "because he was, within one year before his apprehension, the most mighty Geraldine that had been of the Earles of Desmond, his predecessors; for it is certainly reported that he had 8,000 men, well armed, under his command at one time; all which he employed against his lawful Sovereign. And secondly, a notorious traytour, because, &c., &c. So far had the rancour of malice corrupted his venemous heart! &c., &c."

From the presence of Sir Robert Cecyll, the prisoners were led back to their cells in the Tower, the Earl under sentence of death, with "the fingers of the Lords tingling to hang him;" and Florence, to commence a series of letters, petitions, expurgations of his whole past life, and *the incessant prayer to be brought to trial*, destined to outlast the lives of every man who had been, or then was, his accuser.

As naturally as Browne had had recourse to Carewe, on the first tidings of Florence's restraint, Donal had betaken himself to O'Neill, who, seeing that Florence was removed from all further possible co-operation in the national cause, and seeing the whole Sept of the MacCarthys without a leader, and Desmond disposed rather to the neutral policy of Florence, at a time when the arrival of the Spaniards was looked for hourly, readily received him again as MacCarthy Mor; for the same reasons he met with no opposition from the O'Sullevans, and so at once resumed his old title, and the country with it.

The storm so long impending burst at last. On the 21st of September, 1601, John Meade, the Mayor of Cork, despatched a series of couriers to the Privy Council, to the Lord Deputy, and the Lord President, conveying the intelligence that at that moment of writing, the Spanish fleet was sailing into the harbour of Kinsale. A multitude of letters and despatches followed to the President, to the Privy Council, to Cecyll, and to the Lord Deputy, with all the rumours that had instant birth, of the various Irish Chieftains, who were repairing hourly to the Spanish camp.

"*The* MAYOR *of* CORK *to the* LO: PRESIDENT.

" Rᵗ Honᵇˡᵉ. This very hower about six a clock in the afternoon of this day being the 21ˢᵗ of Septʳ. came a post to me from Kinsale, aduertising of

55 shippes seen this afternoon hard by the Old Head of Kinsale, which I
suspect are our enemies; and the wind serves them well for this harbour or
Kinsale, and so in hast,

"J. MEADE, Maior."

"1601. *Sept*ʳ. 23.   MEADE *to* CAREWE.

" Amonge their men is one Teige McCartey, and one Farsinge, whome
in my memoire, hath served Florence McCarthy; my harte wisheth your
speedie returne.

" Among them is one Cormac McFinin (MacCarthy) a chief leader."

"1601. *Sept*ʳ. 23.   SIR JOHN DOWDALL *to* CECYLL.

" Uppon their arrivall they specially demanded for Florence Mac
Carthy.

" They demanded where Florence McCarthy was, and James Fitz
Thomas; the Sovereign answered they were in the Tower of London; upon
which answer the man turned back again to his General."

"1601. *Sept*r. 24.   ORMOND *to the* PRIVY COUNCIL.

" This Cormac McFinin Carty named in the Mayor's letter is said to be
Florence McCarthy's servant: and Don Morrice is Cousin Germain to the
late Earl of Desmond, who was slain in his, rebellion in the time of my
government in Munster (1583)."

Christopher Galway, examined by the Mayor of Water-
ford, says that on board the Spanish ships are, Archer, the
Spanish Archbishop of Dublin, Darby McCarthy, and Cormac
McCarthy, who are called Captains.

"1601. *Nov*r. 7.   H. POWER *to* CECYLL.

" Donell (Dermot Moyle) McCarthy Florence's brother is guide of the
forces under Tirrell sent by Tirone, they will be 4000 men at their
joining."

The evil destiny of Don Dermutio Carty, the writer of
the Spanish letter alluded to some pages back, had led him to
attach himself to the ill-fated expedition of the Spaniards; he
fell into the hands of Carewe on the surrender of the fort of
Rincoran, and the reader will scarcely need to be told what
next happened to him.

"1601. *Dec*r. 23.   CAREWE *to* CECYLL.

" Don Juan de Aguila was lately hurt in the face with a splinter of a
stone broken with a great shot, the wound not great.   The Spaniards discipline the Carbry rebells after their manner, and arm them with corselets,
with taces down tothe knee.   As yet no other septs of the Irishry of

Munster are in rebellion but the Carties, and their followers, and the chief among them is Florence's brother, and cousin germains. *If he had been now at liberty he would have had above* 3000 *to have followed him,* whereas all that are yet joined with Tirone are not above 500 at the uttermost. In my former letters I wrote unto you that Don Dermucio Cartie, a servante of Florence's, was taken, and since executed. Of late we understand that Don Carlos Cartie, another of Florence's followers, and a captain, is dead of a wound received in the great sally upon our artillery the 2ᵈ of this present."

"*Decʳ.* 28. CAREWE *to* CECYLL.

" I thank God that James Fitz Thomas and Florence are in England; they were the heads of the English and Irish in Munster, and upon them two the whole province would have relied, and no doubt but a general defection would have ensued, by the example whereof it is very probable that the other provinces, in the like manner, would have taken example, for the corruption of this kingdom is universal, and it is a rare matter to find a loyal subject in it. I have in Corke Irish letters sent unto Florence from Tirone and others, which will confirm his former treasons, wherewith your honor is already acquainted; when I may have a time to start thither I will send them unto you. As yet in Munster there is none gone into rebellion, but Florence's kinsmen, and followers, and those which in former times did ruin his fortune. In the king's pay that are entertained there is O'Sullevan Beare, who hath 200 foot, Donogh McCarty 100, his brother Florence 120, O'Donevan 100, and Felim McCarthy 100, in all 620."

Well might Sir George Carewe "thank God that FitzThomas and Florence McCarty were safe in the Tower !" The first inquiries of the Spaniards on arrival were for them, and when they heard of their apprehension, "they were seized with consternation, and knew not what counsel to take." The history of this attempt of Spain to assist the native Irish against the forces of Elizabeth, has been too circumstantially written by historians, English and Irish, to need further account of it in these pages. The reader knows how, under the walls of Kinsale, the defeats of Bagnal, Harrington, and Clifford, of the Pass of Plumes, the contemptuous chase of Essex out of Munster, and a multitude of minor overthrows, and flights, fightings-in-retreat, and feats of footmanship were avenged! Well we know how, after one of the most marvellous marches on record, the forces of O'Neill and O'Donnel were united ; how the wisdom of O'Neill was over-ruled by the chivalry of O'Donnel ; how the Irish army, urged by incessant entreaties of Don Juan, marched out one early morning in the darkness to attack the English camp ; how their intention had been betrayed ; how, missing their way in the dark, and becoming separated, the foremost bodies found themselves unexpectedly in the face of a force already awaiting them, and how, attacked in their disorder, they instantly broke and fled! Irish writers, humbled and astonished at this sudden and disgraceful overthrow, have been accustomed to believe that there existed some cause for it, hidden and enigmatical, which time might eventually clear up! It suggests itself that Spanish archives may contain this painful secret. Spanish archives may indeed discover to us why, after enticing the Irish under the walls of Kinsale, with a promise of breaking out from its defences, and attacking the English in the rear, whilst they should be engaged by the Irish forces, Don Juan remained motionless within his trenches; but they can reveal no more than this! They cannot tell us why the Irish, of whom the Four Masters say truly, "previous to this day a small number had more frequently routed many hundreds of the English, than they had fled from them in the field of battle, in the gap of danger (in every place they had encountered) up to this day." The history of this rout and run of Kinsale is fairly told in two lines, by O'Sullevan Bear! in one sentence by the Earl of Thomond! "Ita panico terrore," says O'Sullevan, "omnes perculsi sunt, vel potius divina vindicta fugati." "Manifest was the displeasure of God," say the Annals of the Four Masters, "and misfortune to the Irish on this occasion! The prosperity, chivalry, dignity, and renown of the island were lost in this engagement."

Never since the days of Strongbow had there been so gratifying a chapter added to the glorious narrative of English victories! "The Irish enemy," says Stafford, "consisted of 6,000 foot and 500 horse! Of these, 1,200 were left dead on the field, and 800 were hurt, many of whom died that night! And on our side *one man was killed, three officers and five or six common soldiers hurt!*"

Such was the *battle* of Kinsale! "The Earl of Thomond had read in an old book of Irish prophesies that this great victory was to be! I beseech the reader to believe me," concludes the English historian, "for I deliver nothing but truth."

Thunder and lightning had incredibly wasted 16,000 of the Queen's soldiers in the defiles of Munster. Lord Thomond's Irish prophet betrayed the counsels of O'Neill, led his army astray in the darkness, and thus,—with a brilliant performance of footmanship, and the fall of the English soldier,— finished for another half century the question of the nation's liberty and religion!

. It might have been expected that after the failure of the

Spanish expedition, the native Irish would consider their cause as lost; and, in fact, all further opposition to the President was for a time trampled out in Munster; but the country of O'Neill remained, as hitherto, defiant of the Queen's authority, and the centre of a large national force ready at any moment to burst again into Munster. Furthermore, the pride of Spain had been deeply wounded! O'Donnel had been received with honours little less than royal at the Spanish Court, Don Juan was in disgrace, and every friend of the cause of Ireland was urging the King to send a second expedition before the enthusiasm of the Irish should subside into hopeless submission. Confidential persons, chiefly ecclesiastics, were sent from Spain to ascertain what resources might yet be available for another attempt; large supplies of arms and money were forwarded to O'Neill, and distributed by him amongst the Munster chiefs, who were ready at short notice to renew the struggle.

After the battle of Kinsale, the slaughter of Sir Richard Græme's cornet, and the hurting of the Queen's six common soldiers, Donal and his Munster forces ran with the rest, and was so fortunate as to reach the fastnesses of Desmond, so "unsuitable for service by Her Majesty's forces." When the rest of his countrymen were regaining courage, from the causes we have mentioned, a sudden burst of sunshine, through one of the blackest of storm-clouds, brightened the particular fortunes of Donal. Owen M'Eggan, the Pope's Bishop of Ross, called by Carewe "a traitorly priest; than whom a more malicious traitor against the Crown and State of England never breathed," arrived in Munster, bringing with him a large amount of treasure, of which Donal had his fair share, but—worth all his treasure to Donal—he brought also a certain document from His Holiness, a Bull!—(Pontifical Letters Patents)—*the Legitimation of Donal!*

The priceless value of this document no one could tell better than he, who had been considered all his life through little better than a kerne for the want of it! Who could now dispute his title as M. C. Mor? But even in the first moments of his rejoicing he had no desire for his father's Earldom, now canonically his own; nor can we feel any great surprise at Donal's ignorance of the value of this exalted rank; for the late Earl, his father, had been, in this respect, scarcely wiser than his son. "With his new honor," says the learned Windele, "he never felt comfortable; his haughty followers despised it, and him for its acceptance, and he soon after renounced it; but it was only again to assume it, as

occasions far between served, or made it expedient." Donal's
first act as MacCarthy Mor was to procure a force to ensure
his authority; for this purpose he took into pay Tirell and
400 bonies, and with them he made such preparation as occurred to him for the second coming of the Spaniards.

But the hope of Donal had brief life; no second expedition came from Spain; all prudent men quickly began to send
in their submission to the President, and to solicit the Queen's
mercy; and Donal, "bearing a good affection towards the
Lord President, and relying much also on the Governor's
kindness," hastened to place himself, his title, and all his
pastoral wealth—which was considerable, however come by
—in the hands of Sir Charles Wilmot. Donal's simplicity
upon this occasion stood him in the stead of a master-
stroke of policy; for he presented himself in his own person,
without any capitulation or protection, before the Governor,
"who, perceiving his loyal simplicity"—and his present of
5,000 cows, besides sheep and garrans in great numbers—
"would take no advantage against him, but gave him all
countenance, and contentment that his place could afford."
The good affection which Donal bare to Carewe, Carewe bare
to Donal; and like Sir Charles Wilmot, he thenceforward gave
him all the countenance his place could afford.

The two following letters resume the interrupted romance
of the adventures of Donal; they also convey tidings of the
death of Florence's brother, and the tardy and useless outbreak of the sons of the late Sir Owen, Florence's cousins.

DERMOD MOYLE MACCARTHY.

Of all the MacCarthys in arms against the Queen's government, none was so inveterate a foe to English rule in his
native country as Dermod! he was brave, and able, fondly
attached to his brother, and uniformly guided by his judgement. Carewe would have us believe that Florence used
him, and ever put his life in peril upon trifling occasions, for
his own selfish purposes. It seems never to have occurred to
him that amongst these rebel Irish such a thing as natural
affection could exist; much less that the more active hand of
the younger brother should consent to be guided by the
abler mind of the elder, from any motive but selfishness on
one side, and stupidity on the other. His conception of
human nature was singular! The man shut up in a solitary
cell in the Tower, denied the sight and speech of his fellow-
creatures, would, he doubted not, seem to be *glad*—nay stick
not to swear it—that his only brother should have lost his

life in an accidental fray with his own relatives and allies!
Florence may have pretended many surprising things; he
pretended "to love, honour, and respect me (Sir George
Carewe) as much as any man living;" he pretended that "he
had great faith in my word! great respect for my honour!"
that he believed every word of Carewe's professions of friendship for him! that he knew Sir Robert Cecyll to be the best
of his friends and patrons at the time when he knew also
that these two men had found a man to poison him! all this
he pretended, but he never, as far as we know, pretended to
be glad of his brother's death!

"1602. *April* 13. CAREWE *to* CECYLL.

"The bonies in Munster do begin to shake, thinking that now I am at
leisure to hunt them: divers of them make suit unto me to have my pass
to depart the province; which courtesy I will not deny a Devil that is
weary of my company; and when they return to their dwellings, let every
particular Governor look to his charge! for I will forbear no means un-
sought to rid my government of strangers.
"Even as I was writing this letter Dermond Moyle McCartie,
Florence's brother sent to the Bishop of Cork to entreat me to receive
him into the Queen's mercy; but he is a wicked traitor, yet the Queen can
get nothing by him, for, as I think, he has no inheritance; to kill or take
him will be difficult; but I am sure he shall not long live in Munster,
which is but an ease for a time; for upon every occasion banished men
return and make new fires; the best way to root out such rebels is large
rewards; for a good bag will perform more service than the sword upon
such fugitive traitors; but of the Queen's purse I dare not be too bold.
Donell McCartie, bastard son unto the Earl of Clancar, upon the arrival of
the Spaniards assumed unto himself the name of McArtie More, now
finding his hopes to fail him, makes humble suit to be received to mercy,
and promiseth that if the Queen would bestow upon him the lands which
once she assigned to his portion (which by her letters she willed to be
assured to him) he would quiet all Desmond; which were a good service,
for to appease it by force will be very difficult, by reason of the nature of
the country, which is all mountainous; and when he is humbled, and the
country in subjection it will be very little beneficial to the Queen; for no
Englishmen will dwell in it. The letters he had were taken from him in
a house, which he had, by Florence McCartie; wherefore if his motion be
liked of, I beseech you to cause searches to be made for the copies of it,
in the Counsell book, or with the clerks of the signet; he hath not an acre
of land to loose, and the prosecution of him will be chargeable to the
queen; upon his reduction all the buonies will presently depart; but I dare
not deal in this business, or receive him until I have direction out of
England, lest I should offend, whereof I am fearful, so rest
"Your honours all wholly as
"you have bound me,
"GEORGE CAREWE."

"1602· *May* 29. CAREWE *to* CECYLL.

"Kerry and Desmond are wholly reduced, which happened by a good
blow which S^t. Chas. Willmott gave O'sulevan More, whose son and heir,

Florence's nephew, was then in action. This service was performed by the help of one of Osulevan's men's brothers called Dermond Osulevan, and Donell McCartie, bastard son to the Earl of Clancare, he took out of his country 5,000 cows which hath made Osulevan's son unable any more to give any bonaght, as he did, and utterly wasted that country; the reason that moved Dermond Osulevan to draw this draught, and Donell McCartie to join in it, was the fear the one had that I would hang his son, which was his pledge in Castellmayne; and the hope the other hath that her Majesty will be pleased to give him the 28 plowlands which she gave him at his being in England, and afterwards taken from him .by Florence McCartie. In my opinion the queen may do well to bestow that rough and mountainous land upon him, unfit for our honest men to dwell upon; and I find him honestly inclined to live a subject, who when he is a rebel will at all times be able to carry 1000 men at his heels, to do mischief, and I do verily believe that that small portion of land, which was his father's, will continue him loyal, whereby all Desmond will be contained in obedience. I am sure he will be a suitor for it in England, in the which I wish him good success, for I know it will prove beneficial to the service. Dermond Moyle McCartie the thirteenth of this month was slain by some of O'donovan's men commanded by Fynin McCartie his cousin-german. McCartie Reoghe came also unto the ending of the fight; the cause of his mischance was the carrying away of certain cows from McCartie Reoghe tenants, which was followed by Fynin McCartie, one of St Owen McCartie's sons; and in the first encounter Dermond Moyle was shot; whereupon his men fled, and on both sides not above twelve men hurt and killed; now that he is dead every one strives to have thanks for it, which I plentifully bestow upon them; but I assure you they were sorry for it, which appears by concealing his body, in forswearing that they cannot tell where he is buried; fearing (as indeed I pretended) that I would send his head to Corke. Florence will seem to be glad that his brother is gone and will not stick to swear it; but thus far let my credit prevail with you, that Dermond was his greatest hope to work his enlargement, by doing mischief in Ireland; he had a far better wit, more valiant, and of loose men better beloved and followed than Florence; and by him Florence hoped to establish his fortune .both when he was a rebel, and since he was a prisoner," &c., &c.

Thus does Carewe pay unwilling tribute to the merits of Dermod. " He was valiant, of good wit, and much beloved!" He might have added that he stood higher than any of the minor chieftains then in action, in the estimation of his party, as was proved but few days after his death. When Owen McEgan the Pope's Nuncio came from Spain into Ireland to breathe new fire into the smouldering embers of the actions he brought two letters from the Spanish monarch, beside, treasure to be divided amongst the leaders who had bonies in pay; a considerable portion of this treasure, and one of these Royal letters was addressed to Dermod! The treasure was given to his widow ; the letter was with honour returned to the Spanish monarch, and not improbably by the hands of Dermod's widow, who took her departure at once for Spain.

"1602.   *July* 19.

" The re-examination of Ellyn-ny-Connor vic Fyneen, taken before me the President of Munster; who &c., sayeth :—
" That the King wrote into Munster by the Patache, but two letters, one of them to O'Sulyvan, the other to Dermot Moel McCarty, Florence's brother; but because Dermot was slain, Owen McLigan, who brought the letters, kept Dermott's letter. What was written by the king to other men she knoweth not, nor yet the contents of those two letters aforesaid.
" That the Conde of Caraçena, (who by the Irish is called Earl of the Groyne) did also write unto O'Sulyvan ; but what it contained, or whether he wrote any more letters, she knoweth not.
" That Ellyn ny Donnough (wife to Dermot Moel McCarty) is gone into Spain to be a suitor unto the King for relief, in consideration that her husband was slain in his service.

"   GEORGE CAREWE."

" SIR GEORGE CAREWE *to the* PRIVY COUNCIL, *Jan*. 22, 1602.

" It may please Your Lordships,
" Understanding that the sons of Sir Owen McCarty, and Donogh Reagh McCarty brother to Florence in the Tower, had retired out of Beare into the strength of Carbery with their creates and followers, to the number of 400 fighting men, I commanded this bearer Captⁿ Taafe with the 400 of the Rising out, together with his own troop of horse, and 400 of Sir Edward Wingfield's foot, to draw into those parts, and to endeavour the best service he could upon them, whilst the other forces were busied in Beare ; wherein it pleased God to give him good successe ; for the 5ᵗʰ of this present his foot entering their fastness these Carties before remembered gave them a good skirmishe, and put his men in route, whereof many of them were slain ; which he seeing, being with his troup upon the skert of the woods, charged them into the same, and slew four horsemen of theirs ; whereat their foot amazed, fled ; which Owen McEggan (the Pope's Nuncio, and his Bishop of Ross) perceiving with a drawn sword in one hand and his Portas (his Breviary) and Beads in the other, with 100 men led by himself, came up to the sword, where he was slain. Sir Owen McCarty's sons who formerly had been humble suitors unto me to be protected, and were refused, did now again importune to be received unto the Queen's mercy ; at which time Captⁿ Taafe, not knowing of the good success that our forces had in Beare, and having formerly received instructions from me, after a blow given them, to receive them if it were humbly sought, did accept of their submissions, and hath brought them with Donogh Reagh, Florence's Brother, to me, by which means all the whole country of Carbery, being the largest scope of land of any Lordship in Munster, is clearly reduced, and at this hour no one Traitor remaining in action in it, &c. &c. Touchinge Cormocke McDermond his treasons are manifest, more odious, and more in number than Florence McCartie's. I beseech your Honor that his son at Oxford may be restrained; he is a youth of great expectation among the Irish, (elsewhere he says his father loved him as his own life) and will be exceedingly followed ; and being at liberty would prove as dangerous a Traitor as the father, &c."

It was not without design asserted in an earlier chapter of this volume that " the Irish chieftain in sending his children from him for education in any English school or college

gave a hostage to his rulers!"   On receipt of this letter from
Carewe Cecyll instantly wrote to Oxford to have the son of
Cormac M⁰ Dermod sent up to London, that he might have
him under his own custody. After a while Cecyll wearied of
the charge of his maintenance, and sent him back to Oxford.

One of the earliest cares of Carewe, after the return of
some tranquillity to his province, was to rid himself of the
children whom at an earlier period of his proceedings he had
been so anxious to get into his power as pledges for the conduct of their parents. These were the sons of Florence, of
his brother Dermod, and of Pierce Lacy. These "whelps"
were of no further use, and he was impatient to be relieved
of the burthen of their maintenance. "Well he knew that in
the course of nature these children must within few years
grow into rebels;" but if not allowed to kill them, he had at
least no wish longer to cumber the Queen with their support.
Florence's wife claimed hers; the others were orphans; the
fathers of both had been killed in rebellion.

The name of Florence's wife has not been, during her
husband's difficulties, brought under the reader's notice. Alas!
a painful narrative must accompany the future mention of
this lady. She applied to the President for letters of recommendation to England, whither it was her intention to
repair; and the terms in which the letter of Carewe is worded
leave no room for doubting that by means of threats, and
promises respecting her property, and her children, he had
long since obtained so powerful an influence over her that he
had been able to use her as a spy upon her husband during
the whole period of his stay in Ireland. Upon the occasion
of Florence's first imprisonment, 14 years before, she had, in
defiance of the Vice-President and the Queen, hastened to
England to afford him such consolation as she might, and to
urge upon the Queen a tearful suit for his freedom; and
Florence had repaid her affection by withdrawing his own
petition for leave to return to his country, because she "was
big with child, and he would not leave her."

Now again she followed to his prison, to present herself and her four children to the husband she had betrayed!
The first time she fled after him with a single female attendant, at dusk! following, without question, a servant who was
to conduct her, as best he could, through Munster and over
sea to her husband. Now she bore the President's letters to
Her Majesty's Principal Secretary, as a "poor gentlewoman
who had ever withstood, and repugned as much as in her lay,
the undutiful courses of her husband; and as one whom *he*

*had ever found very 'faithfully and truly affected to the State,
and willing to give the best 'furtherance to Her Majesty's service, either by intelligence or any other means."* These might
be inducements to Cecyll to welcome her to the Court, but
scarcely to her husband to desire her company. What reception she met with from him we shall presently see in his own
words; in the meantime he took his young children to share
and cheer his prison life, and thenceforward Lady Ellen
became a suitor to the Queen and her successor for restitution
of portions of her father's lands, for pensions, small gratuities,
and petty monopolies for herself; never again for her husband!

" 1602. *Dec*ʳ. 16. *From the* LORDS *to the* PRESIDENT *of Mounster.*

" And first touchinge the enlargement of the children of Florence
Mac Carthy, Dermott Moyle (Florence's Brother) and Pierce Lacy, which
children were first restrayned as pledges for the loyaltie and subjection of
their said fathers. For as much as the cause of their imprisonment is for
the most part now removed, and the danger cleared (the one of the said
fathers being in the Tower and the other two slaine in actual rebellion)
you shall understand that Her Majestie is well pleased, the rather for
ease of her charge (unlesse you find other cause to detain them) that they
shall be enlarged uppon good securitie to be taken to Her Majestie's use,
as well of some Lordes, or Cheefe Gentlemen of the countrie that are of
power to restrain their insolences, if when they come to age they should
follow the steppes of their fathers, or attempt anie thing prejudicial to the
State, as alsoe of some marchante or inhabitant of Corporate Townes that
are meniable to the lawes.   " &c.   &c.   &c."

" 1602. *Jan*ʸ. 31. CAREWE *to* CECYLL.

" It may please your honour. This poor gentlewoman the la: Ellen,
the daughter and heir of the earl of Clancarty, and the unfortunate wife
of Florence, having obtained the Lord Deputy's license for her repair into
England, hath desired my letters in her favour to your honour, that inasmuch as her father's living is now in Her Majesty's disposition, and not
accrued to Her Highness by any attainder or other disloyal means, but by
his own meer gift and surrender, and that she hath ever withstood, and
repugned (as much as in her lay) the un lutiful courses of her husband,
your honour would be pleased therefore to be a mean to Her Majesty for
some competent living for her towards her maintenance; being no longer
than during her life, and the state of her father's lands to Her Majesty
being perpetual, which I humbly beseech your honor to vouchsafe her, the
rather that I do know, not only that which she suggesteth to be true, but
also have ever found her very faithfully, and truly affected to the state,
and willing to give the best furtherance to Her Majesty's service that
she could, either by intelligence or by any other means, as by Patrick
Crosbie (who is well acquainted with all that concerneth her cause) can at
large be declared unto your honor. And so I humbly leave her to your
honourable consideration and remain ever as I am bound

" Your honor's most humble ready to serve you
                                        " GEORGE CAREWE.

" Cork, the last of Janʸ 1601/2."

The reader has seen the skill with which, in the instance of Stafford's rude sketch of Florence, the President could, by a few simple touches, give animation to that dreary likeness; he is now presented with a finished portrait, by the same hand, of Sir Owen O'Sullevan, Florence's brother-in-law, so often mentioned in these pages; it is drawn with evident care and much art, but is in the style of Sir Warham St. Leger, and like that great artist's sketch of Sir Owen MacCarthy Reagh, is famous rather for its vigour than its resemblance :—

Letter to Sir R. Cecyll, *dated* 13 *April* 1602.

" O'Sullevan, as Crosbye can tell you, was the inwardest with Florence, of any man in Ireland; his wife will confess no less unto you, and she hath said (which I know she will not deny) that he was the worst counsellor that her husband and had to incite him to treasons; but I must confess unto your honour I did not then believe her, nor hitherto was I ever deceived in any man of Ireland birth but himself, for I took him to be one of the honestest men in this realm : Such another Simon I never saw, or a more smooth, perfidious, dissembling knave ! let your honour be assured that I will plague him soundly, &c."

Similar to this was his spirited profile of two other Irishmen, relatives of Florence—his cousin, Cormac McDermod, Lord of Muskerry, and the Lord Roche, his uncle.

" The most cankered subjects that under-hand support the rebels, are the Lo : Roche, and Cormock McDermod; Roche is a brain-sick foole ! but the other is a subtile fox, under the habitt and pretexte of a subjecte, workinge more villainy against the state than he were able to do if he were in rebellion !"

We know that with tract of time, and the incident change of language, phrases are oftentimes bent aside from the precise signification which they may have borne when originally used. We may, without venturing to meddle with the portrait of Cormac McDermod, suggest that the above sketch of the Lord Roche may not have been intended in so severe a sense as it now bears ! " Brainsick foole !" may possibly have meant no more than "a gentleman of sentimental tastes, a scholar addicted rather to the imaginative, than to the practical pages of literature !" In this sense the character given by the Four Masters to this nobleman would be in accord with the expressions of Carewe.

" The Roche, (say the annals) *i.e.* Maurice, Son of David, died in the month of June of this year (1600). He was a mild, and comely man, learned in the Latin, Irish, and English languages. His son, *i.e.* David, took his place."

CHAPTER XVI.

WE come now to the only scandal in the life of Florence; the
single letter which dwells painfully in the minds of his
countrymen. Irishmen are jealous of the loyalty of their
forefathers; but loyalty to the English Government was not,
in the days of Florence, loyalty to his race and nation. They
are prepared to look with indulgence, though not precisely
with admiration, upon the process of diamond-cutting, as
carried on by artists of so much celebrity as Cecyll, Carewe,
and Florence. They understand promises passing amongst
such men, in a diplomatic sense, that is, in the sense in which
they were made and understood by Sir Robert Cecyll; they
know that a man fencing for his life may be driven to make
many feints, and, in a measure, to adapt his attack and defence
to the style of his adversary; but they recognise limits within
which such contest must be restrained! And there has long
been a painful impression, derived from the letter about to be
laid before the reader, that their countryman exceeded these
boundaries! that when hardest pressed, his submissions included something more than words and professions; certain
actions not consistent with the faith and loyalty due to
his country! It will be a relief to Irish readers if this painful
impression can be removed; if the following letter can be
expounded to them as it was interpreted by Cecyll, to whom
it was addressed.

Though a close prisoner in the Tower, Florence was kept
perfectly acquainted with all the events passing in his native
country. With what interest he must have heard of the arrival
of the Spaniards; with what anxiety he must have watched
their early proceedings; and with what shame he must have
learned *the great battle of Kinsale*—the details of which were
as well known to him as to the author of the Pacata Hibernia—
the massacre of the English soldier, and the headlong flight of
the Northern Chieftains, the reader may imagine! He may
imagine also the contempt with which he must have heard
that the Spanish Commander, with a large fleet, an open sea,
no great scarcity of present victuals and ammunition, a

friendly population on all sides of him, and the knowledge
of reinforcements on their way, had chosen to surrender and
depart! All this was known to Florence as speedily as it
occurred! He had watched the effect of these events upon
his countrymen; he had seen universal stillness and depres-
sion follow them; and presently, with new promises, with a
generous supply of treasure and arms from Spain, the elastic
spirit of the nation spring again to action. A new expedition
on a much larger scale than the former, was promised, and all
Irish matters seemed to have, as nearly as possible, fallen
back into the condition in which they had been in the spring
of 1601, when Carewe sent him, with his pardons and protections, to the Tower! It seemed not unreasonable to hope
that Cecyll might be induced to send him again to Ireland,
on the old errand, to recover his country from Donal, to withdraw his Sept from action, and to do such service to Her
Majesty as no one but he could do. All that was needed for
this result was a revival in the ministerial mind of a belief
in his loyalty, and hence this letter:—

" 1602. *Aug.* FLORENCE Mᶜ CARTHY *to* CECYLL. *Tower of London.*

" It may please your Honor.
  " I have of late delivered Mʳ. Lieutenant a letter to your Honor,
wherein I did partly acquaint you with mine opinion concerning Ireland,
whereof my discoursing with him brought me to remember an important
piece of service that may be done for Her Majesty, which I am, and was
ever, willing to perform, as appeared hitherto by my works, and now by
all that I can think, or study.
  " Having, as soon as I was able to carry arms, served Her Majesty
against the old Earl of Desmond, with three hundred men at mine own
charges; with which, and with one English Company, I chased him out
of the strengths of Desmond into his own waste country, where all his
people were driven to forsake him; himself being kept afterwards by
Gory Mᶜ Swinye, until some of my men killed the said Gory, whereby the
Earl was killed within a week after. Upon due information of which services, Her Majesty hath not only bestowed a thousand marks in money,
and one hundred marks a year upon me, but also showed me ever that
favour, and countenance that gave me more contentment than any reward; since which time no man can say that I have spent my time, followed or sought anywhere, but to Her Majesty and the State here; *mine
unwillingness to go into Ireland last, being well known to your Honor and to
Sir John Stanhope;* where, upon my landing, without charge or means to
do service, I have, by the advice, and warrant of such as governed there
then, allured from the rebels some of their best companies, which I joined
with as many of my own as were furnished; none else acknowledging
Her Majesty; and maintaining forces in the country abroad then, when
all the English Companies, nor her greatest subjects there, durst not enter
Desmond, upon all that country people and seven hundred Connaught
buonies I recovered with five hundred, in spite of all the rebels, that

strongest country they had, and overthrew all those forces that assisted, and joined with James and the rest upon all occasions, which wild unruly people and buonies of that country that I found in action, I contained ever since from helping, aiding, or assisting the rebels anyway.

" Afterwards the Lord President, presently on his coming, having written very earnestly for me—although myself and my country was in the power of Connaught buonies, and that I knew nothing could make me more odious to them, and endanger my life, or my leading a prisoner to Tireowen, then to go to him—yet knowing it to be beneficial to Her Majesty's service, I came to him presently, because it would be thought, otherwise, that I had favoured the rebels, which would make others to stick to them, and join with them, whereas by trusting myself into the Lord President's hands upon his letter, it did assure all men there, that I was for Her Majesty, and encouraged all the rest to come in, and trust his Lordship ; where having satisfied, and assured him of my best endeavours for Her Majesty, when he told me that nothing was better for Her Highness' service, then to put the Connaught men out of Munster, I cassired presently three or four hundred of them that I had ; and endeavoured ever since to drive them all away, by making war upon them when he came from Limerick against James Mᶜ Thomas and the rest; whereby they could not take entertainment of James, nor help him ; and while he was in hand with James and the rest of the rebels, I wrote still to him of their weakness, assuring him that he should have no resistance, and that I would vex the Connaught men on the other side, and contain all my country people and neighbours from aiding or assisting them ; caused also my nephew O'Connor of Kerry to deliver his Lordship, the use of his Castle for Her Majesty's service, which was his best means to weaken James Mᶜ Thomas, and the lord Fitz Morice, and drive them out of their countries ; and his bridge, by the which he sent a garrison into Kerry.

" After the coming of which garrison, whereby I had their help to defend me, I came to him myself, and delivered him mine eldest son as he desired ; *and having had Her Majesty's protection renewed unto me about a month before my commitment, which I have ready to show, without any clause to hinder it by my pardon, or anything else,* together with *my pardon that was brought to me within four or five days after, whereby they would help me if I had offended ;* yet because I kept myself in the rebellion, and ever since, in such sort as *no matter can be found against me,* I am contented to refuse, and renounce the benefit of my said pardon and protection, if ever I have joined, by word or deed with Tireowen, James Mᶜ Thomas, or any of the rebels, or helped, aided, or assisted, any of them ; or if ever in all my life, myself or any other for me, to my knowledge, wrote anything beyond the seas, or was ever privy to any practices thither, or from thence ; which I have already, in like sort, renounced before your Honor, at my commitment hither, knowing not then that the chief commanders of the Spaniards that came afterwards, and such of my country as came with them, should fall into the hands of the State there, out of whom had been wrested and informed hyther, if I had anything to do with them.

" As all which services, carriage, and offer (*no matter also being against me*) are sufficient proofs of my loyalty, so shall your Honor find that my daily study now in this calamity, to do Her Majesty service, and mine endeavour here hence to procure more, and better service to be done—if I may have scope first to work it, and when it is to be done, some show of favour to put my friends in hope of future favour, and to encourage them to do for me—shall as well, or better, satisfy Her Majesty and your Honor for it for ever after.

" And for the service whereof I wrote now last, which concerns the importantest place in Ireland, where the Spaniards could neither be besieged, nor beaten out of it, which is the city of Limerick, where father Archer was in the last rebellion, and had taught him, by some of that city, a sure and secret way to surprise the Castle of Limbrik that commands the north gate, and bridge of the inner, and strong part of that city, by the which one may bring as many as he will into the city; which way to surprise it, with all other circumstances concerning the same, I have acquainted M^r. Lieutenant withal, and delivered him a note thereof for your Honor, which I was very glad to remember, for Her Majesty's sake, because father Archer being now in Spain, it will be the first thing that he will propound, and his chiefest motive to bring them; but now I have taught your Honor to prevent that danger, which is not the chiefest service that I am minded, and most desirous to cause to be performed for Her Majesty, nor any other, but that which may be done against Tireowen's own person; who at my last being here, hath not only caused all the buonies that he sent into Munster to create a skurvie kearne, that is said to be my wife's base brother, Lord of my country, and to establish him in the possession thereof, but also, when he came into Munster himself, would presently employ all the Connaught buonies that were there with the said bastard, to dispossess me, until, with much ado, Maguyre, that was O'Donell's cousin germain, and other gentlemen of the north, for O'Donell's sake, with all the gentry of Munster that were there, got him to stay until they sent for me; and being come to parley with him, upon all the assurance that could be devised, when he saw that no persuasion, nor offers that he could make me, could procure me to deliver him my son for a pledge to be in his action, he did not only countenance the said bastard to quarrel with me, and call me still before him a " damned counterfeited Englishman, whose only study and practise was to deceive and betray all the Irishmen in Ireland;" but also the best conditions that could be obtained for me was to leave that bastard possessed of the two best castles in my country, and to stand to the order of bishop Mc Cragh, and others with him, for the Signorie thereof; with which, nor with any thing else he would not be (have been) satisfied, until he had dispossessed me for him altogether, if he were not (had not been) driven to depart suddenly, upon advertisement that the Earls of Ormond and Thomond gathered great forces to meet him.

" For the compassing of which service against his person I do not think that any hath better means and knowledge, nor men of better ability and sufficiency to perform it than myself; wherof none, nor none other of the birth of Ireland, in mine opinion, is so sufficient for the performance thereof as Morogh Nymart, who without exception is the most exercised commander, and of greatest skill, experience, and reputation, for that country's wars of any mere Irishman. He is my foster-brother, son to my foster-father, that was chief commander of my father's footmen. When I was committed hither before he fled into the north; where being followed by some four hundred soldiers, he served old O'Neyle, for whom he gave Tireowen a great overthrow at Carriglyeh; afterwards he maintained O'royrk in his country for awhile; and understanding of my enlargement served Sir Richard Byngham, who sent him, and his soldiers, pardoned, into their country; he, and a younger brother of his that keeps a hundred men about him also, are now, as I hear, joined with O'swlivan-bere. I am persuaded, if I had knowledge how things stand there, and sufficient messengers to employ about it, I might get Captain Terel and his buonies cut off, or beaten out of Munster; but because I do not think him a man of any great moment, and that it would be a hindrance to the other service of greater importance, I do not think it best for the Queen, knowing that if I procure Morogh ny-mart and such others as I think good, to go into the north this winter, and *work the rest to come in*, that Terel and his buonies will not stay there: for the effecting of *this* service that I do intend, I must presently send for messengers of those that are best learned and spoken in that language, and of special trust, credit and authority, to persuade any gentlemen; which country hath two sorts of people that are of greatest ability, and authority to persuade that country gentlemen, which of all other sorts, and sexes, doth most distaste and mislike the State, and government of England; whereof the one, which are the priests, are by no means to be trusted with my service for Her Majesty; of the other, which are the Rimers, some may be trusted only by those gentlemen whose followers they are by lineal descent, and of whom depends their living; of which sort I will employ one of special trust and sufficiency for the effecting of this service.

" I wrote in my last letter to your Honor myne opinion, that the Spaniards will come into Ireland; but I do not assure myself of their coming this harvest, because I am persuaded they will endeavour, by reason of their experience there last, to come stronger, and with more means, which will hardly be provided but with time. Also O'donell, that hears daily how things stand in Ireland, understanding that Tireowen and the rest kept themselves hitherto, will not perhaps be very earnest now to hasten them. Knowing the advantage that rebels have to help themselves in winter, when all kind of flesh there is in season; the nights long, the rivers flowing, and the weather cold and rainy; and if, as I think, they will conclude to come for the north and Connaught, I am persuaded they will endeavour to bring gallies; which, as they know, and as Odonell will tell them, will be very necessary, and available for them, both for the shallow bays about Gallway, and all the islands there about, and to beat away the garrison of Loughfeavyll, and command that arm of the sea betwixt Ireland and Scotland, whereby they may have what they will from thence; but now they can hardly bring, nor use gallies, knowing by experience how subject to storms that coast is henceforward; which may make them take the beginning of summer, both to bring and to use gallies all that season for their first, and necessariest services, and also to provide more means and forces in the mean time.

" It may be also that Don John del Agila who is, perhaps, a wise man, and a skilful commander ! learned much of the state of that country at his last being there, and weighed what forces came against him, and what oversight hindered him, and viewed Cork, and saw the weakness thereof; whereby he knows if he come upon the sudden thither, with any good forces, that he will hardly be kept out; as also that if he have Cork, not only Youghill and Kinsale will be his presently, but also the Lord Barry, who dwells near it upon a Neck of that haven, and his country along the haven up to the gates thereof, and Cormuk Mc Dermod, whose country comes to the gates also, and dwells within three miles thereof, together with Mc Carthy Reogh, the Lord Roch, and Mc Donogh, whose countries are within eight or ten miles thereof, and John Fitz Edmonds that dwells upon that haven, besides many others that dwell thereby, must all, with their countries and people, be subjects to him; the knowledge whereof, by his last being there, may haply induce him to come for Cork in the beginning of winter; imagining that the weather then will be unseasonable, and discommodious for any fleets or forces to be sent here hence; that besides the discommodities of winter for such a purpose, especially in that country, the lord Deputy hath neither town, country, or any other means or succour, to besiege him, nearer than Waterford or Limerick; and that in the spring his succour will be as ready to relieve him as any other to annoy him; which is all that I can guess, or think, of their proceedings; and if I can hear anything that may help me to guess, or judge what course they are like to take, I will advertise your Honor thereof; in the meantime, wishing, as I have been heretofore the chiefest causer of cutting off the Earl of Desmond, that I may be now the chiefest procurer of cutting off this greatest traitor; beseeching God to preserve and prosper your Honor.

"I rest ever,
"Your Honor's most humble & bounden,
"fflor Mᶜ Carthy.

"*Indorsed.* To the Right Honᵇˡᵉ his very approved friend Sʳ. Robert Cecill, Knight, Principal Secretary to the Queen's most excellent Majesty and of her Higness' most honorable Privy Council, &c."

On the receipt of this letter Cecyll wrote to Carewe:—

"You shall understand that Florence MacCarthy of late hath been very desyrous to write to me, of whose wordes, though I know well what accompt to make, yett I thought it nott amisse to send you a coppye of that I receaued, because you may see how probably the witty knave can argue."

It is evident that this letter, kept amongst the State Papers in London, has been seldom seen by Irish scholars; that it has been carelessly read, and never understood. It is the only solicitude of the author of these pages to set the fame of his relative right with his countrymen. What phrase would best designate his conduct towards an authority which had singled out, in an especial manner, *his inheritance for "dissipation,"* because it was larger than the English Government thought it safe for any native Irishman to possess, because the Queen was jealous of the rights and chiefries of the heads of Septs, and because the undertakers coveted it, and *himself for proscription,* because he was mere Irish, and the ablest, most accomplished, and most powerful of his race, is no matter of concern to his biographer. But to remove from the reputation of this distinguished Irish chieftain a blemish which his countrymen have seen cast by their own scholars upon his good name—which they have seen with pain—for though they had no access to the documents which would have protected him, they knew that fifty years of captivity had been the penalty of his opposition to English rule in his native country; to remove this reproach is of *much concern* to this writer; nay, it has been his chief concern, whilst—at the invitation of the Venerable Charles O'Connor—he has employed himself in compiling this biography.

The charges brought against Florence, and solely founded upon this letter, are two ; and it is surprising that there should not have been more! These two have been distinctly stated by a scholar who, better than most men, knew the gravity of the charges he was making, by the late learned Dr. O'Donovan, who must have made them with regret, for he thought highly, not less of the learning than of the loyalty of Florence to his countrymen.

In his translation of the satire, entitled " The Tribes of Ireland," by Angus O'Daly, he has written at page 24, " The celebrated Florence MacCarthy wrote a letter to the English Government, when he was confined in the Tower, *advising the bribery of the bards to bring over the gentry to the English interest; and there can be but little doubt that it was at his suggestion our author was employed to write this poem !*" He boasts that " *he was the chiefest cause of cutting off the Earle of Desmond.*"

For the purpose of reply to these charges, this letter of Florence may be analysed as follows :—

1st. It contains general professions of his desire at all times to serve Her Majesty.

2nd. A narrative of his early services, and his father's, against the old Earl of Desmond.

3rd. A declaration that he had allured the bonies in Munster into his own service, and thus prevented their taking bonaght with the rebels.

4th. That he had kept his own followers out of action.

5th. That, to please the Lo : President, he had discharged his bonies.

6th. That at the time of writing, he held in his possession *the Queen's protection for his personal freedom from arrest, and her unconditional pardon for all past offences,* and was ready to produce them.

7th. The discovery to Cecyll of a secret passage into an Irish Castle.

8th. Offers to do service against O'Neill.

9th. Offers to drive Tirell and his bonies out of Munster.

10th. He proposes the employment of Rymers !

11th. His opinion of when the Spaniards would next come to Ireland, and *where* they were likeliest to land.

Of the above eleven propositions this author needs only to observe, in general terms, respecting all but the 2nd, 7th, 8th, and 10th, that the reader has, in the course of these pages, been himself a witness of the conduct of Florence, and seen with how much, or how little loyalty to the Queen, of disloyalty to his own people, Carewe considered that

conduct to be consistent. All the professions of desire to
serve Her Most Sacred Majesty were of the nature of the
incence daily offered to the old lady, "whose divine loveliness
and matchless wisdom ravished the world." Relative to the
graver charge of having taken credit to himself for cutting
off *the Earl of Desmond*, the reader must be reminded that
there were many Earls of Desmond—four, if not five—in
Florence's time ; through careless reading of his letter, he is
understood to claim merit from the English Government for
having caused the overthrow of James Fitz Thomas, the
Sougaun Earl (no blame could attach to him for aiding to
overthrow any other Earl of Desmond if he had chosen), or
in other words of having betrayed the national cause in the
late "Holy Action." Had he done this he would have done
an act of detestable baseness! had he even boasted of doing
it he would have exceeded, to the detriment of his fair name,
the wide limits allowed to the range of political veracity in
those days! but neither did he do it, nor did he boast of
having done it! His boast was that he had been the chiefest
cause of cutting off the *old Earl of Desmond*, that is of Gerald
the 16th Earl. This old Earl was in rebellion for purposes
of his own; for no national cause, except in so far as all
rebellion was for the national cause. He was the hereditary
foe of the MacCarthys, on whom his ancestors had imposed
humiliating tribute of beeves, in token of superior force! and
between whom, notwithstanding innumerable intermarriages,
intermittent warfare had been carried on, from sire to son, in
all time since the year 1272. Of the cutting off of this old
Earl Florence boasted, as his ancestor and namesake, Finin
of Ringroan might have boasted, and, unless he was an
exceedingly modest Irishman, no doubt did boast, of his
great victory at Callan, when he utterly cut off John Fitz-
Gerald, the ancestor of the FitzGeralds of Munster, his eldest
son, eight barons, fifteen knights, and other English nobles
(besides an ancestor of the Lo: Barry), "after which the
Desmonds did not dare to put plough in ground for eight
years."

There can no stigma attach to Florence for his serving
against this old Earl of Desmond, which would not have
attached with ten-fold disgrace to James FitzThomas, the
Sougaun Earl himself, who was in arms with Florence at the
same time, for the same purpose, and who in a letter to
Ormond, made the same boast, to prove—as Florence was
endeavouring to prove—his past loyalty to the Queen.

"It is well known to your Lo: he wrote, I have shown

my willingness in service against my uncle, and his
adherents, whereby I have been partlye meane of his
destruction." Florence has suffered detriment because in
this, as subsequently in his recovery of his country from
Donal, and his expulsion of the bonies who had been living
at loose quarters in Carbery, his interests chanced to coincide
with the policy of the English Government, and the convenience of the President of Munster, at the time. Having
recovered his country he filled all his castles with weaponed
men; and, although he kept his followers from open action,
and thus secured tranquillity in Desmond, he so neutralized
the availableness of the Queen's small force, that—to use
Carewe's expression—"had James FitzThomas but understood his business better," he might with little difficulty,
with his 8,000 men have captured Carewe, and Cork, and
the 1,700 men-by-the-poll, who formed his sole protection.

As for Florence's assertions that by his hiring bonies he
had prevented James FitzThomas, and other rebels from
having them,—like his former boast that he had enticed
several companies away from O'Neill himself,—they were
doubtless true; it is evident that these men were either
loose Connaught men, every man's money, or Munster men,
his own born followers whom, as he was raising as large a
force as he could, to recover his country, it was natural that
he should hire, and appropriate! and as for his declaration
that when Carewe was about to attack FitzThomas, he met
with no opposition from him; and that upon all occasions
he overthrew these forces who assisted and joined Fitz
Thomas, this means that he allowed none of the Geraldines,
any more than he allowed the President's Sheriffs, or the
soldiers of the Governor of Kerry, to set foot within his frontiers.
The overthrow of the men who joined the Earl, meant, mani-
festly, the expulsion of Donal, and his bonies out of Desmond! If, whilst affording to FitzThomas all the encouragement in his power, and probably as great supplies as he
needed of cattle and corn, from the fertile country of
Carbery, he called him and O'Neill, rebels, and arch-rebels;
if there had been any accidental deflection from the narrow
path of a rather perilous veracity; the reproach to him for it
should have come from Cecyll, not from any of his countrymen, in those days, or in our own.

To these minor cabinet affirmations of Florence's letter
Irishmen will offer no very grave objection; but proposal
the eighth has been considered a more serious matter.
Florence positively revealed to Sir Robert Cecyll the exist-

ence of a secret way into a castle at Limerick! which castle commanded the north gate and bridge: which secret was known to Father Archer, who was then in Spain, and to others of the city! By the knowledge of this secret (which no English spies, in or out of Limerick, could ever have discovered,) Cecyll might, when the Spaniards, by direction of Archer, should have landed at Limerick, and by means of the said secret way have captured the city (from which, by no other means than by the way they had entered, "could they be beseiged, or beaten out of it")—have brought as many as he would into the city, and by this way, surprise it! Risum teneatis?

Presuming that the Privy Council might fail to esteem this *secret* as an equivalent for his enlargement, Florence prepared to offer nothing less than the suppression of all rebellion in Ireland by the suppression of O'Neill, the Arch Rebel! not indeed by any of those *curious means* by which so many had before offered to suppress him; not by *" drawing a Draught upon him,"* or aiding Sir Geoffry Fenton *" to find the axe to cut down the great oke,"* which he was at that time in search of, but by sending a great warrior, Morrough-ny-Mart, his foster-brother, the late commander of his father's foot forces (and of his own), into the north, where he had already served, who would, with such others as Florence thought good, go thither this winter. It must be admitted that this scheme of Florence against the person of O'Neill becomes perceptibly mistier, and more shadowy as its development proceeds; and it must have struck Cecyll as very inferior to the offers to which he was accustomed. What Morrough-ny-Mart was to do becomes at each paragraph less clear. His leading his free lances into the north was evidently with intent to oblige Tyrell to hurry out of Munster to protect Tirone! but was he, with his own 400 bonies, and the 100 of his brother, to attack, in his own country, the man who had overthrown Marshal Bagnal and 4,000 of the Queen's best troops, and who could, probably, at short notice, summon 10,000 followers to protect him? Scarcely this! and careless reading of Florence's proposal could alone lead to so absurd an interpretation of his meaning.

Morrough-ny-Mart was indeed to lead his own and his brother's army into Ulster, and having been himself recently converted to serve the Queen, he was to *persuade O'Neill and the others to come in!* that is—persuade them to seek reconciliation with Her Majesty. But this warlike demonstration of Morrough was to be seconded by other means; slow cer-

tainly, but ingenious, and effective! And this leads to the
gravest of the charges against Florence, namely, that so
distinctly made by Dr. O'Donovan, that "he advised the
Government to bribe the Bards to bring over the Irish
Gentry to English interests; and that with this intention, he
employed his hereditary chief bard of Munster, Angus
O'Daly, *to write a venemous satire against all his countrymen,
promiscuously, throughout every province in Ireland!*" This
would indeed have been a remarkable way of "bringing
over the Irish Gentry to English interests!" and it does not
appear to have presented itself to the mind of Florence
when he was writing. The real functions intended to be
performed by the bards are clearly explained in the letter:
they were to aid Morrough-ny-Mart in the conversion of the
gentlemen of Ulster from rebellion, and persuade them to
come in! "Knowing—says the letter literally—that if
I procure Morrough-ny-Mart, and others, to go into
the north this winter, and work the rest to come in, Tyrell
and his bonies cannot stay in Munster! and *for the effecting
of this service*—that is, to work the *rest* (all others in arms
for the same purpose as Tirell, viz., all other gentlemen,
followers of O'Neill) *to come in*—to effect *this, I do propose to
send the bards*, &c. &c., and especially one of trust, and
sufficiency to persuade any gentlemen, &c." Or,—to render
Florence's letter a little more perspicuous than Cecyll probably found it—the importantest service he proposed to do
Her Majesty, against the person of O'Neill, was (if allowed
to return in freedom to Ireland!) to despatch his foster-
brother into the north to persuade O'Neill to submission;
and at the same time he would employ certain Rhymers to
work his followers to come in also! But Dr. O'Donovan
adds, "there can be little doubt that Florence caused the
satire on the Tribes of Ireland to be written!"

What Florence wrote the reader has before him! He
made his proposal to Sir Robert Cecyll in the month of
August, *sixteen hundred and two*, and his design was to make
some *present* offer that might lead to his enlargement! Had
he proposed by his influence, to introduce loyalty into Ireland by a bardic education of Irish chieftains, and to employ
for this purpose a class of men "who of all other sorts and
sexes did *most distaste and dislike the State and Government of
England*," who should make excursions through the country
to satirize every Irish gentleman along their route, Cecyll,
who had already expressed a very uncomplimentary opinion
of his intellect might again (and with better cause this time)

have called him " a vain fool! and a malicious one also,"
but would scarcely have sent him back to Munster to begin
these proceedings.

" The Tribes of Ireland," which Dr. O'Donovan has so
learnedly edited, and translated, is a venomous satire or
Aeir which, according to bardic belief, was powerful to bring
blotches to the cheek, nay at times, to cause the death of the
parties satirized. Angus O'Daly in the year 1617, that is
fifteen years after Florence made this cast for his freedom, when
O'Neill was no more in Ireland, Cecyll himself forgotten in
the Foreign Office, Ireland tranquil—because helpless—and
neither King nor Privy Council caring an old song about the
Gentlemen of Ireland, or their bringing over to English interests, set out on a poetical excursion from Fidnach-of-the-
Relics in Leitrim, with intent to traverse the four provinces,
and bespatter with ridicule, and contempt, every chieftain
along his way! This was rough education for the Gentlemen of Ireland, and its political purpose not very obvious!
unless it was that he designed to bring all his countrymen
into contempt by contrasting the generous open-handed hospitality of the undertakers, with the mean and stingy housekeeping of the native Irish. His sarcasms turned, without
exception, upon the sorry fare that was furnished him as he
proceeded, and it is surprising to see in what variety of language he could express his affliction at the spare or un-
savoury diet laid before him. His chief sorrow was, however,
the want of butter for his bread. From Connaught, through
Leinster, and Ulster, he pursued his way, ever singing of the
cold kitchens, and bare larders of his countrymen, befouling
all, without fear or favour, with mockery and insult—bringing
over the Irish Gentlemen to English interests—till his steps
brought him to the borders of O'Donnel's country; there he
paused! he heard the hissing effervescence of the poison of
his Aeir within his own breast, and was seized with sudden
terror! He thought of Teige Dall O'Higgin, whose tongue
had been cut out, and wife and child murdered, for satirizing
the Sept of O'Harra! " Were I to satirize the whole human
race—he said, after a while—O'Donnell could protect me!
Speak I but one evil word against O'Donnell not all the sons
of Adam could save me!" And he passed on his way and
was silent till he arrived in Munster, and amongst the homes
of the Sept of Florence.

The reader will presume that if any of the Clan Carthy
be attacked it will be Florence's evil wishers, Donal Pipi,
and Donal his base brother-in-law, whom in a moment of

2 B

great anger he had called a Skurvy Kern! And if any spared, it would be his chief friends and followers, O'Sullevan, MacDonogh MacCarthy, and MacCarthy of Muskerry!

It was far otherwise! The Roches were the first insulted, the O'Sullevans the next, (both of them his near relations,) and then each branch of the MacCarthys in the order of his travel.

> " *Flattery* I got for food
> In great Musgraidhe of Mac Diarmada,
> So that my chest dried up from thirst
> Until I reached Baile-au-Cholaig."

" Musgraidhe, now Muskerry—says Dr. O'Donovan in his note on this passage—a Barony in the county of Cork. The chief of this territory was sometimes called MacDiarmada, as being descended from Diarmaid Mor MacCarthy." What could this poet have expected, other than he got from the Lord of Blarney Castle?

> " At Easter I was in the house of Mac Donogh :
> He was my friend ! My girdle he tightened :
> His people and feast were such
> As if Easter were Good Friday."

" This McDonogh was one of the powerful chieftains of the MacCarthys, who was seated at Kanturk in the Barony of Duhallow (J. O.'D.)."

> " Bread, without being drowned in butter,
> And much chaff in its body—
> In order to make me thankful,—
> This was my fare at Ceapach !"

" Ceapach, now Kippagh. This was one of MacCarthy's houses—(J. O'D.)." It in fact belonged at the time to Florence himself; and we shall shortly witness his efforts to rescue it from his plunderers.

> " In Desmond, above all other places,
> They deserve to go to Heaven.
> On account of their fasting for their crimes !
> They should go dryfooted in !—"

What Angus O'Daly omitted to write, but would have written if his wit had but equalled his desire to bring over his countrymen to English interests, has been supplied, after an interval of 250 years by a poet of our own days (Clarence

Mangan) who certainly was not bribed by any descendant of
Florence to write it.

> " The Clan Carthy are vain, but as deep as a churn;
> They grasp all you have, and give words in return.
> What good deeds you do them are written in water;
> But injure them once, and they doom you to slaughter."

To these bardic compliments to the chief gentlemen of
his Sept the writer of these pages will add but one more;
indeed the only one more added by the Bard himself; it is
to an irritable Tipperary gentleman of the name of
O'Meagher.

> " A large fire in the house of O'Meagher,
> Men and meat beside it,
> A large caldron of fermented wine grapes,
> Under which O'Meagher's cow calves."

On this mystical passage of the poem Dr. O'Donovan remarks, in elucidation, " this is a touch of satire which was
felt by the Feadhmanac as directed against the dignity of
his master and namesake."

This lay of O'Meagher's caldron, and his cow, concluded
the musical tour of the Munster Minstrel. Suddenly, and
fearfully the Aeir worked its destiny.

Instead of sharing the bard's indignation at the meanness
of his entertainment, the followers of these penurious chieftains rather took it amiss that the inhospitality of their lords
should be thus made matter of publicity. When Angus had
said his last word against O'Meagher, "a servant of trust
of Muintir Mheachair, seized with a sudden fury, stood up,
and thereupon made a fierce thrust of the sharp knife which
he held in his dexterous right hand," into the ill provided
store chambers of his person, and thus finished satire and
satirist! and no more was heard of bardic tuition in English
loyalty!

But why attribute this exposition of the unprovided larders
of the Irish Chiefs to the orders of Florence? When this
poem was written he had spent 15 years in London prisons,
and he well knew that it was something very different from
the songs of Irish rhymers that was needed to procure his
freedom. Had he chosen to give up his property in Carbery
and Desmond, he might have spared the reputations of his
kindred, left O'Meagher's cow to calve where she pleased,
and saved his chief bard from the sharp knife, and the dex-

trous right hand of the Tipperary Feadhmanac. Could we even suppose that he could derive any satisfaction from the malignant incantations of the bard, he would surely rather have sent him to Molahiff to satirize a blemish upon the comely English countenance of Browne—who continued to hold *his* Signory, though not without loud brangle of protest and litigation, and appeals of Florence to the Privy Council against him, and his letters patents, as well those granted to his father as those renewed and amended for himself—than to the castles of his best friends and supporters!

With unfeigned respect, at all times, for the opinion of a scholar so learned as Dr. O'Donovan, who served the literature of his country so loyally and so well, the writer of these pages may at least say that he finds nowhere discoverable any evidence, either documentary or inferential, that Florence employed O'Daly to write this satire. No enemy of his was satirized; no friend spared; no advantage could possibly accrue to him from it; and no one will suppose that gratuitously he would make any effort to gratify the undertakers at the cost of the credit of his friends, relatives, clansmen, and fellow-countrymen!

Florence's opinion respecting the coming of a fresh expedition from Spain, and the port at which it might be expected, could not fail to attract the notice of Cecyll; it was the result of able reasoning, and might "*almost* (as Carewe once said) persuade him that Florence was dealing plainly with him." But the Spaniards were then to come for the north, and Connaught! and not to land at Limerick after all! Could Father Archer have forgotten the secret passage into the castle, which commanded the north gate and bridge, and from which, had he once introduced the Spaniards there, they could not be besieged or beaten out? What value would Cecyll be likely to set upon the secret that was to enable him to drive them out, when it was made so plain to him that they could have no intention of going in?

There was a new King in England: the clear-sighted, fearless, high-hearted, majestic woman who had ruled England for close upon half a century, was no more! and in her Florence had lost a friend!

There were new rulers in Ireland; the Felon of the Dublin jury was withdrawn from Munster; Florence was in the Tower; and the wide domains of Desmond and Carbery were open to public scramble, to the operation of private enterprise, and of letters patents. Donal Pipi, who was still fretted by the bonds he had signed with Sir Owen, was eager to resign his lands to the King, and resume them from him, if he could but any way escape the forfeit of £10,000 to Florence; but Barry had it already in design to bestow upon himself certain commodious portions of these very lands of Carbery. Lady Ellen was claiming a considerable tract of her late father's country, and certain small pensions besides. Browne was of course at Molahiff again, with promise of new letters patents adapted to altered circumstances, but in uneasy tenure, for Florence had begun a vigorous legal resistance, destined to outlive the Browne now flourishing, and the Browne yet in the cradle. But loudest of all was Donal now once more descended from his dignity, but in remarkable treaty with the Government, which, during a long course of years he had served, as the reader has seen. His petition was of surprising tenour, but he was in high favour after his present to Sir C. Wilmot of the 5,000 cows captured from his chief followers the O'Sullevans.

It has been more than once mentioned that in the estimation of the Irish, bastardy within the first degree is not always considered a bar to succession; Donal, more particularly since his reception of the Pope's Bull, had adopted this national view of the accidents of life, hence his petition to the King was for letters patents—such as had probably never issued from a royal chancery before—to confer upon Donal MacCarthy, the son of the late Earl of Clancar, unlawfully begotten, with remainder to the heirs male of his body, unlawfully begotten, all that the said Earl had left him by will, and which, through the good offices of the Lo: President of Munster, had been restored to him by Queen Elizabeth!

" 1604. March 2. Barry Court.

" My most honorable Lord, I have briefly written to your Honour how that I despair to benefit myself by his Majesty's favour extended towards me by your Lordship's means for a lease of the lands of Dermod Meah Mc Cartie and Fynym Mc Owen; for divers do oppose themselves against His Majesty's title to the same, especially Mc Carty Reoghe, who now intendeth to repair thither, hoping by some means to frustrate the good courses here taken in that behalf; for by my means, and to my charges of three hundred livres in buying of evidences & otherwise, an office hath been found for his Majesty of a good deal of land as yet in the possession of the said Mc Cartie and others. But I hope that as your Honor hath been the mean for me in obtaining of my suit in that behalf, so now you will prevent Mc Cartie in obtaining any thing there in prejudice of his Majesty's right; but referred to follow his suits here, as shall be agreeable to ordinary courses of law. I have a bordering neighbour (I mean S^r. John Fitz-Edmonds) who is now intended to make a surrender of all those lands which he possesseth (amounting to the number of three plowlands) to his Majesty, only to defraud such as have best right to those lands; and among the rest meaneth to have part of my ancient inheritance passed; wherefore I beseech your Honour to be a mean that every man's right be always saved; otherwise great inconveniences might arise, and a number of ancient English gentlemen prevented of their right. We have here a daily expectation that by your honorable means there will be a reformation of the extortion of Government's troops, soldiers, Sheriffs and cessors, who do altogether impoverish his poor kingdom, and commonwealth, and that His M^y. will be pleased to take some other course for the better establishing thereof, to the increase of his Highness' revenues. Which, leaving to your honorable regard, With the remembrance of my humble duty I do evermore remain

" Ready to do your Honor every service

" BARRY BUTTEVANTE.

" To the Honble. my very good Lord the Lord Cycell, Principal Secretary to the King's most excellent M^y. and one of his Highness' most honorable Privy Council.

" Lord Barry to my Lord from Barry Court."

All these petitioners were attended to in their turn, but not before the claims of Lady Ellen, Florence's wife, upon the pity and the justice of the King, had been acknowledged. On her repair to England, and towards the prison into which her loyalty had cast her husband, and which she affected a wish to share, she had brought the disgraceful letter of recommendation from Carewe, which the reader has seen. As the price of her loyal intelligence she had received from Queen Elizabeth a pension of £100 per annum. She now made suit for portions of her late father's lands, and for some gratuity in her great distress. Her petition was received favourably. Under date of 21 June we find a doquet.

" An annuity of £150 p^r. an^m. to the Lady Ellen Mc Carthy daughter to the Earl of Clan Carthy in Ireland, during her life, provided that the payment hereof do not begin before certain letters patents of £100 annuity granted her by the late Queen be first cancelled, and that annuity of £100 presently to cease, and this to begin from the Annunciation last.

" King's Letter.

" To grant to Elline Cartie daughter and sole Heiress of the last Earl of Clancarthy, without fine, part of the lands of the said Earl, not yet in charge, and not 13 quarters of land in extent; to hold for life with remainder to Teige MacCarthy her son and heir apparent, and his heirs males, like remainder toher other three sons, Donal, Cormac, and Finin ; the reversion to remain on the Crown.

" 16 April 4th of James 1st."

At the same time, when the above favour was shown to his wife, Florence was himself on the point of obtaining his freedom, not indeed to return to Ireland, but at least to live amongst his fellow-creatures; for Sir Thomas Vavasour K^t. Marshal of the Household, under whose charge he was, "procured from the Privy Council, to further his liberty on good securities, to continue within ten or twelve miles of London, but Sir George Carewe (now in England) heard of this from Sir Richard Boyle, and got the Lo: Chamberlain to charge Sir Thomas Vavasour to give it over." The K^t. Marshal sent in his bill of charges, and Florence continued his prisoner.

"*Pell Records.* S^{ir} THO^s. VAVASOUR, K^t. *Marshal of the Household.*

"Second of March by order 26 February 1604. To Sir Thos. Vavasour K^t. Marshal of his Highness' Household the sum of £248 for the diets of Sir Anthony Standon, Florence McCarty, and George Gwynne, late prisoners in the Tower, and from thence removed, and committed to his charge, at several rates and times, according to a certificate under the hand of the said K^t. Marshal. By writ dated 24 May 1604."

The first of the petitioners to obtain notice, after Lady Ellen (for Barry obtained none), was Donal Pipi, who had at last made up his mind to incur the risk of Florence's claim upon him for the ten thousand pounds due for his breach of covenant. He had probably ascertained that the English lawyers considered the bonds, so often alluded to, as null, in that they were in opposition to the spirit of Imperial policy, if not to the letter of English law. This probably Florence had also discovered, for Donal's petition was granted, and Florence, as far as we know, made no claim on his cousin for the penalty.

It has been stated that the persistent policy of the English Government through several reigns had been "to dissipate the large estates of the Irish Chieftains," and at the same time to abolish the *Rights* and *Chiefries*, as trenching upon the Royal prerogative, tending to uphold the independence and power of the Chiefs, and to keep the Septs in union. To effect the former purpose every plausible pretext for confiscation was ruthlessly seized, and greedy adventurers were always ready to risk the slender outfit with which they had come to seek their fortunes in Ireland—nay life itself, some of them—to obtain grants of land thus confiscated, which they were not able to cultivate when they got them, nor in times of trouble, to defend.

Royal letters patent were ever at the service of these enterprising men, who, for rents to the Sovereign, varying from threepence to a penny per acre, made to themselves signories of from five to ten thousand acres. They indeed bargained to introduce English ploughs, and Protestantism, loyalty, and civility, so many, and so much, to the Signory. And in ordinary times they struggled on, with help of the Queen's horsemen for their protection, in such manner as the reader has seen, hunting such men as Donal and his loose swords into bogs and woods, but occasionally seeing their own cattle feloniously running before the fugitives, the winter nights illumined by blazing homesteads ; and not seldom were these professors of civility themselves knocked on the head by the barbarous people whose lands they were endeavouring to form into model farms.

The abolition of rights and chiefries was sought by means of less violent nature. Royal invitation was made to all heads of Septs, to secure to their children uninterrupted succession to their domains, by delivering them into the hands of the King, and receiving them back as gifts from the Crown, to be held by English tenure. Tanistry, or collateral succession, was, in favour of such chiefs as accepted these terms, abolished, and with it all the rights and chiefries so offensive to the pride of the Sovereign. These cessions and receptions of Irish estates were of frequent occurrence ; they held good usually for the first succession, and were neglected afterwards ; Tanistry resumed its course, and the sons of deceased chiefs patiently submitted to see their uncles or elder cousins precede them, and to wait till the old usage called them, in the course of nature, to succeed. Not only was election within certain limits resumed, but the rights and chiefries were resumed with it. Sir Donogh, the father of Florence, succeeded his elder brother, putting aside Donal Pipi the son, and heir by English tenure ; and how resolutely *he* vindicated his rights and chiefries, in spite of all letters patent, and all murmurings of the cessors of the county, and of the Cork jurors, the reader saw in an early chapter of this book, when Florence, then but 12 years of age, and his cousins, the sons of Sir Owen, were sent out with kerns and galloglass to collect spoil from refractory followers, who were disposed to profit by the Queen's right to the chiefries, ceded two generations before.

An interesting light is cast upon the subject of these cessions, by Irish chieftains, of their countries to the Kings of England, by a passage in the will of Sir Cormac McTeig, whom Sir Henry Sidney had called "the rarest man that ever was born of the Irishry, and whom he wished to see nobilitated."

It may have occurred to the reader as surprising that

chieftains who left sons should not have made an effort,
towards the close of their days, to secure to them the succession for which their estates had been purposely surrendered,
and placed, on re-delivery, on a tenure so tempting for parent
and son to maintain! The will of Sir Cormac removes all
surprise on the subject! It was matter of *conscience and
religion* with the dying Chief to make restitution for a wrong
which he or his father might have done. The laws of
Tanistry were on all other points held sacred between chieftain and follower. No conscience could be at rest under the
violation of this, the most important of all, as it regulated
the rights, not only of the different members—all nearly
related in blood—of the family in which the chieftainship
was hereditary, but upon it depended the most valuable
right of the entire Sept, viz., that of the election of their
chief.

The Lordship of Muskerry was one of those Irish Chief-
tainships which had been surrendered in the manner we have
described; and, had the tenure been respected, the eldest son
of Sir Cormac would have succeeded to it. It was no
opposition in this great branch of the MacCarthys which
interfered with the course of English law. When Sir Cormac
was settling all his worldly affairs, and had to make known
his last will and testament, he first declared, "Cormocke
Ooge, my son, is my lawful and undoubted heire of my body
lawfully begotten!" He then proceeds, "Item Where there
is a patente paste unto me of the manors, castells, townes,
lands, and tenements of Moycromyhe, Carickedrohidd, Castell-
more, Blarney, and the reste of the castells, towns, hamlets,
&c., of the whole countrey of Muskry, &c. My will is, *for
conscience sake*, that Kallaghan McTeige, *my brother*, shall have
and enjoye the whole lordshipp of Muskry, together with all
the manors, towns, and hamlets thereof (excepte the manor
of the Blarney, and Toyhoney-blarney, with the appurte-
nances, and th'other lands hereafter devised) to have and to
holde the said lordshipp of Muskry as aforesaid, and the
lands, &c., unto the said Kallaghan McTeig during his natural
life. The remaynder after his decease, *unto my nephewe*, Teige
McDermod, during his naturall life: the remaynder *after his
decease* to *my son* and heire, Cormock Oge, &c."

Donal Pipi allowed no scruple of *his* conscience to inter-
fere with his testamentary arrangements. He was succeeded
by his son in the possession of the lands, *but not as a chieftain*.
The reader may have noticed that Donal's predecessors had
been always mentioned as *Sir* Cormac, *Sir* Donogh, *Sir* Owen;

not that they had received knighthood from the Queen, or the Lord Deputy, but because *knighthood accompanied the Tanistry,* as it often did the priesthood! But Donal Pipi was never styled Sir Donal; he was the eighth and *last* MacCarthy Reagh by Tanistry! With him utterly ceased this princely and time-honoured title! His son, and the heirs male of his body lawfully begotten, were henceforth *Esquires,* if he, and they, and the gentlemen of Carbery, then or now, but knew what that meant!

" 1606. *July* 2. *The Report of the* LORD CAREWE, LORD CHIEF JUSTICE, SIR ROGER WILBRAHAM, *concerning* DONNELL M⁰ ARTY.

" May it please your Lordships, We have examined the petition of Donel M⁰ Carty (Donal Pipi) touching his offer to surrender the country of Carbry to his Majesty, and to accept the same by letters patents, to hold the same by English tenure of His Majesty.

" We have also considered of many objections made against his suit by Florence M⁰ Carty now prisoner, and upon consideration hereof we are of opinion That it is not inconvenient for His Majesty to accept a surrender, and to grant the same by His Majesties letters patents, (receiving some small rent for an acknowledgement) to hold by Knight's Service in Capite, by one whole Knight's fee, and hereby to extinguish the custom of Tanestry.

" Yet because the country of Carbry offered to be surrendered, as the pretended inheritance of the petitioner, is a large territory; wherein we are of opinion there are, or have been, divers freeholders, and many of them have by attainders forfeited their estates to the Crown, and some other have sold their rights to others, and yet out of some of these not grown to the crown the petitioner and his predecessors may have rightfully some rents and duties, We think it meet before the petitioners surrender be accepted, That by indifferent commissioners and jurors there be a presentment in Ireland, what lands, duties lawful and sufferable services the petitioner hath in them in demesne or service, and what belongeth to His Majesty or other freeholders; and upon return thereof, (certified of records, whereby each parties right may appear) then, and not before, we think convenient to accept the petitioner's surrender, and to grant to him, and the heirs males of his body, such portions of lands, and other duties, and lawful services as by presentment shall be found to be the petitioner's right (not being His Majesties nor growing out of His Majestie's lands or escheats, or any such as hath been granted from the crown to any person,) if it shall be so thought good to the State there, otherwise to certify their opinions to your Lordships, how much, and in what manner, the same were fit to be granted.

" And for securing His Majestie's titles and all stranger's rights, a provision is meet to be incerted in his letters patents to be granted to the petitioner, with liberty of court-leet, half felons goods, waif and stray, and such other inferior privileges as have been usually granted to other lords, and with a covenant that he shall erect twenty four freeholders at the least for service of jurors.

" Which things observed, we think it a beneficial thing to His Majesty, and the country, to have this country reduced from Tanestry to an English tenure, and peaceable course of inheritance.

" Touching the second Article of his petition desiring toleration of the King's royal composition of 80 livres yearly in lieu of cesse ; we think convenient that be preserved; and hold it not convenient to grant him other toleration than other lords or gentlemen, that pretend like poverty have, least by his example others should be encouraged to like suits.

" All the rest of the articles against the Lord Barry, Lady Norrys, and others, are in effect only petitions for justice, wherein we see no inconvenience, if it please your Lordships, to recommend him to the Lord Deputy for the speedy righting of his just complaints against all subjects, saving the undertakers, and such others whose titles have been heretofore hard, and discussed. All which we humbly submit to your Lordships wisdoms. 2 July 1606.

" G. CAREWE.   " J.￮POPHAM.
                                          " ROGER WILBRAHAM."

"DONAL BASE SON OF THE EARL OF CLANCAR. 1605.

" From Patent Rolls of James 1st. Grant of the King to Donal Mac Carthy, natural son of the late Earl of Clancar, of Castle Logh &c with remainder to Donell his reputed son, and his heirs males, for his late services and loyaltie, recommended by our late President of Munster.*

" Ordered to give him all lands left him by his late Father, 28 Ploughlands, all of which the late Queen Elizabeth granted to him by Patent of 21 June 1598. Also together with the Castle Loghie 7 ploughlands, thereunto adjoining, with remainder &c to his reputed son Donal borne before marriage."

We are now taking leave of Donal and his fortunes, and it is impossible to part with him without expressing some satisfaction at the prosperity which closed a career of some celebrity, and great vicissitudes. The reader has seen that he had done many actions little in accord with the customs of an advanced civilization; his birth, his education, the urgency of his position, and the rough times in which he lived are, in part, accountable for this. He was frank and fearless, and though quick to deeds of violence was free from the falsity and meanness which stained the characters of many of the much greater men with whom he was all his days in contention. He was certainly not devoid of ability of a certain kind, and his education appears to have been zealously and attentively carried on by his father's kerns and servants. The first we hear of him on his entry into public life is that he had broken from Her Majesty's Castle of Dublin! and the next, that he was roaming through the wilds of his father's country, the terror of all men! How he was the especial mark of proscription by Herbert, and the Vice-President Sir Thomas Norreys, how he was hunted by Browne with the Queen's horsemen, and how in spite of

---

* The estate thus secured to Donal and his reputed son, and his heirs males was about five thousand acres.

them all, he maintained his freedom, hovering about the homes of the undertakers, now with forty loose swords, and now with but half a dozen, the reader has seen. To use a homely phrase, to each of these gentlemen Donal gave fully as good as he got! He robbed Herbert's man; he burned Browne's farms; " he roamed through all wild places—said Norreys—a Munster Robin Hood, whom it would be well if Her Majesty would take into her service and pay." Later he chased Essex and his flower of nobility out of Munster, with as much speed, and as contemptuously as he would have driven a prey of cows; and, whilst, under favour of O'Neill, he was MacCarthy Mor, and in effect ruler of Desmond, he proved himself an active and daring leader. Carewe spoke truly of him when he said that he would have been a more formidable commander of the power of his Sept than Florence.

Had Florence been kept in England, or taken prisoner by Carewe in the early days of the rebellion, Donal would at once have been accepted in his place, and immediately have joined his force with that of FitzThomas and the bonies; and had they not all been as great idiots as Florence, the Queen's Army—three thousand men, all counted! seventeen hundred available for service—and Her Majesty's Lord President, would have been fortunate, if, like the undertakers, and their English labourers, they could—however shamefully in the opinion of the Earl of Ormond—have fled away, and found shipping at Limerick or Waterford, and carried their civility and loyalty back, where they would have been better appreciated, but seemed to have been less wanted, and Donal, like innumerable Donals before him, might have styled himself King of Desmond. But these contingencies were not within Donal's destiny: Ireland was pacified, and remained so for the long period of forty years. Donal retired to his domains at Castle Lough, secured to him (and his unlawful issue) at the intercession of Carewe, by the King's grace (and his father's will), where for the rest of his days, he extended his hospitality yearly to the English tourists to his native lakes of Killarney.*

* " I know not whether it be worth the while to mention such small matters as these, to wit."—CAMDEN.

It is said that in the " Lake Hotel " which is built upon the ruins of Castle Lough at Killarney, there is preserved to this day a feather bed, sole souvenir of Donal, which is made of the plumes collected by order of that chieftain, in the pass of Barnaglitty.

" Blame me not for mentioning these things considering that the

These peaceful days were alas! not of long duration. About the middle of the century all the laborious work of English civilization was again undone; war was once more everywhere; and, in due time, again came a new pacification for another half century, and a new revision of the Lex Agraria. The reader curious to know how it fared with the unlawfully begotten offspring of Donal of Killarney, and of all other MacCarthys mentioned so often in the preceding pages, will find them duly calendared, each one with the name of the lands of which he had for a brief while repossessed himself, "in the returns of persons indicted of Treasons at the assizes of Youghal, August 2, 1642."

A new name, the first of a coming multitude, was at this time added to the list of the invaders of Florence's patrimony in Carbery. The following petition from Lord De Courcy to the Privy Council shows how simple, and expeditious was the process by which the estates of the prisoner were dismembered. All the country of MacCarthy Mor was instantly occupied; the Queen's claim to it was supposed to be unquestionable; but this attack of De Courcy, like that of Rogers and Popham, made years before, in the time of his first imprisonment, was upon his hereditary private property, actually bought from a previous Lord de Courcy, by his father Sir Donagh. Florence's protest against this fresh spoliation follows quickly upon the petition of De Courcy, and is his first passage of arms in the great legal war which occupied all his energies during the remainder of his long life. There were found many quickly to follow in the path of the new assailant, and it will be seen that Florence was nothing daunted either by their numbers or their influence. His early acquaintance with law and lawyers, and the peculiarity of his own character, which was admirably suited for the subtleties of litigation, now enabled him to contest with patience, with untiring perseverance, and ultimately with success, against a host of enemies.

Owing, in part to his first long imprisonment, and probably also to his requirements during his rule in Desmond, when he had many hundred bonies in his pay, he had been compelled to lease, and mortgage great portions of his lands in Carbery, so that when these lands were seized by the greedier of his neighbours, the holders of such leases and mortgages naturally fell back upon him for their money or for compensation, so that each such transaction was attended

gravest historians have recorded such like matters more at large."— CAMDEN.

with a double suit, and his whole property became a mass of entanglement and confusion, which might have bewildered a mind with less training, or less natural disposition for such pursuits. Quickly following upon the petition of De Courcy and before Florence could have time to offer any explanation upon the matter, arrived a despatch from Ireland, more likely to aid the cause of the claimant than the arguments on which his suit was founded; it was from the Earl of Thomond, now Lord President of Munster, to Cecyll, now Lord Salisbury. The noble writer informed the Minister that "the Jesuits and Traitors were giving out with great joy that Florence was to be set at liberty! He never did good unto this province, or ever would; but sought ever to infect it with traiterous actions." The letter of Florence in reply to the suit of De Courcy, not only disposes of that case, but reveals matters so extraordinary concerning his capture by Carewe, as to be incredible were they not addressed to the Minister who had perfect cognizance of every circumstance of that arrest. Quite as extraordinary is it that, as Florence was made prisoner by Carewe, so does he appear to have been kept a prisoner by the sole will of that arbitrary personage.

" 1607. *July* 24. LORD DE COURCY *to the* EARL OF SALISBURY.

" Right Honble. and my very good Lord, my bounden and most humble duty always remembered: It may please your honorable good Lordship to be advertised that by virtue of letters from the honorable Lords of the Council, directed upon my humble suit to Her late Majesty for examining of my right to the Lordship and Seigneurie of Coursie's country, and for restoring me (upon proof thereof) to the Castle of the Old head of Kensale, being one of my principal manors I have been by order of the late Lord Lieutenant of this kingdom and the Lord Clapton (Sir Geo. Carewe) then Lord President of this province, established in the possession of the same; for that my right thereto, and to my Lordship, was well proved and found by inquisition recorded in his Majesty's Exchequer. Yet, Right Honble good Lord, I am let to understand that Florence Mac Cartie (now in restraint there) being driven to his hard shifts, doth set forth that he is interested in the said Castle of the Old head, and to my manor of Ring Roane, and so doth hope to have some one there that hath more money to spare than good employment for, to hold and take the same from him : and lately the said Florence hath demised the said Castle of Old head to one Bellew, who lately repaired here hence towards the said Florence. I am an humble suitor to your honorable good Lordship that as I have felt and had your Lordship's former favour in my causes, that while my deserts shall serve the same, your honorable good Lordship do continue your honorable favour towards me; and that upon no untrue surmise or complaint of the said Florence, or any for, or by him, I may not be removed from the possession of the said castles, and the lands belonging to them, until that by order of Law the same be evicted against me, or myself

present to make answer, and defence to my title. And so presuming upon
your honorable good Lordship's favour I crave pardon for this my boldness, and do most humbly take leave
          " Cork the 24ᵗʰ of July 1607.
          " Your honorable, good Lordship's most humbly to command
                                        " JHO: DE COURCY.

    " To the Right Honᵇˡᵉ and his very good Lordship the Earl of Salisbury,
one of His Majesty's most Honᵇˡᵉ Privy Council."

    " *Limerick*, 1607, *Sept*ʳ. 19ᵗʰ.   *The* EARL OF THOMOND *to the* EARL OF
                              SALISBURY.

    " My honored, good Lord I wrote to your Lordship some fifteen days
past; since which time I received letters from my Lord Deputy and
Council, wherein he writes of the going away of Tyrone and Tyrconnell;
and a letter to me in private, the copies of both I send to your Lordship
hereinclosed. Your Lordship may see how my life is shot at by these
malicious traitors; for my own part if I had a hundred lives I could never
bestow them better than in God's, and His Majesty's service; and if these
men of the country be taken at the first there will be the less danger.
While we have priests and Jesuits so rife as they are, true subjects shall
never remain in quiet in these kingdoms; the Jesuits and priests, and
those that have been traitors do give out with great joy that Florence
Mᶜ Carty shall be set at liberty! he never did good unto this province, or
ever will; but sought ever to infest it with traiterous actions; for it hath
been ever his study. O Sowleuan Bear is reported to come out of Spain
into England; this man my Lord Clapton knoweth to be the arrantest,
and maliciousest traitor, to his power, that ever this kingdoms bred. If
these two should come into the province they would do nothing but kindle
rebellion, and never show good example, but be opposite to all good subjects, and all Civil proceedings. I have sent for all the nobility, and better
sort of this province, to settle all things in the best sort I may; what shall
be done, and proceeded upon, I will advertise your Lordship of. The
Towns and country are so given to priests and Jesuits, being altogether
ruled by them, as I never saw them more obstinater, and unsweeter in
mind than they are now. The want of the forts and citadels, believe it
my Lord, is a great hinderance to the service &c.
                                        " THOMOND."

    Sickness and ill usage which at last began to render the
style of Florence's letters more plaintive and more indignant,
did not impair its vigour! He was as ever, ready for his old
enemies; with a clear memory of all past passages between
them, and with fearless front to meet all new ones. His
challenge to the Lords of the Privy Council to prove aught
against him, was as defiant as formerly, as was also his repeated complaint that he had never yet been so much as
called before them to give answer to the charges on which,
by their decree, he was still held prisoner! The following
letter reveals by its language of anger, and aversion, what
Florence understood by his wife's " good affection to the

English State, and readiness ever to aid Carewe, by intelligence or otherwise." These letters leave nothing hidden or overlooked, nothing that his biographer needs supplement or explain! The attempts so constantly made to bribe him with promise of liberty if he would abandon his property to men in power; the frequent shifting him from prison to prison, seeking, as their disappointment grew upon them, ever those that were the most unhealthy; the sufferings he endured in consequence, and, before long, the death of his eldest son in one of these jails, are all so clearly related, that the letters, as they follow each other to the Minister or the Privy Council, are as ample as an unbroken diary.

"1608. *June.* FLORENCE Mᶜ CARTY *to the* EARL OF SALISBURY.

" Right Honᵇˡᵉ.

" Such is my hopeless and healthless state, (being in a consumption that with extreme pain weakened me and will shortly end my life) as I had not troubled your Lordship if it were not for this gent Mʳ. Harbert Pelham, unto whom (in my first trouble here) I leased certain lands which my father that purchased, and myself enjoyed quietly above 50 years, as Mʳ. Pelham did these 16 years, until my long trouble and the general opinion of the continuance thereof until my life be lost, encouraged the Lord Coursie to dispossess him wrongfully of the castle of Rinroin, and 5 or 6 ploughlands; by whose example the Lord Barry (that now, in my trouble, dispossesst me wrongfully of other lands) endeavours to dispossess Mʳ. Pelham also of 7 ploughlands, without any more right or colour than the Lord Coursie had to Rinroin, which was, above 50 years past, sold to my father, and afterwards to myself by Gareth, the old Lord Coursie that sold the rest of his lands to the merchants of Kinsale, and others whereof none is dispossessed but we; which lands he doth not challenge for any defect in the purchase, nor as heir to the old Lord Coursie—for if he were a lawful heir the title had not been denied him, for the which he was driven to procure a new creation—and having no colour to the lands, Sir Richard Boyle (that brought me to all this trouble) taught him one of his tricks, wherewith he gets whole countries there; which was to get a grant of the said old Lord Coursie's intrusions, that died about 10 or 12 years past when he was above 100 year old, and being of good years succeeded his father at such a time as no man's livery was sued for, when there was neither sheriff, nor justice in Mounster; but every lord governing his own country; which device avails not much against others more than to trouble them, until they agree to give him some little composition; as of late, one Geoffrey Gallwey a merchant of Kinsale, that hath as much of that land as I or thereabouts, agreed with him for 22ˡⁱ. 10ˢ.

" The Lord Barry's challenge being idler; who upon a lease of concealed lands that he had, got some of his own people and followers, that he empanneled, to find an office for the attainder of one Fynyn McOwen, that at the very first coming of the rebellion into Mounster was killed by some of the rebels; under colour of which office he disinherited his poor children; and challenges my land, and Mr. Pelham's; which if any will say that Fynyn McOwen, or any for him, did ever hold, enjoy our challenge, we are contented to loose it; being about 60 years past, bought by

my father; and possessed by him, and by me, ever since; whereunto if
Fynyn McOwen or any other had any challenge, no doubt but Mr. Pelham
should understand thereof in 16 years that he enjoyed it; which being
truly the state of his cause, I hope your Lordship will further him to such
letters as may establish, and maintain him in the possession of his right.

"Touching myself, although I am like to end my life here now, it
could never appear in 7 years that I have been restrained, that ever I had
anything to do with any foreign nation, or favoured the rebels which I
did rather hurt by alluring some companies from them, overthrowing some
of their forces, and recovering the strongest country they had; and although Captain Flowre (by burning my castles, killing my tenants, taking
away 1400 cows, and following me 30 miles) constrained me to fight with
him some 10 days before the Lord Carewe came—which was the cause that
made me procure a pardon—yet I came presently to my Lord and, (cas-
sireinge by his advice those companies that I had) informed him still of
the state of the rebels, assuring him that he should have no resistance,
and caused my nephew to deliver him his castle of Carrigifoyll, that stood
commodious to annoy them; of all which he informed your Lordship then,
as appeared at the late Lord Trērs, when I was sent over, where your
Lordship confessed that I was good in the rebellion time; at which time,
when I recovered my country, and was there without any pledges, hostages
or sureties bound for me, who doubts but that I would then (if I could be
thereunto persuaded) join with the rebels ? which if I *had*, why should not
her late Majesties pardon avail *me* as it availed them ? or if I could be
touched for any such matters, who can imagine or think that I would (at
the late Lord Trērs aforesaid, before your Lordship and the rest) refuse
my *pardon and protection, which I have still*, if ever I aided, assisted or
joined with Tireowen, James of Desmond or any of them, or did write
beyond seas, or was privy to any matter or practise thither, or from
thence.

"Yet notwithstanding I have been ever since these 7 years restrained
without so much matter as might bring me to be questioned withal, being
first brought into suspicion—and letters procured here hence, upon informations drawn there by Mr. Boyle, and other informations procured by
other friends from LoghFoyle, for Sir Valentine Browne's sons, that
coveted those lands, which with long trouble, suit and charges I cleared
here; and with great charges, loss and danger I recovered there, from
rebels—and afterwards committed; when my tenants being spoiled of 500
cows by certain officers and soldiers of Sir Charles Wilmott's, the Lord
Carewe was thereupon wrought to give me some hard speeches, and (upon
an imagination or fear of any discontentment for those spoils and speeches)
persuaded by Sir Charles, and Boyle, to commit me; but no cause nor
colour could be had for it; until one Blake of Cork a tailor that dwells
here in London, was brought to complain of me for a challenge of 22ls for
the which he committed me ; Boyle, that could do most with him, persuaded
him to send me hither, and to write still against me; at whose coming
over, being at Boyle's instigation incensed against me *for clearing myself
to discredit him*, as he said, *he was also aggravated against me by the wicked
woman that was my wife!* whom I saw not, nor could abide in almost a
year before my commitment; who being wrought, and recommended hither
against me, came to me to the Fleet, and desired to stay with me; which
when I refused, she made my Lord Carewe believe that I railed of him,
and all his friends, and caused him to get me sent hither; although I spake
not, (as God judge me) of any of them, as she confessed to some afterwards; and having gotten this gent Mr. Pelham to deal with his Lordship,

his answer to my letter was, "*that he so misliked my justifications* as I should never have liberty, before I confessed my faults and submitted myself;" which if I would do, he would further my delivery; yet being still followed by my sister, and friends, he was in the end reasonable-well contented, which when Boyle that was here, perceived, he came to the marshalsea to see me, and told me my Lord Carew was my friend, and that I should be discharged; but if himself were mine enemy he said he had some of my country that could accuse me : to whom when I said there was none that ever said, or could say so, and defied him to find any, he made my Lord Carew believe that I stood upon such defiance and terms to clear and justify myself, as I would utterly discredit him if I were enlarged; and there withal he, and Thomas Browne, Sir Valentine's youngest son, devised letters here from some undertakers and others that were in Ireland, against my liberty, which Browne preferred to the Council; of which device I never had intelligence until some of them in Ireland (unto whom they did write to acknowledge those letters) sent me word, to clear themselves thereof; by which devices my liberty was then crossed, and the Lord Carew so incensed against me ever since, as when Sir Thomas Vavasour obtained of your Lordship to further me to liberty, upon good sureties to continue within 10 or 12 miles of this city, my Lord Carew got the Lord Chamberlain to charge Sir Thomas Vavasour to give it over.

" And to find some matter against me Captain Nuce came to offer me money from Coronell Jaques that he did owe me ; which when I refused, one John Mathewes came in July last to offer me liberty for money, and to persuade me to write to Jaques for that money, who (when I refused, and offered what money my friends in Ireland could make up, and to stay here until they paid it) gave me over; whereof (when in September after, news came of Tireowen's running away,) a matter was made to get me sent hither, where being restrained without sight of the air ever since, I am fallen so diseased as my life shall be shortly lost, that will more prejudice His Majesty and the State than myself, because I can do them such service as none else of all Ireland can do, or hath such means to do as I have, which I hope will move your Lordship to preserve my life; for the which is no hope nor help except it proceed of your Lordships honourable inclination, and consideration ; for if any do go about to speak for me, whosoever can do most with him shall be wrought to charge and persuade him to give it over; neither is there any (in respect of your Lordship's former favour toward me) that I had rather be beholden unto for my life than unto your Lordship; at whose hands I will both deserve it well, with the service that I can do now, and rest ever ready to perform therewith what may be acceptable and beneficial unto your honourable Lordship.

" My humble request therefore is that it will please your Lordship to further that I may be confined here in such sort as your Lordship shall think fit, whereby I may have some hope of the preservation of my life, and recovery of my health. And if the informations of my adversaries, or anything that was inferred against me, brought me to be suspected or mistrusted, I have two sons, the one of 12 years of age, and the other of 10 years, whereof I will not only deliver one into the Lord President of Munster's hands, and keep the other to school here, or deliver both where your Lordship will appoint; but also find sufficient sureties besides, for my continuance within what limits your Lordship and the rest of the Councill shall set down. *Beseeching your Lordship to consider that none other was ever tossed thrice to the tower and restrained 7 years without so much matter as might bring him once to be questioned withal! and in the end turned to end his life, languishing in a close prison, much less any that no cause nor colour was had to commit him but a challenge of 22ˡⁱ, as is known to all Ireland, and to all the Englishmen there; nor none that had the queen's pardon and protection was ever refused here to have the benefit thereof, which (although I have) can no way avail me,* if my life be thus lost, which (hoping your Lordship will commiserate) I leave to your honorable and favourable consideration, resting

" Your Lordships most humble and bonden
" to be commanded
" FLOR: Mᶜ CARTHY.

" To The Right Honble, His very approved good Lord the Earl of Salisbury, Lord High Treasurer of England."

Florence was not the only sufferer by what he termed Boyle's tricks. The Earl of Ormond had in a letter to Cecyll from Kilkenny, enclosed notes showing how " one Crosbye, and Boyle have been the means of overthrowing many of Her Majesty's good subjects, *by finding false titles to their lands, and turning them out.*" These complaints had reached the Queen, and it required all the ingenuity of Cecyll to screen him from her anger. He did so for Carewe's sake, though he concealed not from him his own opinion of the man he was protecting.

" Boyle, he wrote, is accused by Crosbye, for I know not what of cosining and concealing! one barrell little better herring than th'other! Let me know therefore whether you wold haue him fauoured or no; trewly the fellow seems witty!"

" 1608. *Dec. To the Right Honᵇˡᵉ the* EARL *of* SALISBURY, *Lord High Treasurer of England.*

" The humble petition of Florence Mac Cartie, prisoner in the Tower :—
" Humbly shewing his being restrained here close at the first when he was sent over, *and after his removing from the Fleet, about three years, which brought him so diseased, as his life was hardly preserved in the Marshalsea, where he was afterwards kept three years and seven months, until he was, about three years past, removed thither again and kept close ever since,* to the undoing of him and three young sons which he maintains; his eldest son being dead here; and himself grown so diseased, as he never enjoyed his health any long time ever since.
" Forasmuch as your suppliant *is by the late Queen pardoned,* and that the Lord Viscount Roch, O'Sulivan More, and the White Knight are bound for him.
" He therefore humbly beseecheth that it will please your Lordship of your honorable and accustomed favour towards him, so far to commiserate his life, now in his extreme misery, and dangerous diseases, as to *further his removing to some* other prison, in hope that his life may be preserved, and he shall ever pray for your honorable Lordship."

2 c 2

" My chefest hope consisting in your Honor's favor, which makes me persevere in importuning your Lordship when now my misfortune encreases, mine adversaries (whereof some that entered into condicions to me) doethe endeavour to have me kept until my life be lost in this close prison, where I was wrought divers times, and now last upon John Mathew's his offer of libertie unto me for money, for the which (where no offence nor matter can be made thereof) my punishment hathe been very great, being kept close here above a yeare; which brought me so extreme sick the last winter, as I was never well since, nor have no other hope but to end my life shortly, if I continue thus after my long troble, which hathe altogether worne me both in body and mind; whereunto I was brought for no cause or matter that could ever appeare these seven or eight yeares past that I have been restrained, *when all the most suspected persons of Ireland, both for Rebellion and foraine practices, were here at libertie, and are freely in their countries;* Although your Lordship acknowledged (when I was sent over) that I did well in the rebellion time, and that I refused then before your Lordship the benefit of my pardon if ever I helped or aided the rebels, or meddled with anie foraine nacion, *yet I am not only restrained ever since without being called to answer, or charged for anie thing,* but alsoe my life is sought by way of close imprisonment, *when neither the late Queene's pardon that I have, nor the king's gracious clemencie that helped the chefest offenders of Ireland, nor the benefit of lawe avayles me, but that my long restraint these seven or eight yeares, without anie matter to be had against me,* cannot but give your Lordship sufficient light and knowledge of my cause; and that my being so often wrought hither, where now I have been kept close these four yeares alreadie, with all the miseries that I sustained, will move (to commiserate my unfortunate life) your Lordship, unto whom I have been long known, and much bound, by whose honorable favour I was maintained and dispatched when I was a suitor; and my life was preserved since my troble; for when there was order to bring me back from the Marshalsea, your Lordship upon my petition furthered me to a warrant for my staying there, without which I had not lived; and since my coming hither it hathe pleased your Lordship (upon my petition by my son) to write for my good usage, and of the permitting of some to me, which was my best helpe to preserve all the life that is left me in this close and solitarie calamitie; where (knowing your Lordship's just and honorable inclinacion and disposicion) I lived in hope that time would bring your Lordship to the true knowledge of my cause; until the long continuance of my close restraint brought me so diseased and distempered, and so weak and melancholick as I doe not hope to live: And now I doe not desire libertie, or that your Lordship should be trobled to deal or speake therein; *My humble request being onlie that it will pleasure your Lordship to extend your Honorable favour for the preservacion of my life, by furthering my removing to some other prison, where I may live among men,* in hope that my health may be recovered, and my life preserved.

"ffLORENCE M^c CARTHY."

From bad to worse! This man, ever discontented, ever flourishing Her late Majesty's Pardons and Protections before the face of the Privy Council, ever murmuring against the salubrity of H. M's. prisons, ever fancying that every gentleman-undertaker in Munster is robbing him, ever obstinately declaring that no charge had ever been brought, or ever could be proved against him, ever striving by his justifications to bring discredit upon the late Lo: President of Munster, and his friend Mr. Boyle, as if his arrest, and the alienation of his lands had been contrary to honour and justice, now afflicts the feelings of His Majesty's Hon: Privy Council by making this unavoidable incident, the death of his son in prison—a child that was always sickly, as was well known by the constant impossibility of delivering him as a hostage to the Lo: President of Munster, in the days of his father's rebellious practices—a subject of petition, and fresh discontent! And with disrespectful irony solicits that, as he is dying of numerous diseases where he is, and as he has—ever ready to be shown—the *pardon* of Her late Majesty, he may, through their Lordships' *extreme 'favour, be sent to some other prison!* where he may live amongst men! and so have hope to preserve his life!

CHAPTER XVII.

FLORENCE'S TREATISE ON THE EARLY HISTORY OF IRELAND.

ALTHOUGH the mind of Florence might seem sufficiently occupied with the incessant struggle with a host of enemies, and his spirits wearied and worn by the many humiliations which ever beset the man who falls from dignity and riches, into poverty, it is gratifying to perceive that he could fight against the melancholy of his own thoughts, as courageously as he did with his plunderers. That a man of education would be naturally driven to books to comfort him in the dreary solitude of a prison, where " *he was kept so close as none might come to him, and he was without sight of the air,*" is what would be expected; and if the period of his captivity were prolonged, that the mind, concentrated by determined effort upon certain subjects, to enforce the exclusion of others, should seek further relief in the recreations of literary composition, is equally natural. Florence was a fair scholar, understanding various languages, and certainly better acquainted than any man of his age with the traditionary history of his country. That he was a clear and forcible writer of the English language, that his letters are, at the least, in as good grammar as those of Cecyll, and as logical as Carewe's, will not be disputed. That he understood those Irish MSS. which abounded in his day, and the style of which, from immense antiquity, was daily becoming more and more obsolete, he has proved by his frequent reference to them. That he had "much cultivated Spaniards, and the Spanish language," St. Leger wrote, as a grievance against him, to England, 20 years before! and that he maintained uninterrupted intercourse with agents in Spain he himself declared, both to Cecyll and Sir Thomas Norreys. That he had a competent knowledge of Latin can be scarcely doubted, for Latin was the language with which even the minor provincial Irish chieftains, who, like Bryan O Rork, were too barbarous to understand English, communicated both orally and in corre-

spondence with the Lords Deputies, and other English
authorities, when such gentlemen possessed the learning to
qualify them for the intercourse. The greater portion, nay,
in all probability the entire multitude of learned works which
the reader will see shortly referred to by him, existed in his
day probably only in the Latin tongue! That Florence
possessed in his Tower cell many rare volumes we have the
clearest evidence. Carewe asserts that he borrowed from him
certain volumes when he was engaged in composing his tomes
of Irish Pedigrees, which are now preserved at Lambeth.
Colgan makes mention of books—which Dr. O'Donovan re-
cognizes by internal evidence as "The Annals of Inisfallen"—
in the possession of the Illustrious Florentius MacCarthy,
Prisoner in the Tower; and Dr. O'Donovan traces to an old
copy of "the Book of Invasions;" to certain "Munster Annals
not now accessible;" and to a copy of "the War of the Gaels
with the Gauls," as well as to the Annals of Innisfallen,
many references in the writings of Florence.   Dermod
O'Connor in his version of Keating's History of Ireland, speaks
of Florence as "a reputable author called Florence Mac-
Carthy, who has delivered down the transactions of Ireland
for many ages."   Besides these various works, chiefly Irish
MSS., which we know Florence to have possessed, many
scores of volumes must have been within his reach, to enable
him to write the treatise presently to be brought under the
reader's notice.

   With such acquirements, and with such resources, in the
9th year of the second period of his captivity, and when close
prisoner within the Tower of London, Florence composed a
most remarkable Treatise on the Antiquity and History of
the Mythic ages of his country, which after lying lost to sight
for 250 years, has recently been edited and published, by the
late Dr. O'Donovan. That learned scholar declared to the
author of this Biography, that in all this national lore, the
learning of Florence left all his own acquirements a long way
behind. The writer of these pages transcribed this Treatise
with great exactness, for the use of the learned editor, and to
him he wrote at the time, " the letter throughout is distinct,
clear, and firm as print; it is without a blot, and exhibits
only two or three amendments. What minute characters
the large hand of the writer could form, and with what
certainty and precision it could trace line after line in fault-
less parallels, and with intervals so minute that there seems
upon the page but a sharp, slender thread of white encircling
each word, may be judged from the fact that three pages,

and twenty-one lines of a sheet, foolscap size (more correctly folio size,) sufficed to contain the whole of this long letter."

This Treatise was addressed to the Earl of Thomond, whose name has so frequently occurred in these pages, and who had, since Florence's imprisonment, given his daughter in marriage to Cormac Oge MacCarthy, Lo: of Muskerry, Florence's cousin. This nobleman whom Cecyll in his correspondence with Carewe, ever mentions with a sneer, but whom he afterwards appointed Lord President of Munster, was not indifferent to the pretensions of his countrymen to an early and unrivalled civilization, and to a matchless antiquity in their pedigrees. There is preserved at Lambeth a valuable collection of the descents of every noble family of Milesian race, collected for this Earl—it has been said, "by paid spies, and for purposes of spoliation"—no proof is offered of his having been influenced by any motive so base. The reader has seen that in a recent letter to Cecyll, Lord Thomond had declared that Florence was fit to be kept in restraint; that he was too dangerous to be allowed to return to his native country! later we shall see him with a generous inconsistency lending his name—with responsibility of £500 —as surety, with other noblemen, for Florence's liberation from prison, and liberty within certain range of London. The opening paragraph of Florence's Treatise attributes to the antiquarian tastes of this nobleman, the suggestion which caused its composition.

"At your last being in England I understood of your being studious of the antiquities of our nation, wherein (altho' my memory is much decayed in almost nine years extreme endurance) I would be glad to do any service to so ancient a nobleman of the nacion." Then commences the History of Ireland from the coming of its first inhabitants from Greece, the Terra Cethim! a few years (500) after the universal Fludd. Next follow the migrations of the successive races that settled there, the synchronisms of its incidents with the better known histories of a multitude of Monarchs, and Mythic heroes, displaying almost as much learning as the erudite O'Flaherty himself. He continues his narrative through the invasion by the Normans, down even to the period of James the First and that distinguished Scottish Knight "who thought the Irish fitter to be rooted out than to be suffered to enjoy their lands."

The Treatise concludes with a passage which is the more interesting as it proves the writer's familiarity with the oldest of our Irish MSS., which were written in the Bearla Feini,

and which all our most eminent scholars, for nearly a century
and a half, have acknowledged their inability to read.
Florence's critical observation on these writings, is unosten-
tatious proof of his intimate knowledge of his native language.

"Those (writers) that were learned, who wrote about
1,000 or 800 years past, although their language is now out
of use, wrote more copious and elegant, to whose books, if
this king were anything affected I think His Majesty might
best have them." "This much—he concludes—of the nacion
(being all the service that I am able to do y^r Lo^p) I thought
it fit to acquaint y^r Lo^p withal, before I end my life in the
languishing torture of this close prison, where since my commitment I have been threese tossed, without any matter to
chardge me withal, and where so long as God will spare me
life, I will rest y^r Lop^s most humble and faithful to be commanded."

To this letter is appended a memorandum in the Irish
language by a certain Conor O'Kinga, who had made a copy
of it. "Let every one—he says—who shall read this treatise,
join to pray for him who copied it ; and moreover that God
may redeem Finghin MacCarthy, who set this forth (composed the Treatise) from the imprisonment and bondage in
which he is detained in the Tower of London.

May God Almighty have mercy on the souls of both !"

From all this learned speculation Florence was soon to
fall back to a style of composition with which for more than
20 years, he had been familiar, to letters and petitions to the
Minister, and the Privy Council ; to turn from Alexander the
Great, Gathelus, Cecrops, Pharao Cingris (his maternal
ancestor) Moses, and innumerable demigods, to Sir George
Carewe and Sir Robert Cecyll !

Year after year was passing ; the long period of his first
imprisonment was already exceeded by this second, and
Florence must have seen that unless he could bring his mind
to part with his Irish possessions, he would *never* regain his
freedom ! the only alternation that successive years brought
with them in his lot, was a change from one of the King's
prisons to another. Thrice, to use his own words, was he
thrown back into the Tower, and without any matter alleged
against him. When his health gave way, from the severe
discipline, and ill climate of that prison, he was allowed the
indulgence of a change of air, and some human fellowship, in
the Marshalsea ! No sooner was his health recruited than his
enemies, men determined to break his stubborn resistance to

their designs upon his lands, obtained his recommittal to the
Tower.

Although the liberty of Florence could no longer have
any connexion with the political condition of his country, his
detention in an English prison had become of immense importance to two descriptions of persons ; the one, Undertakers,
determined to wrest his vast territories from him at any cost,
for distribution amongst themselves ; and the other, men in
favour with the learned Monarch then on the throne of
England ; men in power ready to sell their influence to the
best bidder ; as ready to traffic with Florence for his freedom
as with M. C. Reagh, or de Courcy, or Barry, for the continuance of his restraint ; nay, for his confinement in the most
unhealthy of the King's prisons, in order that by such torment
he might be driven to despair and submission. In the year
1611 this iniquitous struggle was at its height.

Happily the lawyers, ever the most faithful of his allies,
were more powerful than the robbers ; and the greediness of
Scotch favourites provoked occasional opposition in the higher,
and no less greedy English officers of State. His enemies
acted in perfect union, and with unscrupulous cruelty ; but
Florence preferred the miserable lot of continued imprisonment, to the denuding of himself and his children of the last
remnants of his property. It would appear from the tone of
his letters to Cecyll at this time, that something of the good
will of other days had been regained. Florence has some
acts of kindness to thank him for (probably a change of
prisons), and is not without hope that a skilful exposition of
the baseness and cupidity of his oppressors—men well known
to the Minister—and of his own wrongs, may lead to some
further proofs of his affection. It is sufficiently obvious that
if Florence had been willing to humble himself to Carewe,
and be silent upon his *justifications*, which so deeply offended
that personage ; to satisfy Sir James Hamilton, and to com-
pound with Lord De Courcy—as from the circumstance
of that nobleman's consenting to be surety, with others, for
his freedom, it would seem he had been in some treaty to do
—and, in short, have applied for letters patent to divide his
estates amongst the Lo : Barry, his cousin M. C. Reagh, Sir
Richard Boyle, and the other enterprising colonists mentioned
in his letters, he might about this time have obtained a fresh
pardon and protection, which, if they would but have been
respected, till he could regain the fastnesses of Desmond, he
would doubtless have known how duly to appreciate in
future.

"1611. *Marshalsea, 27 Nov.* FLORENCE Mᶜ CARTY *to the* EARLE OF SALISBURY.

" Right Honorable,

" I hold myself so much bound to your Lordship as I desire much, and wish myself able to make known my thankfulness for your favours, which I will rest readier to deserve with all the service that shall ever lie in me to do your Lordship, unto whom only (as I always seek) I must have recourse, by reason of the wrong that is now offered me for lands that my father and myself purchased of Gareth, lord Coursie, and enioied about 60 years, which, above 20 years past, I leased to Mr. Harbert Pelham; whereof he is now dispossessed by this Lord Coursie, who alleging himself to be the said Garrith, Lord Coursie's kinsman, obtained of the late Queen his intrusions, wherewith he vexed a great while the burgesses of Kinsale, and the other purchasers, and wrought so now with the tenants that held my land of Mr. Pelham, as he got the possession thereof without any resistance, and is come over for letters to surrender, and pass the same by patent. Also when my cousin Mᶜ Carthy Reoghe (taking advantage of my restraint) came hither, with intent (by surrendering the country of Carbrie) to defeat me contrary to his agreement, and bond of ten thousand pounds, wherein he is bound to me, Sir James Hamilton came and brought Sir James Sempel to me, where *(upon their undertaking to procure me my right of Mac Carthy)* I entered into covenants to give them the one half of whatsoever they recovered for me, they being to pay me £100, and bound likewise by covenants to me that I should have the one half or moiety of what they obtained of the King's Majesty, or recovered or got of Mac Carthy, or by any means in that country; but when Sir James Hamilton perceived how far Mac Carthy was friended he brake with me, and dealth with him, of whom he got such interest as he intends not only to keep me from having anything, but also to dispossess all the gent. and freeholders in that country, together with Sir John Fitz Edmonds, and Mʳ. Walter Coppingēr, and many English gent. that holds a great deal of land there; to which end he hath written over now to Sir John Greham, and others that are joined with him in this matter, to have the King's letters sent over unto him, with intent to join himself pattentee with Mac Carthy, unto whom he is by their agreement to give but 60 plough lands, with certain rents and cheferies, that he had in that country, which I thought good to acquaint your Lordship withal, being *so restrained as I cannot resist him;* although my right is apparent, as appears by Mac Carthy Reoghe's own bond, and by Sir James Hamilton's covenants; which if I had not, the Lord Carewe, Sir Robert Gardner, and Sir Roger Wilbraham, who are best experienced in the government of Ireland, knows there was never any country holden by Irish custom, that came in question before the state, but they gave their several portions to such as were best interested therein, to hold by English tenure, according to justice and equity, as was ever thought fit and necessary by the State, unto whom, or to such as your Lordship will think fit, I am willing to submit myself and my right, having here Mac Cartie's bond, and Sir James Hamilton's covenants, which I would show to Sir Roger Wilbraham, or to any that would relate unto your Lordship the state of my cause; humbly beseeching your Lordship to stay the King's letters in their behalf, and that I may have your Lordship's furtherance for the obtaining of letters to the Lord Deputy and Council, to make stay of the surrender and proceedings of Mac Carthy Reoghe, and Sir James Hamilton, until your Lordship be made acquainted with all, and until my cause and right be heard, and known; the rather that the

said country of Carbrie is such, and the matter so great, as it is not fit that
any thing should be done therein without your Lordship and the rest of
the Council's knowledge; as it is well known to the Lord Carewe, who
knows what a number of gent and freeholders hath their livings there,
and what a great number of Englishmen are planted and seated there,
more than in any other country of Ireland; which will breed a great deal
of suit and trouble to the state here, and there, if Sir James Hamilton do
get any interest of Mac Carthy reogh therein, which with the King's
letters patents thereupon will be his colour to trouble them. And for the
Lord Coursie (by whom, his chief friend against me, Sir James Hamilton
wrote now for the King's letters to defeat me,) he hath been here with me
oftentimes to offer me composition for my land; which I refused, and we
have been since before the Commissioners, by whom our cause was referred to the order or arbitrament of two indifferent friends, learned in the
law; since which time he laboured, unknown to me, a certificate for letters
into Ireland, to surrender my land, and take it by patent, and now refuses
to stand to the order. My humble request therefore is that it will please
your Lordship to stay the Lord Coursie's letters to pass my land by patent,
until the matter be ordered by those unto whom the Commissioners referred it, or by themselves, or until he recover it by due course of law in
Ireland, where I will send mine evidences to be showed, being persuaded
(when the burgesses of Kinsale and all the other purchasers doth still enjoy
their land,) that myself alone ought not to be dispossessed of mine, for the
which the Lord Coursie cannot say nothing to me more than he can say to
them, but that *they are at liberty to defend theirs, and I so restrained as I
cannot speak in the defence of mine,* which encouraged Mac Carthy reogh
to keep five ploughlands wrongfully of my portion of that country; and
O'Donovan, and the lord Barry, and to dispossess me now in my restraint
of a great deal of my purchased lands, that was all upon my father's death,
about 35 years past, found by office for Sir William Drury, Lord President
of Munster, whose ward I was; which office is recorded at Dublin, and all
the land specified therein, yet the long continuance of my restraint, and
hopeless state bred such an opinion in most men there that they think they
may take, and keep anything that was mine; which I humbly beseech your
Lordship to redress, by directing some course for what liberty your Lordship shall be pleased to further me unto; I have since my commitment as
is known to the Lord Carewe, procured sureties, the Lord Viscount Roche,
O'Sulivan Moore, and the White Knight being bound in great bonds for
me; and now upon knowledge of your Lordship's pleasure that I should
find sureties here, I have procured the Lord of Hode (Hoath), and the
Lord Coursie, that is in controversy with me for land, together with Mr.
Henry Hudlestone, (Sir Edmond Hudlestone of Essex, his son and heir,)
and Mr. John Thrill, a Sussex gent. of good living, humbly beseeching (in
respect they are now after the tearme to depart shortly,) that it will please
your Lordship to appoint any to take their bond; wherein referring me
to your Lordship's honorable and favorable consideration. I rest ever
Y^r Lo^ps most bounden and thankful to be commanded.

"ffloRENCE M^c CARTHY.

"To the R^t. Hon: his most approued good Lo: the Earl of Salisbury,
L^d. High Treas^rer of Engl^d."   .

In the month of December of the same year the Lady
Ellen was as busy as her husband, seeking protection from

the loyal settlers in her father's country.   Her property had
fared as badly as her husband's.   It had been coveted, and
parcelled out amongst the Undertakers, who, after Florence's
arrest, had settled like a cloud of locusts on the lands of
Desmond.

The reader has seen that she obtained the King's order
for thirteen quarters of her own inheritance, but those who
pretended previous claims, or any claims, to this land, frustrated all her attempts to get possession of it.   The King
found it easier to relieve her present wants with a gift from
his exchequer than to recover her lands for her; her petition
procured her a dole of forty pounds.

" *To the Right Honorable the* EARLE OF SALISBURY, *Lord High Treasurer
of England.*

"The humble Petition of the Lady Hellen Cartye,
"Shewinge unto your good Lp: that whereas the Petition having
hertofore a small annuytie out of the'xchequer during her own life only:
and out of her desire to provyde for her poore children who are destitute
of all relief, she became an humble suito̔ to his Ma^{ty} for pte of her
father's lands in Ireland; and after four yeraes suite here, toher exceedinge greate charge, she obtayned a graunt from his Ma^{ty} of 13 quarters of
her father's lands, and therupon (wholly relyinge on that poore estote) she
made away her said anuytie, towards the satisfacc̃on of her creditors, and
for her owne presente reliefe, wch done, and havinge prosecuted suites
both in England and Ireland, a longe tyme, to her greate charge, in hope
of the recovery of the said 13 quarters of lande, according to his Ma^{ts}
graunt, was notw^{t}hstandinge, at length frustrated therof, by such as had
former graunts of the pmisses, to her utter undoinge.
"Now, lately, she cominge over hither in hope of some other releif,
was bold humbly to laye open her poore estate by her li̅es to your Lp, and
in regard of her sicknes, and want ever sithence, she was not able
to followe yo̔ Lp to sollicyte her suite, and now her extreamityes
are such as necessity doth enforce her tobecome an earnest suit to
yo̔ Lp   Beseechinge yo̔ good Lp in yo̔ goodnes and com̃yserac̃on
of her miserable estate, to vouchsafe unto her Lycence for the
transportinge of certen tonnes of Beere out of this kingdome, as to yo̔
Lp shall seeme meete, towards the releevinge of her wants, wch will be
piudiccall to none, and therefore she hopeth (in regarde his Ma^{ty} hath
solely her father's lands, and yo̔ sup^t beinge the last of that howse) to
charge his Maty for any releif, yo̔ Lp will conceave the same a matter
reasonable for her, wherby she shalbe enhabled to recover her pention
againe; and will never trouble his Ma^{ty} or Yo̔ Lp hereafter but contynually to pray for your L^{ps} health and happiness long to contynue."

"1611.   *Dec^r.* 26.   *Warrant of Gift of* £40 *to the* LADYE ELLEN CARTYE.

"James, &c.
"To the Treasurer and Undertakers of Our Exchequer greeting!
Whereas upon the humble petition of the Ladie Elyne Cartie, we are
given to understand of her great necessitie and present want, in com-
miseration whereof, out of our Royall disposicion, we are pleased to

bestowe on her the som of £40 of lawfull money of England ; wherefore we will and command you out of the Treasure in the receipt of our Exchequer, to pay or cause to be paid for throughout to Ladie Ellen Cartie or to her assigns the som of £40 to be taken unto her, as of our free gift, and reward, without accompt, imprest, or other charge to be sett upon her, her executors, administrators, or assigns, for the same, or anie part thereof.   And these our Letters shall, &c., &c.

"Given, &c., this 26th day of Decr, 8th of our Reign of England, France, and Ireland, and Scotland."

In the month of December, 1611, there was issued a docket "to pay to Florence MacCarthy, now prisoner in the King's Bench, the som of £3 weekly, until His Majesty's further pleasure." Thus matters trained on for three years longer; frequent indulgence of change of prison; till at last, after a confinement of fourteen years, there broke upon the prisoner the sunny prospect of some limited degree of freedom : not the freedom to return to Ireland, but to walk the streets of London unrestrained! but what mockery of freedom was this!   In Ireland he would have been a great lord, "infinitely embraced by his countryman.'   As Tanist to M. C. Reagh, and actual M. C. Mor, he would have been a more powerful chieftain than any of his ancestors had been for 400 years! and after the overthrow of the northern Earls, the greatest of Irish race, or of any race in Ireland!   To be allowed to go back to Munster would have been real freedom, but to train around and across London and its suburbs, twelve miles of a galling chain, one end of it fast fettered about his ancles, and the other bolted in the Tower walls! to be allowed, like a winter-fly, to crawl about in such sun as shines in London!   This was such freedom as the brigand gives to the traveller, for whose ransom he is waiting!   But such liberty as this was, it enabled him to frequent the inns of law, and the houses of great men, as he had done to good purpose twenty-five years before.   He had been called upon to find sureties for the large sum of £5,000, for his not straying more than twelve miles from London ; these sureties were readily procured from amongst the noblest of his countrymen, but even then the small indulgence was made matter of such tardy concession, that he needed to write, and beg, as an especial favour that "he might be furthered to that little liberty that was granted or intended for him."

"1624.   *July* 28.

" According to His Majestie's pleasure and direction at Oatlands the 5th of this present, under your hand concerninge Florence MacCarthy I have taken bonde :—

" Of The Earle of Thomonde,
    The Earle of Clanrickarde,
    The Lord of Delvin, } In £500 a-piece.
    Sir Patrick Barnewall,

" Of Sir Randulp McDonell,
    Sir Donell O'Brien,
    Dermott McDonogh MacCarthy, } In £250 a-piece.
    David Condon,
" And of Florence in £2000.

" The condicion is in *hæc verba*, ' That whereas Florence MacCarthy of
Desmonde, Esqre in the Kingdom of Ireland, is upon humble suite made
to His Majestie, released out of the Tower of London (where he remained
prisoner) and confined to the cittie of London.   If, therefore, the said
Florence MacCarthy shall not depart out of the realme of England without
His Majestie's Lycence first had and obtained, nor travaile above one
daie's jorney from the cittie of London, without Lycence under the
hands of six of His Majestie's Privie Councill, that then the obligation
bee voyde, &c.

" And soe I rest.'

" July 28, 1624."

" EDMONDES.

" 1614.   *Oct.* 15.   FLORENCE M^cCARTHY *to the* EARL OF SOMERSET.

" Right Honorable,

" Although I have many suits for my living, and certificates from the
Earl of Thomond, the lord Carew, the Lord chief justice of Ireland and
others, to prove my right to sundry parts of my lands, whereof divers, by
taking advantage of my restraint, did wrongfully dispossess me, I
resolved, notwithstanding, to forbear importuning your Lordship and to
rest, as I do upon your honorable favour, and expect your lordship's best
leisure, as I have done since I entered my sureties at the Lord Deputy's
departing.   But now understanding that those that dispossessed me of my
lands, doth daily devise sundry ways to keep it, and to strengthen themselves therein, as also some of it, which I recovered here this last summer
of Captain Henry Skipwith, for the possession of which I had the Lords
of the Council and the Lord Deputy's letters, is now lately, by permission
of the said Captain Skipwith, or his wife, entered into, and taken from
me, by one of that country called Lord Coursie, whose son sues here now
to the lords, and is like (in respect that I cannot speak for myself, nor
defend my right,) to obtain letters to keep it; whereby your Lordship may
see that my restraint disables me to defend, or keep my own, and hinders
me from recovering my right, which I humbly beseech your Lordship to
consider, and that it will please your honorable lordship so far to commiserate my long endurance, with the loss of my living, without which I
cannot maintain my poor children, as to further me to that little liberty
that is granted or intended me, upon the sureties I entered, which the
Lord Deputy certified to be the best assurance that I could tender, whose
bonds of £500.), that I shall not depart this realm, nor go above a day's
journey from this city, without his Majesty's and the Council's licence, the
Clerk of the Council hath these four or five monthe, which I leave to your
Lordship's honorable consideration, resting ever

" Your Lordship's most humble and faithful to be commanded,

" FLORENCE MC CARTHY."

· " October, 1614."

The result of this petition was that after fourteen years
of restraint Florence was allowed to go out from his prison,
and enjoy such freedom as the conditions of his sureties permitted. How he employed this period of his liberty, which
lasted without interruption for nearly four years, we shall
presently see ; evidently his legal suits throve the better for
it. The great contest of his life was, as it had been for 30
years, with the Brownes, whose ally was no longer the Lo :
Barry, but the Lo : De Courcy ; the struggle had lost nothing
of its bitterness, and gained in the subtlety of its tactics by the
change. Three years after Florence had left his confinement,
a great and united effort was again made to send him back
to one or other of the prisons, from which, with so much
difficulty, he had obtained his liberty. An order suddenly issued
from the Privy Council—at whose application appeared not,
nor for what purpose was it specified—that there be prepared for
their Lordships an official *abstract of all such matters as were on
record concerning Florence MacCarthy!* Simultaneously with
this abstract, and so similar to it in design as to render it but
little doubtful at whose influence the abstract itself had been
called for, was laid before their Lo⁵ : an affidavit of a certain
Teig Hurley, a Carbery man, a born follower of Florence, and
formerly his servant. His communication is rigorously of
the type of that famous letter of John Annyas! indeed so
wonderfully like it in the recital of the writer's personal experiences as to suggest the suspicion that not the conglomera-
tion only of his recollections and adventures, but the biographical portion also was literally copied from the actual
manuscript of that romantic epistle. Teig, like Annyas, " had
wrestled with his Beble!" and there "seen the fallacy of the
creed of his youth, of the policy of Papistry." Sir Valentine
Browne and Lord de Courcy had done for him the good office
which Sir Owen Hopton had done for his Tower prototype.
The " matching with an English woman of the same faith"
was an improvement on Annyas's mere conversion ; and her
want of dower, and otherwise her inferior merits and condition, proof of the sacrifice he had made, and of his readiness
to endure much for his new principles.
     The precise purport of Teig's affidavit it is difficult to
discover ; but its value is undeniable, for the details incidentally afforded by it of Florence's prison life, his curious
interviews with men who could appear abroad only in disguise ;
men who still believed in Spanish expeditions, and whose
trust was that the illustrious Don Florentius, MacCarthy
Mor, would one day again awaken the slumbering spirit of

national enterprise, and again "take the opinion of the gentlemen of Munster upon the nation's liberty and religion." This affidavit of Hurley is an archæological treasure; and although it might puzzle a justice of the peace to discover what it proved against Florence, it is a lively picture of Irish genius, Irish faith, and Irish diplomacy, with a national oversight of the want of a perceptible object or intelligible design for its composition. The idea of Florence's flight away from his property into Spain, was worthy of Teig Hurley! Could Florence have carried Carbery and Desmond with him, he would never have seen the outside of His Majesty's Tower of London. Had he been inclined to fly, it is to be presumed that Browne, Barry, M. C. Reagh, and at need a score of undertakers, would as willingly as his own four men, who skulked about from the Sugar Loaf, in Thames Street, to the Boar's Head, in Ludgate, have accompanied him, and seen him safely through the perils of the watchers of the Custom-house, and of the Justice of the Peace, and not have left him till they had seen him safely on board ship for Flushing, or Dunkirk, or Damme, in Flanders; and that the only persons living who would have opposed his evasion would have been his friends, who must have had to contribute £500, or £250, as it might be, in virtue of their bonds, to console the English nation for losing such a subject.

No such correspondent as Teig Hurley existed in the world; none had ever been, except John Annyas, the Irish-man! and he, alas! had been prematurely removed from the world of letters and of politics! but so similar was this com-position of Hurley, in graces of style and delicate intricacies and superfluities of ingenuity, to the famous letter of his countryman, that it might pass for his.

The abstract demanded by the Privy Council, though con-taining nothing but what the reader has seen in endless repetition laid to the charge of Florence, is yet here offered to his notice, that he may perceive how completely all these old Irish enmities of a certain David Buttevaunt, and others, had faded out of official memory, and how incorrectly it was pos-sible for the archivists of the Foreign Office to make an abstract on which might depend the liberty and fortunes of gentlemen whose biography was scattered over half a cen-tury of their records.

"1617. *March* 27.

"An abstract of such things as are found in the Office of His Majesty's Papers for business of State concerning the actions and proceedings of Florence Mc Carte.

" First it appeareth by the 16th Book of the business of Ireland, Anno 1594, fol. 99, under Sir William Fitz Williams his hand, being Lord Deputy of Ireland, and Sir Thomas Norreys, upon the confession of one David Buttevant, that the said Florence Mc Carte had near correspondency with Sir Wm. Stanley, and one Jaques, who sent over hither Patr. Cullen to kill the Queen, and was executed for the same, and was to be only servant of the said Florence; it also appeareth thereby that the said Florence and Jaques were sworn brothers.

" By a letter written from Sir Nich. Browne, the 4th Decr. 1594, it is thus written, ' I know him to be suspicious and subtle, a great briber to his power, friended by some great men of Ireland, who have procured him favourable countenance with some of great calling in England; an importunate suitor, and indeed the only dangerous man in Munster, having been brought up and in league with James Fitz Morrice, Dr. Saunders, Sir Wm. Stanley, and Jaques.'

" By a letter of Sr. Gefferey Fenton's, anno 1595, he sets him out to be ' the fittest head of a faction, when time should serve for it; and that being always Spanish, he sold all his patrimony to purchase the old head of Kinsale, so greatly desired of the Spaniards for a landing place,' and in divers other letters from Sir Gefferey Fenton in '96, there are very earnest advices given ' to lay hold on him, and to keep him in safe-guard for being so dangerous a man, and so wholly Spanish.'

" There are divers letters directed unto him, whereof the originals (as it seemeth) remain with my lord Carewe,—for the copies are here found under my lord Carewe's hand,—directed to Florence Mc Carte, from the Earl of Tyrone, and O'Donel, and divers other rebels; the tenor whereof are these as followeth. (They are printed in the Pacata Hibernia.)

" It appeareth by a letter written from his agent Mac Donagh, addressed to the King of Spain, by his direction, that he made proffer of his service to the said King. The letter is dated in Jan. 1601.

" Signed,   Tho. Shelton.
" Testified by my lord
" Carew.

" It appeareth by other papers that are collections of his actions and intentions, that he was combined with Desmond in his rebellion, and had prepared forces to have served with that party in the action.

" That immediately before the Spanish intended invasion he departed into Ireland, married the daughter of the Earl of Clincart, and by that means got from that Earl and from Sir Owen Mc Carte, some places of the greatest strength in Munster and most tending upon Spain.

" That there passed Curriers betwixt him and Jaques, that notable traitor; and that Patrick Cullin, who should have killed Queen Elizabeth, went betwixt them.

" That he pretendeth to come lineally from the Kings of Munster, who were expelled upon the conquest of Ireland; and to be both Mc Carte More, and Mac Carte Reo, and so to have command upon all the Lordships that do lie one upon another above three score miles together westward, next towards Spain.

" This that followeth is since His Majesty's coming to the Crown.

" It appeareth by a long relation made by one Teag Hurley, a servant to Florence Mc Carte, that when he would have gone into Ireland he intreated him to stay, and promised he would employ him into Spain, in the third year of his Majesty's reign.

" That at the same time he being in the Marshalsea, a seminary priest

coming out of Spain, had continual recourse unto him in the habit of a
poor Frenchman, and had secret conference with him from morning to
night a long time together; and he sent the said priest into Spain for
money, and another of his servants to Brussels. The said Teag heard him
design how he will escape (upon the receipt of the money which he hoped
for) out at a window in an upper chamber in the Marshalsea.

" That upon his sending to Brussels, there came over unto him one
Francisco, brother to the traitor Jaques, to help Florence to money, and
upon some other treacherous intentions, which were known only to
Florence, and his men, as Teag Hurley sayeth, and which the said Francisco was so afraid to have discovered that, meeting with Captain Newse
who knew him, invited him to a banquet and poisoned him; for the which
he was committed to the Tower.

" That Jaques being prisoner in the Tower, he did write letters in
ciphers to Jacques, and sent them by this Teagh, whereof he knew not the
contents. That about a year and a half since he employed one man into
Spain, and another in the Low Countries.

" This information upon the oath and under the hands of Teagh
Hurley was set down the 27th March, 1617.

" *Indorsed.* An abstract of Florence Mᶜ Cartyes treasons and intentions from 1594 till 1617."

" 1617. *March* 28th.

" A relation of divers criminal articles against Florence Mᶜ Carthy,
alleged by Teig Hurly of the country of Carbry, sometime the said
Florence's servant, and confirmed by his oath on the 28ᵗʰ of March, 1617.

" The said Teige affirmeth that about 27 years past, he being a native
of Carbry by the father's side, and his mother of Barrye's country, and
entreated by the said Florence Mᶜ Carty to his service, went with him as
his footboy into England, and staid with him no longer than one quarter
of a year; from thence went to travel into Spain and Germany, and so
from one kingdom to another, for the space of 16 years; and then arrived
back in England, being in the service of one Sʳ Thos. Beadle, whom he
followed in France and Italy for two years; and coming into London he
found Florence Mᶜ Carty, in the Marshalsea, whom he often visited whensoever he came into the city, being his old maister. The said Florence,
upon his visiting of him, would be very inquisitive of the state, strength,
and wealth of the Spaniards, and how he heard them converse and talk
of him, or of his imprisonment, or if he could attain his liberty, in being
in Spain whether the king of Spain, or the Spaniards would make much of
him ? or be glad of his enlargement ?

" The said Teig seeing his own time spent but in travel, and that to be
no means for his future good, and likewise conceiting that the old proverb
might be verified in him, viz. ' a young serving man, an old beggar,' resolved to repair into his own native country; with which intent, coming
to take his leave of his restrained maister Florence; the said Florence entreated his stay, with a great deal of earnestness; telling him that in his
service he should not want means, which he himself daily expected, and
that he would employ him into Spain; being the third year of his Majesty's
reign of England. To which promise the said Tieg gave credit, and stayed
well near a twelvemonth, expecting both means and employment from him;
but in the mean time the said Florence did change his resolution in employing the said Teige, as aforesaid into Spain.

" About a quarter of a year before the said Teige's coming into Florence's service, one Richard O'Connell, a seminary priest, by birth from Irrelagh in Desmond (his ancestors being constables of Ballycarbry, the principal seat of Mc Carty More) came out of Spain into France, and from thence into England, where he, disguised as a Frenchman, did lodge with Florence's men Cornelius, *alias* Cnoghor O'Rorke, and Dermond Mc Finn O'Haugelin, in the house over against the Marshalsea door, being the sign of the Crowne, at one M^r. Goodchild's; and every day for the space of a fortnight or 3 weeks came in that habit of a poor Frenchman into the Marshalsea to Florence, where he would continue sometimes from morning to night in private conference.   The cause of knowledge of the said Richard's being so disguised, and of his frequenting the company of Florence, was his own confession in his often telling the said Teige that he would send him after the foresaid Richard into Spain, and also the confession of both of his men, and of the good man of the house who knew him not to be priest, but took him to be a Frenchman.   But the said Florence would often tell Teige that he expected his quick return of Spain, with money, and for his hastening would send the said Teige after him, yet after altered his mind, and sent him not, but sent another of his men called Dermond Mc Fynn O'Haugelin into Spain; and sent his other man Cornelius O'Rourke into Brussels, to confer with Lieutenant Jaques, who was his great friend.

" Dermond being in Spain for a quarter of a year, returned into Ireland, missing his expected purpose of getting money from O'Sulivan Beare; and the priest likewise, who went over for the same purpose, failing thereof, the said Dermond came to Florence into England; by whose message from the priest he was put in hope daily to be relieved with money, the want whereof only detained him from flying into Spain.   To which purpose his plot for his escape was, that after the money being received, he should obtain (to effect his intent) a more convenient chamber from the under marshall, M^r. Richardson, being the highest in the house, and looking eastward upon the Bourdenn, where he thought to make his escape out of a window; his four men Cornelius O'Rourke, Thomas Hanloane, Dermond Mc Fynn and Tieg Hurly being ready without to receive him.

" His other man Cornelius, that went to Jaques, after a month's time spent in Brussels, returned into Dover, being the harbour from whence he took shipping, and so came back to Florence, without interruption, and brought him, as a present from Jaques, a sword which as the said Tieg saith, was disguised with a broken and rusty hilt, but was in fashion between a sword and a rapier, with a back, and of a good length.   This Cornelius had told and assured his maister Florence, that Thomas Francesco (who was brother to the forenamed Jaques) would be with him within a month after, and obtain money for him in London, which the said Thos. Francesco performed partly, in coming privately to London.   And afore the month's end, every day Cornelius O'Rourke would duly watch at the Spanish Ambassador's house, expecting news from Francesco; who the second or third night after his coming to town, late in the evening walking as private in the street, and in as disguised a manner as he could, it was his fortune to meet with one Capt. Newce, who formerly had been of his acquaintance in the Low Countries; and being exceeding fearful that he should be discovered, had no shift to prevent his discovery, but bid him to a banquet, in his chamber; to whom the said Captain Newce went, and there received such a poisoned entertaintment that all his hair and his nails fell off, and thereof complained to the Council; whereupon Thos. Francesco was apprehended, and put into the Tower; where, remaining for the space of half a year, and no matter proved against him (none knowing his intent, but Florence and his men) upon the earnest suit of his wife, to the Council for his liberty, he was enlarged, and not daring to go into the Marshalsea, he and his wife went over into the Low Countries.

" The said Tiege doth moreover affirm that Mc Gwyr coming out of Ireland in a disguised manner, came into London, Florence being then in the Marshalsea, and having through the favour of the Keeper the liberty to go abroad with his keeper, one Richard Lawson, and hearing by one of Mc Gwyre's men that one would speak with him, the said Florence going with him into the King's Arms, a tavern, and this Tieg Hurly with him, they found the aforesaid Mc Gwire in merchant's attire, with two men more in his company, and talking privately together; he craved Florence's advice how he might with security safely get out of England ; who gave him all the counsel he could, which was to go to Dover, and carry his horses with him to avoid suspicion, which conference the aforesaid Tieg overheard. And they after meeting twice or thrice, and Mc Gwyre staying in London two days, went to Dover, and there left his horses, assuring that within one month they would return, praying their horses to be well looked unto, as the said Tiege did afterwards hear.

" Who likewise affirmeth that the same year, about the spring time, there came out of Spain one Owen Mc Tieg Merigeh, who having been a notorious rebel in Ireland, and despairing of pardon fled over into Spain with O'Sulivan Beare, where being entertained into the King of Spain's service, he was made his *prisoner* (pensioner ?). This Owen Mc Tiege came into London, and two or three times visited the said Florence in the Marshalsea, and kept continually with his men; and after he had stayed there for the space of a sennight or thereabouts, having placed a son of his (whom he had brought with him out of Spain) with Florence, by the means and procurement of Cornelius O'Rourke he obtained out of the Custom house a pass, and went for the Low Countries, being accompanied by the said Cornelius to Gravesend. The aforesaid Tiege's cause of knowledge was, that during the time of the said Owen's abode at London he kept him daily company, as the rest of his fellows did. And as concerning the said Owen's son, whom he left with Florence, about a quarter of a year after he died of the plague at the forenamed Goodchild's house.

" The foresaid Tieg likewise affirmeth that expecting means and employment from Florence, he staid after the sending away of his men aforesaid, and half a year after Jaques, his brother's enlargement, but then finding Florence's word to be no payment, and his expected hopes failing him, he was fain to come back again, and prostrate his service in a poor habit, and pennyless, to his former kind maister Sr Thos. Beadle, whom he served for a whole year afterwards ; and when voluntaries were going to serve in the Low Countries out of England, after the year's end, the said Tiege went into Flanders ; but before his going, took leave of Florence, who was removed from the Marshalsea to the Tower ; to whom he could not have access, because he was close prisoner. But hearing, by one of his men, that the said Teig was going away, sent by his man Dermond McFinn a script about the breadth of two or three fingers to him, to be delivered to Corronell Jaques in Brussels, written in characters, the contents were unknown unto the said Tiege; but after the delivery of the letter to Jacques, he examined the bearer, what countryman he was, and after he told it him, he asked whether he would live there as a soldier? The said Teig answering his intent was to serve in the wars, he told him he would be a means to enter him into the King's list, and should be in pay, which he performed. Then the said Tieg serving for four years together in Captain Driscoll's company, under the King's colours, forsook the place, and came back again to London, and found his old maister Florence in the Marshalsea; whom he visited, and told, for anything he could find, he was not the better used in the Low Countries for *his* sake; upon which the said Florence grew strange towards him; and he, finding his unkindness, supposed it might proceed out of a suspicion of him; and then he became servant to the Lord Courcy, who was then in London, and in suit with Florence; who hearing thereof, imagined he should be discovered in his plots, the Lord Courcy being his adversary; and spake in the presence of divers and namely of one Donogh McDonell McCarthy, that he was sorry that he had not better rewarded his old servant Teig Hurly; and said he would give him the office of sergeantship, or overseer of his lands of Cariggenassy. Upon which report, the said Donogh coming where the lord Courcey and the said Tieg his man, were, told the Lord Courcy in his ear that he ought not to trust him; for Florence meant to do him good in conferring that place upon him. The cause why Donogh bore him, the said Tieg, malice was, one Vallentyne Browne, son to Sr Nicholas Browne, then being in England, following his suit for abatement of part of his Majesty's rents, the said Tiege used to come to him; and one day being in his chamber, the aforesaid Donogh, in great want, came to borrow some money of him; Tieg, knowing his intent, and the ill affection he bore the said Vallentyne, and the Lord Barry in Ireland, to whom he did some wrong, rounded Mr Browne in the ear, and warned him not to lend him any at all! The said Vallentine having a boy, Donogh McFynnyn Carthy, a near kinsman to the aforesaid Donogh McDonell, who overheard the said Tieg's warning, revealed the same to his cousin. In revenge whereof he thought to put the Lord Courcie in suspicion with him; but the Lord Courcie hearing of Florence's proffer told the said Tieg he should be preferred into a great Office by Florence; to which the said Tieg replied, 'My lord, there is an old proverb in the Spanish 'Palabras y plumas el vento los lieven,' as much to say, as 'The wind bloweth away words and feathers,' knowing that Florence would perform no more to him in that promise, than formerly he had done in divers others. Afterwards hearing the said Tieg resolved absolutely to serve the Lord Courcie, or the said Vallentine Browne, spake to him himself, entreating him not to do it; and to stay with him in London, which Tieg denied; and so came over with the Lord Courcie; after which service for a time, hearing that Vallentine Browne came over into Ireland, prostrated his service to the said Vallentine, where he served for the space of four years and a half. In which time having a scruple in his conscience of the grounds of his religion, perceiving it rather founded on policy than on the word of God, he was converted from papacy to the true service of God; wherein continuing, and desiring to match with one of the same belief, he married an English woman, without the knowledge, or advice of the said Vallentine Browne; whose purpose it was to have preferred him to a better match. Whereupon the said Vallentine being sorry, and displeased that he had so cast himself away on one that brought him not any means, and himself likewise having none, would give no countenance to the said Tieg; upon which dislike he went away to Carbry, and there lived with his brethren for two months; and upon his wife's friends entreaty, both by word of mouth and letters, to come to them, he went into England, and about a fortnight in Wiltshire.

"After which time the said Tieg going into London to see Florence, hearing he was for doing to him many injuries, and especially for altering his religion, to which the said Tieg answered. ' For any cause of injury, I have assuredly done you none; but for my religion, I think, maister, if you were not so old in your error, you would be of my religion too, as well as I,' these and a great many of other speeches passing at that time, and this was in August last past, 1616. But frequenting the said Florence's house, and lying in one bed with one of his men, called Thomas O'Hanloane for the space of three weeks, for some two or three days in that time the said Tieg, as his former custom was, came to Florences chamber to visit him, and still found him and his men absent; which he wondered at; but conceived not the cause, until one day coming thither early, he found one John O'Voleghane, Cnogher O'Voleghane, and Tieg Mc Cormock, all three Desmond men born, and one of them brother to the Franciscan friar Tieg O'Voleghane, all being new comers out of Ireland. The said Tieg Hurly bade them welcome, and was inquisitive of news out of Ireland; and asked them when they came into London, to which they answered some two days since. That very night coming into his lodging, where the aforesaid Thomas and he did lie, (being at the Boar's Head, without Aldgate) the said Thomas came late to his lodging, about 11 of the clock at night; where Tieg Hurly asked him where he had been so late? and he answered, 'with his maister;' and after other discourse he made relation to him of some friends of his that were two or three days in town, and were bound for beyond sea.

" What friends of mine—said Tieg—that have been here so long and would not acquaint me with their being in town? What dare they not walk the streets? or are they friars? or men ashamed of any of their actions?

" John Entlea is one of them—quoth Thomas.

" Then—quoth Tieg—what a devil should John here?

" He is here, and Tieg O'Voleghane, the Franciscan friar, with him! said Thomas.

" O, is it so? I know—said Tieg—it was to keep them company. Florence was missing this two or three days out of his chamber!

" It is true! said Thomas, although I was not with them, they did all five that came over, dine at the Boar's Head, within Ludgate, and Florence with them there, and they think no man can better procure them a pass from the four Maisters of the Custom house, than yourself, in regard you are acquainted there!

" I assure you there is nothing I can do for them, but I will do it ; said Tieg; but yet believe me, it is hard for me to undergo such danger ; and how may I effect it?

" Nothing said Thomas, but instead of Tieg O'Voleghane, let your name serve for the Friar, and it will prejudice you nothing!

" And then after many persuasions to that purpose, the said Tieg, Thomas, and John Entlea, went to the Custom house, where there was gotten one pass in the name of Tieg Hurly, and John Entlea.

" This Franciscan friar, the said Tieg saw in Ireland before this time, and knew him to have been collecting of monies within the counties of Corke and Kerry, under pretence of mending an abbey within the county of Kerry, called the Abbey of Ircelagh; under colour of which work, the said Tieg saw him going up and down the country, and levying of monies, having some masons working of a few stones, only to colour his intent, and blind the people with a seeming zeal of mending a work so charitable; and thereupon through the devotion of many well-minded men, he obtained a good purse of money, wherewith he has taken his journey into England, and from thence beyond seas.

" After the receipt of the pass out of the Custom-house, they went to the friar's lodgings in Thames Street, as he takes it, being the sign of the Sugar-loaf, *where he saw the friar with Donell and Cormock, Florence's two sons;* the friar's brother, called John O'Voleghane and Cnoghor O'Voleghane his kinsman; with whom the said Tieg there broke his fast, and warned the friar to make as much haste as he could away; and being so far engaged for him hastened him still. And after that, the very self same day, the said Tieg, and John Entlea, went to Billingsgate to provide a little boat to go down to Gravesend; and the said Tieg procured the Boat; but the tide serving not till night; in the evening went the friar, Tieg Hurly and John Entlea into the boat; on landing at Gravesend they took a chamber. The next morning the said Tieg and John Entlea went to inquire what ships were going for the Low Countries; and hearing certainly that there were in the harbour two barks ready to go, the one bound for Dunkirk, the other for Flushing, the said Tieg and John came back to the friar, and told him of these two ships that were immediately departing, and wished him pack away. The friar answering, I will go in the ship to Dunkirk; but Tieg told him it was unlikely he should have allowance to go in that ship, having in his pass but to arrive at Damme in Flanders; and that it were convenient for him to go into Flushing; but the friar's inclination being towards the Spanish shore, still resolved to go into the ship of Dunkirk; and with that resolution they went to the water's side! A boat then being ready with passengers to go to the Dunkirk bark, the friar stept into it; the searcher standing on shore asked him whither he was going? or where his passport was?

" He answering, here it is! delivered him.

" The same which the Searcher reading, This bark, quoth he, goeth to Dunkirk, and your pass is to Damme in Flanders.

" With that they cried, come ashore—you shall not go there.

" Whereupon the Searcher grew very angry, and told that the State was much abused by such dealing; and presently carried him to a Justice of the Peace; and was there examined what the reason was that he intended to go, contrary to the effect inserted in his pass?

" He made answer that he was unacquainted either with Damme or Dunkirk, but his business being to the Low Countries, he desired to arrive there in any place, and that he was desirous not to lose his passage.

" You shall not then go into Dunkirk ! said the Justice of the Peace.

" And with that cold comfort they parted, and came to their chamber; whereupon they consulted what was best to be done; and then the friar, more dismayedly than he had any cause given, bewraying his guiltiness by his outward changing of colour, began to suspect the Searcher would follow, and search what he had about him; which Tieg perceiving, advised him if he had anything that might endanger him, he should do well to hide it in the chamber; who told him he had his book, and two letters that were folded like wrapt sheets of paper, without sealing or superscription, which they put between the hanging and the wall; being formerly sewed up in John Entlea's doublet; which being done, the said Tieg went out upon the quay, where he met with the former Justice of the Peace, who demanded of him where his company was?

" And he answered, they were in their chamber taking a pipe of tobacco; for getting no leave to go, it behoved them not to walk on the quay.

" One of the standers by said that there was another bark going for Flushing; whereupon the said Tieg came back, and told the friar thereof, advising him to look boldly, and to intreat the Justice to let him have his pass back again to London, if he would not let him go! upon which admonition he went out, and met the Justice, whom he intreated with a great deal of fear (his heart failing him to look aright on the Justice), whereupon *he* looking on *him* said, I know not what to think of you! but I have nothing to say to you!

"After which words he took boat, and went to the ship. And this about middle of August, 1616.

"About a sennight before the departure of the friar, one John Meogh, being son to Meogh the pirate, was by him employed into the Low Countries to Capt. Cnoghor O'Driscoll; upon whose coming to him the said Captain went into Spain.

" And ever sithence the said Florence doth run in the score; *having his three sons with him in England, not allowing them breeding, learning or education,* ready upon the receipt of means, to be gone, having in his company, as his servant, one Donogh-ne-buille, a man of his own country of Carbry, and a very good linguist; also one Donogh Mc Tieg Duffe is gone into Spain, about a year and a half since from him, and is a Carbry man; and also Cormock Mc Calloghane, being a Desmond man, served him for a quarter of a year, and was by him then employed into the Low Countries.

" All these before mentioned allegations, the said Tieg hath sworn by the holy evangelist to be true, and in witness thereof hath hereunto set his hand, the day and year first above mentioned.

" TEAG HURLY.

"A note of all Florence Mc Cartie's men, and employed by him :—

" Alive O'Falvy
" Tieg Mc Cormock Carty, }
" Cormock Mc Calloghane, } Desmond men.
" Donogh-ne-buily, a Carbryman.
" Thomas O'Hanloane, of Meath.
" John Meogh, of Kinsale."

CHAPTER XVIII.

As the years of Florence's captivity roll on, his petitions become fewer, the complication of his legal suits greater, and his success in them—probably owing to the opportunities which his liberty gave him of more frequent interviews with his legal advisers, and his friends about the Court—more marked. We at last perceive that his petitions begin to fix the attention, and excite the sympathies of the Privy Council. It must be borne in mind that the property of Florence accrued to him from two sources of very dissimilar title, and unequal validity. One, the large hereditary estates left to him by his father, which, fortunately for him, had been officially surveyed, and attested on oath, at the inquisition held after the death of Sir Donogh. This property at the time of Florence's arrest, escaped, by some miraculous chance, from confiscation. The Queen made no claim to it, or to any portion of it, and the law could only view as interlopers and trespassers all who, like Popham and Rogers, in times past, and De Courcy now, turned out his tenants, or intercepted his rents.

The second source of his wealth was, as the reader has seen, that large portion of the Earl of Clancar's country settled on him as marriage goods with his wife, and the remainder of the Earl's country (with exception of a moderate estate left by the Earl's will to Donal, and the Countess's third, during her life), *given to him* by Queen Elizabeth. Relative to these latter vast possessions was the contest of Florence's life with the Brownes and others. The dispute with Donal Pipi had been of an entirely different nature, viz., whether Donal, by placing Carbery under the English law of succession, could make void Florence's hereditary right as Tanist.

The suit with Browne—already more than once *finally* settled by legal judgment—was still an open contest, and so continued for at least 20 years longer. We shall see that although Donal was permitted to surrender his lands to the King, and thus free them from the operation of Tanistry, he

was by no means allowed to leave all to his son! The Chieftainship was abolished, the Demesne lands were divided
between him and Florence and the sons of the late Sir Owen,
after allotment of some small portions to remoter claimants;
and Donal's eldest son fared as might any eldest son of any
entailed property, with precedence of his brethren under the
new division of the estates.

Although the grand contest of Florence was with the
Brownes, he by no means neglected the recovery of those
minor parcels of lands of which the usurpers were men of less
influence, and the parties—mortgagees, lessees, and others—
injured in common with himself, were persons of consideration.

"1617. *April* 10*th.*   *To the Right* Hon^*ble* *the* LORDS *and others of His
Majesty's most honorable Privy Council.*

"The humble petition of Florence Mc Carty.

"Showing that where the late Earl of Clancarty, at his being in England, mortgaged unto your suppliant about 30 years past, before he married
his daughter, for a £190, a place, and certain lands called Twoh Irilagh,
and Dromhumfrey, which was by your suppliant that enjoyed it quietly,
mortgaged afterwards to M^r. Harbert Pelham, by whose tenants it was
holden; and after your suppliant was committed and sent hither, the Earl
of Tyrone caused those lands and place to be delivered to one of that country
called Donell, that untruly alleges himself to be the late Earl of Clancartie's
Bastard, who thereupon brought to Tyrone, out of that country, as many
men as he could, *with whom he was at Kinsale* when he was overthrown;
and being afterwards pardoned, *holds ever since those lands* that was not
demanded nor sued for by any, by reason of your suppliant's restraint;
and where also certain small parcels of your suppliant's lands, which is
worth but about £30 a year, called Anagheilly, Lahharde, Culmoe, Bally-
ahir, Eaglais, Ballytrasny, Turpin Fahagh, and *Ceapagh*, was in your suppliant's restraint, possessed by certain farmers and tenants of that country,
for mortgages made, as they allege, by your suppliant's predecessor, the late
Earl of Clancarty, which land is still holden by them, or by others of that
country people, unto whom they passed their mortgages.

"He therefore humbly beseecheth, in respect that your suppliant was
since his trouble driven to satisfy M^r. Herbert Pelham, your suppliant
himself being dispossessed of that land, and never paid, nor satisfied of this
money that he disbursed for it; and that he is ready to pay what mortgages
shall appear to be due upon those other small parcels, That it would please
your honorable Lordships to grant him letters to the Lord President of
Mounster, that he, and the lord Chief Justice of the Common Pleas, that
dwells there, and the Chief Justice of Monster, or either of them, to hear
and examine this matter, and to certify unto your Lordships the state
thereof, whereby your Lordships may thereafter take such order as your
suppliant may be restored to his right, And he shall ever pray for your
honorable Lordships.

"Florence Mc Cartie's Petition to the Council."

"Copy of a letter from the Privy Councillors to the LORD DEPUTY *of Ireland, in behalf of* FLORENCE Mᶜ CARTY, *April* 10, 1617.

"After our very hearty commendations to your Lordship. Humble suit having been made unto us by Florence Mᶜ Carty, for our letters of reference unto you, for the examination of a complaint made by him, as well concerning a place and certain lands called Twoh Irilagh, and Drom humfry, formerly mortgaged unto him by the late Earl of Clancartye, of £190, and since mortgaged again by the petitioner to Sʳ. Herbert Pelham, and lastly during the troubles in that kingdom, dispossessed of, and given by the Earl of Tyrone to one Donell, as a pretended bastard to the said Earl of Clancarty, who still detaineth the same, upon that pretence, as also touching some other parcels of land mentioned in the petition, about the yearly value of £30, possessed and held by certain farmers and tenants of that country, who allege that the same were passed unto them, in mortgage by the said late Earl, as by the petition will at large appear; We have been moved hereby to pray, and require your lordship, the rather, for that the petitioner alledgeth that these inconveniences are fallen upon him by means of his restraint here, and offereth to redeem any mortgage whereof any of his lands stand justly charged, to take notice of the petition; and upon full and due examination of the parts thereof, to certify unto us the true state of the cause, together with your petition touching the same, that such further order may be taken as shall be just. And so we bid you heartily farewell.

"From Whitehall, this 10ᵗʰ of April, 1617.
     "Your lordship's very loving friends,
          "GEORGE CANTERBURY.   "RALPH WYNWOOD.
          "Wᵐ. WALLINGFORDE.   "JULIUS CÆSAR.
          "JEAMES HAY.   "EDW. WORCESTER.
          "THOS. SUFFOLK.   "GEORGE CAREWE."
          "THOS. EDMONDES.

The adversaries of Florence might have taken warning when they saw that even in these minor cases the prayer of the suppliant attracted the notice of the Lords of the Privy Council sufficiently to obtain from them letters to the Lord Deputy of Ireland, to cause enquiry to be made into the truth and justice of a petition of Florence! this was new language: a few years ago it would have been judged in Ireland as little less than revolutionary. In former days, when Florence petitioned their Lordships to cast their eyes upon certain documents which he held out to them; certain gracious pardons of Her Majesty for his past faults; certain solemn promises made in Her Majesty's name that his personal liberty should be held sacred, it was answered that he was "a vayne fool!" Words that at once tranquillized the minds of all the undertakers in Munster.

The following interesting paper,* an able summary of

* The compiler of this life is indebted for the transcription of the above document to the kindness of Eugene P. MacCarthy, Esq., an assiduous

Florence's transactions with the Brownes, written by himself about the time that Hurley and his employers were making their grand attempt to bring matters of State policy once more to their aid against him, contains several details relative not only to these matters in dispute, but to the intrigues of Boyle, and the story of the debt to Blake, the tailor, which the more timid or shame-faced of his adversaries offered to the world as the cause of his arrest. This trumpery subterfuge was utterly beneath the notice of Carewe, he never condescended to adopt it. The assertion that "Carewe had protested to Sir W^m. Taaffe that he had rather than Two thousand pounds he had not committed me," made by Florence whilst Carewe—Lord Totness, was still living, may have been, and it is a pleasure to believe that it was, true.

"*Copy of an original paper at Muckruss, endorsed 'Florence M·Carthy More's own statement of his transactions with the Brownes,' written between 1616 and 1620.*

"The late Earl of Clancarthy, called Mac Carthy of Desmond, and my father called Mac Carthy of Carbery, being long since descended from two brothers, the Earl when his son died in France, wrote to me that then attended here the late Queen, whom I served in the Earl of Desmond's rebellion, to go over and marrie his daughter, but before I went, the Earl (upon occasion of lands of his that Sir Valentine Browne brought in question) came hyther, where he got me bound in £6000 to marrie his daughter, and recovered his lands. Then Sir Valentine wrought Mr Secretary Walsingham to deal with the Earl for marrying of his daughter to a son of Sir Valentines, whereupon the Earl sent me word to marrie her, and being threatened by M^r. Secretary he promised to conform him to his will; but when it was known here that I married her, M^r. Secretary procured letters to commit me, and the Earl was driven to mortgage these lands that he recovered, to Sir Valentine Browne for £560, whereof he then passed a Patent for color to keep it. When the Earl died, I being before enlarged, sued here Sir Valentine's son for these lands, which cause the late Queen referred to her Privy Council and learned Counsel, who when they considered of his Patent and of an ancient Deed, that I shewed, by which the s^d Earl's lands were entayled before his time, they concluded that if the s^d. Earl had surrendered his lands as he alleged (which was all his color to keep it with his Patent), being but tenants in tayle, his surrender was of no force, but during his own life, and that those lands by right were mine, who was enjoyned to pay him his money and has the late Queen's letters to enjoy and pass those lands by Patent which a little before was taken by the Rebels, whereby the Earl of Tirowen's appointment they placed one Donell, son to Donell O'Donoghue, of that country, who untruly alleged himself to be the late Earl of Clancarty's bastard, and spent all his time in their rebellions with the Earl of Desmond and Tirowen, with whom 800 of the rebells forces were left there, which (when I went here hence) I over

Irish scholar, a valued contributor to our historic literature, and a no less zealous antiquarian.

threw and recouered from them those lands, whose inhabitants I brought
to be subjects, which was the best and the greatest service that was done in
Munster for the late Queen, for whom I kept forces at my own charges in
the field, when no body else (out of the towns) acknowleged her and never
offended, but fighting once with Captn. Flower and others that burnt two
Castles of mine, killed my tenants and spoiled them of 1200 cows : immediately after the Lord Carewe came thyther to govern, unto whom I
came and informed him still of the state of the rebells, caused my nephew
(O'Connor Kerry) to deliver him his castle that was comodious to annoy
them, and delivered my son as a pledge, as he desired, to his Lordship,
who, for my fighting with Captn. Flower protected me still, procured me a
pardon and assured me of a good Patent of my lands, to which end he had
of me the late Queen's letters first granted me when I recovered these
lands here of Sir Valentine Browne's son, that (since the wars commenced
there) was here in England, from whence he wrought M^r. Boyle now Lord
Boyle, to work the Lord Carew against me, and to draw sundry informations, which being sent from divers parts of Ireland hether, Sir Valentine
Browne's son followed here, until letters were procured to commit me then,
but afterwards upon an imagination of my discontentment for the spoiling my tenants by his Captains, and speeches that he (Sir G. Carew) gave
me, he resolved to commit me, for which he could find no matter until one
Blake of Corck a taylor that dwelt here was brought or came (God knoweth
how) to complain of me for a bond of £121, whereunto I entered many
years before for a gentleman of Ireland (that was here a while), upon
which complaint the Lord Carewe committed me until I found sureties to
answer it, and sent for me again and told me openly that he committed not
for that nor for any other matter, but least any discontentment should
move me to offend the Queen or hurt myself, promising to stand my friend,
and that I should not be restrained long, and protested to Sir W^m. Taaffe
that he had rather than £2000 he had not committed me, which he w^d not
have done, had he not seen the figure of discontentm^t in my face; and
because that he durst not trust me there any more, he sent me over hither
where I was no sooner sent than Sir Valentine Browne's son went over and
passed those lands, that with long suit and great charges, I recouered
before from him here, and there from . . . . the with
endangering my life and those of many men . . . means of quarrells also
of the (marginal note—the original MS. is broken and defaced here in a
few places) holden by the supposed bastard who got the possession first by
the Earl of Tirowen's means, and afterwards of a patent by the sinister
practices of a wife that I had, who got it passed in his name to have it
sold for her, whereof he being Patentee, defrauded me of it, and some other
parcell is holden by freeholders and farmers of that countrie, alleging small
mortgages of the lands . . . . . . but all theirs and the bastards is
but little and of little value, which they would deliver up if M^r. Browne,
who had the chief substance of all the demesnes, was caused to take his
mortgage and deliver up the land, according to the late queen's letters
upon her Privy Council and learned counsels orders for it in my behalf;
these are that which I chiefly challenge. The Earl of Clancarthy's rents,
seignories, chieferies and duties which was his chiefest living, being by his
Majesty given to Sir Henry Power, who sold it to Sir Thos. Roper. Myne
own father Mac Carthy Reagh, that enjoyed, and died seized ofthe Signory
of Carbery, and was by the custom of that country, succeeded by his
second brother, Sir Owen Mac Carthy, whom Donal the late MacCarthy
of Carbery succeeded, by whom the Demesnes and the most part of the
rents and chiefries thereof was mortgaged, and made away; upon whose

death, I being to succeed him, petitioned to the Lords, who referred it to the Lord Carewe and Sir George Wilbraham, that certified my petition to be true, and that I had good right; Yet because that custom is misliked by the State there, they thought best that all should be divided, and I to have a large portion thereof in recompense of my right; which being shewed to the Lords, they gave order that the King's Majesty should be moved for his gracious letters in my behalf for the same, as appears upon the same certificate which I have: my said father also puchased certain lands, (whereof when he died seized), sundry offices recorded in Dublin were found before Sir William Drury, Lord President of Munster, that had my Wardship, which lands being by me enjoyed after him; the countries were all waste after the late wars, and I restrained close in the Tower, divers of that country people entered thereupon and keep it, upon what color they please to devise; for which I sued to the Lords of late, which they referred to the Earl of Thomond, the Lords Carewe and S^t. John, that was Chief Justice of Ireland, who upon sight of one of those offices, certified in my behalf, whereof I had no benefit yet, being before I could have it thither by Sir Robert Staunton, which of my father's inheritance whereof I have such Certificates, Offices, and Evidences, as they cannot be denied me, is with the rest afore mentioned, all the Estate I had there. (Marginal note—'the statement is here nearly illegible.') "

The abstract and the letter of Hurley, though they did not affect the decision of the Privy Council in the matter of Florence's law suits, operated swiftly, as they were expected to do, upon his freedom. After four years' enjoyment of liberty upon sureties, he was suddenly, without cause assigned, hurried back to prison. Some time elapsed before he could discover the motive for this extreme proceeding, and in the early days of his indignation, and under much suffering, he petitioned the Privy Council! His petition was in the tone of the petitions of the last 20 years! "*that he might forthwith be called before their Lordships, if there be any matter against him!*" Before long what Mr. Secretary Nanton refused to tell him, was discovered for him by one or other of his friends at Court: he then learned that not only had all his past career been re-examined, but that one of his own servants had made an affidavit against him of recent acts which, it was hoped, would be considered treasonable. Understanding, probably, more clearly than any one but an Irishman could do, the main purport of the singular composition of Teig Hurley, he at once threw back the most dangerous of the charges upon the deponent's present master; declaring that Browne and his servant had conspired, with equal folly and malice, to entrap him into treasonable intercourse with a friar; that the said friar was an emissary of Browne, who, and not he, was guilty of this breach of English law.

It was the custom of Florence, and had been through the

periods of both his imprisonments, when he petitioned the Privy Council, to write at the same time to one or other of the Ministers—to Lord Burghley, or to Cecyll, or as now, to Lord Zouche— a more detailed, and outspoken exposition of his wrongs, or hardships, which, and not the more restrained and submissive letter to the Lords, was meant to be the subject of deliberation, in the matter of his petitions.

"Abt. 1619 Nov.*

" *To the Right Honble the* LORDS *and others of His Majesty's most honorable Privy Council.*

" The humble Petition of Florence Mc Carthy,

" Showing that whereafter many years restraint he petitioned for his liberty, which the King's Majesty referred to the Lord Deputy of Ireland, who with divers of the Council there being here, then certified in his behalf, and that he could not offer better security; whereupon it hath pleased His Majesty, and your Lordships above 4 years past, upon bonds of the Earls of Thomond and Clanriccard, and the Lords of Delvin and Downeliffes, and other Knights and gent of that country, to confine him about this city, where he hath ever since (without giving any occasion of offence or suspicion) lived in great want, being then abridged of 3^li a week for his diet, and 20^s a week for clothes, that his Majesty allowed him; and by divers of that country dispossessed of his lands in his long restraint, whereof they took advantage, and being out of hope of obtaining the allowance that he had of His Majesty, and advised by his friends (because he had no means), to sue for some of his lands, he hath, lest he should be driven to be troublesome or chargeable to His Majesty, petitioned to your Lordships, by whom it was referred to the Earl of Thomond, the Lord Carew, and to Baron Denham, who certified what course they thought best to be taken by your Lordships for his relief, whose certificate he could not show nor make no use thereof, being about 20 days past sent for by M^r. Secretary Nanton and committed to the Gatehouse.

" He therefore humbly beseecheth, in respect that your suppliant, who by his carriage and trial these four or five years upon sureties, did rather expect more liberty, is already worn with imprisonment and very sick of an ague, and an extreme cough, and destitute of any means to maintain him and his children, who are ready to starve, that it will please your honorable Lordships that he may forthwith, before he perish in extreme misery, be called to answer before your Lordships if there be any matter against him, or else that he may be suffered to live confined upon his sureties, as he hath these four or five years past, and get some means of his own to maintain him and his children so long as your Lordships shall be pleased to keep him confined.   And so shall ever pray for your honorable Lordships."

" 1619.   *June* 24.   FLORENCE M^cCARTHY *to* LORD ZOUCH.

" Right Honorable,

" I cannot but acknowledge myself much bound to your Lordship that vouchsafed, before the cause was known, to deal so effectually with M^r. Secretary Nanton for me, which I will rest ever ready to deserve with my

best service; and because M^r. Secretary was then put in hope to have
matter against me I suspended ever since to trouble your Lordship until
I understood from thence what was pretended against me, which I am moved
(having in the beginning found your Lordship my best friend) to acquaint
you withal, who (I hope) will be as willing to friend me in the end, when
(now it is known that there is no matter against me) your Lordship may
best prevail for me. About 3 years past a man of M^r. Brownes (that holds
the best part of my lands) being here, met a friar and a householder or
farmer of that country, and when he told them that he was with me, they
wished that they had also seen me; which M^r. Browne's man told me, who
(suspecting that M^r. Browne employed that friar to make some matter
against me) assured his man that if any friar or priest came to me I would
bring him in question : about a fortnight after, that man told me that they
were gone out of this land; whereof M^r. Browne (imagining that I had
spoken to them) got an information made, and endeavoured to get some of
the Council there to prefer it hither; which when he could not, he got it
sent to one here that kept it about a year, until M^r. Secretary Nanton (unto
whom myself and my cause was unknown) was persuaded to commit me
thereupon ; of this information (although I had intelligence from thence
about two years past) I took no care, knowing that I who saw not, nor
spake not to any of them, could not be touched withal; and judging that
I should not be committed again upon an information of mine adversary
that holds my lands, after my being by his Majesty, and the Council, upon
the Lord Deputy of Ireland's certificate, and upon bonds of the Earls of
Thomond and Clanriccaird, the Viscount of Downeliffes, the Lord of Delvin,
Sir Daniel Obryen, Sir Patrick Barnewell and divers others, confined about
this city, where I have lived in great want, being then abridged of 3 pounds
a week for diet, and 20 shillings a week for clothes, that His Majesty
allowed me; and by divers of that country dispossessed of my lands, in
my long and close restraint, whereof they took advantage ; and being,
because I had no means, advised to sue for some of my lands I petitioned
to the Lords, who referred it to the Earl of Thomond, the Lord Carewe,
and Baron Denham, that certified my right to above 500 pounds land a
year, purchased by my father, whereof I could have no benefit, being within
a few days after committed hither, *where I have remained above seven months*
without means to maintain me and my children, when by my carriage and
trial these 5 years past, upon those sureties I expected more liberty *after*
18 *years endurance without being ever called to answer or charged for anything.* The information whereupon I was now committed, if it were of
any probability or substance, had neither been rejected by any of the
Council there, nor kept still here from the King and Council's knowledge ;
and the said friar that is well known to M^r. Brown, who may have him if
he will, being there in the country, and the other that was with him committed long since, and I contented to lose both liberty and favour if any
can justly say that I saw or spake to any of them, or wrote to or by any
of them, or saw or spake to any friar or priest from thence since my commitment, or kept or maintained ever any while I was there before; whereof
when M^r. Secretary (that at my commitment was promised matter against
me) finds nothing, he now alleges reasons to restrain me at the request of
another, who is desirous to have in this prison my life that he hath already
worn in prisons. It should seem that M^r. Secretary Nanton of himself
was indifferently inclined to discharge me, for to a friend, that at the
intreaty of Sir Thomas Roper dealt with him, he answered, that if the
Lord Chancellor that joined to commit me, would join with him he would
be contented to enlarge me; now to my petition he says that for reasons to

2 E

him known he may not in his duty discharge me! but will further me to obtain the means that I had at His Majesties charges; And because I see no reason why His Majesty should be put to unnecessary charges for me and my children, and I by my restraint, hindered of those means of mine own that is (as aforesaid) certified for me, and myself without any cause kept here, to shorten my days, after the trial that hath been had of me these 5 years past upon those sureties, bonds which the clerk of the Council keeps; My humble request is that it will please your honorable Lordship to be a mean that I may be suffered to enjoy that little liberty that His Majesty and the Council granted me upon those sureties, if there be no matter against me, and to deal effectually with Sir Robert Nanton, for by the Lord Chancellor's answer to a petition of mine, I gather that all stands in Sir Robert, with whom I doubt not but your Lordship will prevail, your credit being greater with all men than his that works Sir Robert to re- strain me. And your Lordship shall find that I will thankfully by my service deserve your favour, which I leave to your Lordships honorable consideration, resting ever

" Your Lordships most humble
and faithful to be commanded
" FLOR: M^cCARTHY.

" To the Right Honble. His very approved good Lord,
the Lord Zouch, Lord Warden of the Cinque ports
and one of His Majesties most honorable Privy
Council."

On the 4th of December, 1619, there was an Order in Council for the release of Florence MacCarthy from the Gate- house.

Five years more passed away, and although we have no evidence that Florence made any progress in the many suits which had now become the sole business of his life, he yet enjoyed his freedom—freedom within the limits of the metropolis, and as ample social enjoyments as his straitened means would allow. His constant complaint was of poverty, of utter destitution, caused by the plunder of his property during his many years of restraint. As long as he was an inmate of the King's prisons, he was allowed four pounds a week for his maintenance and clothing. This was the precise sum he paid for his enlargement, for as soon as the prison doors opened to him for his exit, his Majesty's purse closed. Yet from his own frequent petitions we learn that when portions of his property were to be recovered by the clearing off of mortgages, the money was never wanting! These were mysteries to all but himself and his lawyers. New loans might liquidate old ones; times were improved, and even Irish property had grown to be of some value in an English market.

In 1624, Florence was again in his old quarters in the Gatehouse! The Earl of Thomond, one of his sureties, had

died, and instantly they, to whom his actual restraint, or the
power of using the threat of restraining him, was of advantage in the ruthless contest with him, and whom he always
mentions as " the continuers of my restraint," called the
attention of the Privy Council to the circumstance; and,
precisely at that moment—whether by adverse stellar influence,
or by design—came a letter from the Lord Deputy of Ireland
to Mr. Secretary Conway, raising again the alarm of danger
to the State from the continuance to him of such liberty as
he had been enjoying. " Florence MacCarthy," said that
mischievous letter, " a man infinitely adored in Munster, and
a person of consequence now in England under good securitie, and [fytt to be restrayned there!" Again with this
dangerous man to the Gatehouse!

Mr. Secretary Conway, like every Secretary for the last
36 years, was seized with an aguish shiver at every such
sentence from Ireland. " Florence M°Carthy, infinitely adored
in Ireland!" After 25 years of absence! These few words
of the Lord Deputy cost Florence as many months of incarceration; for under plea of defective securities, the Privy
Council ordered him to be detained in prison. He was compelled to allow time for this official panic to subside before
he could venture, with any hope of success, to petition again
for his enlargement. New sureties were found: and this long-
suffering and unsubdued man, now over 70 years of age,
again sues, and again obtains his suit, for his liberty; but not
until there had been forced from him piteous complaint of the
inhumanity to which he was subjected, and another fruitless
prayer, " that he might be called to answer if there might be
any matter against him!" For 24 years he had made the
same petition, and with the same result. He was, though
he had probably never been informed of it, " a *prisoner at
discretion!*" " Sickness and ague, and extreme cough, and
children ready to starve," were all conditions of imprisonment on such terms.

Only too soon will the reader be shocked by discovering
the name of the chief mover in arresting and shutting up
" an old man, over 70 years of age, in a little narrow room
without sight of the air, where his life was endangered," and
keeping him there in spite of illness for a year and a half!
for the present let the motive for this cruel and needless
restraint be supposed—as indeed doubtless it was with some
of the Lords of the Privy Council—the price fairly owing
for "being infinitely adored in Munster."

The sternest trial of Florence's long life was reserved for

its last years. His entire career had been a series of disappointments ; the mere accessories to his great fortune, noble birth, illustrious alliances, which to other men would have been as an ornament and rich inheritance, were to him the most fatal of the many gifts which nature had bestowed upon him; his personal accomplishments, the charms of address and speech which had caused him to be "greatly embraced by the brute sort of his countrymen," and at times scarcely less so by the members of Her Majesty's Privy Council, and her Principal Secretaries ; his prudence and wisdom, had all received bad names, because they were his, and were openly pleaded as just causes for his suppression. His marriage, for which he had paid the heavy penalty of eleven years of captivity, turned out a lasting and bitter sorrow! But worse than kingly descent, grace of person, charm of manner, worse than a host of adversaries and a treacherous wife, was in store for Florence as years rolled on, and old age was overtaking him. It has been seen that when the wife, who had been ever *so ready to show her loyalty by affording intelligence of her husband's treasons*, presented herself to him in his English prison, he took his children from her to share and console his prison life. The mother of these children he spoke of as the wicked woman who *had been* his wife! He mentioned her but twice during the many years of his long life afterwards; and it is probable that they never again met. It would seem that his sons lived with him through the period of their boyhood, in the various prisons into which he was thrown. In one of these prisons the eldest son Teig "the yonge childe who—as we were informed by the Bishop of Clone—after his countrey's manner, was used amonge the people as a yonge Prince, caryed abowt the contrey with three nurses, and six horssmen." This child—imp, as he is called by the Bishop —(imp means, according to Swift, a puny Devil! The Rt. Rev. Father could not have known this ; he must have thought it meant benighted little Papist!) This whelp, as Carewe styled him, escaped, and caused much misery! He died in the Tower!

Florence's three remaining children stayed with him, receiving from him such education as he was himself competent to give them ; according to the severe mind of Teig Hurley "they received neither breeding, learning, nor education," and indeed it is probable that they were earlier familiarized with the subtleties of litigation, bargains for court protection, and the intrigues of a fallen national party, than with the ingenuous arts, and the accomplishments befitting their years and condition.

As these young "devils" grew up to manhood, and their
characters developed, one of them at least, Donal, now the
eldest son and heir, wearied of prison life, rushed out into
the great world, and profiting by his father's consideration, at
least so far as to procure his admission into high society,
married, contracted debts, and at the outset of life became
hopelessly involved in money difficulties, and lived in constant
terror of his creditors. His first resource was to become a
petitioner to the Privy Council, and an angry adversary of
the Brownes; in all this there was nothing to destroy absolutely the good feeling between him and his father; nay, the
vigour with which he entered into the contest with the
Brownes might have excited Florence's admiration, and
strengthened his affection for him; but Donal had acquirements which he had not gained from his father, and which
must have excited in the heart and conscience of Florence
the utmost contempt and abhorrence.

In the pedigrees of the MacDonels, as well as those of the
MacCarthys, Donal is always mentioned as having married
Sarah, a daughter of the Earl of Antrim, a friend of Florence,
the nobleman so often referred to as one of his sureties; he
did so; but it is asserted in some pedigrees that he was previously married to Joan, a daughter of Malcolm Hamilton.

This may be a mistake, founded upon a mutilated passage
in a letter of Donal's, which will presently be laid before the
reader; but whether Donal's intimacy with the Hamiltons was
the natural consequence of a marriage into their family, or
merely arose out of the transaction of the marriage of the
Archbishop of Cashel's daughter, it is apparent that he had
contracted a very intimate alliance with them, to extort—with
whatever ultimate purpose between the parties—from his
father, the estates of the late Earl, his grandfather, which
he pretended were unlawfully withheld from him.

It may be in the reader's recollection that as far back as
the year 1611, Florence, in one of his letters of bitterest
complaint to the Earl of Salisbury, had exposed the treatment he had received from a certain Sir James Hamilton, who
had gone to him in his prison and offered to procure his
liberty, and also to secure his succession to Carbery, on the
condition that he would give over to him half of the lands
he should thus recover; but finding Donal Pipi bent upon the
surrender of his lands to the King, thus to ensure his son's
succession to them, and that his influence at Court was great,

he left Florence, and carried the terms of his bargain to him. From that day he became one of Florence's most bitter enemies. If it be true that Donal married a relative of this man, it would the most readily account for the direction which his iniquity took when hardest pressed by the misery of his position. His first proceeding was to conform to the religion of the Court; his next to demand of his father "to pass to him his living, and deliver up his evidences;" his third effort in the pursuit of fortune can be fitly told in no language but his own.

Few of the minor traits in the character of Florence evince so clearly the moderation and benignity of his nature, his self-respect, and the control he had gained over his emotions, as the forbearance with which, in the following letter to Sir Edward Conway, he relates the behaviour of his unworthy son.

"1625.   *To the Right Hon: the* LORDS *and others of His Majesties Most Hon. Privy Council.*

"The Humble Petition of Florence MacCarthy prisoner in the Gate House.

"Sheweth that *after fourteen yeares rest within the tower,* he was by his late Majestie about ten yeares past, confined upon bonds of the Earles of Thomonde and Clanrickarde, Westmeathe and Antrim, and others of good livinge; and being by divers of that countrie (in his long and close restrainte) deprived of his lands, whereof he could not recover by being disabled to prosecute his case by his confinement, he petitioned to his late Majestie for libertie whereby he might recover means of his livinge, which was referred by your Lordships to the Lord Willmot, the Lord Docura and others of the Council there; upon whose certificate your Lordships concluded that he should have his libertie, and His Majestie's Letters to have his living, which he followed, until upon the late Earle of Thomond's death it hathe pleased your Lordships to committ him until he had found other securitie for him; although the Earle of Thomonde did by his bond bind him and his heirs, whereby his son, this Earle of Thomonde, is still bounde for him, he hathe for your Lordship's satisfaction, procured the Earle of Ormond to be bounde, and the Earl of Clanrickarde (whereof some question was made) to signifie that he will continue still bounde for him; He therefore humblie beseechethe your Honorable Lordship as well to commiserate his age, *being above seventy yeares,* and long endurance these 24 yeares without being charged for anie matter, as to consider the triall that (without anie charges to His Majestie) hathe been had these ten yeares past uppon his suryeties of him, whoe now *since,* for noe cause, is *seventeen or eighteen months here in the Gatehouse,* tohis great suffering, where now he hathe no meanes to maintain him and his children; and in respect that his late Majestie gave orders for his libertie, that such great surieties are bound for him, and noe matter against him, that it will please your Lordships to give order for his enlargement and he shall ever pray for Your Honor's Lordships.
                                        " fflor: M^cCARTHY."

" 1625. *March* 12.   *To the* R^t. Honble Sir Edward Conway, K^t., *Principal Secr^y to the King's Most Excellent Majesty and one of H. M's Most Honb^{le}. Privy Council.*

" It may please your honor. The endeavours of the continuers of my restraint these 24 years, without ever being called to answer, or charged for any matter, hath been such as made me fearful, and doubtful of all men, which moved me (that was desirous to make my cause known to your Honor) to entreat M^r. Andrew Windsor to learn whether any dealth against me with you, whose honourable answer (that I cannot but take very thankfully) encouraged me to trouble yor Hon^r. My Father-in-law, and Predecessor in the Signorie and lands of Desmond, the late Earl of Clancar mortgaged certain lands to Sir Valentine Browne, of whose son (when after the Earl's death he refused to take his money and deliver it) I complained to Queen Elizabeth, upon whose reference, her Privy Council, and learned C^o. ordered me that land, which shortly after I recovered from the rebels, and enjoyed until he got some of his friends to inform against me, and to work my commitment; for the which no color was had but to get one to complain of me for a bond of £20, or £30, wherein I was bound many years before for a Gent^n. of Ireland that was here a suitor; upon which complaint I was committed and sent hither, where the late Earl of Salisbury was brought to cause me to be kept close in the Tower *contrary to Queen Elizabeth's pleasure, that knew me well,* whom I served long; and to His Majesty that after his coming, granted oftentimes my liberty, by whom I was in the end, after fourteen years restraint, confined upon bonds of the Earls of Thomond, Clanrickard, Westmeath, and Anthrim, and others; and being by divers of that country, (in my long restraint) deprived of my lands, whereof I could not recover any, being hindered by such as continued my restraint, and disabled to prosecute my cause by my confinement, I petitioned to His Majesty for means, or liberty whereby I might recover means of my living which was referred to the Lords, and by their Lo^s. to the Lo^s: Wilmot, Docrua, and others of the Council there; (in Ireland) upon whose certificate their Lo^s. concluded that I should have my liberty and his Majesty's letters to have my lands, which (although I was hindered by such as continues my restraint) I followed until my son came hither and desired me to pass my living, and deliver mine evidences unto him : which when I refused he protested before divers that he would get such as continues my restraint, to have me committed to the Tower, because the Earl of Thomond was dead, that 'was bound for me, who was shortly after sent for by some of the Lords, and told that the Earl of Thomond, one of my Sureties was dead, and that they would commit me untill I found another. I believe my commitment was wrought by ill-willers that considered not His Majesty's charges, by my restraint, the Triall, upon my Sureties without any charges to His Majesty, that hath been had these ten years past of me, who in that time was driven to sell or mortgage to Sir James Lancaster, Sir Thomas Heuytt, and Sir George Horssey, and others, about £400 land a year, by my being restrained here, about a year and four months, upon the like color, and to follow the effect of my liberty and living; which being concluded to be granted to me, I am, notwithstanding restrained to charge His Majesty, and to undo me ; and being now, by order of the Lords removed to the Gatehouse, until I find further security, the Earl of Thomond, and Sir Patrick Barnewell, two of my Sureties, being dead, *I am here kept in a little narrow close room without sight of the air,* where my life, that *am above* 70 *years of age,* after my long restraint, is much endangered; although the Earls of Clanrickard, West-meath, and Anthrim, with Sir Daniel O'Brien, the Earl of Thomond's brother, and others of good living are still bound for me, with the Earl of Thomond and Sir Patrick Barnwell that by their bonds did bind them and their heirs, yet, notwithstanding, I am not suffered to go under safe custody, or speak to any that would be bound for me; but kept here with-out any allowance of His Majesty, or means of mine own, whereby myself, and two young sons, and servants are like to perish, except your Honor will be pleased to commiserate me; wherein my humble request is that it will please Your Honor to send order hither that I may, under safe custody, be suffered to go speake to my friends, and know whether I shall bring those Sureties to Your Honor, or to whom else Your Honor will have them brought to take their bonds; and I will procure the Earl of Ormond to be bound instead of the Earl of Thomond; and others of sufficiency for Sir Patrick Barnewall, and rest,

"Your Honors most humbly to be commanded,
"fflor. MᶜCᴀʀᴛʜʏ."

The assertion made by Florence in the above letter, that "his imprisonment in the Tower was contrary to the pleasure of Queen Elizabeth, who knew him well," may have been but an opinion of his own; it may have been a fact well known to him. Were it but a mere opinion, it was doubtless formed in the mind of Florence from the treatment he had received from Her Majesty all through his career. With exception of the single instance of the Queen's yielding to the solicitations of Walsyngham—who was eager to promote the rapacious designs of his relative, Sir Ed. Denny, and other undertakers, his allies—and commanding his arrest and imprisonment for his marriage, he could call to mind nothing but benefits received from her, and he was too reasonable to deny that his conduct in that matter had been contemptuous of her authority, and had given to an imperious temper great provocation. It is true that his father had rendered her great services, and had been pronounced "one of the best subjects ever born of the Irishry!" And it is also true that Florence himself had from the age of 12 to 20, borne arms under her commission, and that all his Sept had aided in the suppression of the great Desmond rebellion; but in return for these services she had written her own royal letters of thanks to Sir Donogh; she had, after his death, graciously re-ceived his son at her court; she had presented him with a thou-sand marks in money, and a pension of two hundred marks. She had bestowed upon him a present of a Chiefry forfeited by the Earl of Desmond of a hundred beeves yearly, due from the MacCarthys of Carbery.

Doubtless in the estimation of the Queen and her Ministers, this was a gift simply of so many head of cattle yearly; but far otherwise was it in the estimation of Florence, and the men of Munster! We are informed by the author of the Carbriæ Notitia, that as soon as the FitzGeralds recovered from their overthrow at Callan, and when the MacCarthys began to fall out amongst themselves, "they got the best of it, and imposed on Carbery a most unjust and slavish tribute, called Earle's beeves." The gift to Florence was in fact the remission of this tribute. Shortly before Carewe apprehended Florence, he wrote, "There was due to Gerrot, late Earl of Desmond attainted, upon Carbery, viz., McCarty Reagh's country, 100 rent beeves yearly, which Her Majestie gave to Florence; if he be revolted, the beeves will be the Queen's." The author of the Carbriæ Notitia affords us the last trace of this ancient proof of the superior power finally acquired by the Earls of Desmond, "which (tribute) though, as I conceive, not maintainable in law, is yet tamely paid by the Carbrians to this day (about 1690) for want of unity amongst themselves to join in proper methods to get legally discharged of it."

The universal and repeated testimony of friends and enemies, the assurances of Cecyll himself in the joint letter sent by him and Sir John Stanhope to Florence, when evil reports of him had reached England, prove the kindly feelings of the Queen towards him, whilst the gift of the famous fine due from Barry, and lastly, her Majesty's free gift of the estates of his father-in-law, all of which had, in deficiency of heirs male, reverted to her, may have been sufficient motives to convince him of the benevolence of Elizabeth towards him; in addition to which, his intimacy with so many of the personages who formed her Court, must have procured him accurate information of her sentiments in his behalf.

But there are other reasons which were probably unknown to Florence, which may lead us to his opinion that his second imprisonment in the Tower was not according to the Queen's pleasure; for no sooner was it known that Carewe had laid hands upon Florence, than Cecyll wrote that "*it was not likely Her Majesty would proceed with any severity against him.*" And, evidently that an act so perfidious might not be without some show of urgency for its perpetration, he desired him " to spare not the sending over any proofs" of his guiltiness! The terms also in which was expressed the Queen's approval of the arrest were scarcely as cordial as the President probably looked for. " She accounts it an excellent pledge to have him safely sent hither." Not to the Tower as a traitor, but *hither* to London, out of Ireland, where, if he have the inclination, he cannot have the opportunity of doing mischief!

Furthermore, there was the great scandal of arresting a man who had placed himself within the power of her President, in entire reliance upon her royal parole, " solemnly and advisedly given for his personal freedom without touch." That this act of infamy had made its impression on the Royal mind there is reason to believe ; for as soon as Carewe had sent Florence to England, he arrested also Cormac MacDermod, of Muskerry, of whom he had long had an especial dislike, and he was on the point of sending him also to England. As soon as this was known he was ordered by no means to do so ; but "if his treasons were so manifest, to have him tried at common law ; for," added the Minister, " the clappinge up without trial maye prove scandalous !"

The suspended pleasures of litigation were resumed the minute the prisoner was let loose. New opponents sprung up in his pathway at every step ; not only had he in hand the great struggle with the invaders of his lands, but out of his money transactions in England, his loans and mortgages to raise means wherewith to fight his interminable legal battles, there arose new difficulties, and extortions so iniquitous that the very frauds of the lenders befriended him by enabling him to appeal to the usury laws for his protection. It would seem that every grievance of Florence was a matter of State, for all were addressed to the Privy Council, as if he and his affairs lay without the cognizance of the ordinary courts of law ! and that august assembly ever condescended to examine his complaints, and occasionally, as now, to interpose between him and his oppressors.

" 1626. *May* 15.

" Florence MacCarty by petition sheweth that after his long restraint in the Tower, being confined here at his own charges, one hundred Pound land a yeare was for £450 mortgaged unto Sir Thomas Hewett, unto whom £250 rent was then due of the tenants of the land, for which, when uppon the Earl of Totness and Baron Denham's certificate the Lords of the Council granted him letters, he was by Sir Tho⁸ Willoughby arrested to the counter, and restrained until he condicioned not to seeke for his said rent, and entered into a bond for that with the said Sir Thomas, who also keeps unjustlie from him above £80 of the £450 mortgage that he should pay him for the said lands ; holds a hundred a yeare of his lands for lesse than £400, refusing to take his money and discharge it when it was offered him about 4 yeares past ; and where alsoe Francis Foxe, of London, holds £60 a yeare of the Petitioner's land on mortgage for £200, and refused about 7 yeares last past to take his money and discharge it, he humblie desires, in respect that his use of £25 and £30 a yeare for £100 is within the compass of the statute to bargaine and mortgage being made here, and the rent which is the interest yearlie returned hither, and contrary to His Majestie's proclamation and order in Ireland, that His Majestie would refer it to such of the Privy Council as His Majestie shall think fitt, to call the parties before them, and to order the matter in such sorte as the petitioner may be righted."

" At the Court at Whitehall, 15 May, 1626.

" It is His Majestie's pleasure that the Lord Grandison, Mr. Chancellor of the Exchequer, and the Master of the Rolls, or any two of them doe make due examinacion of this matter, calling before them the parties whom the same concerns, and thereuppon to set down some final order therein, according to equitie and justice."

It is not the purpose of the writer of these pages to glide from the biography of the father to that of the son; indeed it is painful to be forced to bring the name of this young reprobate at all before an honourable reader; but certain of his letters must be presently brought under his notice, for without them it would be impossible to understand the shame and grief of the parent of such a son. These letters betray a baseness so deep, that this author much prefers to leave them to tell their own disgraceful story, which they do with astonishing coolness and perspicuity.

In Donal's first petition to the King's Most Excellent Majesty, there is sufficient evidence in style and composition that his education, at least, had not been so much neglected as Hurley had declared it. There is unmistakeable resemblance to the style of his teacher; the same tenacious claim for "parcels of land left by his grandfather, the late Earl of Clancar;" the same lamentation over straightened means, plundered property, and evil treatment; there is wanting the calm submission of his father, his urbanity towards his adversaries, and his dignity in remonstrance; in place of which is a fiercer handling of the Brownes, and but too little respect for the Majesty to whom his petition was addressed; but well were it if this petition were the only one he ever wrote! if a few blemishes of style, some youthful impertinence, and rudeness of address, were the only faults of the writer!

The reader may be amused to perceive how capriciously time had reversed the positions of the writer and his adversary. Although we were led by Teig Hurley to believe that he owed his conversion from the policy of Papistry to his intercourse with Sir Valentine Browne, we have a plain charge made against that gentleman of having himself turned Papist! and though yet outwardly holding with the religion of the State, yet " *damning* the King, and all his loyal subjects, who professed the true and *Catholic ʾfaith!*" that is

Protestanism ! Donal himself, like Teig Hurley and John Annyas, had wrestled with his Beble, and seen the errors of the faith of his boyhood. Like Teig, he had married a young woman of the same faith, differing only that in his instance she was probably much too good for him; but more unfortunate than either of these converts, he had brought upon him "his father, brother, and the rest of his kindred and friends, as great persecutors of him for his religion, as his other adversaries—whereof he had many—for his land."

The writer of the following letter, a venerable personage, not likely to use severe words at random, knew but the smallest part of the baseness of Donal; the terms he uses concerning him were probably sufficient to express his abhorrence of him, for what he did know; no language but Donal's own could describe the full amount of his baseness :—

" 1628. *April* 10. *Translation of a letter written from Madrid to a Franciscan Fryar called* EUGENIO FIELD, *in the Monastery of Timoleague.*

" Deere Father
" I have received your fatherly letters of the last of December, by which I understand that our beloved son Estranig resides in Dublin. Here both the King and Council are well satisfied with your informacion, and chefly we assure ourselves ofthe constancy of Don Carlos Mac Carthy, Lord of Musqry, of his allies and others, with their resolutions: We likewise see by your letters the small hopes there are of the sonne of Don Florentio Mac Carthy his heir. I am in your opinion in that which you write of his inclination tothe perverseness of Lutherans, and enemies of our quiete. I doe understand likewise that there is no hope of the libertie of Don Florentio, whom God prosper, with all those that are well affected, &c. &c.
" There are less hopes ofthe sonne of the Lord Kierry (who as I have heard is a terrible man) than of the sonne of Don Florentio; but it is no wonder; he having alwaies been brought up amongst the English; but Don Florentio his Sonne is a *Child of Curse*, who is readie, not onlie to destroy his own Father, but alsoe his Mother the land where he was born, &c. &c.
" FLAHREUS TOMONENSIS."

In a letter from Father Bodloch, or Boethius McAgan, dated 26 May, 1630, from Louvais to Mr. Boethius Agan, merchant, Galway, it is stated that " The Archbishop of Tuam died at Madrid on the 18th Nov). The King of Spaine wrote with his own hand news of his death to the Infanta. This Bishop, before his profession, was a great chronicler in the Irish tongue, and learned."

It was this Prelate who but a few months before his death, wrote the above letter to the monk of Timoleague.

Had Donal left no literary trace of himself but his petition to the King, men might have judged the terrible sentence of the Archbishop a mere ebullition of vexation, the angry and rash judgment of a bigoted churchman, or disappointed politician; had this letter also perished, sufficient of the character of Donal would remain to us in his own handwriting. Donal's petition was doubtless backed by powerful friends; but Browne, with less alliance, possessed the hereditary vigour of his race. He despised Donal as an adversary, but was ready, as ever had been his father and grandfather, to meet Florence before King or Council. His petition was quickly followed by the counter-petition of Donal.

" 1630. *April* 22. VALENTINE BROWNE *to the Right* Honble *my most respected noble Lorde, the* LORDE VISCOUNT DORCHESTER *Principal Secretary to His Majestie, and one of his most* Honb^le *Privie Council.*

"These give at Court.

" Right Honb^le I understand by late advertisement from my agent there Edmund Hussey, that my petition (preferred to His Majestie by your Honor, at the request of my Cousin germain Thos. Merry) hath bin referred by His Highness to the Committees for Ireland, reade before them, and considered off, and that their Honors gave orders to refer the consideration of that my honest request (more important a thousand times for His Majestie's general goode in countenancing the plantacions ancientlie settled, than for my particular profit) to the Lords Justices, and Council of this kingdom and that a letter being drawn to that purpose from the Lords Committees was stopt by my Lorde Treasurer, which moveth me to conceive that my ancient adversary (Florence Mac Carty) doeth revive his old cunning sleights, by his misinformacions to gain him som frends about Court; But such ones they must be (in my opinion) that being not truelie informed of the disloyaltie, ambition and danger of that man, will give ear unto his own fictions, commiserat his restraint, (though deserved highly,) and credit the large promises he makes; which here his children and frends spare not to proclaim (to the no small terror of my English plantation,) viz that they will give to one frend or other half my lands or more to recover all from me. I am, in playne terms, at full defiance with them. If I have your Honor of my side to assiste me in my right, derived from the Crown in plantation lands, enjoyed by my Grandfather, & father successivelie, being English, and descended to me. My intelligence from my cousin Merry and agent, doeth ensure me of your Honble Lordship's noble favors, and though unacquainted I embouldened myself thus to troble your Lordship (for which I desyre pardon) and withal humblie entreat your Lordship to persist in furthering my occasions at this present, which you shall find to agree with His Majestie's profit, honor and safetie of this kingdom of Ireland; and my adversary's aimes to tend to the contrary absolutely, however cloked and cullered.

" And further I bind myself hereby to perform fairly whatsoever my said agent shall promise for me: and from time to time (by my thankfulnesse) to endeavour to merit your Honor's good opinion of me that am resolved to approve myself alwaies
"Your Lordship's most humble & devoted Servant
" VAL: BROWNE.
" Ross 22 April 1630."

" 1630.   *Petition of* DANIEL, *eldest son of* FLORENCE MAC CARTHY.

" To the King's most Excellent Majesty,

" The humble petition of Daniel Mac Carthy, son and heir apparent of Florence Mac Carthy, and grandchild and heir (by his mother), to the late Earl of Clan Carr, deceased.

" Sheweth that upon a late petition exhibited to your Majesty on the behalf of Sir Valentine Browne, Baronet, who holds Your Majesty and your loyal subjects, all damned, that profess the true and Catholic faith, openly professed in your Majesty's kingdoms and dominions, however he outwardly professes it, himself being a man divers others ways, for alliances and otherwise, dangerously refractory to your Majesty's laws, customs, civil government, and conformity; whose petition is stuffed only with manifold untruths, false glosses of plantations, fortifications, and pretended services, purchases and grants (as shall be proved) to induce your Majesty to confirm unto him your poor subject's inheritance; which ought to descend unto him from his said grandfather, by an act of the next Parliament to be held in Ireland; for the better preparation of this his deceitful plot he hath obtained from your Majesty a reference to the Lords, and others, committees for Irish causes, who without hearing, or calling your subject or his father (who hath the evidences of the lands in question) thereunto, have concluded thereupon to refer the matter of the said Sir Valentine's petition to the now Lords Justices of Ireland to examine and certify therein.

" May it please your Majesty to be informed, this matter that Sir Valentine would now set on foot, was long since in the time of Queen Elizabeth of famous memory, by a reference from her Majesty to the then Earl of Salisbury, Sir John Popham, then Attorney-General, and other Honourable Commissioners of her Majesty's Privy Council, and learned council of England, and Ireland, decided and adjudged against Sir Valentine's father here in this kingdom; as your Majesty's subject can and will make it appear, though Sir Valentine's father and himself have got those lands since, after his father's commitment, and held it ever since in his restraint, which they wrought *and continued these* 29 *years,* upon misinformations, *without ever being called to his answer,* or they or their confederates to stand to, or at all to prove their misinformations against him; who notwithstanding upon every untrue and unseasonable blast of their misinformation was still locked up from time to time, without any examination, or further ado.   Therefor, in imitation of that royal prince's gracious inclination to Justice, humbly beseecheth your most sacred Majesty to refer back the matter (so well and so anciently decided already here upon mature consideration by those honourable grave personages aforesaid,) to the said Lord's Committees, calling unto them some of your Majesty's reverend Judges to hear, and to be truly informed of your subject's title, and infinite wrongs, and oppressions done him, and his father, by the practices of the said Sir Valentine and his father, and to certify your Majesty of the true state of the said cause; and for the better affecting the same to cause your subject may be righted, and not further hindered of your Majesty's said royal progenitor her royal intent aforesaid, whereby your subject may be enabled to live (who is now for want of means ready to perish) and such a member as Sir Valentine is, and shall be proved to be may, together with his most wicked, divelish, and inhuman practices, be utterly overthrown ! and quite frustrated !

" And your subject, as he is already bound, shall eternally pray for the continuance of Your Most Sacred Majesty's happy reign long over us."

Donal's spirited reply found sufficient favour at court, to bring that long pending conflict—it had lasted half a century, and reached to the fourth generation of the Brownes—to an end! (that is, to one of its ends, the fourth!) not precisely such as Donal and his great friends may have wished, but such as the law must pronounce, if it pronounced at all.

The note of alarm, the antiquated battle cry of Florence's disloyalty, ambition, cunning, sleights, &c., had been sounded too often, it pealed however clearly and shrilly as of old, and with the usual martial flourish of the Brownes. but it fell at last upon ears dull to its influence. The Lo : Viscount Dorchester probably saw little danger in restoring certain Irish lands to an old man who had been for 30 years oscillating between the various jails of London ; and detected little ambition in the man whose chief prayer for indulgence was to exchange the horrors of the Tower for the amenities of the Marshalsea ; little sleight and cunning in the attempt to recover lands worth £1000 per annum, which had been in pledge for fifty years for the loan of £500! One day of Sir George Carewe, or Sir Ro : Cecyll, or Mr. Attorney-Gen. Popham, would have been worth more to the Petitioner than all "the dangers to the English Government" which his genius could invoke.

"1630.   *Decision in re* BROWNE *and* FLORENCE.

"Whereas Florence MacCarthy, Esquire, and one Sir Valentine Browne, Knight, now lately deceased, had severally exhibited unto us and to the Lords of our Privy Council here in England, several petitions concerning the Castles of Cosmaignes, Glaneroght, and Ballicarberie, in the counties of Kerry and Desmond in Ireland, heretofore mortgaged by the Earl of Clancarr unto Sir Valentine Browne, Knight, and Nicholas Browne his son deceased, father and grandfather of the said last-named Sir Valentine Browne, the petitioner pretending the said lands to be purchased by his said father and grandfather for *great sums of money;* that he had several grants thereof from the Crown, did thereupon sue unto us by petition to have the same passed to him and his heirs by Act of Parliament :   And whereas the said matters upon both their petitions were referred unto the consideration of Sir William Jones, K^t. one of our Judges of our Court of King's bench in England, whereupon hearing Counsel on both sides, hath found and certified that the said Earl by two several indentures about 30th and 31st Elizabeth, did convey and assure the lands now in question unto Sir Valentine Browne, the grandfather, and his son, for about £500 *in money,* upon *conditions for redemption* thereof by payment of the monies at any time, and *that their lands are affirmed to be worth £1000 per an^m. and the profit thereof to have been taken for* *the use of the money ever since.* As also that the said Earl had issue only one daughter, who was married to the said Florence MacCarthy, and hath issue now living, and hereupon thought it not fit that Sir Valentine Browne, the petitioner, should be suffered to pass any Act of Parliament to preclude the said Florence MacCarthy's title, but that the said Florence MacCarthy might take his remedy here, or in Ireland, or we should direct the said Judge, *knowing no matter of State that might hinder the same,* as by his certificate now fully appeareth: Now, for as much as the said Earl of Clancarr and his heirs had liberty by the said deeds of mortgage, whereof the counterparts are extant under seal, to redeèm the lands mortgaged, with payment of the mortgage monies at any time, which mortgage monies as appears by the said (indenture?) are for the Cosmaignes and brought only £421 1s. 2d. and £121 13s. 3d., and for Ballicarbry £80, and the said Florance MacCarthy, who married the daughter and heir of the said Earl, is willing to pay all the said moneys accordingly: and *the grants obtained from the Crown are only in nature of confirmations.* These are now therefore to will and require you, that upon payment made of the said sums of £421 1s. 2d., £121 13s. 3d., and £80 by the said Florence MacCarthy unto the heirs of the said Sir Valentine Browne, or to his use, you forthwith deliver the possession of the said mortgaged lands unto the said Florence MacCarthy, or to his assigns; and that due consideration be had of some recompence to be given to the said Florence MacCarthy, for *the mean profit for the time past,* and that you make no composition with the heirs or assigns of the said Sir Valentine Browne upon our commission of grace."

Thus, after the lapse of fifty years since the Brownes had their first dealings with the Earl, was this famous contest decided! Florence had stoutly fought it out under three generations, and now triumphed over the fourth. The sentence to refund the mean profits must have fallen upon the intelligence of Sir Valentine II., if he had lived to hear it, with as much of amazement and disgust as in former days fell the tidings of the gift of the notable fine of £500 to Florence on the ears of Barry.

Family tradition may have informed the young Sir Valentine, who had recently stepped into so cheerless an inheritance, that this great contest had been finally decided three times before! Once in favour of his Great Grandfather, when he obtained his patent! a second time when the unlucky word Heirs was discovered, "where there should have been Heirs Masles," and which carried all the Earl's lands over to Florence's wife. A third time when Florence was captured, and Sir Robert Cecyll at once gave over lands and crops to Sir Nicholas, and promised that amended Letters Patents should presently follow! Tokens of times stormier than England had known for centuries were already perceptible, and if the young Sir Valentine had but the endurance and resolution of his family he might yet hope—if he could but outlive Florence—to see a fifth decision. In the mean time there was no choice but to refund the mean profits, which, if calculated at the reputed value, £1000 per annum of the Earl's lands, for fifty years, must have had a singular appearance as the offspring of the original loan of £622 14s. 5d.

CHAPTER XIX.

IT is difficult to know with what sufficient apology to introduce the three following letters to the reader's notice! Had
they borne the signature of John Annyas, or Teig Hurley,
we should, after previous specimens of the correspondence of
those ingenious and original writers, have been prepared for
their very curious contents. In what mood of mind, or with
what estimate of the understanding and morality of the Lord
Viscount Dorchester such letters were written, it surpasses
ordinary abilities and a common conscience to conjecture!
They are however the genuine productions of Florence's
eldest son, who borrowed a worthy English name only to
disgrace it! they were written during his father's life time;
and nearly all that we have any means of knowing, far more
than we could have any desire to know, of this "child of
curse" is derived from them.

" 1630. *Nov*. 2.   DANIEL MAC CARTHY *to* LORD VISCOUNT DORCHESTER.

" May it please Your Lordship. In England I have eaten most of my
bread, and altho' Ireland challenges my birth, were it not for feare to encur
hatred of the one or be suspected of flattery by the other I could justlye
say and sweare without either lying or flattery that there is no nacion under
the sun I doe more truely affect than England, and English men; but to
avoide the one and the other inconvenience I will onlie refer the further
declaring of my integritye on that particular to God first, who knows best
the secrets of all hartes, and next to my actions and service, when it shall
please God that my Soveraine and the state there may be pleased to employ me. Little is it to be wondered or suspected, that I should be thus
affected to England and Englishmen, for I cannot chuse but be so, without
I were more than beastlie ungrateful, for that since the year 1617 at which
time I entered suite for som few parcells of my birthright, which continued
to my great charge pains and travell unto the year 1627, at which time,
with much adoe, with the favourable furtherance of my Rev^d. & Honble.
frends my Good Lord's Grace of Canterbury, the late Earle of Totness, the
Lord Viscount Grandison, M^r. Endimion Porter, Sir Thomas Stafford and
others, and with the especial grace and favour of my good and gracious
Soveraine that now is, of whose blessed raign God grant long to continue
over us in all happinesse: But my long suite for those parcells, having my
father, brother with the rest of my kindred and frends as great persecutors
of me, for my religion, as my other adversaries (whereof I had many) for

my lands, which they covet, and detaine from me, caused that I became
much indebted.   In the first yeares of my suite I owed a pretty quantity;
and sure, but that I did so, and that I was sorry that some English Gentlemen and others that lent me their money freely and lovingly should lose it,
or anything by me, I should never have had the patience to see out the end
of my suite, with that miserie I endured with it; but my hastie desire to
see all paid their owne made me abide all extremitie, hoping that if I recovered those parcells, as at last I did, I might with them pay everybody;
but deceived I was herein, for though it is now three or four years since, yet
in all that time I received not above £10 of their rents : My brother
whom I appointed overseer over all, hath done with all what he thought
fitt: whereupon I, seeing myself altogether disappointed of the expectacion
I had of making honest satisfaction, therewith made a second suite for some
other parcells of my birthright, hoping if I might recover the same I should
thereby be enabled (as indeed I should) to pay my debts, and present those
my Rev^ds. and Honble. frends with some small token of my gratefulness,
who have so generously, voluntarily and of mere pitty furthered my former
suite, as I said.   For the gaining of which latter parcells I had His Majesties letters in my behalf to the Lord Falkland then Lord Deputie of
Ireland, but could recover none, to my utter undoing ever since.   To renewe
me suite for those parcells, but to marry the Lord Archbishop of Cashell's
daughter [to] Malcolm Hamilton after his Lordship's death, for a small som
of money, and hope of her best frends furtherance of my just suite, but
having failed in most of these expectacions, and like to starve in London
until an honest Gentleman called Mr Thraile that lives in Durham Yard,
did of mere mercie take me into his house, with whom, for money he lent
me, and for half a yeares diet I owe forty pounds or thereabouts, which I
wish to God with all my harte he had, likewise I owe a worthy honest
gentleman and frend of mine called Mr William Northcott of Haine in
Devonshire, within three mile of the cittye of Exeter, about £100, and twice
as much I owe to two other gentlemen and frends of myne, the one called
Capten Thomas Dourich and the other Mr Thos Jay.   These debts and
crosses, together with other small debts I owe, whereof I doe herewith send
your Honor a note, made me fly to this side the seas, but not to shun making
honest satisfaction of such due debts or to deprive anie of their own, but in
hope I might get some money here for that conceite wherewith I might pay
all or most part of my said debts, and to that intent to return suddenlie
again for England, but my expectations here also were frustrated, where
I did not presume to come before I had my Passe granted me by the Lords
there, neither would I ever have come if their Lordships had not granted
me my passe : And now being here I am loath to return till I see whether
I can get something that maie enable me to paye my debts there honestlie,
and gratifye my frends.   Som Irishmen here persuade me to go serve the
French King because he is of alleyance and league with my own Soveraine
Lorde, promising and assuring me not onlie that they will procure that I
shall have intertainment of a Regiment, but that alsoe all Tyrone's regiment or most part of them will follow me, which before I would return back
for England, or take that or anie other course I thot fitt to present to Your
Honble. consideracion, this being a service that to my knowledge hath bin
alwaies laboured, much desired and often attempted, but never as yet effected,
because no good or certen course hath never been taken for the same.   If His
Majestie and the State will be pleased to imploy me herein, or in anie
other service that shall not savour anie way of baseness, or shall not be
against divine or human laws or the qualitie of a Gentleman, I will to the
uttermost of my power, with the hazard of my life effect it, and especially

this of drawing this regiment of Tyrone from serving the Spaniard, to serve the French King, so that I be sure that it be an acceptable service to the King and State, and that His Majestie and the State will vouchsafe to command me thereunto, and accordingly recommend me to the French King that he may grant me the command of a regiment or of soe manye as I shall bring thither. Your Lordship and the world shall see that I will performe the part of a true & loyall subject therein, though to tell Your Lordship truelye I am not all given to warr, valor or killing of men, and had rather undertake to do His Majestie and the State anie other service rather then what belongs to warres. Neverthelesse to do my Soveraine and the State service I will (contrarie to my affection to such exercises) hazard my life : or if your Lordship hold not this materiall for His Majestie's service (though I know if the Irishmen were once brot from serving the Spaniard it would breede a jealousie for ever betweene them) howsoever for my good will I humblie beseech Your Honor so far to comiserat and tender my miserable case, thus banished for debt, and the case of my poore wyfe, from whom I am forced to absent myself, so far as to cause that my father and brother may satisfye my said debts, out hand with those lands and rents which His Majestie caused me to be so possessed of three or four yeares since, called Castellogh and 13 ploughlands, and that some other meanes may be there settled·for me and my wyfe's maintenance, either of my own birthright or yearlie allowance from His Majestie, that I may returne home again to London, from whence I think my absence to long; If it were God's will your Lordship should think fitt to employ me in that occasion of France great care is requisit to be had that the Spanish Ambassador there, or anie Irish or English Spanishlie affected, hear not of the intention or any thing thereof. My integritie and earnest desire and ambition to follow the steps of my ancestors in their services tothe crowne of England, whose actions and loyaltie I will not onlie defend against all calumnies of adversaries that should tax them with the least act of Treacherie or Treason since the first submission of Ireland tothat crowne: witness the records of Tower and Chancery of London, witness more particularly the Patent granted by King Henry 7th to one of them in the 12th yeare of his raine extant now in that chancery: Alsoe my zeal to our church, and tothe observance of God's holy lau, and commandment, wherebye he wills all men to be true loyall and faithful to their natural princes, and therefore not by anie Christian tobe violated: and who ever doeth is, and shall be accursed in my opinion; Lastly the odious conceipt and abominable estimacion I have of that name of Traitor. All which I humblie leave to your góode Lordship's most honble and grave consideracion. Humblie taking my leave I am ever your Honor's truelye devoted in all observance humblie to serve.

" Post Scripta.—One thing more I must refer or present to your Lordship's consideracion is that if I be in France employed I shall be able still to certifye the state truely still of what shall be intended by the Irish or Spaniards against the King and State in Brussels Rome and Maderid, so that, as I said your Lordship will keep secret from the knowledge of the Spanish ambassador, and all such as are of English or Irish either Spanishlie or Popishlie affected, be they of the Council or otherwise, be they suspected or known.

" Calis 2 November 1630.

" DANIEL Mᶜ CARTHY."

"1631.   *Nov*. 11.   *To the R^t Honb^le the* LORD VISCOUNT DORCHESTER
Principall Secretarye to His Majestie, and of the Privie Councell.

" R^t. Honble I am that poore Gentleman that presumed from beyond
seas, in a tedious confused manner to write to your Lordship, humblie ten-
dering my service, with a full and cordial expression of my integritie to
His Majestie, the State & Religion.

" Your Honor received it at the hands of M^r. Thomas Jay my good
frend, who since my arrival told me your Honor's good and noble acceptance thereof, wishing me to present myself to your Lordship to render the
dewtie I am obliged to so noble a disposicion conceived without anie meritt
in me or of myne. But I being a poore Gentleman altogether dejected and
cast down by misery and misfortune, dare not presume myself worthy to
present myself or speake, much lesse to call me your servant, and soe dare not
draw neere to do those dewties, without your Honor will be pleased to give
a gracious admittance to him that may happilye doe your Honor more acceptable service then others that may promise more, and be chargeablie
hired, or then my former letter could induce your Lordship to imagine me
so serviceable. My Lord the ould proverb ever ruleth ' A goulden sword is
sometimes seathed in a leaden seathe.' The reason why I troble not M^r. Jay
now to geve your Lordship notice of me your Honor shall learn upon my
admittance. If your Lordship be pleased to conceive me dewtifull, be
pleased also to acquaint none with my coming to your Lordship, or my
name, be pleased onlie to call me *M^r. George Watts,* who notwithstanding
humblie remain as I am ever

" Your Lordships humble, poore, distressed (in what manner your
honor pleases to esteeme me) readie to do all service to my poore power
                              " DANIEL MACCARTHY.
" Novr 11, 1631."

"1631.   *Nov^r* 19.   *To the R^t. Hon:* LORDE VISCOUNT DORCHESTER *from*
        GEORGE WATTS (*alias* DANIEL MACCARTHY).

" R^t. Honble. when last your Honor vouchsafed me admittance to present myself to your Honor, though far unworthy the favour, your Lord-
ohip then desired me to declare circumstances with the names of such
parties whom the matter concerns. If please your Honor to remember, I
then said as my conscience and zeal enforced me, out of meere dewtie
loyaltie and integritie to His Majestie, the State and religion, and discover
those things that came to my knowledge, which I fear may concern all
more than is imagined, or as yet dreamt of hitherto, for which others not
long since have been like to suffer innocentlie, and as I doe not expecte anie
reward from His Majestie, and the State for what I declare for their service, nor have or can have anie end therein, so on the other side I told
your Lordship my conscience alsoe restrained me from naming parties, least
anie should receive detriment in body or goods, by anie thing that should
proceede from me, which your Honor was pleased to promise me, none
should that I should name, nor myselfe be published for author of this
service; presuming thereon I doe now cite to your Lordship the substance
of what I have to utter, together with the names of so many of the parties
whom it concerneth, as I can at present call to minde, humblie beseeching
your good Lordship upon my knees that you will be pleased to remember
alwaies your honorable promise to me your unworthy poore servant, in
their behalfes, as I shall be both quite disabled, and altogether dishartened

to doe anie service for the future, according my most loyall intent, neither (under favor) must suddaine notice be taken of things; onlie an undelayed fortifying and securing of all those places as I shall name.

"The Partie. {
The partie by whom I came to knowledge of what shall now followe, was one Condon, an Irishman in a Towne called Burbrook in Flanders, this somer was twelvemonth as I take it.

"The Irish, their plott to be tould {
Certen Irish their plott to sack, burne spoil and kill a whole new planted Towne of English, of great trading, where he said they were sure tohave armour for a thousand men, and money to maintain them a good while; as also the sacking and spoiling of all the new planted English townes through the whole province of Monster and totake and fortifye Limebrick a cittie there, and make it their residence of State, being neere the center of Ireland, and at hand for the discontented of all partes to repayre to, and for that two winds serves thence to Spaine and back, and manie from England.

"The Parties undertakers herein both temporall and spirituall both openly and underhand both living and dead. {
First Condon's own chefe and kinsman called M^r. David Condon, who though he be one of the meanest among all the rest, was chefe actor or hatcher of this plott. The names of the rest is as followeth.

"According to Condon's relacion The temporall, openly so soon as things were executed and otherwise. {
1st. The Lord Kierry deceased M^r. McDonogh, al^s Dermond Mac Carthy, deceased. The Lord of Muskree, that lives.

" M^r. Morrice Roche the Lord his son & heir.
" M^r. John Power, son and heir to Sir W^m. Power.
" M^r. Edmund Fitz John Gerald of Ballymarter.
" M^r. O'Sullevan Beere, besides divers I remember not.

"The temporal underhand assistants for as many as Condon knew, who said he was sure there were others. {
The Lord Earle of Barrymore. The Lord Sarsfield, chefe Justice of the Common Pleas.

"The Spirituall Papists according to Condon's relacion, and as I can remember at present. {
The Archbishop of Tuam called Flahry, resident, and dead since, in Spaine. The Archbishop of Cassell, dead since also. The Bishop of Corke, now living in Ireland, and brother in law to the Lord Sarsfield.

" Robert Fitz David Barry, Prior of Ross.
" Owen Field, of eminence alsoe.
" Richard Connelo, the lyke.
" Philip Holyhan, alsoe one Strang, or Strange, whose christen name I know not, with a far greater rabbel that I cannot remember.
" This is, my Lord, a true relacion of soe much of the discourse happened twixt me and Condon, in Burbrook. I have other things to acquaint your Honor withal, both of passages that shall confirm, in a maner, those things to your Lordship's judgment which are partlie of myne owne knowledge, and partlie of Condon's, and make the actions or practices of others known to your Honor, and when your Lordship is at full leisure to heare, I will imparte, which are much as I can remember, what else shall

come to my knowledge or remembrance your Lordship shall be alsoe acquainted therewith from time to time, and surelye much more was tould beyond seas by many, but I neither remember them, nor what they said, as yet onlie this much I remember, and I thank God I remember it, and I think it is well I doe, and truelye I had remembered the rest had I thot your Lordship would esteeme my accompt; what I remember I humblie, truelye, freelye, and ingenuouslye imparte it to your Lordship, without desire of harm to anie, as your Honor may well perceive, or glorie, gain or reward, or end, but that onlie end, which of all ends I hould myself bond in dewtie and conscience to have alwaies chefe regard unto, which is the preservacion and welfare of His Majestie, the State and Religion. If your Lordship shall be displeased because I have not presented your Honor with these things so soone as I arrived here, be pleased to blaim my dejected state through my manifold crosses and misfortunes, and not my good will or loyaltie, that wanted nothing but a bringer on, being doubtfull and fearfull who to reveale these things unto in this uncerten age, least I should be discovered as author of the service. I humblie crave both your Lordship's pardon and patronage If your Honor will be pleased to make use of me or hould me worthy tobe your Honor's servant, your Lordship shall finde me both faithfull, trustie, and serviceable to my power; and will, if your Honor will give me leave, prescribe a waie without charge to His Majestie wherebye I may be best made serviceable to work in time what may be most acceptable in bringing hidden things to light; for as I said to your Honor that your Lordship nor anie could make me more willing, readie, loyall and faithfull, but far more able your Honor may, which I humblie leave to your Hon[ble] consideracion, whereunto I refer myself, humblie kissing your Honor's hands, taking leave and remaining

"The meanest (doubtless! the very meanest!) of Your Lordship's servants,

"GEORGE WATTS."

"19th Nov[r]. 1631."

It is enlivening to fall in again with the name of our venerable countryman the Arch-Bishop of Cashell. He had but recently completed his earthly pilgrimage, and at the age of one hundred years had departed from many Bishopricks, and many cares—not, it must be admitted, in very favourable repute with churchmen of his own day, or of ours—and leaving it doubtful whether he had not, in his latter years journeyed back over the ground which he, Annyas, Hurley, and George Watts had, with so great travail of conscience, traversed before; whether he had not again fallen into the worship of the scarlet pictures of his youth. The last two years of his life he spent in bed, where it pleased him to compose an epitaph, which in due time was to be, and was, engraved upon his monument. It is itself a monument, ære perennius, of his erudition, and the subtlety of his genius. No learned man of his own day, no one during the two and a half centuries that have passed since, has been able to expound the meaning of this enigma! Sphynx could scarcely do it—in fact has not done it—Never, probably, may its solution be looked for, till "Cashel of the Kings" shall produce such another Archbishop.

Miler left sons and daughters; and of all the curious incidents of a capricious fortune was this, that a son of Florence should petition for "the marriage" of one of these Archiepiscopal maidens! that is that His Majesty would be graciously pleased to make over to him ("for the alleviation of his sufferings at not being able to pay his debts, and present his Rev. and Hon. friends with some small token of his gratefulness"), the royal right to prefer this fairest of his wards in marriage, to any gentleman the most enamoured, or willing to pay the most for the charms of the lady, and the honour of the alliance.

As the reader might expect, the last trace discoverable of Florence is a "petition to the Privy Council!" and the last object of that petition, the "restitution of certain lands which had in his close restraint been entered upon, and kept from him." The document now following is the *last* that has been preserved amongst Her Majesty's State Papers, in the handwriting of Florence; it is undated, and is presumed to have been written in the year 1630. He was at the time in the 70th year of his age, and the 42nd of his captivity. A surprising change had taken place in the nature of the correspondence from Ireland; the host of letter-writers encouraged by Burghley, Walsyngham, and the younger Cecyll, was utterly extinct; they had passed away gradually during the early years of King James. There was no longer any open opposition to English rule; the Irish Chieftains were no longer of importance, or cause of any anxiety; confiscation was stopped for a time, and letter-writing was left to mere officials; and it would seem from the fewness of such documents as now exist, to have nearly ceased altogether.

The countries of MacCarthy Mor, and M. C. Reagh were antiquated geographical divisions of a great province, chiefly to be traced by the *Plots*, or Maps of Nicholas Browne, and others, which the taste of Carewe saved from perishing. The days were gone by when writers like Annyas suggested the policy of English Statesmen towards Ireland; they were succeeded by an entirely new class of men, though precisely of the same instincts, gentlemen of slender patrimony, and of the type of that Northern Knight whom Florence mentioned, as of the opinion that the Irish were fitter to be rooted out, than to be allowed to enjoy their lands; friends of the King, who, as they resided at the court, had no occasion to pursue

their purposes by letter-writing, but who, by the farming of
the fines of English recusants, and traffic with the inmates of
London jails for change of air, and by shrewd bargains with
Irish undertakers, followed fortune, loveliest of the Olympians,
who is represented with eyes bandaged, surely that she may
not see by what means, and by what men her favours are
solicited!

Florence's troubles had for some time past ceased to proceed from political charges; Browne's last letter, and the
Abstract which had once more wakened up the echoes of
the old war cries of Jacques and Stanley, were the last of
his annoyances of this kind. All men's remedy against him,
and his against all men, was henceforth by action at law;
theoretically this process was all that could be desired;
but in effect it was attended with the inconvenience that
although decisions of great legal functionaries might be
obtained, and orders of the Privy Council for their enforce-
ment might, with patience, be also procured, the execution of
such orders for restitution of lands in the picturesque regions
of the remoter parts of Munster, on the borders of the pearl
lakes of Castle Logh and Killarney, by a proprietor who was
forbidden to move more than 12 miles away from Whitehall,
was still a difficulty.

Florence's letters were, however, written in better spirits
than of old; the man who could wrench from the grasp of
the Brownes the Signory of Molahiff, after fifty years of possession, need not despair, even though 70 years of age, of
obtaining his freedom.

"1630-1.   FLORENCE MAC CARTHY'S *Petition to the Privy Council.*

" Shewing that where he hath petitioned to your Lordships for certain
lands of his that (in his close restraint so many years, as it was not known
there that he was alive,) some of his own country people entered into and
keeps, which cause your Lordships referred to the Earl of Thomond and
the Lord Carewe, and Baron Denham, that (a little before your suppliant's
last commitment to the Gatehouse) certified their knowledge thereof, he
therefore humbly beseecheth, in respect that your suppliant doeth not sue
for £1000 lands a year, of his that is kept from him under color of a small
mortgage of his predecessor, nor for his father's inheritance, which upon a
reference from your Lordships is formerly certified to be his right, but for
a small thing as appears by their certificate, that it will please your Lordships to give order that their said certificate may be made known to His
Majesty, to whose gracious consideration he is left by them. And he shall
ever pray, &c. &c.
" (No date,) most probably in 1630-1."

. The reader, hearing that the *last* petition in the hand-

writing of Florence has been laid before him, may have considered the announcement as a note of warning that the *end*
was come, or coming; and have judged that if all sound of
battle have ceased for evermore, then surely the busy hand
that had written so much, fought so well, had stiffened! that
the sharp weapon which had so bravely defended him, had
dropped from it! that his active mind had sunk to rest, and
that the patrimony of Desmond and Carbery was left to other
combatants!   But it is not so!   We have read from time to
time, during the past thirty years, painful accounts of his
health, ruined by unhealthy prisons; how at one time " he
was dying of consumption, and was languishing away," at
another that he was " perishing of sickness, ague, and extreme cough, that he had fallen melancholy and must soon
die!" but when, upon these occasions, the humanity of his
best of friends, Sir Robert Cecyll and Lord Zouch, prevailed
over the sharper discipline of Carewe, Boyle, and the Undertakers, and he was allowed the benefit of change of air from
the relaxing atmosphere of the Tower ditches to the more
bracing and exhilarating climate of the Marshalsea, we perceived at once, by the renewed vigour of his style, a quick
recovery from his various painful maladies.   The absence
from his last petition of any complaint of failing health, and
the energy of the accustomed cry of robbers! afford hope of
life to be prolonged for many years to come.   It is gratifying
to the author of this biography to see nowhere any token of
the coming shadow, and to be able to leave him in the full
possession of mental vigour, in the enjoyment of victory, and
the prospect of great chances yet to come.

Although no more petitions in the handwriting of Florence
are preserved, we do not immediately lose sight of him : his
petitioning continued for several years longer, and with the
customary result—favourable reception in the Privy Council,
orders to the Irish Government " to make enquiry, that justice
may be done," tempests of opposition, thunders of accusation
of treachery, and malignancy, and rebellious practices, from
the Undertakers, and then renewed petitioning!   As late as
the close of the year 1637 this was the precise condition of
Florence and his suits.   One after another all his ancient
adversaries had fallen around him : Barry, the Brownes (three
of them), Carewe, Cecyll, M'C. Reagh had all ceased to
trouble ; but their places had been filled by others ; for the
land remained—and no being was ever yet created with the
perseverance and tenacity of the undertaker—and the owner
of this unluckiest of all the heritages of the world was as

ready to encounter them as he had been to fight their fathers,
and fathers' fathers sixty years before.

This author is indebted to a small volume entitled Lake
Lore, by A. B. R., for knowledge of the existence of the two
following documents : if any further trace of Florence may
be hoped for, it is doubtless in the reports of the sittings
of the Privy Council—numberless enormous MS. folios without index.

"1637. *August* 18. STRAFFORD, *Lord Deputy of Ireland, to* Mr SECRETARY
. COKE.

" Yours of the 9th of the month, and therein a Petition contained, concerns only Mr Florence Mac Cartie.   I believe his suit will appear clamour-
ous ; and sure, if all be true of him they say here, is a person that deserves
no favour having been as false and malevolent to the crown during the
late rebellion, as any other in the province of Munster.   I hear nothing at
all of him ; and to become the solicitor for such a fellow is not at all pleasing
to my nature ; yet, that I may in the least, as in the greatest, give despatch
unto the commands of his Majestie, I have sent the copie of the petition
to *Sir Valentine Browne,* requiring him to send his answer, which I am
confident will be such as will manifest the little right *this cunning old
traitor* hath to anie of the lands he claimeth."

" Mr Secretary Coke to Strafford.
 " 1637.   Octr. 5.
            " &c.   &c.   &c.   Florence Mac Carthy
is left to your Justice."

Although as far back as 1631 Florence had obtained a
sentence for the recovery of all his father-in-law's lands from
the Brownes, we see by the above letters that they were still
withheld from him!   *The commands of His Majesty* were again
sent to the Lord Deputy to cause enquiry to be made into
the matter.   In Ireland there was a new Sir Valentine, and
happily for him, a new Deputy, whose notions of justice were
so peculiar, that he referred the matter for answer to the
very man who still held the lands which by sentence of the
Privy Council were already adjudged to be the property of
the petitioner!

Of the second period of Florence's life in England—about
forty years—fourteen consecutively were spent in the
Tower and other prisons; these, and a few intermittent residences of a year or two at a time in the same abodes, completed the tale of years of his absolute incarceration.   During
the earlier, and probably the much shorter portion of this
time, he was *close prisoner,* when no one from without was
allowed access to him; after this he obtained, subject to
sudden revocations, intervals of comparative freedom, which

he calls his first, or second, or other *liberty*. He might then receive all men from without, who chose to visit him; this, and that he was himself at liberty to go abroad, and dispose of his time as he pleased, subject only to his return at stated hours, we learn from the invaluable affidavit of Teig Hurley. His absolute prison life is not to be supposed spent in a solitary and barred cell, with scant daylight, and prison fare; the probability is that, except under peculiar circumstances, State prisoners were allowed the enjoyment of free intercourse with each other, and certainly whatever attendance and personal comforts their fortunes would allow.

Flórence had not been many weeks in prison before he learned the landing of the Spaniards at Kinsale; nor many months before the tidings reached him of the *battle* under the walls of that old town, the massacre of the English cornet, and the headlong flight of the forces of O'Neill and O'Donnel. Then presently followed great events; the death of Queen Elizabeth; the succession of James; the struggle for power in the Cabinet; the triumph of Cecyll, and the utter defeat of the party which had sought his overthrow! With brief interval followed rumours of a conspiracy by the leaders of the fallen court faction; and within few days, the Tower gates opened to admit an old friend, whose fall had been as great and as sudden as his own—Sir Walter Raleigh!

The history of this conspiracy, or rather this Court intrigue, which precipitated the Earl of Northumberland, the Lords Cobham and Grey, from the Cabinet to the Tower, and brought the two latter, with Raleigh, under sentence of death, is known to the reader. Under this sentence Raleigh was conveyed to the Tower, and there spent about 13 years of reprieve.

We read that "the Earl of Northumberland,* so fortunate as to have escaped the fate of his friends—the Mecænas of the age—had converted that abode of misery into a temple of the muses; that Raleigh was inspired by the genius of the place, and there wrote his 'History of the World!'" Probably inspired by the same genius, or led to seek consolation by the same philosophic direction of his thoughts, Florence beguiled some hours of his own confinement by the composition of his learned treatise upon the mythic history of his country. The subject was akin to a small portion of the great work of his fellow-prisoner; the materials required by both were in part the same, and "the deep research, the chronological

* Lingard. Hist.

knowledge, and acquaintance with Greek and Rabinical writers," displayed in the great work of Raleigh, were none the less requisite for the composition of the learned letter to the Earl of Thomond; in the one case, as in the other, all this erudition was, as Dr. Lingard suggests, most probably derived from versions in the Latin language; and it may not be presumptuous to propose to the judgment of the reader whether, from the ancient Irish manuscripts preserved at that time, and intelligible to Florence, may not have been derived traditions upon such subjects more ancient than have been transmitted by any Grecian writers!

Such community of pursuit, with intervals of dialogue upon the great events passing daily over them, and the past and coming fortunes of Ireland, may have increased the friendship which had existed between these prisoners since the days of Florence's boyhood; and, at least, must have served to beguile many hours of their dreary confinement. But the sympathies of Florence were not limited to the interest he took in the sorrows and pursuits of his companions in misfortune, or the intrigues of English statesmen. About the same time that Sir Walter Raleigh was sent to the Tower, O'Neill came, in the company of the Lord Deputy Mountjoy, to London, and was presented at Court. During the whole period of his rebellion, the Irish Chieftain had been in correspondence with James, and the men who now formed part of his Privy Council. Fenton had, years before, written " Tirone receiveth letters from the King of Scots : Scotland beareth up this rebellion."

Now on the throne of England James could desire no more rebellion, and could have little gratitude or encouragement for rebels. O'Neill found his stay in England far from pleasurable, and scarcely safe. Of this great Chieftain's visit to the Court, and of the persons who chiefly sought his presence, we have an interesting description from a man who for hire, or bigotry, constituted himself a spy upon him and them, a certain Robert Atkinson, not improbably a kinsman of the Priest of the same name, who had been in treaty with Cecyll to poison O'Neill a short time before—presented himself before a notary public, and voluntarily related as followeth :—

"That at his Majesty last being at Hampton, where he was a suitor, he saw one called Father Archer, a Jesuit, alight from his horse whereupon he was well mounted. at the Earl of Tirone's lodgings at Kingston, whom he forthwith saw introduced by one of the Earl's servants, and conducted up to his lodging wherein his Lo. then was, and thither Archer often afterwards frequented, as he had formerly done at the Earl's being lodged at Chelsea; somewhiles following the Earl to Court, and in company keeping of those Irish Knights and gentlemen which are in the Tower, and Sir Christopher Plounkit, Sir Edward Fitz Gerald, and others of that nation, in divers kinds of apparel, sometimes like a courtier, and otherwhiles like a farmer, or chapman of the country. Him he well knew in Ireland, where he saw him as chief commander over the Irish troops of rebels, horse and foot; for his own guard commanding as many as himself pleased, and for any murders, burnings, spoils, or other bloody actions that were to be exploited upon any of the English nation or favourers of the English government; called commonly the Pope's Legate, and Arch Priest over all others in the Provinces of Leinster and Munster; and also the ONeill's, or of others called Tyrone's, confessor, as he had been the Arch Duke's confessor of Austria; and in England is said to be the Earl's massing priest, daily to execute his function of a Jesuit for masses, absolution and such like, as for others the Knights and Irish gentlemen with whom he is conversant however near unto the King's court they may happen to be lodged.

" At Kingston also he often saw in company of the before named Knights and gentlemen in the Tower, and that are their countrymen at liberty, a secular priest called Father Hussey, well horsed and in their company, with feathers in his hat, as gallantly attired as any knight in the court; for whose apprehension the Hon. George Hume, Chancellor and Treasurer of the Exchequer, directed a warrant to one William Atkinson, a kinsman of this relaters, howbeit this relater for some friendly respects he bare unto some of the Knights in whose companies it was intended he should have been apprehended (whereof there might have occurred discredit and trouble), gave such forewarning thereof to one of the Knights as he escaped. Archer is in stature somewhat tall, black, and in visage long and thin, born in Kilkenny."

There can be little doubt but that Florence—if at the time, in one of his periods of *prison liberty*—was amongst "those Irish Knights and Gentlemen who were in the Tower," and who repaired to the Earl of Tirone's lodgings to have conference with the Irish chieftain, and with *the tall, thin-visaged black man* who had cost so many English lives, and so much English treasure; and who thus with matchless audacity ventured in these fanciful disguises to walk the streets of London. The flight of O'Neill, the *Dissipation* of Ulster, and the execution of Raleigh, were the chief great experiences of Florence's after life. How the interval from his liberation to the period when the last trace of him is lost to sight—22 years—were spent, his letters and petitions have made accurately known to us.

When Mr. Secretary Coke wrote to Lord Stafford in his behalf, Florence was but two or three years short of 80 ! It would have been nothing wonderful if he had lived these two or three years : this would have carried him to the year 1641, and then he would have seen the events of 1601 reacted with a scrupulous fidelity of imitation. He would have seen " the Irish again aspiring to their ancient nobility

and liberty!" a new O'Neill rush from his northern home to
"do all the hurt in his power to all who did not join him!"
He would have seen "Munster to a man in arms," every
MacCarthy again in action, and chief amongst them the sons
of Donal Pipi, the son and grandson of Teig O'Norsey of
Gleanachroime, and the reputed son of Donal of Castle
Logh! There was a new rush of undertakers from castle
and homestead! Loyalty and civility crowded to the port
towns in search of shipping! and, as the Bishop of Cork in
former days, so the Bishop of Down now, was the first to
write—it must be allowed with less composure than his
predecessor—the tidings of the coming of · the new arch
rebel!

As all these things were to be, it may be permitted to express the hope that Florence was spared to see them; and
that, with all his old energies rekindled, he could see, not
far before him, the day when he should again recover his
country, and rule Desmond from the Mang to the mountains
of Beare and Bantry! and Carbery from Carrig-o-Glaveen
to Misenhead; when O'Sullevan, and the Gentlemen of
Desmond would again lay on him the title of MacCarthy!
and when he would—to do Her Majesty great service—again
repair to the camp of O'Neill to consult on the matter of
the nation's liberty and religion!

And if, at the age of four score, he was compelled to
submit to the lot of all born of Adam, we may trust that
the sentence of St. Leger, which for fifty years had been his
reproach, proved to him, in his last hours, a sacred and
joyous truth, that "he was firmly attached to the old
religion."

The following document contains what little can be
further gathered of the fortunes of Florence's offspring! we
have their existence for three or four generations, and then
their unaccountable disappearance. We are informed that
the sons of Randal of Castle Logh were bred to low trades!
that they sank into pauperism, as in those days of ruthless
confiscation, sank the noblest families of Ireland in such
multitudes as to have formed a peasantry of nobles! In
the land whose social scheme, for two centuries, provided
that men should live with their heads in the mire, and their
heels in the air, where all that is ancient, all that is historic,
all that is noblest in blood is undermost, such a fact is not
surprising! but it would seem that even the low trades have
done with them! for no trace is any where discoverable of
them at the present day.

FLORENCE'S DESCENDANTS.

" By a Decree of the Court of Claims made the 28th July 1663 the 15th of Chas: II, the sev[l]. lands of Pallas, Muckruss, Cahiruane, Castle Lough and sev[l]. other denominations of land &[c]. &[c]. were restored to Dame Sarah Mac Carthy otherwise Mac Donnel, daughter of the Earl and sister to the Marquis of Antrim, and the widow of the *then* late Dan[l]. Mac Carthy-more, the eldest son of Flo[ce]. Mac Carthy more and the Lady Ellen Mac Carthy, the Earl of Clancare's only daughter and heiress, and to the eldest son of the s[d]. Dame Sarah and Daniel, viz: to Florence Mac Carthy more, the s[d]. Sarah, Daniel and their son Florence being decreed by the Court to have been innocent Papists and as such the s[d]. sev[l]. lands &[c]. were then restored by s[d]. Decree to Sarah and Florence, as the same had been settled on her the s[d]. Sarah and her issue by the marriage settlem[t]. entered into between her and her late husband, Dan[l]. Mac Carthymore, to whom s[d]. lands &[c]. belonged in fee, *this* second Flo[ce]. Mac Carthy (the son of Daniel and Dame Sarah) sold Cahirnane to Maurice Hussey in 1684, he (Florence) was married to Elinor FitzGerald, daughter of John FitzGerald, Knight of Kerry and died without issue, and was succeeded by his brother Charles Mac Carthymore, who was the Governor of Carrickfergus for K: James in 1690 and was married to Honora Burke the daughter of Lord Brittas. By Patent of 23[d] July 1605 K: James I granted Castlelough with the lands thereto attached, to Donald Mac Carthy base-son of the Earl of Clancare, this grant was in all probability for the separate use and benefit of Mac Carthy-more's wife, without the controul of her husband Florence, as may be strongly inferred from some papers of this Florences statement of his transactions with the Brownes which will be found in the appendix hereunto annexed, Castlelough however continued in the possession of the Mac Carthymore family until the reign of Chas: II when the then Flo[ce]. Mac Carthy more, Dame Sarah's son, granted Castlelough and other lands to his cousin-german, Denis Mac Carthy, whose son or grandson shortly after the accession of George II sold Castlelough to Colonel William Crosbie.

" It appears that the Lady Ellen Mac Carthy and her husband Florence Mac Carthy more had two sons, Daniel Mac Carthymore the eldest, and a second son called after his father, Florence, this Florence, the youngest son, married Mary daughter of O'Donovan and was the father of Denis Mac Carthy, to whom Castlelough was granted by Mac Carthy more in the reign of Charles II. Denis Mac Carthy married Margaret Finch, an English lady of distinction and by her had two sons, viz: Florence, his eldest son who followed James II to France and was there father of Charles Mac Carthy living in 1764 and *then* in the French service and of several other children, and of Justin Mac Carthy his second son who remained at Castlelough and by Catherine Hussey daughter of Col[l]. Maurice Hussey of Cahirnane was father of Randal Mac Carthy of Castlelough, who sold in Geo: II reign to Crosbie. Randal had several sons who were bred to low trades, and were *all uneducated paupers*, some of them now living.

" Charles Mac Carthy more (the second son of Dame Sarah and her husband Dan[l]. Mac Carthy more and the successor of his eldest brother) was married, as has been mentioned to a daughter of Lord Brittas and by her, was father of Florence Mac Carthy more, married to Mary Mac Carthy daughter of Charles Mac Carthy Esq of Cloghroe, a collateral branch of the Earl of Clancarthy's family who forfeited in the reign of James II. This Florence Mac Carthy more died early in the reign of Geo: II his son Randal Mac Carthymore became a protestant and married Agnes Herbert eldest daughter of Edward Herbert of Muckruss by Frances Browne, youngest daughter of Nicholas the second and sister to Valentine the third Lord Kenmare. By her, he was father of Charles the last Mac Carthymore, who was an Officer in the Guards, and enjoyed but a small part of the great Estates of his ancestors or predecessors, wᶜh were dissipated partly by their imprudence but principally by the different revolutions in Ireland, and their persevering loyalty to their Sovereigns; they however escaped forfeiture except during Cromwell's usurpation; they were restored by a Decree of Innocence in Chas II reign to a remnant of their Estates, the part settled on Lady Sarah Mac Donnells marriage, but which has been since materially lessened by subsequent Sales. The last Mac Carthy More died in 1770, and under his Will and a Settlement with the Representative of his heirs at law about 40 years ago, the present Mʳ. Herbert of Muckruss his cousin-german, is now seized of the Earl of Clancare's or the Mac Carthy More's rights and the Estates on or near the Lakes of Killarney, which the last Mac Carthy More passed or had pretensions to at his death in 1770.

"Florence Mac Carthymore in 1684 conveyed the lands of Cahir-nane on the Lower lake to Maurice Hussey. This Florence was eldest son of Daniel Mac Carthy More and Dame Sarah mᶜDonnell and was grandson of the first Florence and the Earl of Clancare's daughter. He also granted Castle Lough to his Cousin-German Denis MᶜCarthy another grandson of the first Florence. In 1738 and '40 Hussey's sons sold to Arthur Herbert.

(Egerton MSs 116).

It now remains but to pen the last paragraph of this Life of Florence! to add the few words that his Biographer had selected for his Epitaph, in case he had been compelled to chronicle his demise. "They were written, as Sir William Herbert once said, by myne enemies, and they serve to myne ornament!"

"HE WAS A MAN INFINITELY ADORED IN MUNSTER!"

THE PEDIGREE OF MACCARTHY MOR.

This, and the two following Pedigrees are extracted from the " Irish Family History " of Mr. R. F. Cronnelly, though not without some doubt of their absolute accuracy.* They are the only ones here introduced because the only ones to which frequent reference is made in the foregoing pages. Some of the marriages of the MacCarthys Mor, and Reagh are inserted to show the frequent alliances of these families with the Fitz Geralds, and the near relationship between Florence and the so-called Sougaun Earl of Desmond. It was not to the purpose of Mr. Cronnelly, nor is it of this writer, to enter minutely into all these alliances; it may suffice to assert, on the authority of Lodge, that of the Earls of Desmond the 2nd, 7th, 8th, 12th, 13th, 14th, 15th, and 16th, chose wives for themselves and their sons from one or other of the great branches of the MacCarthys Mor, Reagh, and Muskerry; and gave their daughters in exchange to them.

_____

* " Irish Family History ; being an historical and genealogical account of the Gaedhals, from the earliest period to the present time ; compiled from authentic sources by Richard Francis Cronnelly (Irish Constabulary Force), in two volumes. Vol. 1.

" Dublin, printed for the author by N. H. Tallon & Co., 1 Upper Sackville Street, 1865.

" Amidst the laborious duties of a calling adverse to all literary pursuits, and in precious hours abstracted from a scanty and too needful recreation, during intervals between the wearisome patrol of the streets of a crowded metropolis and the duties of a Police Court, the author of these family histories collected, with immense research, and arranged in admirable order, a great amount of documentary, and traditional genealogical materials, which had, notwithstanding the labours of the late learned Dr. O'Donovan, and other modern Irish scholars, floated about unconnected, unappropriated, and intractable, until his time. Mr. Cronnelly was a hard worker, and had hoped, in another volume, to conclude the great labour which he had undertaken, and to place before his countrymen all that was accessible of the authentic pedigrees of the Milesian race. Death, which within a brief period, had removed so many of our Irish scholars, and amongst them O'Donovan, O'Curry, Petri, and Windele, has called away also Mr. Cronnelly, in the mid-hour of his laborious day, when resting between the work he had accomplished, and the work that lay before him !"

The same precisely, and upon the same authority, may be said of the Lords of Kerry, of whom the 2nd, 3d, 5th, 6th, 7th, 8th, 9th, 15th, 16th, 17th, and 18th, intermarried with the MacCarthys. Were it not that it would necessitate the introduction of long complicated genealogical tables, it might be shown also how closely related Florence was to *all* the mere Irish families of the South of Ireland, in and out of rebellion, as well—by endless intermarriages—with all the branches of his own Sept, as with the O'Sullevans, the Knight of Kerry, the Earl of Thomond, the O'Donoghues, Lord Roche, O'Connor Kerry, the O'Mahons, with the Lord Barry himself, (more intimately, and more frequently than with most of the others) and finally, with Dermod O'Connor the Bony! with the White Knight! and—if seven generations had not absolutely worn out all trace of the kindred—with Sir George Carewe himself! for Donal Caomh, A.D. 1311, the 7th in ascent from Florence, had married a daughter of Carewe Marquis of Cork! Few Pedigrees can (it is to be hoped) show such alliances, in one generation, as Florence's with the three names last on the list foregoing!

The great current of Florence's descent had rolled down with full and majestic flood from Milesius unto him. In the course of ages its mere overflow, and stray waters, had sufficed to form numerous noble streams which in their wanderings, had mingled with many remote genealogies. Florence's enemies, who so carefully traced his descents, and reproached him with "the coming of his house out of Spain," concealed the fact that Her Sacred Majesty Queen Elizabeth herself derived her descent from an ancestress of his! and thus also "came out of Spain." Saba, the daughter of Tadg MacCarthy King of Munster, was twice married; her *second* husband was her cousin Cormac Muimnach, King of Munster; from them lineally descended Florence. Saba's *first* husband had been Dermod O'Brien King of Thomond, the great grandson of Brien Boroime; from this marriage proceeded not only the main stream of the O'Briens of Thomond, but, by marriages, several generations of O'Conors, DeBurghs, Plantagenets, Mortimers, Richard II., Edward IV., Elizabeth the wife of Henry VII., Henry VIII., and finally the illustrious Lady whose glorious reign was so much troubled by her Irish cousin.

103. Saerbrethach or Justin= A.D. 925.

Carthach = from whom the Sept name.

Tadg, King of Eoghanacht Caisil.　　　　Muireadhach = King of Desmond.

Saba = 1st. Dermod O'Brien.
　　 = 2nd. Cormac Muimhnach.

Donogh, King of　　　　Cormac Muimhnach, = Sarah, or Saba, McCarthy, his
South Munster.　　　　　King of the two　　　cousin, widow of Dermod
　　　　　　　　　　　　　Munsters.　　　　O'Brien, King of Munster,
　　　　　　　　　　　　　　　　　　　　great grandson of Brian
　　　　　　　　　　　　　　　　　　　　Boroime.

Dermod Mor-na-Cille Bain, = 1st = 2nd Petronilla de Bloet.
King of Cork and Desmond,　　　|　　　|
born 1098, slain 1185.　　　　　　　No issue.

nal Mor-na-Curradh, = Cornac, rebelled and　　Tadg Roe-na-Sgairte, from whom the
eated the English in |　　slain 1177.　　　　branch of Tadg Roe.
5.

rmac Fionn McCarthy Mor, = Donal Oge, who flourished in 1203, alias Gud, FROM
n 1170, died 1215.　　　　WHOM THE MCCARTHYS REAGH, AND THE MCCARTHY'S
　　　　　　　　　　　　　OF GLENNA-CHOIM.

onal, King of = Margaret, da. of　　Donogh　　Dermod, from = Donal, from
esmond, born |　Nicholas Fitz-　　Cairthanach,　whom the　　whom the
204, ob. 1302. |　Maurice, 3rd Lord　King of　　McCarthys of　Clan Donal
　　　　　　　　of Kerry.　　　Desmond.　　Dunhallow.　　Fionn.

Donal Oge, born = Dermod of Trallee, ancestor of the
1239, ob. 1307.　|　McFinin Carties; slain 1325.

Cormac Mor, = Honoria, da. of Maurice FitzMaurice, 6th Lord of Kerry.
born 1271.　|

rmod Mor, first　Finin of　　Eoghan,　　Donogh, ances-　Donal, = Joanna, da. of
rd of Muskerry,　Ringrone,　founder　　tor of the　　b. 1303, |　Maurice Oge
born 1310,　　1350.　　of Cosh-　　McCarthys of　ob.1371. |　FitzGerald, 4th
ob. 1367.　　　　　　　maing.　　Ardcanaghty.　　　　|　Earl of Kildare.

Tadg-na-Mainistrich, =　　Donal MacCarthy Mor,
or of the Monastery, |　ob. 1409, s. p.
born 1413.

Donal MacCarthy Mor, born 1373 =

Tadg Liath (the greybeard) =

Cormac Laighrach, born 1440 = Elinor, da. of 9th Lord of Kerry.

Donal an Druimin =

lg =　　　　Catherine = Finnin　Honoria = 16th　Donal, Earl = Honoria, da.
_|　　　MacCarthy Reagh.　Earl of Des-　of Clancarr |　of 15th Earl
therine = to the　　　　mond.　　　　　　|　of Desmond.
h Lord of Kerry.　　　　　　　　　Donaldus Nothus. |

Tadg, Lord Valentia, s. p.　　Ellen = Florence McCarthy Reagh.

PEDIGREE OF THE MACCARTHYS REAGH.

107. Dermod Mor-na-Cille Bain, = 2nd = Petronilla de Bloet.
King of Cork and Desmond, | |
born 1098, ob. 1185. | No issue.
Donal Mor na Curradh =

Cormac Fionn McCarthy Mor.   Donal Oge, alias Gud = flourished 1203.

Donal Maol =

Donal Caomh, = da. of the Marquis of Carewe.
(the handsome)
1311.

7. Donal Glas, Prince of Carbery =   CORMAC DON, FROM WHOM THE McCARTHYS
OF GLEANNACHROIM.

Donal Reagh = Johanna FitzMaurice.

nogh of   Donal Glas,   Cormac-   Eoghan.   Dermod-an-Dunaidh (1) = Ellen, da. of
iskene,   ob. 1442.   na-Coille.   1452.   Tadg, Lord
1452.   Muskerry.

(2) Finghin = Catherine, da. of Thomas FitzGerald, 8th Earl of Desmond.

(3) Donal = Ellinor, da of Gerald Fitzgerald, 8th Earl of Kildare.

Finghin = Catherine,   (6) Donogh = Johanna, da.   (4) Cormac = Julia, da. of   (7) Owen.
da. of   of Maurice,   na-haoine.   Cormac
Donal an   and niece of   Oge Laidir,
Druimin,   James, Earl   Lord Mus-
MacCarthy   of Desmond.   kerry.
Mor.

Donal-na-Pipi = Margaret, da. of Thomas,
ob. 1612.   eldest son of James, 15th
Earl of Desmond; sister of
James, the Sougaun Earl.

Many children and descendants.

FLORENCE = Ellen, da. and   Dermod Moyle = Helen, da. of Tadg
heiress of Donal,   O'Donoghue of
Earl of Clancar.   Glenflesc.

nal Mc = Sarah, da.   Charles = da. of 17th   Florence.   Tadg, *eldest son, died in his*
rthy **Mor** of Earl of   Lord of   *boyhood in the Tower of*
Antrim.   Kerry.   *London.*

NOTE.—The chieftains of this branch succeeded in the order numbered above.

107. Dermod Mor na Cille Bain, = 1st to   = 2nd to Petronilla de Bloet.
King of Cork and Desmond.

Donal Mor na Curradh =

Cormac Fionn MacCarthy Mor.   Donal Oge, alias Gud =

Donal Maol =

Donal Caomh, or the = da. of the Marquis
handsome, Prince of   Carewe.
Carbery, 1311.

Donal Glas, Prince of Carbery, from   Cormac Don = obtained frc
whom the McCarthys Reagh.   father the
                                                                        tory of Gle
                                                                        chroim.
                                                                        1366.

Felim = called Chief of Gleann-a-chr

Tadg, called of Dunmanway =

Finin, or Florence =

Dermod-na-Glac = Ellinor, da. of Sir Cormac, Lord of Muskerry.

Tadg-an-Fhorsa Ist = Ellinor, da. of Roderick McSheehy.
or of the Forces,
MacCarthy Duna.

Tadg-an-Duna Ist = da. of Brien McOwen McSweeny.
Chieftain of Gleann-
a-Chroim.

Tadg-an-Fhorsa II. =   Dermod =   Eoghan, from whom th
                                                     Carthys of Ballinodie.
Tadg-an-Duna II., = 1696.
in whose time was   Dermod, or Jeremy, =
confiscated the ter-   restored to his lands
ritory of Gleann-   by act of grace 1684.
a-Chroim.

               Denis of = Betsy Donovan.   Cormac Glas = Angelina H
Felim =   Dyeragh   of Ballina
                                                                  Castle.
Dermod =   Mary = Edmund Schuldham,   Denis = Catherine Crowl
                        Crown Solicitor, to
Tadg =   whom she took the   Daniel =
                       lands of her grand-
Jerry an Duna =   father Dermod.
                                      Denis =   Daniel =   Justin,   T
Charles = lately deceased.   S.P.

    Sir Charles, late =   William,   Felix,   Daniel, = Harriet, da. c
    Governor of   now living.   S.P.   author   miral Sir Hom
    Ceylon.   of this   ham.
                                                           work.
Richard.   Charles.   Florence Strachan.

PEDIGREE OF H.S.M. QUEEN ELIZABETH.*

104. Carthach = from whom the Sept name of the MacCarthys.

Morrogh =   Tadg =

Donogh.   Cormac Muimhnach =   Saba† = Dermod O'Brien, great grandson o
                                                Brien Boroihme.
             Dermod, of Kilbahin,
             King of Desmond,   Tirlogh = da. of O'Fogarty.
             FROM WHOM FLO-
             RENCE.   Donal Mor = da. of MacMorogh.

        Mora = Cathal-Crov-deargh O'Conor, King of Connaught.

             Hugh O'Conor = da. of O'Farrel.

             Una O'Conor = Robert de Gernon.

        Hodierne de Gernon = Richard de Burgh.

        Walter de Burgh = Mahaut de Lacie, Countess of Ulster.

        Richard de Burgh = Margaret de Burgh.

John de Burgh = Elizabeth de Clare, da. of Gilbert, Earl of Gloucester.

William de Burgh = Matilde Plantagenet Lancaster.

Elizabeth de Burgh = Lionel, Duke of Clarence, son of Edward III.

Philippa de Clarence = Edmund Mortimer, Earl of March.

Roger de Mortimer = Eleanora Holland, da. of Thomas, Earl of Kent.

Anne Mortimer = Richard, Duke of York.

Richard II, Duke of York = Cecile Neville, da. of Raoul, Earl of Westmoreland.

Edward IV. = Elizabeth Woodville.   Richard III.

Edward V, *s. p.*   Elizabeth = Henry VII.

enry VIII A. = Catherine of Arragon.   B. = Anne Boleyne.   C. = Catherine Seymo

        Mary.   ELIZABETH.   Edward VI.

---

* From the Généalogie de la Maison MacCarthy.

† " Saba, ou Sara MacCarthy, qui par son mariage avec Dermod O'Brien, Roi d
Munster, ou des deux Momonies, décédé à Cork en 1120, a transmis le sang des MacCarthy
la plupart des maisons souveraines de l'Europe, &c. Elle épousa en secondes noce
ormac Muithamnagh, Roi des deux Momonies, son cousin-germain."

"GLEANN-A-CHROIM, OR THE VALLEY OF HOSPITALITY."

In a manuscript family pedigree, in the possession of the author of this memoir, (a document a little in the ornate style of John Annyas,) composed in the year 1784, and attested by Dr. John Butler, Bishop of Cork, and by a multitude of MacCarthys, O'Driscolls, Hurleys, and others, it is stated that—

"Gleann-a-chroim is situate in the west of East Carbery, and county of Cork; wherein were many fertile flowery plains, and flourishing verdant woods, environed with a ridge of hills, the most pleasant, and romantic, nature could intend for sheltering, and watering a spot designed to yield all the pleasures, and desirable necessaries of life, that could be procured in that wholesome climate. Upon the said Demesne were built several spacious houses, besides two strong, and stately castles, viz., that of Togher, and the other of Dunmanway, where the chieftains respectably, and alternately, displayed their liberality; so that they were remarkable for their hospitality; in so much so that no gentleman in Munster, of whatsoever ability, was accounted equal to them in that of housekeeping, for which they got the name of MacCarthy-na-Feile, or the Hospicious."

So far the pedigree! but long beyond this document in elegance of style, and fervid eulogy of the loveliness of "Gleann-a-chroim, the Valley of Hospitality," is a poem in the Irish language, preserved at Manooth, amongst the collection of Irish MSS. made by the late Dr. John Murphy, R.C., Bishop of Cork. It is the composition of Donal-na-Tuile, a Munster Meliboeus, who flourished in the year 1696, and had himself been an eye-witness of our Mantuan confiscations. It must be admitted that the style of Donal—like that of the *Bearla Feine*, or primeval language of the Bards—is now and then a little conjectural as to its precise sense and import; the benevolent reader is therefore besought to pardon certain transpositions, and free version, without which the writer of this memoir must have relinquished the endeavour to lay before him any portion of Donal's pastoral. The poet first sings of the virtues and the death of his chieftain—

"Tadg, son of Tadg, the powerful Lord of Crom, the hawk of hospitality, the valorous heir of heroic deeds; in whose heart was neither guile, deceit, nor falsehood! he was a generous, hospitable, wise, pious man, till the messenger of death attacked the king of the blood of Cashel, the pure

white-spirited Carthy ; and now silent lies the Lord of Crom-
-in-the-vale, beneath a flag in the glebe-land of Barran!
bitter are the tears we shed for the fall of MacCarthy, flower
of the field of Eibher!!"

From his lamentation over the loss of his chief, the poet
passes " with showers of bitter tears " to a celebration of the
past glories of the race of Tadg. " Its ancient free princes
surpassed all the nobles of Inisfail in generosity ; they were
animated with impetuous valour ; they studied not deceitful
deeds, nor treachery; but they had true generosity without
guile, one towards another! They were a people accustomed
to bestow wines, and tender beef, and holiday dresses! They
were graceful, and beneficent ; their strongholds were filled
with beautiful women, and quick-slaying cavalry viewing
them ; mirth, playing on harps, poems, and songs were at
their feasts; their women were prolific, and accomplished;
silken—chaste—white were the slender bodies, and sedate
the eyes of their maidens!"

But this bright picture was not without its shadows—
fleecy clouds—which, to the dazed eyes of the bard, seemed
but an additional inundation of light and glory: " Hilarity,
drunkenness (occasional) were at their festivals! loud
sounded the song of bards! louder the shouting, and roaring
of cripples, and large bodied vagrant flatterers contending ;
and of soothsayers, and gamblers in mutual discord!"
Breaking away abruptly from the memory of these faded
glories, Donal turns, with bitter wrath, upon the " impius
Miles,"—whom he calls a barbarous spoliator!—and to the
desolation of his native valley.

" Red is the anguish of Fodhla! Fiercely and cruelly,
did the foe spring upon us! the black-thorn, no less than the
green apple, tore they up with impetuous violence! they left
us not a twig, nor a crooked stick—capable of receiving a
graceful shape! not an acorn! nor a hazel nut! nor so much
as a red berry! The foreign host destroyed utterly each
fertile-bright-mansioned-hill of Tadg of the fair-branching-
tresses of the race of brave Oluim, and Eibher! Nor can
this vale boast any longer of playful calves in folds, nor
herds of flocks, nor of sweet milk which used to be drained
incessantly from the milk vessels in the meadows! Were I
not exhausted by grief and sorrow my poem would run
beyond the compass of the memory of hundreds! Weep
with me, I beseech you, over this vale which is now so bare
and treeless!"

That the encomiums of Donal on the hospitality of the

family of his chief were not wholly undeserved, we have the testimony, in homely prose, of the author of the Carbriæ Notitia, and of Smith, in his history of Cork and Kerry. "To the North thereof, says the former, we shall find Dunmanway, a small village well situate on the banks of the river Bandon, fortified with an old castle; and to the North thereof the Castle of Togher, a large strong pile. This tract belonged to Teig-a-Downy (Tadg-an-Duna) one of the ' best branches of the MacCarthys, and always reckoned the best *Scologes* (or housekeepers) in Carbery." "A second branch of this family, says Smith, possessed a tract called Glawnacrime, being the parish of Fanlobus, now Dunmanway; near which place they had their residence *in a Castle lately demolished by Sir Richard Cox.* This family was famous for extravagant hospitality, a... practice formerly much applauded in this country. The last (chieftain) of this house was called Teig O'Downy, who besides the forenamed castle, had another, which is still standing, called Togher."

In the time of the grandson of Florence MacCarthy, and when the title of Earl of Clancar, or Clan Carthy, had been restored in the branch of the MacCarthys of Muskerry, "It was often—says the author of the Carbriæ Notitia—disputed by the followers of these great men which branch of this family was the principal or chief! MacCarthy Mor (Florence's grandson) alleges that he, having the name and title, and being likewise, by his Grandmother, heir to the last Earl of Clancar, ought to be acknowledged chief without dispute.

To this the others answer that by the father's side (which is chiefly regarded in Ireland) he is younger son of Mac Carthy Reagh, and ought not to exalt himself above the chief of his house; that an Irish title and name must be governed by the Irish law of Tanistry, which, like the royal law Salique in France, will not admit women to inherit estates, and principalities.

MacCarthy Reagh alleges that he is the eldest branch of this noble family, which by the law of Tanistry ought to be preferred; that he is a degree nearer of kin to the common ancestor Donal-Mor-ne Curradh, King of Cork, than any of the pretenders; that (the present) MacCarthy Mor is but a younger brother of his house.

But the Lords of Muskerry say that *because* MacCarthy Reagh is the eldest branch of this family, that is, the first that separated from the common stock, he is *therefore* excluded from the inheritance till all the later branches are lopt by death . . so by the law of England a brother shall be preferred before an uncle, and an uncle before a great uncle; so that by both laws, the nearest of kin to him that was last seized shall be his heir."

At the time of these disputes no voice ventured to plead aloud for the right of the Sept itself to determine, as from time immemorial it had done, who should be its ruler, and recognized head! The right of the Sept to elect its chief could admit of no question. Florence, on the extinction of the elder male branch of the MacCarthys in the person of his father-in-law, had been "*unanimously, and solemnly chosen by all the Clergy, Nobility, and Gentry of Munster, to be Mac Carthy Mor.*" As head of his race, his rights extended not only over the fourteen Lords of Countries enumerated by Sir W. St. Leger, but over the Chieftains of Muskerry, who, in submission to the most princely of all the chiefries of M. C. Mor, were bound to obey his Garemsloeg, or *Rising out*, and "to send 30 Galloglas when he made his war." These rights would, by the usual custom of Tanistry, descend to Florence's children; first to his eldest, and then successively to his other sons; and neither by M. C. Reagh, nor by Mac Carthy of Muskerry, was any appeal admissible to proximity of blood to any recent M. C. Mor. Could the claims of Florence's descendants have been set aside, who can doubt which of these great branches were the worthier to assume the place left vacant by the extinction of the elder branch? The Lords of Muskerry were subordinate to the main branch! MacCarthy Reagh, Prince of Carbery, paid tribute to none! his rights were in all respects, identical with those of the chiefs of the elder branch; he did not even receive the rod of inauguration from MacCarthy Mor; but, as did that chieftain himself, from one of his own followers! He, too, had the regal right of *The Rising out;* and not one of his followers paid tribute to any but to him!

Nor, in the adjustment of these Sept claims, could the rights of another branch,—less indeed than most of its kindred in wealth and territory, but equal to the highest in dignity,—be overlooked! MacCarthy Reagh was descended from the *eldest* of the sons of Donal Caomh; from the *third son of the same prince* descended the MacCarthys of Gleanna-chroim, (the ancestors of Tadg of the fair-branching-tresses). Like their brothers of Carbery, they knew no superior! and though they had no followers, and received no tribute, they paid none! and were not bound to attend the Rising out of MacCarthy Reagh, much less of MacCarthy Mor! Side by side with their elder brothers, and allied with them by innumerable intermarriages, they dwelt in the territory originally assigned to them in the beginning of the 14th century : they submitted spontaneously to the political influence of the MacCarthys Reagh, and appear to have had no ambition but to prove their claim to the designation of *na-Feile*, the hospicious, and to be the best of *Scologes*, or housekeepers, in Munster.   If MacCarthy Reagh could justly claim precedence of the house of Muskerry, so could the MacCarthys of Gleanna-chroim ! .The issue of the dispute was that King Charles bestowed his honours on whom he pleased; the Lords of Muskerry became Earls of Clancarthy, and the descendants of Florence, as long as they had visible existence, continued to bear the title of MacCarthy Mor, and to prove themselves the head of their race, and the legitimate chieftains of these Earls, by the same means by which they proved themselves the chieftains of the fourteen Lords of Countries enumerated by Sir Warham St. Leger, that is, by the exaction of yearly tribute—in token of dependence—of " certain parcells of beefe, porke, and butter," and the exercise over them of all such other rights and chiefries as were not expressly abolished by English law.

SUPPLEMENT.

OTHER DRAUGHTS.

IF Hugh O'Neill had employed one of his Gallogologhs to split the head of Sir Geofrey Fenton with his axe; or the heir apparent, or presumptive, of the Lord Dunsany, "with promise of his place, and honour for his reward to cutt off his Lordship;" or some sanctimonious lunatic to find his way into the privacy of the Lord Deputy, and "being taken by him by the hand, and seeing that he had his quilted coat laid aside," to plunge a dagger into his naked breast; or,—ascending in devilry as he ascended in imitation to a loftier model,—employed the chaplain at Theobald's to mix deadly nightshade in the chalice offered to the lips of Her Majesty's Principal Secretary of State, in the most sacred act of his religion, he would have approved himself to posterity as an able disciple of the illustrious statesmen who, in the 16th century, laboured so strenuously to civilize our wild forefathers!

In the language of the time, "to do Her Highness good service," usually meant to murder somebody! and how many or how noble were the lives purchased, and paid for with money out of the Queen's exchequer may never be known in this world! No life was so often put to price, no assassination so frequently undertaken as that of O'Neill. During the whole course of his rebellion every man was welcome to the Minister, or the Lord Deputy, who, to save his own neck from the rope, or, "to do his country good service," had a project for ridding the Queen of this arch-rebel. Atkinson and Annyas were miserable men who consented to do murder to save their own lives: Cecyll might have hired a hundred, or a thousand such in the streets of London, who would have done it for a less consideration. The characters of such men are so saturated with infamy that they will endure no additional drop of evil fame; hence must the full ignominy of all crimes in which they had employers, or accomplices, be borne by the latter. The meditated destruction of an English fleet, and the murder of the Queen, are enough for the reputation of Annyas; the betrayal to the scaffold of Tichbourne, a brother-priest, ample for the fame of William Atkinson; the projected poisoning of Florence and O'Neill is superfluous for *them;* it remains for appropriation, at the disposal of future biographers of the statesmen who employed them. From the correspondence now about to be laid before the reader, it will be seen that Sir Robert Cecyll has not the entire credit to himself of suggesting or conducting *all* the *practises* "to serve his country, and spare the effusion of Christian blood," by cutting off the arch traitor.

August, 1598, the date of Sir Geoffery Fenton's letter, was precisely the period of the famous "Jorney of the Blackwater," when the writer himself, in company with the Lords Justices, was shivering with terror in Dublin, in hourly expectation of the coming of O'Neill, and his victorious followers. "The great oke" was never in more vigorous luxuriance than when this trembling functionary was in quest of the axe to lay it prostrate. Let the reader turn to the narrative of the Jorney of the Blackwater; and he will see in what condition to strike down the monarch of the forest, were the Council of Ireland, at the time the following letter was written.

"SIR GEOFFRY FENTON, AND THE GREATE OKE."

"1598. *Augs*⁴ 4. FENTON to CECYLL.

". . . for the other greater matter mencioned in yᵒ̃ Loˢ tre, thoughe I know yt wilbe difficult to draw one dogg to byte of an other, and more despat to fynde an ax to stryke downe at one blowe, a greate Oke that hath growen upp in many yeres, yet I will cause the forde to be sownded, to see yf theire may be founde a passage that waie. When yᵒ̃ ho: shall write to me of theis matters of seruice, or in any other cause that may concerne myne owne pticuler, and that yō do send those tres in the gẽnall packett; yt may please yō to endorce the direction of the packett to me, so shall I take owt myne owne tres, and delyer the rest tothe Ll: justices."

In February of the year 1601 O'Neill was, if possible, more

an object of terror, than in 1598; for the Spaniards were coming; the same silvan simile served the men who were next ready to take up *the service* which had been essayed so often, and so fruitlessly. The great Oke had still grown, and its mighty limbs now overshadowed Munster; the axe was not yet taken from the mine, the arm was not yet shaped that was to strike down that noble tree; to commit murder upon that able and hated rebel!

" Lord Dunsany and the badd Graff."

"1601. *Feb^y* 10. Lo: Dunsany to Sir Ro: Cecyll.

" . . . In the meane I thoght y^t my dutie to signifie this muche unto yo̊), that in the seruice of cutting of a badd graff, wch when I tooke my leaue of yo̊) I promysed to sett a worke, I haue assaied many waies. Butt whate for the difficultie and daunger of the attẽpt, and for the distrust of requitall in eny pporc̃on, of a seruice of that consequens, I fownd myne endeuor styll frustrat; butt nowe to my greater comfort and hope, I procured (wth all circumstance of secrecy and othes,) the mater to be broken to one of gretest nobilitie, spirit, and valure amongst them; promisynge unto him the place and hono̊) for his reward whose ambition tooke the sooner, and faster hould thereof, because his birth dooth in a sort warant him to s̃ceed, as beinge lineally descended from the cheefe house; and for as muche as y^f the matter take wished-effect, som̃ others might labor for ye honor of the proiect, yt may please yo̊) to understand y^t. Henry Oge McHenry McShane is ye man, beeinge linealy descended from Con O'Neyle. *This my proceedinge I haue imparted to my Lord Deputie, wch I hope in God will take effect! !*"

In August 1601 Queen Elizabeth who, as Cox informs us, was but too often penny wise, and pounds otherwise, brought her mind to make a great, and costly effort to extinguish the Irish rebellion, "which had almost reached that sum at which Her Majesty estimated the worth of the realm of Ireland"— the army had increased from 7 or 8 to 16 or 17 thousand foot; and from 2 or 3 hundred horse to as many thousands. With this force the Lord Deputy Mountjoy resolved to attack O'Neill in his great fastnesses, and to force the dreaded pass of the Moiry; thither he marched, and *there* was fought many a sanguinary skirmish; for O'Neill had, as usual, *plashed the*

ways, and erected earthworks, and placed his best men to
guard them. The weather was stormier than had been
known for 20 years, and the English soldiers perished faster
by exposure and want, than by the sword; but Mountjoy
persevered; and having forced his way several miles within
the pass, built forts to secure the ground he had won. O'Neill
retreated, and the Deputy was enabled to lead his troops to
the famous fortress of the Blackwater; the old castle was in
ruins; he built a new one; and it is gratifying to know that
the first constable to whom it was intrusted, was the gallant
Captain *Sir Thomas* Williams! That brave man had had a
soldier's revenge for his former ill luck; for he had met his
old enemy in a fair field, and after a hard fought day had
beaten him. In the camp of Carrickban, on the 25th of July,
he had received the honour of Knighthood from the sword of
the Lord Deputy. It were well for the fame of Mountjoy if
he had written nothing to Cecyll but the journal of that
arduous, and eventful campaign, the account of his visit
to the scene of Bagnal's disaster, and the prowess of Sir
Thomas Williams! but from the camp of Carrickban went
also the two following letters:—

" THE LORD DEPUTY MOUNTJOY, AND ONE WALKER, AN
ENGLISHMAN AND LONDINER."

"23 *Aug*. 1601. *The* LORD DEPUTY *to* SIR R. CECYLL.

" S^r, when I planted the garison at Armaghe, I apointed
Sir Henry Dauers to comaund the same in the absence of Sir
Francis Stafford, both because I found him best able for that
service without any newe charge unto Her Maty, hauing horse
and foote of his owne in enterteynement, and that I sawe he was
extraordinarely desyrous to take that oportunity to bee actiue,
in hope therby to deserue Her Mat's fauour and good opinion.
I aduised him to be often stirring with his forces upon the
rebells, and with all to-practise what possibly he could deuise
upon the person of the Arch traytor Tyrone; and he assuring me that he would leave nothing unassayed, that in his
iudgement might tend toye perfecting of that woorke, within
a few days after found one Walker, an Englishman and a Londiner, newly come ouer, who brake with him tobee employed
in that same busines, alleaging that he knewe yt tobe a
seruice tending greatly tohis countries good, and for that
cause, and to aduaunce his owne fortune, that he was come

resolued to kill Tirone, hauing plotted the maner howe to
doe yt. Sir Henry was desyrous tobee made acquainted with
his plott, but Walker refusing to discouer it, under pretence
tokeepe yt the more secreate, he pressed him no furder there-
about, and the rather for that Walker desyred no other help
or furtherance from him, but tobe put without the guards in
the night, and so left totake his fortune. *Sir Henry imparted
this offer of his to me, and I wished him to giue way to yt, as I
have done to divers others, and may not refuse the like to any, for
yf any one speed it is enough, and they that misse loose nothing
but themselves ;* but because this Walker coming afterwards to·
Tirone did not effect what he had undertaken, though (as
himself sayth) he was much made of, and had once drawne
his sword with purpose to kill him, tho under pretence to do
great matters in his quarrell I thought fitt at his return to
our camp to apoint Mr. Marshall and Sir George Bourcher to
examine him, and he confessing unto them, that Tyrone
would haue sent him into Scotland, which seemed tobe the
more probable, by reason he was with Randall McDonnell,
and by him sent to Sir Arthur Chichester to Carrickfergus,
and from thence to Sir Fra: Stafford at ye Newry, and so to
ye camp again to mee, I comitted him *close* prisoner, and sent
him to the Newry, wishing Sir Francis Stafford further to
examine him, and doe nowe send him in bands unto you Sir,
whoe can best judge of him, and may hapley learne more of
his intent and disposition, by reason his frends are dwelling
there in London, than we here can find the meanes to doe.
I am sorrie I should be troublesom toyou in a matter of this
nature, because for myne owne part I confess I thincke the
man little better than frantick, though such a one was not
unfitt for such an enterprise; Yet considering it might otherwise proue dangerous to myself, or toy^e gentleman that sett
him awoorke, I presume you will hold me excused, and conceave that I haue reason to so doe, for myne own discharge.
And so Sir I comend you tothe grace of God.
"From the Camp at Carickbane
     this 23^d Augst. 1601.   " Yours to doyou Service
                                                  " MOUNTJOYE.
" The Maior of Chester is written to, to send
     you this prisoner; and the copie of this
     his lre herewith sent, will shew ye discre-
     tion of ye man."

2 H

" 1601. *Augt.* 22. *From* THOMAS WALKER, *close prisoner at* y⁸ *Newry, to the* R*ᵗ*. *Hon: the* LORDE MOUNTJOYE *Lorde Deputie of Ireland, deliuer thesse.*

" Rᵗ. Honᵇˡᵉ.

" I your Honour's pore petitioner, a prissoner till my truth haue had her triall, which I trust inGod will not belonge, since I understand youre Lordship hath sente into England aboute me, doth beg for his sacke, whoe hath fashioned us to his one similitude and likenes, yᵗ your Honor will not see me hunger for wante of meanes, My good Lorde I speake this in all humillity, for them I sente to for my meanes, feares by sendinge to supplie my wants, least they be allso brought in troble for me; thus in the worlde's eie I seem hardly thought one, when had I had a souldier's harte, as I wanted not his forwarde minde, and not given place unto effeminate thoughtes, forgettinge how I promised to my God, yf it woulde please him to send his Angell to conducte me saffe, and give me fauor in the presence of Tirone, I would not feare to smitte him, weare his garde aboute him, it had not bin so whith me as it is; And to see Godes mercie towardes me that daye! he had no garde to speake on, neither had he on a quilted coate, only a blacke fresse gerkin which beinge unbuttoned I might see his naked brest, I having my armes redelivered me by his own com̃andement. He tooke me twisse, in that shorte time I was whith him, by the hande, sayinge I was wellcom tohim, and toulde me by those wordes, I was the fortunatest man that ever came unto.him, for had not my horsemen bin the honester, sayde he, they would have sore wounded thee, but had my foottmen. mett thee, thoue hadest never come alive before me—thus before and after I was most mithily preserved by the Lorde, and persuade myselfe it is ,tosome good end; wherfore His name be praysed, whose mercie endureth for ever. And my good Lorde when I am found an honest man towardes my countrie I will shew myselfe a true servante to youre Honor, in givinge youre Lordship toknoue what I have herd and seen in my travells, meanwhille I will laye it up in my harte, till I may have accesse unto your Lordeshipe Yett ernestly beseechinge youre Honor for Gode's sacke to shake offe by littell and littell the harde conseate youre Lordship, whith good reason hath of me, for God that knowes my harte, knowes it is free of that maculated spott, I am a foolle to speake thus much, but alas! hath not the sillie asse, that is beaten for his stumblinge, sence to knowe in what he made his Lorde a faulte? A littell beare whith me good my Lorde, for I have wrotte this in my teares, and whatsoever I have sayde or done, hereafter God willinge I will give a reason for it: but it will seem foolish for a time—thus fearinge to overlaye youre Honors patience whith copiosnes of wordes, I will surceasse; Comittinge youre Honor tothe saffe keepinge of the Allmithie, that his stronge arme maye be ever whith youre good lord-ship to your liues end.

"From the Prisson of the Neurie

"Satterdaye the xxijth of August 1601.

"Youre Honor's true servant whille liffe lasteth.

"THOMAS WALKER."

Another year was drawing to its close, and the great oke still flourished! under its majestic branches armies encamped, and Irishmen still dreamed of the freedom of their country. Cecyll was by this time accustomed to see the dagger dropt, and the poison spilt, but as long as 3,000 English angels were at his command he had no cause for despondency. Walker had succeeded no better than Atkinson, Sir Geoffry Fenton than John Annyas, the Lord Deputy Mountjoy than Lord Dunsany. In the next attempt—the last with which we shall weary the reader—the Minister took the matter in hand himself; he found his own man, and made his own bargain. The usual course of such transactions is reversed; hitherto the offer stood in the writing of the assassin, now it flashes forth in the authoritative words of the Minister himself.

"1602. Decr. HER MAJESTY'S PRINCIPAL SECRETARY AND RICHARD COMBUS.

"Answeares to certayne articles of Richard Combus:—

"To the first, wherein it is desyred that the enterprise (whereof you and I had conference) be keept from the Counsell of Ireland. You may be sure, that none shall know it but the Deputy himself, whom her Ma^t hath putt in trust wth her kingdome, and of whose secrecye and wisdome she hath approoued experience.

"To the second. That the Governour of Carickefargus, be made party to it, it is all verie well liked, because he is a wise gentleman, and a commander of those places, wch lye most convenient for retrayte after the enterprise. But because it may be uncertayne, to what place he shall first come for retrayt, he shall haue a tre dyrected to him, and others, her Mat^s comanders, cap^{ens} and officers, whomsoever, to receaue the partye into their proteccon till advertisem^t. be sent hethe).

" To the third. For her Ma^{t's} tre to be written to McDonnell before hand, she will in noe sort yeild to the same.

" To the fowerth. For my writinge tohim, or assuraunce by bond to you, if you will send upp a draught of ether, I will signe them if I like their forme ; if not, I will draw an other in such forme as I thinke convenient, whereuppon you may proceed if you like it.

"Lastly (because we may each of us understand one and other, and that I may not discreditt my iudigm̃^t. wth the Queen, and my creditt wth you that trust me,) I think it not amisse to toutch theise two poynts followinge :—

" First, if your meaninge be, that Donnell Gorran must haue libertye to passe into Tyrone wth any numbers, at wch all those that know not the cause, will exclame and wonder, if *then** it should soe fall out, that he should not performe this, but that the least addition of strength or opinion of strength, should be conceaued to be added to the Traytor by this tolleration of *his* goinge ower to *the Traytour* (wch but for this end should never be suffered) *in such case untill the effect thereof shalbe shewed, itself, much* advantage would be taken against my counsell *all* wch beeinge in the hands of God, *as it may lack success* though he weare never soe well *disposed*, so will ye disgrace *be much greater to me y^t. haue ben the adviser, if the Q : shold receaue ye scorn to let him go wth any forces, and he then tourn on thother sydes, or show y^t he neuer went but to serve some other tourn.* In wch respect, because you did not perticulerly sett downe whether he meane to goe in, privately and do *only* desyre to haue such an assuraunce, as if he shew it when he hath done, it may be sufficient to procure the proteccon of her Ma^{t's}. forces if he come for retrayct, or whether he meane to goe in wth nombers (in shew, to serve the Traytor) thereby to amuse him, and yet because he feares her Ma^{t's}. forces, would *troble him doth desire some tre to her ministers* to lett him passe wth *his* nombers, I doe desyre to know his meaninge by your next certificate *in this point. In these respects I think fitt to let you know* that if he can goe in wthout her Ma^{t's}. dyrection to her Governours, for letting him passe (whereof there wilbe much varietye of censure, *as I would not*

---

* The words in italics are in Cecyll's handwriting.

care though he went wth neuer soe many.) *But* if he must needs carrye some, and cannot passe without her Ma^ts. tolleration, then had they need tobe verie feau he caries. As I shall therefore heare from you, you shall haue a tre to the Gouvernour of Carickfargus, wch beeinge sent privately to him, by some trusty person, there may be some course taken, between them for his safetye, and yet noe shew made but that he doth come in agaynst his will.   Thus much I thought good to lett you know, because the Governour must presently be acquaynted, wth the reason, if he cannot passe w^thout his tolleration.   Where otherwise, noe man should need to know it in Ireland, till it had been done, and then he mought haue had about him such a tre, as should haue been sufficient, to haue procured him a welcome, and a safe retrayct, *when ye enterprise was past, and yet he should not haue doubted to be discouered, seeing no body cold tell it but myself.*   The other matter wch I thinke fitt to lay before you, is this: that when the Proclamation was made, the Traytor was in his pryde, and then 3,000li had been well bestowed, to haue saued three hundred thousand ; but now that his hart is broken, and he allmost a wood kerne, for me to ingage my word for more then was offered, weare lacke of discretion ; for be you sure of this, that beeinge perswaded, as I am in my conscience, that it is not unlawfull to practise, the death of a declared, a proscribed Rebell, that whatsoever you shall receaue my hand for, I will see discharged, though I sould my shirt of my backe. And therefore, Sir, proceed in the matter, as you please ; and for the Proclamation, doe not much buyld uppon it; for much tyme is past since it was divulged.   But be you assured of this, that if by this draught, Tyrone be slayne or taken, there shalbe payed to your disposition 5,000 English Angells (a gold coin, varying in value from about six shillings and eightpence to ten shillings—Halliwell).   And this is the substance of all my answeares, *who, as I am desirous to do my country service herein, by sauing ye effusion of much Christian blood, whereof he will be ye aucthor whilst his lyfe lasteth, so I am jelous of ingadying you, or any man, uppon any promises wch I will not pforme to you as I will do these by God's fauor really.*"

THE JORNEY OF THE BLACKWATER.

"Doubtless," writes Camden, relative to the defeat of the English at Armagh, "since the time they first set foot in Ireland, they never received a greater overthrow!" or, in varied phrase, the fairest opportunity Ireland ever had of ridding her soil, at one sweep, of Normen, Palemen, and undertakers, was after the great fight under the walls of the fort of Blackwater. That day the valour and skill of an Irish chieftain almost achieved the freedom of his country; but, astonished at the very magnitude of his success, he lacked the decision to close "the barbarous hand" into which that great prize had fallen. The rebellion of 1598 had long been foreseen by English statesmen; yet, so great was the Queen's aversion to the enormous charge attending the ordinary government of Ireland, that her Ministers shrank from urging upon her the additional outlay requisite for any considerable increase of her army.

As early as April, 1594, Sir George Carewe had, "from his lodging in the Minories," written a long letter to Cecyll to prove, not that rebellion was imminent,—for that he presumed the Minister saw as clearly as he did,—but how a rebellion, to be successful, ought to be, and, no doubt, would be, conducted. His opinion of O'Neill was this :—"Tyrone having had his education in our discipline, and naturally valiant, is absolutely, and worthily reputed the best man of war of his nation. The most part of his followers are well-trained soldiers, using our weapons, and himself the greatest man of territory and revenue within that kingdom; and at this present, by reason of his great alliance, and, as well for friendship as fear, the absolute commander of all the north of Ireland."

The warning of Carewe met with little attention : some trifling supplies were sent to the army in Ireland; but when the rebellion broke out, the whole force there consisted but of 10,082 foot, and 521 horse, of which number about a third were mere Irish, "ready,—to use the Queen's words,—to run away and join the enemy against her."

In 1595 Sir Henry Russel, the youngest son of Francis, Earl of Bedford, succeeded Sir William Fitz-Williams as Lord Deputy of Ireland, and, "foreseeing a storm of war arising,' applied for reinforcements, and an experienced commander to be sent from England to his assistance. It was time! for the plans of O'Neill were ripe : he had assembled an army of 1,000 horse and 6,280 foot, not of the wild kerne of his own country, but of "expert soldiers, who had been trained and exercised to their arms, and had already served in the wars of the Low Countries." No sooner did the tidings reach him of the coming of Sir John Norreys, with 1,300 old soldiers who had served in Bretagne, than he at once burst into rebellion, and seized the Fort of Blackwater, which commanded the passage into the land of Tirowen. On the arrival of Norreys he was compelled to relinquish his prize; but not until he had wasted the surrounding country, and burned the town of Dungannon and his own house in it. The Queen's army was stopped at Armagh for want of provisions; a garrison was placed "within the metropolitan church" of that city, and the troops led back to Dublin, where, by proclamation, O'Neill was declared a traitor, by the name of Hugh O'Neil, grandson of Mathew Fardareugh, *i. e.* the Blacksmith. Jealousies broke out between Norreys and Russel: the former entered into treaty with O'Neill, which led to a series of short truces: during which Russel was recalled, and a new Deputy, the Lord Borough, "a sharp-witted man, and full of courage," was appointed in his place. Norreys had expected that high post for himself: he sickened of the disappointment, and shortly after died of chagrin. O'Neill had again possessed himself of the Fort of Blackwater, and the Deputy at once led a force to recover it. He succeeded, strengthened its fortifications, and returned to Dublin, having confided the command of it this time to a gallant officer, of the name of Williams. Tyrone again led his "companies" to that Fort of evil omen, and the Deputy again marched to its relief. In mid journey he was stricken by sudden illness, and died, leaving the army without a leader, and Ireland without a governor. Williams, though his small force was half famished, and sickness was amongst them, refused to surrender the Fort. The garrison had eaten their last horse, and were living upon "grass that grew upon the bulwarks." O'Neill had surrounded the place on all sides, and "swore by his barbarous hand, that as long as he could get a cow from the English Pale to feed his companies, he would not leave it." In the meantime Ormond, the same who, fifteen years before, had trampled out the great rebellion of Desmond, was appointed Lieutenant-General of the army; and, until the Queen could make up her mind to the selection of a new Deputy, the civil government of the country was placed in the hands of Adam Loftus, Archbishop of Dublin, Sir Robert Gardiner, and two or three others, with the title of Lords Justices; and never were the destinies of a nation confided to men more pusillanimous! The purpose of the following narrative is less to relate the fortunes of the Fort of the Blackwater, though a hero commanded within it, than to tell what happened under its walls; how the grandson of the blacksmith kept his "great oathes;" what the Lord Justices thought of it; and what Queen Elizabeth thought of *them*. Yet the gallant conduct of the officer who commanded the garrison well deserves its own share of notice; and, therefore, before entering upon "the disastrous journey of Armagh," we will present the reader with the account of one day's assault, and the hero's speech, which—after the usage of times heroic—preceded it.

" 1598. *Aug*[st] 20th. *A Book on the State of Ireland by* FRANCIS COSBIE.

" After this mishapp His Honor seeing no possible means to accomplish his desier except he had been able to have had another convenient army to have landed at Loghfoyle, and soe to have sett uppon Therle Traytor on all sydes, victualled the Fort [of the Blackwater] placinge therein as Counstable a valyant gentillman named Cap[n] Will[ms], with som ccc soldiers, and after brake up campe and retourned to the Newry, where making but small aboade, drewe towards the Cavan in Owreylies country, and there placed Sir Christopher S[t]. Lawrence commander of certaine companies there laide in garrison, and then repayred to Dublin; and there not contynuinge long, for that he considered the proportion of victualls left with Capt[n] Williams at the Forte was neerehand consumed, drew thetherwards again with as much expedi̅c̅o̅n̅ as might be; and even the same day he cam to Aramagh Tiroane's forces had beleagered the forte, and in the ende the most valyantest men in his retynewe undertooke to wynne the same; for that they had pfect intelligence that the warde was not onely sick and unserviceable for the moste pte, but all their victualls consumed; and so advauncinge themselves upp upon their scaling ladders gave a most wonderfull and bould assault; contynuinge the same very long wth greate resolucion, as well in their fighte, as contynuallye supplyinge of fresh men in the places of the slayne, hurte, and wyckened; and with great lyklehoode they had wonne the same at that instant if they had met with a cravynne, as they buckled wth a man of worthe; for the worthie constable Capt[n] Williams, when he saw the enemy first approaching to him with so great a resolucion, and assured of their intente, comforted his soldiers in the best manner he might, and tould them that now it was the tyme to shew themselves as beseemed men of their places fighting in the right of their Prince and country, wch if it were their fortunes to w[th]stande the enemies first assaulte, their natures and cowardyse was suche that either they would recule or fight in greater feare, to his and theire advantadge; not doubting of the victory, by the help of God, wherefore hee wished them in generall, as well the whoole y[t] was verry few, as the sick psonnes that could stand up and but advaunce their weapons, and to do theire duties in that measure, as was fitting for soldiers in theire case, the sight of wch woulde be a terror to the enemy; and remembrynge lykewyse what reputacion they should get either lyvinge or dyinge like men: where on the contrary pte, no more was to be expected at thenemies hands, if they should pvaile against them, and shame and infamy for ever if either they shoulde yeld their bodies as psoners, or by force to be taken by them lyke a sheepe going to the shambles, and therefore, said he, pull up your harts, for this hand of myne havinge a linstock therein, shall give fyer to this traigne, and bothe blowe youe and myself up into the skyes rather then those miscreants shall enioy this chardge of myne !   Upon wch every man that was able to stand and hould a weapon beinge anymated to doe their best, uppon those former speeches, cryed out We will dy with honor to the last man.

"Then the Enemy being advaunced to the top of the wall as aforesaid, and covetinge by all means to enter, were in that manner receaved by the soldiers that the ditches were filled with their dead corpses; yet stood they to it right manfully, untill they sawe that the soldiers, contrary to their expectacions, purposed to fight it out to the last man, and for to make their payment sterlinge, the two feild peeces planted in very necessarie places w^thin the forte, and charged wth muscet shot paid them their hyer bothe comynge, stayinge, and retournynge; and glad they were (although it is a custome among them to carrye away as many dead corpses and maymed men as they may), yet for all their cunninge they left xxxiiii behind them in the ditches, wth all their ladders, and some furniture, for a witness they had come there; but I ensuer you there was a nomber slaigne and hurte that were conveyed away, and very few of the warde either slaigne or hurte. Upon the next day the Lo Deputy drewe towards the forte, and at his arryvall made an oracion to the constable and soldiers greatlie commendynge boath him and them for their good service; and after he had victualled the forte; and supplyed the same with fresh and able soldiers, he stayed there not long."

The Irish chieftain attempted no more assaults, but vigorously set about digging trenches around the fort, and thus cut off from Captain Williams the hope of future sallies, and the capture of his enemy's mares. These trenches are described as works of amazing magnitude, such as had never yet been seen in Irish warfare; they were more than a mile in length, several feet deep, "with a thorny hedge on the toppe," and connected with vast tracts of bog; every approach to the unhappy garrison was "plashed," and rendered impassable for artillery, as the English afterwards found to their heavy cost; and the Irish forces so distributed, that a battle, under every disadvantage, must be fought by any army coming to relieve the Fort. O'Neill was too good a politician not to be informed of the exact state of the country, the resources of the Lords Justices, and the impossibility of their opposing in any effective manner at one time more than one division of his forces. Camden informs us that "the state of Ireland was at this time very much out of order, for all Ulster beyond Dundalk, except seven garrison castles—namely, Newry, Knockfergus, Carlingford, Green Castle, Armagh, Dondrom, and Olderfleet, and almost all Connaught, were revolted." If any man could have extricated the Government from its miserable plight, it would have been Ormond. "Vir magnæ strenuitatis et audaciæ." Yet even he looked with dismay upon the unequal struggle before him. "The times," he wrote, "are more miserable than ever before." If our wants be not speedily supplied, the whole kingdom will be overthrown." "The garrisons everywhere at this moment are ready to starve." "The soldiers run away daily, though I have hanged many of them in the maritime towns."

"And now to drawe an ende of this my raw intelligence," writes Francis Cosbie, "Cap^n Williams, before rehearsed, lying longe in that unhappye forte w^thout any reliefe but suche garrons and horses as he by pollicy could attayne unto for the suffycinge of himselfe and hungry ward, acquainted the estate with this their woeful misery ; who, havinge as well regarde of theire distresses, as the saffety of that great bulwarke, sent for the Lo: Liefteñant-Genl to Dublin ; where, after debating what course was best to be held, in the ende concluded that Sir Henry Bagnall should have the general command of this expediçõn."

Such was, indeed, the result of the much debating, and greatly contrary was it to the opinion of the civil members of that Council ; they, after wringing their hands in utter consternation and indecision, had written home for advice and help ; and, could they have had their way, they would have desired Williams to make the best conditions he could, and surrender the Fort ; but the soldiers overruled them. Bagnal cried shame upon the timidity which would bring dishonour upon the army, and insisted upon an instant march to re-victual the fort, and drive O'Neill from before its walls. And then was taken the fatal resolution of dividing the English forces into two bodies ; one to march without delay to the Blackwater, and the other to proceed against the Cavanaghs. It was the wish, nay, the earnest prayer, of the Council, that Ormond himself should undertake to deal with O'Neill ; but it chanced that Bagnal and O'Neill were bitter personal foes ; O'Neill had married the Marshal's sister, and out of that alliance had sprung a mutual feeling of deadly hatred. Bagnal entreated Ormond to allow him to meet his enemy, and it was so decided. The rest of this interesting story will best be told in the language of the parties concerned in it. They passed through the various phases of panic, shame, repentance, and recrimination; and, fortunately for us, disastrously for themselves, they wrote long letters under each transition.

"1598. Sir Geof^y. Fenton to Cecyll. *June 11th from Dublin.*

"The last truce expired the 7th of this monneth, and w^thin ii daies after, Tyrone made this devesion of his forces ; one pte he sent before the Blackwater, wch now he holdeth envyroned, swearing by his barbarous hand, that he will not depte till he carry the forte ; another pte he thrust into the Brenny, and at this pnte assalteth the castle of the Cavan there promising not to leave the place so long as he can gett a cow out of the English Pale to feed his companies."

"1598. *June* 17.   THE LORDS JUSTICES *to the* PRIVY COUNCIL.

"Where in the forefronte of this tre we made mencõn of the forte of Blackwater, and how yt is blocked by the Traytor Tyrone, not mencõning then for how long tyme it was vittled, wch is but tyll the last of this monneth at the furthest, and forasmuch neither the trayto^{rs} force can be removed, nor the place releeved wth vittles, but by the cuntenance of an army, yt standing so far in the mayne land, as there is no comõdity to succor it by water, wee doubt, that thorow these extremities, yt may receave suche disaster as wee shalbe sorry for ; and yet not hable to remedy yt."

"1598.   *June* 18, *Dublin.*   ORMOND *to* CECYLL.

"You write that you of the counsell wear sensible of my lacks; I confess hit is no small hart grefe unto me to hold the place I do, and to want the meanes whearbye I shold be inhabled to perform that I most desier against the traytors.   I protest to God the state of the scurvie fort of blackwater, which cañot be longe held, doth more toche my harte then all the spoyles that ever wear made by traytors on myne owne landes.   This fort was always falling, and never victualed but ons (by my self) without an armye, to her Majesties exseding charges.
"Your most assured and loving Friend,
"THOMAS ORMÕD ET OSS."

"1598.   *July* 7.   SIR G. FENTON *to* CECYLL.   *From Dublin.*

"Touching the Forte of Blackwater being the second place now holden for Her Mat^y in Ulster, I dowte the nexte newse I write to yor Hono^r thereof wilbe that that place wilbe forced by the Rebells, and either the garrison putt to the sword, or dryven to quitt the place upon suche condicõns as they cann make for their owne saffety."

"1598.   *July* 22.   THE LLs JUSTICES *to the* PRIVY COUNCIL.

"The Forte of Blackwater is yet helde wth greate honour and resolucõn by that valyant Gentⁿ Capten Thomas Williams, whoe comãnded it ; and althoughe Tyrone have lately bent his whole forces to surprize it, and have lost many men still about yt, whoe have blocked them in on all sydes of that forte, yet that worthie Captain dothe still defende himselfe and the place ; and as wee understande hathe latelie by some stratagem issued forthe, and besydes killing of 2 or 3 principall men of Tyrones hath gotten divers horses and mares of theires into the forte, which as we are enformed is victualled yet for a month ; and we hope that upon the Lo. Leeutenants coming hither his Lo will have an honourable care for the reliefe and supplye of that servitor, and the risk of the soldiors in that forte (who have hitherto with suche hono^r and resolucõn preserved yt for Her ^Ma^{tie} from the many assaltes used by the rebell to gett yt) wherein wee will assist His Lo wth o^r best advise and furtheraunce."

"1598. *July* 24.　Sir Geff. Fenton *to* Cecyll.

"The Forte of Blackwater holdeth out still, notw^thstandinge Tyrone hath lyen afore it above a moneth, and hath spent the most parte of that tyme in plashinge of passes, and digginge deepe hoales in the Rivers, the more to distresse the armye that should come to releeve yt. Cap^n Thos. Williams coḿandethe in the forte, hath done many worthy s^ervices in defence of yt as well by soundry sallyes, wherein he repulsed the traytors and slew some of their best men, as by many rare stratagems by wch he hath draiven into the forte many of their horses and garrans, wch stande him and the garrison in good steade for foode : The Gent^n deservethe great coḿendaćons, to whom if yor Hono^r wolde p̄cure a ĺre from the LLs acknowledging his good s^ervices yt wolde comfort him muche and give others incorageḿ^t."

"1598. *Augs^t*. 2.　The Lords Justices *to the* Privy Council.

"It may please y^r LLs to understand that uppon consideraćon had of the forte of Blackwater wch yet holdeth out as we are informed, thoughe with great extremetie, and comparinge likewise the state of Leinster endaungered in ev^ry p̄te by the rebells of the same province and ayded by forces from Tyrone, as in o^r laste former letter wee have written, Sir Henry Bagnall the Marshall is now to drawe into Ulster wth p̄te of the armye consisting upon 3500 foote by polle, and about 300 horse, to revittle the Blackwater; and wth an other p̄te of the armye I, the L. Lieften͡sant Genl wth such fewe companies as remayne am to attend the p̄secution in Leinster.

"The daye appoynted for the Rendevoues for the Ulster armye is the 16th of this month; when all the companies are appoynted to assemble at Ardye, and from thence to marche to the Newrie, and so to the Blackwater; the successe and accydents of wch Jorney shalbe advertised to yor lls as they shall fall out; wch wee pray God to p̄sper to Her ^Mties Hon^r, and the saffetie of the armye, onely we understand that Tyrone hath plashed the waies, and digged deepe holes wth other trenches and fortificaćons to ympeache the armye betweene Armagh and the Blackwater."

"1598. *Aus^t* 14.　The Ill Newse out of Ireland.

"The 12te of August thay cam from the Newry to Armaghe : The 14th of August theye sete forwardes towardes the Blackewater with 4000 footemen and 350 horses.

"Capt: Percy and Cap Cosbey led the firste regiment of foote, being 2000 ; Cap Percy was hurt : Cosbey slaine; and almoste all the regimente slayne.

"Sr Henry Bagnall ledd the second regiment, being of 1000, he was shott into the hedd, slayne, and moste of the regimente.

"Sir Calistianes Brooke ledd the horses, being 350, was

shott into the belly, and thought to be slayne. Abought
2000 footmen slayne, and

Cap : Cosbey	Cap Banke	Cap Bourke
Cap. Evans	Cap Petty	
Cap Morgan	Cap. Henserve	
Cap Turner	Cap Bethel	
Cap Leighe	Cap Fortescu	
Cap Streete	Cap Harvey	
Cap. Elsden	Cap Molmarey Orrely	

William Poule Commesarey a vollentarey, slayne
Jaymes Harrington, soone to Sir Henry Harrinton
Maximilaan Brooke taken or slayne,
Mr Counstable a vollintarey gentelman slayne."

"1598. *Augs*ᵗ 16. THE LLs JUSTICES *to the* PRIVY COUNCIL.

" It may please yʳ LLps at the L. Lieftenants last being heare wch was
at the tyme of oʳ last dispatch to yʳ LLs of the 2ᵈ of this mouneth : uppon
conferment had in counsell touching the distresse of the Blackwater, and
the revitlinge thereof. The Mrshall beinge also present at that consultacõn and sent for expressly by the L. Lieuteñant, som of us were of
opinion that the hazard were too greate to adventure so many of Her
Mₐᵗⁱᵉˢ forces as were thought requisitt to be employed in that expedicõn;
yelding this reason amongst others, that the forte being valued at the
highest wos noe way comparable to the loss, yf tharmy shold receve any
disaster in the attempt; But when wee saw his Lo, and the Mʳshall
stande so muche uppon the honor of the service, alledging how greatly yt
concerned Her Mₐᵗⁱᵉ in Honʳ to have the forte releeved, we left to themselves the resolucõn, wishinge, by waye of advice after they had determyned yt shold be attempted, that the L. Lieftenant wold undertake the
matter in pson; alledging amongst many other respects, that in that case
his Lo. might drawe wᵗʰ him many of the nobilitye with their followers,
wch wold greatly strengthen the accõn, and besides his psence in the field
might move Tyrone, eyther for feare or for som other respectes, to give
way to him, whereby the service might be pformed with less daunger.
And before this consultacõn havinge considered thorowly of the pills in
this enterprize of the forte, and the difficulties to accomplishe the same,
the Lo Lieutenant and oʳselves jointly together wroate to the Mʳshall,
lyinge then upon the borders, and wth all sent our specyall tres to bee
conveyed by his meanes to the Capⁿ of the Blackwater, advisinge him to
consider howe he might make his composicõn with Tyrone in tyme, to the
most honʳ he cold for Her Maᵗʸ, and best saffety for himselfe and the
garrison their; but the Mʳshall stayinge these tres in his owne hands, did
not send them to the forte; but brought them back agayne with himselfe,
affirminge how dishonorable it wold be to hold that course; and that he
knew by good intellegences that the forte was yett in case to hould out ;
and that he had tryed by stratagem to send some vittles into them. In
our advice wch wee gave to his Lo. for undertaking the service in his owne
pson, wee putt him in mynd that the prosecucõn of Leinster might bee
commytted to som other duringe his absence : But his Lo. and the Mŝhall
agreeing afterwardes, his Lo. tooke upon him the matters of Leinster, and

left to the Mšhall the accõn of the Blackwater; who accordingly came to
Armagh the 13ᵗʰ of this mouneth, wthout any loss, other then the takinge
of Capᵗᵉⁿ Ratcliff prisoner, and some 4 or 5 others cutt off in the straight
betweene Dondalk and the Newry, who stragled after the armye, and did
not march under the saffety thereof: and the next day, beeinge the 14ᵗʰ
of this psente, th army dislodginge from Armagh with purposs to pass
further to revittle the Blackwater, the rebells of the North havinge way-
laide them there, in places to ouʳ disadvantage roase owt with their mayne
forces to stopp their passage; where after a sore tryall made by the army,
stryvinge to put the rebells from the advantage of theire place, our forces
were repulsed with a greevouse loss, both of the Mšhall himselfe with
sundry other pticular Capⁿˢ with their coollors, and also a great nomber
of the souldiers; the resedue that remayned (except som of the Irish who
rann to the rebells) retyred to Armagh as the next place of succor they
cold gett, where they remayne in the church there, awayting for soch
comfort as men in so great a calamity may expect. These heavy newes
were brought to us this day by Capⁿ Charles Montague who having the
second place of chardge of the horsemen in the service, and beeinge appoynted by the consent of the Capⁿˢ (as he affirmethe) to adventure thorow
thenemyes countrey to come to us, hath made declaracõn to us of this
lamentable accident in this summary manner, wʰ herewith we send to yʳ
LLs under his hand. A matter soe greevouse to us, in respect of soe
greate a dyminucõn of Her Mᵗʸˢ forces in so daungerous a tyme as this,
and to have soe greate a pte of the armye (beeinge 1500 men, as Capⁿ
Montague reportethe) cooped by in the church of Armagh envyroned round
aboute with the rebells, as we cannot but feare farr more daungerous
sequells, even to the utter hazard of the kingdome, and that owt of hand,
yf God and Her Maᵗʸ prevent them not: for we assure ourselves that upon
this accident in the North the whole combinacõn of the reste of the rebells
in all ptes of the Realm will grow mightely prowde, and will not spare to
take the opportunitye of the tyme, and pursue this success at Armagh to
their best advantage in Leinster, Connaught, and all other places of the
realm. And they know as well as ourselves that we are not hable wthout
psente succor owt of England to fetch off those poore distressed companies
that are in Armagh, who (as Capⁿ Montagu reportethe) hath vittles to
serve them for 8 or 9 daies, and not further; wthin wch tyme wee have no
meanes to reskew them from thence by force, nor after that tyme to releeve
them with vittles; wch being a most lamentable distress to us, wee have
now signified the same to the Lo. Lieftenant Generall, who as we heare is
at Kilkenny, praying his speedy repayre hither upon this heavy occasion.
This encounter at Armagh was the 14ᵗʰ of this psente, and the report
thereof brought to us this daye about 9 in the morninge; since when we
have bin busie to send owt many dispatches into sundry ptes of the realm
to prevent daungers, and contayne the people as moche as in us lyeth; and
have specyally written to the Lo Lieftenant Genˡ to haste hether with all
speed to thende to consider with him of the pnte daunger in all ptes, and
howe Her Maᵗʸˢ forces, that are left, wh. are wholly under his chardge, may
be employed to the moaste saffety of the realme, and pservacõn of that wh.
remayneth. But under yoʳ LL's honorable reformacõn, and in all humble
dischardg of oʳ duties, wee wishe that Her Maᵗʸ were thorowly enformed
of the daungerous estate of this realme, as well as for want of forces, by
reason of this defeate as for lack of skillfull and experienced comãnders;
and pticulerly this desaster of Armagh having taken awaye the Mshall,
wh. place is in Her Maᵗˢ disposicõn, wee humbly wishe that som well
chosen pson beeing of good understanding in the warrs may be sent from

thence owt of hand, to supply that office, to thende that by thassistaunce
of suche an officer Her Mats intiall services may bee carryed in that course
wh is requisitt agaynst so many prowde rebells in sondry ptes of the realm.
And though the Lo Lieuteñant bee now absent from hence wherebye wee
cannot comunicate with him in this and other things as were meet, yett
yf his Lo were here, wee doubt not but he seeth reason to be of our
opinyon that inasmuch as the distresses of this kingdom are devided into
many ptes, and every pte hathe his pticuler daunger, that that necessity
presseth to have a further assistaunce in the proceedings of the warr, and
a subsistinge authority to be joined with his Lo. unless Her Matie wold be
pleased to settle the whole government entyrely in one man's hands, wh.
for our ptes, wee wishe, for the avoydinge of many confusions, growinge
in the mayne government, now that the aucthoritie is devided, wch it is
not unlyke wold be better redressed, yf the supr authority were reduced
into one man's hand, as Her Mas deputy; the consideraçon whereof we
humbly submytt to yr Lo. grave advice.   Onely and lastly beseechinge yr
LLs with all the dutye and carefulness we can, that tyll a Deputye may
come a Mrshall may be sent with suche other assistaunts for the warrs as
yor LLs shall think requisitt, and that also a further force of men may be
sent owt of hand, the certaine nomber whereof we cannot otherwaies
lymitt then according the greatness of our daungers: and that such as
shalbe sent may be trayned men, well weaponed, and consistinge of hable
bodies, to be able to beare owt the toyles of this hard service.   This choiss
of a Deputye, or in the mean while some good assistaunts for the warrs, to
be assigned and sent owt of hand with forces, the longer yt is deferred
the more will it encrease the daungers of the realme, for that boath
thennemyes will multiply, and insult, knowinge how weake wee are, as
well in commanders as in men; and the subjects that yett stand will take
yt for an occasion of discouragement when they see soe small means to defend
them.   Suche further advertisements as wee shall receave of the desaster
of tharmy in the North, or of any other matter occurringe in any other
ptes shall be signified to yor LLs with the beste speed we can, being most
greeved that this wicked land will not yett yeld better matter to advertise to
yor LLs.   And so beeing greatly fearfull that Tyrone in the pryde of this
success will bend some daungerous attempts against the Newry, Dondalk,
Knockfergus or other frontyer places of importaunce, wee most humbly
take our leve

"In great haste at Dublin 16th August, 1598,
"Yr LLs most humbly at commandment,

"Least Tyrone might use further violence to those distressed companies in Armagh we thought good to send a Pursyvaunt to him wth or lre, the copy whereof wee send to yor LLs herewith, having directed the Pursyvaunt to learne the true state of the soldiers, with other instrucõns wch was our chefe purpose in sending him to Tyrone."

"AD. DUBLIN
"ROB. GARDENER
"ANTHY ST LEGER
"H. WALLOP
"GEFF. FENTON

"1598. 16 *Augs^t*. THE LORDS JUSTICES AND COUNCIL *to*
TH'ERLE OF TYRONE.

" We have taken knowledge of the late accident hapned
to pte of Her M_a^{tes} forces employed in Ulster, only for vitlinge
of the Blackwater, and that many of them are retyred into
Armagh, where they now remeyne : we thought good upon
this occasion to sende to you on their behalfè ; thoughe wee
thinke that in y^r owne consideraçõn you will lett them depte
w^thout doinge them any further hurte : wee are to put yo^u in
minde howe farr you may incense Her Maties indignaçõn towardes you if you shall doe any further distresse to those
companies, beeinge as you know in cold bludd ; and on the
other side howe farr you may move Her M_a^{tie} to know a
favôrable conceite of you by usinge favor to these men ; and
besides your auncient adversarye the Mshall being now taken
away wee hope you will ceasse all further revenge towardes
the rest, against whom you can ground no cause of stinge
against yo^rself, being employed by Her Ma^{ty} in theis Her
Highness' services. Thus much we thought good to sygnifye
unto you, and by waye of cawtion to admonishe you, to
avoyde to pvoke so mighty a Prince upon such a matter as
to distresse her servitors in cold bludd.—To this ende we
have sent this bearer the pursyvant, by whom wee expect
yor answere. At Dublin 16 Augustj 1598

" AD. DUBLIN, CANC.
" RO. GARDENER
" H WALLOPP.
" GEO BOURCHIER
" GEFF FENTON

" *To Therle of Tyrone.*"

" 1598. *Aug_{st}* 17. THE LORDS JUSTICES *to the* PRIVY COUNCIL.

" It may please y^r most hon^r LLs. Albeit we have now joined with
the rest of this council in a lre to y^r LLs sygnifying the most wofull and
greevous accydent of the Marshall's death, and defeating of that army, yet
fearinge greatlie least that blame might bee ymputed unto us wch we have
not deserved, we have made most humbly boulde in our own dischardge to
troble y^r LLs wth these fewe lynes *in private* from o^rselves : we hope y^r
LLs do well remember, howe absolutelie Her most excellent Majestie hath
left the managing of all the marshall affaires in this realme totherle of
Ormond L^oLieuten⁹ant Gn^{rl} ; and wee lymitted onelie to the administraçõn
of civile justice ; not havinge to deale with so muche as the distribuçõn of
the treasure sent. Nevertheless, as by all former dispatches yor LLs might
pceave wee have not fayled to bend our whole studie in assisting his Lp[:]
from tyme to tyme, and at all tymes with our best advise in any of his

affayres concerning Her Ma^{ts} services:　And touching the victualling of
the forte at Blackwater, yt is well knowen to all this table, uppon con-
sultaĉon had thereof, howe muche agaynst our advise and myndes the same
was undertaken.　We alleadged the difficulties to pform yt, the chardge
and exceeding troble that yt wold bee, both tothe soldiers and miserable
contry, and lastlie the great pril and imynent daunger wch yt wold bringe
the whole realme into (yf yt were undertaken, and tharmy defeated) as
now yt hath don.　Yelding our opynion that yt were more convenyent and
far more salfe, rather to quitt that forte wch might have bin don wth good
condiĉons, beeing of little worthe in respect of other places, and easy to be
built agayne, with good convenyency, and thre or four daies stay of tharmy
whensoever they should pceed northward—and therefore to defend the
Pale beeing the hart, and in a manner all that is now left of the whole
body, untill Her Ma^{tys} resoluĉon had bin understood here for a full and
throughe psecuĉon of these warres, wch hetherto had byn so exceedinge
chardgeable unto Her Higness.　This wee urdged with suche vehemencye
as was offensive to som, howbeit all the reasons and pswasions wch we cold
use would not drawe his Lp and the Marshall from their intended purpose
to victualle yt, wch beeing so determyned by him who had the disposing
of those causes absolutelie in his own hand, and no power in us to alter yt,
we then wyshed, and urdged muche that his Lp would himselfe undertake
that service, beeing of so great ymportaunce, and then alleadged two
reasons which did especiall move us so to advise his Lp.　The first was
that wee knew yf his Lp wold goe himself in pson he shold bee accompanyed with the moast pte of the nobilitie, and their followers, with many
other gent^n voluntarie attendaunts, whereby he shold bee a farre better and
greater armie then otherwise he cold sett out with the marshall : Thother
was that yf yt came to that extremytie wch now (alas !) yt hath don, wee
thought the great Rebbell would have had more reverence and regard to
his Lps pson place and calling then (we were sure) he wolde have tothe
M^{r}shall, agaynst whom he bare a deadlie hatred.　Yett his Lp beeing
either unwilling or unable to endure that troblesome jorney, answered us
that himselfe could not be spared from the service in Leinster, wch he
wolde attend.　And havinge so resolved, layed that other service upon the
Marshall, who spedd unfortunatelie therein, tothe losse of his owne lyfe,
and a great pte of that Army, except the horsemen, whereof as wee understand, none perished, the distresse of the rest, now invyroned bythe
Rebell at Aedmaghe, and apparent pill of this whole state.　The L. Lieutenant returning then to Kilkenny hathe there and thereabouts remayned
ever since, as yett he dothe ; the Leinster rebells beeing nevertheless exceedingly encreased, and daily burning preying and spoyling the contrye,
having alredy possessed themselves of all the Queenes County called Leix,
some three or four castles at the most excepted, which cannot long hold out.
There they possesse the lands so dearly bought by Her Majesty and her
pdecessors, and doe even in peaceable manner enioye the goodes, and cutt
downe and gather the cornes of thauncient English gent^n of that country ; to
the great discomfort of all our naĉon remayning in this wretched contry, (the
lyke sturre have they alreadv bego^{9}n in Offaly, called the King's county,
and the lyke ende, in all lykelyhood, will they make there ; the Rabbel of
them being nowe by this disaster so encurraged and encreased as they doe
even what they list w^{t}hout controlm^t.)　A greate pte of the county of
Kildare they have alredy spoyled and burned, and daylie advertisem^{ts} we
have of there entraunce into the county of Dublin, and of their purpose,
even this day, as we understand, to make heade even towards this citie ;
to wch God knoweth they may make an easie approach, yett have wee, to

encounter their comynge, sètt out this present mornyng the nomber of six or seaven hundred of cittizens and others to ympeache their purposed approache. This (and worse than wee have saide) is the state of Leinster. For Connaght, howe muche this blowe hathe weakened yt, and strengthened the Rebbells of that Province, yor LLs may conceave : and Mounster not free from infection, very lykely to brust out, and this is now the state of this poor and most miserable lande !

" Thus muche in effect have wee in divers our former private l⁹res foretould, and sygnified to yor LLs, and this doe wee now agayne in dischardge of our most bounden duties declare to yor LLs. Wee have noe meanes left in us to help o^rselves, and the remnant of Her Ma^{ts} poore subiects here, onely this wee besche Thalmighty God soe to styrr upp the hart of o^r gracious Soveraigne hir most sacred Mat^y as yet at leingth (and allmoste to late) she will behold o^r miseries wth the eyes of compassion ! thinke uppon a present course touching the forme of this government; and speedily undertake a Loyal and stronge psecution agaynst these vile ungratefull Rebells, otherwise shall not wee bee hable to render any other account to Her Highness then that her Realme is lost. We have in all hast by two sev⁹al messingers acquainted the Lo Lieutenant wth this callamytie, desyring his speedy repayre hither, wth suche forces as hee may make, and convenyentlie spare, at whose comynge wee will use all o^r beste meanes for the bringing off the rest of tharmy now remayning in Ulster, wch wee thinke wilbe very weake : and so wth o^r prayers we comende yor LLs to God's most blessed ptection

" From Dublin the xvijth of August 1598
     " Yo^r LLs most humbly at comandm^t
      " AD DUBLIN
       " RO GARDENER

 " For her M_a^{ties} Affayres
To the Honorable the LLo: and others
of hir M_a^{tis} most Honorable Privie Councell
Haste, Haste, Haste, Haste, Haste.
Delivered to the sea: on Fryday at 10 of the clock
in the fornoone, the 18 of August
     " AD DUBLIN."

   " 1598. *Augs*^t 24th. ORMOND *to* CECYLL.

" S^r—Although I know the jointe tres written to the LLs there from th LLs Justices myself and the Councell here, of the late accident happened to the Marshall in the north will com to your hands : yett the losse of our syde being since delyvered to me by several men, as appeareth in the enclosed notes, I thought fytt to sende the same to you ; whereby yt appeareth that our losse, God be thanked, is not all so greate in the slaughter of the men as was first reported ; though to greate and shamefull as yt is ! Our newe men sente over for supplies never offered to fight ; but, as their leaders saye, ranne awaye most cowardlie : castinge from them their armour and weapon, as sone as the rebells chardged them. I finde by examyninge this matter that wante of goode direction was the cause of their overthrowe; for the armye were putt to sixe bodies, and marched so far asonder as thone of them could not come in tyme to seconde nor help thother; whereof I warned the Marshall to take speciall care, before he went hence. In the middest of this feight there were 2 or 3 barralls of powder putt a fyre in the Battayll, which blewe upp and hurte divers of our men; wherew^th the traitors were encoraged, and our men dismayed. Hit is very necessarie, uppon the sendinge over of forces, to sende trayned men that have seene som service, consideringe that they conte to be presently ymployed, and can have no longe tyme to be dysciplined here. Fewe or none of the newe supplies brought backe their armes; soe as the proporc͠on of munic͠on to be sent hether hath nede to bee the greater. I wish the leaders of those that shall come were men of experience in service, whereof I doubt not you will have that considerac͠on that is fytt. And so for this tyme I committ you to God's blessed protection.

" Your veray loving
" And assured Frend,
" Thomas Ormōd et Oss.

" From Dublin the 24th of August, 1598.

" I do sende you hereenclosed the copie of a ĩre wch p̃re^etelie I receaved from the constable of Her Majesty's house of Dongarvan."

" 1598. *Sept* 4.   The Lords Justices *to the* Privy Council.

" It maye be that some dislyke may growe uppon a ĩre wee thought to send to Tirone upon the first reporte of the accident at Armagh. And though at that tyme wee had som reason to hould that course, yett uppon better deliberac͠on *wee revoked the letter* and wold not suffer yt to bee sent; having this device at the first that the letter shold bee but a coollor to send to see the state of the companies wth direccion that yf there were anie possibilitie to fetch off those companies, the letter shold not be delivered; which was accordingly p̃formed, and wee have at this p̃sente the ĩre in our handes, which is true upon our creditt

" Ad. Dublin.   Ro. Gardener.
" F. Wallop.   Anth^r St Leger.
" Geff. Fenton."

"*Sept*" 15.   ORMOND *to* CECYLL.

"The LLs Justices might have written more advisedly
then to say the hole army was overthrowne; truely hit might
have beñ so, yf God had not letted hit; for there disorder was
suche as the lyke hathe not beñe amonge men of anye understanding, deviding tharmye into six bodies, marchinge so farr
asonder as one of them could not second nor help thother till
those in the vangard wear overthrowen. Suer the devill
bewiched them! that none of them did prevent this grose
error.   Sir, for that I understand the LLs Justices wrote over
to you after this disaster that hit was not there act to send
the Marshall, but that it was a plott sett downe betweene him
and me, I have thoght goode for profe of the contrary, to
send you the inclosed notes which I pray you to make knowen
to Her Majestye in my discharge; being lothe to troble you
farther at this tyme I committ your guiding to God.
     "From Ratothe the 15 of Septēber, 1598.   .·
                "Your fast assured loving frend,
                        "THOMAS ŌRMŌD ET OSS.
"The bearer was with the Marshall when
    he was slayne, who can tell you how
    ill owr companies were placed, not
    beeing able to com̄ to help one another
    I pray you afford him your honourable
    favor."

"*Sept*" 12, 1598.   THE QUEEN *to the* LORDS JUŚTICES. ·

"Wherein [the arrival of Sir Richard Bingham] we knowe
that you and our cousin of Ormond, our Lieutenant, will find
great ease in every way.   It beeing neither fitt nor possible
that you shold spend your bodye in all services at all tymes,
and yet we must pleynely tell you that we did much mislike
(seeing this late accōn were undertaken) that you did not
above all other things attend yt; therebye to have directed
and countenanced the same.; for yt were strange to us when
allmost the whole force of our kingdome were drawn to hedd,
and a mayne blow like to be stroken for our honor, agaynst
the cappytall rebell, that youe whose person wold have better
daunted the Traytor, and would have carryed with yt another
manner of reputacōn, and strengthe of the nobilitie of the
kingdome shold employ yourself in an accōn of less importance
and leave this to soe meane a commander.

" Wherein [in the matter of the Blackwater] we may not passe over this fowle error to our dishonor, when you of our counsell framed *such a letter to the traytor after your defeate, as never were read the lyke either in'forme or substance for baseness! beeing such as we persuade ourself yf you shall peruse yt agayne when you are yourselves that you will be ashamed of your own absurdities, and gryeved that any'feare or rayshness shold ever make you aucthors of an acc͠on so much to your Soveraign's dishonor and to the increasing of the traytor's insolency.* For other things past wee have well observed, That all y͏ʳ Jyourneys and attemptes uppon the northe have had theise successes that not only our armyes have come backe wᵗʰ losse or doeing nothing, but in their absence other parts of our kingedome have ben left to be spoyled and wasted by the rebells; and thoughe the unyversallytie of the Rebellion may be used as a reason of the mischiefe, yet it is almost a miracle that wᵗʰ the charges of an armye of eight or nine thousand men the provynciall rebells of Leinster and Wexeforde and other places should not be mastered.

" POSTSCR :
"Synce the wryting of this łre we have understoode that y͏ʳ łre wᶜʰ wee heard from yoᵘ was sent to the Traytor by y͏ᵘ hath synce ben stayed *by accident,* whereof for our owne honor wee are very gladd, thoughe for y͏ʳselves the former purpose still deserves the same imputac͠on.
" At Greenwiᶜʰ the 12th of Septᵇʳᵉ 1598."

THE TOWER EARL OF DESMOND.

When Ireland was in a blaze of rebellion, the extensive palatinate of the Geraldines in the possession of Fitz Thomas, Desmond occupied by Donal and his Connaught bonies, and the city of Cork, with a circuit of little more than a mile, nearly the sole possession left to Her Majesty in Munster, Sir Robert Cecyll allowed himself to be persuaded that it would be a master stroke of statesmanship to take from captivity a prisoner whom the English Government had deeply injured, a man of great ability, supreme knowledge of his countrymen, and with unbounded influence over them, and to send him to Munster, that he might withdraw the most powerful of the Irish Septs from rebellion, and rescue the greater portion of the province from the insurgents in whose hands it then was. The success of this scheme was immediate, and complete : within six months the whole of

Desmond, Carbery, and Muskerry were reduced to an acknowledgment of the Queen's authority, and to obedience to Florence. His Sept, with few exceptions, withdrew from action, his castles were filled with fighting men from his own followers, and neither Geraldine nor the loose swords who, during the recent years of his captivity, had infested the country, dared to set foot within his limits. Thus far the scheme of the English Minister was eminently successful; but it was found to be attended with certain inconveniences, not foreseen previous to its accomplishment. The Geraldines, driven out of Carbery, drew nearer to the Presidential City; Cork was surrounded; and the royal army of Munster,— 1,700 men by the poll,—in no little danger of assault, and capture.

When Florence MacCarthy quitted London, he left in what might be called his English home,—although of late years he had been allowed, under heavy recognizances, and subject to hasty recall, occasional out-of-door residence,—in Her Majesty's Tower of London, a cousin many years younger than himself, James FitzGerald, son of the great rebell, the 16th Earl of Desmond, who had had his abode in that historic fortress from his childhood. When surrounded by difficulties, —chiefly attributable to that master stroke of the statesmanship of Sir Robert Cecyll,—and emulous of the fame gained by that prosperous adventure, Sir George Carewe urged upon Her Majesty a repetition of the policy of her Secretary: he solicited the liberation of young FitzGerald from the Tower, who, he assured Her Majesty, would, on his mere appearance in Munster raise the blockade of Cork, lure back every follower of his house to loyalty, cause the surrender of every castle to Her Majesty, put an end to rebellion in Munster, send the Sougaun Earl's head to London, and not impossibly O'Neill's with it. Strange to say, the project, though so near akin to that of the English Minister, found not a single supporter! every one opposed it, and none more vehemently than the Queen; but Carewe held firmly to his proposal, and less resolute minds gave way before him. James FitzGerald was taken from the Tower and conveyed safely into the hands of the President. How he landed at Youghal; what his reception was in the first instance;—*and in the second!* how he captured the castles; brought back his followers; extinguished the Irish rebellion; these and the other performances of his brief career in Munster, as also his unobserved return to London, and his early death there, are all familiar to the reader of the Pacata Hibernia: so much of his life concerned the Lo: President, and hence, so much of it has become part of the history of Ireland; but there are many other traits of this youth which had no interest for Carewe, though much for Sir Ro: Cecyll.

Although heedfully nurtured from his infancy; watchfully shielded from the rude influences of the outer air; spared the excitement of the society of noisy companions of his own age, country, and condition; withheld from the fatigues of such exercise as youth is so recklessly inclined to; suckled by Mrs. Fethergill—with the assistance of Mr. Roberts—upon physick; swathed in comfortable plaisters; soothed to slumber upon cushions of vyletts and waterlillyes; his mind disciplined by selected schoolmasters; and his conscience freed from the fetters which had enslaved his ancestors for five centuries, probably for ten; this young Norman captive was ever a source of uneasiness to his great benefactress Queen Elizabeth, and his attached friend Sir Robert Cecyll! Never had training, diet, drugs, schoolmaster, Thames atmosphere, and Sir Owen Hopton met with more signal success! We learn that when this interesting young patient was sent to Ireland to extinguish the rebellion there, to reduce the followers of his house to loyalty, to punish the pretenders to the Earldom of Desmond, and to the crown of Ulster, and with nearly unlimited control over an expenditure of five hunded pounds a year, the utmost fault that could be found with him by the undertakers, who fancied that his "teeth were always watering" for the recovery of the 600,000 acres which had belonged to his father, and now formed their Signories, was a tendency to extravagance! In all other respects, we learn from the English historian of his career in Ireland that " *he was too good to live amongst such traitorly followers.*" With fear and trembling in the heart of the English Secretary, with ill humour and misgiving in the mind of Her Majesty, and the ill-suppressed ridicule of the courtiers, the gates of the Tower were thrown open for the exit of its prisoner, and the young FitzGerald, bewildered by his recollections of the past and the prospect of the future, "not knowing whither to turn him—if into tyme past, beholding a long misery ; if into the present, such a happiness in the comparison of *that* hell*,*" &c., &c.—was declared *free !* From the generosity of Sir Ro: Cecyll he received a gift of a hundred pounds sterling, " for the purchase of *armour !* and necessaries for *the sending away of his nurse !*" And then, sustained by the affectionate ministry of Dr. Noel, his physician, and provided with a selection of comfortable drinks and appliances by Mrs. Fethergill, in the pleasant company of His Grace Miler M'Grath, the Archbishop of Cashell, and under the indulgent custody of Captain Price, he was conveyed by gentle journeys to Bristol, and thence, having shipped his horses and *armour*, set sail with his nurse for Cork.

The reader shall now see more in detail what had been the training from infancy, through boyhood and youth, and what the energy of mind and body of this " Puer male Cinctus," this slovenly Cæsar, who was " to go, see, and subdue" Munster.

" 1583. *Novr.* 17. THE LORDS JUSTICES *to the* LORDS *of the* PRIVY COUNCIL, DUBLIN.

" Post scriptum

" Our verie good LL. for that we acompt Desmond's sonne here in the Castell to be a prisoner of greate chardge, and that manie escapes haue ben made hearehence, (thoughe not in our tyme,) we wyshe, for the better assueraunce of hym, that Her $M_a$tie mighte be pswaded to remouve hym hence unto the Towre of London, wch notwthstandinge, we leue to yo^u LL's graue consederacõn."

" 1584. *July* 9. *From* TREASURER WALLOP *to* SIR F. WASLYNGHAM.

" My Lo: Deputie hath sent the Erles of Desmond and Clancarty their sonnes to the Courte, by tow of my men, whome I beseche yo^u to dischardge as sone as they com to the Courte wth them.

Decr. 25th, 1588.

" The Demaundes of Sir Owyn Hopton Knight Lavitenannt of Her Majesties Tower of London, for the Diette and other chardges of Prisonñs in his custodie from the Nativitie of Our Saviour Christe laste paste 1588 till Thannunciacõn of our Blessed Ladye the Virgyn, then nexte followinge, beeinge won quarter of a yeare, as heerafter is pticulerly declared—

" James Fitz Garalde

Imprimis For the Diette & other chardges of James Fitz Garrolde from ye xxvth of December MDLxxxviij till ye xxiv of March then nexte followinge beein xij weeks at xx^s the weeke for himselfe   ...   . xiij^{li}

It^m For his Appell at xxx^l. the yeare... ... ... vij^{li}. x^s.

It^m For the dyet of his Scholemaster at xx^{li}. the yeare ... v^{li}.

It^m For the wadges of his Scholem^r at xiij^{li}. vj^s. viij the yeare iij^{li}. vj^s. viij.

It^m For the wadges of my servant attending on him at v^{li}. the Yeare   ... . xxv^s.

               Somma ... ... xxx^{li}. 0. xx^d.

Bill sent in by Sir Rich^d. Barclay, Lieut^t. of the Tower.

For physick furnished by Mr. Fethergill, for Mr. FitzGeralt, the 12th daye of June, 1596.

Inprimis A pourgation with Syrop of Angoustome & other iiij^s.

Syrops for vij morninges ... ... v^s.

A Bolus of Cassia and Rubarb	v^s.
A laxative powlder for ij doses	iiij^s.
A Plaister for the Backe	v^s.
A Linyment for the syde, con̄ iiij oz	ij^s.
A Quilte for the hedd	vj^s. viij^d.
A coolynge Oyntmente con̄. vij. oz	xij^d.
A coole Julep to take at all times	v^s.
Syrop of Vyletts & limons demi^{ld}	iiij^s.
A Quilte for the backe	v^s.
Laxative cinrans compounded with Rubarb iiij^{ld}... ...	v^s.
For iij Cordyall Drinkes with bezar	iiij^s.
Cinnamon water one pynt	v^s.
Aqua cælestis one pynt	x^s.
Consurve of barberys & others	iij^s iiij^d.
Consurve of Roses	iiij^s.
The Julep as before	v^s.
A Compound Syrop &c.	iiij^s.
Acornes & barberys for a Stitch	vj^d.
A Compound Electuary to take at Morning Con̄ 7^{ld} ...	v^s.
Soundry distilled Waters with Syrop of Vyletts and limons contayninge a pottle	vs. iiij^d.
Another pourgation with Rubarbe	iiij^s.
Sewger-Candye a Quarterne...	x^d.
Manor Christi iiij oz	iiij^s.
The Julep agayne as before	v^s.
Another Coulde oyntmente Con̄ iiij oz	ij^s.
The Cordyall drinke agayne as before	iiij^s.
Syrop of Vyletts iiij oz.	ij^s.
A box of pfume for theares...	vj^s.
A bolus of Cassia & Rubarbe	iiij^s.
An Aperitive Julep for the Lyver	v^s.
Pills for hedd and stomack for soundry tymes	v^s.
Diaphalma ℥iiij	xvj^d.
Syrop of Vyletts & lemons to take every morninge Con̄: viij oz	iiij^s.
Consurve of Waterlillyes, of vylets & of borax for soundry tymes contayninge V̄j ouz.!	iiij^s.
A Julep to drincke after the Consurve	iiij^s.
A fomentacōn for the syde	v^s.
A compound oyntmente for the same	iij^s.
A Bathe contayninge mãy ingredients	x^s.
An Aperitive to take yt all tymes	v^s.
Another box of perfume as before	vj^s.
A plaster for the Stomack	
A pfume for the hedd	
A Laxative drinck for Soundry tymes	
An electuary to take in the mornynge	*
A Syrop to drinck after yt	
Rubarb to stepe in a drinck	
A drinck for the Rubarbe	
A Glister	
A Fomentacōn for the Stomack	iiij^s.

* These prices not visible owing to the folding, and fraying of the paper.

A confortable oyntmente for the Stomack... ... ... iijˢ.
An Oyntment for the hedd ... ... iiijˢ.
A powder for the same ... ... iijˢ. vjᵈ.
A lixiˡir for the same ... ... ijˢ.
An oyle for theares ... ... ijˢ.
A Quilte for the hedd ... ... vˢ.
A pfume to ayer the same ... ... iijˢ.
Another Glister ... ... vˢ.
Aperitive Syrops for v mornynges ... ... vˢ.
A pourgation with Rubarbe & manna ... ... vˢ.
Losangis for the hedd, stomack and backe jˡᵈ ... ... xˢ.
A confortable powder to be taken before meate ... ... vˢ.
A Julep to take at all tymes... ... ... vˢ.
          Summa totalis ... ... xiiijˡⁱ. xvjˢ. vjᵈ.

" I receaved all theis things above written according unto the severall perticulars.

                                        " J. FitzGerald.
    " William Burghley,
    " Buckehurst.
" Ro : Cecyll."

" 1593. *June* 17. *From* James FitzGerald *in the Tower of London, to the R* Hon: Sir R. Cecyll.

    " Honorable Sʳ,
    " Let it not be offensiue, I besech you, to be troubled with the lynes of an unknowne stranger, who though yong in years, yet being old in miserye, taught therby to apprehend any meanes of favour whersoever vertue may move compassion. My hard fortune and my faultelessness I hope ar nether unknowne unto you; howe only by being born the unfortunate sone of a faulty father, I have since my infancy never breathed out of prison,—the only hellish torment to a faithfull hart tobe houlden in suspect, when it never thought upon offence,—the favour and comfort which I have alwaise receyved from my especiall good Lord yoʳ father, hath, I verily thinke, ben the preserver of my sorowfull lyfe, which er this would els have pyned away with greef : And nowe in his Lordship's absence, I am therfore inbouldned to solicitt yoʳ Honor, as a worthy branch of soe true, noble, and vertuous a stocke; hoping to find the same favorable inclination towerds me which his Lo : hath alwaise shewed. Lett me then humbly entreat and obtaine att yoʳ Hoˢ handes to further my hũble request which I shall this day make unto yoʳ honorable assembly at the Counsell table, and soe fur as it shalbe thought resonable and convenient to lett it be cõmẽded to Her Mᵃᵗⁱᵉ. If you shall afford me any favour heerin, soe furr as so unhappy a man shalbe able to doe you service, assure youʳselfe to have made a purchase of a most faithfull and thankfull hart. Thus praying for the preservation of yor health, and daily increase of Honor, I humbly take my leave.
                    " Yoʳ Honor's ever to comand,
                                        " James FitzGerald.
    " Frome the Towre, this xvij of June, 1593."

" 1598. *April* 20. FENTON *to* CECYLL.

O'Neill openly declares to his friends,—
" I do assure you all upon my creditt and as I wold haue yo͡ hereafter
to beleeve me and be directed by me, that thErle of Desmond's sonne is
escaped owt of the Tower of London by meanes, of the Lieften͞t of the
Towers daughter, who is gonn wth him, and arryved in Spaine, where
they had such acceptanc and entertainem͞t as seldome hath ben hard of
tobe in that kingdome afforded to a man of his yeres; and further I do
assure you that before a monneth do pass, yf wynd and weather do serue,
wilbe in Mounster wth great forces, both of men, municon, and treasure;
the lyke whereof I do expect, wth assurance to myself, and therefore
comforte yo͡selves."

" 1600. *Aug͞t*. 30͞th. THE L͞d. PRESIDENT CAREWE *to* SIR RO: CECYLL.

" Who so knoweth this kingdome and the people will confesse that to
conquer the same and them by the sword onlie is opus laboris, and almost
may be said to be impossible, and I do verylie beleve that all the treasure
of England, wilbe consumed in that worke, except other additions of help
be ministred unto ytt. The fayre way that I am in towardes the finishinge
of the heauye taske wᶜh I undergoe I am affrayd wil receyve some speedye
and roughe impediment, unlesse my aduyse in sendinge of the yonge
Desmond hether may be followed; the good wᶜh by his presence wilbe
effected hath bene by me so often declared as I holde ytt needlesse to
trouble yow wᵗh reiterations of the same : the danger that may ensue if
he should proue a traitor (wᶜh I suppose tobe the motiue of his detention)
is no more then the malice of a weake rebell, who can neuer be so great,
by reason of his education, wᶜh hath bene in simplicitye unaccustomed to
action, together wᵗh his religion, as this countrefaict Earle, nourished in
uillanie and treasons, and the greatest piller (Tyrone excepted) that euer
the Pope had in this kingdome, and farther, if this traytor were taken or
slayne, yet the rebellion is not ended; for these Mounster rebells will
establishe another Robin Hood in his roome, and so in sequence, as longe as
there is a Geraldine in Ireland. As sone as the bruict was divulged that
he shoulde be sent unto me, I found such an alacritye in his followers as
an immediate sight of a present quiet did represent ytself unto me, ...
Sir beleue me all the perswasions in the world will not preuayle to induce
them to serue against James Mᶜthomas, much lesse to do anythinge upon
his person, before they see his face.
" If God be pleased, for the good of this country, to direct her Mᵃᵗⁱᵉˢ
counsayles to send him hether, I do humblye beseche yow to moue her that
he may come (or not at al) as a free man, wᵗhout any marke of a prisoner,
and that he may enioy the name and tytle of an Earle. What land is most
conuenient for him to have, and least dangerous if he should be ill disposed,
I haue heretofore at large deliuered my opinion ; and also how easie it is
to prevent any harme he may do if he be enclined to do ill.
" GEO CAREWE."

" 1600. *Sept͞r* 24. CECYLL *to* CAREWE.

" Nowe is the hour come that you shall receave the pson ofthe Earle of
Desmond, soe called here by courtesye alredie, and soe resolued by hir
Mᵃᵗⁱᵉ to bee, as maie appeare by the pattent you receave ; onlye this is the
dyfference, that her Mᵃᵗⁱᵉ will see som imprest of other mens promises
before she geve him plenary satisfaccon ; wherein I pteste unto you noe :

one thinge hathe made hir more to sticke then the doubt wch she hath that there wilbe noethinge don for him worthie of soe greate a favour. For the matter I must owne and speake to you my opinyon, yt you and I have made a greate aduenture to presse and importune for a thinge soe subiect to ill successe, in a tyme when most thinges are iudged by effect, and shall especially be applyed untoe us ; because the mallice of som, and the igno-raunce of others have taught them this odd sentense to hinder any thinge (they wold not have, or understand not,) by saying, ' Yea butt he maie proove a rebell hearafter.' I praie you thearfor when you have him, take this counsayl of me ; whensoever you fynd any cause toe doubt him, never feare toe laie holde of him ; for therin we will never blame you, butt we will take yt for a thinge that was necessarie, quoniam ipse dixit.
"Robt Cecyll."

"1600.   Septr 28.   Cecyl to Carewe.

" You must knowe that notwithstandinge all the poore credytt I had I cold not disswade hir M^a^tie from deferrynge to signe Desmonds pattent, allthough I did laye before hir howe infinit advauntage and oportunitie wold be loste ; but yt pleased hir to be stille fyxed that she wold see som-thinge effected before she did absolutelie geve him the title ; still layinge before me what a scorne she shold receave yf he shold effect nothinge ; and then Tyrone might laughe att her doble, as he hath don alredy att the cominge in of Sir Arthur O'Neil, whome he called ' Queen Elizabeth's Earle that cannot comaund a hundred kern.'
" Robt Cecyll."

MEMORANDUM BY SIR ROBERT CECYLL.

" A note of ye somes that have ben delyvered by me to the E of Desmonds use.

" One C^li. to M^r. Lieftenant when he was first dyscharged out of ye Tower, whereuppon himselfe and his followers lyved at D^r. Nowel's.
" One other C^li. delyvered to himselfe in ye presence of Cap^n Pryce at my house at ye Savoy for ye provyding of armor and apparell and neces-saries for the sending away his nurse and syster.
" Ten pounds delyvered him at ye Court.
" One C and iiij^xxli delyvered to Cap^en Pryce for his charges.
" For his charges into Ireland.
" Twentye Pounds dely^d to Moryce Shehan for his use.
" Ten pounds to ye B^p. of Cashell.
" Thirty pounds to John Pore.

(PROBABLY HEADS OF SERMONS TO BE PREACHED BY MILER M^cGRATH.)

" 1600.   To the EARL OF DESMOND.

" 1 Touchinge his dysposinge in marriage.
" 2 Touchinge his servantes and retinewe.
" 3 That he contayne himself moderate in matters of Religion &c.
" 4 That he at his first cominge do fashion himselfe in some convenient measure agreeable tothe Irish nacion.

" 5 Several cawtyons for thè frugall managinge of his estate.

" 6 Particuler admonitions tohold himselfe humble, gratefull and loyall towardes her M^{atie}.

" 7 Priuate instruc͂ns for his present and future course of lyfe in generall, and in ͣpticuler for his correspondence, and his dependencye here, and in Ireland."

" 1600. *Moyallo, Octr.* 21. EARL OF DESMOND *to* CECYLL.

" My pen not daring to presume to approach the piercing and resplendent Maty of my souueraynes eyes, I have imboldned my self to commend my humblest service and affection by you, under her royall person my best frend, to whome Right Honorable I am not to fill paper wth those blandishments of ceremonies that I know is continwally sounded in the eares of such as y^r Honor is, but onely beseech you to moue her Ma^{ty} to looke into her selfe and foorthe of that to behold me, and then I doubt not, as she shall finde, that she hath doon much, so gathering all circumstances, and examining all objections, I am tied not to performe a little ; and howsoeuer my performance of seruices may be great in common opinion, yet for myne owne parte, I shall hold them far short of that infinite. obligation wch I owe, and therefore wth the still layinge of the ernest of my vowes and thankfulnesses, lett me advertise you of my progress since my departure from you. Uppon Mondaye the 13th of October wee sett sayle from Shirehampton for Corke, where wee, having so fair a passage as the honest gentleman this bearer can tell you, the Master and Saylers saied they neuer for this tyme of the yeare knew the lyke ; wee held our course for the place appointed by your honors instructions ; but I, that was so sea sicke as whilest I liue shall neuer loue that element, being two dayes and a night at sea, besought them to lande me any where ; so being not able to reach Corke, a tuesday at night beeing the 14th of this month wee fell in at Yoghal, where, that y^r honor may know the trueth of my proceedings, I had like, comming new of the sea, and therefore somewhat weake, to be overthrowen with the kisses of old Calleaks, and was receiued with that ioy of the poore people as dyd well shew they ioyed in the exceeding mercy hir Sacred Ma^{ty} shewed towards me. From thence we went to Mr. John Fitz Edmonds house at Clone, where wee had a great deale of cheere, after the contrey fashion, and shew of wellcome, from thence to Corke (where I humbly beseech your Honor to take notice of this I write) for that Towne, as Cap^{en} Price can wittnes, Coming thether three or fower howers before night, wee could not gett lodging in a long tyme, neither place to send my cooke to provide supper for us, untyll I was fayne (except I would goe supperless to bedd) to bidd my self tothe Mayors house, a lawer, one Meagh, who if he haue no better insight in Littleton then in other observations of his place for hir Maties seruice, maye be well called Lack Law, for it was much a doe that wee gott any thing for money, but that most of my people lay without lodging, and Cap^{en} Price had the hoggs for his neighbours. From that towne, wch hath so great a charter, and I feare me so littell honesty, I cam to My Lord President to Moyallo, where by some of my well-willers I am put in very good hope that with My Lord President's fauour, and the helpe of her M^{aties} forces I shall gett Castellmayne, wch if it so happen shalbe the ioy of my next advertisement. The people came many unto me uppon my landing, as the Lord of the Decis, and many else of the best quality, whome I tooke hand ouer head, and preached to them hir Highnes' clemencie towards one, of wch there could be no truer exemple

then my selfe—and besought them if they bare me any affection, to ioyne
with me in shewing their thankfullnes wth myne to do her Highness service, wch they haue promised faythfully wth their mouths, and I pray
God tobe truely settled in their hearts; and my selfe harteles when I think
the contrarie.

"Thus y^r Honor hath heard the discourse of this my hitherto travayles,
crauing, according to my deserving, the continuance of your fauour w^{ch}
hath brought me to the height of that wch now I am. My best frend, next
yr Honor and my Lord President, the Lord Archbishop of Cashell putteth
me in very great hope, that wee shall shortly performe our greatest taske,
I meane the killing, or taking of James McThomas, wch once accomplished,
and therein the warrs in this province ended, I shalbe very glad to attend
upon your Honor, untyll wch tyme I shall not be my self,—And for
Mr Crosby I do find such good in his counsayle and readynes to advance
her Highnes' employements, that I hold my selfe, amongst a number of
bonds, so tied to y^r Honor for sending him with me, as I do assure my selfe
all our businesses will succeede the better for his company. And so beeing
all in very good health, I take my leaue.

" Yo^r Honor's in unfayned
Seruiceable affection
" DESMOND.

" Moyallo ye 21th of October 1600."

" 1600. Octr. 21. P. CROSBY to CECYLL.

" It may please Yo^r Ho^r, on Monday the xiij of this instant thEarle
of Desmond wth his retynue, and attendants were embarked at Bristoll;
and arrived at Youghall the next day aboute vij of the clock at night.
At whose entry into the town there was so great and wonderfull
allaccryty, and reioicyng of the people both men, women, and children,
and so mightie crying and pressing about him, as there was not onlie
muche a doe to folloue him, but also a great nomber outhrowne, and
ourun in the streates in striving who should com first unto him; the like
wherof I neu hearde or sawe before, nor woulde think it coulde eu be,
except it were aboute o^r Prince. Indeed I haue often read that upon
thelleccon of a kinge the people genllie woulde crie Kinge H, King H,
or otherwise, according to his name, so likewise (though unmeete to be
don to a subiect) the harts of the people: Ye the very infants, hearing
but this Desmond named, coulde not contayne them selves from shewing
thaffeccon they beare to his house. I assure yor Honor it was not like
the crie made toRich the third at Baynardes Castle.

" The next daie there came flocking unto him from all pts of the
contrey LLs, Gent: and comons both to congratulat his comyng, and to
offer their service, and attended him that night toClone, M^r. Fitz
Edmonde's house. The next daie to Cork, and so on Thursday to Mallow,
to my Lo President, where he was entertayned, and a certen course taken
for his estate, and whither all intelligences doe com, and the people doe
resorte from all places.

" The twoe plotts both for Castlemange and th usurping Eale are nowe
in hand, and wthin theis twoe daies a jorney wilbe undertaken to see what
good may be don both in them, and in other things; I hope, and I doubte
not, but all will doe well, and that very shortlie untill the profe wrought
may be had, My Lo President will not suffer me to depte, but must attend
the successe of his jorney.

" I knowe yor Ho^r. will looke to here of the yonge Earle's carriadg since his depture thence (my self being still wth him) wherein I must say (as I love to tell yor Ho^r truth) that of his owne nature and disposicõn he is both honest, faithfull, and dutifull, and very willing to doe her Mate service ; but I see so muche alreadie touching thexpences, and other things as I doe not think fitt that either him self, or any of his owne people shoulde holde the raynes of his bridle ; but the same to be cõmytted to others, of whom there hath bene had good triall, both of their fidelitie tothe state, their knowledg ofthe countrey, and sufficiencie to pforme the acte, whose vigillant care and circũspeccion oũ him wilbe suche, as they will not onlie not suffer him to run any other then an even course (where-unto I must sweare him self is very well inclyned) nor pmitt any badd resorte unto him, that may any way corrupt him, either in his religion or otherwise : but also by their councell and advice wilbe good assistants unto him for the managing of his causes, wthoute whose helpes he cannot but erre ; for neither his yers, his experience of the worlde, or knowledg of the countrey can warrant the sufficient dischardging of so waightie matters.   Yet I am psuaded (in respect he is so tractable and towardlie) that it wilbe easy to carry him to all good courses.   This I assure yor Ho^r wilbe the way to make him to doe that wch is expected, for w^ch, as you are alreadie growen famous in this province and in most pte of the kingdom, and have purchased the prayers of a nomber of people, so I doubte not but her Maty shall have great cause to gev you thanks for the same, as for one of the greatest services (considering thiniquity of the tyme) that eũ was don her in this kingdom.

" Touching this bearer Cap^n Price I say that although he be noe great doctor, nor any ofthese curious stately followers, yet I assure yor hon^r he is an honest plaine gent^l : and as discreete and carefull of his chardge as eũ I saue any ; I would he had the lik still about him to hold the helme so he could speak the languadge.   The Archbushop is very good if he could still contynue wth th Erle, but he cannot be alwayes wth him.   Thus muche for this tyme, hopeing tobe the next my self, or at least to send you better newes, and in the mean while, and for eũ wilbe

" readie to live and die in Your Service,
"P. CROSBIE.

" From Mallow the xxjth of October, 1600."

"1600.   Octr. 22.   MILER MAGRATH, *Archbishop of Cashell, to* Sir Ro : CECYLL.

" . . .   But howe soeũer the successe shall proue, there is agret apa-rance of gladnes and good will shewed in every place wher the yonge Erlle of Desmond came, Corke only excepted, whosse magistrates seemed not to be glad of any tinge, that might induce mor streinght or possibiliti in the Englis gou^lment then to be as it is, nor so muche it shelfe. .   but what shewe the comon sort ther, and eu^ly sort; from the cheffest, to the loest, in other places, doe make uppon his cõminge, I doe referr it to the honest berer his report, and the fruits thereof shall very seortly (God willinge) make the same manifest—the yonge Erlle was not 48 howres in the land when sure promisse was mad to hym of Castellmayn tobe deliu^lred tohym ; for wch purpose his Lo and my selffe were suters tomy Lo President, to giue us a cõpanei of horsmen to goo thether to make present triall of that promiss ; but his Lo ueisly consideringe hou warfuly traytor's promisses shulde be trusted, toght fitest tosend a trusti man from Desmond tomake proffe of the promiss, then to go in pson; wherupon John Pouer is sent, be whome we expte good newes this night or the next. The next day afther John is departure others came to Desmond makinge sure promisses of 124 (James McThomas) to be delivered (or at the least) discoued to hym wthin few dayes accordinge tothe first plott."

"1600. *Novʳ.* CECYLL *to* CAREWE.

"—— I have mooved the LLs to uryte untoe the Cittye of Corke about the lewde usage of the yonge Erle of Desmond, to whom I have sente this copye that he maie be comforted; for indeed Capten Price sware untoe me that all this was trewe wᶜʰ is urytten, he being bye."

"1600. *Decʳ.* CECYLL *to* CAREWE.

" I praie you Sir privatlie fynde meanes toe discouer weare yt possible, yf yong Desmond can be so vayne as toehave anie purpose to marry the widowe Norreys; yf he have, and yᵗ he will confesseyt, tell him freelie yᵗ her Maᵗⁱᵉ will in no sorte allowe of yt; not in respect of anie unwoorthines in her, butt because hir Maᵗⁱᵉ looketh att his hands to fetche all light for his accõns from hir, and not topresume for other respects, wherof she is not ignoraunt, nor anie waye allowethe him toe bynde himselfe. I praie you Sir, use this wth secresye and discrecion."

" 1600. *Octʳ.* 1. CECYLL *to* CAREWE.

". . . I thinke Castlemang wold be a veray acceptable pleasure tothe Queen, and an argument that myght be used to the world that the Queen getts somthinge by him good for herselfe, as well as for him. As for his expenses lett him knowe he must lyve frugallye, and within £500 yerlye, till hee bee seated, and lands given him. He maie alsoe be tolde that he shall com over when he hathe don anie good, and marrye in England, whither yt seems he longs to retorne; and I assuer you in my opynion, he will never muche lyke an Irish lyfe, for he is tender and sicklye; but tyme will shewe.

"I praie you Sr remember good pleadges uppon the White Knight whylst thinges are prosperyinge well; for yt is saide you wilbe cosened bye him at laste. You cannot please the Queen better then that som of the principal knaves of name be hanged—It is said that Cahir can delyver Dr. Craghe when he list: It wear well tryed to impress yt uppon him, not as the doer, but under hand; for he can doe yt with a wett finger, and it will make him irreconsylable. Lett Dermod's wyfe have som maintenance, and contente the Archbishop with good wordes; for he doeth speake veray well of you, whatsoever he thinkes, and in this matter of Desmond maiebe suerly trusted—God send yt well! and som act to ppose to followe, that maie visiblye stopp the mouths of thoes that here laughe att yt as our plott —I shall never ende but that my sleep surpriseth me, and therefor beare with this raphsodye.

"At Courte 1 Octʳ. 1600.

"Your's al Solito
"Robᵗ. CECYLL."

" Right honnorable
" The dutye that I owe unto that Sacred Matie that hath raysed
me from nought tobe her creature (in which tytle I doe onely hold my
selfe happie) maketh that the least defect, which might be a hindrance
unto the aduancement of Hir Highness' Seruice, soe greuous unto me,
that I come soe farr short, of intymatinge myne humble thanckefullnes, for
soe exceedinge a mercy, as the greatest seruice which I might doe euen to
the sacreefysinge of my lyfe, weare but tooe litle for her gratious fauour
towards me.   Not withstandinge, lest your Ho should hold your expec-
taton of my indeuours as altogeather frustrated, may it please youe tobe
aduertised, sithence my last letter unto your ho, Thomas Oge, who was
constable to James Fitz Thomas in Castlemayn, yelded the same unto me,
whereof I tooke possession by my seruant John Power, the xiiijth of November, and kept it for som few dayes, untill it pleased my uerie good
Lord, the Lord President to haue it yelded unto his owne hands, to whome
I comaunded it should be deliuered, and his Lordship is now possessed of
it.   When it was perfectly knowen in Ireland that I landed, James Fitz
Thomas his company that remayned, dispersed them selves, and him selfe
being sicke, kept him close in solitarie places, for which cause I sent my
spialls to trackt him out, who brought intelligence yt he was kept in
Arlough, untill the verie first night that I came to Kilmallocke, at w^{ch}
tyme he was conueyed from Arlough by a few horsemen to one Morris
Powers house, as they informed ; but I hope by my spialls shortly to finde
his trackt, if he be within Mounster; and the sooner to bringe him to an
end, I, with the aduise ofthe Lord President, sent his Los protection to-
geather with my letters for Dermot O'Connor, hopinge that he, with the
assistance of my truest frends myght finde out the Sougan in his most
secret den; and for Dermot's most safety in his trauell to come with a few
company to this prouince the Lord President sent his letters in yt behalfe
both to the Gouernor of Connagh, unto the Earlls of Clanrickard and
Thomond, safely to conduct Dermot with some fyftie men through their
Gouernment to this province; who after receauinge his protection, jorneyd
hitherward as farr as Gortnishygory xxiiij myles from Lymbrick, and was
there murdered by Theobold Bourke alias Tybot ne Longe accompanyed
with 300 men.   Some saith this murther was comitted for that he tooke
prisoner James Fitz Thomas (and I hold it the chefest cause, howsoeuer it
may be disguised) whereby the Irishry were weakned, and feringe that he
wold doe more seruises against them, as I doubt not, your Ho shall understand by My Lord Presidents letters, who is as much greued with this
indignitie offered tothe State, as I am, yet I finde my self the more greued
for that his cominge hither was procured by my Lord President's protection and my letters; the reuenge whereof I referr to your honnorable consideration.   Now I humbly beseech youe to consider my estate which is so
dessperat in this kingedome that my person is not heere secured by these
inhabitants great or litle, nor able to doe any seruice by reason I want
meanes to execute it.   I dooe desyre noe perpetuitie of hir Highnes charges
towards me (but of hir fauor) neither doo I desyre tobe here (God is my
wittnes) for any respect except to doe hir Matie true seruice.   If I had
knowledg of James Fitz Thomas where he were, I haue no comaund of
force to take him, except I shold send to the garrisons to joyn wth me;
and what oportunitie is lost in that tyme, I referr to yor Ho^s discression.
Let any man imagin himself in this state that I writte to youe I am in,
and I will demand noe more then he wolde, in the lyke condition.   I find

2 K

my Honnorable good Lorde kinde unto me, but I am contemptible unto the contry, in regard that they see my meanes under my Lorde not soe much as a privatt captein's, to follow the reblles, if there were present occasion of seruice, nor in their good carriage to geve soe much countenance as a farr mener man then a Earle; so as I do not at all, at least uerie litle, partici-pate of the Italyan proverb Amor fa molto, argento fa tutto. I hope your Ho: holds yor resolution for James Fitz Thomas, Pyerce Lacy, and the Knight of the vallei's lands, that I shold haue it, for Mc Morris his land my honnorable good Lord hath an assured tytle to it, and he that wth your Honor's fauor gott me to be intytled as I ame, I shall neuer be soe ungratefull as to possess any thinge of his, for it cannot be but his gifte, and the worlde can binde me no more then I am. I humbly beseech youe that these obstackles, that hinder the abilitie of my euer-willinge seruice-able testimonies, may not make youe expect those performances of my dutifull prosequtions that their suply might giue youe iust cause to expect, except youe send directions to inhable me, otherwise lett me haue leaue to come into England, which howsoeuer youe procure her Highnes to make me great here, I protest, if it be put to my choyce I shall allways hold tobe there best, and soe will I imbrace it. The latter end of your letter maketh me to desyre the knowledg of that honnorable personage whome her High-nes hath thought of my unworthynes for, which with expectation of reso-lution of your Ho, in all these my expressions bythis bearer, myseruant, yelding many thanks for yor infinett fauors, and hauing noe offeringe of my loue to send youe but the Sugan's aunciient (his standard) which this bearer shall present youe I rest

" Your Ho in all humble and faithfull affection
" DESMOND.

" Moyallo the xviijth of December, 1600."

" Decr. 21. DESMOND to CECYLL.

" R^t. Hon. Sithence the writting of my lr̃es, Thomas Oge hath brought unto me Piers Lacyes two sonnes. I do fynd him the trueste follower I haue, since my coming ouer. Whereof I beseeche yor Honor to consider in behalf of his dylygence to do her Matie service, and his affection to me. And thus I humbly take leaue, and rest Your Honor's as I will and ever protest.

" DESMOND.

" Kyllmallock the xxjth of december, 1600."

" 1601. Jany. 14. JOHN MEADE, MAYOR OF CORK to the PRIVY
COUNCIL.

" I received another l^{re} from y^r. Ho:^s directed to me, and the Aldermen, wch lr̃e did contayne that yor Ho. were informed that the young Earle of Desmond whou lately came hither, was, wth his company, very hardly intertayned here, and not well accomadated wth lodgings, or other neces-saries : the truth is R^t. Hon^r. that upon his repaiere hither yit did not appeare unto me by sight of his Pattent or in any other manner, what aucthority he received from her most Excellent M^{atie} (albeit I hold the favours bestowed by her Matie uppon him a most rare psident of her Highnes wonted gracious clemency) and where he hath landed at Youghill, he did not repaire to the Lord President, being then at Mallo, but came hither first, and therefore yt may please yor good Ho. to be advertized that

I did feare it might be offensive to entertaigne him, or any other, not putt in aucthority by her M$_a$^{tie}, with any publique wellcome, at the gates of the Cytty, or otherwise, w^{c}h is onely used to the L Deputy, Lo : President; or such as are aucthorized by her Highnes. And yf Ihad knowenn it were her Ma^{ts} pleasure, my good will should never want to countenaunce ani wth that measure her Highnes would expect, were yt signified unto me by lyne, lr̃e, or otherwise, from my Lord President, or any in aucthority. But R^t. Hon. althoughe I hope well of the dispotion of the young Earle, yet I did feare thuse of some of his auncestors whou have challendged courtesies for duetyes, and soe might intangle this Corporaĉon wth newe customs, w^{c}h onely depends of God and her most excellent Matie, and of no other peere, or pson whatsoever. Yet for private kindnes there wannted none ; for I assure your good Ho : that the young Earle's officers did send to bespeake one of Mr. Skiddy's house, for some private affectõn betwixt them, wherby I expected the same should haue bene readdie for his Lp ; but by meane of certayne provaunt and pvision of the garrizons w^{c}h was kept in the said house, the same was not so soone reddie as his Lp came hither, wheruppon I entertaigned him at my poore house, while his lodging were a making reddie ; and when he had remayned an houer or two in my house, his officers would not accept of the former lodging, and thereuppon I was fayne to lodge him at one Phillipp Martell's house (being an Alderman of this Cytty) being th usuall lodging of th arle of Ormond, and where Sir Warham St. Leger, here lately in com̃ission, did lye ; and the Lo cheefe Justice of England at his being here ; and being of the principallest houses in this place ; and notwithstanding that the self night of his Lo^{ps} repaiere hither, there came alsoe 400 of the Walshe soldiers sent hither for supplies, wth the lodging of w^{c}h th officers were much troubled, yet all his company w^{c}h came to the Bayllies of this cittie to demaund lodging, were harboured sufficiently, and lodged wthout making of any paym^t for the same, neither would anie of them repaiere unto th usual Innes ; and yf any were unlodged it was for waunt of demaunding the same of th officers appointed here for those causes. And concerning his supp the truth is I expected his steward and others had pvided for him the first night of his repaiere hither, and ment to have entertaigned him to deinner the next daie ; but that his Lop came of himself wth his trayne whou had the best provision I could affourd. And his Lop being at supp complayned of the waunt of horsses, and he would not beleeve but that the cittie could affourd sufficient horses for him and his troupe, w^{c}h I truely answered that all the horsses of the towne, except a few garrans for wood, were stollen awaie this last rebellion, and out of use : for that the cittizens durst not traivaile abroade, and withal I gaue him the best advyse I could, to send to the Lo^s and Gentle adioining for horsses; and his L^p called for pen and inke to urite unto my Lord Presid^t: and I thinking that he ment to uriet by way of complainte for not furnishing him wth horsses, praied his Lo^p of God's will to acquainte me with his meaning, and that I would endevo^{1} to see him provided to my power; and he said his lres were for her M$_a$^{ties} service, and required haste ; whereuppon I psently dispatched them awaie at midnight by a messenger of the Cittys, and collected the keis, being devided among the Aldermen, by custome used here since King John's tyme, and I receaved the next morrow an answere, the contents of w^{c}h I have dilligently endevoured to observe (at w^{c}h conference Capt^{en} Price was not present) and that was all that past betwixt the Earl and me touching anie lres ; protesting before God that he never writt lres to yor Ho in my house, but wee did passe the tyme in merym^t, and in no such matt^{rs} of waight, w^{c}h were to be used with gravity and secrecie. Onelie he writt those few lynes to the

L Presid^t, sitting at the table, accompanied wth me, and diverse others after supp; and I marvaile greatlie that of such small and publique conference these matters were informed against me, as rather became mere indiscretion and childishnes in me if I were faulty, then anie witt or sense, beseemyng the place I now carrie or my pfession of lawyer. And albeit I cannot make ostentacōn of discretion, or other sufficiencies fitt for the place I now beare, wch was involuntaryly cast uppon me, being a burden of greate care and chardge, yet there is no waunt of my love and zeale to serve her Matie, according my most bounden duty; and to extend my poore power to entertaigne such as are in her Princely favor, whome God Allmighty long may blesse and prospr against all her enemyes whatsoever! And soe not doubting but the L President hath, and shall have occasion to make like repte of my willingnes in her Ma^{t's} service as occasion shalbe here ministred, I most humbly take leave.

" From Corck the xiiijth of January, 1600.
" Yo^r ho: Lps most humbly a comaund
" Jo Meade
" Maior of Corck."

" 1601. Jany. 25. Cecyll to the Earl of Desmond.

" Wherin becaus I have fallen in to ye subiect of marriadge, and y^t I see youe take hold of some words of myne concerninge a disposicon of matchinge you in England, in wch poynt you desier tobe satysfied, who shalbe ye pson I have; I have thought good to make you this answere. Fyrst that yt proceeded from a disposicon wch I did noate in yor selffe, when you were in England, to bestowe yor selff to hir Maties likinge, wth som English psone, wch was the reason that I have both gon about to ppare hir Maties mynde to suche a course for you, as alsoe to consyder wth myselff in pticuler wher to fynde suche a match for you as shold in all circumstances answere the publique respects of hir Mats service, and above all thinges the satisfacčon of your owne mynde, and your desieres. But my Lo. I must entreate you to consider that in a matter of mariadge, shee is of smale valyewe whos frends wilbe contented to have hir name used before ther bee likelyhood of an affeccon of your pte, although in this generall sorte above mentioned, I have ben contented (as an argument of my care and affeccon towards you) to forthinke where wilbe most necessarie for you, soe as I can only for your satisfaccon make this (remark) that shee is a maid of noble familie, between 18 or 19 yeres of age, no courtier, nor yett ever sawe you, nor you her. Wherwith I praie you remayne satisfied till you shall fynd occasion herafter, for further consideracons, to repayre into England, at wch tyme (with tyme enough) this matter maye be thought of.
" Robt. Cecyll."

" 1601. April 30. Cecyll to Carewe.

" I am veray gladd y^t thEarle of Desmond is heer; he is well used, and shall have the same some wch growes bye the Lendynges, but not by the apparell; att the least he shall not knowe soe muche, because he is every daie lookynge for more then his allowaunce. Other newes heare are none but y^t the Queene is well, and goinge to Greenwich.
" Robt. Cecyll."

" 1601. *Avgt.* 31. DESMOND *to* CECYLL.

" My Most Honored Sr. It is no smale greefe unto me that I cannot
attend hir Matie, nor so often accompanie yor Honor as in all affection I
would; for in both those courses only, under God, my hopes doth rest; but
before I begin these fewe lines of my demongstrating necessities I knowe
not whither to turn me, if into tyme past, I behold a long misery; if into
the present, such a happines, in the comparison of that Hell, as maye be a
stopp to anie farther incrochement. Yett pardon you this my
humble sute, who wahinge wth my self hir Maties liberallyty unto me, and
yor honorable fauours towards me, that I maye not be distastinge to either
in ouerpressinge receaued bounties. I haue heere inclosed sent yor honor a
note of a sute whereof no disbursement shall growe foorthe of hir Highnes'
purs, but an encrease of £20 yearly tohir cofers, wch by the aire of yor
breathe unto hir sacred Matie, and the blessednes of hir graunt, maye supplye these my wants, wch neuer hereafter shall importune you. If it be my
misfortune not to haue it, soome other shall, and where can hir Highnes
charity more perfectly shine then uppon hir humble creature who hath
receaued life from hir, and grace by you? wherein as you haue begun wth
me, so I may not herein find you wanting tome that submitts all his ends
to yor likeing, and in all humblenes doth rest much assuredly bound
toyou.

"DESMOND."

" Greenwich this last of August 1601.

" I do heere that yor honor shalbe ernestly solicited for certaine lands
in Ireland, espetially James Fitz Thomas' Lands, I beseech yor Honor not
to procure anie graunt to anie boddy untill the land wch shall stand at Hir
Highnes fauour to bestowe uppon me be passed."

" 1602. *Jan^y.* 14. *The* LORD DEPUTY *and* COUNCIL *to the* PRIVY
COUNCIL.

" . . . As your Ll^s. haue directed, upon notice of the decease of the
Erle of Desmond, the company allowed for him is discharged; save what
yt hath pleased you to continue tothe Archbushop of Casshell, the Erles
sisters, and John Power."

" 1602. *Jan^y.* 17. WILLIAM POWER *to* Sir Robt. CECYLL.

" . . . And least my lr̃es haue not come to yor Hon^{rs}. hands, and that
the best freind I had, the young Earl of Desmond (whom yor Hon^r had
raised) is lately dead (as it is credebly reported) so as nowe I am altogether
destitute of any freind there to countenance my honest desart, &c.

" The late unfortunat young Earle of Desmond hath left here four poore
sisters; the Lady Roche best able of them, but of meane estate, to live;
and the rest, albeit hauing some annuity of Her Majesty, yet for the
smalenes thereof are much distressed, wthout any other freind or meanes to
help them. You have been a father unto him (as himself often told me)
and I think yor Hon^r should add much to your immortall fame, tobe so
unto them in pcuring Hir Ma^{ts} most gracious goodnes towards them for
their reasonable matching there, or here.

" Cork 17 Ja: 1601.

" Yo^r Hono^r humble dependant

" W^m. POWER."

CONCLUSION.

Lest by inadvertence the reader of this biography should confuse the politics of the 16th century with those of the 19th, and lest certain passages of doubtful loyalty to Queen Elizabeth detach themselves from the time and circumstances to which they belong, and settle like burs upon the skirts of the writer, who has had to travel through much rough country, it may be permitted to him to assert that his intention has been entirely restricted to the century over which this history extends; and to appeal to his reader whether— in the interest of honour and morality—any language less severe than that which he has occasionally used would be applied by himself to the conduct of men whose actions, as herein represented, have been revealed to us by their own letters, and the letters they have written of each other.

This author will also crave permission to remind his reader that even at the present day—when essaying the experiment of conciliation—England sends the noblest of her nobility, and the ablest of her statesmen to rule in the place of convicted Felons; and Irishmen seeing the best, where they had formerly seen but the worst qualities of their rulers, have felt their anger give way to wonder that seven centuries of the basest annals on human record should be the history of the occupation of their country by a people reputing themselves just, and magnanimous,—that even now, in this century of experimental truce, it is excusable in the descendants of those families which at the beginning of the 16th century held large possessions in the south of Ireland, to wish to know how it came to pass that at the close of it they find their estates in the hands of strangers, and their ancestors paupers! It may be also expected that some notice be taken of the question so often asked "why the Irish have been for the last two centuries so difficult to please, so reluctant to be quiet, *now that their country is so comfortably settled?*"

It is presumed that the perusal of the foregoing pages will have satisfied to the utmost all curiosity on both these subjects.

FINIS.

INDEX.

Laine, Monsieur, 313, 314.
Lawne, river, 3, 223, 319.
Leyne, Dermod, 59.
Leicester, Earl of, 65, 66.
Leighe, Captain, 477.
Lea, river, 229.
Lingard, Dr., 202, 444, 445.
Lishin Castle, 296, 297, 298.
Littleton, 493.
Loghlene Castle, 3, 223.
Lodge, 450.
Loftus, Adam, Archbishop of Dublin, 67, 471, 479, 480, 481, 483.
Lucas, Mr., 106, 107.
Lyston, Gerote, 284.

Magnes, John.
MacCarthy, Sir Donogh, vii., 1, 2, 4, 5, 6, 9, 10, 11, 21, 93, 95, 119, 140, 143, 376, 381, 410, 414, 424.
MacCarthy, Florence, v, vi, x, xi, 2, 4, 5, 6, 7, 8, 12, 20, 23, 24, 27, 28, 29, 30, 35, 37, 40, 47, 48, 55, 56, 57, 58, 60, 62, 64, 65, 68, 69, 75, 76, 78, 81, 83, 87, 88, 89, 90, 92, 93, 96, 100, 102, 104, 114, 116, 124, 126, 131, 133, 136, 141, 146, 151, 153, 159, 179, 182, 183, 186, 191, 192, 194, 195, 208, 209, 211, 216, 226, 227, 228, 229, 230, 231, 232, 233, 234, 235, 237, 238, 240, 211, 212, 215, 248, 258, 263, 264, 266, 372, 273, 283, 384, 288, 289, 290, 301, 303, 308, 309, 311, 312, 314, 315, 326, 327, 332, 333, 334, 336, 340, 342, 344, 353, 358, 364, 372, 374, 375, 378, 381, 382, 383, 390, 397, 401, 419, 428, 429, 431, 432, 441, 443, 445, 449, 459, 462, 486.
MacCarthy, Dermod Moyle, 2, 191, 237, 241, 297, 298, 315, 337, 338, 347, 351, 353, 354, 355, 356.
MacCarthy, Ellen-ny-Donogh, 354.
MacCarthy, Donal Mor ne Curradh, 143, 163, 193, 458.
MacCarthy, Finin, of Gleannachroim, 104, 106, 109, 111, 112, 113, 223.

MacCarthy, Teig O'Norsie I., 103, 110, 111, 112, 113, 223, 447.
MacCarthy, Teig O'Downy 1st, 113.
MacCarthy, Teig O'Norsie II., 113.
MacCarthy, Sir Owen, 4, 5, 12, 18, 21, 22, 23, 29, 39, 43, 55, 56, 59, 98, 99, 100, 112, 131, 133, 134, 135, 143, 357, 372, 376, 402, 411, 414.
MacCarthy, Mr. Charles, 70, 233, 238, 260, 263.
MacCarthy, Cormac M'Finin, 347.
MacCarthy, Sir Cormac M'Teig, vii, 1, 9, 15, 43, 376, 377.
MacCarthy, Cormac, 347.
MacCarthy, Finin of Ringrone, 143, 163, 364.
MacCarthy, Felimy M'Owen, 112, 134.
MacCarthy Don Morrice, 347.
MacCarthy, Donal-na-Pipi, 5, 21, 22, 23, 29, 30, 36, 39, 59, 83, 84, 100, 103, 131, 132, 133, 134, 135, 175, 218, 223, 238, 260, 277, 313, 315, 353, 362, 369, 372, 373, 375, 376, 377, 378, 379, 394, 395, 401, 410, 414, 421, 442, 447, 458.
MacCarthy, Donal, base son of the Earl of Clancar, 37, 46, 50, 71, 72, 73, 85, 87, 88, 89, 98, 116, 122, 123, 146, 147, 148, 149, 154, 159, 161, 162, 163, 178, 179, 180, 182, 180, 100, 191, 193, 200, 208, 210, 212, 215, 216, 218, 219, 220, 229, 232, 235, 264, 265, 270, 271, 272, 273, 274, 275, 276, 277, 278, 281, 292, 308, 309, 312, 314, 331, 332, 346, 350, 351, 352, 353, 366, 369, 372, 373, 376, 379, 380, 381, 411, 412, 413, 448, 485.
MacCarthy, Donal, reputed son of Donal, 379, 447.
MacCarthy, Lady Ellen, 2, 34, 55, 58, 60, 61, 62, 75, 77, 81, 82, 125, 143, 150, 156, 183, 187, 314, 326, 355, 356, 373, 374, 375, 396, 397, 402, 413, 432, 448.
MacCarthy, M'Teig, little, 106.

PRINTED BY HARRISON AND SONS, ST. MARTIN'S LANE.

WS - #0026 - 030221 - C0 - 229/152/29 - PB - 9780282867355